INTRODUCTION TO

Physical Anthropology and Archaeology

Charles A. Weitz

Temple University

INTRODUCTION TO Physical Anthropology and Archaeology

Prentice-Hall, Inc.
Englewood Cliffs, New Jersey

To my parents, Sidney and Catherine Weitz

Library of Congress Cataloging in Publication Data

Weitz, Charles A
Introduction to physical anthropology and archaeology.

Bibliography: pp. 335–342.
Includes index.
1. Somatology. 2. Archaeology. I. Title.
GN60.W46 573 78-26719
ISBN 0-13-492637-4

Printed in the United States of America

10 9 8 7 6 5 4 3 2 1

Cover photo of Monkey Temple in Varanasi, India, by Linda Bartlett, Photo Researchers, Inc.

Part-opening photo credits: Part One: David Brill, National Geographic Society Photograph; Part Two: George Holton, Photo Researchers, Inc.

Chapter-opening photo credits: Chapter 1: Jacques Jangoux, Peter Arnold Photo Archives; Chapter 2: Miguel Castro, Photo Researchers, Inc; Chapter 3: Pro Pix, Monkmeyer Press Photo Service; Chapter 4: Brian Brake, Photo Researchers, Inc.; Chapter 5: Nancy Nicolson, Anthro-Photo; Chapter 6: Jen and Des Bartlett, Photo Researchers, Inc.; Chapter 7: George Tames, *The New York Times*; Chapter 9: Courtesy of the American Museum of Natural History; Chapter 10: Gerhard E. Gscheidle; Chapter 11: United Press International Photo; Chapter 12: Courtesy of the American Museum of Natural History; Chapter 13: Paul Mangelsdorf and R. S. MacNeish; Chapter 14: George Gerster, Photo Researchers Inc; Chapter 15: Bernard Wolff, Photo Researchers, Inc.

Prentice-Hall International, Inc., London
Prentice-Hall of Australia Pty. Ltd., Sydney
Prentice-Hall of Canada, Ltd., Toronto
Prentice-Hall of India Private Limited, New Delhi
Prentice-Hall of Japan, Inc., Tokyo
Prentice-Hall of Southeast Asia, Pte. Ltd., Singapore
Whitehall Books Limited, Wellington, New Zealand

Outline

Contents

9 Principles of Genetics 175

10 The Study of Human Diversity 191

PART TWO ARCHAEOLOGY 215

11 Introduction to Archaeology 217

12 Early Hominid Cultures 233

Preface

As students take their seats at their first class in human evolution, most have little idea of what lies in wait for them. They have barely an inkling of the true complexity of physical anthropology and archaeology, their methods and data. But most beginning students have enrolled in the course because they are curious: They want to know who our ancestors were, what all those fossils that have been uncovered in Africa mean, and what past cultures were like. My goal in this book has been to keep this curiosity alive and well by making the field, with its ambiguities, controversies, and contributions, interesting and easily accessible to students.

There are many ways to write an introductory textbook, and perhaps this one is best described as an "uncluttered" approach. A conscious decision was made to keep interruptions in the text and diversions on the page to a minimum. I have long believed that all the distractions and motivational extras in the world are no substitute for an interesting, clear, concise text.

I have taken special care to make apparent the sequence of biological and cultural change in a series of time scales and in a step-by-step treatment in the text. But today, it is generally accepted that a recounting of these sequences alone is not enough. Students must also understand something of the process of change itself. One of the most helpful frameworks for understanding biological and cultural change is that provided by ecological principles. I have taken care, where it is appropriate, to emphasize the dynamic nature of human interaction with the rest of the biosphere.

An ecological explanation helps students understand the diversity of information from other fields upon which archaeologists and physical anthropologists have come to rely. More than just providing students with relevant data from primatology, paleontology, genetics, or geology, this text shows how archaeologists and physical anthropologists use ecological theory to integrate information from these fields into their work. In so doing, it has not sidestepped controversies. The temptation to bias the presentation in favor of one particular view is resisted. Instead, the arguments and evidence used by proponents of different views are presented clearly, and the decision to emphasize one or another is left where it belongs—with the instructor.

An important part of making evolution interesting to students is to give them a sense of just what a tenuous endeavor it often is to move from guess to hypothesis to theory, as excavation and research add to what we know. Therefore I have included ample discussion of research methods and have tried to structure the coverage so that students can see the relationship between evidence and hypothesis.

General Plan and Organization

The text is divided into two parts. The first, consisting of Chapters 2–10, covers physical anthropology, and the second, which includes Chapters 11–15, covers archaeology. The last chapter of the book focuses on the theme of disease as a selective agent to show in detail how human cultural and biological evolution can influence each other. Although it is clearly recognized that the distinction between biological and cultural evolution is arbitrary, I feel that this organization allows introductory students to understand better how concepts, research, data, and theory unique to each field are linked together.

The section on physical anthropology begins with a chapter designed to give students a thorough overview of the field and the basics of natural selection. Chapter 3, a presentation of the principles of ecology, serves as a foundation for discussions of change in later chapters. This chapter is followed by a consideration of primatology (Chapters 4 and 5). Both anatomy and behavior are introduced, as well as how information from the study of primates has been used by physical anthropologists to interpret different aspects of hominid evolution. Topics of popular concern in this section include a discussion of ethological and sociobiological interpretations of primate behavior. These two chapters are followed by an explanation of the nature of fossils, geological time, and the primate fossil record (Chapter 6). Pliocene-Pleistocene fossils, and the controversy surrounding their interpretation, are discussed in Chapter 7, and *Homo erectus* and *Homo sapiens* fossils are considered in Chapter 8. A final section in Part One is concerned with explaining genetics (Chapter 9) and modern human variation (Chapter 10). Genetics is introduced at this point primarily because it is more relevant to understanding the biological nature of living human populations than to interpreting fossils. Part Two opens with an introductory archaeology chapter written to give students an overview of how excavation is carried on and the nature of archaeological theory. The next three chapters (12–14) deal separately with the Paleolithic Age, the invention and spread of agriculture, and the emergence of complex societies. In this text, the traditional lithic terminology is used, simply because of its general familiarity. The problems some archaeologists have attributed to this typology are presented clearly in the text, although most are avoided by defining precisely each lithic term geographically, temporally, and culturally.

The chapters covering agriculture and the emergence of complex societies stress the hypothesis-testing approach to archaeology. In both chapters, major theoretical statements are presented first. Then, the theories are assessed in terms of the archaeological data from different parts of the world. This is designed to provide students with clear examples of the dynamic features of archaeological model building.

The last chapter (Chapter 15) focuses on human disease, because of its growing interest to medical anthropologists and because it illustrates the manner in which human biological and cultural evolution are linked. The prevalence of certain disease types and their selective impact on human biology are traced within the temporal and cultural frameworks presented earlier in the text.

Learning Aids Within The Text

Illustrations

In the preparation of this text I have included numerous photographs and illustrations so that readers can visualize what is being discussed in the text. Because this need is especially strong in the chapters on the primates and primate and human evolution, these chapters are lavishly illustrated. In all, the book contains 75 charts, graphs, and drawings and over 50 photographs.

Chapter Summaries

Rehearsal is an important part of long-term learning. With this fact in mind, I have concluded each chapter with a summary of the major points that should be remembered from it.

Glossary and Bibliography

As each new important term is introduced in the text it is defined. A glossary at the end of the book redefines each term for the student, and a bibliography contains references to all of the material cited within each chapter.

Supplements to the Text

The text is supplemented by a study guide and workbook for the student and an instructor's manual and a test bank for the teacher.

The study guide is divided into four parts: a study outline, a list of key terms and concepts, a pretest consisting primarily of multiple-choice questions on the most important points covered in the chapter, and a study outline, consisting of questions of varied sorts that ensure that the reader has learned the material covered in the chapter at a greater depth. Immediate feedback is provided by having the answers to all questions provided in the margin of the workbook directly next to the question and by keying them to the page of the text on which the material appears, so that a reader who misses a question knows immediately where to look to rehearse the material.

The test item file consists of some 750 multiple choice questions. It is available, as is the instructor's manual, free upon adoption. The instructor's manual consists of an overview of each chapter, a group of resources for classroom discussion, a list of paper topics, and a film list keyed to appropriate sections of each chapter.

Acknowledgments

The aim of this text is to present simply, clearly, and completely theory, method, and data in physical anthropology and archaeology. These are ambitious goals in fields of such complexity and rapid change. The strategy adopted in the preparation of this text was to bring together a number of experts in the various stages of publication. A large number of people worked cooperatively to produce an easy-to-read and up-to-date product. While my name appears on the title page, all of these people deserve recognition for their contributions.

I wish to thank Stephen Graff, who assisted me in the pursuit of relevant literature and who provided the much appreciated legwork necessary to assemble the data and visual aids that form the basis of this book. I wish to thank the writers who coordinated the data, along with my notes and outline, and produced a first copy of each chapter: Jared Becker, Ernest Kohlmetz, and Elaine Schechter. I want particularly to express my gratitude to Mary Pat Fisher for her extra effort and lively writing. I also wish to thank the reviewers who kindly read and provided thoughtful comments on early drafts of the chapters: Leonard Greenfield, Temple University; Richard Jantz, University of Tennessee; Ellis R. Kerley, University of Maryland; Gery Moreno-Black, University of Oregon; Frank J. Orlosky, Northern Illinois University; and Anthony Zavaleta, Texas Southmost College. Stan Wakefield, who handled the review process and the marketing, has been extremely helpful in all stages of the project and also deserves my thanks.

The contributions of technical experts must also include those of Cheryl Mannes, editorial assistant; Nancy Perkus, permissions editor; Alan Forman, photo researcher; Florence Silverman, art director; Susanna Lesan, copy editor; and Nancy Myers, manufacturing buyer. Ruth Kugelman provided the research base on which the book was begun. Patricia Quinn, production editor, deserves special thanks for her diligence and skill in giving the manuscript the attention it needed at crucial stages. To each of these individuals I express my sincere thanks.

In large measure, however, the creation of this book must be credited to my development editor, David Crook. He tirelessly edited the initial versions of each chapter and then re-edited each of my rewrites. Through long stretches of the past year, he worked night and weekends on the innumerable small details that sometimes seemed to engulf the entire project. I am grateful indeed for his comments, guidance, and perseverance.

My wife, Velma, deserves special appreciation for her patience during those frequent episodes when the book took precedence over family life.

CHARLES A. WEITZ

INTRODUCTION TO

Physical Anthropology and Archaeology

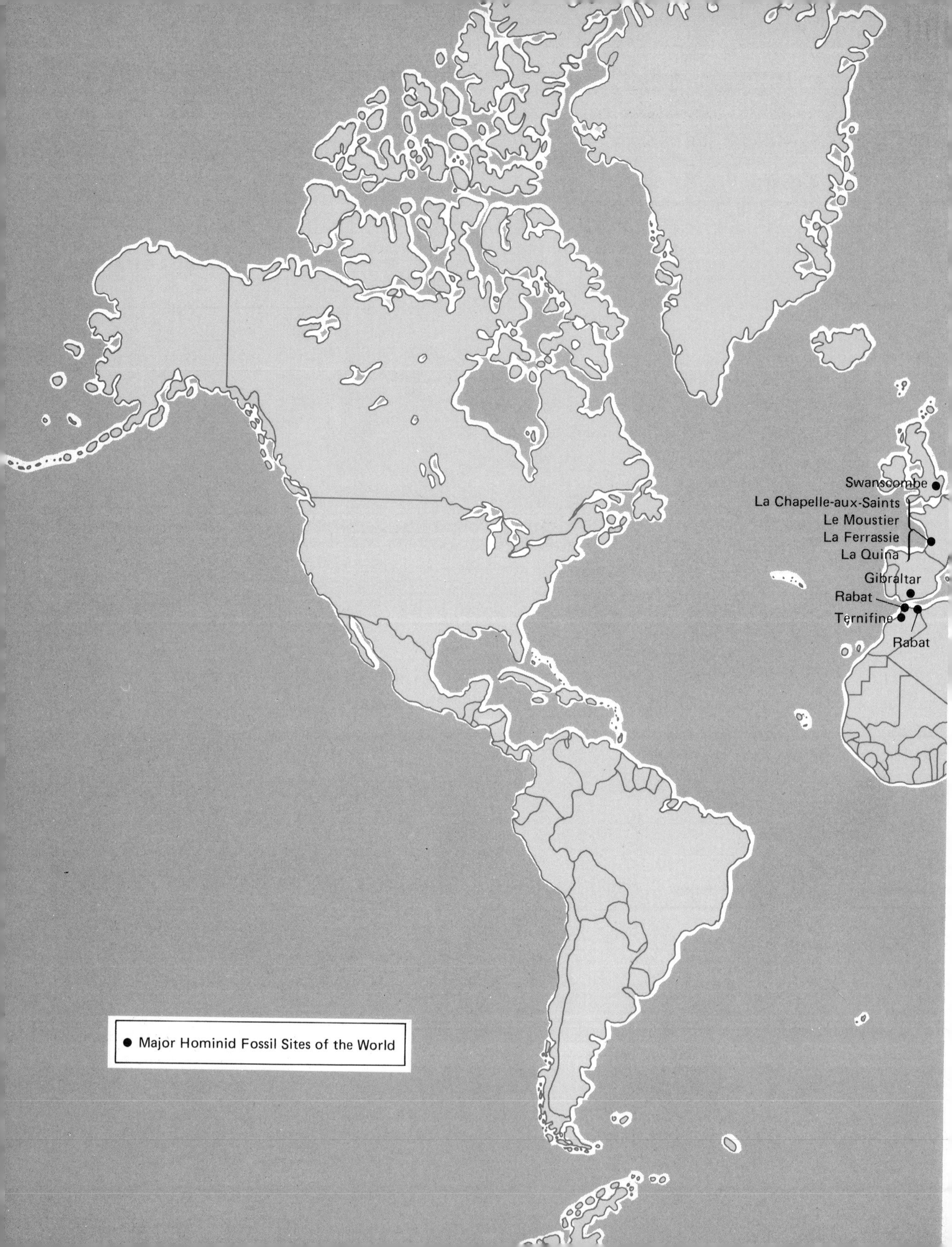
Swanscombe
La Chapelle-aux-Saints
Le Moustier
La Ferrassie
La Quina
Gibraltar
Rabat
Ternifine
Rabat
Major Hominid Fossil Sites of the World

Neandertal
Heidelberg
Ehringsdorf
Monte Circeo
Saccopastore
Spy
Vertesszöllös
Krapina
Petralona
Vallonet Cave
Shanidar
Mount Carmel
Hava Fteah
Chou-kou-tien
Lantian
Yuanmou
Hadar
Omo River
Koobi Fora
East Turkana
Lothagam
Laetolil
Olduvai Gorge
Solo
Broken Hill
Kromdraai
Makapansgat
Sterkfontein
Swartkrans
Taung
Saldanha

1 Introduction to Anthropology

PEOPLE have long been curious about the origins and nature of the human species. Many societies have developed beliefs about the creation of humans and their place in relation to the rest of the natural—and perhaps supernatural—world. The organized study of human beings—*anthropology*—has existed as a distinct field of inquiry for over 100 years. Only within the past few decades, however, has anthropology graduated from being a quaint subject that studied the "strange" artifacts and customs of little-known or remote peoples to a systematic attempt to explain human cultural and biological variability.

Modern communications and a world war that carried Westerners to far corners of the earth brought Western technology to isolated people and at the same time made Westerners aware that people once thought to be exotic are very much a part of the real world. As anthropology turned to questions of more direct significance to modern industrial life and adopted a more systematic, scientific approach to human social life everywhere, it acquired an established place among American academic disciplines that it had not had previously.

The Anthropological Approach

Anthropology is somewhat like sociology, history, human biology, and many other disciplines as well. What sets it apart from these ways of looking at humanity is its attempts at holism and relativistic comparison. It is an attempt to understand the origin, evolution, and present diversity of human biology and culture.

Holism

Anthropology is an immense subject. It is the most inclusive of any academic discipline, for it seeks to encompass not only all that is known about human beings around the world but also the history of their gradual evolution from small mammals that lived almost 70 million years ago. It covers all that is known of culture—the learned ideas and beliefs that characterize human groups as distinct from other primate groups—and of human biology as well. This takes anthropology through time and space into fields as diverse as paleontology (the study of fossils), anatomy, primatology, economics, archaeology, linguistics, genetics, religion, art, and political science, to name a few.

Anthropology tries to pull all this information together and organize it in some systematic fashion. For instance, anthropology makes inferences about the earliest humans by studying isolated living populations. It also compares the way of life of remote aborigines with that of urban city dwellers, and the behaviors of monkeys and other nonhuman primates with those of humans. It is this all-inclusive scope—called *holism*—that gives anthropology its unique character. Holism is an attempt to incorporate all of this knowledge into a meaningful understanding of humanity.

This claim of holism is more a goal than a reality, however. There is no overall framework—for example, no single theory of how culture works—that all anthropologists would happily use for explaining their data. Different kinds of anthropologists see things from very different points of view. Furthermore, increasingly specialized training has produced a generation of anthropologists who communicate primarily with those in their own subdisciplines. Still, the concept of culture ties together all anthropologists, whether they are interested in social relationships,

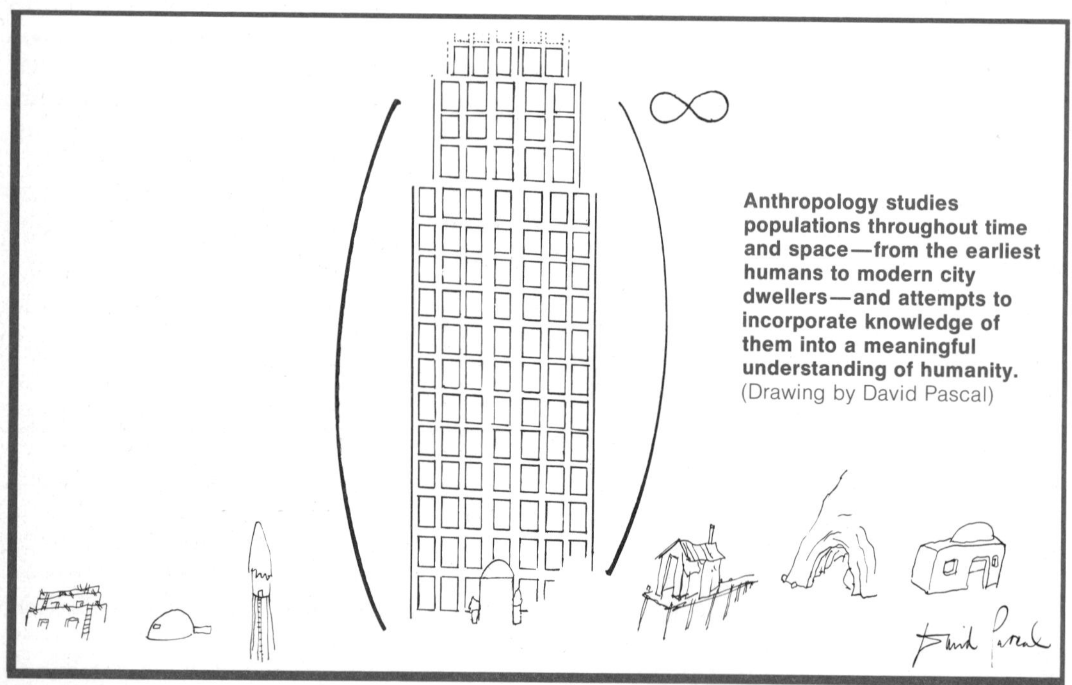

Anthropology studies populations throughout time and space—from the earliest humans to modern city dwellers—and attempts to incorporate knowledge of them into a meaningful understanding of humanity. (Drawing by David Pascal)

linguistics, archaeology, or physical anthropology.

Traditionally, there was a continuum in anthropology, ranging from those who emphasized biology to those who emphasized culture. At one extreme were those who tended to view humans basically as biological organisms whose behaviors are largely determined by genetic and environmental factors. They analyzed human groups in the same terms by which other organisms are studied: inherited traits, local food supplies, climatic changes, and other features that affect biological survival. At the other extreme were those who saw humans as unique creatures who have asserted their independence from most biological factors by their genius for cultural solutions—houses to modify the effects of climate, tools for manipulating the environment, and political organizations to maintain social control. Today this division is not as important as it once was, since both physical and cultural anthropologists are using more of the same concepts and approaches. As we will see, the main subfields of anthropology continue to be informed by work done in the others, and attempts to integrate the whole field continue to appear.

Relativistic Comparison

In addition to holism, there is another unique aspect of the way anthropology looks at the human condition. This is *cultural relativism:* the attempt to understand and evaluate each cultural system in terms of its own internally consistent logic. Before the need for relativism was recognized, visitors to cannibalistic tribes, for instance, were appalled at their "immoral" practices. They were judging cannibals by their own society's moral code, by which it is unthinkable to eat human flesh. But later anthropologists made an effort to be less culturally subjective in their observations. They tried, for instance, to accept the fact that some cultures consider cannibalism acceptable behavior. Instead of condemning it, they tried to determine what functions cannibalism serves for the groups that practice it. *Ethnocentrism*—the tendency to judge other cultures by the standards of one's own culture—became the devil to be exorcised in every introductory anthropology course.

By the middle of this century, however, it became apparent that anthropologists could not completely free themselves from ethnocentrism. No matter how much they tried to immerse themselves in other cultures in order to understand them better, they were inevitably influenced to some extent by their own society's ways of looking at things. A certain amount of ethnocentrism seemed to be essential to the functioning of any social system, including their own. And in trying to explain their experiences to those back home, they found that they were obliged to translate them into terms which had significance in their own culture. Having to do so destroys the efforts to treat cultural systems in their own terms. Thus, anthropologists continually search for the most appropriate method of translating what they know about a culture into concepts that are meaningful in their own. Only by doing so are they able to offer insights into the operation of our own cultural system.

Another difficulty, which is potentially very serious, is that by attempting to explain objectively the function of practices which seem inhumane to us, anthropologists may seem to be approving them. Infanticide, for instance, can be explained in terms of its biological and social functions. To condemn the practice would require the kind of value judgment that anthropologists have long avoided. However, some anthropologists feel that they must make it clear where they stand on such matters. The question of how to do so without sacrificing relativism is a critical dilemma which anthropology has not yet resolved.

Anthropology and Other Disciplines

Anthropology occupies a central position in any liberal arts curriculum because it serves to link the humanities, natural sciences, and social sciences.

The *humanities* include art, languages, music, philosophy, and history. Anthropological research and interpretation extends into all these areas, often taking them into sectors of time and space that would not otherwise be described. In art, for instance, anthropology has contributed a great amount of information about the folk art of cultures outside Western traditions, as well as data on the role that art plays in society and culture. And in history, archaeology (a branch of anthropology) has pushed our understanding of extinct peoples back into the shadows of prehistoric times, before written records were kept.

The *natural sciences* upon which anthropology draws for some of its explanations include biology, ecology, chemistry, and geology. Chemical analysis, for instance, helps anthropologists figure out how old fossils and artifacts are. Geology contributes knowledge of the environments within which humans evolved. Ecology—the study of the relationships between living things and their environment—clarifies how human populations and the rest of nature influence each other. And biology is a rich source of concepts and information about human anatomy, physiology, variation, evolution, and behavior. The exchange is not just a one-way process, however. To these sciences, anthropology brings knowledge of how human activities have changed human biology. It also provides its special humanistic viewpoint—a fundamental concern for understanding and explaining human cultural differences.

Anthropology is most commonly listed as one of the *social sciences.* It deals with topics covered in a number of other social sciences—economics, psychology, sociology, political science, statistics, law, geography. Anthropology overlaps with geography, for instance, when it studies the links between culture and environment. It coincides with psychology—the study of individual behavior—when it looks at the relationship between culture and individual personalities and actions. And over and over again, anthropologists have pointed out that law, economics, and politics are parts of integrated cultural systems and cannot be fully understood unless the rest of these systems are described and explained.

Sociology cuts across some of the same territory as anthropology. But its subject matter is more limited, and its methods different. Traditionally, sociology has been concerned with Western societies, whereas anthropology studies societies and cultures everywhere in the world. Sociologists tend to isolate only certain influences on group behaviors—such as age, sex, income level, social status, and educational background. By contrast, anthropologists try to look at everything that may affect how people in a certain culture behave. This includes not only the factors listed above, but also the environmental setting, the group's survival strategies, its religious beliefs, its history and political organization, and so on. Sociologists run surveys with questionnaires and statistical samplings that reveal the relationships between certain variables (such as divorce, income, and educational level). By contrast, anthropologists try to figure out how a whole culture works by making in-depth studies. They may also compare features of one culture with those of others to see if there are any regularities in the ways humans tend to approach various facets of social life—sex, incest, adolescence, and so on (Fried, 1972). *Cross-cultural comparison* is one of the hallmarks of anthropology.

Subdisciplines

Anthropology is commonly divided into four subdisciplines: physical anthropology, archaeology, linguistics, and cultural or social anthropology. The major distinction traditionally has been between the first—the study of humans as biological animals—and the last—the study of humans as creatures who are unique because of culture. This is no longer necessarily the case, as we have seen. Archaeology is closely tied to cultural anthropology in its attempt to reconstruct life ways prior to written records. But it also works with fossil remains and biological concepts in reconstructing history. Linguistics is perhaps the most independent of the four subdisciplines because its body of data has distinct boundaries. As you will see, all of these branches are in a state of flux, revising their traditional methods to help them get at the heart of the questions that people are interested in today.

Physical Anthropology

Physical anthropology, the study of the biological aspects of human existence, was once a rather static science. Its nineteenth-century practitioners spent much of their time measuring people in the effort to group humans into races according to head shape and various other traits. The initial concern was to describe the variation of a few features in modern and ancient populations. Today, however, physical anthropology not only describes the variation of hundreds of features—from blood protein composition to limb length—but also encompasses the entire history and nature of human biological change. This new anthropology represents an enormous expansion in scope.

We can begin to make sense of the diversity of the field by thinking of physical anthropology as the study of the events and processes of human evolution. An event can be described as the appearance in the fossil record of any of the traits that characterize a species in different stages of its evolution. These events take place within a geological time frame and occur much more slowly than the events we read about in the papers. By placing thousands of fossils together in the correct time sequence, physical anthropologists have begun to reconstruct the history of our evolution.

An ideal picture of how we evolved would be complete in every detail, including a vivid

Physical anthropologist Donald Johanson uses an air scribe to clean sandstone from around the fossil skull of a child that lived 3 million years ago in East Africa. (David Brill © The National Geographic Society)

description of the climates, plants, and animals comprising ancient environments. The actual picture is far from ideal. Crucial periods early in the history of our evolution are almost completely unrepresented by fossils. For instance, during the period from 14 to 5 million years ago, our humanlike ancestors began to walk upright on their hind limbs. But we have no fossil leg bones or pelvises from this time. In fact, the known primate remains from this period are a single tooth. We do, however, have a fairly complete record of the human evolution during the past 3 million years. Geologists and a host of other specialists have developed techniques for determining prehistoric precipitation, geography, flora, and fauna. But for a complete understanding of how these features affected past human evolution, much more data must be collected.

The present is also a valuable source of clues to the past. By studying the anatomy and behavior of the other primates, physical anthropologists can reconstruct how fossil species (including the earliest humanlike creatures) probably moved and, to some degree, how they may have behaved together in social groups.

Physical anthropologists want to know more than what happened; they are also curious about *why* evolutionary events occurred as they did. They are interested in what evolutionary processes have been responsible for the events. The most important source of this knowledge is living human populations. Analysis of how the frequency of various physical traits in human groups is shifting in response to changing environments and cultural practices can provide analogies to evolution in prehistoric groups.

Physical anthropologists who study modern human variation face the problem of distinguishing environmental action on an individual during his or her lifetime—such as the effects on the body of growing up in a cold or a high-altitude setting—from those that are truly the result of inherited factors. Researchers must also separate the cultural influences on human biology from those of the natural environment. Cultural beliefs and values can shape the process of reproduction and therefore influence the course of evolution. Physical anthropologists have come to understand human variation as the consequence of enormously complex interactions with both the environment and culture.

The study of the interaction of biological and cultural factors has led to some unique contributions. For instance, Carleton Gajdusek, of the National Institute for Neurological Diseases and Stroke, won a Nobel Prize in 1976 for applying physical anthropological and epidemiological methods to the study of a progressive neuromuscular disease called kuru. The disease occurs among a group of New Guinea highlanders called the Fore. He found that kuru has a cultural component—the eating of uncooked diseased brains in the course of ritual cannibalism. The virus is then transmitted to those who eat the brains. Gajdusek discovered a genetic factor as well. Although cannibalism is a common practice among highland New Guinea peoples, the disease occurs only among the Fore highland groups. This fact suggested a genetic susceptibility to the disease. Gajdusek's discoveries are important because some progressive muscular disorders found in the West—such as multiple sclerosis—may also be studied in terms of the cultural and genetic factors involved.

Archaeology

Archaeology overlaps both physical and cultural anthropology. But it exists as a distinct discipline with its own subject matter and methods. It can be defined as the study of the history, life styles, and processes of change in prehistoric human cultures. For the most part, archaeologists examine what happened in human societies before they began to keep written records. Recreating what life was once

Archaeology students make a site survey at the Pyramid of the Sun, part of the monumental architecture of Teotihuacán, a city state that dominated much of Mesoamerica from about A.D. 200 to 500. Excavations at this site have added a great deal to our knowledge of the rise of cities and states. (Marilu Pease/Monkmeyer)

like in the dim past and understanding how it changed is like trying to put together an intricate jigsaw puzzle in which most of the pieces and the picture of the completed puzzle on the box cover are missing.

Generally working without written records, archaeologists use the most durable scraps of human activities as clues. Occasionally these are well-preserved buildings and implements. But more often, evidence consists of such objects as bits of broken pottery, flakes from ancient stone tool making, charred animal bones around an ancient hearth, and slight changes in vegetation or soil patterns caused by prehistoric farming. Archaeologists try to relate these material remains to the behaviors of the humans who left them behind. To do so, they systematically survey, dig up, date, classify, and then interpret the remains.

Interpretation of what went on in the past was once just a matter of organizing bones and artifacts into historical sequences. Long-inhabited sites with many layers built up over the years often reveal, for instance, that one kind of pottery was gradually replaced by another kind and then still another. Archaeologists were at first content merely to catalog these sequences. But in the "new archaeology," scientists analyze a variety of data as clues to the actual activities of the humans who left these traces. In following the spread of early human tribes, for instance, archaeologists analyze tools, indications of environmental conditions, and the remains of animal prey for information on the changing role of hunting.

Among other surprises, archaeologists have found that the appearance of tool-using humans in North America seems to have coincided with the disappearance of many large game animals. One hundred species of mammals—including mammoths, giant beavers, and giant ground sloths—suddenly became extinct about 10,000 years ago. In evolutionary terms, this was not long after the first humans seemingly made their way to the continent from the Far East, probably by way of a land bridge at the site of the Bering Strait. Were humans responsible for these mass extinctions? Had they developed hunting techniques—such as surrounding herds with fire or running them off cliffs—so wasteful that they wiped out their prey? Or was it something else—a major climatic change, perhaps—that killed so many so fast? We are not yet sure. The "Pleistocene overkill" theory is still under investigation, as are many other theories about how our ancestors lived from day to day and changed over the centuries.

To analyze and interpret their finds, today's archaeologists call on a battery of specialists. Analysts range from zoologists who examine deer antlers to determine what times of year a site was occupied to scientists who can tell from minute grains of pollen how old a site is, what kinds of plants once grew there, and what the climate was like. Interpretive models may also draw on the work of economists, ecologists, statisticians, geographers, cultural anthropologists studying modern primitive populations, and even physicists. Growing numbers of archaeologists are unearthing vast quantities of materials at sites around the globe, guided by a desire to find and record as much data as possible before the evidence is destroyed by advancing industrial civilization. The result is a dynamic field undergoing explosive growth. We now know far more about how humans once lived than we did even a few years ago.

Linguistics

Thanks to the work of linguists, scientists who study language, our understanding of this central aspect of social life is also increasing. Anthropological research into language is expanding in many directions at once.

Some anthropological linguists are busy recording languages that will soon become extinct because they are spoken in vanishing cultures. Others are trying to find ways in which all languages are similar. These findings may suggest something about humans' basic capacity for using vocal symbols to communicate with each other, as well as the fundamental structure of the human mind. Other linguists focus on differences, rather than universals, in languages. These, they think, reveal fundamental differences in the ways people of various cultures perceive life. Some languages, for instance, have no way of expressing neat divisions of time into past, present, and future, as ours does. Our vocabulary and grammar reflect a linear view of time—and perhaps an obsession with it—that is by no means universal. People of other cultures are obsessed with other kinds of details. Indians* of northern Canada, for instance, have not 1 word for

*In this text we will use the term *Indian* to identify aboriginal peoples in the New World—in North, Central, and South America. We do, however, recognize the fact that some people prefer various other terms—especially *native American.* We choose *Indian* from among the list of possibilities as the one term that applies everywhere in the New World.

Anthropological linguists study the form and use of spoken language, as well as nonverbal systems of communication that are characteristic of various social groups. (Klaus D. Francke, Peter Arnold Photo Archives)

"ice," as we do, but at least 13. Since it is important to them to know whether a stretch of frozen water will support a foot traveler or a dog sled, they are careful to categorize these kinds of ice in their verbal communications (Basso, 1973).

However linguists approach it, language is a key element in the study of culture. Fieldworkers obviously need to know a people's language before they can learn much about them. Models developed for the study of language can also be used to study how whole cultures work. For anyone patient enough to record and analyze its intricacies, language is a rich source of information about everything from the patterning of kinship relations to how other domains of culture are perceived (Fried, 1972).

Cultural Anthropology

The fourth subdiscipline, cultural anthropology, is the most familiar of the branches, the one which people usually think of when the word "anthropology" is mentioned. But, given its diversity, it is also the hardest of the four to define.

Cultural anthropologists themselves do not all agree on what it is they are studying. Culture—one of their principal subject matters—is variously defined as a worldwide striving toward "civilization" through the accumulation of practices and beliefs; a unique pattern of beliefs that shapes personalities in each society; a local system of ideas and practices that are functionally integrated; an unconscious structure that generates ideas and behavior; a system of shared symbols that come into play in social interactions; and a system by which people adapt to their environment. Cultural anthropologists work with the concepts culture and society. Those who focus on the interaction of individuals, and the institutions such interaction creates, sometimes stress their particular focus by referring to themselves as social anthropologists. In this text, the emphasis is on culture as an idea system, but the concept of society is absolutely essential to all of the chapters dealing with social organization, such as kinship and marriage, non-kin groupings, and politics and leadership.

Underlying most definitions of culture is the basic assumption that groups of people—Samoans, Americans, members of an Eskimo tribe—come to share a set of understandings about how their society works and how one should behave in it. These un-

Cultural anthropologists study people's understandings about how their particular society works and how to behave in it. Here, the men of a Hoti Indian family in Venezuela inspect the bamboo used to make blowguns with which they will hunt monkeys and birds, and boys of the Ibo of Nigeria dance around a masked figure at their New Year festival.
(Jacques Jangoux, Peter Arnold Photo Archives; Peter Buckley, Photo Researchers)

derstandings in turn affect the ways in which people behave—how they choose marriage partners, build houses, organize politically, procure food, communicate, worship, divide labor, maintain social control, express themselves in art, and so on. Since these beliefs and behaviors may be quite different from one group to another, anthropologists usually see them as products of the local culture rather than as basic aspects of human nature. In each society, though, members tend to accept their own way of looking at things as the norm. In the United States, for example, we "know" that older people need to be retired (and thereby lose the opportunity to contribute their knowledge and skills to society). But in some other societies, the aged are respected for the knowledge and wisdom they have developed over the years.

Collecting information about "strange" practices was the central concern of anthropologists during the early years of the discipline. This concern frequently appeared to be separated from any understanding of one's own culture. The information they gathered fascinated and amused the folks back home. But today a crisis of sorts is facing the field: there are very few "unknown tribes" left to describe. The cultures of many peoples are rapidly becoming extinct. In some cases, contact with Westerners has introduced diseases for which their bodies have no built-up immunity. Measles, tuberculosis, smallpox, mumps, and other introduced diseases have decimated many primitive* tribes. And as more technologically advanced peoples have pushed into the environments that once sus-

*We use the term *primitive* here to indicate, in general, nonliterate peoples who live without permanent dwellings and by means of simple technology—hunting and gathering of food.

tained them, hunting-and-gathering tribes have been relegated to the most barren settings or resettled in communities that are inadequate for their needs and desires. This disruption of their traditional life style and food supplies has created severe vitamin and mineral deficiencies and, in some cases, destroyed their social structure. As a result of such pressures, the aboriginal population of Australia, for instance, plummeted from 250,000 at the turn of the century to no more than 40,000 today (Lévi-Strauss, 1967).

Elsewhere, though, formerly primitive populations are reproducing rapidly and becoming part of a growing and restless third world. In Latin America, Asia, and Africa, people are increasingly aware of the more technologically advanced nations and of their own lack of power and material wealth. They resent being the objects of anthropological studies, and they express ambivalent feelings about Western technology and ideologies.

To deal with the first crisis—that of extinction of primitive peoples—cultural anthropologists are speeding up their attempts to gather information while they may. Data on how the remaining primitive tribes live provide invaluable clues to the primitive life ways of ancient humans. Observation techniques are therefore being sharpened and made more systematic in the urgency of capturing this information before it is lost forever. At the same time, however, many anthropologists are turning to the study of the far more numerous urban cultures.

The second crisis has serious implications for world harmony. Third world cultures feel that anthropologists from technologically advanced nations are more interested in maintaining the status quo than in helping them develop and join the rest of the political and economic world. This feeling is due to the fact that the study of colonial peoples by anthropologists often stresses traditional systems rather than situations of change and unrest resulting from colonial administration. In the face of this distrust—and of the extinction of their other subjects—many Western anthropologists are turning to a study of their own culture instead. When they do so, they find it hard to maintain anthropology's traditional distinction between the anthropologist and the group being studied. Instead of the perspective of a culturally alien observer trying to be a participant, studies of Western culture have the peculiarly self-reflective point of view of participants who are trying to be observers.

French anthropologist Claude Lévi-Strauss (1967) suggests another alternative: invite third world anthropologists to come study us. This solution might reveal things about our own "strange" customs that are hard for those of us who have grown up with them to see. It might revise anthropology's established use of alien peoples as subjects and permit a more meaningful interaction with the third world.

The fact that there are so few isolated peoples also requires another change in cultural anthropology as it was practiced in the past. Traditionally, in-depth studies described a single social group, in and of itself. But such isolated pictures no longer reflect the whole situation. In Brazil, for example, even the most remote Indian tribes in the Amazon jungle have been affected by the new trans-Amazonian highway and by the policies of government agencies appointed to deal with Indian societies. They also are influenced by the influx of commercial enterprises that have begun to exploit the natural resources of the region. When anthropologists describe village life in these remote areas, they can no longer ignore the effect of these regional influences. This methodological problem is even more acute in the developing countries. There, the lives of people whose parents or grandparents were members of more isolated cultures are now touched more directly, not only by regional economic and political developments but by world events as well. As a result, it is increasingly important that analyses of cul-

The telephone booth in the marketplace in Jedda, Saudi Arabia, is a relatively new addition, one that is indicative of the modern communication systems that are becoming regular features of developing nations all over the world. (Kent Reno, Jeroboam)

tural systems take into account the wider social systems in which they are encapsulated.

Although the days of describing remote tribes are coming to an end, anthropology is needed now more than ever before. All over the world, modern communication systems are bringing a flood of information about other cultures to mass audiences. Anthropologists' perspective and knowledge of these cultures can help to interpret the information and build understanding between peoples. There is also hope that in coming to understand other people better, we will learn something about ourselves—perhaps that our behaviors are to some extent the result of local choices rather than inevitabilities of human nature or of the "right" way of doing things.

In addition to serving the public, anthropologists are also in demand by international organizations. As the third and fourth worlds begin to organize and assert themselves, the major powers need to learn more about these people's life ways, heritages, and points of view. Cultural anthropologists' new studies of urban cultures may also contribute to programs of development and planning.

Instead of being simply a science *of* humanity, anthropology is becoming a science *for* humanity. In all its branches, anthropology is being drawn into the serious questions of the day—the effects of unequal distribution of wealth, of genetic engineering, of loss of cultural identity, of technological impact on the environment, of racial strife, of sex-role stereotyping. Instead of simply observing and describing interesting details of the human scene from afar, anthropologists are becoming aware of the serious implications of their research for people's lives. Sensitive topics are now being handled with greater care than they once were. The American Anthropological Association, for instance, is very concerned about information collected by anthropologists and how it is disseminated to the public. The result may be a science that is at the same time more systematic and more humane.

Summary

1. Anthropology is the study of everything human—from our biological origins to how our cultural systems influence our behaviors.

2. Anthropology cuts across the entire liberal arts curriculum, taking other disciplines into sectors of time and space that might otherwise be neglected; it studies people from all times and in all places. It also distinguishes itself from the subjects it overlaps by its *holism* (all-inclusiveness) and its *relativism* (considering people in terms of their own cultures). But some of its own branches and points of view do not mesh well with each other. And in some serious matters, anthropologists feel that they must reveal their value judgments.

3. There are four main branches of anthropology: physical anthropology, archaeology, linguistics, and cultural anthropology.

4. Physical anthropologists traditionally studied a limited range of biological variations in living human populations. But now they study as well the events and processes by which humans have evolved.

5. Archaeologists study extinct human cultures. Using durable fragments of human activities as clues, they devise theories about how people behaved and changed before they began to keep written records.

6. Linguistics—the study of languages—has been adopted by some anthropologists as a way of understanding how cultures work. The language that a people uses may reveal many features of their social life.

7. Cultural anthropologists generally study the understandings about human life and the external world that people in every human group learn from those around them. This understanding—that is, culture—tends to shape everything they do, as well as their beliefs and attitudes. Cultural anthropologists have traditionally studied the "strange" (to us) ways of "exotic" peoples. But today the cultures of these remote and primitive peoples are vanishing as they are touched by the industrial world. The focus of anthropology is, therefore, shifting to urban cultures elsewhere and at home.

PART ONE

Human Biological Evolution

2 An Introduction to Physical Anthropology

PHYSICAL anthropology presently focuses on three central questions: (1) Through what stages has the human species developed to the form that we know today? (2) What is the mechanism that has caused these changes to occur? and (3) What is the nature of ongoing change in living human populations? The organizing principle of physical anthropology is *evolution*—biological change over time.

Because we are human, living within our own limited time span, it is often hard to appreciate the enormous amounts of time involved in evolution. Humans have existed in approximately their present form for the last 40,000 years. Although this may seem like an incomprehensibly long period of time, 40,000 years is but an instant in the millions of years that humans have been evolving and in the billions of years that life on earth has been evolving.

Within this vast time span, nothing has been static. The number and variety of life forms have been changing all the time. This change has not occurred randomly; it has followed a pattern. But it was not until the nineteenth century that the major mechanism of evolution was recognized by naturalists. And Charles Darwin, more than any other, brought to light the nature of this mechanism.

The History of the Theory of Evolution

Early Views of Nature

Theories of evolution were not new when Darwin published *On the Origin of Species* in 1859. In fact, the idea of evolution itself had evolved for over 2,500 years before Darwin's time. Aristotle (384–322 B.C.) believed that new forms of life could arise from old forms. Some kind of intelligent design, he felt, was directing these transformations toward an ideal form. Everything in nature could be arranged in a scale according to how close it came to the ideal. Humans were closest to the ideal, and inorganic matter was farthest from it.

Early commentators of the biblical history of creation were strongly influenced by Aristotle's ideas. Their readings of the Book of Genesis allowed room for the possibility that new species could arise from those first placed on earth by God. But in the seventeenth century a more literal reading of Genesis became accepted not only in the church but also among scientists and lay people in general.

According to the new church doctrine, every form of life now on earth had been shaped during the original creation and had stayed unchanged into the present. The extinction of a species was inconceivable. As in Aristotle's theory, however, all nature was arranged in a scale of perfection. This hierarchy was called the *Scala Naturae,* or the Great Chain of Being. Humans, because of their ability to reason, were placed at the top of the Chain, closest to the divine. Monkeys and apes were placed just below humans, but above simpler animals, plants, and inorganic matter.

The concept of slow change from one form of life to another was not part of this world view, not only because species were thought to be permanent, but also because the world was believed to be only a few thousand years old. In the seventeenth century, James Ussher, archbishop of Armagh, set 4004 B.C. as the date of creation. His date and the *Scala Naturae* were generally accepted until the nineteenth century, although they did not go completely unchallenged.

During the Middle Ages, there was little interest in firsthand observation of nature. Scientific writers were content to base their writings on classical authorities. But in the seventeenth and eighteenth centuries there was a renewed interest in observation. This interest was sparked to some extent by the insistence of the English philosopher Francis Bacon in his book *Novum Organum,* published in 1620, that the *inductive method* be followed in scientific inquiry. This method was a system of reasoning from the facts of observation to generalizations based on those facts. These generalizations, or *hypotheses,* were to be tested by experiment and gradually refined into natural laws.

The inductive method became popular among scientists and gave tremendous impulse to research. First among the observers who followed Bacon was the great Swedish naturalist, Carolus Linnaeus (1707–1778). Linnaeus was intrigued by the steady flow of unknown plants and animals into Europe, a result of greater global exploration. His research led him to develop a *taxonomy,* a system of naming plants and animals and placing them in a series of categories each more inclusive than the one below it. This taxonomy was set forth in the classic *Systema Naturae,* published when Linnaeus was only 28.

Linnaeus's work shows a remarkable blend of traditional belief and brilliant insight. He was the first to classify human beings with monkeys and chimpanzees, showing his awareness of the close physical similarity among them. He did not, however, speculate about a common ancestry. At first Linnaeus accepted the idea that the species were fixed in form. Later, however, he felt that new forms could arise. But it was his earlier view that was well known, and it reinforced the traditional religious notions about natural history. In the long run, however, his taxonomy helped those who followed to see the relationships among different life forms and organize the evidence of evolution.

During the eighteenth century, this evidence was being gathered rapidly in the fields of geology, paleontology (the study of fossilized remains), and comparative anatomy. In speculations that foreshadowed Darwin's theory to a remarkable degree, the Comte de Buffon (1707–1788) drew on this new knowledge. He believed (1) that variations within a species occurred, (2) that the best-adapted individuals would survive in the fight for survival, and (3) that species had evolved from one another. Natural history, he asserted further, must have unfolded over a much longer time span than was generally thought. But because Buffon changed his mind on some of these issues several times, his views were not influential at the time.

Jean-Baptiste de Lamarck (1744–1829) also believed that species evolved from one another. He, however, carefully supported the notion with a comprehensive roadmap of evolution—a sequence of organisms arranged from the least to the most complex. In this scheme a simple common ancestor had gradually given rise to higher forms, until the present diversity of life was reached.

Lamarck is chiefly remembered today not for this bold evolutionary idea, but for his discredited theory that acquired traits could be inherited. He believed that organisms in the course of their life acquired certain characteristics that better adapted them to their surroundings. These traits were then passed on to the next generation. In this way, the characteristics of a species were altered slowly. Lamarck's theory now has few supporters because no one has been able to prove that acquired traits can be passed on.

During the later eighteenth and early nineteenth centuries, geologists were digging up vast numbers of fossils. They found that few living species existed in the fossil record in their present form. To reconcile this evidence of evolution with church doctrine, Georges Cuvier (1769–1832) proposed a theory called *catastrophism.* According to the theory, the earth periodically had been swept by violent upheavals such as floods and volcanoes. These catastrophes killed all existing species, trapping and preserving their remains as fossils. Divine creation then populated the earth with an entirely new set of species, the remains of which were preserved in the next catastrophe.

The English geologist Sir Charles Lyell (1797–1875) was not convinced by catastrophism. His studies of rock layers and the geological processes responsible for them convinced him that there had been no supernatural interventions, and that if any catastrophes had occurred, they were local. In his *Principles of Geology,* published in 1830, he set forth the theory of *uniformitarianism.* According to this theory, the earth always had been shaped and still was being shaped by geological forces such as volcanic action and erosion. These forces acted slowly over long periods of time. This theory directly conflicted with the idea that special divine acts had from time to time radically altered the makeup of the earth.

Because geological forces act so slowly, Lyell reasoned that the earth and the fossils preserved in it must be millions of years old. Although some thinkers before him had felt that the earth was actually older, there had been no way of proving it until now. Lyell's study did much to convince other scientists of the earth's great age and provided the time frame that would be needed for Darwin's theory of evolution by natural selection.

Charles Darwin's Theories

Linnaeus, Buffon, Lamarck, Lyell, and many others contributed important parts of the theory of evolution. But it remained for Charles Darwin (1809–1882), the brilliant observer and generalizer, to put the pieces together in one theory. Darwin not only presented a forceful case that evolution had occurred, he also presented a theory, natural selection, to explain and account for evolutionary change.

Two of the Galápagos islands. Darwin was puzzled by the diversity of life forms in the uniform climate here. (Miguel Castro, Photo Researchers)

Darwin's work was distinguished not only by his ability to generalize but also by the quantity and quality of the evidence with which he supported his hypotheses. Most of his observations were made during his five-year voyage around the world aboard H.M.S. *Beagle.*

We can now see two stages in Darwin's solution to the question of the origin of species. First, he had to show that evolution had taken place—that species evolved from previously existing species. Second, he had to describe the mechanism that caused this transformation of species. On his voyage he managed to solve only the first part of the problem, though the observations he made served as a base for the solution of the second part (Eiseley, 1961).

When the *Beagle* reached South America, Darwin made many long trips into the interior. He noticed as he traveled south from Brazil that certain animal species were replaced by forms only slightly different from those further north. To him, these animals seemed to be local variants of the same species, not the products of separate and independent acts of creation. In Argentina, Darwin found the fossils of huge creatures that shared many features with armadillos living in the area at the time. From this and other evidence, he concluded that new species must emerge from older species that are very similar in form. Lyell's uniformitarianism also seemed correct. Because the fossil forms shared so many traits with the living forms, Darwin discounted the conventional view that episodes of creation had from time to time repopulated the earth with wholly new species.

Although Darwin did not work out the mechanism of evolutionary change on his journey, he found baffling clues in the Galápagos archipelago, a group of volcanic islands in the Pacific, 600 miles west of Ecuador. Darwin had hoped to continue his study of fossils there, but the islands turned out to be cinder heaps newly risen from the ocean floor. So instead of digging for fossils he set to work collecting specimens of animals, plants, insects, and reptiles. Just before Darwin had to leave the islands the vice-governor of the islands pointed out to him that certain animals showed only a slight variation in form from one island to the next. Darwin had not noticed this fact himself, but in the few days before his ship sailed he confirmed it.

The finches, in particular, interested Darwin. They differed greatly in the structure of their beaks. Some had small beaks, like those of warblers. Others had stout, straight beaks, like those of woodpeckers. In all there were 14 distinct species, none of which existed elsewhere in the world.

Darwin had seen this kind of slight variation in form earlier in South America. As he had approached the Galápagos, he had concluded that different climates and natural surroundings somehow molded organisms into different appropriate forms. But here in the Galápagos there was no variation in climate: One island was exactly like another. Yet variation in form persisted (Eiseley, 1961). What, then, had caused the original finch ancestors to diversify in a uniform climate?

Natural Selection. Darwin was to ponder this problem for 20 years after his return from the voyage. His first set of clues came from studying the breeding of domesticated plants and animals, some of which, he observed, bore little resemblance to their ancestors. In order to focus on what caused this change, Darwin turned his attention to domestic pigeons.

He found that when pigeon breeders developed a new strain, they bred only those pigeons with the traits they desired. The breeders followed the same procedure with each following generation—mating those who had features closest to the desired type and eliminating those who did not have features close to the desired form. The products of several generations of this human-directed, artificial selection differed considerably from their ancestors.

Darwin observed that individual variation occurred in natural populations as well as in domesticated ones, and he reasoned that some sort of *natural selection* must cause evolutionary change. He used the term *natural* to mean that the selective process does not occur by human choice, as is the case with the artificial selection process used by breeders. Some force in nature allowed certain members of a species to reproduce and discouraged others.

Darwin continued to look into the available literature on the subject of variation. He happened to be reading Thomas Malthus (1766–1834) when he found the insight he needed. In his "Essay on Population," Malthus, an economist, foresaw a "struggle for existence" among future humans. He projected a vision of future generations of humans racked by problems caused by an ever-increasing population with a limited food supply. Darwin immediately applied this idea to nonhuman populations. In nature, he observed, populations tend to increase their numbers. If every breeding pair produced two young to replace it, population size would remain constant. However, most organisms known to Darwin produced many more than two offspring. Some of these died quickly because they were born with fatal defects. Others were killed by predators. Still other members of the population died before they could reproduce because they lost out in the competition for limited resources such as food and water.

In each generation, he concluded, a slightly higher percentage of the well-adapted individuals survived. And as the characteristics favoring survival are passed on gradually from generation to generation, they become more common. The unfavorable traits become less common because the individuals that have them are less likely to survive. Over many generations, these slow alterations would produce major evolutionary changes.

In 1859 Darwin published these theories in his classic work, *On the Origin of Species.* He was spurred to publish his findings when Alfred Wallace (1823–1913), another English naturalist, reached many of the same conclusions on his own and communicated them to Darwin in a letter. Darwin's concept of natural selection can be broken down into five major points:

1. Organisms produce more offspring than can survive to reproduce.
2. Since the number of individuals in a species is more or less constant, there must be a high deathrate.
3. Individuals vary in their characteristics; they are not identical.
4. Variations that make individuals more suited to the environment will ensure their survival. Those organisms that survive will pass on their characteristics to future generations.
5. Future generations will possess and continue to modify the adaptations that came about by gradual changes in their ancestors.

The Descent of Humans. Darwin stopped short of applying the concept of natural selection to human beings. He realized that humans had evolved from more primitive forms and that these same forms probably also gave rise to the apes. But, preferring solitude and peace, he let others defend evolution in the enormous controversy with the church and conservative scientists.

Twelve years after publication of the *Origin,* Darwin finally set forth in *The Descent of Man* (1871) his position on the question of human ancestry. Drawing on comparative anatomy, Darwin described the probable common ancestor of humans and apes as a "hairy, tailed quadruped, probably arboreal in its habits." Ultimately, he said, humans descended from minute organisms living in the dim obscurity of the past (Darwin, 1871).

Darwin based his conclusions on three arguments. First, he believed that nature forms a continuum from simple to complex forms, with human beings as the most complex. Second, he gathered evidence from comparative anatomy to prove that structural similarities linked human beings closely to some animals and more distantly to others. And third, he believed that the mental, emotional, and even moral qualities of human beings also exist in animals, though to a lesser degree.

In time, new evidence modified but did not disprove Darwin's theories. When he first published his theories, however, his concept of evolution and its application to humans were weakened by two flaws. First there was very little fossil evidence of forms that were ancestors of humans to show that humans had evolved. And second, nothing was known about how traits are passed on from one generation to the next. Since Darwin's time, research into genetics has given insights into inheritance. And excavation carried on by physical anthropologists and others has brought to light more and more fossilized remains of the creatures that once populated our evolutionary past.

The Rise of Physical Anthropology

The ability to describe the human body precisely was developing rapidly while Darwin was piecing together his theory of evolution. When the *Origin* generated a desire to find fossil evidence of our ancestors, *anthropometry,* the study of the measurements of the human body, proved basic. In order to place one fossil in relation to others, exact comparisons were necessary.

Physical anthropology emerged from anthropometry in the eighteenth century. Its purpose was to find certain physical characteristics by which all living humans could be grouped into races. Linnaeus had established four basic groups on the basis of skin color and geographic origin. But because skin color was shown to fall into an infinite number of intermediate shades, it was not a useful criterion of race. In the early nineteenth century, Johann Friedrich Blumenbach (1752–1840) stressed the shape of the skull in addition to skin color, hair, and body build. He began the science of *craniometry,* the descriptive analysis of skulls. Later anthropometrists refined the science by taking into fuller account certain facial angles and skull contours.

By the end of the nineteenth century, dependence on measures of the skull came under strong attack. Several scientists pointed out that certain head shapes were common to many widely separated groups of people, as were many other physical features. Brown skin, small size, and narrow heads, for instance, typified not only Iberians, but also Berbers, Sicilians, and southern Greeks (Voget, 1975).

In this country, physical anthropologists have developed better methods of measurement, and, as we shall see, they began to develop ways to study previously unexplored aspects of anatomy. The effort to define racial groups did not make much progress. There were almost as many different ways to group humans as there were physical anthropologists. By the end of the nineteenth century, however, the skills of anthropometry were proving valuable in another area.

Fossil Evidence for Human Evolution

A major weakness of Darwin's theory, as you will recall, was the lack of fossil data. The first well-publicized find of fossil humanlike remains was a skeleton found in 1856 in a cave in the Neander Valley of Germany. This so-called Neandertal skeleton presented a striking contrast to modern humans, and for a time status as an ancestor of humans was denied. The volume of the skull, or cranial capacity, was small, and enormous brow ridges made it seem more animal than human. Proof that humans had evolved from primitive forms would have to wait for something more convincing than this.

Excitement was great in 1891 when *Pithecanthropus,* commonly called Java Man, was discovered. The cranial capacity of this skull, placed at 900 cc, was 300 cc greater than the highest recorded for the gorilla and not far below the minimum for modern human skulls. These and many other measurements led, after much debate, to the conclusion that *Pithecanthropus* fell somewhere between all known apes and the Neandertals, the remains of which had been turning up in greater numbers at various sites in Europe.

During the twentieth century, as we shall see in Chapters 7 and 8, thousands of human and humanlike fossils have been uncovered. The task of describing and comparing this material often fell to anthropometrically-trained physical anthropologists. Today more and more physical anthropologists specialize in interpreting the human fossil record. This material has strongly confirmed Darwin's belief that we have evolved from an apelike creature.

The Contribution of Genetics

The second major weakness of Darwin's theory was his inability to explain how traits are inherited. Unfortunately, he was unaware that an Austrian monk, Gregor Mendel (1822–1884), had solved the problem in 1865. But Darwin was not alone in passing over Mendel's work. Mendel's findings gathered dust in a few libraries until 1900.

The early geneticists, building on Mendel's work, tended to explain all variations in nature in terms of large-scale mutations—sudden changes in genes, the factors that Mendel suggested controlled physical traits. These scientists paid little notice to any role for natural selection in evolution. Instead, they believed that some unknown force directed a series of mutations to bring about rapid change in a species.

Population Genetics and the Synthetic Theory of Evolution. By the 1920s Darwinian evolution and Mendelian genetics seemed to be in direct conflict. Darwin had identified the whole population as his unit of study. Mendelian geneticists, on the other hand, focused on individuals. The study of *population genetics,* however, began to resolve this impasse in the early 1930s. Biologists took a new interest in Darwin and applied modern statistical and experimental methods to the level at which evolutionary processes work—the *population.* A population is an interbreeding group of relatively similar individuals that share the same environment. It was therefore recognized that the pool of genes held by the population as a whole was the right thing to study in order to understand evolutionary change.

Population geneticists explain evolution as change in gene frequencies over time in the gene pool of a population. Natural selection increases the frequency of those genes that help the organism survive to reproduce. In addition to change shaped by environmental factors, two other models of how changes in gene frequency can occur were constructed by population geneticists: *gene flow* and *genetic drift.* Both are random processes of evolution that do not necessarily adapt the organism to its environment. We will discuss these processes in more detail in later chapters.

How do today's scientists explain evolution? Surprisingly, there is general agreement on a theory of evolution that combines, or synthesizes, the theories we have just discussed (natural selection, Mendelian genetics, mutation theory, and population genetics. This combination is called the *synthetic,* or NeoDarwinian, *theory of evolution.*

The New Physical Anthropology

Up until the 1950s, physical anthropology was mainly descriptive in nature. For over a century it had been refining ways of measuring and thereby describing the human body. At the end of the nineteenth century it had begun to apply this expertise to the description of our fossil ancestors. Today, the traditional descriptive work continues, though it is a much smaller part of the field. Bones and teeth have been of continuing interest to physical anthropologists, but new techniques have expanded the traditional descriptive range. X-rays, for example, have made analysis of the internal structures of teeth and bones possible. Physical anthropologists also study body composition and build as well as human growth. Much of their descriptive work continues to be of value to designers who need to know the range of human variability for human engineering projects such as public transportation.

Despite physical anthropology's limited, descriptive scope in the early years and the fact that relatively few persons have specialized in the field, it has become highly diversified in its approach to human biology.

The synthetic theory has been a major force behind much of this change. Before this theory, physical anthropologists could compare in great detail the bones of every known human ancestor with one another and with those of modern humans. But they had little idea of how to study the evolutionary processes involved in changing from one form to the next. The synthetic theory provided the chance to apply a refined knowledge of how evolution works to the study of humans. As you will see, physical anthropologists have begun to study mutation, genetic drift, gene flow, and natural selection in modern-day human populations. They presently use the mathematical models of population genetics to analyze patterns of variation in traits such as blood type. They are also studying the anatomy and behavior of monkeys and apes for clues to our own evolution. And, finally, physical anthropologists, seeing fossils through the eyes of population geneticists, now regard them as the remains of members of ancient populations and apply insights gotten from studying modern populations.

Today the work of physical anthropologists can be divided into three basic categories: paleoanthropology, primatology, and the study of modern human variation.

Paleoanthropology

Paleoanthropology, or human paleontology, is the study of fossils relevant to the evolution of humans. Fossils supply the only direct evidence of what our ancestors looked like and how they walked and ate. Only fossils could have told us that the rate of human evolution has not been constant. Bursts of change have followed periods of relative stability. And only fossils could have indicated the general sequence of our bodily evolution. Fossils have shown, for instance, that our legs took their present shape long before our heads did.

The search for fossils can be quite difficult. In recent years workers combing the Afar Desert of Ethiopia, one of the world's most desolate areas, have had to endure constant 120° temperatures. Excavators sometimes have to deal also with volatile political situations, almost inaccessible sites, and a shortage of funds needed to carry on their work.

As they interpret the fossil record, paleoanthropologists try to identify the forces that have effected the evolution of humans. In doing so, they look for both biological factors (interaction with the physical environment) and cultural factors (interaction with the social environment), both of which have influenced the changes in the human body.

Any attempts to explain the course of biological evolution must take into account the development of tools, hunting, fire, and the construction of shelter, all of which, in effect, created a new environment. When humans began to change their environment, they profoundly affected their own biological evolution. Moreover, certain biological changes were probably so closely linked with the development of culture that elements of both evolved at the same time. Early increases in brain size and complexity probably resulted from the selective advantage of toolmaking. Yet more complex tools would have been impossible without the intellectual power to design and make them. Because the interaction between culture and biology can be so important, excavators must look carefully for both kinds of evidence as they dig.

Once a fossil has been uncovered, paleoanthropologists must try to place it chronologically in relation to other fossils. Only then can they make further inferences about the sequence of change through which our ancestors have gone. Establishing the correct sequence can be tricky. On what basis, for example, can we say that a given fossil is closer than another to modern humans? Scientists have tried to answer this question by defining features common to all members of our *lineage,* the line of our descent from the earliest human-like animals. But lists of such features are always controversial, as is their application to actual fossil remains.

Aside from defining humanness, two kinds of problems hinder the interpretation of fossils: (1) The fossil record may be incomplete, and (2) dating may be inaccurate or impossible.

Though large gaps remain in the fossil record, evidence is being gathered more quickly than ever before. Fifteen years ago the known remains of *Ramapithecus,* possibly a transitional form from apelike creatures to those more closely resembling humans, consisted of about a dozen fossils. Now there are close to 40 fossils (Simons, 1977). Despite the recent deluge of new data, however, fossils of humanlike forms dating from between about 4 to 8 million years are limited to a few teeth. This period is especially crucial because it is possible that during this time the human lineage was diverging from that of the apes. Fossils from this span would be extremely welcome and could very well be uncovered in the near future.

Incomplete fossils add to the problem because guesswork is necessary in reconstructing them. Bones that have been deformed by geological processes or are fragmentary invite misleading interpretations of both their relation to other fossils and their function in the animal.

Before the development of modern dating methods, paleoanthropologists had no way of determining the absolute age of a given fossil. If two fossils were found in different layers of the earth, scientists could only say that one was relatively older than the other. As we will discuss in Chapter 6, modern techniques can now determine the age of a rock with a margin of error of only a few percent, making possible an accurate time scale for the evolution of all life from its beginnings. Other methods such as flourine and nitrogen dating allow scientists to pinpoint whether two fossils found near each other are of the same age. Each of these latter methods can, however, be used only to date materials from limited time ranges, and only under certain geologic conditions. To compensate, new methods are continually being developed.

The enthusiasm generated by paleoanthropologists such as Louis Leakey and his son Richard has led to the excavation of a great many humanlike fossils. There has been a particularly substantial increase in information for the period between 2 to 4 million years ago. Quite often, new pieces of evidence require changes in our theories about how humans evolved. This makes paleoanthropology one of the most dynamic and intriguing subfields in anthropology.

The Study of Primatology

Primatology is the study of our closest nonhuman relatives—the great apes, monkeys, and primitive animals called prosimians. It is the only possible source of certain kinds of information about our ancestors. *Comparative anatomy,* the systematic comparison of bodily structures, provides the knowledge necessary to reconstruct entire animals from fossil fragments. It also supplies a basis for inferences about the nature of the creatures living in periods unrepresented by fossils. By observing how the other primates eat and move, we can better interpret from fossils how our more apelike ancestors performed these functions. Finally, by looking closely at what other primates do, we can identify not only those behaviors that all members of the order share, but also those that are unique to humans. By isolating what makes us different from the

Beatrice Gardner, a primatologist, teaches symbols to Washoe, a chimp who showed many of the elements of linguistic communication. (Photo courtesy of R. A. and B. T. Gardner)

other members of the primate order, we can make progress toward a definition of what it means to be human.

Comparative Anatomy. The history of human evolution is the history of cumulative change. Thus, the physical traits that we call human are really modifications of an already elaborate primate inheritance. To get a sense of our origins, we must be able to separate primate characteristics from the traits that are unique to our lineage. We can begin to do this by comparing our anatomy with that of the nonhuman primates. Dissection, for example, has supplied detailed information on the anatomy of gorillas and chimpanzees. Anatomists also have exact knowledge of the bodies of modern humans. This anatomical knowledge is essential to understanding whether a given fossil leg bone, for example, belongs to a human ancestor, an ape ancestor, or a common ancestor.

Anthropologists and comparative anatomists often try to reconstruct the appearance of extinct animals from incomplete fossils. This kind of reconstruction can be done only by anthropologists who know enough about anatomy to be familiar with the muscles and soft tissues of living animals.

Comparative anatomy gives us one picture of how the various members of the primate order emerged. In the 1960s a new approach to understanding evolutionary relationships between living primates was developed. Researchers began to compare the structure of hemoglobins and serum proteins in different primates. By assuming that the changes in these molecules have occurred at a constant rate through time, some researchers feel that they can estimate how long it has been since the primates last shared a common ancestor. The *phylogeny,* or history of the evolution of a group of genetically-related organisms, constructed by Vincent Sarich and Allan Wilson in the 1960s agrees in most respects with that put together on the basis of the fossil record. They have found, for instance, that human blood molecules are most similar to those of apes, confirming their status as our closest relatives.

The Significance of Primate Behavior. If we were to encounter one of our early ancestors on the street we would judge its humanity more by the way it acted than by the way it looked. We would want to know, for example, whether the creature could speak or had a primate communication system of sounds, postures, and facial expressions. Behavior, in effect, has become just as important as anatomy as a criterion of classification. By understanding the relationships between anatomical structure and behavior, paleoanthropologists can make inferences about the locomotion and feeding habits of a fossil animal. Unfortunately, the important aspects of social behavior do not fossilize. For these behaviors, we must rely entirely on our knowledge of living primates. If today's nonhuman primates share certain behaviors with humans, the inference can be made that our humanlike ancestors also possessed them.

When relating modern primate behavior to animals that are no longer living, anthropologists have always recognized the need for caution. It might be attractive to suggest that the animals we call *Ramapithecus* behaved exactly like chimpanzees. But we must realize that these are two different animal forms, each with its unique biological and behavioral characteristics. Therefore, living primate behavior can only be used as a broad model for what might have been.

Today, anthropology's knowledge of primates comes from two kinds of studies: field and laboratory. In the field, observers record what animals do—when, where, and for how long. They also note how animals behave in groups and how individuals and groups respond to one another as well as to changes in their environment. Back in the laboratory, workers ideally can refine these observations under controlled conditions. Manipulation of environmental conditions, impossible in the wild, is the basis of laboratory work.

Sociobiologists are pursuing another line of research into primate behavior. These scientists assume that any persistent behavior in a population must increase the chances that its members will survive. Behavior, like physical features, will survive only if it increases the organism's chances of survival. Sociobiologists therefore study the behavior of primates with an eye toward its adaptive value.

Primatology and a Definition of Humanness. In the course of observing nonhuman primate anatomy and behavior, a central goal has been to define what makes us different from them. The intense study of primates in recent years has shown that many attributes once thought to be unique to humans are widespread among the primates. In the past, humans were often distinguished on the basis of their ability to use tools and communicate with symbols. This definition had to be modified, however, when researchers observed that chimpanzees also use tools and communicate with symbols. Jane Goodall saw chimpanzees using twigs to get termites out of mounds. Recently chimpanzees and gorillas have been taught American Sign Language, a type of symbolic system. They have learned the meanings of these symbols, used them to convey meanings outside the context in which the symbols were first learned, learned some grammatical rules, and expressed new meanings by putting the symbols together in new combinations. We have therefore come to understand that our uniqueness lies more in the way we rely on certain basic primate behaviors than it does in having unique characteristics.

The Study of Human Variation

The study of how contemporary populations differ from one another is the third major area of physical anthropology. Research in this area has sought to understand the processes of evolution in human populations.

Much of the early work in physical anthropology consisted of descriptive studies, not only of the ancestors of humans but also of living groups. Variations in body build and tooth and skull shape were described in populations around the world. The motivation behind a great deal of this work was to define races by discovering the physical traits shared by the members of each race. Though this concept of race is now discounted by most experts, descriptive studies have made, and continue to make, significant contributions to our knowledge of human variation. Today, in fact, researchers often test theories about the process of evolution in particular cases by drawing on data from the descriptive studies.

Humans vary physically from each other in an almost infinite number of ways. Some human characteristics are controlled by a small number of genes *(simple genetic traits)*. Many more are controlled by a large number of genes *(complex genetic traits)*.

The structure of certain proteins is the result of simple genetic control. Only a few genes control the making of the amino acids that combine to form proteins such as hemoglobin. One or more of these genes may exist in an alternative form that produces a protein with a variant structure. Chemical analysis of the blood reveals which form is present. Because simple genetic traits are either present or absent, it is easy to map their frequency. By charting such traits, human biologists are able to study the action of mutation, genetic drift, gene flow, and natural selection in human populations.

Complex genetic traits, such as height or skin color, are controlled by the interaction of a large number of genes. The study of these traits is complicated further by the fact that the environment often strongly affects how these traits are expressed. Poor nutrition, for example, may hinder growth. Good nutrition might allow an organism to grow to the upper limit of its genetic potential. The genes, in effect, set limits in complex traits, within which environmental change can occur.

The most basic problem in the studies of complex traits (sometimes called human adaptability studies) is to sort out the effects of genetic control from those of the environment. Take, for example, traits among populations exposed to high altitudes over the course of thousands of years. Anthropologists have found that high-altitude dwellers tend to have larger chests, greater lung capacity, and slower skeletal growth than is typical of sea-level populations (Lasker, 1969). Recent research has shown that these traits are related to long-term developmental adjustments to the low-oxygen content of the air in the mountains. They probably are not caused by genetic factors.

Osteological Studies. Anthropologists can also, to a limited extent, study variations among prehistoric human populations by analyzing their bones. This study is called *osteology*. Like the rest of physical anthropology, this kind of human variation study has been influenced deeply by the interest in population genetics and the mechanism of evolutionary change.

For decades before the mid-1950s, osteology was a mainstay of physical anthropology. The anthropometrists of the nineteenth and early twentieth centuries, using their calipers and measuring tapes, generated a huge mass of data. They were interested not only in making racial classifications but also in tracing the evolution of racial groups through time.

Modern osteologists have begun to apply the synthetic theory, and population genetics in particular, to their studies. New models are making it possible to describe ancient populations in statistical terms. Because sex and age usually can be determined from bones, it is possible to calculate sex ratios, average life span, and birth and death rates for prehistoric populations.

Patterns of disease, which often leave traces in the bones, also are being studied. Variations in height and robustness, resemblance between parents and offspring, and differing forms of soft tissue can be inferred from bones as well.

Bones also carry a surprising amount of genetic information. Some dental characteristics, such as shovel-shaped incisors, are thought to be simple genetic traits. Blood type, another simple trait, may be learned by close analysis of pieces of bone. Because these traits are much more easily studied than complex traits, osteologists can use them to begin to reconstruct certain aspects of ancient gene pools. As in modern populations, the effects of gene flow, mutation, and genetic drift can be identified, though to a much lesser degree. Since only a portion of a population's original characteristics remains in its bones, evidence for any conclusions is limited.

The study of the skeletal hallmarks of age, sex, and other characteristics also have application in forensic (legal) medicine. Physical anthropologists who specialize in osteology are frequently called upon to make identifications in medical-legal cases.

The Present Evolution of Human Beings

For millions of years, nature molded the genetic makeup of human beings. But when our ancestors began to develop culture, they began to organize the environment to suit their needs. By modifying the effect of the environment, human beings began to exert control over the direction of their own evolution. In fact, some people argue that culture in the twentieth century has completely neutralized natural selection. Although this is an extreme position, most scientists agree that modern technology has a great impact on human biology.

The link between biology and culture has never been more apparent than in modern, industrialized societies. Our technology helps implement important social values. Our desire to ensure a healthy life to everyone, for instance, has stimulated the growth of medical technology. Phenylketonuria, a disease that causes severe mental retardation, is now known to be controlled by a single mutant gene that prevents the body from processing protein normally. All children presently born in America are screened for this disease. If they have it, it is easily corrected by diet. The possessors of the gene that controls the disease suffer no disadvantage in the environment our culture has created for them. They survive and reproduce as well as anyone else.

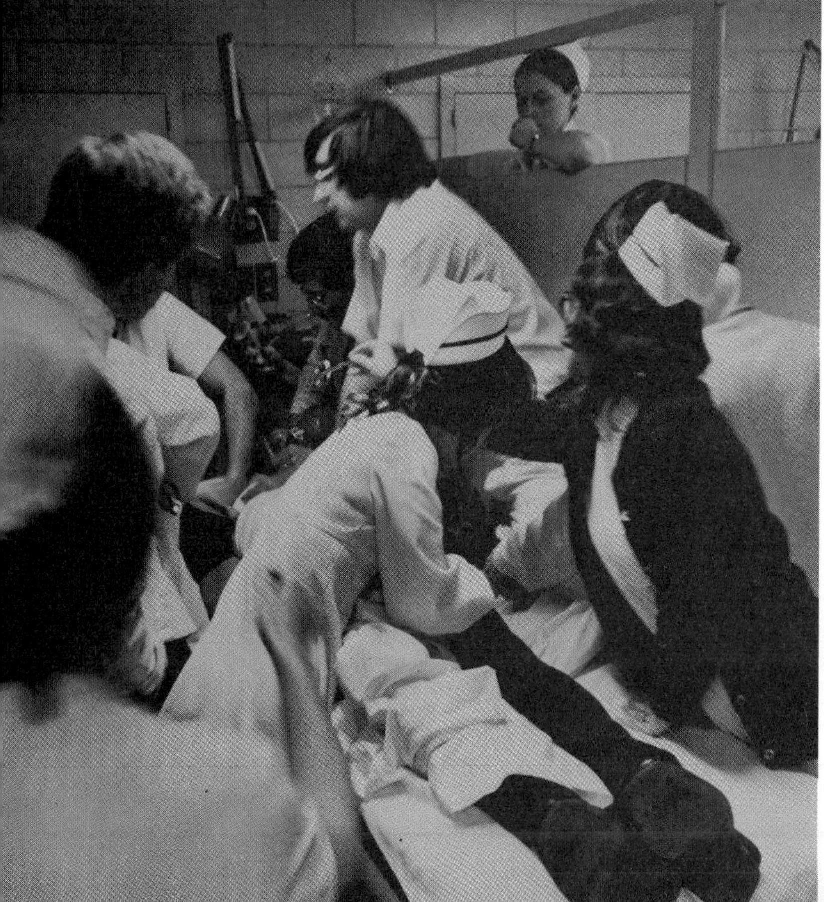

To an increasing degree, culture is replacing nature as a selective agent. Here medical technology allows a victim of a cardiac arrest to survive. (Dan Budnik, Woodfin Camp)

The biological result of our ability to treat the disease is an increase in the frequency of the gene within the population.

Most people are aware of the great advantages of petrochemicals such as pesticides. By allowing us to control insects, they help produce the abundant food supply upon which Americans have come to depend. Yet it is also true that many pesticides can cause mutations or cancer. Many scientists feel that the potential effect of these chemicals on human biology will be significant unless they are controlled. The petrochemical industry argues that by controlling use one runs the risk of limiting food production.

This is the kind of dilemma that will confront us more and more as we gain fuller control over nature. As we reduce nature's impact, it becomes increasingly possible to direct our own evolution. But in so doing, we assume a tremendous responsibility in applying values to decisions concerning survival. Resolving the problems posed by the use of pesticides in agriculture is but one of the biologically significant dilemmas of modern society.

Summary

1. *Physical anthropology* is the study of the events and processes of human *evolution,* the change of human biology over a period of time.

2. The idea that one form of life can evolve from another dates back to early Greek thinkers. Church doctrine of the seventeenth century, however, arranged nature in a hierarchy of unchanging species, called the *Scala Naturae.* In the eighteenth and nineteenth centuries, Linnaeus, Buffon, Lamarck, Lyell, and many others worked out parts of the modern theory of evolution.

3. Darwin, however, first put the pieces together in a single work *(The Origin of Species),* demonstrating that evolution had taken place and describing the mechanism responsible for this change.

4. *Natural selection* is the mechanism of change Darwin described. Individuals compete for survival. Those with certain characteristics survive to breed while those with other traits are eliminated. As the traits favoring survival are passed on from generation to generation, they gradually become more common, and unfavorable characteristics become less common. Over a long period of time, these gradual changes produce major evolutionary trends.

5. Darwin could not explain how traits are passed from one generation to the next. Nor could he cite fossil evidence that humans had evolved from more primitive forms.

6. Early physical anthropologists became adept at measuring variations in the human body in the unsuccessful attempt to define the characteristics of racial groups. Later they became involved in the search for, and analysis of, fossil evidence of human evolution.

7. Mendel and the early geneticists explained inheritance in terms of processes occurring within the cell nucleus.

8. *Population genetics* applied statistical and experimental methods to the level at which evolutionary processes work—the *population.* Population genetics interpreted evolution as a change over time of *gene frequencies* in the *gene pool.* The combination of two random models of change—*drift* and *flow*—and Darwinian natural selection, Mendelian genetics, and mutation theory is called the *synthetic theory* of evolution.

9. Today, the work of physical anthropologists can be divided into three basic categories: paleoanthropology, primatology, and the study of human variation.

10. *Paleoanthropology,* the study of fossils relevant to human evolution, attempts to place fossils in the correct time sequence and

identify the biological and cultural influences on human evolution.

11. *Primatology,* the study of nonhuman primates, is a unique source of data about how structure relates to function in fossil bones.

12. The *study of human variation* attempts to trace evolutionary processes in modern human populations. Both *simple* and *complex genetic traits* are studied. *Osteology* attempts to study the same processes in ancient populations by analyzing bones for genetic and demographic information.

13. Today, culture is replacing nature as the agent of selection, and as nature's control is reduced, it becomes increasingly possible to direct our own evolution.

3 Ecology, Adaptation, and Evolution

As physical anthropologists began to study human evolution, they found it necessary to define precisely the relationships between humans and the environments in which they live. Human biology, they discovered, is influenced not only by nonliving environmental features such as temperature, sunlight, and precipitation, but also by the living features—the organisms with which humans share an area. Microorganisms that depend on human hosts for part or all of their life cycle, for example, often cause serious illness. Certain plants and animals are particularly important because they serve as food: They provide the energy the body needs to move, grow, and reproduce.

Among humans and many other animals, these environmental relationships are complicated by nonbiological, learned behavior. Among humans, this behavior is especially elaborate, and forms a network of values, symbols, and organizations commonly referred to as *culture.* Culture structures perception of the environment, production of the material necessities of life, division of labor, and the procurement and distribution of food. By manipulating the environment through our culture, we can change it radically. Such changes may have great effects on the human body and its evolution. Shelter and clothing can alleviate the stresses of climate. Agricultural technology can reduce forests to grasslands and produce gardens out of deserts. Industrial technology, while making us able to exploit almost all of the world's environments, also produces byproducts that can be devastating to the survival of many life forms, including, possibly, our own.

Any environmentally-oriented study of the human condition, therefore, must see humans as both cultural and biological beings. Often, however, human culture and human biology have been studied separately. Each, in turn, has been further subdivided into many specialized fields. The study of human culture is approached by sociology, economics, history, geography, law, and religion in addition to anthropology. One need only look at a list of social science and humanities departments at a university to see how diversified knowledge of human culture has become. The same tendency occurs in the study of human biology. Genetics, cytology, physiology, epidemiology, and many other specialized approaches have diversified the field considerably.

These specialized studies have produced enormous amounts of information. Unfortunately, this information is not always accessible to others. Each discipline tends to have a special set of assumptions, theories, techniques, and jargon that often makes the communication of knowledge among disciplines difficult. Anthropology is no exception to this tendency, though the special task of explaining human biological and cultural evolution has always led some anthropologists to try to unify many of these subfields in one body of theory. One of the most promising of these unified approaches is ecology. *Ecology* is the study of relationships among all aspects of living and nonliving environments. It provides a theoretical umbrella under which it is possible to bring the environmental sciences, the biological sciences, the social sciences, and evolutionary theory. Because scientists in specialized fields are beginning to use the same principles and concepts, there is a growing body of ecologically-oriented information that can be applied by anthropologists to the understanding of human evolution.

Ecological Definitions of the Environment

Ecologists make a basic distinction between the *abiotic* (or nonliving) part of the environment and the *biotic* (or living) part of the environment. The abiotic environment includes features such as temperature, precipitation, humidity, soil types, and solar radiation. The biotic environment includes all living things, from the smallest microorganisms to the tallest trees and the largest animals. Because we are concerned here with humans and human evolution, we will focus on the abiotic and biotic features of *terrestrial* (or land-based) environments, rather than on *marine* (or sea-based) environments.

Abiotic Features

Because ecologists are interested in the relation between the living and nonliving things in an area, they study those abiotic features of an area that affect the biotic features. Not all the abiotic features of an area affect the life that exists in it to the same degree. Some elements of the soil, for instance, may not be used directly by every organism to carry on its life function. Of those abiotic features that do affect life forms, some may be more important than others in determining how well living organisms can survive in an area, and, indeed, whether they can live there at all. Abiotic features, by their scarcity or overabundance, structure the *biotic diversity*—the number of different kinds of life forms in an area. Two basic principles are used to understand the effect of abiotic features on biotic diversity.

The first principle was developed in the 1840s by Baron Justus von Liebig (1830–1873), a German chemist. Basically, it states that the number and diversity of life forms depend on the essential geophysical element that is present in the least quantity. This principle is sometimes referred to as Liebig's Law of the Minimum. This law was modified slightly in the early twentieth century to allow for the fact that the abundance of one factor may offset the scarcity of another. Today, most ecologists study the interaction of factors that limits the diversity of life (Boughey, 1973).

The second principle was developed in 1913 by V. E. Shelford (1877–1968), an American animal ecologist. He studied a whole range of factors that are as harmful to life forms when they are overabundant as when they are too scarce. He theorized that each abiotic factor can be limiting to life in both high and low concentrations. Between these extremes lies a range—sometimes called the limits of tolerance—in which life forms normally exist (Boughey, 1973; Valentine, 1973).

The abiotic features that most commonly affect the diversity of life include temperature, precipitation, soil composition, wind, solar radiation, and, less often, fire.

Temperature. Most organisms, plants included, have fairly narrow temperature ranges within which they are able to carry out vital life processes. Among animals, mammals have the broadest temperature tolerance because of metabolic characteristics that permit them to maintain constant body temperatures in a number of different environments. In humans, death will occur rapidly if internal temperatures fall to 82°F or rise to 106°F. But with protection in the form of clothes and shelter, our range has expanded to include almost every terrestrial ecosystem in the world.

Precipitation. Hail, sleet, rain, and snow comprise another limiting factor. Because all living things are made up of large amounts of water (80 percent of human weight is water), it is essential that access to water be fairly continual (Shepro, Belanarich, & Levy, 1974). In environments with too little water, life forms are scarce. However, abundant water does not necessarily ensure an abundance of life. In cold, wet environments life may be just as scarce as in hot, dry environments. Because both warmth and moisture are so essential for life, the most diverse terrestrial ecosystems are those of the tropical rain forest.

Solar Radiation. Ultimately, the sun provides the energy for all life on earth. Green plants convert solar radiation by means of photosynthesis into carbohydrates, proteins, and lipids, all of which are stored in the leaves. This energy is then consumed by animals, which are incapable of using solar energy directly. In the Arctic and Antarctic, the absence of sunlight for long periods of time restricts the amount of plant life. This in turn limits the diversity of animal life.

Soil. Soils vary in terms of texture (determined by the proportions of silt, sand, clays, etc.), acidity or alkalinity, moisture, air, mineral content, and the amount of organic matter. Because the growth and reproduction of plants depend on these soil characteristics, the diversity of plant life varies from soil to soil. Moisture is a very important feature. In dry areas moisture evaporates quickly, leaving behind minerals in the topsoil. The fertility of these soils can be maintained over long periods. In more humid areas, however, where water filters down to the water table, minerals are drained away from the topsoil, making it less fertile.

Wind. Differences in the frequency and speed of winds can change the effects of both moisture and temperature. In a dry area wind can blow away fertile topsoil. Wind currents can also dry an area so that the effect of precipitation is minimized. Air currents also make the effective temperature colder than the actual temperature. Life forms are therefore scarcer in cold, windy areas than in areas that are just cold.

Fire. Started by lightning and volcanic activity, fire has probably long been a common feature in many environments. Indeed, the biotic features of some environments are structured by the presence of fire. In the chaparrals of the American west coast, the seeds of some cone-bearing trees are not released until the cones have been partly destroyed by fire. The burned areas of the ground then form fertile beds in which the new plants grow well. Naturally, the effects of fire will be made worse by the presence or absence of other abiotic factors, mainly moisture and wind.

It should be obvious in our discussion that single limiting factors are less common than are interactions of factors that limit life. The scarcity of life in the Antarctic and Arctic is due to a combination of cold temperatures, high winds, sometimes low moisture, and the absence of solar radiation for long periods of time. Deserts are created by the lack of moisture, easily leached soils, and, sometimes, drying winds.

Microenvironments

As already pointed out, if humans had no clothes or shelter, they could only live in the tropical and subtropical areas of the world. The fact that humans are biologically best adjusted to these areas may reflect our origins in tropical regions. We can survive in temperate as well as in extremely hot and cold areas only because we can use culture to restructure the environments in which we live. Environments that have been changed in this way are often referred to as *microenvironments.* Interestingly, the microenvironment that we try to create is tropical. The warm reindeer-fur clothing that arctic Laplanders wear in winter gives very effective protection against the cold, even when people remain still for hours in subfreezing temperatures. The human microenvironment inside the fur clothing is such that temperatures next to the skin are the same as they would be in a tropical environment (Schollander et al., 1957).

Humans are not the only animals that create microenvironments. When birds build nests or moles burrow into the ground, they also create microenvironments. Humans, however, have the greatest potential for environmental modification and tend to rely on their microenvironmental adjustments more than on biological adaptability.

The Biotic Hierarchy

Ecologists arrange the biotic environment in a series of categories, each of which includes all the categories below it. (See Figure 1.)

The Individual. At the most basic level the focus is on the individual. The study of the growth and aging of the individual, its interactions with organisms in the same group and with those in other groups, and its functioning in relation to abiotic features is sometimes called *autecology.* These characteristics are used to define an individual's environmental *ecospace*—the biotic and abiotic range within which the individual can live (Valentine, 1973). Although each human has an ecospace, no two ecospaces are totally identical because the genetic factors involved in sexual reproduction give each individual a unique biologi-

Figure 1 The biotic hierarchy.
A group of interbreeding individuals living in the same area make up a population. The populations in a definable area make up a community, which, along with all other communities, is part of the biosphere.

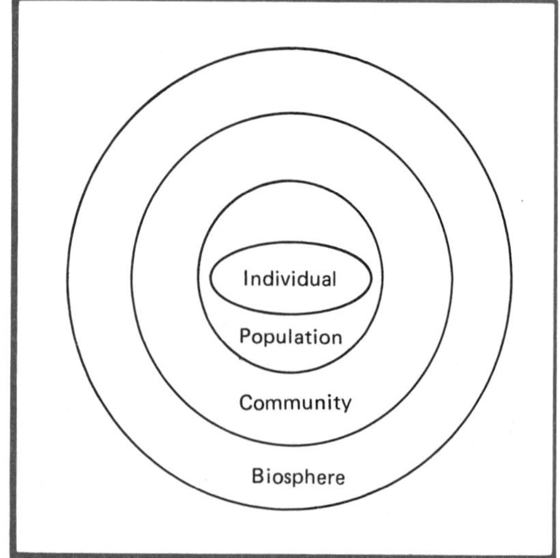

cal nature. Each individual's metabolic activity, immunological system, and bodily proportions (height, weight, muscle mass, amount of body fat, etc.) are unique. In addition, the interaction between heredity and environment that occurs as humans develop gives each individual a unique behavioral profile. Since these factors are part of the definition of *ecospace,* some humans' ecospaces will be better suited to cold environments, others to hot environments, and still others may be poorly structured in both environments. The fact that each individual has a slightly different potential for surviving in different environments is important to evolution. As you have learned, individual differences in survival and reproductive capacity are the basis of biological evolution by natural selection.

The Population. Closely related individuals are studied as a *population*—a group of animals living in the same area and mating almost exclusively with each other. This causes them to be reproductively isolated from other animals in the same environment, although they may mate with members of similar populations nearby.

The makeup of populations is not static. They grow when the birthrate is greater than the deathrate, remain the same when the birth- and deathrates are equal, or decrease when the deathrate is greater than the birthrate. The biological characteristics of their members may change as the result of evolution, and a single population may even give rise to several new ones.

Population ecology studies the interactions of the population as a unit with other populations in the same area, as well as with the important abiotic features of that area. A population can be defined in terms of its *econiche* (*niche* for short). The niche is the sum of all the interactions occurring between a population and its biotic and abiotic environments. The BaMbuti Pygmies, for example, live in the Ituri Forest of Zäire. But their niche is defined on the basis of their interactions with other biotic populations living in the same area. Because the BaMbuti hunt elephants, the interaction between elephants and humans becomes part of the niche definitions of both populations (Turnbull, 1963). Niches are also defined by the population's interaction with abiotic features. The abiotic features of the Ituri rain forest include heat and moisture. The interaction between these abiotic features and the BaMbuti's biology and behavior has produced a number of anatomical, physiological, and cultural traits to cope with these stresses (Austin, 1974). These responses thus also become parts of the BaMbuti's niche structure. The concept of niche is dynamic, in that the niche is defined not only by the presence of biotic populations or abiotic features, but also by the interactions between them.

Often an ecological population is confused with the more familiar term *species.* Unlike the ecological definition of a population, the concept of species is not defined in terms of any particular set of environmental conditions. A species is simply a group of animals whose shared biological background permits individuals to mate with each other and produce fertile offspring. Animals of different species cannot mate to produce fertile offspring.

The makeup of a species, like that of other classification categories, is arbitrary and not without ambiguous boundaries. Two groups of animals that are able to produce offspring are sometimes classified as different species. In some cases, two animals such as horses and donkeys are classified as different species because their offspring (mules) are sterile. In other cases, two groups can be classified as different species because they are geographically isolated from each other or because their behavior normally prevents them from interbreeding, or both. Desert and savannah baboons exist in separate ecosystems, normally do not interbreed, and are distinguishable on the basis of certain physical and behavioral traits. Yet when members of the two species do interbreed, as sometimes happens in zoos, they are completely fertile and produce fertile offspring. Scientists are aware of the ambiguities of the species category, but for the sake of discussion are often forced to make judgments about the limits of the category that are open to question.

In some cases, an ecological population can be the same as the concept of species. This occurs when the term *species* is applied to a group of animals who all live in a certain area and breed only with one another. Koala bears are found only in eucalyptus forests in Australia (Pianka, 1974). Due to its reliance on the fruit of particular eucalyptus trees, the koala has a limited geographical range and occupies a fairly well-defined niche. Because koalas breed only with other koalas, they meet the criterion of reproductive isolation and therefore fit the definition of a *species* as well as an ecological population.

Humans, on the other hand, are located throughout the world in a great many diverse environments. Each local human population has a unique niche structure because its biological and behavioral characteristics are understandable only in terms of the specific biotic and abiotic circumstances that exist in its area. Boundaries between local human populations generally are maintained by cultural, rather than by geographic, mechanisms. Culture often defines the pool of potential mates. The social rules of the BaMbuti pygmies, for example, make it more likely that they will mate with one another than with the neighboring Bantu populations. At the same time, in all human populations there exist circumstances that encourage, or even force, neighboring populations to exchange mates. It is not uncommon for Bantu males to take pygmy females as wives. Thus, while mating among humans tends to be localized within the population, this practice is far from universal. Exchange of mates between local human populations maintains the broad biological unity that is the basis for classifying all humans as the same species. The species category *Homo sapiens* is a biological term that applies to all humans, regardless of the environment in which they live. It does not address itself to the biological diversity that exists within the species. The concepts of niche and population allow us to talk about this diversity in environmental terms.

The Community. As we study populations we come to realize that they do not exist in isolation from one another. Indeed, the same interaction that makes one population a part of the niche definition of another creates a web of life forms, each of which affects the others directly or indirectly. Ecologists call a group of interrelated populations that exist in a definable area a *community.*

The interaction of a biotic community and the physical environment of an area is often referred to as an *ecosystem.* Ecosystems are commonly described in terms of some dominant feature. In marine ecology, coral reefs are usually discussed as an ecosystem and separated from tidal ecosystems or from open-sea ecosystems. In terrestrial ecology, ecosystems are often described by their plant life (forest ecosystems, grassland ecosystems, etc.). Ecologists recognize that these categories are somewhat arbitrary. Grasslands grade imperceptibly into deserts. But the ecosystem concept is useful for describing relationships that exist in areas whose characteristics are familiar to most people.

The Flow of Energy. One way of understanding the organization of an ecosystem is to look at the feeding relationships that exist within it. All energy available to life forms originally comes from the sun. Plants alone can use the radiant energy of the sun by combining simple inorganic compounds (such as water, CO_2, nitrites, sulfates, and phosphates) to form organic compounds. Plant eaters break down the energy compounds in plants into forms they can use—carbohydrates, proteins, and lipids. These broken-down compounds are recombined to form the animal's cell structures. They also provide the energy needed to drive the animal's vital processes. Energy stored in animal cells can, in turn, be broken down to provide the energy needs of other animals.

The simplest way to discuss a community's food relationships is to organize its populations in a *trophic hierarchy*—a series of categories each of which is broadly defined in terms of how its members get their energy. Because plants directly use solar energy they are often referred to as *producers*. Other organisms are called *consumers*. *Herbivores*, animals that eat only plants, make up the primary consumer trophic level. *Carnivores*, animals that eat only primary consumers, make up the secondary consumer trophic level. Some ecosystems include third and even fourth levels of consumers. Both are sometimes called top carnivores and rely on secondary consumers for their food. Finally, *decomposers* such as bacteria break down the remains of organisms, making basic organic and inorganic compounds available to plants once again. (See Figure 2.)

Not all of the energy that is available at one trophic level is absorbed by the one above it. Only 10 to 20 percent of the food energy that was in the plants eaten by a herbivore is finally stored in its cells. And the energy that is finally stored in the carnivore's cells is only 10 to 20 percent of the energy that was in the cells of the herbivore.

Because so much energy is used at each level to get energy from the one below it, the supportable *biomass*, the total mass of living tissue at a given trophic level, is reduced. Thus, the biomass of the herbivores in an ecosystem is less than the biomass of the plants; the biomass of the carnivores is less than the biomass of the herbivores; and the biomass of the top carnivores is always less than the biomass of lower carnivores. Ecologists estimate the biomass of any one trophic level as roughly 10 percent of the biomass of the level below it.

Although the trophic pyramid is a useful way of remembering basic food energy relationships, it is an ideal representation of what actually exists. In reality, many animals participate at different levels in the trophic pyramid. Consequently, the image of a food

Figure 2 A representation of a trophic pyramid.
Note that the energy at each level is about 10 percent of the level below it.
(After M. A. Little and G. E. Morren, Jr., 1976)

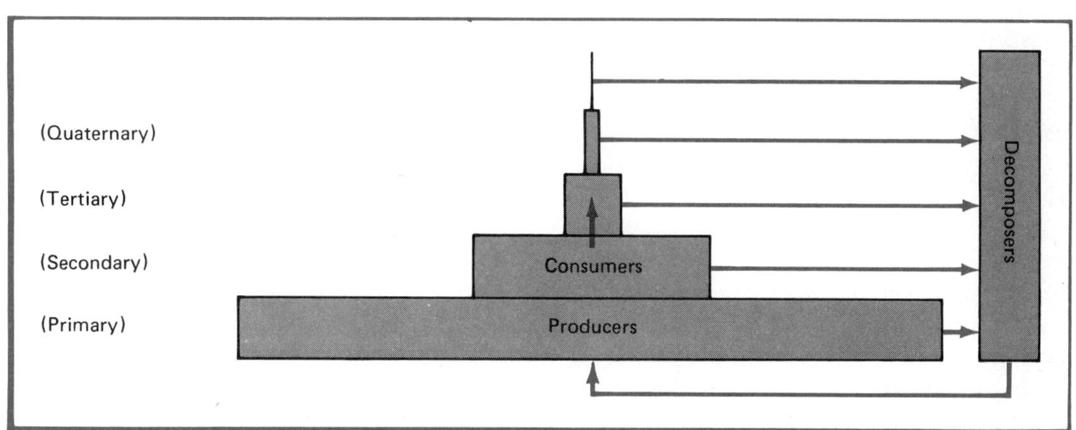

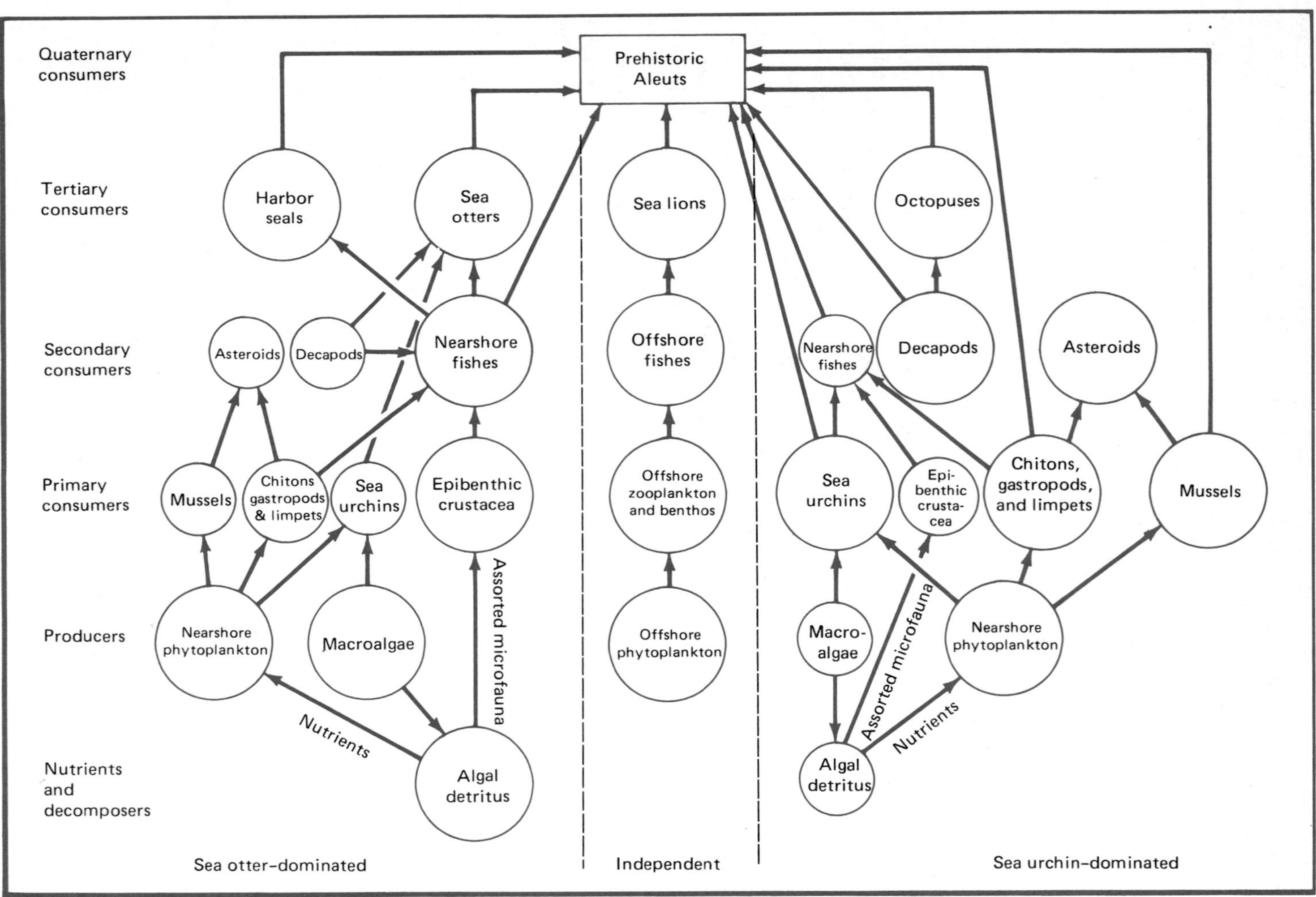

Figure 3 The food web of the prehistoric Aleuts

web is often used. Humans are a good example. In many environments, they tend to be both primary and secondary consumers. They eat both plants and animals. In some cases, they may be third- and even fourth-level consumers because they also eat other carnivores. Prehistoric Aleuts, for instance, made use of almost all the food chains in their environment. By eating chitons, they were secondary consumers. By eating nearshore fish, which are secondary consumers, they became third-level consumers. Finally, by sometimes eating sea lions, which eat offshore fish, the Aleuts became fourth-level consumers. (See Figure 3.)

The Biosphere. One final level in the biotic hierarchy remains: the *biosphere.* It is the sum total of all the material and energy involved in living systems on the earth (Salthe, 1972). Often, however, it is divided into the world's two major ecological domains—the sea and the land. The marine biosphere includes all the communities that inhabit the sea, and the terrestrial biosphere is made up of all land-dwelling communities. Except to note in passing that the biosphere concept helps us to understand the interactions between ecosystems, we will not be concerned with what occurs at this level.

"What do you mean, you're going to work your way up the food chain?" (Bill Maul)

Adaptation and Evolution

Evolution is the study of how and why changes occur in life forms. The traditional unit of evolutionary study is the population. Individuals do not evolve, at least in the genetic sense. Even though a person's anatomy and physiology may change during development and aging, the genetic composition remains the same throughout life. The genes we are born with are those that we will pass on to the next generation. However, the individuals that make up a population do not all survive into adulthood. Those that do will not all have the same number of children. As a result, the genetic composition of the population changes from one generation to the next. This process of change, called *adaptation,* allows the population to respond biologically, or *adapt,* to changes in the biotic and abiotic environments.

Because populations are part of ecosystems, any attempt to understand adaptation and evolution must be based on the sort of ecological relationships we discussed in the first part of this chapter. The most important concept here is the niche, the population's position within the interactions that take place in an ecosystem. If ecosystems were stable throughout time, and biotic and abiotic interactions remained the same, the niche of each population within the community would never change. Indeed, the niche structure of some animals has remained constant throughout enormous amounts of time. Seahorses have remained almost unchanged for tens of millions of years. However, such permanence is unusual, because the abiotic features of the earth are continually changing.

The ability of niche structure to respond to changes depends on the specialization of the population. If the population has a very specialized diet and its members show little variation, its ability to adapt to environmental change is limited. The koala bear depends almost entirely on the eucalyptus tree for its food. If a change in the abiotic environment decimated the eucalyptus population, the survival of the koala would be threatened.

Humans, however, occupy an extremely diversified niche. If one food source is eliminated, human populations can switch to a different source. And humans rely on learned behavior for a great part of their interactions with the biotic and abiotic environments. Learning makes human niche structure more flexible than that of other animals. This flexibility has two great advantages. It permits us to exploit diverse ecosystems, and it reduces the number of individuals that die as the population adapts to environmental change. Populations that have depended on biological adaptations (including our early humanlike ancestors) have lost those individuals who could not adjust to environmental change.

Selection

The mechanism by which populations biologically adjust to a changing environment was first suggested by Charles Darwin. Darwin recognized that individuals that make up populations differ in their biological and behavioral characteristics. In ecological terms, their ecospaces (personal interactions with the environment) are different. As the environment changes, the ability of individual ecospaces to adjust to the new circumstances varies. Some individuals possess biological and behavioral characteristics that permit them to survive in the changed environmental conditions. Others do not. Because the characteristics of the survivors will be different from the characteristics of those who do not survive, a new set of biological-behavioral interactions with the changed environmental conditions will emerge, reflecting the attributes of the survivors. The population's niche will have changed, or evolved, as a consequence of changes in the environment.

Darwin thought that selection operated primarily through differences in mortality. That is, individuals unable to adjust to the new environment would not survive to reproduce. However, modern neo-Darwinian biologists see that differences in fertility may also play an important role. An environmental change may not be severe enough to cause the immediate death of unadjusted members of the population. Instead, they may have fewer children than the better-adjusted members. Since (1) the biological and behavioral characteristics of many animals are inherited from their parents and (2) the better-adjusted individuals will contribute more offspring to the composition of later generations, the number of individuals with advantageous traits in the population will gradually increase.

Normally, evolution by natural selection occurs slowly over hundreds of generations. But there are a few cases in which selection has transformed a species almost instantaneously, compared to more usual rates. One of the best-studied cases is the phenomenon of industrial melanism among certain light-colored moths in England. One of these moths, *Biston betularia,* is known to have had a light color in the early 1800s, which permitted it to blend into the pale lichen-covered tree trunks of its environment. In 1848, less than 1 percent existed as dark variants. As industry developed during the course of the century, soot darkened the tree trunks. When this occurred, the birds that ate the moths were able to find the light ones more easily on the darkened trees. Generation by generation, fewer of the light-colored moths were able to survive and reproduce. The dark-colored moths, because they were camouflaged against the dark trees, survived and reproduced in greater numbers. By 1898 about 95 percent of the population consisted of the dark variant. Since the moth produces only one set of offspring a year, only 50 generations were required for the frequency of dark-colored moths to increase 95 times in the population (Kettlewell, 1961).

Two generalizations apply to the process of evolution. The first is that evolution is *opportunistic.* Selection cannot create wholly new anatomy or physiology; it can only operate on the individual variations that already exist in the population. Characteristics that may prove to be useful in new environmental circumstances must be possessed by some individuals in the population before natural selection can operate on them. Black moths could not have become the most common form in industrial England unless some members of the original population possessed the color. In the new environment, made up of sooty trees, the black moths had an advantage that permitted them to survive better and reproduce more than the white-colored moths. If the combination of characteristics necessary for survival in new environmental conditions does not exist in the population, then the population will become extinct.

Evolution is also irreversible. Selection molds a population whose interaction with other niches and with its abiotic environment permits its own survival. After a set of biological and behavioral characteristics has become common among the members of a population, the former set of adaptations will not return, even if environmental conditions revert to the original state. Any single trait can be reversed by selective breeding, but an entire series of traits cannot be recreated.

Random Evolutionary Forces

Selection produces a population whose members are adapted to the environment. The entire process of natural selection occurs in response to, and is therefore oriented toward, changes in the environment.

Two other evolutionary phenomena also produce biological change, but they occur without influence from the environment. They produce changes that may or may not be adaptive. The first of these is called *genetic drift.* In all sexually reproducing populations, particularly small ones, the genetic composition of one generation varies from that of the preceding generation, due to certain random processes. There exists an easily calculable chance that some of each individual's genes will not become part of the germ cells that will create new individuals. The smaller the number of offspring that one has, the greater the chance that this will occur. Thus, in small populations there is a good chance that some genes may be lost from one generation to the next. Although genetic drift does cause changes in the biological makeup of the species, it is thought to be more important in the evolution of small local populations.

The second kind of random evolution is called *gene flow.* When members of a local population exchange mates with a nearby group (as often occurs among humans), genes that control traits that have evolved in one ecosystem may be acquired by members of the other. If the gene continues to spread from one population to the next, the biological nature of the species may also begin to change.

Although both drift and flow give a certain amount of biological variability to the population, the new variants are also subject to natural selection. A trait does not spread by way of gene flow unless it offers an advantage (or at least no disadvantage) in new environments. New gene combinations arising from the action of genetic drift do not persist unless they make survival easier for their possessors. Thus, natural selection in the long run is probably the most important of the evolutionary processes.

Ecosystem Evolution: The Creation of Diversity

Normally, the number of niches in an ecosystem gradually increases. Usually, the creation of new niches is less rapid in harsh environments (those with severely limiting abiotic features) than it is in environments with few abiotic limits. In harsh environments, niches tend to be more broadly defined. More plant and animal species are part of each niche. For example, only a limited number of primary consumers, each depending on a number of different plant resources, can be supported in such areas. Second- and third-level consumers, such as human hunters and gatherers, eat a large number of different foods (as we saw in the Aleuts example) and also have small populations. The low precipitation of deserts and the extreme cold of the Arctic thus reduce diversity and keep the number of possible niches low.

In areas where there are few abiotic limiting factors, however, a variety of plants exists, thereby permitting a great diversity of animal life. Each of the many consumer populations is small and specialized for eating particular plants. Likewise, each member of a large number of small, carnivorous populations feeds on a relatively small number of prey species. Diversification is more rapid in this dense matrix of life because there are more potential niches.

Speciation

As a population evolves in response to changing environmental factors, one of two evolutionary pathways will emerge. The population may persist as a single biological unit through time. The biological characteristics of its membership may change from generation to generation because of individual differences in fertility and mortality, but each generation is directly descended from all earlier ones. This unilinear evolutionary pathway is referred to as *anagenic evolution* (Dobzhansky, 1962). This type of evolution has characterized the human past for at least the last 1 million years. In the other case, the original population may split into two or more distinct biological units. This type of evolutionary pathway, which is responsible for the creation of biological diversity, is called *cladogenic evolution* (Dobzhansky, 1962). Cladogenic evolution is most likely to occur among populations whose interactions with the biotic and abiotic environment have been successful enough to produce an increase in their number and ecological range.

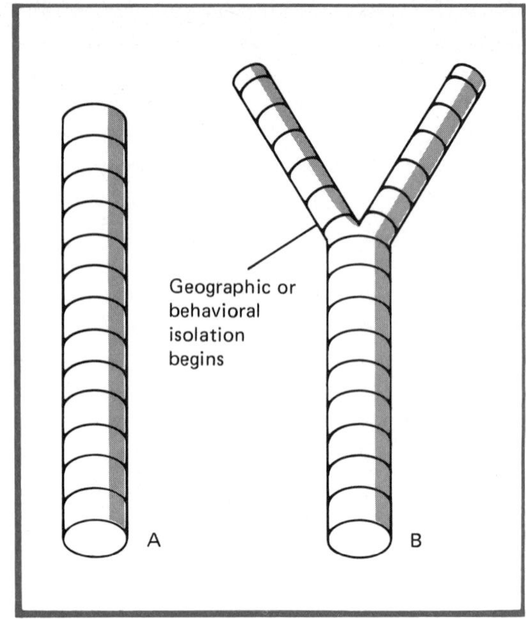

Figure 4 **Anagenic and cladogenic evolution.** In anagenic evolution (A), the population evolves as a single group. In cladogenic evolution (B), speciation divides the original population into two or more separate populations.

When two or more populations diverge, and new niches are created, the populations may become reproductively isolated from each other. When they are no longer able to reproduce, *speciation* is said to have occurred. There are two basic ways in which speciation can occur. It can begin when part of an expanding population moves to a new area, thereby creating a physical separation between the new and old groups. This is referred to as *allopatric speciation.* It can also begin when parts of an original population no longer interbreed, though they coexist in the same area. This divergence is known as *sympatric speciation.*

Allopatric Speciation. The emergence of two or more distinct econiches, whether due to behavior or to geographic separation, is a necessary condition for speciation. Before allopatric speciation can occur, individuals must migrate into a new area and establish a subpopulation. This subpopulation at first tends to exploit the new ecosystem in the same way that the original population exploited the original area. In doing so it may find itself in direct competition with other populations for the same food resources, or it may find that the new area lacks some or all of the food sources that were in the original area. If the migrant subpopulation is to survive, it will have to establish new relationships with the unique biotic and abiotic features of the new environment; that is, it will have to develop a new niche. Selection will begin to favor those individuals whose characteristics either minimize competition with other species or allow them to overwhelm competing populations in this new ecosystem and establish themselves in their place. The amount of biological divergence between the original and migrant populations depends on how different the two ecosystems are. The greater the difference, the more radical the divergence of the two niches.

Sympatric Speciation. In sympatric speciation, behavioral isolation can produce an effect comparable to geographic isolation. Rather than migrating, a subpopulation modifies its behavior, thereby creating a new niche in the same ecosystem. Using the same food resources at different times of the day is a common way this can occur. Many of the most primitive primate populations have survived because at night they use the same food resources that more advanced primates rely on during the day. Changes in courtship behavior can also lead to niche divergence. Such behavior in many fish, reptiles, and birds is designed to excite females before mating. If environmental forces cause a change in courtship behavior, it may not evoke the proper female response, and reproduction will not occur. The two populations separated in this fashion begin to develop distinct niches that do not overlap.

The Role of Reproductive Isolation. Though two subpopulations may gradually diverge in their differing niches, this process is not enough to cause speciation. *Reproductive isolation,* the absense of interbreeding between two populations, must be maintained over a long period of time for speciation to occur. Humans are distributed throughout the world in numerous subpopulations, yet we remain a single species. In part this is because we rely on culture to reduce the differences between environments, thus reducing differences in selective pressures. It also occurs because human populations are not reproductively isolated from one another. Obviously, a small population of Eskimos in the Arctic is not likely to interbreed with every other human population in the world. However, because they exchange mates with neighboring groups, and because these groups exchange mates with their neighbors, and so on, there is created a web of genetic relationships that binds all human populations together into a single biological entity. Because of this, no human population is reproductively isolated from others long enough to become a separate species.

Thus, the following steps are essential to cause speciation:

1. Behavioral or geographic separation must occur.

2. The niche structure of the two populations must begin to diverge.
3. The two populations must become reproductively isolated.

When members of the two populations are no longer capable of interbreeding, even if contact is restored, speciation has occurred.

Evolutionary Trends

Adaptive Radiation. The fossil record sometimes shows the emergence of a great many species, seemingly at once. This rapid speciation is called *adaptive radiation.* It often occurs in environments where there are many potential but unoccupied niches. It can be inferred that the 14 different finch species discovered in the Galápagos islands or nearby are the result of adaptive radiation. A single ancestral population gave rise to subpopulations that exploited various niches in the islands. Today, one of the tree finch species has a parrotlike beak and is basically vegetarian. Another climbs trees to hunt insects in the cracks of bark. Still others have become ground feeders (Boughey, 1973). The behavior and biology of these subpopulations have gradually

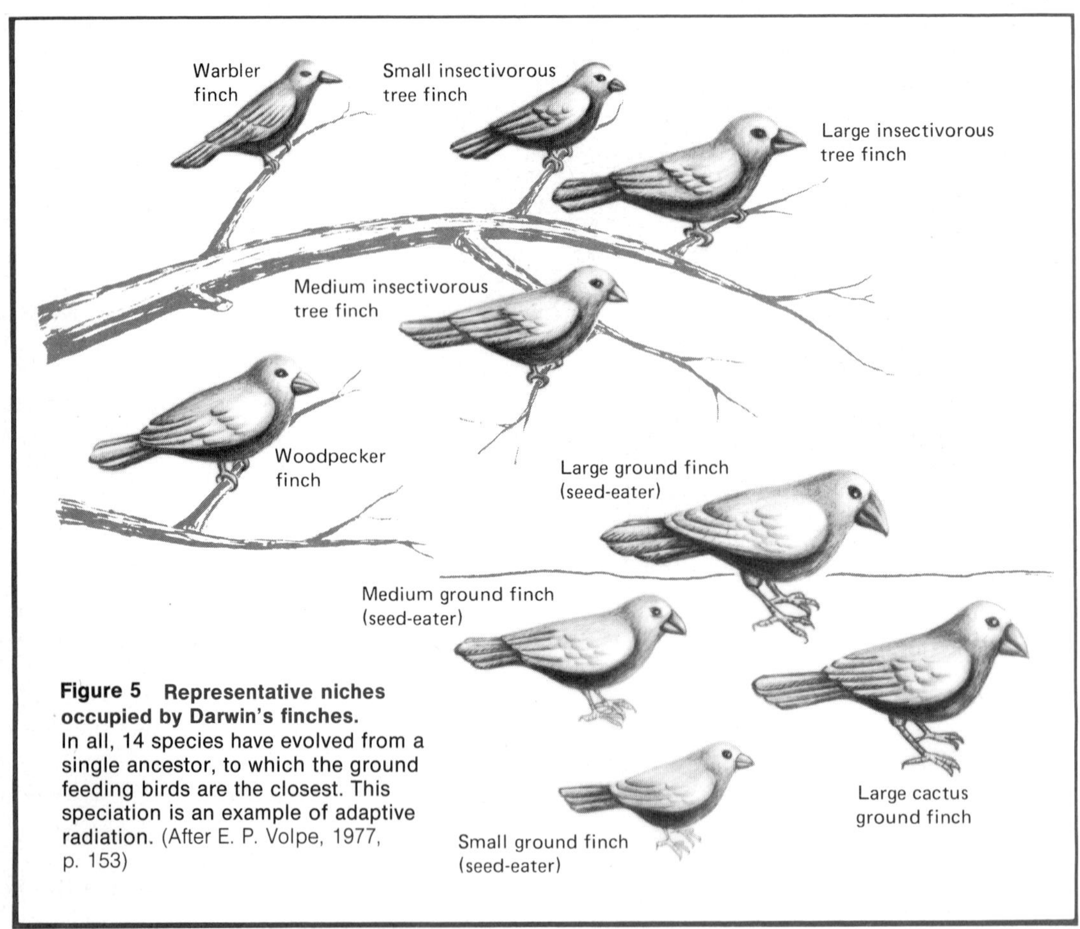

Figure 5 Representative niches occupied by Darwin's finches. In all, 14 species have evolved from a single ancestor, to which the ground feeding birds are the closest. This speciation is an example of adaptive radiation. (After E. P. Volpe, 1977, p. 153)

become specialized for particular food resources. These behavioral characteristics eventually caused reproductive isolation and, in this case, a type of sympatric speciation.

A comparable event may have occurred when the earlier primates began to adapt to living in trees. The fossil record shows that in a very short time a large number of anatomically specialized populations developed. This is taken as evidence that a large number of different arboreal niches were exploited, explaining the subsequent emergence of many different arboreal primate species.

Parallelism and Convergence. In widely separated but similar environments throughout the world, certain plants and animals have numerous similarities. The existence of these similarities can be explained as a result of one of two long-term evolutionary trends: parallelism or convergence.

Parallelism occurs when two closely related species or groups of species begin to exploit similar but geographically separate ecosystems in similar ways. Parallelism occurred in the evolution of the primates as the North and South American continental plates drifted away from the European and African continental plates, splitting similar species into two groups. Each one independently began to evolve its own highly efficient arboreal adaptations. Today the biological and behavioral characteristics of the New World monkeys inhabiting the rain forests of Central and South America parallel those of the Old World monkeys, which live in the rain forests of Africa and Asia.

Convergence occurs when two unrelated species or groups of species independently evolve similar biological and behavioral characteristics because of the similarity of their niche structure. Whales, porpoises, seals, and sea lions are mammals that are evolutionarily more closely related to land mammals than they are to fish. Yet, because they occupy a marine niche, their physical and behavioral characteristics have converged with those of more traditional marine vertebrates such as fish. These similarities are therefore the result of different biologies making similar adaptations to similar environments.

Even though a whale's flippers and the fins of a fish perform similar functions, their structures are different. Such structural similarities, deriving from different evolutionary origins and occurring as a result of convergent evolution, are called *analogies. Homologies,* in contrast, are similar in structure because of common ancestry, regardless of function. The whale's flipper, a bird's wing, and the human arm all share certain similarities. The number of bones in each of these organisms remains the same. However, the structure has been modified in each case to perform a different function.

Coevolution. In some cases, two populations undergo *coevolution:* They become so dependent on each other that any changes in one niche immediately redefine the other. Sometimes the association is so close that the extinction of one causes the extinction of the other. Such a link may have existed between the now extinct dodo bird and the *Calvaria* tree in Mauritius, an island in the western Indian Ocean. The dodo bird ate the seed-bearing fruit of the tree. As it did so, only trees with seeds encased in a thick-walled covering survived. This casing protected the seeds from the dodo's digestive tract. Unfortunately, these casings made germination impossible without the bird's help. As the fruit and its seeds passed through the bird's gizzard, the tough casings were reduced to the point that germination could take place after excretion. When humans exterminated the last dodos in 1681, they removed the only natural means of preparing the *Calvaria* seeds for germination. In 1973, only 13 ancient, dying trees remained. Now, however, the *Calvaria* population may be restored by mechanical preparation of the seeds (Temple, 1977).

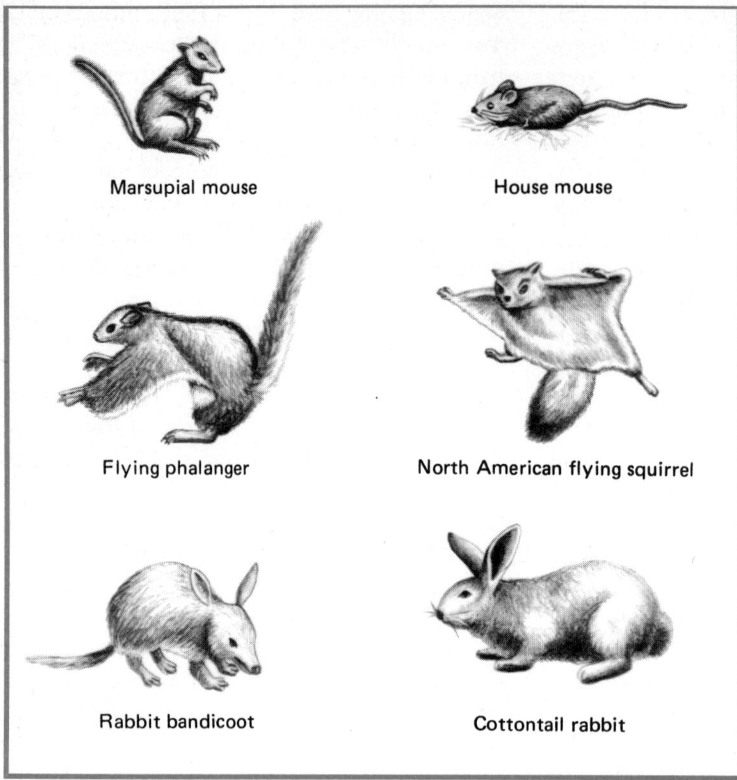

Figure 6 **Adaptive radiation and convergence among the Australian marsupials.** The marsupials have radiated into a number of species, many of which resemble unrelated animals adapted to similar niches in other parts of the world. (After E. P. Volpe, 1977, p. 176)

The Human Impact on Ecosystem Evolution

In this chapter we have for the most part discussed ecosystem structure and evolution as they occur without the impact of human culture. Some scientists feel that during the long period when humans were hunters and gatherers their impact on ecosystems was minor (Watson & Watson, 1969). But today human agricultural and industrial technology has major effects on many of the ecosystems of the world.

Human exploitation frequently disturbs the tendency of ecosystems to evolve more efficient uses of energy. Energy efficiency increases naturally as ecosystem diversity increases. As more species evolve, the energy captured by the ecosystem increases and is utilized more by the organisms of the ecosystem. An ecosystem exploited extensively by humans, however, tends to have fewer species.

For example, groups that farm in the tropical rain forests of Yucatán burn off dense, highly diversified vegetation and introduce only one or two plant crops. The farmers not only destroy the vegetation but also limit the amount of food available to plant-eating animals. Thus, plant and animal species become less abundant. Furthermore, if animals compete directly with humans, the animals may be systematically exterminated. The natural tendency of agriculturalists to reduce the ecosystem's diversity is directly opposed to the natural tendency of the ecosystem to increase its diversity. In effect, agriculture diverts energy away from an intricate trophic hierarchy and into crops, which permits large numbers of humans to live in areas that would normally support only a few hunter-gatherers.

In less mature temperate and grassland environments, the soil is rich enough to permit continuous agriculture over long periods of time. Unfortunately, not all ecosystems can sustain long-term human exploitation. Very mature ecosystems, such as tropical rain forests, are quite fragile. Soil nutrients are easily leached out of the thin topsoil, and crop productivity can decline dramatically after only a few years. Under these conditions, human populations usually abandon the plot and repeat the same cycle nearby. Given enough time (somewhere between 7 and 15 years), normal plant diversity will be regenerated on the abandoned plot. However, as the population in such areas increases, the amount of time a plot is permitted to lie unused is reduced. If such fragile soils become overused, the ecosystem produces less energy than is required by humans, and a population catastrophe can occur. This is often given as an explanation of the collapse of the classic Mayan civilization (Ricketson & Ricketson, 1937).

Industrial societies have an even greater capacity to reduce ecosystem diversity. At the basis of this great potential is a reservoir of fossil fuels, such as oil and coal. Gasoline permits a single farmer to plant and harvest enor-

Figure 7 The effect of agriculture on the human ecosystem. To the left, before agriculture, land areas could support only about 10 million people, primarily hunters and gatherers. Today, agriculture supports 4 billion people on 10 percent of the original land area. Agriculture diverts energy into livestock and crops, forms in which humans can use it efficiently. (Adapted from Brown, 1970)

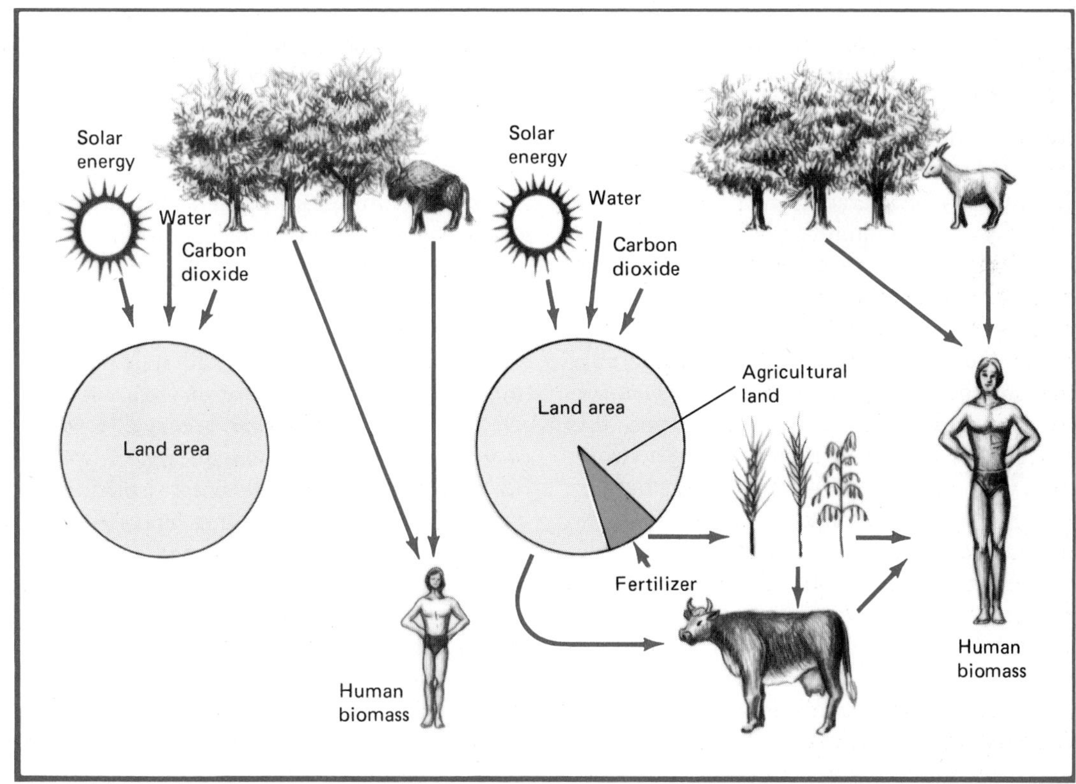

mous quantities of food. The soils of these areas can be continuously rejuvenated by using petrochemical fertilizers. The benefits as well as the drawbacks of industrialized agriculture will be discussed in another chapter.

Summary

1. Human evolution is influenced by the nonliving and living features of the environment. The relationship between humans and the environment is complicated by *culture*—an integrated network of values, symbols, and organizations—because it changes the environment and its effect on our own evolution. *Ecology* provides a theoretical umbrella under which the environmental, biological, and social sciences can be integrated with evolutionary theory.

2. Ecologists divide the environment into *abiotic* and *biotic* features.

3. Abiotic features include temperature, precipitation, solar radiation, soil, wind, and fire. Ecologists study those features that by their scarcity or overabundance influence the *biotic diversity,* the number of different kinds of life forms in an area. Essential abiotic features set limits of tolerance, outside of which life forms cannot exist.

4. Through culture, humans change abiotic conditions to create *microenvironments.* The reindeer-fur clothing of the Lapps, for example, recreates a tropical microenvironment within their cold climate.

5. Ecologists arrange the biotic features of the environment in a series of progressively more inclusive categories: the individual, the population, the community, and the biosphere.

6. The sum of the individual's interactions with other organisms and abiotic features, its *ecospace,* is studied in *autecology.*

7. *Population ecology* centers on the population—a reproductively isolated group of closely related individuals living in the same area. Its interactions with the environment make up the population's *niche.* Both the *population* and the *species* are groups of reproductively isolated individuals. Species, however, is not defined in terms of a set of local environmental conditions.

8. A *community* is a group of interrelated populations that coexist in a definable area. Together their niches make up an *ecosystem.* One way to understand the ecosystem structure is to trace the flow of energy through its *trophic* levels. *Producers,* or plants, store solar energy in their leaves; *herbivores,* or primary *consumers,* get their energy from plants; *carnivores,* or secondary consumers, eat herbivores. Finally, *decomposers* recycle the basic compounds for reuse by plants.

9. The *marine* and *terrestrial biospheres* are made up of all the communities in the sea and on the land.

10. The population is the unit of evolutionary study. As its biological and genetic makeup shifts in response to the pressures of natural selection, it is said to *adapt* to the environment. The more specialized a population's niche, the more limited is its ability to adapt to new environmental conditions.

11. As a population evolves, it follows one of two pathways. It may persist as a single biological unit through time *(anagenic evolution)* or undergo *speciation* and split into two or more distinct units *(cladogenic evolution).*

12. *Allopatric speciation* occurs as a result of expansion into a new area; *sympatric speciation* results in the behavioral isolation of groups living in the same area. Speciation occurs most rapidly in rich environments, which hold many potential niches.

13. Evolutionary trends include *adaptive radiation, parallelism, convergence,* and *coevolution.*

14. Agricultural and industrial technologies often decrease the diversity of ecosystems, increasing their fragility and decreasing the efficiency with which they absorb energy.

MOST people do not give too much thought to our closest animal "relatives," the primates. We tend to think of them in terms of the monkeys or apes we see in zoos. However, *primatologists* (scientists who study the biology and behavior of primates) have shown that this group, which includes the prosimians, monkeys, apes, and humans, is highly diverse and very versatile. As we mentioned in Chapter 2, the work of primatologists has been used to assist in the interpretation of our evolutionary past, as well as to define (both biologically and behaviorally) the uniqueness of humans. Surprisingly, though, scientists began collecting detailed knowledge about the biology of primates only about a century ago. Studies of primate behavior began systematically only after the end of World War II. Even today, however, detailed information on the behavior of many primates is lacking.

This chapter will review the history of our knowledge of, and attitudes toward, primates and describe the different types of primates that are living today. We shall also introduce principles of classification and show how they are used to organize the primates. Along the way, we shall indicate how different groups of primates are distinguished from one another. We shall use this technique to show the traits that humans share with other groups, as well as to isolate those features that are uniquely ours.

The History of the Knowledge of Primates

Humans have always been fascinated by the other primates. Past civilizations were aware of their almost-human qualities long before evolutionists began to suggest that we shared a common ancestry with the apes.

Over the ages, nonhuman primates have been the objects of ridicule as well as worship, superstition as well as scientific observation. That they should provoke emotional reactions in humans is not surprising, for in many ways they remind us very much of ourselves. Today, scientists are probing the physical and social characteristics of primates for clues to our own biological evolution and behavioral background. But present attitudes toward nonhuman primates have emerged from a long and checkered history.

Egyptian tomb painting of Hapi, a guardian spirit of the dead. (Brian Brake, Photo Researchers, Inc.)

Ancient Conceptions of Primates

Early civilizations in India, Mesopotamia, and Egypt were aware of many types of primates. Langurs and macaques were native to India, and although no primates lived in Egypt, a variety lived in the surrounding areas—Mauretania, Libya, and lands to the south. These primates reached Egypt as objects of trade and as tribute payments before 4000 B.C. (McDermott, 1938). Primates and images of them reached Mesopotamia from Egypt beginning about 3000 B.C., because there was much trade between the two countries. In all three of these cultures monkeys were sacred.

Monkey Worship. Religious statues of the hamadryas baboon have been dated as far back as 3500 to 4000 B.C. in Egypt. To the ancient Egyptians the baboon was the symbol and the representative of Thoth, the god of wisdom, learning, and magic. Thoth was also god of the moon. Female baboons were sacred, because their monthly menstrual cycles were thought to be regulated by the moon. The baboon was also associated with time-keeping. This idea was based on the belief that during the two annual equinoxes baboons cry out regularly once an hour (Morris & Morris, 1966).

Some living baboons were considered more sacred than others. Baboons were believed to have taught Thoth the sacred hieroglyphics or sacred writing that he used in his role as a scribe for the gods. So temple priests gave a pen-and-tablet test to baboons to see which ones could write. The animals that in the opinion of the priests passed the test were most sacred. Accordingly, they were housed in the temples and fed the finest wines and roasted meats.

Baboons were believed to play a role in the afterlife. Along with three other guardian spirits, a god named Hapi, depicted with a human body and the head of a baboon, was thought to protect the dead when they appeared for their final judgment before Osiris, god of the dead (Morris & Morris, 1966).

In Mesopotamia monkeys were cult animals sacred to some god, though their exact religious meaning is unclear (McDermott, 1938). Representations of unidentified monkeys suggest that early artists found these exotic animals amusing as well as sacred. A limestone slab found in front of a temple, for instance, shows a monkey sitting at a table and serving drinks from a bowl to the members of an all-animal orchestra.

The hanuman monkey, a larger langur, has been worshiped in India for thousands of years. Originally it was seen as the representative of a god who guarded villages. Every new settlement immediately put up a statue of the monkey god Hanuman to ensure his protection (Morris & Morris, 1966).

Indian reverence for monkeys has been furthered by the epic legends of the noble god Rama, described in the *Ramayana.* Hanuman and his monkey followers performed many heroic feats to help Rama rescue his wife from the king of the demons. Grateful to Hanuman for these and other services, Hindus still protect and worship their primate descendants. The sacred langurs are cared for in temples by priests. Monkeys are graciously tolerated, even when they do great damage to gardens and orchards. And until recently, if any visitor thoughtlessly killed a hanuman monkey, the outraged Hindus considered it their sacred duty to avenge his death by killing the visitor (Morris & Morris, 1966).

Early Scientific Studies of Primates

In contrast to the cultures that viewed primates religiously, the ancient Greeks and Romans made attempts to study monkeys and apes from a scientific point of view. They examined and dissected primate specimens and compared them with one another and with humans in attempts to classify them. Their understanding of primates, however, was always hindered by the tendency to interpret them as if they were some form of humans.

The great Greek philosopher and naturalist Aristotle (384–322 B.C.) was the first to attempt a scientific description of primates. Unlike many other writers, he apparently examined actual specimens. Aristotle's classification scheme was very simple. He divided the primates into apes, baboons, and monkeys. His primate family did not include humans, though Aristotle noted that these three creatures were similar in some ways to humans. He did not suggest that these likenesses had anything to do with a common ancestry.

Although Aristotle's classification scheme left too much out, his description of the Barbary ape in his *Historia Animalium* is fairly accurate. He noted striking likenesses between ape and human facial features (nostrils, ears, teeth, and eyelashes), breasts, distribution of hair, arms, and arm movements. But one aspect of Aristotle's description later caused much confusion. He wrote that dissection of such creatures showed their internal parts were just like those of humans. In fact, they are not. This incorrect assumption was shared by other writers of the time, and the error was not pointed out until the sixteenth century (McDermott, 1938).

It was not until several hundred years later that Galen (A.D. 129–199), a Greek physician at the Roman court, made a significant addition to knowledge about primates. Although Galen was mainly interested in studying how the human body worked, he could not study it directly. Instead, he was forced to rely mostly on dissections and experiments with similar animals—especially monkeys—because dissection of humans was largely forbidden. Although he was aware of five different kinds of primates, he preferred the Barbary ape for his physiological experiments because it had the most upright, human posture. In the course of his dissection, he made up the most complete body of anatomical information since Aristotle. Like Aristotle, however, he wrongly assumed that the internal organs of monkeys matched those of humans. And, like Aristotle, Galen saw likenesses between primates and humans, but did not suggest that there might be any relationship between these two forms of life. Galen did, however, make valuable contributions to the knowledge of anatomy and physiology. He discovered, for instance, that the brain controls the muscles and nerves (Morris & Morris, 1966; McDermott, 1938).

The Middle Ages

During the European Middle Ages scholars retreated from firsthand scientific observation. They considered Galen's works to be authoritative statements to be copied and studied but not improved with new research. As a result, little was learned about primate anatomy and physiology for 1,500 years. Speculation replaced analysis and centered on ape behavior and intelligence, which always were judged by human standards. Apes came to be thought downright evil. Their tendency to remove parasites from one another's fur, a social behavior known as grooming, was cited by one writer as proof that these "monstrous beasts" relished unclean food and would even feast on the vermin they picked off one another's heads. Since captive monkeys were known to bite, scream, and behave aggressively when provoked, they were thought to have evil dispositions (Morris & Morris, 1966).

Despite their revulsion toward monkeys and apes, medieval Europeans nonetheless had to admit some disturbing likenesses between themselves and these hairy creatures. They therefore searched for some distinguishing human trait that would clearly set them above the apes. Christian theologians gave an answer: reason. Reason was believed to be God's gift to humans alone when He created all forms of life. It was believed that monkeys could only mimic or "ape" humans.

Growing Awareness of the Primates

Although ridicule of primates continued well into the nineteenth century, anatomical knowledge of them began to increase somewhat during the late Renaissance. In the sixteenth century, a brilliant Belgian physician, Vesalius (1514–1564), renewed Galen's efforts to base studies of comparative anatomy on observation rather than on reading. He showed that Galen's long-accepted descriptions of human anatomy were inaccurate, because they were based on dissections of monkeys. Although this claim was fiercely attacked, it led to more careful studies of human anatomy. Soon it was impossible for scientists to overlook the differences between primates and humans.

In 1699, Edward Tyson, an English doctor, dissected a chimpanzee for the first time. He found that his specimen resembled humans in 48 ways, and monkeys in only 34 ways. Because it was not exactly like humans or monkeys, Tyson decided that it must be an "intermediate link" between the two.

During the eighteenth century taxonomists tried to classify the primates then being discovered in exotic lands. In 1735 Carolus Linnaeus published his *Systema Naturae.* In this work he made the revolutionary suggestion that humans, monkeys and chimpanzees, and sloths (now not considered primates) could be grouped in the same order—*Anthropomorpha*—on the basis of their physical similarities. He did not mean to imply an evolutionary relationship among these animals. In accordance with beliefs of the time, this grouping mirrored the pattern of the original creation.

During the nineteenth century awareness of the variety of primate types increased greatly. Confusion over how the various primates looked and acted was gradually cleared up as more of the creatures were shipped to Europe for study and classification. Among them was the gorilla, the one great ape not previously examined by Western scientists. At the same time, precise studies of the chimpanzee and orangutan pointed up their physical similarities to each other and to humans.

Darwin used a large amount of primate research in *The Descent of Man,* published in 1871. In this book he stated the theory that he had only hinted at in *The Origin of Species:* Humans are similar to the apes because both have evolved from the same remote ancestor. Darwin held that the physical, mental, and moral differences between humans and their animal relatives are only a matter of degree. A careful observer of the behavior of animals, he noted that they seem to be able to feel a degree of jealousy, devotion, and happiness. He remarked that monkeys used sticks and rocks as tools and that the more complex primates had a sense of curiosity, the ability to do simple reasoning, and a means of communicating with each other.

The Victorians reluctantly began to accept some of Darwin's ideas. The study of primates was therefore changed by two new attitudes. Since primates were now to be considered relatives, Victorians wanted to learn all they could about them. But to avoid disgracing themselves by acknowledging their "poor relations," the Victorians tended to exaggerate the "higher" qualities of the apes (Morris & Morris, 1966).

Studies of Primate Societies. Although anatomical studies of the nonhuman primates have not stopped, twentieth-century primatologists are more and more studying primate societies. A growing number of systematic studies have allowed modern primatologists to gradually do away with the cloud of superstition and emotion that has obscured the nonhuman primates.

Many of the early studies of primate social behavior emphasized their aggressiveness, hostility, and homicidal tendencies. This violent behavior was apparently a result of overcrowding and artificial grouping in the zoos where primates were first studied. The first scientist to try to organize the principles of primate social behavior, Sir Solly Zuckerman, noted that the atypical sex ratio of baboons in the London Zoo was causing them to behave aggressively. Male hamadryas baboons generally collect harems, and in the colony at the London Zoo there were 39 adult males and only 9 adult females (Zuckerman, 1932).

Primatologists quickly gave up studying zoo populations and began to study monkeys in special primate laboratories. In 1930 Robert and Ada Yerkes, for example, began studying chimpanzees at a one-acre compound in Orange Park, Florida. Although the compound was a more natural setting, it was still far from ideal. The pine trees within it, for instance, soon died from all the climbing and branch-breaking that went on.

During the 1930s primatologists finally began taking to the field in order to observe the social behavior of primates in their natural environments. C. R. Carpenter began the trend with his lengthy observations of howler monkeys in Panama, spider monkeys in Central America, and gibbons in Thailand. These were the first really good field studies of primates.

World War II interrupted research, but in the 1950s both laboratory and field studies went on briskly. Harry Harlow and his colleagues at the University of Wisconsin studied the psychology of infant rhesus monkeys in experiments using dummy mothers made of terry cloth and of wire. In the field Irven De Vore and Sherwood Washburn did landmark studies of the organization of baboon troops. Meanwhile, Japanese observation of macaques was yielding new insights into the ability of these primates to adopt learned behavior. Recent studies, such as those of Jane Van Lawick-Goodall (1971), have begun to produce in-depth social studies of single primates.

In many areas our knowledge of the primates is still very scanty. But today there is general agreement among scientists that we humans belong to the biological order Primates.* We share this classification with about 200 other species. We are all thought to have evolved from a common mammal ancestor about 70 million years ago. This ancestor was probably a small insect-eating creature that spent its life in trees. Diverse primate lines, some of which are now extinct, have radiated from this remote ancestor through varying niches in varying ecosystems. But all still show a degree of anatomical, behavioral, and biochemical similarity. In this section we shall look at how the living primates are classified to see where we stand in relationship to the rest of the primate order.

What Is a Primate?

It is not as easy as it might seem to define the characteristics of a primate. Scientists do not agree on the boundaries of this biological grouping. Some experts include in the primate order the tree shrew, a small Southeast Asian creature that looks like a skinny squirrel with a long snout.

Others argue that the animal does not share certain traits common to primates. But when it comes to defining exactly what these shared traits are, taxonomists run into problems. Primates are not like marsupials, for example, which can be identified on the basis of a single characteristic, their pouches. On the whole, living primates are distinctive only for an anatomical and behavioral pattern that has enabled them to live in a variety of environmental settings (Buettner-Janusch, 1973).

*When capitalized, the word *Primates* (pry-*may*-teez) refers to the order.

Physical Characteristics

Primates can be defined in terms of certain physical traits that they share to some degree. Some of these characteristics are not unique to primates; they are also possessed by members of other orders. The original primate ancestor inherited these *generalized,* or primitive, *characteristics* from its mammal forebears. Features such as the five digits on primate hands and feet are homologous to the basic structure of front and hind paws of other mammals. As they adapted to new environments, the primates evolved certain *specialized characteristics,* such as grasping hands. Primates are, therefore, defined not by a single trait, such as the marsupial's pouch, but by a set of physical traits, or "evolutionary tendencies" (LeGros Clark, 1965). The generalized characteristics of primates are:

1. A primitive limb structure. The generalized skeletal features include a five-finger, five-toe pattern *(pentadactyl).*
2. A simple tooth pattern with grinding molars. This "conservative" pattern contrasts with the very specialized teeth other mammals have developed. The canine teeth of carnivores, for example, are specialized for tearing flesh, and the tusks of elephants are specialized for uprooting.

The specialized characteristics of primates include:

1. *Prehensility* (the ability to grasp) of hands and sometimes feet. This, like most of the other specialized characteristics, evolved as an adaptation to an *arboreal,* or tree-living, existence.
2. A collarbone capable of supporting flexible sideways movements of the arms.
3. Flat nails at the tips of the digits (fingers

and toes) and sensitive touch pads underneath. These features aid in an arboreal habitat by allowing grasping instead of clawing. In some primates, a claw (called a "toilet claw") appears on one of the digits.

4. A thumb that is mobile and can be moved opposite some or all of the other fingers, a trait called *opposability*. This ability allows the more complex primates to manipulate objects with their hands. Other mammals grasp objects with their teeth.
5. Changes in the senses of smell and sight, coupled with a flattening of the face. The olfactory (smell) center of the brain is progressively smaller in higher primates, as they depend more and more on sight. The visual area of the brain and the anatomical structures for seeing are increasingly emphasized, for this sense is most important in exploiting an arboreal niche. The muzzle of early mammals is replaced by a smaller nose with a less protruding mouth. The eyes are shifted toward the front of the face. These changes allow *stereoscopic vision,* in which images from each eye overlap to form a three-dimensional picture. Tree dwellers need this ability in order to judge distances from limb to limb. Many primates can see a broad range of colors as well. The high visual acuity of higher primates contributes to their ability to manipulate objects as well as to better eye-hand coordination.
6. Enlargement of the brain, especially the cerebral cortex, which directs the higher intellectual functions. The brain is large not only in size but also in relationship to the rest of the body.
7. Complex reproductive strategy. This strategy includes a longer gestation period and greater efficiency in getting nutrients to the fetus. A smaller litter size results from these changes. The period of dependence by infants on adult caretakers is also lengthened, adding more opportunities for social learning and intellectual growth.

Although all primates share these physical characteristics, they vary in the degree to which they express them. In general, primates in whom these characteristics are the least developed are called "lower" or "simpler" primates. These characteristics are most developed in the "higher" or more "complex" primates.

Social Characteristics

Defining just how primates behave is even more difficult than defining their physical characteristics. Primates rarely live in isolation. Most are organized into groups in which both sexes and all ages are represented. The interactions between individuals are structured by a *dominance hierarchy* (ranking by social power) that is based on age, sex, and individual differences. Behavior is, to a great extent, learned within the context of the troop; it is not totally instinctive, as in other animals.

There are, however, huge differences among the behaviors of lower primates, monkeys, apes, and humans. A definition of primate behavior that is too general does not distinguish the order from other mammals. A system of communication, cohesive social grouping, and social ties among individuals, for instance, mark the behavior of primates and other mammals as well. More specific definitions, however, may fit certain primates but not others. For instance, to say that all primates learn social roles by living within a social group is to ignore some of the prosimians. Few of them form social groups that are even relatively permanent (Dolhinow, 1972b). We can, however, make the general statement that primates display social behavior that is similar to that of other mammals, but, particularly among the higher primates, it is much more elaborate and sophisticated.

Consider communication, for instance. We now know that animals other than primates can communicate using signals of posture, movement, scent, touch, and vocalization.

The information sent in these signals can be quite complex. A honey bee, for instance, can communicate in its waggle dance complicated directions for finding food. In this dance, all the essentials of a flight to the food are mimicked in miniature. Humans cannot only explain where food is to be found but can also discuss emotions and abstractions through the use of language. Other primates cannot talk, but the higher ones can communicate a wide range of emotions and signals. They use facial expressions and gestures, as well as the methods used by other animals.

Where Are Primates Found?

Because of their culture and technology, humans can survive in all kinds of climates and terrains. The range of nonhuman primates is not nearly as wide, but is still very broad and diverse.

Geographical Distribution. As you can see in Figure 1, all of today's nonhuman primates live fairly close to the equator (within 35 degrees). The only primates living in the western hemisphere are the so-called *New World monkeys,* which inhabit Central and South America. Most primates are found in the eastern hemisphere. The *Old World monkeys* live in Africa and Asia. Various groups of the primitive primates called prosimians are found in these areas too, as are the anthropoid apes. Gibbons and orangutans live in the Far East, and our closest "relatives," chimpanzees and gorillas, live in western and central Africa.

Habitats. As we discussed earlier, most primates have evolved specializations for life in the trees, and most still tend to live in or near trees. A few primates, however, spend some or most of their time on the ground in *terrestrial* habitats. These primates are mainly found in steppes or savannas, where trees are sparse, or in forest clearings.

In South America there are no terrestrial primates. New World monkeys live in tropical rain forests, swamp forests, or lush secondary growth forests, where vegetation is growing back in natural clearings made by humans.

In Africa many primates (including chimpanzees and gorillas) live in the moist, warm, tropical rain forests. Trees there are so big and so dense that they house different species of primates at different levels. Guenons and some other monkeys prefer secondary growth in abandoned clearings in the rain forest. Some chimpanzees and gorillas live in drier mountain forests. Vervets, patas, baboons, and sometimes chimpanzees are found in grassy, semiarid, wooded steppes and in woodland savannas, where grass is tall and trees are 20 to 50 feet high.

In Asia primates live mostly in high forests, though a few live in mangrove swamps. Macaques can tolerate the colder climates of temperate zone woods in China and Japan. Heavily furred Japanese macaques, for instance, get through the winter by eating bark from bare trees. And in India some primates are thriving in human-dominated environments. The sacred hanuman langurs live in the trees surrounding villages; rhesus and bonnet macaques sleep on top of houses, temples, and railroad stations.

Classifying Primates

It would be impossible to study or understand the enormous variety of living things and their evolutionary past without some means of organizing them. Scientists have therefore arranged the primates, like all living things, in hierarchical categories called *taxa.* The organization of taxa, or *taxonomy,* that we use today is based on the system invented in 1758 by Linnaeus. He grouped organisms according to their anatomical features. Organisms that shared most or all of their physical features were placed in the same category. The fewer the number of features any two

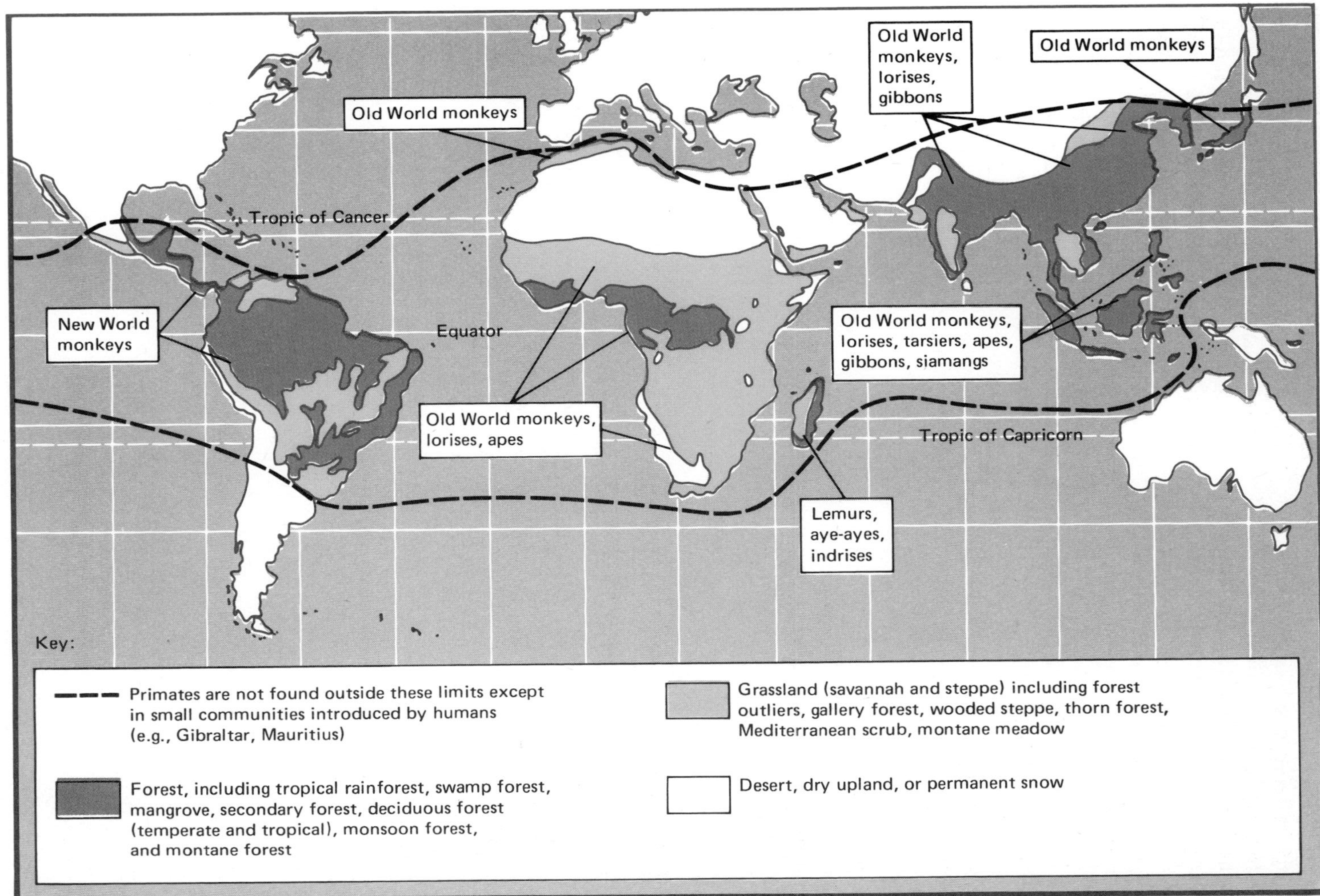

Figure 1 **Distribution of nonhuman primates.** (After Napier & Napier, 1967)

species share, the more likely they are to be placed in different categories.

Taxonomy in its modern use also reflects evolutionary relationships. The system takes into account to some degree the *phylogeny,* or evolutionary relationships, of the various species. Orangutans, chimpanzees, gorillas, and humans, for instance, are classified together into a single superfamily, reflecting the present belief that they diverged rather recently from a common ancestor.

Taxonomic Categories. The modern classification system has 21 categories. But for our purposes there are 12 important categories to remember. They range from species to kingdom, as shown in the boxed example. Each category is a subset of the one above it. A *genus,* for example, is a grouping of similar species; a *subfamily* is a grouping of similar genera (the plural of *genus*). There is no subfamily given for humans because there is only one living species and one genus in our line.

The basic unit in this taxonomy is the *species* (though subspecies are often recognized). As you learned in Chapter 3, a species is a group of organisms that can interbreed to produce fertile offspring like themselves. Members of a species are reproductively isolated from members of other species. This modern definition replaces Linnaeus's notion that a species approximated an ideal established by God.

Species are labeled by two Latin names. According to Linnaeus's system, the first is the genus. It is capitalized. The second is unique to the species and is not capitalized. The familiar chimpanzee, for instance, is called *Pan troglodytes. Pan* is the name of its genus. The term *troglodytes* is used to name the particular species. Some genera, such as *Homo,* contain only one living species *(Homo sapiens).* Others may contain more. *Pan* includes two: *troglodytes* and *paniscus.* Each of these species only breeds within itself. Yet they are anatomically similar, so they are both grouped in the same genus.

Although every effort has been made to bring these classifications in line with real rather than imagined similarities among organisms, the categories are arbitrary and artificial. The taxa we use are imperfect representations of the variety that actually exists. There is no such thing as the primate order in nature—it is simply a category invented by scientists to sort their data. As a result, scientists are always arguing about what the categories are and which animals belong in them. At one time, for example, the family *Pongidae* included gibbons as well as orangutans, chimpanzees, and gorillas. On the basis of recent evidence, however, the gib-

The Taxonomic Standing of Humans

Kingdom: Animalia
Phylum: Chordata
Subphylum: Vertebrata
Class: Mammalia
Order: Primates
Suborder: Anthropoidea
Infraorder: Catarrhini
Superfamily: Hominoidea
Family: Hominidae
Subfamily: ———
Genus: Homo
Species: *Homo sapiens*

bon has been taken out of *Pongidae* and placed into a family of its own, the *Hylobatidae.* A set of rules—*The International Code of Zoological Nomenclature*—is used to resolve ambiguities of classification. But since new information about living animals is always being discovered, many categories are constantly being revised.

Other Factors. Anatomy does not always clearly reflect the degree of biological relationship between two species. Sometimes the physical appearance of two animals that are in fact distantly related may be very similar as a result of convergent evolution. In addition, the fossil record may not provide clear evidence of the phylogenetic relationship between two animals. Since the 1950s taxonomists have come to use two other factors to verify apparent relationships: behavioral characteristics and *serological* (or blood serum) characteristics.

Behavioral Evidence. Use of behavioral evidence in classification depends on our ability to link certain behavior with taxonomic status. This has been done successfully with some vertebrates. Song patterns, for example, have been used to classify bird species. And studies show that gestures, vocalizations, and other behavior patterns do not vary much among primate groups of the same species (Dolhinow, 1972a). At the genus level, too, behavioral similarities are being discovered.

As our knowledge of primate social behavior increases, behavior may become a more useful classificatory criterion. However, all primates share the same sort of general behavior pattern. For this reason, it is difficult to distinguish biological relationships on the basis of behavior alone.

Serological Evidence. Compared to behavioral studies, serological data have been of far greater importance in the creation of primate taxonomies. Since the 1960s researchers have been comparing various proteins in the blood to see whether the biochemical characteristics of living primates show the same degree of relationship suggested by anatomical features. It is assumed that primates having similar blood proteins may be relatively closely related. Fewer similarities suggest more distant relationships.

To construct a biochemical taxonomy of the primates, researchers have studied blood serum molecules from a number of primates. The similarity of structure among these molecules is determined in a number of ways. One method uses *antibodies,* proteins formed to protect the body from biochemical structures, such as disease microorganisms, not normally found there. Most commonly, the antibody to a specific blood protein is created by injecting the protein into another animal, often a rabbit or a chicken. The foreign protein differs in shape from that performing the same function in the injected animal. As a result, the animal's immunological system reacts to the invading protein as a foreign substance and creates an antibody to help eliminate it. This antibody is then injected into a number of species related to the animal from which the original protein was extracted. If the intensity of the reaction between the antibody and the protein is similar in any two of these animals, it means that the structure of the protein is also similar. This protein similarity is then taken as evidence of a close biological relationship.

Vincent Sarich (1968) has applied this immunological technique in his study of the blood protein *albumin* among the primates. He isolated human albumin and injected it into rabbits, which then produced an antibody against that protein. The intensity of the reaction to the antibody was naturally greatest when tested with human albumin. Chimpanzee albumin reacted less strongly when tested with the rabbit-developed antibody, macaques still less strongly, and New World capuchin monkeys least strongly of all. This, of course, suggests that the structure of human albumin is more like that of the chimpanzee albumin than it is like those of the macaques and the capuchin monkeys.

Because of the great evolutionary distance between humans and rabbits, however, the antibody produced by the latter does not react differently to proteins that are very similar in structure. It reacts, for example, in the same way when tested with chimpanzee albumin as when tested with gorilla albumin. Thus, it is impossible to determine which of these two species possesses albumin more similar to that of humans. For a finer level of discrimination, the human protein may be injected in a more closely related species, such as macaques. The antibody produced by macaques does react differently to chimpanzee albumin than to gorilla albumin. This result suggests that chimpanzees are most closely related to humans.

A second approach breaks down a protein into its basic amino acid parts. Functionally similar proteins in different species are then compared in terms of the amino acids they contain. It is thought that closely related species have the fewest number of amino acid differences, and more distantly related species have the greatest number of differences. Such studies have been carried out on hemoglobin, the oxygen-carrying protein of the red blood cells. Although this method is more direct than the immunological approach, it provides data that are often difficult to interpret.

Taxonomies developed by the two approaches differ, and the results obtained by either approach also vary if the protein is changed. Analysis of serum albumin generally agrees with the classification scheme based on anatomy. It identifies our nearest "relatives" as the great apes (chimpanzees, gorillas, and orangutans), followed by the Old World monkeys, the New World primates, and then the prosimians.

Comparisons of the amino acid structure of primate hemoglobins also generally support the classification based on anatomy. But it muddles some relationships. The hemoglobins of baboons are as different from human hemoglobins as are those of the prosimians, despite the closer relationship between baboons and humans indicated by anatomical studies (Buettner-Janusch & Hill, 1965).

Despite its limitations, most taxonomists agree that the biomolecular approach, when integrated with anatomical data, can be a valuable aid in the classification of primates. Biomolecular evidence has also led most primate taxonomists to place the gibbons in a separate family. It has also helped to confirm that the African great apes—chimpanzees and gorillas—are more closely "related" to humans than is the Asian great ape, the orangutan.

Distinguishing the Living Primates

Now that we have looked at the basis for taxonomic distinctions, we can begin to sort out the primate taxa. The taxonomy we will use is summarized in Table 1 (see pp. 64–65). It differs in a few ways from others in current use, but there is no single taxonomy that is universally accepted. Note that it does not include the tree shrews in the primate category, as mentioned earlier.

In this overview of the primates we shall progressively isolate the characteristics that define humans. We have already looked at the generalized characteristics that we share with the other primates. Our distinctive human traits will come into focus as we move through increasingly narrow taxonomic categories to *Homo sapiens*. Along the way, the major taxa into which humans fall will be distinguished from those into which they do not fall.

Distinguishing Prosimii from Anthropoidea

Prosimians are the least complex of the primates. They are distinguishable on the basis of certain primitive characteristics thought to have been possessed by the earliest primates. Some of these traits are also found among nonprimates, especially those in the order Insectivora, which includes shrews, moles, and hedgehogs. In both prosimians and insectivores the sense of smell, for instance, is very well developed. This trait is less emphasized in more complex primates in favor of sight. The eyes of prosimians are placed at the sides of the skull. Because there is a limited overlap in the fields of vision, three-dimensional sight is not fully developed in many species.

In addition to their retention of primitive characteristics, prosimian species also have many specialized characteristics. These characteristics are adaptations that have allowed prosimians to live in new areas and avoid competition with anthropoid populations. Many, for example, have developed specializations for nocturnal, or nighttime, activity. These adaptations (such as huge eyes) have cut down on their competition with diurnal, or day-living, creatures. Varying patterns of evolution have created prosimians as unalike as the tiny froglike tarsier and the large bearlike indri. The characteristics that distinguish prosimians from the higher primates are:

1. Either of two primitive adaptations to movement in the trees: (a) modifications for clinging to vertical limbs and leaping from tree to tree (as in the tarsiers): long hindlimbs, strong hindlimb muscles, skeletal arrangement to support a vertical posture; (b) modifications for very slow climbing on all fours (as in the slow loris): short limbs, arms almost as long as the legs, mobile hip and ankle joints for hanging, short tail or none at all.
2. Ability of fingers to act in unison; inability to act separately. This arrangement allows powerful grasping, but not manipulation of objects, as in the anthropoids.
3. Claws on some digits instead of nails. These claws are called *toilet claws,* because they are used for cleaning dirt and parasites from fur and skin.
4. Primitive arrangement of the pads on the fingertips and toes. These pads aid in clinging to vertical surfaces. In more complex primates, the pads are smaller and little more than thickened skin.
5. Eyes set apart at a greater angle than in anthropoids.
6. Adaptations by some prosimians to nocturnal life. These include enlarged eyes and loss from the eye structure of retinal cones, which respond to bright light and allow color vision.
7. Large, mobile ears that can scan for sound.
8. Well-developed sense of smell. Some have *olfactory muzzles*—snouts with bare, moist tips, curved nostrils, and a tethered upper lip, attached in such a way as to allow little facial expression. The sense of smell is less emphasized in the anthropoids.

Figure 2 **Distinguishing Prosimii from Anthropoidea**

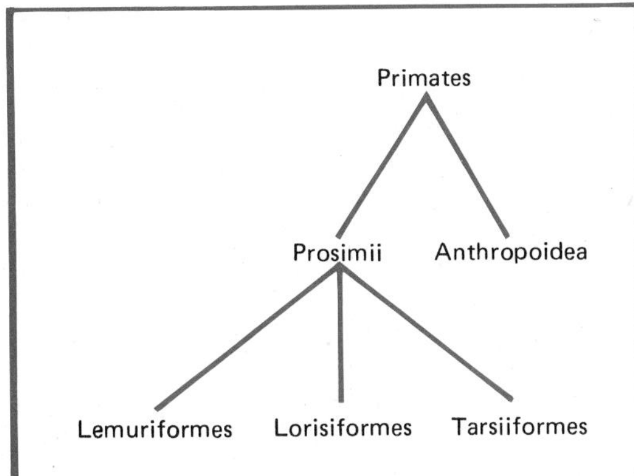

Table 1 Taxonomy of the Primate Order

Suborder	Infraorder	Superfamily	Family	Subfamily	Genus	Common Name
Prosimii (prosimians)	Tarsiiformes				Tarsius	Tarsier
	Lorisiformes	Lorisoidea	Lorisidae	Lorisinae	Loris Nycticebus Perodicticus Arctocebus	(slender lorises) (slow lorises) (pottos) (angwantibos)
				Galiginae	Galago	(galagos)
	Lemuriformes	Lemuroidea	Leumuridae	Lemurinae (true lemurs)	Lemur Hapalemur Lepilemur	(lemurs) (gentle lemurs) (weasel and sportive lemurs)
				Cheirogal-einae (small lemurs)	Cheirogaleus Microcebus Phaner	(dwarf and mouse lemurs) (mouse lemurs) (fork-marked mouse lemurs)
			Indriidae		Indri Lichanotus Propithecus	(indrises) (woolly indrises) (sifakas)
		Daubentonoidea			Daubentonia	(aye-ayes)
		Ceboidea	Cebidae (cebid monkeys)	Cibinae	Cebus Saimiri	(capuchin monkeys) (squirrel monkeys)
				Alouattinae	Alouatta	(howler monkeys)
				Aotinae	Aotus Callicebus	(night monkeys and douroucoulis) (titis)
				Atelinae	Ateles Brachyteles Lagothrix	(spider monkeys) (woolly spider monkeys) (woolly monkeys)

Anthropoidea (anthropoids)	Platyrrhini (New World monkeys)			Callimiconinae	Callimico	(Goeldi's monkey)
				Pitheciinae	Pithecia	(sakis)
					Cacajao	(uakaris)
					Chiropotes	(sakis)
			Callithricidae		Callithrix	(marmosets)
					Cebuella	(pygmy marmosets)
					Leontideus	(golden lion tamarins)
					Saguinus	(tamarins)
	Catarrhini (Old World primates)	Cercopithecoidea (Old World monkeys)	Cercopithecidae	Cercopithecinae	Cercopithecus	(guenons, talapoins, vervets)
					Cercocebus	(mangabeys)
					Cynopithecus	(black apes)
					Theropithecus	(gelada baboons)
					Erythrocebus	(patas monkeys)
					Macaca	(macaques)
					Papio	(baboons)
				Colobinae	Colobus	(colobus monkeys and guerezas)
					Nasalis	(the proboscis monkey)
					Presbytis	(leaf monkeys; langurs)
					Pygathrix	(douc langurs)
					Rhinopithecus	(snub-nosed monkeys; Tibetan langurs)
		Hominoidea (hominoids)	Hylobatidae		Hylobates	(gibbons; siamangs)
			Pongidae	(pongids)	Pongo	(orangutans)
					Pan	(chimpanzees)
					Gorilla	(gorillas)
			Hominidae	(hominids)	Homo	(humans)

9. Relatively large olfactory lobes in brain. There is less cortical area than in anthropoids, and ratios of brain size to body weight are smaller.
10. Dental specializations: the upper front teeth, or incisors, are very small, and the canine teeth (pointed teeth between the incisors and the grinding teeth) are large. The lower incisors and canines project forward in many species to form a *dental comb* for grooming the fur. (Adapted from Napier & Napier, 1967; Rosen, 1974; Campbell, 1974)

The Prosimians. There are three major *infraorders* in the prosimian suborder: Tarsiiformes, Lorisiformes, and Lemuriformes.

Tarsiiformes. The tarsier is the only remaining member of the once large *Tarsiiformes* infraorder. These tiny creatures, which live in Borneo and the Philippines, are equipped with a very long tail and hindlimbs for hopping from branch to branch. Their huge eyes and the pads at the ends of their fingers add to their strange froglike appearance. The special pads help them cling to smooth, vertical surfaces. Tarsiers can walk on a vertical sheet of glass. During the day they sleep clinging to a vertical branch. They wake at dusk and spend the evening hopping from tree to tree looking for insects and lizards to eat.

Lorisiformes. Nocturnal primates, *Lorisiformes* are divided into two distinct types—lorises and galagos—according to their locomotor patterns. Lorises are found in subsaharan Africa and in Asia. They are adapted to slow climbing and creeping. This movement is made possible by a very powerful grasp and strong muscles. Lorises can hang by one hindlimb while reaching for food. Insects seem to form the bulk of their diet, but they will eat almost anything from flowers to young birds.

The slender loris is a slow climber and creeper. This form of locomotion, together with the loris's large eyes, adapt it to a nocturnal, arboreal niche, reducing competition with other animals. (San Diego Zoo Photo)

Galagos, by contrast, leap gracefully through the trees, taking long kangaroolike hops with their strong hindlimbs. Their shorter forelimbs are used to grab hold of branches when they land. They can easily leap from one vertical support to another. Galagos range from the size of large mice to the size of large rabbits. Like the lorises, they are *omnivores,* that is, they eat both plants and animals (Buettner-Janusch, 1966).

Lemuriformes. The *Lemuriformes,* which include lemurs, the indrises, and the aye-ayes, are found primarily on the island of Madagascar, off the southeast coast of Africa. They have developed many variations because of the lack of competition and predators. The members of one genus, the mouse lemurs, are smaller than a mouse; they are the tiniest living primates. The largest members of the infraorder are the indrises, which measure over three feet from head to tail. Most Lemuriformes are active during the day and at dusk, but some are nocturnal. Most are completely arboreal, different species living at different levels in the same trees.

All lemurs are wonderful acrobats. They can leap great distances, sometimes to the smallest of branches, swinging themselves up gracefully at the end of the jump. Their ability to do so is due not only to their musculature but also to unusually well-developed binocular vision. Unlike other prosimians, the lemurs avoid animal foods and seem to be highly social. Among other prosimians, only females and infants live together. But the lemurs live in troops of up to 60 members and sleep huddled in small groups with their tails wrapped around one another (Buettner-Janusch, 1966).

These ring-tailed lemurs are spectacular arboreal acrobats who move almost nonstop throughout the day. Like other Lemuriformes, they have prehensile hands and feet and nails on their digits. (Russ Kinne, Photo Researchers)

The Anthropoids. The anthropoids, too, are a diverse suborder. But they are characterized by their own shared set of specialized adaptations. These adaptations mainly allow a more effective use of arboreal environments. Forward-facing eyes permit stereoscopic vision among the anthropoids, and the visual centers of the brain are complex, allowing integration of large amounts of visual data. Depth perception and quick reaction to visual cues are essential to tree-living. Anthropoids also possess color vision, which aids in depth perception and the sighting of brightly colored fruit in trees. Adaptations for grasping and handling objects are crucial to life in trees, as well. Finally, the characteristically high brain-to-body ratio of anthropoids increases their ability to survive by agility and learning. These qualities are more appropriate in the trees than are the specializations of terrestrial animals for attack and defense, such as large horns, tusks, and claws (LeGros Clark, 1965).

Distinguishing Platyrrhini from Catarrhini

Within the suborder Anthropoidea, there are two infraorders: *Platyrrhini,* the New World monkeys, and *Catarrhini,* the Old World primates. The most important traits that distinguish these two groups are:

1. Distinctive locomotor pattern. New World monkeys usually run along branches on all fours. While feeding at the ends of small branches, they spread their weight between their hands, feet, and tails. Old World primates are more likely to leap from tree to tree, swing by their arms, or walk on the ground.
2. Tails. All New World monkeys have tails, some of which are prehensile. Although some Old World primates have tails, none are prehensile.
3. New World monkeys lack ischial callosities, which are tough pads of skin on the

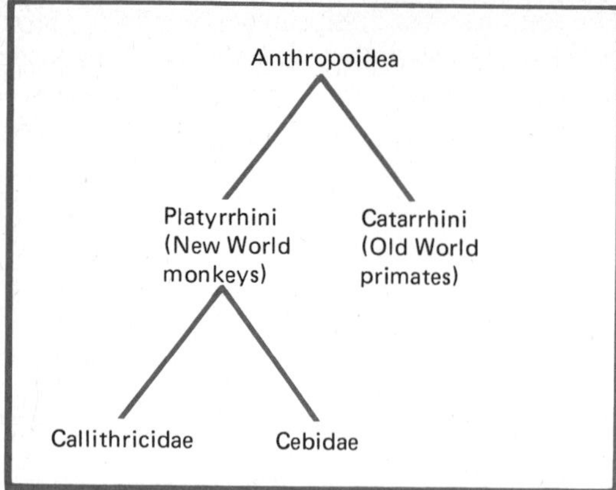

Figure 3 Distinguishing Platyrrhini from Catarrhini

rump that allow the animal to sit on tree limbs for long periods of time.

4. New World monkeys have flat noses with round nostrils and a broad fleshy area between them. Old World forms have nostrils that project and point downward.
5. New World monkeys have a $\frac{2.1.3.3.}{2.1.3.3.}$ dental pattern (like that of the prosimians). On each side of the jaw there are two incisors, one canine, three premolars, and three molars. Marmosets, an exception, lack the third molar. Old World forms have one less premolar, top and bottom. (Adapted from Rosen, 1974; Napier & Napier, 1967; Campbell, 1974)

The New World Monkeys. The New World monkeys live throughout the heavily forested regions of Central and South America. They are divided into two families: the Callithricidae, which include the marmosets and tamarins, and the Cebidae, which contain six subfamilies. Most New World monkeys belong to the Cebidae.

Most New World monkeys seem to spend their lives in the trees. The woolly titis, for example, live only in the smallest branches of the highest trees. They do not come down, even for water. Apparently they get enough moisture from the flowers, fruits, and nuts they eat. But the more highly evolved capuchins, which are commonly known as "organ-grinder monkeys," sometimes leave the forests to steal fruit and vegetables from farms. Squirrel monkeys, too, will sometimes come down out of the trees to catch insects.

Locomotor patterns vary among the New World monkeys. Some walk on all fours, both on the ground and on tree limbs. Others, like the spider monkeys, are best at moving in an upright position. They do so by swinging from their arms, which are longer than their legs. Spider monkeys use their strong, prehensile tails to swing and to grasp limbs as they pick fruit. Reportedly, they can jump as far as 30 feet.

We know very little about the social behavior of most New World monkeys because

A strong prehensile tail frees this spider monkey's hands and feet for a variety of uses. Though, like other New World monkeys, its thumbs are not fully opposable, its long limbs and flexible digits adapt it to a largely arboreal life. (D. J. Chivers, Anthro-Photo)

they live in thick jungles, high in the trees, where they cannot be observed easily. They have been seen in troops of up to 30 and in family bands.

Old World Primates. Within the Old World line, there are two superfamilies—*Cercopithecoidea* (or Old World monkeys) and *Hominoidea* (humans, apes, gibbons, orangutans, chimpanzees, and gorillas). The major differences that have evolved between these two groups are:

1. Most species of Old World monkeys have tails; hominoids have no tails.
2. Old World monkeys are generally smaller than hominoids.
3. Old World monkeys have prenatal development of ischial callosities. Most hominoids are not born with these rump pads, although they may grow after birth.
4. Old World monkeys have a shorter life span than the hominoids.
5. Old World monkeys have smaller brain-size to body-weight ratios as well as less complex brains than the hominoids. The cerebral cortex is especially well developed in hominoids. (Adapted from Napier & Napier, 1967; Rosen, 1974)

The distinctions here are somewhat more finely drawn than the others we have made. This is because both superfamilies are included in the same infraorder, a sign of their similarity of anatomy. They are more closely related than, say, members of suborders or infraorders.

The superfamily Cercopithecoidea contains a single family, which can be divided into two subfamilies, the Cercopithecinae and the Colobinae. The most numerous genera in the Cercopithecinae are: (1) the arboreal monkeys of the genus *Cercopithecus;* (2) the mostly arboreal mangabeys, or *Cercocebus;* and (3) the terrestrial macaques and baboons, *Macaca* and *Papio.* Langurs are the most common genus in the Colobinae subfamily.

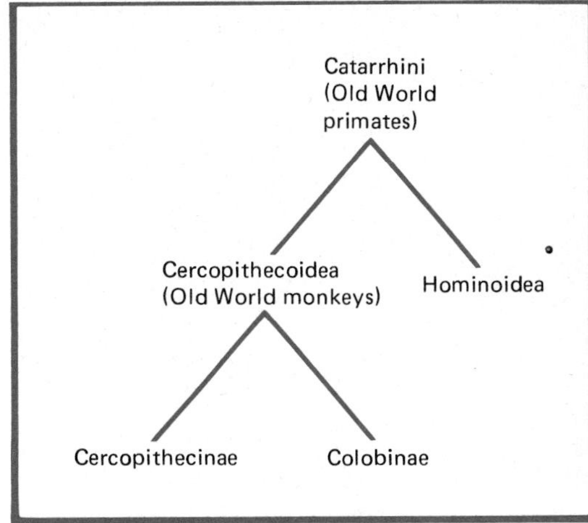

Figure 4 Distinguishing Cercopithecoidea from Hominoidea

Guenons. The cercopithecine monkeys, or guenons, are widely distributed in Africa. Although they live mostly in trees, some species come down to feed on the forest floor, in plantations, in open bush, and in savanna country. They live largely on insects, fruits, and vegetation, but will sometimes eat birds, eggs, and even small mammals. They seem to live in small groups made up of a dominant male and a small harem of females and their children.

Mangabeys. The long-tailed mangabeys, who are sometimes seen with cercopithecines, spend much of their day on the ground. Though they possess some adaptations to life in the trees, they also have some of the traits of terrestrial primates. Their hands, for instance, are more like those of the terrestrial baboon than those of totally arboreal primates. They live mostly in the swampy forests of Africa.

Baboons and Macaques. Though classed as separate genera, baboons and macaques are closely related. If they mate, they can sometimes produce fertile offspring (Buettner-Janusch, 1966). But they inhabit different ranges. The baboons live in Africa and the Arabian peninsula. The macaques range from India east to Japan. They both live mainly on

Savanna baboons. The large canine teeth and mantle of fur around the neck are unique to males and aid in aggressive displays before predators. (Irven De Vore, Anthro-Photo)

the ground, though they sleep in trees. Both have developed finely controlled hands with precision grips that function like ours.

Since terrestrial animals are much easier to watch than those that move in the treetops, the social behaviors of baboons and macaques have been studied fairly well. Baboons live in highly structured troops of 10 to 100 members. Within the troop a clear dominance hierarchy reduces tensions and provides protection from predators. The threat of predators may be the reason for their extreme *sexual dimorphism* (different physical forms for the two genders). Male and female arboreal monkeys, who face few predators and rely on their agility for fleeing, look pretty much the same. But among the ground-living baboons, the males are specialized for defense on the ground. They may be twice as big as the females, and they can put on impressive threat displays with their huge canine teeth and their great ruffs of fur at the neck (Eimerl & DeVore, 1965).

Langurs. Among these slender, long-tailed, Asiatic monkeys, group organization is not

These common langurs are arboreal leaf-eaters. Most Old World monkeys have tails (none of which are prehensile), ischial callosities, and a fully opposable thumb. (Irven De Vore, Anthro-Photo)

as important to defense. They often feed on the ground, but prefer graceful flight into the trees rather than an organized show of force. Langurs sometimes live alone and sometimes in troops. In troops the relationship between males and females is not well defined. The status of females is high when they are paired with a male. But when their infants are born the mothers seem to drop out of the status system altogether. When dominant males are found near temples, they form harems (groups of females) and actually chase away other males (Hrdy, 1977).

Distinguishing Humans from the Apes

The Apes. Finally, we shall look at the differences that divide us from the Hylobatidae (gibbons), and our closest relatives, the Pongidae (chimpanzees, gorillas, and orangutans). A list of the anatomical traits distinguishing these two groups from hominids is as follows:

1. Limited bipedal walking. Although pongids and hylobatids are better than any other nonhumans at walking bipedally in a semierect posture, they do not do so for long periods of time.
2. Short thumbs. As a result, most pongids and hylobatids have a limited precision grip.
3. Ridges of bone directly above the eyes. Pongids lack a forehead.

Figure 5 Distinguishing humans from the apes

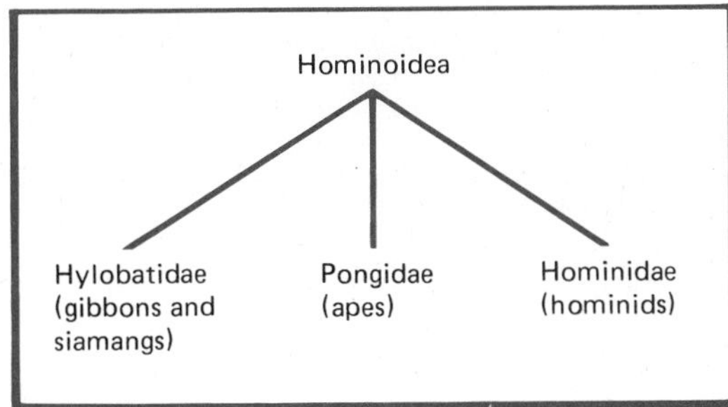

4. Teeth specialized for a diet that includes massive quantities of fruit and vegetation. The canines, used to open fruit and strip plants, are large and projecting. To hold their heavy teeth and support the chewing of such bulky food, pongids have massive jaws that jut forward. A bony *simian shelf* buttresses the inside of the front part of the jaw. Large cheek bones and, in males, a ridge of bone called a *sagittal crest* at the top of the skull, anchor the strong chewing muscles.
5. Lower brain size-to-body weight ratio than among humans, who have the most complex cortical structure of the hominoids.

Gibbons. *Brachiation,* the hand-over-hand arm-swinging that some monkeys use is developed to the highest degree among the gibbons. In contrast to the highly developed hindquarters of clingers and leapers such as the tarsier, the gibbon's shoulders and long arms are powerfully developed and flexible. Its legs are short and relatively weak. Although the gibbon uses its long fingers as a hook when it swings, tucking its thumb out of the way, the thumb is long enough so that it is able to touch the other fingers. Gibbons spend most of their lives in the trees of southeast Asian rain forests. They do not come down often to drink from springs or to feed in the bushes. Although they rarely move on the ground, they sometimes walk bipedally along branches, standing almost erect and using their long arms for balance (Campbell, 1974).

Gibbons of the same sex do not get along very well. Troops are therefore small, usually made up of a male, a female, and up to four offspring. Sexes are equally dominant in the relationship, and they may take turns grooming each other. The males alone, however, patrol the area. They engage in frequent yelling and chasing confrontations with other gibbons who have moved into their territory (Napier & Napier, 1967).

Orangutans. These red-haired pongids live

in the forests of Sumatra and Borneo. Like gibbons, they are largely arboreal. Adapted for brachiation, these animals possess long arms and powerful, mobile shoulders and hands. But because of their larger size, they are not swift and graceful like the gibbon. Instead, they move cautiously, holding onto overhead branches with their hands while trying to find footholds below to spread their weight. On the ground, they walk quadrupedally, with clenched hands and feet Napier & Napier, 1967).

By capturing orangutans for zoos, humans have reduced their numbers in the wild to only a few thousand. Orangs have no other known predators. Quiet and lethargic, they look very much like orange-bearded men, as travelers have described them for centuries. Orangs can oppose their thumb to the other four fingers in order to pick up small objects, feed, and build simple nests.

Very little is known about orangs' behavior in the wild. They seem to live mostly in groups of two to four, though males often live alone. One of the few aggressive behaviors scientists have been able to observe is their habit of dropping or throwing sticks in the direction of people who are watching them.

Gorillas. Despite their intimidating appearance, gorillas are generally peaceful animals. Grown males, in an upright position, measure 6 feet and weigh up to 400 pounds, making them the largest of the primates by far. Gorillas live in a variety of environments in equatorial Africa. Their habitats include low rain forests, woodlands with low trees and lots of undergrowth, bamboo forests, mountain forests, and open mountain slopes up to elevations of 13,500 feet. They are vegetarians, eating a great quantity of stalks, vines, bark, leaves, bamboo shoots, roots, and, in some subspecies, fruit.

This young orangutan displays agility that will disappear during adulthood. Orangs are structurally adapted for brachiation, but large size and weight make cautious climbing a must. (Irven De Vore, Anthro-Photo)

This lowland male gorilla displays its usual form of locomotion—knuckle-walking. The sagittal crest on top of the skull anchors the massive jaw muscles needed to process enormous quantities of vegetation. (San Diego Zoo Photo)

Gorillas look for food on the ground. They walk quadrupedally on the soles of their feet and on their knuckles, which have tough pads to take this punishment. This form of locomotion is called *knuckle walking.* Adults and juveniles have never been seen swinging by their arms through the trees. Tree-climbing is more common among infants and females than among adult males. Though gorillas rarely walk bipedally, they do stand on their hind legs during their chest-beating display. This is part of a ritual sequence of behaviors, including vegetation-uprooting and foot-stamping. The display seems to be an elaborate bluff designed to intimidate an opponent, for an angry gorilla will rarely fight.

Behavior within the troop is peaceful, too. The dominant male acts as leader and protector for a stable group of 5 to 30 gorillas. Since the sex ratio is one male for every two females, many young adult males live alone, occasionally joining existing troops for short periods. At night the troop sleeps in nests made on the ground or in trees. New ones are made each day, perhaps because the gorillas invariably defecate in them during the night (Napier & Napier, 1967; Eimerl & De Vore, 1965).

Chimpanzees. The chimpanzee resembles the gorilla anatomically, but not in size, for a chimp is only a third as big as a gorilla.

Chimpanzees are native to Africa. Like gorillas, they have adapted to a variety of environmental settings: tropical rain forests, savannas, hilly woodlands, forested mountain slopes, and secondary forests. They stay in the trees for 50 to 75 percent of the day and sleep in nests built in trees at least 15 feet above the ground. Though they occasionally eat meat, fish, ants, and termites, their diet is mostly vegetarian: fruits, leaves, nuts, bark, seeds, and stems.

While in the trees, chimpanzees swing by their arms for short distances. They often use their feet, as well, to hold on to limbs. On the ground they move quadrupedally, knuckle walking as gorillas do. Often they stand on their hind legs to see better. But only occasionally do they run or walk bipedally, to carry objects or to put on a display. They have flexible hands and use them to groom themselves, build nests, use crude tools, and, in captivity, even to paint pictures.

An adult female chimpanzee inspects her hand in the course of leaf grooming. Note that the relatively short thumb allows only a poor precision grip, a trait common to all pongids. (Richard Wrangham, Anthro-Photo)

Chimpanzees do not form the rigidly hierarchical societies some other primates have developed. They are together only temporarily, in groups of 2 to 48. There is no one pattern that characterizes these groups, nor is there a clearcut dominance structure. Individuals, particularly siblings or mothers and their offspring, do, however, form close and lasting ties to each other (Van Lawick-Goodall, 1971). Social interaction includes juvenile play, adult grooming, noisy group displays, and communication (Napier & Napier, 1967; Eimerl & DeVore, 1965).

Summary

1. People have long been interested in the higher primates. In their likeness to humans, these primates have sometimes been the object of worship, scorn, and amusement.

2. Scientific curiosity about primates began with the Greeks. Aristotle and Galen generated most of the early anatomical information about primates. During the European Middle Ages, interest lay dormant, and there was a tendency to view primates moralistically as evil creatures. By the nineteenth century enough information about primates was available to permit scientists to think of a common ancestry for monkeys, apes, and humans.

3. During the twentieth century, *primatologists* have demonstrated the diversity in behavior and biology of the primates. Studies of primate societies were conducted in laboratories, controlled environments (such as compounds), and natural environments. As a result, there is now general agreement that humans belong to the biological order *Primates* and share certain characteristics with other species in this order. The *generalized characteristics,* the primitive traits possessed by the earliest primates, include a primitive limb structure and a simple tooth pattern. *Specialized characteristics,* adaptations developed in the course of primate evolution, include prehensility; a collarbone that permits flexibility in arm movements; nails instead of claws; touch pads; an opposable thumb, which allows a precision grip; reduction in the number of teeth; emphasis on sight rather than smell; high body-to-brain ratio; and more complex reproductive and caretaking (of the young) strategies. Behaviorally, primates emphasize social learning and may organize into complex troops.

4. Primates have been grouped according to anatomical features into hierarchical categories called *taxa.* The organization of taxa is called *taxonomy* and is based on the system developed by Linnaeus. The basic unit in this taxonomy is the *species.* Today taxonomy also takes into account *phylogeny* and *serological* and behavioral characteristics.

5. The order Primates is divided into two suborders: *Prosimii* and *Anthropoidea.* The former consists of the least complex of the primates and includes the three *infraorders Tarsiiformes, Lorisiformes,* and *Lemuriformes.* The anthropoids are characterized by a shared set of specialized adaptations that allow more effective use of arboreal environments and by a high brain-to-body ratio. The suborder is divided into the infraorders *Platyrrhini* (New World monkeys) and *Catarrhini* (Old World primates).

6. The New World monkeys are divided into two *families:* Callithricidae and Cebidae. They are primarily arboreal, and because they live in dense jungle areas, little is known about their social behavior.

7. Within the Old World line are two *superfamilies: Cercopithecoidea* (Old World monkeys) and Hominoidea (humans, gibbons, orangutans, chimpanzees, and gorillas). The former superfamily consists of one family, which is divided into two subfamilies: Cercopithecinae (guenons, mangabeys, macaques, baboons) and Colobinae (langurs). The superfamily Hominoidea is divided into three families: Hylobatidae (gibbons), Pongidae (chimpanzees, gorillas, orangutans), and Hominidae (humans). The gibbons and orangutans are farthest from the human pattern while chimpanzees and gorillas are considered to be our closer "relatives."

5 Primate Behavior

AFTER painstakingly removing a fossil molar from the rock in which it has been embedded, paleontologists can describe its form in detail and compare it with other fossil molars. But how can they reconstruct the animal's diet and its method of food-getting? A fossil shoulder joint also is found. What can it reveal about how the animal moved? Questions about simple behavior such as eating or moving can only be answered by studying the teeth and limbs of contemporary descendants of the fossil creature and by watching how these animals eat and move.

How did our apelike ancestors forage and live together? In families? In bands? To what extent could they communicate? Complex behaviors like these do not correspond to specific structures in the body—a set of teeth or leg bones, for example. As a result, they leave few if any traces in the fossil record. So for clues as to the complex behavior of our ancestors, we must study ourselves and the other living primates. It is particularly revealing to search for basic similarities between the behavior of humans and that of the great apes (chimpanzees, gorillas, and orangutans). These similar behaviors probably did not emerge independently in each evolutionary line. More likely, they were present, in some form, among our common ancestors. During the last 15 to 20 million years, the many evolutionary descendants of this ancestral group probably also have possessed these behaviors, so that they are present in all living great apes and humans.

In this chapter we shall examine two kinds of primate behavior. The first consists of anatomically based activity called *first-order behavior.* Feeding and locomotion, for example, are made up of hundreds of mechanical actions that are structured by the size and shape of different bones. *Second-order behavior* consists of interactions between individuals and between populations—hunting together, communication, and social organization, for example. Although these types of behaviors depend on the movement of muscles, bones, and teeth, they are structured by the function of the brain, and are either learned (as in the case of humans and many primates) or programmed genetically. It is possible to get an idea of the gross brain structure of extinct primates by studying their skulls, but it is impossible to guess at the type of behavior these structures controlled. The relationship between brain structure and behavior is so complicated that we are barely beginning to understand it in living animals.

We do know, however, a great deal about the behavior of living primates. Some primatologists are trying to link behavior with the ecosystems in which different primates live. In this way, it may be possible to associate behaviors of living primates with those of extinct species living in similar ecosystems.

Primate Behavioral Systems

Fieldworkers observing a group of primates see an enormous number of details. To make sense of this information, anthropologists break up what they see into groups of related actions. Sets of activities that have a functional relationship to each other are called *behavioral systems.* Information about a first-order behavioral system is found through dissection of muscles and bones and observations of behavior in the field. In this way function is assigned to structure. Information about second-order behavioral systems involves knowing the age, sex, and relationship of the participants, the environmental setting, and the relation of the behavior to previous and later behavior. Behavioral systems are arbitrary concepts. In real life, first- and second-order behaviors are integrated into the nonstop activity seen by the primatologist. In the next section we shall look at two of the main first-order behaviors: locomotion and feeding.

First-Order Behaviors

Locomotion

Most primates spend some or all of their time in trees. But not all of them use the same pattern of locomotion. Locomotion depends partly on the evolutionary history of the species and partly on the animal's niche. Some primates have adapted to the small top branches of trees, others to the middle parts. Still others live only partly in trees and spend much of their time on the ground. Finally, a few primates spend all of their time on the ground.

Primatologists often distinguish four major locomotion patterns among the primates: *vertical clinging and leaping, quadrupedalism, brachiation,* which are shown in Figure 1, and *bipedalism.* But the distinctions are not hard and fast. Although each kind of primate has a preference for a certain pattern, they all display a great range of locomotory behavior. For instance, all primates are capable of moving about on all fours. And most monkeys and every kind of ape can stand and sometimes walk upright.

Vertical Clinging and Leaping. Some prosimians have developed modifications that allow them to rest clinging to vertical tree trunks and to leap with their hind legs from one tree to another. In these animals the hindlimbs are greatly lengthened and strengthened in comparison to the forelimbs. Elongated heels make the back feet effective levers for spring-

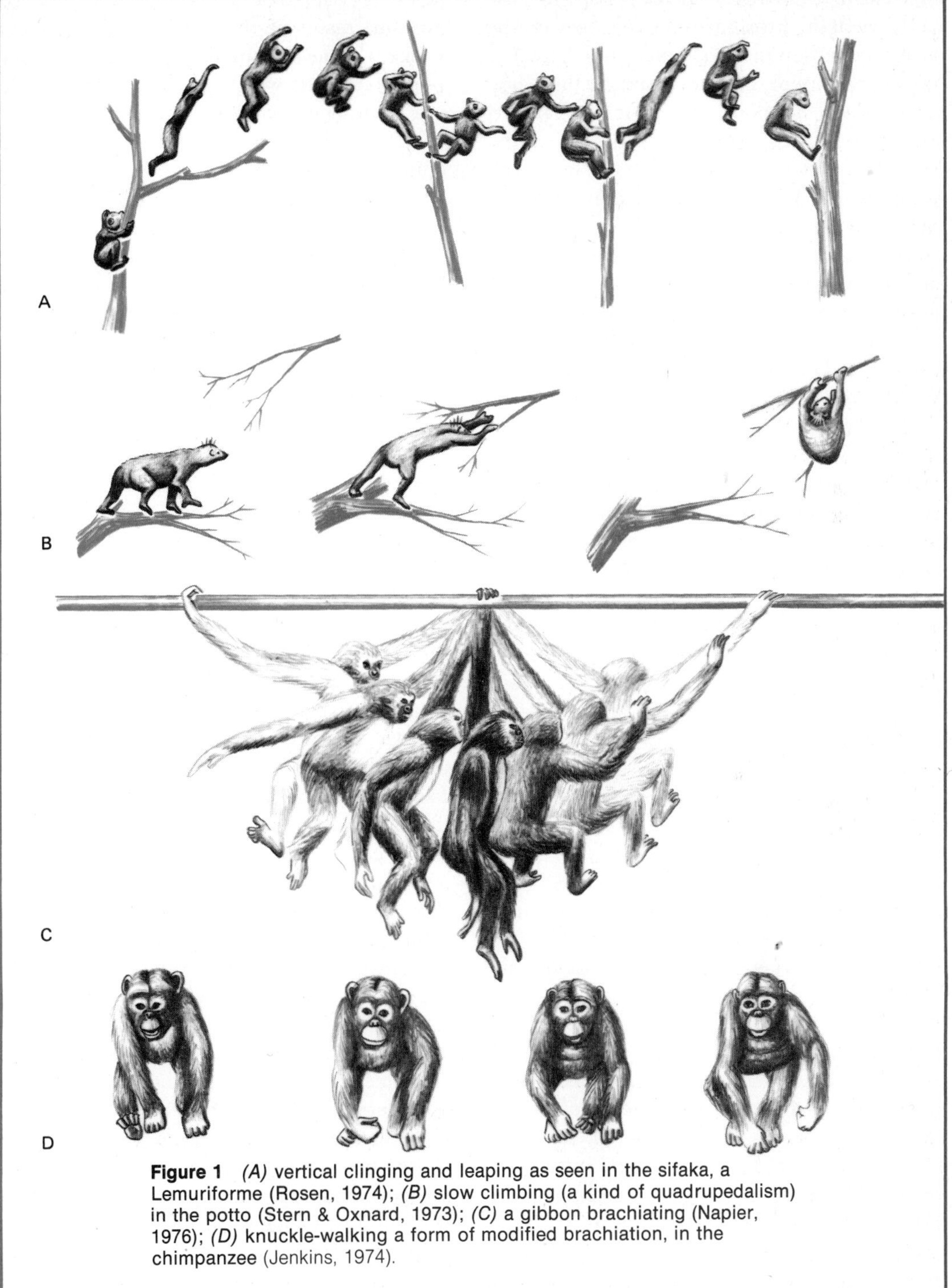

Figure 1 *(A)* vertical clinging and leaping as seen in the sifaka, a Lemuriforme (Rosen, 1974); *(B)* slow climbing (a kind of quadrupedalism) in the potto (Stern & Oxnard, 1973); *(C)* a gibbon brachiating (Napier, 1976); *(D)* knuckle-walking a form of modified brachiation, in the chimpanzee (Jenkins, 1974).

ing. The forelimbs play a part in propelling the body when the prosimians move slowly on the ground, for then they walk quadrupedally. For rapid movement on the ground, they hop using their hindlimbs (Napier & Napier, 1967).

Quadrupedalism. Primates have evolved many ways to use all four limbs in locomotion. In *slow climbing,* the method used by lorises and pottos, at least three of the four limbs are always in contact with branches above.

Some of the Old World monkeys, many New World monkeys, and some lemurs run or walk palms down along the tops of branches. Some terrestrial species, such as macaques, mandrills, vervets, and baboons, walk with only their fingers touching the ground. The fingers are bent back so that the second joints bear the animal's weight.

Semibrachiators use their arms to hang from branches or to swing themselves along. These primates can grasp with their feet, and some of the New World monkeys can also grasp with their prehensile tails. At other times these animals move on all four limbs.

Despite differences in how they use their hands and feet in moving, most quadrupedal primates are very agile. The spinal column between the pelvis and the chest is extremely long and flexible. This is an asset to those species who move rapidly through irregularly spaced branches, as well as to the slow climbers, who wrap themselves around trunks and branches (Eimerl & Devore, 1965; Campbell, 1974).

Brachiation. Bodily flexibility is lessened among the brachiators. Evolutionary emphasis has been placed instead on efficiency of swinging by the arms. In *true brachiation,* the arms alone are used to swing hand-over-hand through the trees and to provide momentum for bridging large gaps from limb to limb. In *modified brachiation,* the arms play the major role in locomotion, but they are sometimes assisted by support from the legs. On the ground, many of these animals are knuckle walkers. The chimpanzee, for instance, supports part of its weight on its knuckles, which are equipped for this with tough, callused pads. The gibbon is a true brachiator; gorillas, chimpanzees, and orangutans are modified brachiators. Like the other primates, these animals can move in a variety of ways. Gibbons, for example, can walk bipedally along branches if arm swinging is not practical (Schultz, 1969).

Evolution of the brachiators has favored overdevelopment of the arms and shoulders in relationship to the legs. This is especially pronounced in the gibbon and the orangutan. Emphasis on arm swinging has also decreased flexibility in the trunk, for it is not used much in this type of locomotion. Three of the lumbar vertebrae, flexible in quadrupeds, are stiff parts of the ribcage in the gibbon.

Bipedalism. Many primates occasionally walk on their hind limbs. But only humans can straighten their hind limbs for a completely upright posture.

Like the great apes, hominids probably never developed the extreme specializations for brachiation that gibbons did. But the fairly inflexible spines and the strong shoulders of the great apes and humans suggest that at some point the hominids may have shared with the gibbon an ancestor with some ability to brachiate. Our closer similarity to the great apes probably means that the common ancestor of living hominids (humans included) was a modified brachiator. But hominid adaptation to a terrestrial way of life led to structural refinements allowing bipedal locomotion (Buettner-Janusch, 1966).

Unfortunately, no fossils exist that can show the beginning of bipedalism. But skeletal comparisons of living primates with living humans suggest that at least six changes were needed to allow the body to balance and move on two feet.

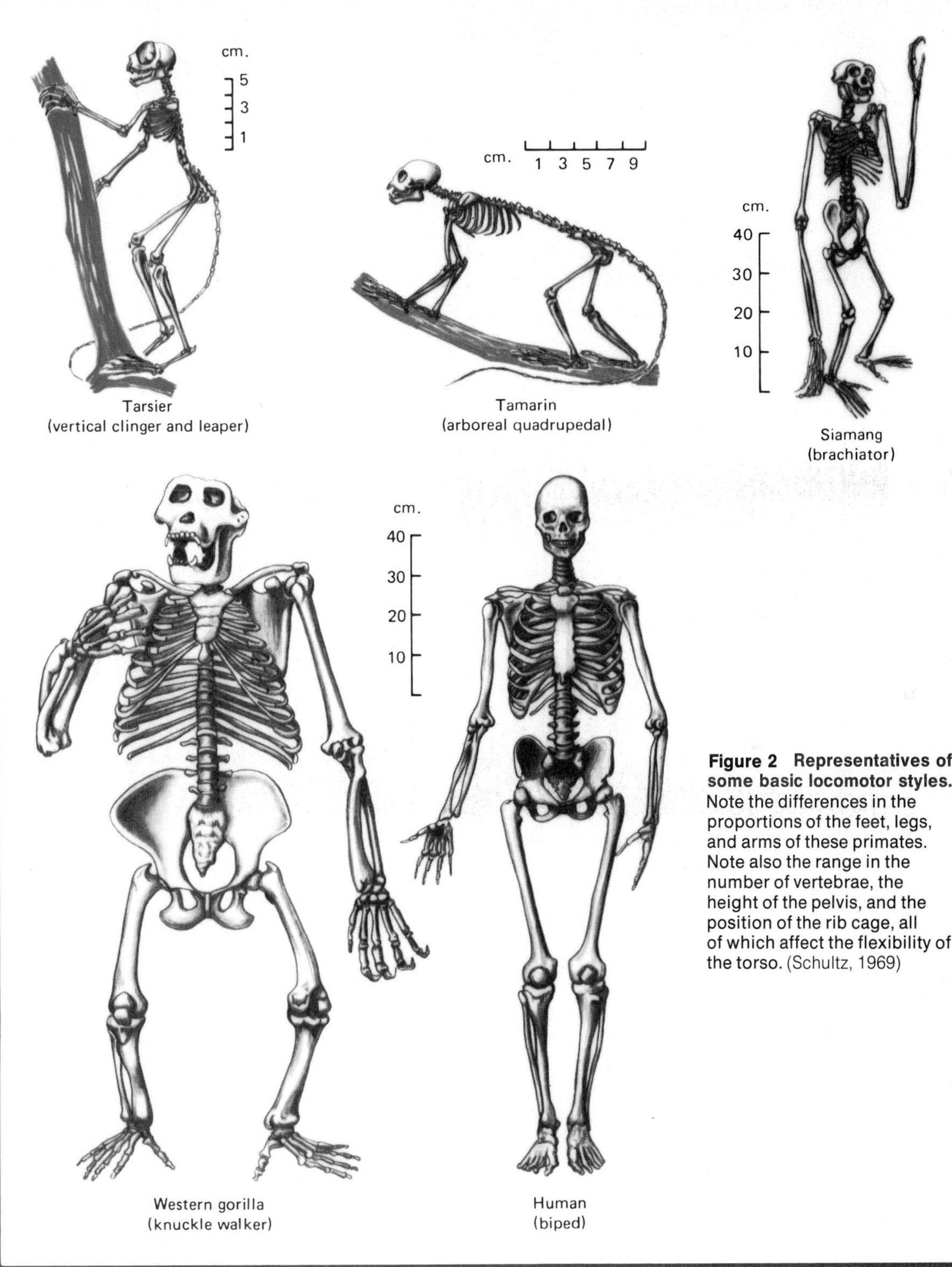

Figure 2 Representatives of some basic locomotor styles. Note the differences in the proportions of the feet, legs, and arms of these primates. Note also the range in the number of vertebrae, the height of the pelvis, and the position of the rib cage, all of which affect the flexibility of the torso. (Schultz, 1969)

1. The hole in the base of the skull through which the spinal cord passes (called the *foramen magnum*) must have shifted forward to better balance the head's weight. In other primates, the foramen magnum is more toward the rear of the skull.
2. The lumbar vertebrae were reduced in number and lessened the strain on the lower back. An *S*-shaped curve developed in the lower spine so that the torso became positioned directly above the pelvis, instead of in front of it.
3. The human ribcage is flatter than that of the semibrachiators, thus making front-to-back balance easier. As a result, the vertical axis of the body weight is close to the supporting spinal column.
4. The top part of the human pelvis, the ilium, became wider to act as a base for the torso. Among the quadrupeds, the pelvis is a pivotal point for attachment of the leg bones and muscles. The human ilium is also shorter and bends back, bringing the plane at which weight is transferred from the spinal column to the pelvis closer to the plane at which weight is transferred from the pelvis to the upper leg.
5. The bones of the upper and lower leg became larger and thicker to support the weight placed on them.
6. The foot became a strong platform for bearing the weight of the body when the other foot is lifted. In humans, the big toe is shifted up alongside the other toes, where it cannot be opposed to them for grasping, a crucial adaptation for arboreal life.

Feeding

How and what a primate eats are reflected in its hands, teeth, jaws, facial muscles, tongue, and digestive system. But physical anthropologists, who apply their knowledge of living primates to fossil primates, are especially interested in the teeth and jaws because these are most often preserved as fossils. Fossil teeth contain a wealth of information. They can be used as indicators of how close the genetic relationship is between one species and another, because the shape and number of the teeth evolve more slowly than other bodily structures. The teeth also provide information about the extinct animal's size, diet, and ecology. To make inferences of this kind about fossil primates, anthropologists must draw on their observations of how tooth structure and diet are related in the living primates.

Like those of most mammals, primate teeth vary in shape and perform different functions. At the front of the jaw, the *incisors* are used to seize and cut food. Behind the two incisors most primates have a *canine* tooth on both sides of the upper and lower jaws. This is used to grip food and to hold it in the mouth during chewing. As you can see in Figure 3, behind each canine, most prosimians and all New World monkeys have three *premolars,* and the Old World monkeys, apes, and humans have two. Behind the premolars almost all primates have three *molars.* Both premolars and molars have *cusps,* or points, that aid in grinding and cutting food.

Diet affects tooth structure by selecting for those forms that most efficiently process the animal's food. Because small animals require more food energy, their teeth must be able to break down proportionately more food than those of larger animals. The teeth of primates that eat high-energy foods, such as fruit or meat, need to be less efficient and wear-resistant because they process less food than the teeth of leaf-eaters, for instance. Finally, the physical properties of the food itself also affect tooth shape. Tough, hard-to-digest foods such as seeds or nuts require molars with pronounced cusps and a large surface area. Primates adapted for leaf-eating and insect-eating have relatively longer cusps and larger grinding surfaces than fruit-eating primates (Kay, 1975).

Although tooth shape and size are strongly influenced by diet, the selective forces at work are often other than dietary. Gorillas have

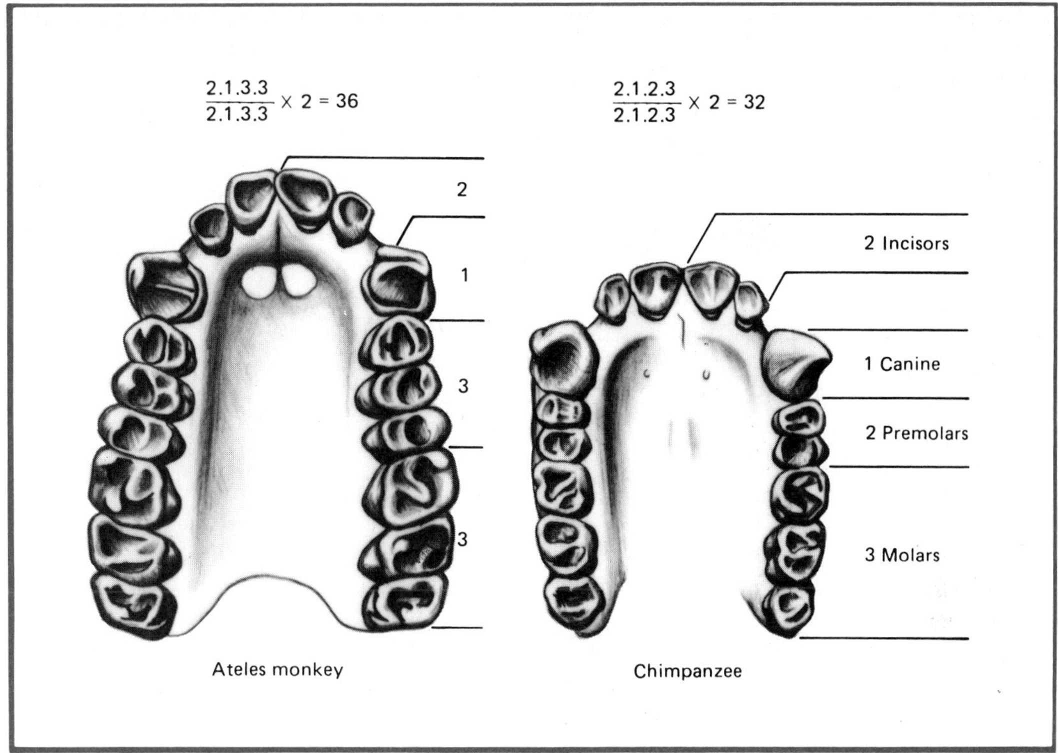

Figure 3 **Reduction of the dental formula in the primates.**
The mammals from which primates evolved probably had a total of 44 teeth. But prosimians and New World monkeys, such as the Ateles, whose lower teeth are shown here, have a total of 36. In Old World primates, including the chimpanzee (shown here) and humans, among others, the total is reduced to 32.

large canines, yet never use them for hunting or killing other animals, as they are exclusively vegetarian. Instead, the large canines seem to have evolved as part of threat gesturing. Many prosimians possess forward-projecting incisors that are used not for biting food, but rather for grooming.

The variety of functions for which primate teeth are adapted is best understood in dietary terms. Therefore, in our discussion of dentition, we will speak in terms of major dietary groups. In each case it will be useful to refer to Figure 4 as you read.

Insect-Eaters. These primates must grind their food finely in order to make it digestible. The incisors are peglike and broadly spaced in the insect-eaters' upper jaw. Below, they are thin and set close together. Both sets of incisors stick out beyond the plane of the face. The crests of the molars are sharp and high, and in many insect-eaters these cusps are connected by ridges that serve as excellent shearing edges.

Leaf-Eaters. In primates that live primarily on bulky vegetable foods such as leaves and stems, both teeth and stomach are adapted for improved digestion of the high-cellulose diet. In general, the incisors are small and the cheek teeth, the premolars and the molars, are large. Leaves are easy to remove from trees,

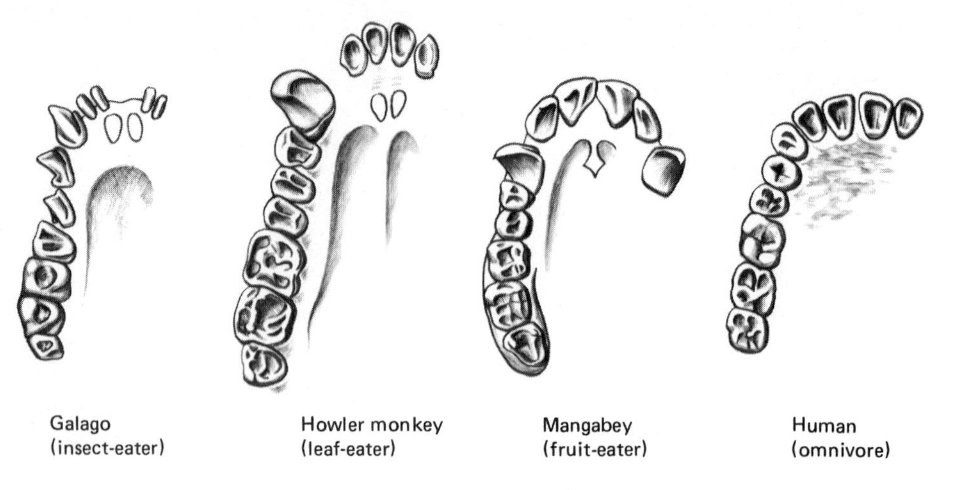

Figure 4 Dental pattern of respective primates.
The galago, an insect eater, has peglike incisors and three-cusped molars with high cusps and deep trenches. Like other leaf-eaters, the howler monkey has small incisors and cheek teeth with a large grinding surface and high cusps. Fruit-eaters such as the mangabey have broad incisors, possibly an adaptation to the hard fruit these monkeys crack with their teeth. Their cheek teeth are designed for crushing and have lower cusps than those of leaf-eaters. In humans and other omnivores, the incisors and molars are closer to the same size than in other primates. (Swindler, 1976)

but difficult to chew. Molars are broad, with a large number of extra shearing and grinding surfaces, because leaves must be ground into small bits before the stomach can begin to digest them. The stomach and intestines of a leaf-eater are enormous, for the animal must gorge itself on energy-poor leaves to survive. Langurs and colobus monkeys, both primarily leaf-eaters, have to eat so much that at times their food and digestive tracts make up a fourth of their total weight (Eimerl & De Vore, 1965).

Fruit-Eaters. Fruit can be digested in larger pieces than can insects or leaves, so the shearing molars associated with breaking down food to small particles are reduced in primates whose diet is based on fruit. After it is cut, fruit is prepared for eating primarily by crushing, but since it is soft, crushing structures, too, are reduced, compared to the molars of leaf- and insect-eaters. Some frugivores (or fruit-eaters), such as the *Cercocebus* monkey, have large chisel-shaped incisors for cracking hard fruits. In general, however, the teeth of fruit-eaters are small in proportion to body size (Kay, 1975).

Omnivores. These animals have few dental specializations. Their incisors, canines, and cheek teeth all perform several different functions, thereby increasing the range of food omnivores can eat. Humans, for example, eat meat by tearing it with their incisors. They also use their incisors to bite fruit. At the same time, vegetable material is ground by molars and premolars. Among humans, many of the more specialized functions of teeth are taken over by tools, so we do not need our teeth to kill other animals. In addition, we often prepare food before eating it, thereby relieving our teeth of the job of breaking down the tough fibrous material in vegetable foods. The use of tools and food preparation has had a significant effect on human dental evolution, as we shall see in Chapter 8.

The Primate Hand. All primates use their hands for both feeding and for locomotion. In addition, hands are the major exploratory organs of the higher primates. In the course of primate evolution, the sense of touch has gradually shifted from the nose, where receptors are still clustered in living prosimians, to the hand. The Anthropoids depend upon their hands for much of their information about objects in the environment.

The use of the hands in locomotion depends, of course, on how the animal moves. Humans rarely rely on their hands for movement, using them instead to handle and explore objects. True brachiators such as the gibbon depend almost entirely upon their hands, which are modified to provide the best grip as they swing through trees.

Primates use one of two types of grips. All primates can use a *power grip,* simply by bending the fingers tightly against the palm to clamp an object there. Counterpressure from the thumb helps hold the object (see Figure 5). Prosimians tend to rely most heavily upon this grasp, both for clinging to branches during locomotion and for seizing food. A *precision grip* depends upon a refined sense of touch in the fingers, and on separate control by the brain over each finger. It allows the greatest accuracy of control, for here the object is pinched between the thumb and fingers (see Figure 6). Precision grips are most highly developed among the Anthropoids, particularly among the Old World monkeys, apes, and humans. In these animals, the thumb is more truly opposable to the other fingers, allowing greater control over small objects. As you can see in Figure 7, there are many different kinds of primate hands, each one influenced by the locomotor pattern of the animal and its feeding and social patterns.

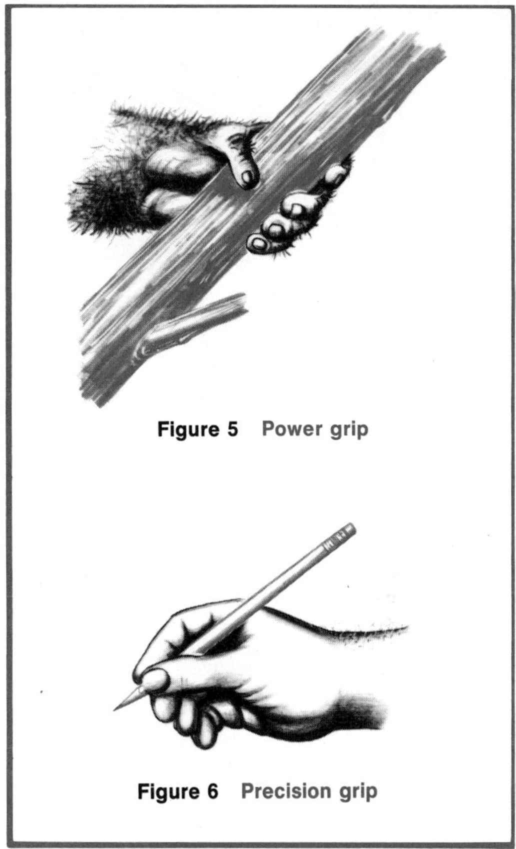

Figure 5 Power grip

Figure 6 Precision grip

Second-Order Behaviors

Anthropologists can study form and function fairly directly in the locomotor and feeding systems. They can measure teeth and limbs and observe how the animal uses these structures to eat and move. The ways the animal coordinates its physical actions in differ-

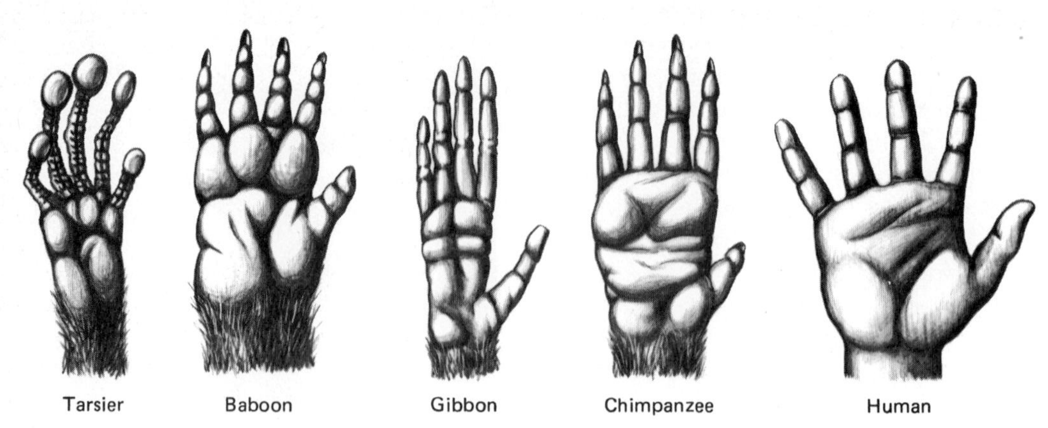

Figure 7 The tarsier, a vertical clinger and leaper, seldom uses a precision grip because its thumb is not truly opposable. Its thumb cannot rotate in its socket to allow contact with all the fingers. Like the gibbon, however, the tarsier is adept at grasping. The baboon, like almost all Old World monkeys, has and uses an opposable thumb. It can control each finger separately, which makes possible a precision grip able to take the stinger out of a scorpion (Campbell, 1974). The gibbon, chimpanzee, and humans can control each finger separately, but the first two, because of their specializations for brachiation, have a more limited precision grip than baboons or humans. The gibbon's hands are long hooks that grip limbs efficiently. The thumb, a possible hazard in the treetops, has become greatly shortened. Humans have a higher degree of fine control over the fingers than do other primates and greater opposability of the thumb. (Schultz, 1969)

ent situations, its interaction with other animals, its communication, and its learning are far less tangible, and much more difficult to study.

The brain controls these aspects of primate behavior. But assessment of behavior in terms of brain structure among living primates is still at an early stage of development. And what is known can only be applied to fossil species insofar as brain structure can be assessed from the skull. The relative size of gross features such as the part of the brain associated with the sense of smell in primitive primates can be observed by taking *endocranial casts,* or molds, of the inside of the skull. Such molds provide a cast of the external parts of the brain. But it is impossible to trace the evolutionary development of internal structures such as the secondary association areas, which in the human brain are responsible for integration of experience and greater complexity of thought. The areas of the brain that probably control most of the complex, or second-order, behaviors (actions that are a part of communication and social interaction) are located beneath the surface of the brain and therefore cannot be reproduced in a cast. Because little can be learned about the internal brain structure of fossil primates, anthropologists are forced to infer what they can about second-order behavior by studying it in the living primates. As you will see, these studies have revealed that humans and the higher primates have an unexpected number of behaviors in common. These results in turn have fed speculation about how our earliest ancestors, newly diverged from the ancestors of modern apes, may have communicated and lived together.

Information Processing in the Brain

The primate brain is larger and more complex than that of the other mammals. Primate evolution has been marked by reorganization and continual expansion of the brain, most of which has occurred in the *cerebral cortex,* the outer layer of the brain and seat of the higher functions. These changes have permitted more accurate sensory perception, especially in the senses of touch and sight, better coordination between sensory input and muscular response, and a greater capacity for learned and flexible behavior.

The most primitive primates rely to a great degree on the sense of smell, though many possess excellent vision as well. As a result, the *olfactory lobe,* the most primitive part of the cerebral cortex, is largest in these primates. As primates have evolved, greater emphasis has been placed on the other senses, particularly vision. The olfactory lobe is therefore largest among the prosimians and smallest among the higher primates. In humans and chimpanzees it is only a tiny projection.

The *motor cortex* sends messages to and from nerves in the muscles. This area controls the conscious movement of body parts. The *somatosensory area* receives messages through nerves leading from the skin, muscles, and bodily organs. Large chunks of both cortices are devoted to the hands and mouth, probably in response to the selective advantages of flexible hands and vocal communication. Experiments show that the size of the motor cortical area devoted to the hand in-

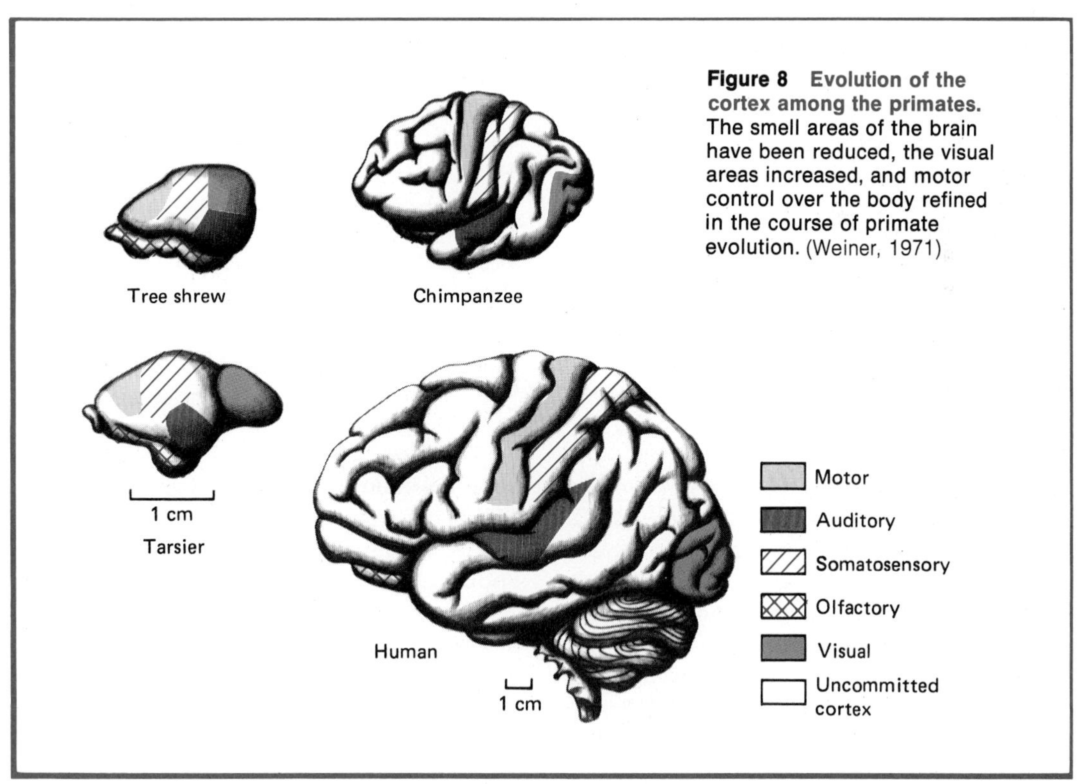

Figure 8 **Evolution of the cortex among the primates.** The smell areas of the brain have been reduced, the visual areas increased, and motor control over the body refined in the course of primate evolution. (Weiner, 1971)

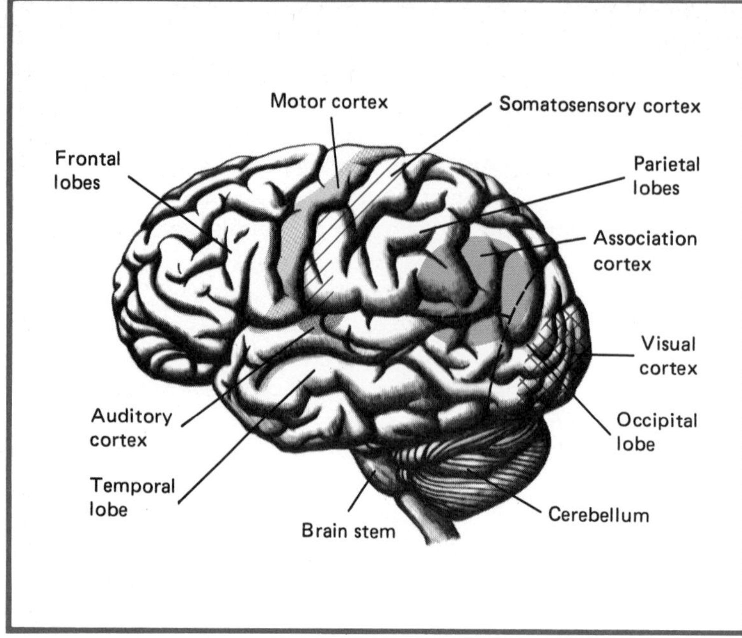

Figure 9 **The left side of the human brain, showing the main parts of the cerebral cortex, together with somatosensory and motor cortices.**

creases from New World monkeys to Old World monkeys to apes to humans (Campbell, 1974; Napier & Napier, 1967).

Analysis of visual images, especially important in moving quickly through a flurry of tree limbs in the forest canopy, takes place in the *visual cortex* of the *occipital lobe.* It is well developed, even in the lower primates. The tarsier, for example, must analyze large amounts of visual information with precision to succeed in its spectacular leaps from one tree trunk to another. Development of visual acuity probably reached a peak among the early apes and remained high in later apes and humans (Napier & Napier, 1967). The number of connections between the visual cortex and other parts of the brain continued to increase, however. Humans' vision is highly integrated with information from the other senses, as well as with motor activity.

As the primates increasingly became adapted to an arboreal habitat, the ability to integrate sensory information with muscular, or motor, responses became vital for survival. Integration of auditory, somatic, and visual information from other parts of the brain occurs in the *parietal lobes.* In monkeys and apes the parietal lobes are connected directly to the sensory cortices. But in humans, a highly developed *secondary association area* complicates the nerve pathways and leads to more elaborate integration and interpretation of experiences. Although monkeys and apes have developed very advanced systems for receiving information from the senses and coordinating them with muscular activities, the application of conscious thought to this process is largely a human specialty (Napier & Napier, 1967).

Good coordination is another adaptation to life in the trees. The *cerebellum,* which lies at the base of the brain, is the center of muscular coordination. It is a primitive feature, but highly developed in all primates, for the penalty for clumsiness in the treetops is a long fall. Muscle responses are largely instinctual in the lower primates. But once again there has been a progressive tendency in primate evolution toward conscious control over muscle responses. This trend takes the form of increasing nerve fiber connections between the cerebellum and the cerebral cortex, a trend that is most pronounced in humans (Napier & Napier, 1967).

The ability of areas of the cerebral cortex to direct other areas of the brain extends to some of the most primitive parts of the brain. The *limbic system,* which can be traced back to our reptile ancestors, translates sensory stimuli into states of arousal, perhaps something like emotions. These states of arousal trigger muscle responses through hormone and nerve impulses. These are usually impulses to carry out basic adaptive activities—caring for offspring, finding food, mating, fighting or fleeing from predators, and so on. The limbic system is common to all mammals. But in humans, interconnections with the higher cerebral cortex make it possible to bring these impulses under conscious control and even to inhibit them. We do not mate every time we encounter a willing partner, for instance. Nor do we grab all the food on the table for ourselves. Learning stored in the higher brain can be superimposed on the impulses of the limbic system, giving us greater flexibility in handling them.

The ability to concentrate on a long-term goal, make plans, and suppress conflicting impulses has been traced to the *frontal lobes.* In contrast to nonhuman primates, who usually cannot concentrate on anything for more than 15 to 30 minutes, humans can spend years planning and working toward a goal. Some anthropologists feel that this ability may have developed with the evolution of hunting behavior, for it is found to a degree in carnivores as well. A human hunter who could not follow an animal or lie in wait for a long time would probably come home empty-handed. Ultimately, the ability to concentrate has played a great part in the development of culture, which in turn has allowed specialized behavior to replace physical specialization as a means of adapting to environmental change.

Methods of Primate Study

The second-order behaviors controlled by the brain features that we have just discussed are studied by primatologists in three ways: (1) naturalistic studies, in which primates are observed in their natural environments, (2) compound studies, in which primates live in special areas that limit their movement, and (3) laboratory studies, in which researchers observe primate social behavior under controlled conditions. Each approach provides a different kind of information and has its own set of limitations.

Naturalistic Studies. Observation of animals in the wild has several advantages over other methods. First, only in the field can the interaction between behavior and environment be studied effectively. Eating habits, group size, and territorial range, for example, are closely linked to environmental factors. Information about these links in living species is vital to understanding the niche of fossil species. Second, fieldwork can best focus on the social group as a whole, rather than on the individual. To a far greater degree than in other animals, primate behavior is shaped by learning within the group. And finally, naturalistic studies can take into full account the complexity of primate behavior. Although lab studies of patas monkeys, for example, have shown that a son's status ranking is affected by his mother's rank in the troop, field studies reveal that rank is actually the product of a much more complex set of social factors (Hall, 1968).

On the negative side, there is a limit to what field observers can find out, even after years of watching. Nocturnal and arboreal species are especially hard to see and follow. And the behavior that observers do see is the result of learning, rather than the learning process itself. Although we have found out, for instance, that wild chimpanzees sometimes kill other animals for meat and that they use a few crude "tools," we know little about how such behavior has developed (Van-Lawick-Goodall, 1971).

Compound Studies. Primate-watching is easier within a compound. Since troop movements are limited by an enclosure or an island setting, many behaviors that would go unobserved in totally naturalistic settings are more easily recorded. But there is one big drawback. Primates are so versatile that they may change their behavior in response to the new environment. The unnaturally boring life and the surplus of males in a two-acre compound in Oregon, for example, probably induced the unusually aggressive behavior noted in one troop of macaques imported from their natural setting in Japan (Alexander & Bowers, 1967).

Laboratory Studies. Scientists can isolate certain important factors in primate social behavior only in the laboratory. Carefully controlled experiments can reveal, for instance, whether physical contact or nursing is more important in the infant's attachment to its mother, the conditions under which certain behaviors are elicited, how behaviors develop as the animal grows, and how behavior is modified. Problems have arisen, however, when experiments have been set up and judged from a human point of view. Experimenters have also tended to overlook the importance of the group and the environment in shaping the individual's behavior.

So far, experimenters and fieldworkers have operated along very different lines. Hypotheses that have come out of field studies are rarely tested in the lab, and vice versa. Although some fieldworkers try simple experiments, such as introducing a new food, a systematic approach and controlled conditions are impossible. Some workers think that lab studies should make more use of the fieldworker's knowledge of the context of behaviors. Experiments might then elicit patterns of behavior instead of a reaction like lever-pressing, which is more typical of the human species (Mason, 1968).

Communication

In field studies, primatologists have learned that primates communicate with each other in a variety of ways, including groups of vocalizations graded according to factors such as volume and duration, facial gestures, and body movements. In laboratories chimpanzees have even been taught to use simplified versions of human symbolic communication, consisting of many, if not all, of the elements of human language.

Primate Communication in Nature. Most primate communications concern the intricacies of group life—domination and subordination, keeping the peace, mating, and caring for infants. Primates communicate not only by vocalizing, but also by signs that can be seen, felt, and sometimes smelled. Although we will consider these modes of communication separately for simplicity's sake, they are often combined into complex clusters that convey subtle variations in meaning.

Olfactory Communication. Scent-marking is rare among monkeys and apes, but prosimians use it to mark their territories. Some rub branches with secretions from special scent glands, and others spread urine or feces. The nocturnal prosimians, who move only within a limited territory, use scent signals because darkness makes visual signals hard to see. Monkeys and apes, however, are diurnal, and their territory is too large and variable to mark with a scent. Among these primates, only the scent of a female in estrus remains as a clear olfactory signal.

Tactile Communication. Although most mammals touch one another with their noses, primates usually use their hands. Grooming is the most common form of communication by touch. Although it does serve to remove de-

Chimp greetings, a form of tactile communication. (Richard Wrangham, Anthro-Photo)

bris and insects from another's fur, grooming also seems to ease tensions in strongly hierarchical groups. Less dominant animals often soothe a potentially aggressive superior by stroking its fur.

In some species, tactile signals frequently are used in greeting. Chimpanzees, for instance, greet each other by embracing, kissing, nuzzling, and caressing. Much of mother-infant communication is carried on with touch signals. Some primates, however, signal hostility by hitting, pulling fur, and biting.

Visual Signals. Visual signals are an even richer form of communication than tactile signals. Primate visual signaling includes varying postures, tail positions, head movements, changes of coat color, and the swelling of sexual areas. But the most intricate shades of meaning are expressed in the mobile faces of the higher primates. Staring—the so-called direct gaze—is a strong signal of domination designed to make a subordinate give way. A mouth opened with the lips concealing the teeth is meant as a threat. But if the teeth are bared in a grimace, the animal is signaling something more like fear and submission.

Auditory Signals. Primates often use nonvocal sound signals, such as shaking branches, slapping the ground, and beating the chest. But the signals in which anthropologists are most interested are vocalizations, for they could resemble the beginnings of human speech.

Like other animals, primates seem to use about 10 to 15 different sound signals. But in the higher primates, these separate signals can

The yawn and exposed canine teeth of a young male baboon signal a threat. (Timothy Ransom, Woodfin Camp & Associates)

A hanuman langur "grimaces," signaling submission. (San Diego Zoo Photo)

be varied to convey greater subtlety of meaning. Among baboons, for example, "barks" vary in pitch, quality, and timing (Hall & De Vore, 1965).

Vocalizations are not chosen at random. They seem to have a direct relationship to the situation in which they are used. For instance, when juveniles are separated from their mothers or find themselves in danger, they make rapid clicking sounds. These vocalizations cut through other background noises and are very easy to trace to a specific location (Jolly, 1972).

The Nature of Human Language. Humans communicate emotions largely by nonverbal means—a raised eyebrow, a frown, an embrace. These signals are strikingly similar to those used by other primates. But in order to describe things and refine our ideas, we use language, which differs in at least five ways from nonverbal signaling and primate call systems.

Openness. Primate call systems are closed. They are limited to a set of fixed signals. The only way to "say" different things is to stick two signals together or to vary the way they are made (loud or soft; many times, or only once). With language, on the other hand, we can easily say things that we have never said before. Language is always open to new meanings.

Discreteness. Each human language is based on a limited number of discrete, or separate, sounds (*phonemes,* such as the sound *m*) and short meaning-bearing sound combinations (or *morphemes,* such as *man*). This makes it possible for us to listen for known sounds instead of being overwhelmed by an infinite variety of them.

Dual Patterning. Human language is both a system of sounds and a system of meanings. The sound system consists of a limited number of sounds, which lack intrinsic meaning but which can be put together in a structured, or grammatical, form to designate an unlimited number of things and events (Hockett, 1960).

Displacement. Animal calls are directly linked to the immediate situation: food at hand, predator nearby, and so on. But human language can be used in contexts far removed from those to which it refers. While baboons may keep on barking "baboo" an hour after a predator has disappeared, they cannot a week later discuss their narrow escape.

Arbitrariness. A final distinction of human language is its arbitrary nature. The word *apple* bears no relationship whatsoever to the juicy object to which it refers. Instead, it is a symbol that has been arbitrarily linked with that object by members of a human group and must be learned by their children (Jolly, 1972).

Teaching Language to Chimpanzees. Though the chimpanzee brain is smaller than the human brain, there are many structural similarities between the two. This similarity has prompted a number of studies of chimpanzee symbolic communication. In human language, vocal sounds act as symbols, which can be put together to communicate ideas or feelings. But no one has ever had much success in getting chimps to say human words. A chimp named Viki finally learned to say "mama," "papa," and "cup." But she had to force these words out in a strained whisper. The human larynx apparently is better adapted for speech than that of the apes (Lieberman, 1975). Instead of abandoning the attempt altogether, recent experimenters have switched to methods that may be easier for chimpanzees. One method uses gestures as symbols. Another uses plastic symbols instead of spoken words.

Washoe and Sign Language. R. A. and B. T. Gardner have capitalized on the chimpanzee's natural use of gestures to teach American Sign Language, or Ameslan, to a chimp named Washoe. After five years of training, she could use 130 word signs and combine them into simple two- and three-word phrases, such as "gimme tickle" and "more drink please" (Gardner & Gardner, 1969).

But has Washoe learned a communication system that meets the tests for human language? Perhaps so. Ameslan is made of cheremes (distinct hand patterns, actions, and locations) rather than phonemes (sound units). But, like language, it is a system of discrete signal bits. Therefore, Ameslan satisfies the criterion of discreteness. Dual patterning is present, too, for the closed system of meaningless cheremes can be built into an open system of meaningful messages. The ability to learn the names of things shows that chimpanzees are able to learn meanings arbitrarily assigned to symbols. Finally, chimpanzees have been able to create new combinations of gestures to express new meanings. On seeing a swan for the first time, Washoe combined the gestures for water and bird, thus showing the potential for openness. Displacement, however, is more difficult to demonstrate among Ameslan-trained chimpanzees. Knowing the sign for an object and repeating the sign do not satisfy the criterion. To be able to know with certainty whether chimpanzees possess this ability requires being able to communicate in one context information learned in a different context. Research is presently underway to find out whether chimps are capable of displacement.

Refining the Definition of Language. As research on the symbolic abilities of chimps has progressed, there has been a tendency among critics to refine their definitions of human language. Some scientists feel, for instance, that chimps lack *syntax,* the knowledge of how the order of words in sentences affects their meaning (Terrace & Bever, 1976). David Premack has tested the ability of chimps to understand the logic behind sentence structure. He thinks that one chimp named Sarah understands structural rules governing sentences. She placed a banana in a pail and an apple in a dish when given the sentence "Sarah insert banana pail, apple dish" encoded in plastic chips, each of which represented a word. Premack reasons that in order to do this task, Sarah must have understood that *banana* and *pail* go together, as do *apple* and *dish,* and that *insert* applies to both objects.

These studies have not demonstrated to everyone's satisfaction the linguistic ability of chimpanzees. Terrace and Bever (1976) would reserve judgment until chimpanzees use lengthy sentences and are able to refer to themselves symbolically. It is not clear, however, whether these new criteria are meant as a definition of language, or as a means of distinguishing human from nonhuman primate symbolic activities.

In any event, it is certain that humans and the great apes share some symbolic abilities. Differences may result from the fact that chimps have brains that organize experiences differently than human brains. Their abilities seem to be enough like ours, however, that they can communicate on a very simple level, using an approximation of our language, not theirs. These findings suggest that the capacity for language may also have existed in our primate ancestors. Why the early members of our lineage alone began to elaborate is a question we shall begin to answer in the chapters discussing hominid evolution.

Social Organization and the Environment

Symbolic potential is just another example of primate behavioral flexibility. In nature, this flexibility is particularly apparent in group organization. At one extreme there is the simple family group, which consists only of a mated pair and their offspring. Orangutan social structure is of this type. At the other extreme are the rigidly hierarchical baboon troops on the one hand and the chimpanzee "neighborhoods" on the other. Organizational form seems to depend more on the demands of the environment than on the species of the primate. The same forms of social organization are sometimes found in different species living under similar ecological conditions (Dolhinow, 1972). And a single species, such as the anubis baboon, may organize differently, depending on its immediate environment (Wilson, 1975).

Social Classification Systems. Anthropologists have proposed a number of ways of classifying primate social groups. One suggestion is to group primates into two types according to their *attention structure:* (1) groups that pattern their behavior on that of the dominant male, and (2) groups that split up in tense situations, with the males remaining behind to face the danger.

A second set of researchers has sorted primates according to the complexity of their social structure. They suggest five grades, ranging from solitary individuals who meet only for breeding, to large groups headed by a single male, with clearly differentiated social roles.

A third suggestion is that primates can be typed according to how involved the male is in social life. In some primate systems the male is solitary. In others a single dominant male drives away other males. And in still others, males of various ages tolerate one another's presence (Wilson, 1975).

Using Ecological Categories. All these classification systems have their merits—and their limits. None can account fully for all the variations in primate social behavior. But the fact that each can be at least partially supported by observed facts shows the complexity of the influences on social organization.

Taking this intricacy into account, we will use a social classification system based on several ecological factors: the kind of environment, diet, and period of activity—night or day.

This framework allows us to focus on how certain aspects of the biotic and abiotic environments affect a primate's group size and its niche structure. Like any other way of typing primates, ecological categories are somewhat artificial. The adaptations of some animals are highly variable and cannot be fit into a single category. But despite occasional examples of category-defying species, discussing behavior in an ecological context allows us to begin to organize a bewildering array of information in a way that clarifies the adaptive nature of social organization.

Nocturnal Primates *Arboreal Insect-Eaters.* These primates seem to be largely solitary. They feed by themselves, and they escape predators by fleeing. Each has a tiny *home range,* the area within which an adult normally moves. The lepilemur, for instance, rarely ranges farther than 50 meters from its nest in the hole of a tree (Napier & Napier, 1967). In all species studied, individual ranges overlap. Though males and females do not usually live together, they may pass each other in their nightly rounds. And during the day these creatures may huddle together in sleeping groups. Otherwise there is often little contact among individuals during their active periods.

But some species also show what may be the beginnings of primate social grouping. For instance, some bushbabies, tiny clingers and leapers, seem to have much more status than others. According to one observer, there are four different grades of males. The most important have many social contacts with females, while low-status males have none (Jolly, 1972).

Diurnal Primates *Arboreal Leaf-Eaters.* Some Old and New World monkeys—most of them semibrachiators—tend to live in medium-sized, harmonious troops of 4–30 members that forage for leaves by day. There is little sexual dimorphism, and troop members rarely try to assert dominance over one another. Intruders, however, are loudly warned away with a chorus of howls. The noise serves to divide the forest into a patchwork of defended territories, areas from which intruders are actively excluded. This kind of territoriality is most highly developed among these primates.

Some anthropologists believe that primates whose diet has little nutritive value, such as that of leaf-eaters, or whose locomotion takes a lot of energy, are relatively inactive and live within a small range, which, however, they strongly defend. Their range can be small because food is plentiful (Jolly, 1972).

Arboreal Omnivores. The third kind of social organization appears in the New World capuchins and titis and the Old World mangabeys and guenons. Their diet consists of not only leaves but also more nutritious shoots, nuts, insects, and small birds (Napier & Napier, 1967). This diet seems to promote more activity, and arboreal omnivores are hard to keep track of as they bound through the trees.

Their social organization seems to be more fluid than that of the leaf-eaters, who remain in small groups. Some forage in small bands or alone during the day but form sleeping groups of up to 100 at night. Others forage in large groups during the day, splitting into smaller groups at night. This flexibility may be related partly to their dietary flexibility. When a fig tree, for instance, is covered with ripe figs, it may also be covered with monkeys. At other times they may be better off foraging by themselves or in small groups.

Monkeys in this group do not tend to set up dawn calls to mark their territory. Instead, they may engage in ritualized or actual fighting with other troops, with loud calling and sometimes biting. Within the troops, too, relationships are less harmonious than among the leaf-eaters. Threats and assertions of dominance often are observed.

Semiterrestrial Leaf-Eaters. The primates we have considered so far do their socializing in the treetops. Those who descend to the ground for at least part of the day seem to form larger troops. But group size in this category—which includes only the sacred hanuman langur of India and the gorilla—seems to be held down by their leaf-eating lifestyle.

Despite their great size, gorillas live like other leaf-eaters—in small groups with small home ranges. These sedentary apes consume great quantities of vegetable matter, but they find it within a home range of about 1½ square kilometers. Ranges of the small, male-led gorilla troops overlap considerably. Males may glare at one another and go through their chest-beating rituals when they meet, but troop encounters are generally peaceful.

Relationships within a gorilla troop also are peaceful. Each is headed by a large silver-backed male. The younger black-backed males are next in status. Despite their fierce appearance, these dominant males are rarely aggressive toward their subordinates, who readily yield their sitting places or the right-of-way on narrow trails. Behavioral signals such as glaring or feigned charges reduce actual conflict (Wilson, 1975; Schaller, 1965).

It is hard to fit langurs into this or any other pattern. Their group life varies with the many environments—mountains, swamps, and human villages—to which they are adapted. In the forests langurs usually live in small male-dominated harems that defend their territory as arboreal leaf-eaters do. But in villages, where many langurs live, bachelor bands may take over the small harems, splitting them up or fighting until new leaders are selected (Jolly, 1972).

Semiterrestrial Omnivores. These primates spend some of the day on the ground in areas of partial tree cover. They include one kind of lemur, vervets, mandrills, savanna baboons, and chimpanzees. The first three usually form troops of 4 to 30 males and females; mandrill, macaque, and savanna baboon troops tend to be larger. Social variations within a species are common, differing perhaps with the habitat. The richer the food supply and the less the danger from predators, the smaller and looser the troops tend to be. Tensions within the large troops are held more or less under control, and resistance to predators is made greater by a highly structured dominance hierarchy. And although the wide ranges of different troops often overlap, they tend to avoid one another rather than fight (Napier & Napier, 1967).

The social behavior of chimpanzees, who share this ecological grade, does not really follow this pattern. They seem to live year after year in large, stable communities of 30 to 80 members. But within their overall home range of 5 to 20 square kilometers, they move about in ever-changing smaller groups. The whole community rarely gets together in one place. Though all know one another well from long and intimate association, the only persistent groups seem to consist of a mother and her young or even adolescent offspring. Other small groups—including bunches of companionable males—form and break up after a few hours or days.

One thing that will draw many group members together is the discovery of ripe fruit. Chimpanzees finding a fruiting tree announce it with a *carnival display* that can be heard over a kilometer away. They drum on tree trunks with their hands and run and swing through the trees until a crowd gathers. But before the eating begins, the adult males go through a ritualized greeting ceremony, which includes embracing, kissing, and shaking hands.

Chimpanzees appear to be the only primates, aside from humans, that share their food. If a limited amount of a special delicacy is located, troop members beg for—and sometimes receive—a share of the find.

Cooperation is evident in their hunting behaviors, for chimpanzees sometimes use subtle signals to organize for group attacks on prey such as young baboons and pigs. Sometimes cooperation extends to other troops whose home ranges overlap their own. Though there is no fighting, tensions may be expressed by excited exaggerations of feeding behaviors. The groups may travel together and even trade sexually receptive females. The estrous females' willingness to copulate with a number of males probably helps to minimize aggression among the males (Wilson, 1975).

Terrestrial Arid-Country Primates. A sixth group consists of hamadryas baboons, geladas, and the large patas monkeys. They are the only primates to adapt to a largely terrestrial life in dry environments, where trees are few or even lacking altogether. In order to find grass, bulbs, seeds, and fruit in their harsh habitats, troops must travel up to 18 kilometers a day.

Though the three species in this category are only distantly related, they all have developed a similar social pattern, which is a small harem consisting of one male and up to nine females and their young. Some primatologists think that this grouping may be a way of coping with the limited food resources. Large troops would have to travel even farther in a day to find enough food to go around. Because predators are few in really dry areas, the presence of a number of males to protect the troop may become less important than the need to find food (De Vore and Hall, 1965). In the patas harems, the single male manages to protect his harem by entering new country ahead of them, acting as a lookout and diverting attacks by cheetahs and wild dogs toward himself (Napier & Napier, 1967).

Though hamadryas and gelada harems forage separately during the day, they often join at night to share sleeping cliffs. Since trees are unavailable for safe sleeping spots, ledges on vertical rock faces may serve as a refuge for hundreds of these primates. Though gelada harems usually look for food separately, they join in large groups to forage when the rainy season brings lusher plant growth (Jolly, 1972).

Terrestrial Omnivores (Humans). The social structure of our forerunners also was very much a product of the environment. If, as many anthropologists believe, our ancestors were apelike creatures that had adapted to life in dry, open country, they may have lived in small groups, joining occasionally into larger bands. Primitive hunting and gathering tribes still follow this pattern, using a flexible combination of foraging in small and large groups, according to the availability of food. Their ability to cooperate in hunting is increased by the absence of active territorial defense mechanisms. Among the primates, territorial defense is found mostly in arboreal rather than terrestrial species.

Learning to be a Member of the Troop

The social organization of the various primate groups adapts them for efficient use of the environment, defense against predators, and satisfaction of other basic needs. It does so by structuring behavior for effective responses in different situations. But how do individuals come to adjust their own behavior to fit into group life? The answer lies in social learning, or *socialization.*

Precocial Strategy

Because primates depend so heavily on learned behavior, anything that aids learning is probably adaptive. The reproductive strategy primates have developed is a good example.

Primates follow a *precocial strategy* of reproduction. That is, the gestation period is long, litters are very small (usually only one infant), and offspring are born physically well developed. In humans, the nervous system is well developed, although the rest of the body is relatively immature at birth. Primates nurse for a long time, reach sexual maturity after a long period of development, and then live a long time as adults. Though the length of these life periods varies from group to group, their proportion of the total lifespan is similar. See Figure 10.

Primates probably follow the precocial strategy as a result of early adaptations to limited food supplies. In environments in

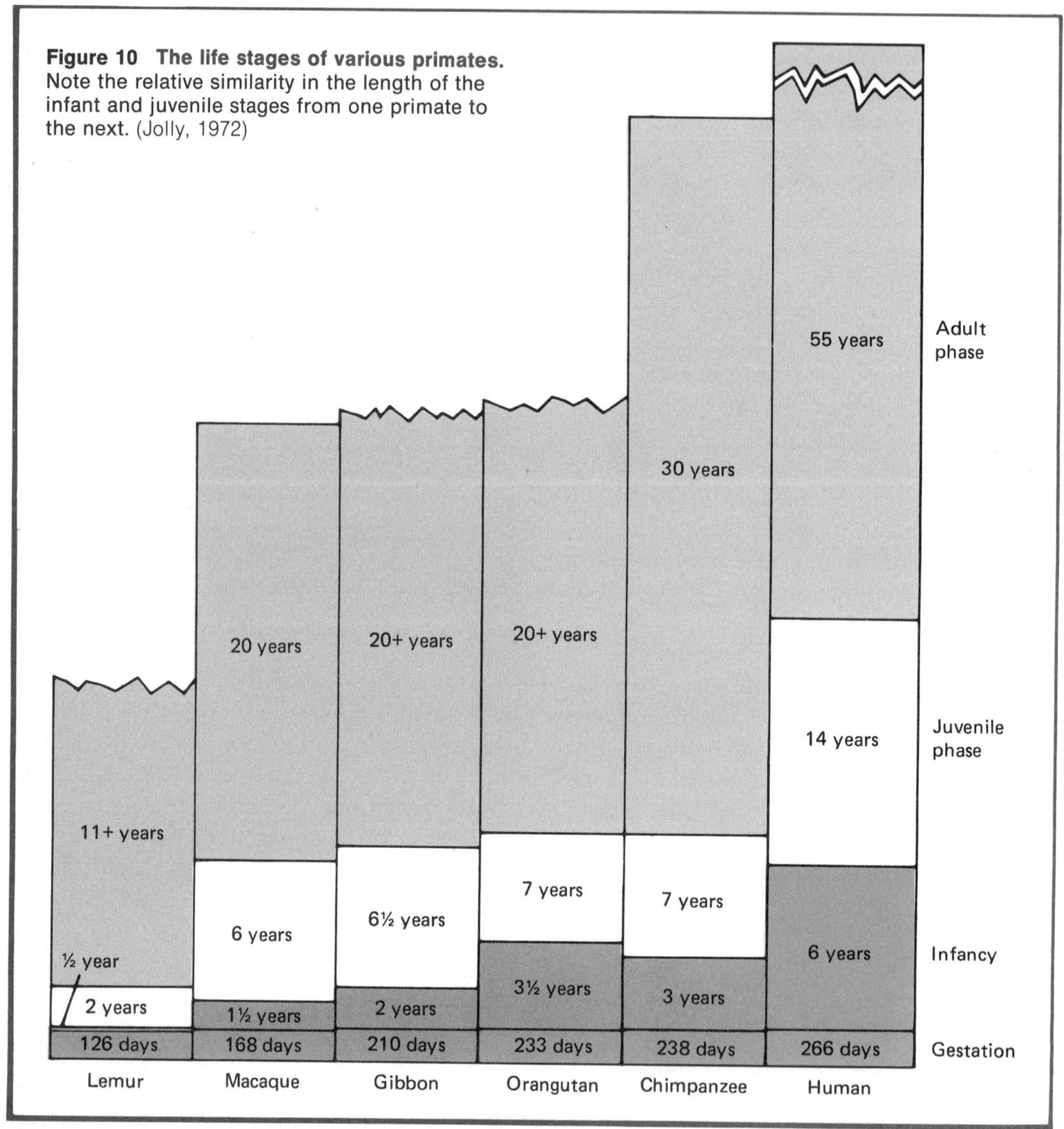

Figure 10 The life stages of various primates. Note the relative similarity in the length of the infant and juvenile stages from one primate to the next. (Jolly, 1972)

which food is plentiful and animals are not crowded, selection will favor those that can raise the largest families and gather the most food. But when animals are competing for a limited food supply and a species population is existing very near the carrying capacity of the environment, natural selection will favor those that have fewer young and therefore consume less food. Large animals—like primates—are more likely to strain the carrying capacity of an environment and are thus under greater pressure to have small litters of young (Martin, 1975).

Small litters and a long period of dependency ensure that each offspring gets a lot of attention from its parents. Not only does this improve their chances of survival, but it also gives them time to absorb a great deal of learned behavior. The environments in which the higher primates in particular have evolved have been characterized by changing feeding relationships and environmental conditions. In such environments, the ability to learn new behavior is an important advantage.

Stages of Development

Socialization occurs mostly in critical sequences of interactions between the mother and the infant and among *age-mates,* or peers. These interactions have been studied carefully in experiments with monkeys and apes that test the importance of such variables as physical contact with the mother. Such experiments may help us to understand early hominid behavior and human development as well.

Infant Stage. The first stage in the young primate's development involves close attachment to its mother. For the first few months of its life the two are in constant contact, because the infant is completely dependent on its mother for food, protection, and transportation.

Infant-Mother Attachment. For the baby, this is a reflex stage. Its behaviors are instinctive responses to specific stimuli, serving mostly to keep the baby in contact with its mother and to help it to feed. When primate young are touched near the mouth, they instinctually turn their head toward the stimulus. Sucking is elicited in the same way. Primate young also are born with the ability to cling to their mother's fur as she moves from place to place.

Experiments run by Harry and Margaret Harlow at the University of Wisconsin show that the cravings for contact and bodily support are even stronger than the food-seeking drive. The Harlows rigged up pairs of surrogate monkey mothers. One was made only of wire but gave out milk through a nipple. The other offered no milk but was covered with terry cloth. Infant rhesus monkeys were separated from their own mothers at birth and placed in cages with both surrogate mothers from which to choose. They invariably spent most of their time clinging to the cloth mother, visiting the wire one only to nurse. Further experiments suggested that infants find this body contact reassuring, especially in new or frightening situations (Harlow & Harlow, 1958).

Mothering. Infant primates are born with reflexes that tie them to their mother. But to what extent is mothering instinctual? Does caring for an infant—suckling, carrying, cleaning, and protecting it, tolerating its clambering and clinging, and gently shaping its behaviors—come naturally? Probably not.

Observations of langurs show that older, more experienced langur mothers are able to keep their infants quiet and contented. Younger mothers, on the other hand, have many more problems. Sometimes they even try to nurse their babies upside down (Jay, 1965). Mothering is apparently learned in part from youthful interaction with a mother and other infants. The Harlows found that rhesus

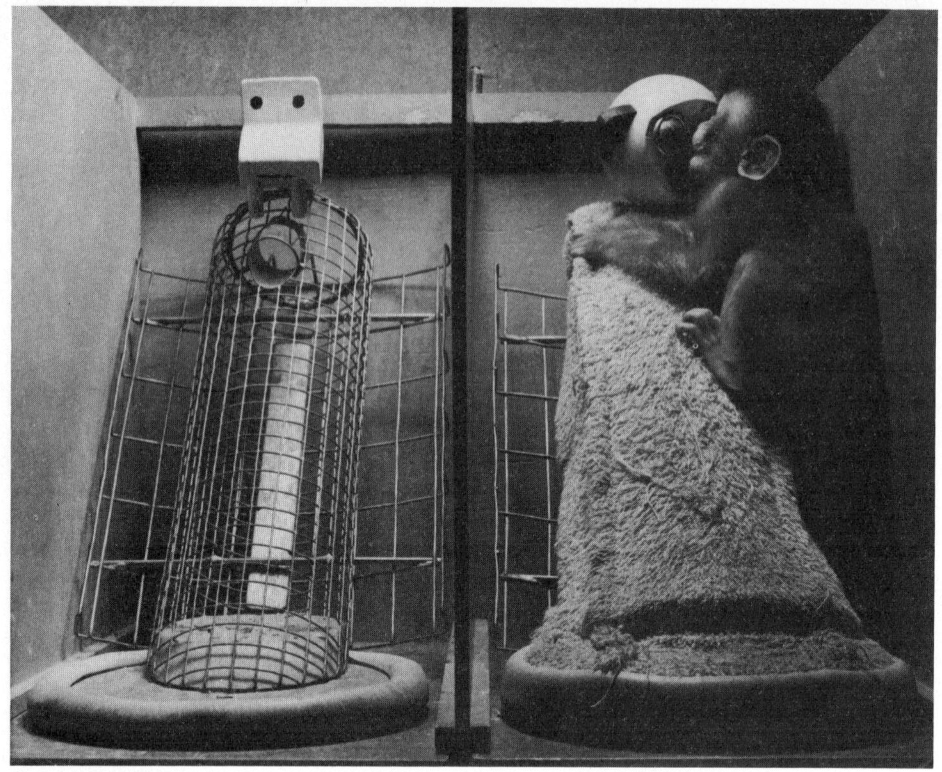

Experiments by Harry and Margaret Harlow show that infant rhesus monkeys have a strong need for the reassurance of bodily contact with their mothers. Here, an infant clings to a surrogate mother made of terry cloth. (Harry F. Harlow, University of Wisconsin Primate Laboratory)

monkeys raised in total social isolation make terrible mothers. When the infants tried to cling, their mothers pushed them away roughly, beat them, and held them to the floor (Harlow, Harlow, & Suomi, 1971).

Fathering. Though the mother is the central figure in the infant's life, sometimes the males also are involved. This varies greatly from troop to troop and species to species. In 3 troops of Japanese macaques that were studied, dominant males took care of the infants when they were about a year old. But in 15 other troops studied, the males rarely or never adopted a parental role. Among baboons, males are protective both of infants and mothers. The dominant males sometimes carry infants around, letting them cling to their belly for up to 20 minutes. Langur males, on the other hand, are indifferent at best. Sometimes they are downright hostile, and are known to kill infants they did not father (Hrdy, 1977).

Late Infant and Juvenile Stage. As the infant grows older, it leaves its mother for longer and longer periods of time and explores its environment. Using the mother as a secure home base, the infant learns to manipulate objects and begins to interact with its age-mates.

Play. Although we humans sometimes regard play as frivolous "monkey business," it serves real adaptive needs for primate young.

For one thing, it seems to aid their physical development. Chimpanzee mothers often play with their babies by hanging them from a branch and giving them pushes so they can swing back and forth. Strength and coordination improve rapidly. Young chimps also spend hours exploring and becoming familiar with the area in which they will spend their lives (Van Lawick-Goodall, 1965).

Play has another important adaptive function: It helps the young learn to interact smoothly with others and thus promotes integration into the troop. Though primatologists long thought that contact with the mother is most critical in socialization, further studies by the Harlows indicate that play with age-mates is equally important (Harlow & Harlow, 1971). Separation from the mother and age-mates can block normal social development in both humans and other primates. But researchers now emphasize that the behavior of both lower primates and humans is rather flexible during their long development period. Individuals can often recover to some extent from early deprivation if they are later exposed to more normal social situations (Clarke & Clarke, 1960).

Dominance Learning. Our best knowledge of dominance relationships comes from the study of terrestrial or semiterrestrial primates. Order within these groups depends largely on recognition of social ranking. Subordinate animals, for instance, usually move away or look away when a dominant animal approaches. In this way, actual fighting and the resulting injuries are avoided. But how do in-

Chimpanzee mother and her 2-year-old son. (Nancy Nicolson, Anthro-Photo)

A juvenile male baboon threatens another, who has sought protection by grooming a dominant adult male. Such interaction probably helps establish dominance relationships in the minds of young primates.
(James Moore, Anthro-Photo)

dividuals learn where they stand in the dominance hierarchy?

Some anthropologists suggest that dominance is learned during play. Wrestling, for instance, makes it clear to young primates who is stronger than whom. If this learning is accompanied by a bit of pain, it will probably be remembered clearly (Dolhinow & Bishop, 1972). It has been found that the social rank of the mother also has a strong influence on the social rank of her offspring. In rhesus monkeys, the offspring's rank seems to rise or fall with changes in its mother's rank (Marsden, 1968). It is also possible that an infant imitates its mother's style of interaction with others, whether assertive or subordinate.

In addition to inhibiting actual fighting, dominance strongly affects the spread of new behaviors through the troop. In a series of experiments to see how new traditions develop among primates, various new foods were set out for wild Japanese macaque troops. In most cases it was the young monkeys who started new behaviors. Some learned to eat candy, and one started to wash sweet potatoes to remove the sand. These new ideas spread first to other young monkeys, then to their mothers, and only gradually to some of the other adults. By contrast, when the leader of one troop introduced the notion of eating wheat, the new behavior was being imitated by the whole troop within four hours. Subordinate animals seem to learn from dominant animals much faster than the other way around (Frisch, 1968).

Adult Stage. In many species, the final stage in the primate life cycle involves complete separation of mother and offspring. At this point the mother instinctually puts distance between herself and her offspring, who finds relations with peers more and more rewarding. Curiosity about the environment also draws young primates away from their mothers. Even after full integration into the larger group, however, separation is not complete in all species. For example, among chimpanzees and macaques mother-offspring relationships continue to be quite strong and may persist for life. Jane Van Lawick-Goodall (1971) saw a chimpanzee mother being rescued by her 13-year-old son from an attack by a low-ranking adult male. And she noted that a socially mature 18-year-old male still spent a good bit of time with his old mother.

Biological Explanations of Social Behavior

To what extent is our social behavior and that of the other primates innate? To what degree are our actions shaped by our genes and therefore the product of thousands or millions of years of evolution? It is easy to see eating and reproduction as primarily instinctual adaptive behaviors that allow the human species to survive. But what about our nobler tendencies, such as altruism? Can these, too, be seen as adaptations to the biological need to survive and reproduce? According to *ethology* (the scientific study of animal behavior) and *sociobiology* (the study of the genetic basis of behavior and its evolution), perhaps so.

Essentially, these schools of thought contend that much behavior is innate. Because it affects the ways in which the organism adapts to its environment, behavior is susceptible to natural selection. Many behaviors, according to these schools, are encoded in the genes. As the organism develops, certain inherited patterns of behavior emerge. To some degree these patterns can be changed or elaborated by learning. But the basic innate behaviors persist because they offer the species a selective advantage.

In effect, the ethologists and sociobiologists are trying to fit behavior—as well as anatomy and physiology—into the Darwinian theory of evolution. They differ, though, in the emphasis they place on the various aspects of the problem. While ethologists concentrate on the interaction of inheritance and learning in behavior, sociobiologists focus on why certain innate behavior has evolved. Sociobiologists are particularly interested in the adaptive function of behavior. Of the two models, ethology allows more room for the modification of the innate tendencies by learning.

Ethology

Ethologists have identified several kinds of innate behavior. First, there are fixed patterns of action. Red squirrels, for instance, display a highly adaptive behavioral sequence for hiding nuts in the ground. They go through these motions whether they have grown up in the woods or in a wire cage. This instinctual fixed action pattern can be modified by learning, however. With time and practice, wild squirrels learn to make sure that as a result of their movements they have completely buried the nut (Eibl-Eibesfeldt, 1968).

Learning also comes into play in the linking of a series of fixed action patterns. In primates, this learning seems to take place during juvenile play, as the young learn what their bodies can do and what the environment is like. The Harlows' male rhesus monkeys reared in social isolation can make some of the movements required for copulation, for these are instinctive. But linking them into sequences that work requires learning that apparently takes place in juvenile play. Socially deprived male monkeys fail because they do not know just where and how to mount the female (Harlow, Harlow, & Suomi, 1971).

Another kind of inherited behavior is triggered by a particular stimulus in the environment, called a *releaser*. The animal reacts to this stimulus in a set way, even though it has no experience of it. Many primates instinctually launch a blind attack if they hear the distress call of a young one. And sexual responses in male primates may be released by the sight of an estrous female's swollen genitals.

Ethological Explanation of Human Aggression. Ethologists have only recently begun to try to apply these concepts to human behavior. Irenaus Eibl-Eibesfeldt, a German ethologist, found (1968) that expressions and gestures used in greeting, flirting, and praying are similar in many different cultures and may therefore be based on innate behavioral patterns.

Some ethologists suspect that aggression may also be innate, but are unsure of the extent. Ethologists point out that children who are deaf and blind from birth display the same aggressive behavior patterns as people who could have learned these patterns from seeing and hearing them. Even in the most peaceful societies, acts of aggression are common, beginning in childhood. We tend to use the same motor patterns to threaten (glaring and footstamping, for instance) and to submit as our primate relatives do. That these patterns are held in common suggests an ancient biological origin. And, as discussed earlier, one area of our brain—the limbic system—seems to be adapted specifically to trigger aggressive responses. Not surprisingly, it is in the most primitive part of the brain.

Eibl-Eibesfeldt thinks that patterns of aggression are handed down genetically because they have adaptive functions. Aggression may promote spacing of individuals so that they do not overburden their environmental resources. Aggression may also establish dominance hierarchies in which the strongest and healthiest individuals emerge as leaders and protectors. But killing an opponent of the same species is not adaptive in terms of species survival. So along with apparently instinctual predispositions to aggression, animals who could kill each other have evolved inhibitory mechanisms that reduce aggression. In dog fights, the dog that recognizes that it will lose adopts a puppylike posture that seems to melt the other's hostility.

Why then do humans go on killing one another? Ethologists speculate that weapons have made it possible for us to kill before appeasing gestures can inhibit our aggression. But our capacity for modifying innate responses by learning, and the pressure of other humans, tend to keep our potential for aggression in check (Eibl-Eibesfeldt, 1974).

Sociobiology

According to E. O. Wilson, a leading theoretician of sociobiology, one of its goals is to find biological, evolutionary explanations for all of behavior. These ambitions are far-reaching. Sociobiologists predict that their work will bring about a reformulation of the various studies of human behavior—sociology, psychology, economics, and ethnics, for example.

Like the ethologists, sociobiologists do not limit themselves to studying human and nonhuman primate behavior. They have, however, suggested a framework for the sociobiological study of primate behavior. Some of the major social traits of primates are traced through various interacting factors back to ancient mammalian behavioral features that survive relatively unchanged. Aggressive tendencies among the males and a strong mother-infant bond are primitive mammalian traits. Newer trends, such as increasing brain size and adaptation to an arboreal environment, have brought about other behavior. For instance, the ability of higher primates to live in complex societies, in which they must respond differently to many different individuals, can be attributed partly to their increased intelligence. Intelligence in turn is linked in evolution to increasingly skillful manipulation of objects with the hands, larger size (and therefore larger brains), improved vision, and increasingly rich systems of communications (Wilson, 1975).

A Sociobiological Explanation of Altruism. One aspect of sociobiological theory tries to fill an important gap in Darwin's logic: If survival and reproduction are the main evolutionary goals, why would one organism risk its own life for another? Is it possible that such altruism defies biological explanation? The sociobiologists contend that it does not. All persistent behaviors have some biological function. Altruism is adaptive, though sometimes in a roundabout way.

It is easiest to see why individuals might sacrifice themselves for their relatives. In helping each other, blood relatives are improving the chances that the genes they share will be passed on. According to sociobiologists, organisms will unwittingly act as though they understand the mathematics involved. As a British biologist jokingly announced, he would gladly risk his life for two brothers or eight cousins. Altruism within the family can thus be seen as genetic selfishness. It acts to improve the genes' chances of surviving, though not necessarily the individual's chances of enjoying a long life.

The theory of genetic selfishness, however, cannot explain altruistic acts toward nonrelatives. To account for these, sociologists have employed the theory of *reciprocal altruism.* A population that socializes its members to believe that helping one another is good improves its overall genetic fitness. This population also finds it adaptive to promote aggressive morality and guilt in order to punish "cheaters" who do not reciprocate (Wilson, 1975). According to sociobiologists, the existence of many major human institutions—schools, churches, legal systems—can be explained by their contribution to reciprocal altruism.

Like ethological explanations, most of the sociobiologists' arguments are still at a theoretical stage. Ultimately, these scientists hope to be able to predict a population's social characteristics by combining statistical data (such as figures on the growth, age structure, and gene flow of populations) with information about the genetic traits of the population.

Summary

1. The activity of animals can be broken down arbitrarily into *behavioral systems.* In our study of primate behavior, we have discussed *locomotion* and *feeding (first-order behaviors), information processing* (neither first- nor second-order behavior), and *communication* and *social organization,* both *second-order behaviors.*

2. The basic locomotory types among the primates are *vertical clinging and leaping, quadrupedalism, brachiation,* and *bipedalism.*

3. Paleoanthropologists are especially interested in the relation between dentition and ecology among the living primates. *Insect-eaters* and *leaf-eaters* must grind their food into small pieces; their *molars* are relatively large and equipped with many *cusps* and shearing surfaces. In *fruit-eaters'* teeth, which are designed for crushing, these features are reduced. Use of prepared foods has brought about a reduction in canines and size of molars in humans.

4. Primate evolution has been marked by an increase in the size of the *cerebral cortex* and its ability to control the more primitive brain structures.

5. The complex behavior of primates is observed in *naturalistic, compound,* and *laboratory* studies.

6. Primates communicate by means of *olfactory signals* (especially important among the nocturnal prosimians), *tactile signals, visual signals,* and *auditory signals. Call systems* are *closed,* or limited to a set of fixed signals, and linked to environmental stimuli. The highest primates—chimpanzees in particular—have been trained to exhibit some of the abilities needed for human language. They can build a set of discrete symbols into a limited range of meanings *(dual patterning),* understand some logic and causal relationships, and display some self-awareness. Research on their ability to refer to things *displaced* in time and space is proceeding.

7. Because primate social organization is complex, a number of plausible ways of categorizing it have been developed. Group structure is more closely related to the primate's environment than to its taxonomic category. Diet, food supply, and the threat of predators strongly affect group size, structure, *territoriality,* and the size of the *home range.*

8. Primates are born well developed, in small litters: a *precocial reproductive strategy.* During their long period of development they become *socialized,* adjusted for group life. Aspects of this process include increasing separation from the mother, more association with *age-mates,* play, increasing physical development, and dominance learning.

6 Fossils and Primate Evolution

WHEN Darwin wrote *The Descent of Man* (1871), direct evidence of human ancestors was practically nonexistent. So he was forced to rely on what was known of the anatomy and behavior of living primates for his speculations about our beginnings. Today the fossil record of human evolution is much more complete and gives us facts that Darwin never had.

Only the discovery and careful study of fossils will tell us about the sequence of changes leading to modern humans. Without a clear fossil record of our divergence from the apes, we shall never know for sure how *hominids* (humans and their direct ancestors) first distinguished themselves from the evolutionary lineage of the great apes. Only by the study of fossils can we test our theories about what earlier primates looked like; where, when, and how they evolved; and under what environmental pressures.

This search for our origins has intensified in the past few decades and has yielded large numbers of fossil hominids. But fossil evidence is still uneven, so that some parts of our evolutionary past are better known than others.

Fossils and Their Interpretation

A *fossil* consists of the preserved remains of an organism that lived in the past. It may be nothing more than a tooth or a jaw or a footprint. Or it may be a fully preserved body, complete with all its soft parts, such as the woolly mammoths found frozen in the Siberian tundra. Unfortunately, however, most fossils are mere fragments, difficult to find and to interpret.

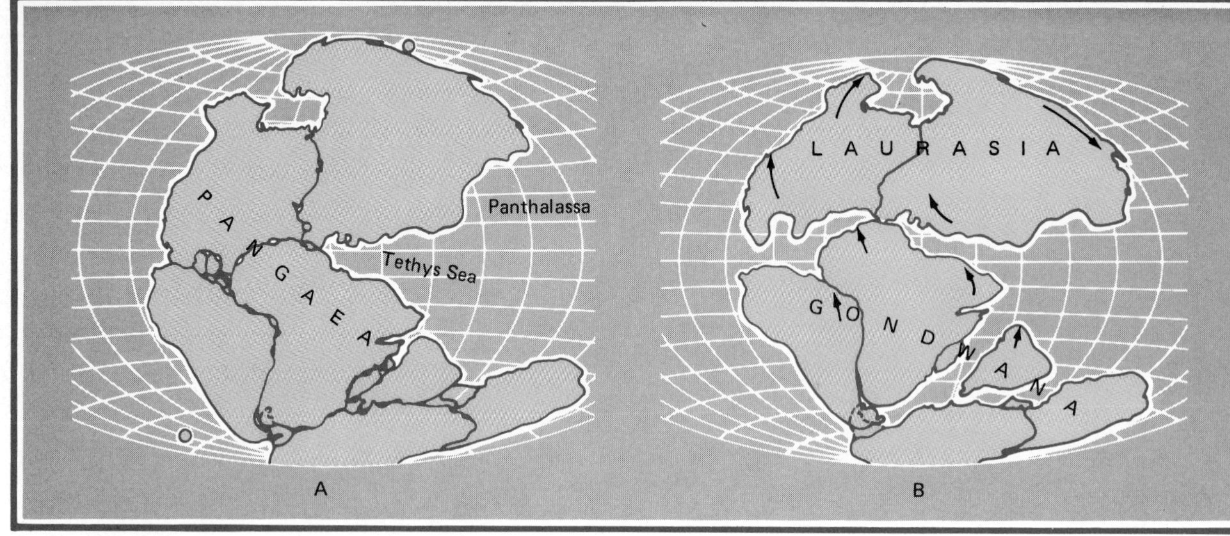

The Formation of Fossils

When a fossil is found, *paleontologists* (scientists who study fossils) need two kinds of information before they can interpret it. The first of these is an understanding of the processes that shaped the earth in that area; the second is an understanding of the processes that preserved the fossil itself.

The Geological Processes. We tend to think of the earth's surface features—hills, mountains, plains, bodies of water—as permanent fixtures in an otherwise changing world. But they, too, are being changed, though very slowly, by the same forces that have always been at work shaping the earth.

Today, a basic assumption underlying the interpretation of fossils is the concept of *uniformitarianism.* As mentioned earlier, it states that events in the past were subject to the same natural laws that are operating in the present. If we find the petrified remains of a shellfish, for instance, we can guess that the shell was covered by sediments, just as shells are being covered now. We assume that processes such as decomposition and the replacement of the shell with minerals in the sediment operated the same way then as they do now.

Understanding these natural processes first requires some geological knowledge about the earth. On a large scale, the earth's continents are made up of fairly thin crusts of rock and soil gradually being shifted about by the movement of molten material plates beneath them. *Plate tectonics,* the study of the movement of the continental plates of the earth's crust, indicates that all land once formed a huge supercontinent, which has been called Pangaea ("all lands"). Pressures in the underlying rock layer apparently caused it to break into 10 large plates and some smaller ones. As these plates were pulled apart, two supercontinents formed—*Laurasia* in the north and *Gondwana* in the south. Further drifting of the plates gradually split the land masses into the continents we know today. Some of the plates eventually collided again. For example, the plate carrying with it the Indian subcontinent pushed into the Asian mainland, thrusting up the Himalayan Mountains. (See Figure 1.)

Geologists think this process of *continental drift* began about 200 million years ago and

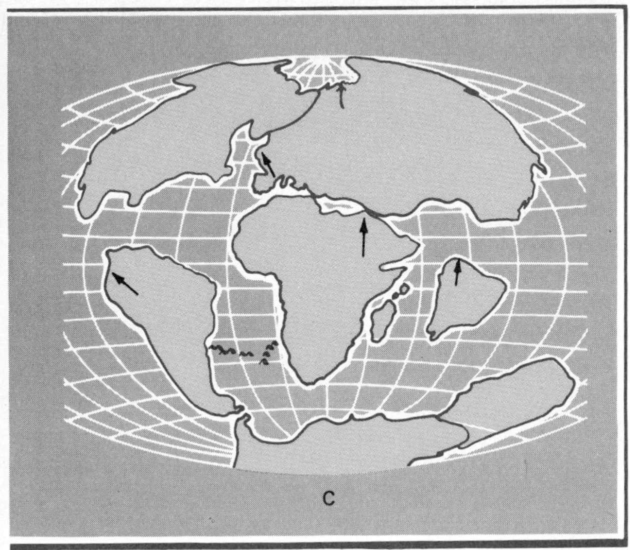

Figure 1 The breakup of Pangaea. 200 million years ago *(A)* all land was part of Pangaea, but by 180 million years B.P. *(B)* Laurasia had split apart from Gondwana, and India had begun its long drift northward. By the end of the Cretaceous period, about 65 million years ago, *(C)* South America had shifted to the west, opening up the South Atlantic, and India had moved far to the north.

continues today at the rate of several centimeters a year. It creates the stresses that now and then cause earthquakes or volcanic eruptions. Knowledge of continental drift is important to our understanding of primate evolution, for areas that are now separated by oceans were once joined in the past. The presence of similar animals or similar fossils in lands that are no longer connected can often be explained by continental drift.

On a smaller scale, all parts of the earth are continually being formed and changed by local geological processes. *Igneous material* is formed when molten mineral matter is brought up from the earth's core (as it does when a volcano erupts) and cools. *Sedimentary material* is the product of the perpetual weathering of the earth's surface. Bits of soil and rock are eroded by wind or water and deposited with organic material in layers in low areas, such as sea bottoms. These deposits may gradually solidify, sometimes preserving traces of plants and animals and patterns such as water ripples or mud cracks. If this sedimentary material becomes buried very deeply by later deposits, the earth's heat or pressure may change it to a third form: *metamorphic material.* Sandstone deposits, for instance, may be changed to a harder form: quartzite.

Each kind of material bears clues to the circumstances under which it was formed. The material deposited in sediments, for instance, shows no change as long as environmental conditions remain constant. If the environment changes, however, different types of material will be deposited. When the earth's surface can be seen in cross-section—in excavations or on cliffs bordering a river—environmental changes show up as *strata* (or layers), which differ in texture, color, composition, and fossil forms. Younger material is always deposited on top of older material. Reading of the layers is complicated by the fact that a number of strata may be turned sideways or even completely folded over by geological upheavals. Upper layers may not be older than lower ones. As a result, geologists must often compare strata with similar layers in other areas to reconstruct the sequence of deposition.

A paleontologist studying this *stratification* can read the layers as clues to changes in the environment. Deposits laid down during very dry periods, for instance, may consist of sharp-sided particles blown from deserts by

Louis Leakey measures strata at the site in Olduvai Gorge where the first relatively complete East African fossil hominid skull was found in 1959. Part of Olduvai's value as a site is that its datable rock layers extend unbroken to about 2 million years B.P. (Jen and Des Bartlett, Photo Researchers)

the wind. By contrast, sediments deposited when the environment was more favorable to plant and animal life may contain remnants of these organisms and rock particles with edges rounded by river and stream action.

Fossilization. When most organisms die, all traces of their existence soon disappear. Their bodies are soon broken down by mechanical and chemical processes and, as we discussed in Chapter 3, by decomposers. Only those that are protected from these processes may survive as fossils. Rapid burial in silt, resin, peat bogs, tar pits, or volcanic ash prevents decay, but coverage by waterbone sediment is the most common form of protection. Creatures that have no hard parts—such as jellyfish—usually decay before this can happen. But shells and the hard skeletal remains of vertebrates may resist decay long enough for burial to occur. Since teeth, jaws, and skulls are the hardest, densest parts of the vertebrate skeleton, they are the most common vertebrate fossils.

Once buried, the hard parts may undergo chemical changes. The few that are preserved without chemically changing are known as *subfossils,* or unaltered fossils. The frozen woolly mammoths are an example. Most fossils, however, are altered by chemicals dissolved in water seeping through the sediment. Some chemicals may completely dissolve the organism, perhaps leaving a *mold* of its shape if the sediment around it turns to rock. Sometimes minerals may seep into the spaces left by decayed organic matter in bones, helping to preserve them. This process is called *impregnation. Petrification,* a third possibility, is the gradual replacement of the original mineral matter by harder minerals. Either impregnation or petrification can literally turn the remains into stone. The fossil that results looks much like the original bone or shell. But it is usually heavier and chemically different, and all the fine details that existed in the original may not be reproduced.

Incompleteness of the Fossil Record. The chances that an organism will be preserved as a fossil and then found by a paleontologist are very slim. So far, we have probably discovered only about 1 percent of the kinds of plants and animals that have ever lived (Sawkins et al., 1974). Because producers form the most abundant trophic level, it is natural that more plants than animals are fossilized. And because humans have been only a small percentage of the animal life on the earth, their fossils are rare. In fact, it is quite possible that we have not yet found the earliest hominids.

There are a number of reasons why the fossil record is so incomplete. Conditions in some areas and times have not permitted fossilization. Some soils, for instance, lack the minerals needed for petrification. Sea creatures have the best chances of being preserved, for sedimentation occurs continually at the bottom of the sea. Usually, land creatures have been fossilized only if their remains end up in an environment where sedimentation is taking place, such as a floodplain, a lake, or an area being covered by drifting sands. Since many animals never reach these areas, certain segments of lineages may not be preserved. And even if an organism happens to be sealed in sediment, and fossilization takes place, the sedimentary rock itself may later be altered by metamorphosis or exposed and destroyed by weathering.

As we have seen, only creatures with hard parts are likely to be preserved, and only their hard parts are likely to be fossilized. Often only a fraction of the original skeleton is discovered. Our only evidence of a creature that may have been the first primate is a single tooth. For all these reasons, the fossil record as it presently exists gives an incomplete and distorted view of the flora and fauna living at any given time in the past. Paleontologists must therefore often work with maddeningly incomplete data. They are therefore always looking for new fossils to expand their knowledge of past animals and plants.

Finding and Excavating Fossils

Our knowledge of extinct life is also limited by the difficulty of locating fossils. Millions of years of sedimentation cover them, often in inaccessible spots. But in areas where weathering or cutting into the earth's surface has taken place, layers of fossils may be exposed. Sand or gravel pits, quarries, stream banks, areas of geological upheaval, and caves may contain exposed fossils. These fossils can simply be picked up or dug out, or, if the site is promising, a major excavation may be organized.

In a big excavation, layers of sediment are removed carefully, one at time. Soil and fossil material is excavated in horizontal slices, or *horizons,* which correspond to natural geological layers. As each horizon is exposed, the excavators draw a map showing the position of any fossils found in it. These maps are invaluable in figuring out whether floods or other forces have placed the fossils where they are, or whether the organisms remained in place when they died.

Interpretation of Fossils

Since the primate fossil record is small, the fossils that are found are subjected to minute analysis. Small details take on great importance in interpreting the age, ancestry, characteristics, and evolutionary relationships of extinct animals known only as fossil fragments.

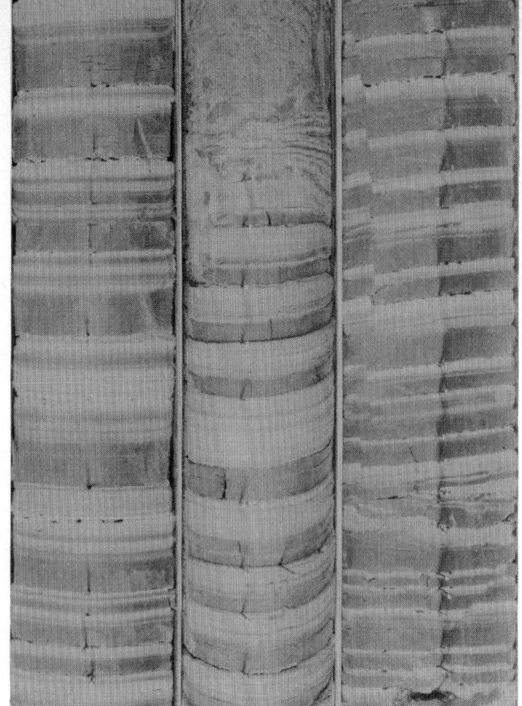

Varves from glacial lakes once located in present-day New Jersey and New York. The light-colored bands were deposited in the summer, the dark-colored ones in the winter. (Courtesy of the American Museum of Natural History)

Dating Fossils. A crucial part of interpreting fossil evidence is dating it, for only after a fossil is placed in a time sequence with other evidence can its place in evolution be assessed. A sequence of events is very important in reconstructing lines of descent, since, of course, descendants are more recent than ancestors. By dating the remains of animals in a site or in a region, we can also learn whether or not they lived at the same time and were therefore a part of the same ecosystem.

Relative Dating Methods. *Relative dating methods* can tell us the age of a specimen relative to another known specimen or deposit. According to the principle of *superposition,* each geological layer was deposited on top of the one beneath it. Therefore, in deposits that have not been disturbed by geological upheavals, fossils found in upper layers are younger than those in deeper layers. During the nineteenth and twentieth centuries, paleontologists constructed a geological history of the earth by establishing the order in which various strata in different parts of the world were formed. The study of sedimentary rock layers and their sequence is called *stratigraphy.*

The age of any layer was given in relation to the ones above and below it. Traditionally, paleontologists could only estimate the absolute age of a fossil by guessing how long it would have taken geological forces to bury the remains in the layer in which they were found. In the nineteenth and early twentieth centuries, paleontologists' estimates of the age of many fossils were far too low. The lack of an accurate time scale hindered early interpretations of our evolutionary history. As a result, the human-like fossils that were being found in Europe seemed too young geologically to be our ancestors.

Fossils themselves can act as clues to the relative dating of sedimentary deposits found in different areas. According to the principles we discussed in Chapter 3, most species change over time and never return to their earlier forms. Layers from two different sites that contain matching fossils are therefore assumed to be about the same age. Some fossils are so common and widespread that they are used to compare the ages of strata at different sites. These so-called *index fossils* are also used to compare the environmental conditions in different geographical areas.

Stratigraphy is still an essential method of relative dating. To it, paleontologists have added several chemical methods. These more precise methods were necessary partly to date different fossils at separate sites and partly because fossils found at the same level in a single deposit may not have lived at the same time. An *intrusion,* caused by a burial, an earthquake, or some other process, frequently places younger remains in the same layer as older ones. Using chemical methods, paleontologists can analyze the composition of fossils found together to determine whether they are actually the same age. While fossils lie buried, they gradually absorb flourine and uranium and lose nitrogen. Chemical and x-ray analysis can show whether two fossils contain about the same amounts of these elements. If not, the fossils are probably of different ages. Unfortunately, differing environmental conditions affect the rate of absorption or loss of minerals. Consequently, these methods can only be used for relative dating of fossils found at the same site.

Another method of relative dating is *varve analysis.* Varves are layers of silt deposited annually in glacial lakes by the water from melting ice sheets. Sequences have been established as far back as 17,000 years for areas that were covered with glaciers for long periods of time, primarily in Scandinavia.

Pollen analysis, or *palynology,* not only provides a sequence by which remains can be dated but also is an invaluable source of data about prehistoric ecologies. Pollen is preserved very well, especially in damp soil. Samples are taken at a site and observed through a microscope. Experts can identify the plants from which the pollen originated and establish regional sequences of vegetational history, some of which stretch back 15,000 years.

Chronometric Dating Methods. Until recently, our ability to date the age of the earth

The excavation of Dragon Bone Hill in Chou-kou-tien, near Peking, China. So-called dragon teeth, which had been sold as medicine in drug stores, led paleontologists to excavate this site in the 1920s and 1930s and find Peking Man, the source of the teeth. (Courtesy of the American Museum of Natural History)

precisely was limited by the lack of any correlation between the way we measure time and the rate at which material is formed into strata. In order to break the continuum of time into measurable chunks, we usually count each revolution of the earth around the sun as a single unit: a calendar year. The problem with trying to measure time in the ancient past is that nothing in the geological record corresponds to our calendar years. Sediments, for instance, are not always laid down in regular yearly bands like tree rings, or at a steady rate measurable in centimeters per year. But scientists have found that certain materials change at a uniform rate through time. In nature, many elements have several forms, each of which is called an *isotope.* Some isotopes are stable, and others are unstable. The stable isotopes do not change over time, but the unstable isotopes, which are said to be *radioactive,* spontaneously change (or decay) into other elements. Decay occurs at a steady rate that can be measured in terms of how long it takes for one-half of the "parent" atoms to decay to atoms of the "daughter" element. The rate is expressed as the *half-life* of the isotope. (See Figure 2.) Unlike chemical changes, these nuclear reactions are not affected by external environmental factors such as heat or pressure. They reflect only the passage of time. These changes can be measured and equated with years to establish the approximate age of fossils. In these absolute, or *chronometric dating* methods, time is often measured backward from the present (set at A.D. 1950 on the Christian time scale). Remains approximately a million years old would be dated one million years before present, or B.P.

Radiometric dating techniques are based on the rate of decay of radioactive isotopes in the rocks surrounding fossil finds. To calculate the age of a rock containing a radioactive isotope, a scientist uses three figures: (1) the initial quantity of the parent isotope in the rock, (2) the rate of decay of that isotope, and (3) the amount of the isotope now present in the rock. The second figure—the rate of decay—is known for most isotopes. The third is determined by laboratory analysis. And the first is assumed to be the same as similar rocks being formed today. These calculations assume a closed system: None of the "parent" or "daughter" has been lost or added to the rock. In some cases, however, this is not a safe assumption. These radiometric methods do not work for sedimentary rocks, because the mineral grains in sedimentary deposits have been weathered from older rocks. It works best for volcanic igneous materials. When datable igneous rocks are found in association with sedimentary deposits (which may contain fossils), the relative time scale suggested by the stratigraphy can be translated to an absolute one.

To give absolute dates to very ancient material, paleontologists must analyze elements that have an extremely slow rate of decay. Uranium, for instance, has a number of unstable isotopes with very long half-lives. They all decay to stable isotopes of lead. Two isotopes commonly used for dating are ^{235}U and ^{238}U. Their half-lives are 713 million years and 4.5 billion years, respectively. These isotopes are often present in common rocks, such as granite. Since they are frequently found decaying together, though at different rates, the age of the rock can be cross-checked by doing separate calculations for each isotope. If the two dates match, they are probably correct. This method is called *uranium-lead dating* and is used to date the oldest rocks found in the earth.

A second form of radiometric dating uses the decay of unstable potassium isotopes (^{40}K) to argon (^{40}Ar), an inert gas. Potassium is found in many common minerals, and its long half-life (1.3 million years) makes it useful for dating very old material. At Olduvai Gorge in Tanzania, for instance, *potassium-argon dat-*

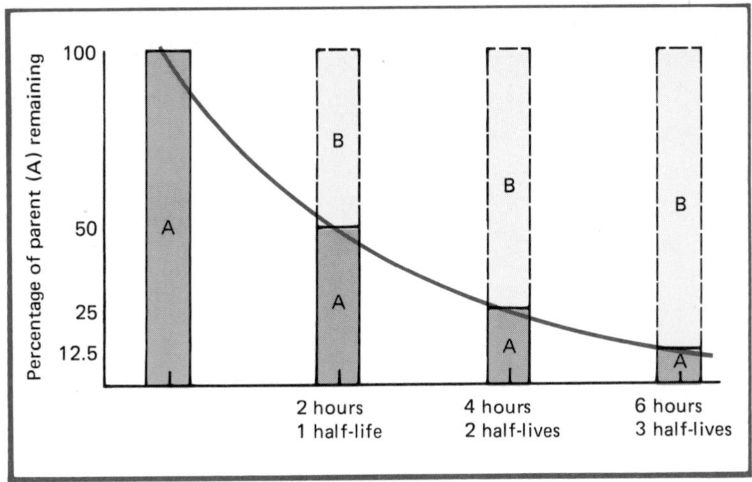

Figure 2 The concept of half-life. One-half of parent isotope *A* remains after one half-life (two hours), and one-quarter is left after two half-lives, the rest having decayed into daughter element *B*. (Sawkins et al., 1974)

ing has been used to date beds of consolidated volcanic ash that buried important early hominid fossils.

Molten rock contains no argon. But as the rock cools, ^{40}K decays at a known rate, and ^{40}Ar is trapped. By determining the ratio of potassium to argon, scientists can measure the time that has passed since the rock was formed. The main problem with this method is that argon sometimes leaks out of the cooled rock, making it impossible to date. Some rocks hold argon gas better than others. Mica, for instance, keeps 80 to 100 percent of its argon; feldspars retain only 40 to 85 percent of theirs (Hole & Heizer, 1973). In addition, not all sites are associated with igneous rock.

A promising method developed in the 1960s—*fission-track dating*—focuses on the short tracks made across a rock by particles of radioactive uranium atoms as they decay. If etched with acid, these tiny trails can be seen under a high-power microscope. To date rock with this method, scientists count the tracks and measure the uranium content of the sample. Because the rate of uranium decay is known, a ratio of the number of tracks to the amount of uranium present yields the age of the rock. The method seems to be reliable for rocks that are 100,000 to 1,000,000 years old. The dates it gives are used to check the results of potassium-argon dating. The two methods together are very accurate. But heating by fire or by geological processes can erase the tracks, posing a potential for error (Michels, 1973).

Fossils found in association with volcanic rocks can also be dated by the orientation of particles in the rock. This method is called *paleomagnetic dating.* In the 1960s scientists discovered that the earth has regularly reversed its magnetic field. For reasons not yet understood, magnetic north and south have sometimes been where they are now, at other times, they have been reversed. About 20 reversals have occurred during the last four million years. As molten rock cools, metallic particles arrange themselves in accordance with the earth's magnetic field, leaving a record of the field at that time. Samples of ancient volcanic deposits and cores from the seabed have been collected from all over the world. Combining the polarity changes and the potassium-argon dates of the volcanic rocks at different levels has allowed paleontologists to chart an absolute time scale for the reversals, which

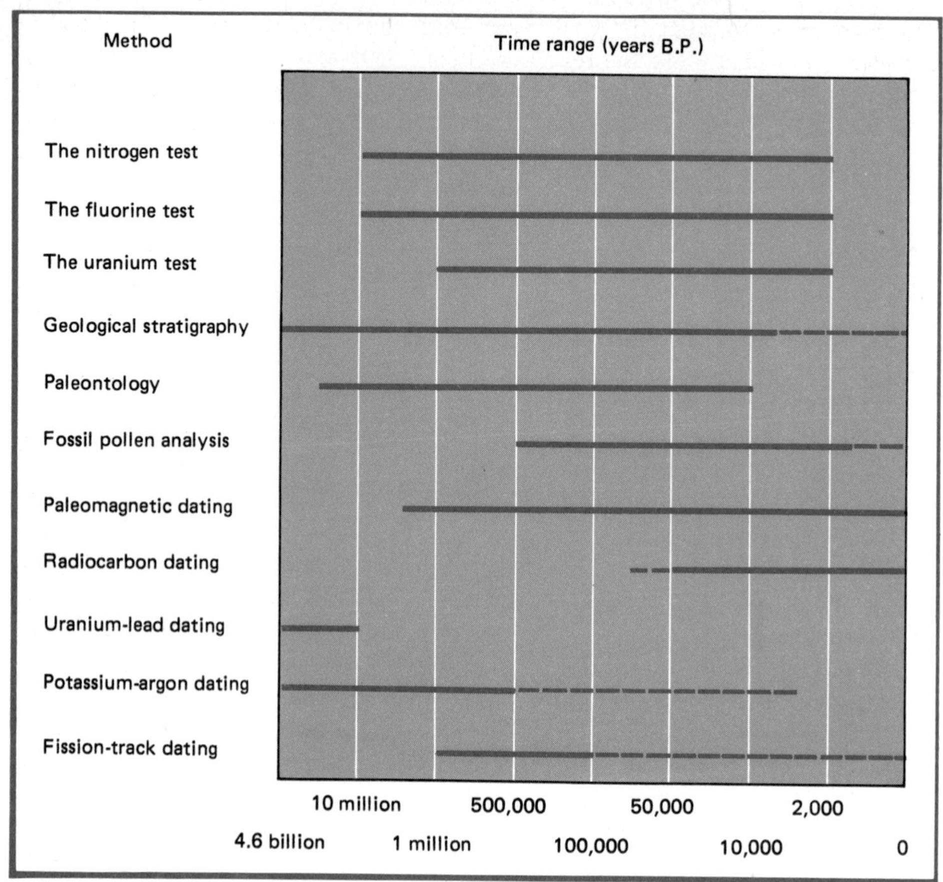

Figure 3 **The range of some dating methods.** (Michels, 1973)

stretch back millions of years. Since the reversals happen very quickly by geological standards, they serve as sharp time markers.

Improvements of chronometric dating have led to continual revision of the geological timescale originally based only on stratigraphy. The new methods make it difficult to fake fossil remains and make it much easier to judge the time relationship of fossils.

See Figure 3 for a summary of the varying time ranges in which the methods we have discussed can be applied. For more recent artifacts and fossils, archaeologists use different methods of dating. *Radiocarbon dating,* for instance, is frequently used to date items up to 50,000 years old. The shortness of the half-life of ^{14}C, the radioactive carbon isotope used, limits its usefulness. We will cover this and other techniques for dating relatively recent remains in a later chapter, where archaeological methods are discussed.

Environmental Reconstructions. In addition to figuring out how old fossils are, paleontologists also try to reconstruct the ancient environment of which the organisms were a part. First it must be determined whether the fossils are *autochthonous* (still surrounded by organisms from their own ecosystem) or *allochthonous* (dumped into a different ecosystem). Predators, scavengers, running water, or wind may have carried the bodies for miles before depositing them in a different habitat. Paleontologists therefore search both the remains and the maps they make of each geological layer for subtle clues to whether the organisms were buried where they had lived. Abrasion marks on bones, for instance, may suggest that they have been transported some distance before being buried by sediment (Behrensmeyer, 1975).

Working from fragments of other flora and fauna and a knowledge of the niche structure of contemporary plants and animals, paleontologists try to reconstruct the ancient ecosystem. For instance, if fossilized palm trees are found, the area was probably tropical to subtropical, for palm trees now grow only in warm regions. Dwarf birches, on the other hand, suggest a very cold climate, for these trees now live only in Arctic or Alpine regions. Vertebrate remains, too, may provide indirect clues to what the region was like. For instance, the presence of animals ancestral to contemporary grazing creatures—such as gazelles—may suggest that the area was once a grassland. Animal clues are not altogether reliable, though, for some animals have adapted to different habitats over time. For example, the ancestors of arctic foxes and polar bears once lived in warm or temperate climates (Thenius, 1973). Nevertheless, environmental reconstructions allow paleontologists to make inferences about the ecological factors that may have influenced the evolution of a species.

Applying Linnaean Taxonomy to Fossils. Because dating methods are becoming more precise, much of the guesswork in paleontology is being eliminated. But figuring out *phylogenies,* theories tracing the evolutionary relationships among a group of organisms, still raises a number of problems. The problem is often further complicated by the scientific names given to fossils. Generally, these taxonomic categories are derived from hypotheses about the relationships between different fossils. Like any other scientific theories, taxonomic categories and the phylogenic theories from which they are derived are subject to revision in terms of new data. In the evolution of primates, including hominids, we are fairly certain of phylogenic relationships from the present back to about 3 million years B.P. But the record of fossils older than that is more fragmentary, so phylogenies and taxonomies suggested for older periods are more controversial.

A second problem is that the Linnaean system, the basis of modern taxonomy, was designed for living species. Species are now defined as populations that can interbreed successfully. But there is no way to tell directly whether two extinct primates could have interbred or not. We have no way of determining reproductive relationships, other than to judge how different or similar extinct animals were in anatomy. For this reason, many scientists make a distinction between *biospecies,* or reproductively isolated populations of living organisms able to breed successfully with one another, and *paleospecies,* anatomically similar extinct animals.

Paleontology creates a third problem by adding a time perspective that does not exist in the classification of living animals. The fossil record stretches back millions of years. When we try to group these extinct forms into families, genera, and species, how many years can each group encompass? There are as yet no generally accepted rules for this. Part of the problem is that organisms differ in their rates of evolution. The evolution of humans has been especially rapid, so that the physical form of hominids has changed more in a shorter period of time than that of other animals.

Until recently, the time dimension was not much of a problem. When there were huge time gaps between groups of fossils that looked different, it was easy to see them as separate species. But as these gaps are filled by new fossil discoveries, it becomes harder to decide where to divide continually evolving animals into distinct groups. Transitional forms—those having some characteristics of an earlier group and some of a later one—are especially exciting to find. But their discovery is usually accompanied by a storm of controversy over where in the existing phylogeny they should be placed.

Naming fossils has posed a fourth difficulty. Taxonomists have worked out careful rules for naming contemporary species. But the excitement of discovering new fossils has led some researchers to give almost every new find a different name on the basis of slight anatomical variations or geographical distance from other finds. They tend to class variants as separate species. For instance, over 60 taxonomic names have been applied to fossil hominids. Having this many pseudospecies greatly complicates the task of seeing trends and relationships in evolution (Simons, 1972; Harrison & Weiner, 1963).

More recently, some scientists have begun to group together anatomically varied fossils in the same category. They use variations among individuals in a living biospecies as a guide to how much variation there may have been in its ancestral paleospecies. Modern gorillas, for instance, are a single species, but individuals vary greatly in size, skull and tooth shape, color, and skeletal patterns. Age and sex are always important sources of variation among the members of a species. The skeletal differences between mature and immature male and female gorillas and orangutans are quite great. Using this model, some paleontologists feel that the variation seen in early hominids may be explained partially as the difference in shape between the male and female of the species.

Reconstructing Extinct Animals. Researchers' views of phylogeny inevitably influence their ideas of how extinct animals must have looked. We have almost no record of the external features of extinct organisms, for soft parts are rarely preserved. At best, drawings and models of extinct creatures can be based on complete skeletons, if they are found. Anatomists can compare these fossils to the structure of closely related living animals to figure out how the bodies of the extinct animals were filled out with muscles and how they moved. Fur, feathers, manes, and skin texture and color, however, can only be guessed at.

In the case of our own ancestors, reconstruction of soft parts is especially difficult, because relatively complete hominid skeletons are very rare. Illustrations and models of our predecessors therefore tend to reflect the scientist's concept of phylogeny, and even the popular evolutionary notions of the day.

The Record of Primate Evolution

We will devote the rest of this chapter to the earliest creatures thought to be primates and trace the beginnings of the evolutionary path that leads eventually to modern humans. Coverage in this chapter will end with the Miocene Epoch, when the hominid lineage may have split off from the pongid lineage. The earliest hominids and the members of the genus *Homo* will be examined in the next two chapters.

The Geological Time Scale

The history of the earth is divided by geologists into four long *eras:* the *Precambrian,* the *Paleozoic* (ancient life), the *Mesozoic* (middle development of life), and *Cenozoic* (recent life). The Precambrian stretches back to about 4.5 or 4.6 billion years B.P., the current estimate for when the earth was formed.

The other three eras are divided into *periods,* which correspond to changing geological patterns—the building up and wearing down of mountains, temperature changes, glaciation, continental drift, the spreading and shrinking of the seas—and also to distinctive plant and animal forms. The two periods of the most recent era, the Cenozoic, are the Tertiary and the Quaternary. These periods are further subdivided into *epochs,* which provide a more precise correspondence with particular life forms or geological features. Table 1 (pp. 118–119) shows the geological time scale that we shall use in this book.

Anatomical Themes in Evolution

As the earth has evolved, a great variety of plant and animal forms has appeared. But despite their diversity, life forms are variations on a limited number of themes. At the broadest level, these themes of anatomical organization are called *phyla.* Our own line developed from the phylum Chordata, characterized by specialized organs and tissues, bilateral symmetry (most structures on one side are duplicated on the other), and an internal backbone. In some members of the phylum, the backbone is a flexible, supportive rod. The others have jointed vertebrae and first appeared in the Ordovician Period of the Paleozoic Era as primitive fish. Later, amphibians and then reptiles developed successful variations on this basic theme, which allowed them to exploit plant life in terrestrial ecosystems. Mammals, representing our version of the chordate plan, emerged slowly in the Triassic Period of the Mesozoic Era, when reptiles were the dominant form of animal life. But mammals mushroomed in number and variety as the Cretaceous Period ended and the Cenozoic Era (the Age of Mammals) began. It was about this time, 70 million years B.P., that the first primates may have emerged from mammalian stock.

The Cretaceous Period (145–65 million years B.P.)

For most of the long *Cretaceous Period,* Pangaea, the land mass that subsequently formed today's continents, was just beginning to break up. Early mammals were therefore able to spread all over the world. Much of North America and Europe was covered by inland seas and swamps, but the land was rising during cataclysmic mountain-building episodes. Because the land masses were grouped near the equator, the climate of all terrestrial ecosystems was probably subtropical or tropical. Changes in vegetation that occurred during this period were very significant for primate evolution. In contrast to the ferns and conifers dominant in the past, *angiosperms* (flowering plants, shrubs, and trees) were becoming abundant. These plants created a number of new potential econiches, which were rapidly occupied. Insects began to use the rich food supplies offered by flowers and fruits. Birds and mammals fed on both the new vegetation and the insects. All of these forms underwent bursts of adaptive radiation as they took advantage of new environmental opportunities.

Some of the Cretaceous mammals were probably small hedgehoglike creatures that ran about on the ground looking for insects to eat (Cartmill, 1975). These insectivores would have seemed insignificant next to the giant dinosaurs that had long been dominant. But when the dinosaurs died out at the end of the period, one of these tiny mammals probably gave rise to the primate line.

Whether this divergence happened during the Cretaceous Period is uncertain. A single molar screened out of sedimentary rubble in Montana is the only evidence that primates may have appeared during this period. The creature to which it belonged has been named *Purgatorius.* Recent finds of similar teeth, toothbearing lower jaws, and a fragmentary

Table 1 The geological time scale. The time divisions are not drawn to a uniform scale. (Flint & Skinner, 1977)

Uniform Time Scale	Subdivisions based on				Radiometric dates (millions of years ago)	Outstanding events	
	Eras	Periods		Epochs		in the physical history of America	in evolution of living things
0							
				Recent or Holocene	0		*Homo sapiens*
		Quaternary		Pleistocene	10,000	Several glacial ages	
					2?		
Phanerozoic				Pliocene			Later hominids
	Cenozoic		Neogene		6	Beginning of Colorado River	Primitive hominids
				Miocene		Creation of mountain ranges and basins in Nevada	Grasses; grazing mammals
575					22		
		Tertiary		Oligocene			
					36		
			Paleogene	Eocene		Beginning of volcanic activity at Yellowstone Park	Primitive horses
					58		
				Paleocene		Beginning of making of Rocky Mountains	Spreading of mammals
					65		
							Dinosaurs extinct
		Cretaceous					
						Beginning of lower Mississippi River	Flowering plants
					145		Climax of dinosaurs
	Mesozoic						Birds
		Jurassic					
					210		
							Conifers, cycads, primitive mammals
		Triassic				Beginning of Atlantic Ocean	
							Dinosaurs

Precambrian	Paleozoic	Permian	Many	250 290	Climax of making of Appalachian Mountains	Mammal-like reptiles
		Pennsylvanian (upper carboniferous)		340		Coal forests, insects, amphibians, reptiles
		Mississippian (lower carboniferous)		365	Earliest economic coal deposits	Amphibians
		Devonian		415		Land plants and land animals
		Silurian		465		
		Ordovician		510	Beginning of making of Appalachian Mountains	Primitive fishes
		Cambrian		575	Earliest oil and gas fields	Marine animals abundant
						Primitive marine animals Green algae
		Precambrian (Mainly igneous and metamorphic rocks; no worldwide subdivisions)		1,000 2,000 3,000		
~4,650		Birth of planet Earth			Oldest dated rocks	Bacteria, blue-green algae

upper jaw in the same area have been assigned to the same genus, but dated to the early Paleocene Epoch. The subtle similarity of their features to those of primates seems to substantiate the theory that at least as far back as the early Paleocene, and perhaps even during the late Cretaceous, this group had begun to distinguish itself from other similiar insectivores. It evolved perhaps in response to competition from rodents who were better equipped to exploit a terrestrial, insectivorous niche. *Purgatorious* and its descendants, it is thought, moved into the trees and gradually shifted away from insect-eating to plant-eating. Consequently, the teeth of early primates have increasingly more rounded cusps instead of the long, sharp cusps of teeth specialized for a diet of insects. This traditional theory, however, has been complicated by new evidence, as we shall see.

The Paleocene Epoch (65–58 million years B.P.)

As the *Paleocene Epoch* opened, the world climate was somewhat cooler than it had been. The continents had begun to drift away from the equator. But although no longer tropical, they were at least temperate. Alaska and Canada, for instance, had plants similar to those now found in the southern part of the United States. The northern continental land mass, Laurasia, was still intact. It was in this part of the world that the first primates probably radiated from the primitive insectivores of the Cretaceous Period (Simons, 1972).

Various common Paleocene and early Eocene fossils, found in both Europe and North America, have been interpreted as early primates. Many scientists now agree that these animals fall into at least three families and can be grouped into the superfamily *Plesiadapoidea.* The status of these groupings, however, is still far from settled. For a diagram of primate evolution, see Figure 4.

One of the three families, the *Paromomyidae,* includes *Purgatorius* and other Paleocene and even Eocene representatives. They are the most primitive of all primates, for their snouts are quite long and their brains very small. But they show the beginnings of certain primate evolutionary trends: flat-crowned molars with low, rounded cusps, a distinctive inner ear construction, and skeletal traits that suggest adaptation to arboreal life.

A second family—the *Carpolestidae*—is similar to the paromomyids. But the premolars of these mouse-sized creatures are highly specialized, with long blades on the top teeth fitting into grooves in the large lower teeth. This tooth structure may have been an adaptation that helped them bite through the tough casings of seeds.

Members of the third family—*Plesiadapidae*—are larger, with bodies like heavy squirrels. (See Figure 5.) They are similar in many ways to later primates. They have unspecialized molars, an ear construction like that of primates, and turned-in feet that may have helped them walk along branches. But in some ways they are more like nonprimate mammals of that period: Their olfactory apparatus is large in comparison to their visual equipment, their brains are small and encased in a flat skull, and they have pointed claws instead of nails. In addition, their first incisors project forward, are unusually large, and have three unique, pointed cusps. These strange front teeth, which may have been good for husking seeds and fruits, are separated from the cheek teeth by a large gap (Simons, 1972).

In some respects, the superfamily *Plesiadapoidea* falls midway between the Cretaceous insectivores and the Eocene lemurs and tarsiers, which were undoubtedly primates. It may represent a transition from a terrestrial insect-eating lifestyle to an arboreal, fruit- and vegetation-eating pattern. But the fossil evidence is too incomplete to reveal whether or not these creatures had begun to develop grasping feet. The idea that

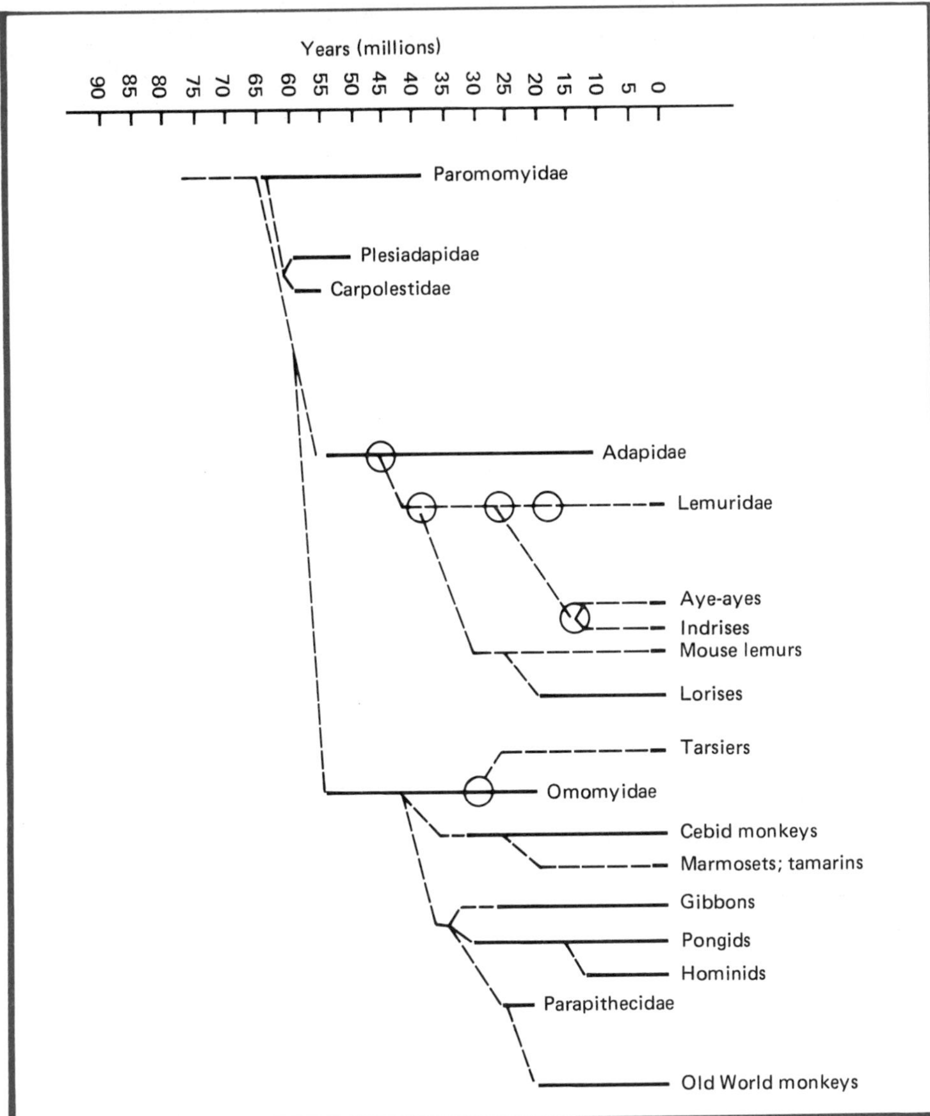

Figure 4 One theory of the evolutionary relationships of selected primate families. Solid heavy lines represent known ranges, and broken lines show the probable relationships. (Szalay, 1976)

they were arboreal is still an unproved theory. And what evidence we do have indicates that some of these creatures had developed specialized adaptations of their own. For instance, the dental pattern of the plesiadapids and carpolestids seemed to be evolving away from the unspecialized dental pattern that characterized later primates. They may, therefore, have sprung from the same ancestor but followed evolutionary paths that began to diverge early in the Paleocene Epoch. Perhaps the only group that is primitive enough to

Figure 5 **A reconstruction of the Paleocene prosimian** ***Plesiadapis,*** species of which ranged from squirrel- to cat-size. (Simons, 1964)

have been a direct ancestor of the modern primates is the paromomyids (Cartmill, 1975; Szalay, 1973).

The Eocene Epoch (58–36 million years B.P.)

The primate trends that began during the Paleocene Epoch are clearly expressed in fossils dated to the *Eocene Epoch* (58–36 million years B.P.). The world was again warm and wet. Laurasia was beginning to separate into North America, Greenland, and Europe. But during most of this epoch, some overland connections must have remained, for fossils of mammals found on both sides of the widening Atlantic are still quite similar. All the southern continents, however, were probably separated from the northern ones by oceans (Simons, 1972).

By this time, all the modern orders of mammals had differentiated themselves from the primitive ancestral stock. Although the Paleocene primates died out, three groups of prosimian-like primates appeared, perhaps as descendants of the paromomyids. Their fossilized skulls, teeth, and limbs have been found in both Europe and America. All had distinctly primate characteristics: relatively large braincases, eyes set close together and surrounded by a bony ring, and grasping feet.

One group, the *adapids,* were probably ancestral to modern lemurs. Most of these medium-sized primates were powerfully built, with strong chewing muscles, a possible adaptation to a diet of tough vegetation. Another group, the *tarsiids,* were ancestral to today's tarsiers. Small, with large eyes, they had elongated ankle bones, which suggest the development of a vertical clinging and leaping form of locomotion.

The third group, the *anaptomorphids,* is a hodgepodge of primates that do not fit into any other family. In general, they seem to have been small nocturnal creatures that ate both insects and fruits with their unspecialized teeth, as some prosimians now do. One of the anaptomorphid subfamilies—the somewhat tarsier-like *omomyids*—is of special interest to anthropologists, for it may have been a direct ancestor of the catarrhines, and therefore of the hominids. The remains of this group have been found in both Europe and North America (Szalay, 1973).

Since the Eocene lemur and tarsiers encompassed a great variety of forms, and since the fossil record of earlier times is so fragmented, scientists have varying interpretations of the evidence. For a long time they went by the theory that a change from a terrestrial to an arboreal life-style was taking place in the primate line. But there is still no good fossil evidence for this, and recent finds seem to call for a more complex explanation. Cartmill (1975) suggests that some of the

Figure 6 A reconstruction of *Smilodectes*, an Eocene prosimian. (Simons, 1964)

primitive insect-eating mammals of the Cretaceous Period began to eat fruit and vegetation as well as insects. During this important adaptive shift, some of the early plesiadapoids, perhaps the paromomyids, may have begun climbing trees in search of fruits, seeds, and leaves, without giving up their taste for insects. They may thus have led dual lives, climbing trees for fruit and vegetation and prowling on the ground for insects. Modern tree shrews still have this mixed life-style and are not specialized for either kind of diet.

The low-cusped molars of the early plesiadapoids were perhaps somewhat better suited for grinding plants than for shearing insects. But they probably managed to crush insect bodies, too, just as small prosimians with similar tooth structure do today. At any rate, it was unlikely that all the plesiadapoids became more specialized for chewing fruit and seeds. Those who did—the *Carpolestidae* and the *Plesiadapidae*—probably branched off from the line that later led to the higher primates. Those who did not develop specialized dentition advanced in other ways instead. During the Eocene Epoch they evolved grasping feet, larger eyes set close together and facing forward (thus making stereoscopic vision possible), and a larger brain for improved visual perception and eye-hand coordination. These changes may have improved their ability to catch mobile insects and to feed at the slender tips of branches without falling.

The Oligocene Epoch (36–22 million years B.P.)

The most extensive radiation of the ancient prosimians occurred during the Eocene Epoch. During the *Oligocene Epoch* they gave up all but a few specialized niches to their descendants, the monkeys and apes. They disappeared almost entirely from the fossil record in Europe and North America, probably because these northern continents became too cool for them as the world climate cooled. Europe and North America were now temperate regions with cold winters. Primates may have been among the animals that retreated across temporary land bridges to areas that were still warm year-round: Africa and South America. For it is here that we get our next glimpse of primate evolution.

Very little is known about primate evolution in South America. According to current theories of plate tectonics, North and South America were rejoined during the Cretaceous Period, when volcanic activity and crustal uplifting created the Isthmus of Panama (Dietz & Holden, 1970). The same types of generalized prosimian forms (paromomyids or omomyids) that gave rise to Old World catarrhines probably also gave rise to the New World platyrrhines (Szalay, 1973). But in both South America and in Africa the evolution of arboreal adaptations occurred independently. As we noted in Chapter 3, this represents a classic illustration of parallel evolution.

Because of our interest in human evolution, our focus from the Oligocene Epoch to the present will naturally be on the Old World. We have not yet found any fossil primates in Africa from periods earlier than the Oligocene Epoch. But it is possible that they evolved from advanced paramomyids or omomyids that made their way to Africa from Laurasia during the Paleocene or Eocene Epochs (Dietz & Holden, 1970; Szalay, 1973). At any rate, the primate fossil record in Africa opens in the Oligocene Epoch with a great variety of advanced forms, suggesting that they had been evolving there for some time.

The richest finds from the Oligocene Epoch come from the Fayum Depression at the edge of the Sahara Desert in Egypt. Now an arid wasteland, it was covered 30 million years ago with lush tropical rain forests and slow-moving rivers. Sedimentary beds from these ancient rivers show that the trees there in the Oligocene Epoch must have been over 100 feet tall (Simons, 1972). The Oligocene primates that may have lived in these great trees were probably transitional forms, somewhere between omomyids and later catarrhines, though scientists are not agreed on how to classify them.

Interpretation of their remains has been complicated by the crudity of early paleontological techniques. Fossils found in the Fayum before the 1960s are hard to date, for their collectors merely noted that they were found in beds now known to contain strata ranging from 25 to 45 million years old. And when the lower jaw of a small primate called *Parapithecus* was discovered in the Fayum in 1908, it was improperly reassembled. For instance, the two halves of the jaw were glued directly together in a V-shaped pattern, instead of the U-shape it would have taken if a missing central piece had been reconstructed. This and other mistakes led to confusing errors in interpretation that persisted until new specimens were found recently. Variously classified in the past as a tarsier-like prosimian, an early ape, or even a possible hominid, *Parapithecus* is now presumed to be an early Old World monkey (Simons, 1972).

The recent finds in the Fayum have led to changes in our interpretation of hominid evolution. Although we once thought that the hominoids (gibbons, apes, and humans) had evolved from monkeys, one current theory holds that the hominoids and the Old World monkeys shared a common catarrhine ancestor (Le Gros Clark, 1965). The Old World monkeys probably diverged from the line by the early Oligocene Epoch, or perhaps earlier, and developed their own specialized adaptations to arboreal life.

In tracing our own ancestors, we shall ignore the monkeys who were developing on both sides of the Atlantic and concentrate on the apes instead. The earliest ape fossil found so far is probably *Oligopithecus,* which dates from about 32 million years B.P. Judging from the size of a fragment of its lower jaw (for this is the only piece of it yet found), it was probably no larger than a squirrel monkey. The pattern of wear on its first premolar suggests that this molar was used as a sharpening edge for a large canine—a feature seen in all Old World monkeys and apes. Its dental formula, 2.1.2.3, also matches that of the higher primates. But its molars are more like those of the omomyids (Simons, 1972).

In the 1960s Elwyn Simons conducted extensive searches of the Fayum site and turned up an almost complete skull of a primitive ape that lived about 28 million years B.P. Called *Aegyptopithecus* ("Egyptian ape"), it was about the size of a fox, and it probably lived high in the forest canopy, eating vegetation and perhaps fruits. Scientists could only guess at how it moved until 1977, when Simons and an associate discovered some of its upper-arm fragments. These indicate that this early ape walked from branch to branch quadrupedally, rather than swinging or leaping through the trees (*Time,* March 6, 1978).

Unlike later hominoids, *Aegyptopithecus* had the relatively long snout and perhaps the tail of its prosimian ancestors. But its eyes are close-set and forward-facing, and its teeth are apelike, with enlarged canines. Its brain, though smaller than that of any living monkey, was nonetheless bigger than that of the earlier prosimians. This combination of primitive and advanced primate characteristics suggests that it is in, or closely related to, the lineage connecting the prosimian creatures of the Eocene Epoch with the pongid line, from which hominids would later diverge. Similarities between *Aegyptopithecus* and *Dryopithecus,* a later Miocene form thought to be a precursor to modern pongids and to humans, underscore the possibility that this early ape may be one of our direct ancestors (Simons, 1972).

Figure 7 A reconstruction of the Miocene pongid *Dryopithecus africanus,* believed by some to have been an ancestor of the chimpanzee. (Napier, 1976)

The Miocene Epoch (22–6 million years B.P.*)*

Although anthropoids from the Oligocene Epoch have been found only in Africa, during the *Miocene Epoch* they apparently spread throughout parts of Europe and Asia by way of a land bridge created between the land masses about 18 million years ago. Monkeys and apes became less and less like each other as their evolutionary paths continued to diverge.

The geological upheavals that created the land bridge between Africa and Eurasia also caused changes in climate and environment. The most important of these was a gradual drying and cooling trend that changed the previously moist tropical forests of Eurasia into wooded grasslands. During most of the epoch the Miocene pongid *Dryopithecus* lived in an arboreal habitat in which the fruit and leaves it ate were abundant year-round. But toward the middle of the Miocene Epoch the drier climate made fruit a less dependable food source, and the larger dryopithecines may have found it necessary to forage for nuts and roots at the forest's edge. These animals most likely were the ancestors of the living great apes and of the members of the lineage leading to modern humans.

The Dryopithecines. A number of different forms are included in the genus *Dryopithecus.* Among the many species into which these primates have been classified are the largest, *D. major,* a 150-pound possible ancestor to modern gorillas, and *D. africanus,* a smaller African species, possibly the forerunner of the chimpanzee. (See Figure 7.)

The success of the rather generalized dryopithecine adaptation can be seen in the long span it survived (some 20 million years—from late Oligocene through the

Miocene and into the early Pliocene), as well as in the vast areas of the Old World over which it spread—Europe, Russia, India, China, the Middle East, and Africa.

The tooth structure of *Dryopithecus* shows a combination of pongid and hominid traits. Like modern apes, it had large canines and a space between the lower first premolar and the canine to make way for the upper canine. But, like humans, it lacked such pongid specializations as the simian shelf (a bony ridge that buttresses the inner part of the lower jaws) and enlarged incisors (used to peel fruit). The shape of the *dental arcade,* the curve of the row of teeth in each jaw, is sometimes a clue to phylogenetic relationships. In modern apes, this arcade is U-shaped. In humans, it is a parabola, since the rows of teeth are not parallel to each other. The arcade of *Dryopithecus* is basically U-shaped, but the rows do form a slight angle. Some experts take this as evidence that the U- and the parabolic shapes evolved separately from the dryopithecine original (Simons, 1977). Finally, *Dryopithecus's* molars had a generalized cusp pattern similar to both pongids and humans, but less specialized than that of modern great apes.

Abundant *Dryopithecus africanus* remains from East Africa reveal certain primitive monkeylike traits. These include reduced brow ridges and a small, monkeylike braincase. (See Figure 8.) Controversy exists over dryopithecine locomotion. While some experts argue that the upper limb and wrist of *Dryopithecus africanus* were suited for brachiation, Le Gros Clark (1965) points to its relatively shorter forearm as evidence that it may have favored quadrupedal running and leaping instead.

Descendants of the Dryopithecines. Among the groups thought to have descended from the dryopithecines is *Sivapithecus.* This primate is often grouped with the genus *Dryopithecus,* but a few investigators (Pilbeam et al., 1977) now think that its dentition shares enough traits with the hominids that it should be placed in a separate genus. Together with *Ramapithecus* it is a possible hominid ancestor.

Gigantopithecus, however, was an evolutionary dead end. An Asian descendant of the dryopithecines, or perhaps of *Sivapithecus, Gigantopithecus* inhabited present-day India and China during the Pliocene and Pleistocene Epochs. This creature's enormous size is indicated by molars and jaws so massive that they dwarf those of modern male gorillas. Estimates place *Gigantopithecus* as tall as 9 feet and as heavy as 600 pounds. Currently, *Gigantopithecus* is believed to have been a ground-living herbivorous pongid, resembling a giant gorilla, and perhaps displaying gorillalike sexual dimorphism (Rosen, 1974).

Summary

1. Only fossils can give direct evidence of the structure, habitat, eating habits, locomotory style, and age of extinct animals.

2. *Fossils,* the preserved remnants of organisms from a past geological age, range from a few fully preserved *subfossils* to the more common *molds* and *petrified* remains.

3. Fossil remains do not accurately represent the original environment. Few organisms are preserved as fossils because most decompose before the necessary rapid burial or coverage by sediments. Of the preserved organisms only parts become fossils, very few of which can be found.

4. In a major *excavation* material is removed and mapped in *horizons,* which correspond to geological layers called *strata*.

5. The interpretation of fossils can include dating them, determining the ancient environment, classifying them, and reconstructing them.

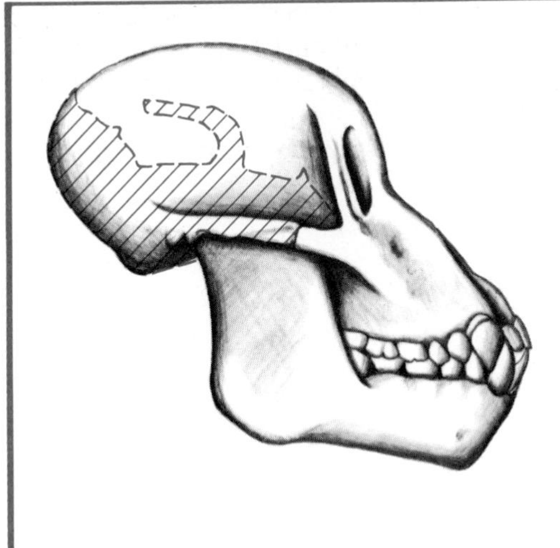

Figure 8 **The skull of *Dryopithecus africanus.*** Its teeth have a mix of pongid and hominid traits, and the primitive brain case is small and rounded, like that of a monkey. (After Robinson, 1952)

6. There are two kinds of dating techniques: *relative dating* and *chronometric,* or absolute, dating. Relative dating, which can show only whether one deposit is older or younger than another, includes *stratigraphy;* chemical analysis of fluorine, nitrogen, or uranium content; *palynology;* and *varve analysis.* Chronometric methods measure a deposit's distance in time from the present. They include radiometric methods such as *uranium-lead* and *potassium-argon dating* and other techniques such as *fission-track* and *paleomagnetic dating.*

7. *Paleontologists,* scientists who study fossils, can reconstruct the ancient environment by comparing fossil plants and animals to present species and their environments.

8. Geologists divide the earth's history into eras, periods, and epochs. Mammals first appeared during the Triassic Period of the Mesozoic Era, but maintained a low profile until the Cenozoic Era began. Then they rapidly increased in numbers and kinds to exploit the bonanza offered by the new flowering plants and the insects that thrived on them.

9. The earliest possible primate fossil is *Purgatorius,* dated to the late *Cretaceous Period* on the basis of a single tooth. Its family—the paromomyids—is better represented in fossils from the *Paleocene Epoch.*

10. In the *Eocene Epoch,* the paromomyids probably gave rise to three prosimianlike primate groups. One of these—the omomyids—seems to have continued the tendency toward unspecialized tooth structure, grasping feet, better vision, and a larger brain, all of which characterize the higher primates.

11. In the *Oligocene Epoch,* primitive monkeys and apes appear in Africa, where they must have been evolving for some time. The monkeys already show specializations of their own. Fossils of *Aegyptopithecus*—a fox-sized arboreal primate with both primitive and advanced traits—suggest that it is on or near the line leading from the omomyids to modern apes and humans.

12. Hominids and modern pongids emerged from the complex genus *Dryopithecus,* whose members had both some unspecialized, as well as some more specialized apelike traits.

7 The Earliest Hominids

FOR thousands of years, humanity has tried to explain its origins. We have answered in myth such questions as Who were our earliest ancestors? How did they live? What did they look like? Today the answers physical anthropologists give to these same questions are constantly changing and often contradictory. New fossils and new dates often trigger intense debate, which may result in new explanations of certain episodes in our evolution. The exciting discoveries in East Africa during the past 20 years, for example, have made our understanding of human origins much more accurate, if less secure than when they were wrapped in myth.

Because fossils do not come out of the ground with a label, we have to develop some standards by which we can judge if a fossil is or is not an ancestor of living humans. The obvious basis for such standards is *Homo sapiens.* Using ourselves as a model, we can list the following standards for classifying fossils as hominids: a parabolic dental arcade, incisors set vertically in the jaw, thickly enameled molars, large brain size, and changes in the shape of the vertebral column, pelvis, lower limbs, and feet to permit erect posture and bipedal movement. Of course, cultural artifacts, especially stone tools, are extremely important signs of hominid status.

We cannot always assume, however, that the presence of modern human traits in an ancient fossil means that it is ancestral to us. Because fossils are often incomplete—especially the older ones—a part of the skeleton that may be important for judging it to be a hominid could be missing. Also, fossils look less and less human the farther back in time we go. Thus, some of the earliest hominids probably had many pongid features. Because the evolutionary lineages leading to modern humans and to the great apes descended from a common ancestor, it is often hard to distinguish fossils of our ancestors from those of ape ancestors. Finally, there may have been many hominid "experiments"—animals that became extinct because others were better adapted to the same niche. Separating the forms that gave rise to later hominids from those that became extinct adds another difficulty.

Ramapithecus

The middle and late Miocene is a period that produced a number of fossil forms, some of which could have been early hominids. Presently, the form receiving the most attention is called *Ramapithecus.* In 1932, G. Edward Lewis, an American graduate student who was searching Miocene deposits about 100 miles north of New Delhi, India, found an upper jaw that impressed him with its large number of humanlike traits. He named the fossil *Ramapithecus,* or "Rama's ape." Rama is a mythical prince and hero of the Indian epic poem, the *Ramayana.* Lewis placed the primate in the family Hominidae, the only living member of which is *Homo sapiens.*

The Miocene Environment

Today our knowledge of *Ramapithecus* is based on the jaws and teeth of some 40 different individuals who lived between 14 and 8 million years ago. Fossils have been found in Kenya, Spain, Southern Germany, Greece, Turkey, Pakistan, India, and China.

Ramapithecus probably lived in subtropical to warm-temperate forests (Simons, 1977) with abundant water, palm trees, and occasional savannas dotted with trees. In India, *Ramapithecus's* neighbors included warthogs, several kinds of carnivores, ancestors of the modern horse, ancient forms of crocodiles and rhinoceroses, and some dryopithecine apes. In Kenya, *Ramapithecus* shared the same sort of environment with rodents, ancient giraffes, rhinoceroses, cattle, dryopithecine apes, and several other primates (Simons, 1972). Much

"Must you hang around with those baboons?"

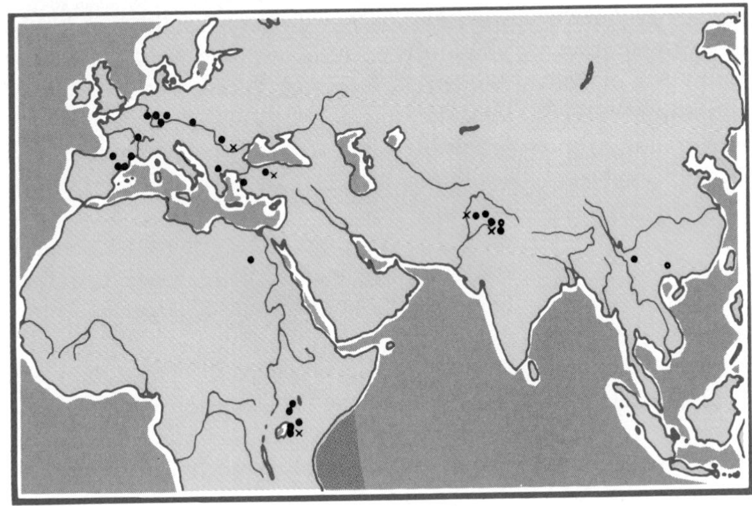

Figure 1 **Distribution of *Dryopithecus* (dots), *Gigantopithecus* (circles), and *Ramapithecus* (crosses).** Both *Dryopithecus* and *Ramapithecus* lived in subtropical to warm-temperate forests, although the Eurasian and Greek sites show signs that *Ramapithecus* may have lived in a savanna or forest-fringe environment as well. (Simons, 1977)

of Eurasia and Greece, however, was drier than Kenya and India. Only at these sites do *Ramapithecus* fossils seem clearly linked with grassland and wooded savanna environments (Simons, 1977). (See Figure 1.)

The Adaptations of Ramapithecus

A drying trend might have caused some dryopithecine apes to get their food in new ways. Simons (1977) believes that as the climate became drier in Eurasia, fruit, which the dryopithecine apes of the tropical and semitropical forests seem to have eaten, became available on a seasonal basis instead of yearround. This may have encouraged some of the Miocene pongids to search for nuts and roots at the forest edge. Indeed, at certain sites in Eurasia, *Ramapithecus* is found in the same deposits as animals that lived in a savanna and steppe environment. The absence of Dryopithecines in these deposits suggests that they may not have been able to survive in such an environment. Unfortunately, it is not always possible to clearly link *Ramapithecus* with a savanna environment. In Kenya, Turkey, and Hungary, they are found in areas with nearby forests. In Kenya, they are found in deposits with forest as well as savanna animals.

Whether *Ramapithecus* lived in the savanna, near the forest fringe, or partly in the savanna and partly in the forest, fossils show the emergence of new dental patterns. The cheek teeth and their enamel covering are larger than those of the Dryopithecines. The teeth also suggest that these animals broke down some of their food by moving their teeth from side to side. *Dryopithecus* probably did not chew this way. Finally, the jaw itself was strong, with internal buttressing in the front.

In a savanna or partly savanna econiche, animals such as *Ramapithecus* with robust jaws and modified molars could have taken advantage of seeds and other small, tough-to-chew foods. Clifford Jolly (1970) has suggested that hominid teeth were, in fact, adaptations to this sort of diet. He has based this "seed-eating" hypothesis on a study of Gelada baboons in Ethiopia. These terrestrial baboons, living in a dry environment, have small incisors and large molars for grinding a diet of seeds, grasses, bulbs, and insects. Their canines are also fairly small to permit effective side-to-side chewing and grinding of seeds. Long canines would hinder this motion. Jolly has suggested that as early hominids moved into more open areas they depended on a diet similar to that of the Geladas. Thus, smaller canines would have made chewing easier. The grinding needed to break down tough vegetation would explain thickly enameled molars and premolars of *Ramapithecus.*

There is some question about the size of ramapithecine canines. Frayer (1974) thinks that they were not really shorter than those of *Dryopithecus.* Simons (1977), however, feels that *Ramapithecus* canines were smaller—about as large as their adjacent teeth. Even if reduction had occurred, however, canines may still have had a function like that of canines in pongids. The pointed form and sharp back edges of some canines may suggest that *Ramapithecus* did not depend totally on tough-to-chew foods. Its incisors retained a cutting edge for tearing food, an edge that the baboons do not have. In fact, some scientists have argued that these slicing incisors point to a carnivorous diet for *Ramapithecus,* but there is too little evidence for any definite conclusions.

Despite the fact that the total fossil evidence for *Ramapithecus* consists of teeth and jaws and does not include brain cases and postcranial remains, scientists have thought about its body and brain size, posture, locomotion, and even social behavior. One worker (Leakey, 1977), judging from the size of the fossils, guesses that *Ramapithecus* was only about 3½ feet tall. Because of its small size and apparent lack of large canines, it could have been easy prey for savanna carnivores. As a result, he suggests, it may have developed a semierect posture, both to see over the tall grass and to permit the aggressive displays that the gorilla and chimpanzee use to frighten off predators. Because an upright posture would have freed the hands, it may also have been promoted by using tools and carrying food from place to place (Leakey, 1977). Clifford Jolly, again drawing on his studies of the Geladas, thinks that the semierect posture of these animals as they feed may be similar to that of the earliest savanna-foraging hominids. This posture leaves the hands free for feeding. Small object feeding requires another well-developed hominid trait—the precision grip. Finally, greater reliance on social behavior instead of teeth and strength for survival may have begun the hominid trend of larger and more complex brains.

Behavior such as group cooperation and food-sharing may have developed as a defense against predators in an open landscape. Open-country dwellers such as baboons are more tightly organized than are forest dwellers, who can flee to the treetops at the first sign of danger. When *Ramapithecus* began to exploit open country, similar group structure may have taken shape. The move to the savanna may also have caused an elaboration of the meat-eating and meat-sharing behavior known to occur among forest chimpanzees (Leakey, 1977).

How Should We Classify Ramapithecus?

There is a great deal of debate as to whether *Ramapithecus* can be considered a hominid. This is natural, seeing the lack of evidence by which to judge. One expert (Simons, 1977) places *Ramapithecus* among the hominids because of its humanlike traits. He argues that the shape of the reconstructed dental arcade is intermediate between that of the Miocene apes and later hominids. (See Figure 2.) The pattern of wear on the molars and the thickness of the bone in the lower jaw, according to him, are more typical of later hominids than of *Dryopithecus* or living apes. Also, the canine teeth and incisors are smaller than those of living apes.

This interpretation is opposed by Frayer (1974), who offers conflicting evidence from certain fossils. He suggests that previous re-

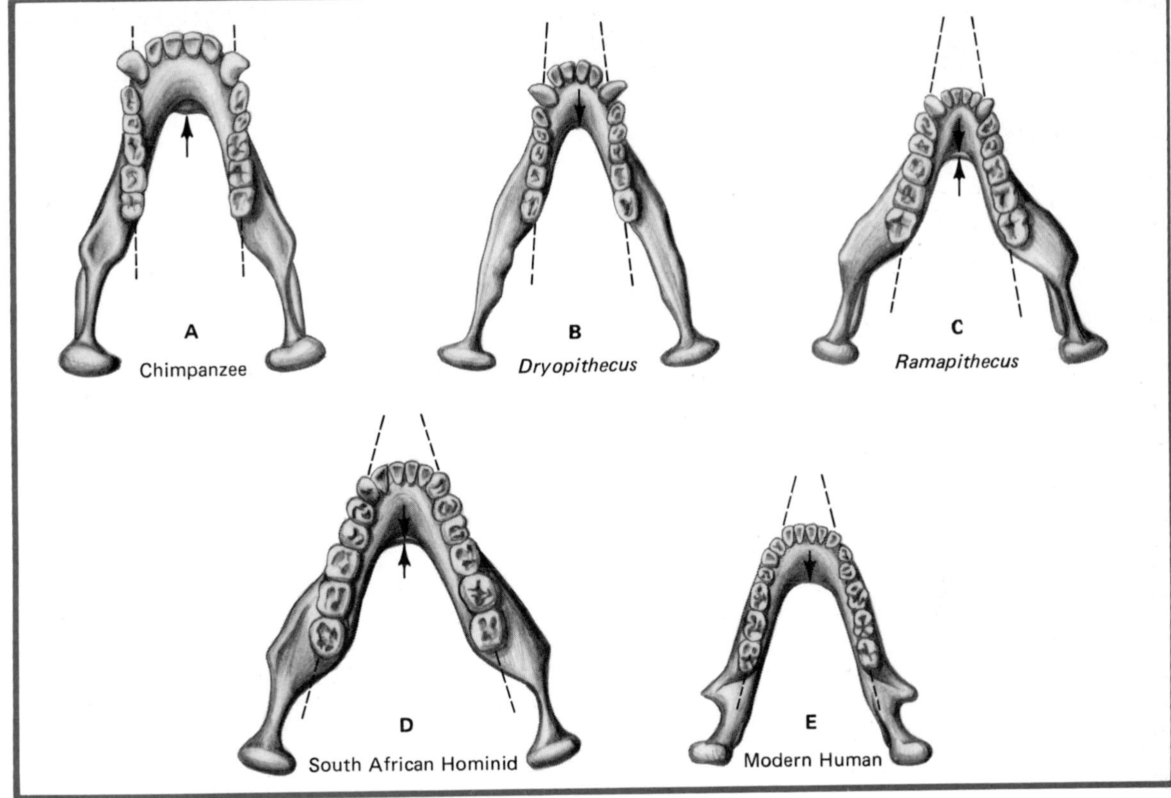

Figure 2 The dental arcades of selected pongids and hominids. *Dryopithecus (B)* is thought to be the common ancestor of living pongids, represented here by the chimpanzee *(A),* and the hominids, including the gracile South African hominids *(D)* and modern humans *(E).* Those who believe that *Ramapithecus (C)* is a hominid think that: (1) the angle of divergence of its tooth rows is closer to that of *D* and *E* than to that of *B*. As you can see, Elwyn Simons, on whose work this drawing is based, holds this view; (2) the canines are not projecting, like those of *A* and *B* but reduced, like those of *D* and *E*. Although the status of *C* is in doubt, by these two criteria, *D* is clearly a hominid. Note also that *D* has rounded molar cusps, like those of *E.* Note, too, the progressive increase in the size of the back teeth, from *B* to *D,* probably reflecting a growing reliance on a diet of tough vegetable material. (Simons, 1977)

constructions of *Ramapithecus's* dental arcade were faulty and that in fact its shape looks more like the dryopithecine dental arcade. He also finds other apelike features, such as forward-pointing incisors, projecting canines, and a gap between the upper canines and the first premolar. And although the canines may be smaller than those of living apes, they are equal in length to those of at least one female *Dryopithecus.* Frayer concludes that *Ramapithecus* differs from the Miocene apes, but not necessarily in ways that place it in the human lineage (Frayer, 1974).

Other experts have fueled the debate by questioning the practice of defining hominids using modern humans as a model (Pilbeam et al., 1977). The advanced primates dating from this period have a mix of so-called hominid and ape traits. Ape ancestors could well have had a number of hominid characteristics, and hominids could have had ape characteristics. Thus, according to Pilbeam, "Extinct hominoids were not identical with, nor, in some cases, particularly similar to living hominoids, and to interpret extinct hominoids as though they were very 'modern' is potentially misleading." Thus, most experts feel that hominids first diverged from pongids during the Miocene, and that *Ramapithecus* had some hominid features. But they do not agree on how to classify *Ramapithecus.*

The Plio-Pleistocene Hominids

Fossil evidence of advanced primates from the late Miocene and the early *Pliocene* periods, particularly in Africa, is thus far very scanty. The Pliocene began about 6 million years ago and ended at about 1.9 million years ago. The Asian fossil record of the early Pliocene provides the remains of the giant dryopithecine ape called Gigantopithecus, living in India and China from about 9 million to 250,000 years B.P. In Africa, during the transition from early debatable hominid forms such as *Ramapithecus* to the earliest undoubted hominids, there is a gap between about 12 and 4 million years B.P. This is precisely the period during which hominid traits such as erect posture and bipedalism are thought to have evolved. When they are found, fossils from this period will for this reason be of great importance. Presently, only tantalizing pieces of the puzzle are available. Among the most interesting finds to date are parts of a jaw from Lothagam, Kenya, dated at 5 million years B.P. and an upper molar from Ngorora, Kenya, which has been dated at about 9 million years old. With cusps similar to those of later hominids and a low crown like that of *Ramapithecus,* it may represent a transitional form (Pilbeam, 1972).

Even the most conservative paleontologists agree on the hominid status of the humanlike creatures that lived in southern and eastern Africa about 4 to 1 million years ago. This span of time includes the Pliocene and part of the *Pleistocene Epoch,* which stretches from about 1.9 million to about 10,000 years B.P. It was marked by cool weather and glaciation. The general agreement about the status of the hominids that lived during this time—the Plio-Pleistocene hominids—occurred only after years of debate and discovery.

The Hominids of South Africa

The first Plio-Pleistocene hominid fossil was found in 1924 in the course of mining operations at Taung in the Cape Province of South Africa. The fossil consisted of a remarkably complete child's skull, unlike any hominid fossil previously known, and a brain cast. Eventually it was sent to Raymond Dart, who was a professor of anatomy at Witwatersrand University in Johannesburg. Although the probable brain size was within the range of modern apes, Dart noted that it was larger than expected in a young pongid 5 to 7 years old. And certain other skull features characteristic of apes were smaller in this skull.

Dart interpreted the mix of pongid and human features as belonging to an animal in a family midway between pongids and humans. In 1925, after looking at the skull for only a few weeks, he announced his findings, naming the fossil *Australopithecus africanus,* or "South African ape." Because Dart was young and had not consulted his more experienced colleagues, his conclusions were strongly attacked. Other paleontologists rightly said that a valid classification could only be based on a mature specimen and that a final decision

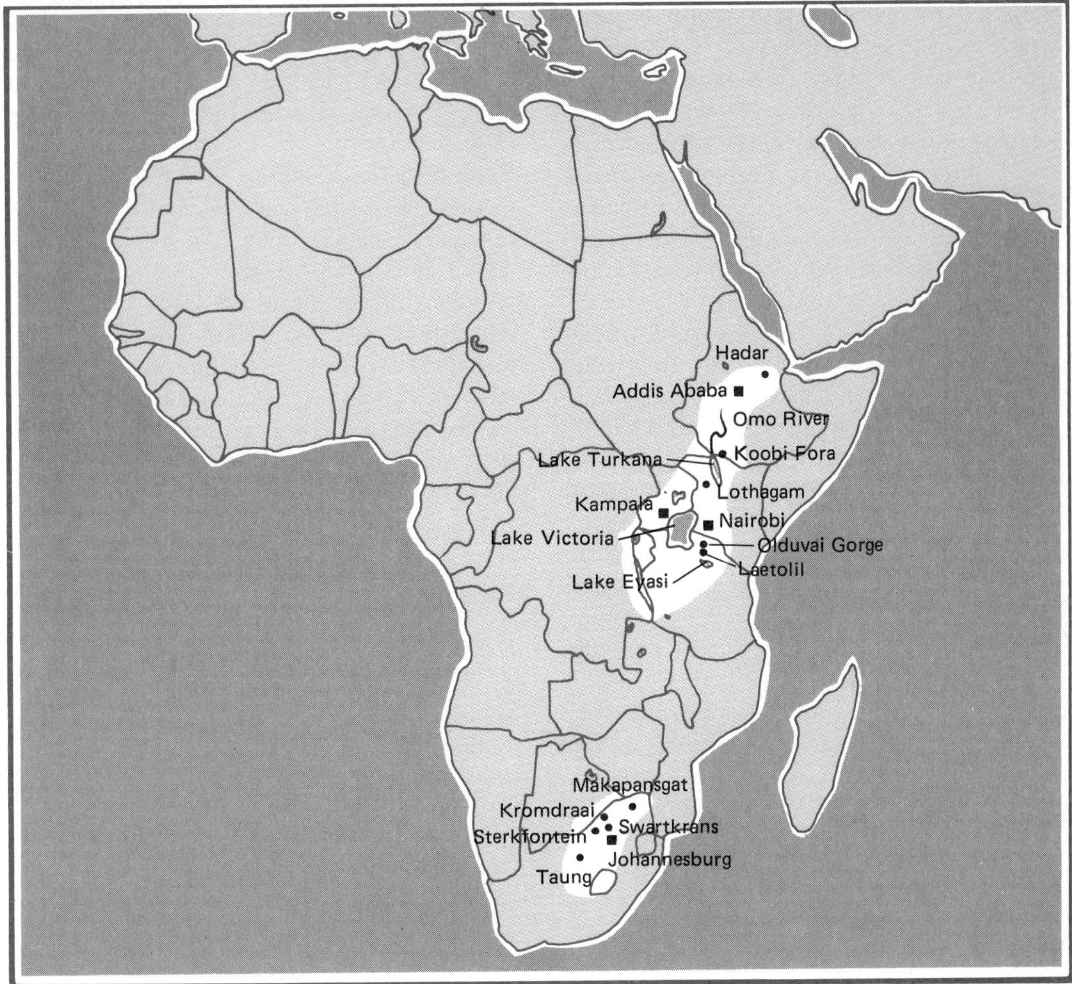

Figure 3 The sites of the major Plio-Pleistocene hominid finds in Africa

would have to await the finding of such a fossil. The Taung child, with its humanlike teeth and apelike cranium, also did not meet the general expectation of what the earliest hominid should look like. Ideas of early human form had been shaped by the fake Piltdown fossil, which had come to light in 1912. This fossil consisted of the jaws and filed teeth of a modern orangutan and the brain case of an Ice-Age human, a fact that was not known until about 25 years after Dart's find.

Robert Broom was the first to find a mature version of the Taung child. An avid amateur paleontologist for most of his life, Broom gave up his medical practice in his sixties to become curator of vertebrate paleontology at Transvaal Museum, Pretoria, South Africa. He had seen the Taung fossil, agreed with Dart's analysis, and begun searching for more evidence. In 1936 miners again made the first find, this time of an adult hominid skull, at Sterkfontein in the Transvaal. Since then, the skulls and some postcranial bones (including a nearly complete pelvis) of several individuals have been found at Sterkfontein.

In the next 15 years Broom and Dart uncovered a rich trove of fossils at several sites. Working in the area near Sterkfontein, Broom found skull fragments and postcranial remains at Kromdraai in 1938, and still other remains at Swartkrans in 1948. In 1947, Dart located more hominid remains at Makapansgat, in the Transvaal, about 150 miles north of Johannesburg. See Figure 3 for the exact locations of these sites, most of which have produced large numbers of fossils since their discovery.

The South African fossils have generally been found in ancient limestone caverns. Limestone, a common rock in the area, is soluble in water. When surface water seeped below the topsoil, it gradually dissolved the limestone, leaving a cavern and a long, narrow shaft that reached from the cavern to the surface. At Swartkrans, the shaft originally opened at the base of a cliff (see Figure 4). Bones lying at the mouth of the opening were washed down the shaft into the cave, where minerals in the limestone allowed fossilization to occur. The resulting material, composed of jagged pieces of bone stuck together in a cementlike matrix, is called *breccia*. Gradual erosion later washed away the cliff, exposed the breccia, and revealed the fossils.

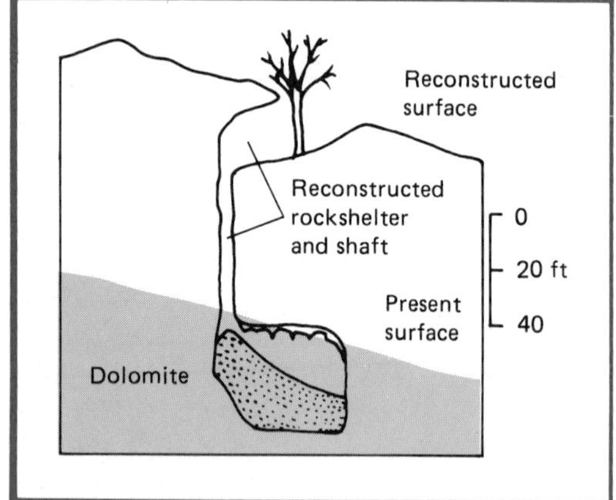

Figure 4 Reconstruction of cavern at Swartkrans. Bones, perhaps of hominids so unlucky as to have become a leopard's dinner, may have collected beneath trees at the mouth of the cave before being washed into the cave eventually to be preserved in breccia. (Reconstruction by C. K. Brain, in Trotter, 1973)

Dart thought that the hominids actually lived in the cave, but C. K. Brain (1970) has made a convincing case for another explanation. He suggests that the bones of the hominids and other animals are the remains of predators' meals. He thinks that, like today's leopards, those of 3 to 1 million years ago ate their prey in trees next to the mouth of caves. After the bones fell to the ground, they were washed into the cave and preserved. The preserved bones resemble the remains of the meals of modern carnivores.

The Ancient South African Environment

Analysis of the breccia deposits reveals that the South African, Plio-Pleistocene hominids had adapted to a drier and more open environment than that in which *Ramapithecus* had lived. One worker (Brain, 1958) has found that the climate at Makapansgat was desert-like—much drier than the climate in that region today. Sterkfontein and Swartkrans were slightly drier, and Kromdraai was wetter. Today the habitat in these areas is open country, with a few trees and wooded areas located along streams. Slightly less rainfall would not have made the area much different from today. Indeed, the breccias contain the bones of baboons and antelopes, both of which are open country dwellers at the present time.

The Fossils

We shall discuss the early African hominids in two large groups: the graciles and the robusts. Scientists do not agree on how to classify the members of these two groups. But grouping the fossils in this way makes it easier to describe them. Later in the chapter we shall consider various theories of the classification and evolution of these forms.

The South African gracile form has been found possibly at Taung and at Sterkfontein and Makapansgat. Examples of the robust form have come from the sites at Swartkrans and Kromdraai. Dates for these fossils are, unfortunately, highly tentative, because the limestone in which the fossils were formed can be dated only roughly with index fossils. Fossil animals found buried with the hominids are sometimes also found at sites that can be dated with a chronometric method. Present estimates place the gracile form at 3 to 2 million years B.P., slightly older than the robust form, which dates from $2^1/_2$ to 2 million years ago (Pilbeam, 1972). See Figure 5 for a summary of the dates of these and other African sites.

The Hominid Skull. For the most part, our discussion of the African hominids will center on the remains of their skulls. Teeth and the bones of the head more often are preserved and are the parts of the early hominid body that distinguish it most clearly from that of modern humans. It is therefore necessary to understand some of the mechanical features of the head and face. In hominids, only the lower jaw, or *mandible,* moves. It carries the lower teeth and transfers to them the force of the chewing muscles. These muscles are attached to the skull above. (See Figure 6.) The *temporal muscles,* which run downward along the side of the head, are anchored high up on the skull. In apes and many australopithecines, particularly in the robust forms, these muscles actually join at the top of the head, where they are attached to a bony ridge called a *sagittal crest.* As the hominids evolved, the crest disappeared and the anchoring areas for these muscles moved back down each side of the skull. Another set of muscles, the *masseters,* are attached to the *zygomatic arch,* an extension of the cheekbone, in front of the ear and are joined to the outside of the lower jaw.

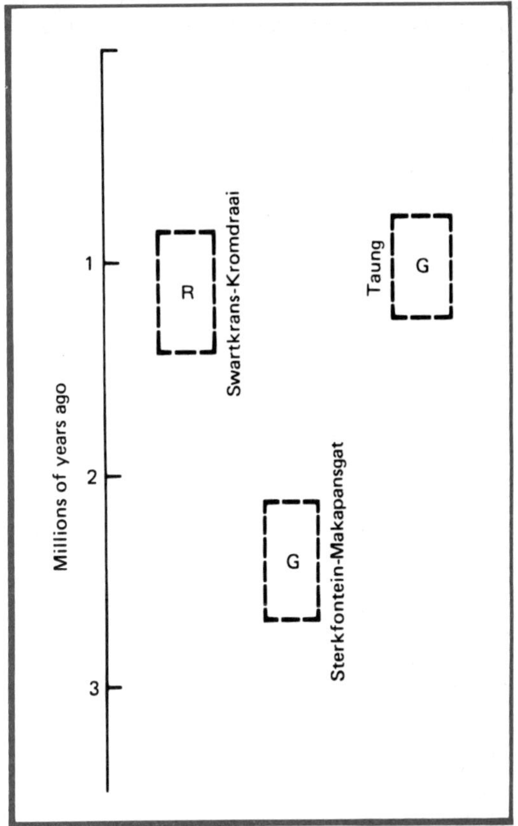

Figure 5 **The age of the early South Africa hominid sites.** Dates are based on relative dating methods, the only techniques applicable to these sites. *G* indicates gracile hominids; *R* indicates robust hominids.

When the food is chewed, two types of forces are used. The first are side-to-side chewing forces. These tend to place great stress on the front of the lower jaw, where the two sides are fused together in early infancy. *Buttresses,* bony structures that strengthen this weak area, are common among early hominid jaws. When a diet of tough foods has required very strong forces, the area has been buttressed with one or two bony swellings running along the inner side of the jaw. When chewing forces lessened, the need for strong internal buttresses diminished, and these were replaced by a weaker external buttress, the chin.

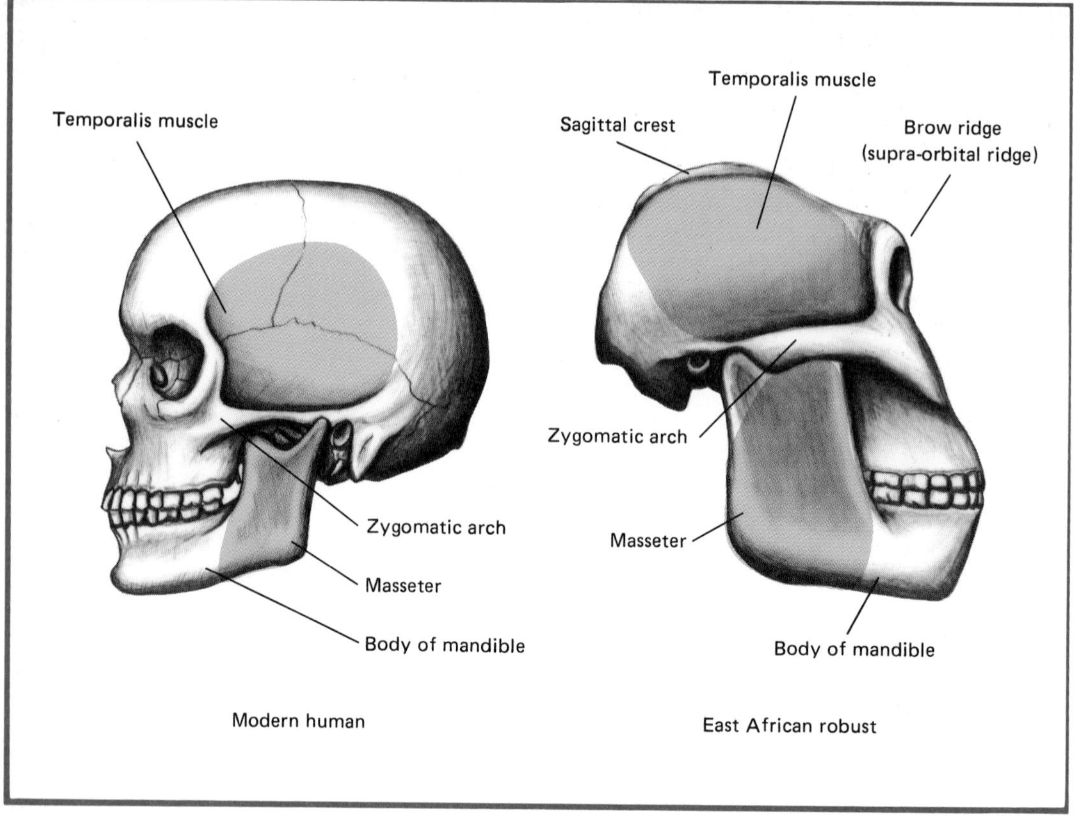

Figure 6 Two hominid skulls

The second type of force is vertical. When the lower jaw closes on food (as in biting), a stress is placed on the upper jaw and transmitted to the face. The thick facial bones and heavy browridges of earlier hominids probably developed as a response to these stresses.

The South African Gracile. Several physical features distinguish this creature from the pongids. A well-rounded forehead (compared to the shallow, flatter pongid forehead) and an elevated cranial vault housed a brain about equal in size to that of modern gorillas. (See Figure 7 for a drawing of the gracile skull.) In proportion to body size, however, the brains of the South African graciles were much larger. A full-sized male gorilla weighs from 400 to 500 pounds and has an average cranial capacity of 500 to 550 cc. The South African graciles were only about 4 feet tall and weighed between 40 and 70 pounds. Their brain sizes, however, ranged from 428 to 485 cc. (Holloway, 1970; Tobias, 1975). The brain-size to body-weight ratio of these individuals is thus far above that of the living gorillas, and is, in fact, within the range of modern humans (Holloway, 1974). In addition, the careful study of brain casts has indicated that the frontal and parietal lobes were more developed than in the pongids. These areas are centers of conscious thought and association. Holloway (1974) feels that these brains were basically human in organization.

The teeth of the graciles are clearly those of a hominid. The incisors were set in the jaw vertically, not at an angle, as in the pongids.

Unlike pongid canines, which are large and projecting, the canines of the South African graciles were short and incisorlike. There are no gaps between the upper canines and the first premolars to allow room for large lower canines. Such a gap is typical of dryopithecine and modern apes. Finally, the dental arcade was parabolic (more like that of modern humans), not the U-shape of the pongids and dryopithecines. (See Figure 2.)

The molar teeth were larger than those of *Ramapithecus,* but not as large as those of the robust forms. Still, the form is very similar to ours: The cusps are rounded and coated with a thick layer of enamel. The specimen from Sterkfontein reveals that the thick protective enamel on the cheek teeth had been worn flat—the result of side-to-side and circular chewing motions. This powerful chewing, designed to break down and process vegetable matter and meat, caused the first molars to wear out before the second wore thin. Fortunately for these early hominids, delayed eruption of the second and third molars kept them in enamel—and teeth—during their rather short lives (Pilbeam, 1972).

The chewing and neck muscles of the graciles were smaller than those of the pongids and the robust form. Little or no sagittal crest anchored the temporal muscles, and the cheek bones were small, a sign of small masseter muscles as well. But although the muscles may have been weaker than those of the pongids, they were probably more efficient, because the gracile's face was flatter. Its jaws were tucked in beneath the braincase. In gorillas and other pongids the jaws are located more to the front of the braincase. As a result, the force of the temporal muscles is applied at an angle more perpendicular to the plane of the teeth. This increases the chewing power of the jaws (Pilbeam, 1972). The wear pattern found on the cheek teeth suggests that vegetable matter was a major part of the gracile's diet.

Tooth wear has been studied for information about the survival rate among the South African graciles. It appears that they, like modern humans, matured slowly, with a long period of dependency on their elders. A prolonged infancy and juvenile stage were followed by a brief adulthood, with only a third surviving 10 or more years beyond reproductive age. The mean age at death was about 20 years, with a maximum age of 40. A mere 15 percent lived to 30 years (Mann, 1968).

Although the gracile form had an upper arm structure suggesting that it was capable of brachiation, it is unlikely that it did so, because it lived in open grassland and was a well-adapted biped. Evidence for bipedalism includes a short pelvis, a curvature in the low part of the spine, and longer legs. A short pelvis lowered the center of gravity in hominids and increased the efficiency of the transfer of weight from the spine to the pelvis and legs. Curvature in the lower back aligned the trunk vertically above the pelvis. Longer legs increased the mass of the lower body, thus lowering the center of gravity.

The South African Robust. Two sites in South Africa's Transvaal have yielded specimens of a much larger, more robust hominid. At Kromdraai, fossil fragments of the skull and postcranial bones of five or six individuals were unearthed between 1938 and 1941. Swartkrans, the other source of robust fossils, was excavated from 1948 to 1952. It contained the largest sample of early Pleistocene hominids. The rich deposits produced pieces of skulls, jaws, teeth, and postcranial bones, as well as some *Homo erectus* remains.

On the basis of a pelvis discovered at Kromdraai, scientists have concluded that the robust South African hominid had a larger body and was probably taller than the gracile form. The robust may have weighed from 80 to 140 pounds. The brain size, too, was larger. An almost complete brain cast of a robust skull from Swartkrans yields a cranial capacity of 530 cc (Holloway, 1970). By contrast, the mean value for the gracile forms is 442 cc. Most likely, the difference is related to the larger body size of the robust form. If so, the brain of the robusts is somewhat smaller relative to body size than is the gracile brain. A brain cast of this same skull shows that the cerebellum (the brain center that coordinates movement) was relatively larger than in the pongids, perhaps a sign of finer control over hand and limb movements (Pilbeam, 1972).

The teeth of the robust form seem to have suited it to a great deal more chewing than those of the gracile. The incisors and canines are like those of the gracile form, but the molars have a greater surface area, and the premolars look more like molars (Pilbeam, 1972). In some cases, the dental arcade looks more like the U-shaped pongid arcade than the parabolic shape of the human arcade.

These large teeth were designed for crushing and grinding, and needed a system of powerful muscles and rugged bony structures on which to anchor the muscles. The presence of massive jaws and cheekbones and the sagittal crest suggest the heavily developed temporal and masseter muscles that once fleshed out these skulls. (See Figure 7.) And a deeper, flatter face than the graciles gave this system of muscles and bone even greater power (Pilbeam, 1972).

On the basis of a pelvic fragment from Swartkrans, it is clear that the areas where leg muscles were attached were similar to those in modern humans. However, differences in the lower pelvis suggest that the robust form was specialized for greater power and less speed in its bipedal movements than the gracile form (Robinson, 1972). Although mainly bipedal, the robust may also have been good at climbing trees (Robinson, 1972). Robinson feels that the robusts walked upright more clumsily than the graciles did. In both groups, however, the orientation of the hip joint, the small size of the end of the thigh bones, and several other features indicate erect posture (Pilbeam, 1972).

The East African Hominids

The first early hominid fossil discovered in South Africa was found by chance. Fortunately, it was sent to a scientist who could see its importance. The discovery of Plio-Pleistocene hominids in East Africa, in contrast, began as an intentional search to find more evidence of the early history of our evolution. Louis Leakey was convinced that he would find this evidence in Africa, contrary to the accepted opinion of the time. He began his determined search of Olduvai Gorge in 1931. (See Figure 3 for the location of this and the other East African sites.) It was not until 1959 that he and his wife, Mary, made their first hominid find, a skull and a shin bone.

Leakey immediately noticed that the fossil was similar in many ways to the robust form of South Africa. However, because of its much larger size, Leakey originally believed that it was unrelated to the South African robusts.

In the years that followed, new discoveries in East Africa seemed to pour forth, with Olduvai Gorge continuing as one of the richest sites. In 1960 Leakey reported a second find at a slightly lower level than the bed in which the original robust hominid had been excavated. Because of its small teeth and large brain, this new fossil seemed to be a gracile form closer to later stages of human evolution. Leakey distinguished it from all the known African robusts and graciles and singled it out as the form ancestral to later hominids.

Another important East African site is the Omo River basin in Ethiopia, north of Lake Turkana (formerly Lake Rudolf). The area had been explored in 1933 by Camille Arambourg, but the fragments he found were not complete enough for classification. Since 1967, a joint expedition made up of French, Kenyan, and American groups, the latter headed by F. Clark Howell, has been making significant finds. So far, the American and French groups have uncovered about 100 hominid teeth, four jaws, and a partial skull.

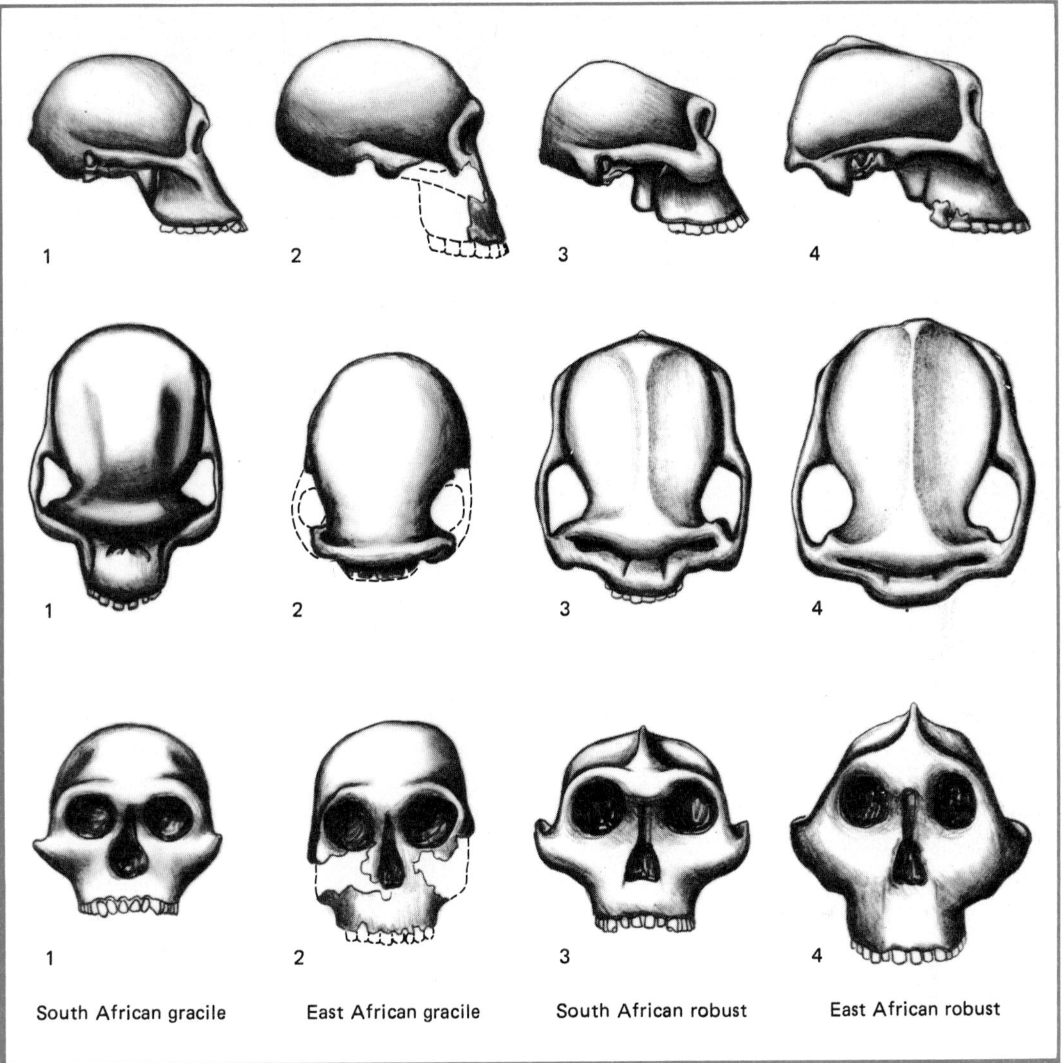

Figure 7 Skulls of the South and East African hominids. Note the following points of comparison: The gracile skulls are much smaller and lighter than the robust skulls, but have a larger cranial capacity. Number 2 has by far the largest, lightest braincase. The top of the skull (the cranial vault) is rounded in the graciles, flatter in the robusts. The graciles have a rounded forehead; the robusts have practically none. A sagittal crest is absent or reduced in #1, absent in #2, present in #3, and pronounced in #4. Crest size is related to the size and strength of the chewing muscles that were anchored to this ridge. Similarly, brow ridges are most prominent in the robusts, whose massive facial structure anchored strong muscles. The cheekbones are thin in the graciles and massive and flaring in the robusts.

In so doing they have widened the known geographical range of the two hominid forms that had been found at Olduvai.

Several other sites have yielded fossils that extend the known time range of the East African forms. The Laetolil beds at Garusi, in the southern Serengeti Plains, for instance, have produced a fossil bearing a strong resemblance to the East African gracile, but dated between 3.77 and 3.59 million years B.P., twice as old as Leakey's Olduvai gracile (Leakey et al., 1976). These fossils are among the earliest of this type. Similarly, finds made at sites along the east bank of Lake Turkana in Kenya by Richard Leakey, the son of Louis and Mary Leakey, have established the presence of the robust form more than 3 million years ago (Leakey, 1973), although dating of this site is in dispute. In 1974 at Hadar, in the Afar depression of Ethiopia, the party of Maurice Taieb and Donald C. Johanson discovered the most complete skeleton of a single individual older than 100,000 years ever found. Dated at 3 million years B.P., this fossil, nicknamed "Lucy," is believed to be a form similar to, although more primitive than, the South African gracile.

Unlike the South African fossil locations, the East African sites lend themselves to absolute dating. Rather than being preserved in difficult-to-date limestone, the East African fossils were covered with lake or river sediments, which exist today in identifiable rock strata. Fortunately, in Pliocene and Pleistocene times, there was a great deal of volcanic activity. During eruptions, the land surrounding a volcano was covered with a layer of ash. Now these layers are distinct markers that are datable with the K-A and paleomagnetic methods. The age of fossils found between two such layers can be estimated with a great degree of accuracy. Olduvai Gorge is a particularly valuable site because it is the product of river action that laid bare a geological record that runs back into the past almost uninterruptedly for 2 million years.

Ethiopian laborers in the party of Donald Johanson sift gravel in the sun-scorched wastelands of the Afar Desert, looking for fragments of early hominid fossils. The remarkably complete skeleton of Lucy, a primitive South African gracile, was found in this area. (David Brill, National Geographic Society Photograph)

The Ancient East African Environment

Most of the East African hominid sites found so far have been close to ancient rivers, stream beds, lakes, or other sources of water. The Olduvai sites, for instance, were once located on the grassy, lightly forested edge of a lake. The hominids found at Omo lived on the banks of a river that changed its course many times. And the Lake Turkana sites are on the eroded sides of a lake in the floodplain of tributary streams.

Hominids probably preferred to live near such sources of water for a number of reasons. Trees and bushes grew near water and provided shade, shelter, and probably food, such as nuts and berries. Trees may have been a handy escape route when hungry predators approached. There is also some evidence that stream beds with gravel bars were a source of raw materials for making pebble tools (Isaac, 1978). The region was wetter and more lushly vegetated than it is today and than the South African sites were during Plio-Pleistocene times. Fossils show that the hominids shared their tree-dotted grasslands with pigs, hippopotamuses, crabs, turtles, grazing animals, and baboons. The hominids were hunters and gatherers who probably ranged over a large area. It is likely that they only camped at Olduvai seasonally. At other times of the year they may have looked for food in other parts of their range.

The Fossils

The East African fossils also can be grouped into gracile and robust forms, although neither is the same as its South African counterpart. Gracile fossils are not as common in East Africa as the robust forms. In East Africa, however, the two forms are often found side by side at the same site and are of about the same age (unlike the South African forms). Dates for the gracile forms range from 3.77 million years B.P. at Omo to about 1 million years ago for transitional forms at Olduvai. The robusts lived in East Africa as long ago as 3 million years, the age of fossils found at Omo and the eastern shore of Lake Turkana. The latest robust fossils date from about 1 million years ago, the youngest of Richard Leakey's finds at Lake Turkana. (See Figure 8.)

The East African Robust. The robust was a highly specialized vegetarian, and most of its points of difference from earlier and contemporary hominids can be linked to an increase in the size of its cheek teeth, probably an adaptation to chewing many small, tough pieces of vegetable matter (Pilbeam, 1972). Its molars and premolars are broader than those of the South African graciles and robusts. In fact, cheek teeth of the two South African forms are more similar in size than the cheek teeth size of East and South African robusts. The size and mechanical efficiency of the chewing apparatus are much greater than those of the South African robust. The teeth are set in a deep, short, and well-buttressed face designed to anchor more powerful temporal and masseter muscles. The alignment of these two muscles is nearly parallel, and brings to bear greater force on the jaws and teeth. (See Figure 6.) The strength of the masseters is indicated by the size of the area on the cheekbone to which these muscles were attached. And the presence of a sagittal crest at the top of the skull shows that the temporals were larger than in other hominids. Though the robust had large brow ridges, it had almost no forehead. (See Figure 7.)

Like the South African robust from Swartkrans, the East African robust from Olduvai has a cranial capacity of 530 cc (Holloway, 1970). The two Lake Turkana robusts that have been measured have capacities of 506 and 510 cc (Holloway, 1974). Examination of brain casts shows some reorganization of the cerebral cortex and expansion of the parietal lobes, areas of the brain that integrate sensory information. Pilbeam (1972) believes that this evidence is not inconsistent with toolmaking ability, though most workers think that the graciles made the first tools.

In East Africa the robusts were comparable to a short but well-nourished modern human, about 5 feet tall (Pilbeam, 1972). Analysis of some pieces of an upper leg bone seem to show that the robust forms stood erect and

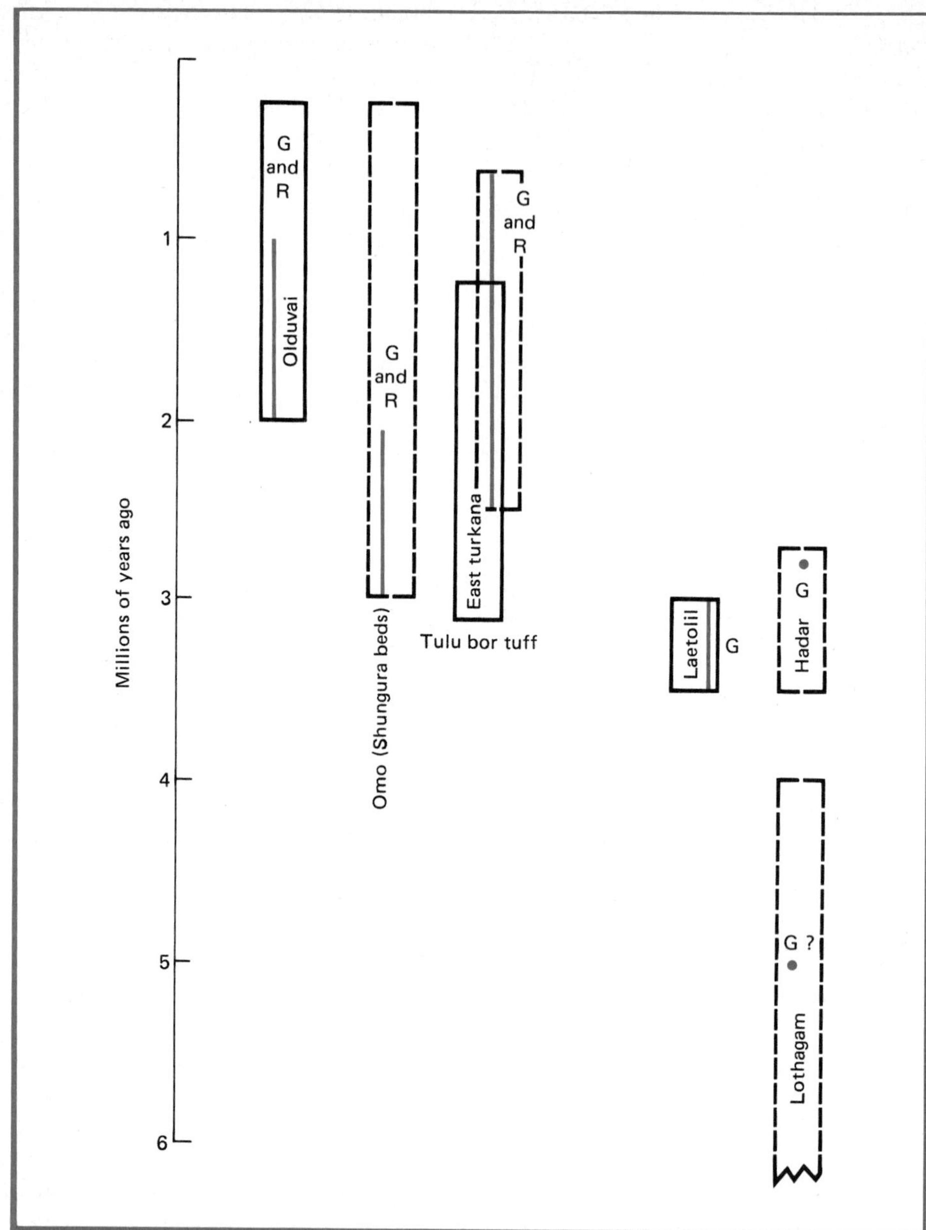

Figure 8 **The age of some early East African hominids and sites.** Solid lines represent dates based on chronometric methods. Broken lines represent relative dating based on index fossils. The color lines show the possible range for the age of the fossils themselves. *G* stands for graciles; *R* for robusts. (Pilbeam, 1972; Leakey, 1978; White & Harris, 1978; Cooke, 1978)

Mary Leakey shows footprints that may have been left by an East African hominid in the bottom of a watering hole 3.5 million years ago in Tanzania. The prints seem to indicate that the animal stood about 4 feet tall and walked slowly, taking steps no longer than its 6-inch long foot. (George Tames, *The New York Times*)

were fully bipedal, though not in the same way that modern humans are bipedal. A major difference may have been that the center of gravity, instead of lying behind the hip joint, as it does in humans, was centered at a point just forward of the hip joint. If this was in fact the case, the East African robusts may have walked with a forward-leaning gait (Day, 1969).

The East African Gracile. In 1964, Louis Leakey and his associates presented their analysis of the first evidence of an East African gracile type. The remains, apparently of a juvenile, consisted of a jaw with teeth, fragments of the skull and hands, and most of a foot and a shoulder blade. The find was exciting because it resembled more modern members of our lineage to a greater degree than any of the other known hominids. The results of dating tests showed that it must have lived alongside the robust form. Chief among its humanlike traits was an estimated cranial capacity of 650 cc. Though the incompleteness of this skull made such measurement imprecise, later finds of the same form at Olduvai have yielded measures ranging from 593 to 684 cc (Tobias, 1975). And a skull (called by its museum acquisition number, KNM-ER 1470) located in East Turkana in 1972 and dated at 2.9 million years B.P. had a brain of about 800 cc. Unfortunately, the dating of this fossil is widely disputed, and it is possibly less than 2 million years old. But if the older date is correct it would suggest a remarkably large-brained gracile contemporary with the earliest-known robust forms.

In many ways the East African gracile looks like the South African gracile. The jaws and teeth are quite similar to the Sterkfontein gracile, with the incisor teeth set vertically in the jaw and the back teeth large in proportion to the incisors. However, the cheek teeth are somewhat narrower in the East African fossils. Postcranially, the two are also very similar. They were about the same size and weight. Both stood 4 to 4½ feet tall and weighed 40 to 70 pounds. The fossil foot and the clavicle of the first find at Olduvai together suggest that the forelimbs and chest of the gracile were proportionally larger than those of modern humans.

Analysis by Napier (1962) shows that the fingers of the East African gracile were more curved and that the thumb may have been a little shorter than in modern humans. Markings of muscles and ligaments on the bone reveal that the creature had a very strong grip. The thumb, although somewhat shorter than in modern humans, was fully capable of circular motion (Johanson, 1976). Study of the same individual's foot has shown that the ankle was somewhat flexed when the creature was standing. Although undoubtedly bipedal, the East (and probably South) African graciles may have stood or walked with a slightly bent-kneed posture. The arms of the gracile fossil from Afar were longer relative to stature than are those of modern humans. However, as with the South African forms, it is doubtful that this is a sign of brachiation. More likely, it is evidence of descent from a brachiating or semi-brachiating ancestor.

Classifying the Early African Hominids

The large number of late Pliocene and early Pleistocene hominid remains collected over the past 20 years in East Africa has added to, rather than resolved, the debate about how the early African fossils should be classified. Though most scientists now agree that these fossils should be placed with modern humans in the family Hominidae, they disagree sharply on how to group them into genera and species. This is mostly a reflection of differing theories about the phylogeny of these animals. For example, scientists disagree as to which form was the ancestor of the later hominids. The opinion of experts on this issue is reflected in the way they name the various forms. Both Louis and Richard Leakey have believed that East African graciles were ancestral to *Homo erectus* and all later hominids. They have therefore classified these graciles in the genus *Homo.* The Leakeys do not favor ancestral status for the South African graciles, or for the South and East African robusts. They place these fossils in another genus, *Australopithecus.* Other scholars disagree with this phylogeny, and prefer to place the fossils in other species and sometimes other genera. Presently, there are three widely discussed theories: the single-lineage hypothesis, the two-lineage hypothesis, and the multiple-lineage hypothesis. (See Figure 9.)

The Single-Lineage Hypothesis

The *single-lineage hypothesis* is concerned with one of the central problems of classifying fossils—defining the range of variations that should be grouped together in the same species. The extent to which members of the same fossil primate species differ cannot be determined from the fossils themselves. To solve this problem, we often use living primates as models. But, depending on which living primate is selected, the degree of difference within a species may be great or small.

Living apes, for example, vary greatly according to age and sex. Using a modern ape as a model would result in a broadly defined species. Among humans, on the other hand, males and females are much more similar. Using humans as the model for interpreting fossils would result in a narrowly defined species.

The single-lineage hypothesis uses living apes as a model and interprets the differences between the gracile and robust forms as resulting from differences in age, sex, or geographic adaptation. According to this theory, modern humans evolved in a direct line from a single group that included all of the Plio-Pleistocene African hominids. For this reason, all the hominids are placed within a single genus and species.

Age. Differences in form and structure due to age are marked among the living great apes. Juveniles not only lack normal adult features such as brow ridges and projecting canines, but are also much smaller than adults. If we judge by the bones alone, young individuals seem gracile compared to the adults. With this fact in mind, some experts argue that it is impossible to know for sure whether the skulls of immature African hominids would have developed into robust or gracile adults. The Taung fossil child, for instance, could just as likely be an immature robust (Tobias, 1974) as

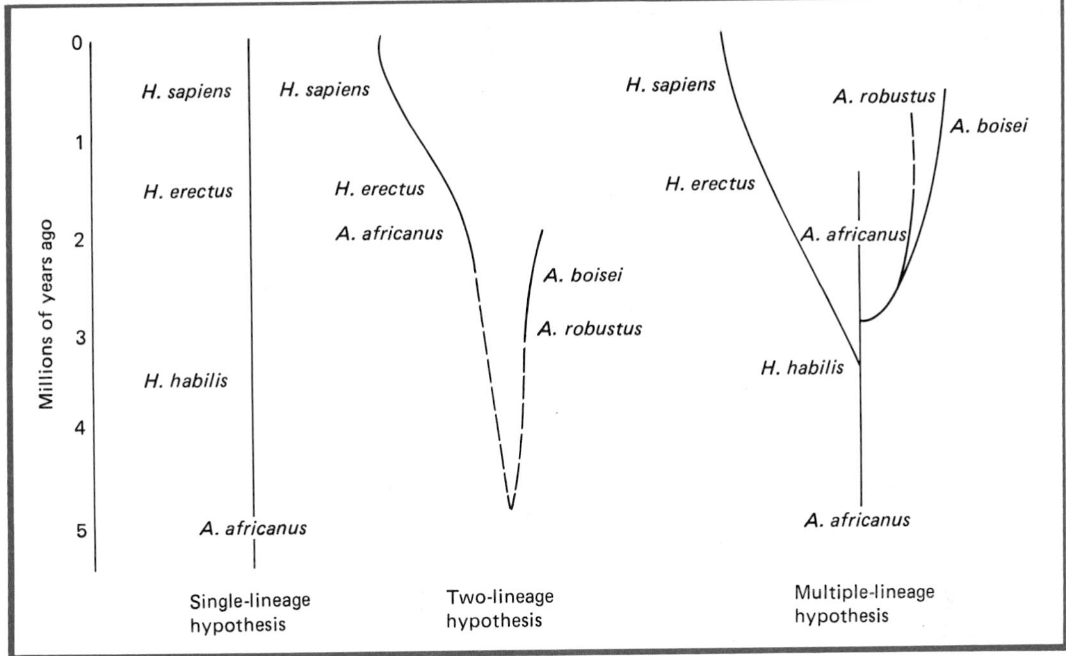

Figure 9 Three theories of early hominid evolution in Africa. Illustrated are: the single-lineage theory (all early hominids are of a single species, varying by age, sex, and geographic location); the two-lineage theory (early hominids are of two groups—the robusts and the graciles, which gave rise to the genus *Homo*); the multiple-lineage theory (the robusts, the South African graciles, and the East African graciles make up at least three separate lineages, of which the last evolved into modern humans).

an immature gracile. For this reason, classification of immature specimens is always guesswork.

Sex. Evidence from the later Pleistocene epoch suggests that as hominids have evolved, males and females have become physically more alike. Thus, the earlier the hominid fossils, the more likely it is that differences in form are sex-related. Consequently, we may unknowingly be using male fossils to draw conclusions about the typical robust, while using female fossils of the same species to stand for the typical gracile. Because of the small sample of Plio-Pleistocene fossils, the true range of variation among the living animals is not known. It is possible, as anthropologist Loring Brace (1973) suspects, that sexual dimorphism accounts for a large amount of the variation seen among the South African fossils. As an added caution against too readily separating early hominids into two or more lineages, Milford Wolpoff (1975) has plotted the frequency of different gracile and robust dental characteristics, particularly canine size. He believes that the results suggest a type of sexual dimorphism comparable to that of modern pongids. However, the variation appears to be greater than that found among living *H. sapiens*.

Geographic Variation. When these early hominids lived, the environments of both South and East Africa were not completely uniform. Parts of each were wetter than other parts. Because of this variety it is thought that hominids living in both areas could have occupied two different niches. As time passed, the differences between the East and South African graciles and robusts in teeth, jaws, and muscles could have evolved as separate adaptations to different niches. This sort of geographical variation has a rough parallel in the physical variations of living humans.

The single-lineage theory has caused paleoanthropologists to reduce the number of species and genera proposed over the years for these early hominids. But many paleontologists feel that the theory does not take into account the nature of the variations. These workers see one cluster of traits (in the robust) that seems to be a highly specialized adaptation to a diet that requires a large amount of grinding and chewing. These experts feel that the gracile tooth structure and facial structures are a separate pattern, more like that of later hominids. Finally, if the recent dates for *H. erectus* in East Africa and China are valid, they suggest that the East African robusts were a highly specialized form living at the same time as *H. erectus,* clearly a direct ancestor of modern humans. If the two forms lived side by side, the single-lineage hypothesis is not correct. In fact, Brace now believes that the earlier Pliocene hominids made up a single lineage, while the Pleistocene hominids evolved in two lineages (in press).

The Two-Lineage Hypothesis

A second theory sees the graciles and robusts as members of either separate species or separate genera. John Robinson (1972), who has classified the graciles in the genus *Homo* and the robusts in the genus *Paranthropus,* attributes the differences in the two forms to a difference in diet. Looking mainly at differences in their teeth, Robinson suggests that the graciles' smaller molars were the result of an omnivorous diet. Robinson also believes that the graciles evolved from the robusts. According to him, the robust kept the more primitive link with wetter environments, while the gracile emerged as the form adapted to a more arid, savanna environment. The robust remained a vegetarian who needed massive teeth to crush and grind its way through a diet of berries and bulbs, roots and shoots, leaves and fibrous wild fruits. The dryness of the graciles' environment, on the other hand, created a scarcity of vegetation and caused it to rely more on animal protein. The gracile was also a toolmaker, who ate meat and perhaps switched some of the work of food preparation from the teeth to tools, according to Robinson.

Extreme wear and scarring on the molars of robust forms lend support to this dietary hypothesis. So does the principle of competitive exclusion, which states that similar creatures can only occupy the same area if they develop mutually exclusive econiches and hence do not compete with one another for the same food supply. Problems with this theory arise, however, when climatological evidence is examined. Soil analysis shows that the gracile sites in South Africa (Sterkfontein and Makapansgat) were indeed drier than one of the robust sites (Kromdraai). But the other South African robust site (Swartkrans) was drier than both gracile sites.

The situation is even more confused when the East African evidence is examined. There, robust and gracile forms seem to have occupied the same sites at roughly the same times. In addition, both groups show considerable variation. The Olduvai robusts were much larger than the South African robusts, and the East and South African graciles differed in ways we discussed earlier. Some experts feel that these differences are the result of specialization in different niches by animals living at the same time. More likely, the differences represent evolution in time. Dates of 2 to 3 million years for the South African sites would place the South African gracile contemporary with the earlier gracile forms from Omo and Lothagam in East Africa. The South African robusts would be older than the Olduvai material and older than the robusts from East Turkana, as well. This being the case, East African graciles and robusts would be later in time than the South African forms.

At one time David Pilbeam (1972) suggested that the apparently older South African graciles and robusts evolved into the younger East African graciles and robusts. He classified the South African graciles as *Australopithecus africanus* (Dart's original classification of Taung), and the later East African graciles as *Australopithecus habilis.* The South African robusts were classified as *Australopithecus robustus.* The later East African robusts were placed in a separate species, *Australopithecus boisei.* Recent redating of the Turkana material to less than 2 million years may stimulate more interest in Pilbeam's hypothesis.

Holders of the two-lineage theory usually think that the gracile gave rise to the robust lineage. They see the robusts as highly specialized herbivores. According to a basic principle of paleontology, generalized forms are ancestral to specialized forms.

The two-lineage theory answers the basic objections to the single-lineage hypothesis. That is, it explains the patterns of variation as evidence of separately evolving lineages. It also explains the presence of the *A. boisei* at the same time as early *H. erectus.* Unfortunately, this theory depends on the acceptance of fairly early dates for the South African material. If (1) the graciles of Sterkfontein are contemporary with the Olduvai fossils, (2) Taung is less than 1 million years old, and (3) the fossils from the Laetolil beds look like *A. habilis* more than *A. africanus,* then three or even four lineages may exist. This possibility is the basis of the multiple-lineage hypothesis.

The Multiple-Lineage Hypothesis

According to this hypothesis, the lineage of East African gracile fossils has many "modern" traits and goes a long way back in time. Louis Leakey is the originator of this theory. Small teeth and jaws, lighter facial bones, and the large brain of the East African gracile are among its advanced features. Louis Leakey felt that it was different enough from the South African gracile to be included in our own genus. He named this form *Homo habilis,* or "handy man."

Most of the *H. habilis* fossils found at Olduvai are relatively late, however. Other paleontologists have therefore suggested that *H. habilis* should be treated as a transitional form of *A. africanus* leading to *H. erectus.* When Richard Leakey excavated an exceptionally large-brained fossil from East Turkana in 1972 and dated it at 2.9 million years B.P., it seemed to document the age of the lineage and to support his father's theory. However, reevaluation of the date suggests that it is probably 1 million years more recent than originally thought. Once again, this seems to leave the proposed "Homo" lineage without time depth, unless Mary Leakey's finds at Laetolil are generally accepted as 3.7 to 3.5 million-year-old representatives of the line. According to the multiple-lineage theory, there are, apart from *H. habilis,* the South African graciles and two robust lineages. The South African graciles would be classified as *A. africanus,* the South African robust as *A. robustus,* and the East African robust as *A. boisei.* Only *H. habilis* was the bearer of culture—the maker of tools and the creator of the oldest archaeological sites in East Africa. The other forms are viewed as more narrowly specialized, without the flexibility of the culture-bearing forms. As *H. habilis* expanded into the niches of the other forms, it gradually won the competition for food and ultimately drove them to extinction.

Presently, the 1470 East Turkana fossil is not firmly dated enough to be used to support the antiquity of *H. habilis.* Evaluation of the Laetolil finds by other scholars is just beginning. The prospect of an early, large-brained, humanlike ancestor is attractive. In the absence of dated early fossils, however, we cannot say with certainty that a separate *Homo* lineage did exist.

Evolutionary Trends in The Early Hominids

All of the early hominids seem to have occupied niches in the same tropical savanna ecosystem. Just how many different niches there were among these hominids is a question of how many lineages one believes existed. Theoretically, each lineage must have been adapted for life in a unique niche.

The earliest hominids shared a set of adaptations that we associate with "humanness." These included large brains essentially human in organization, small canines, and erect bipedal movement. If more than one hominid species is proposed, then we must explain why divergence of the ancestral econiche occurred. Let us assume, correctly or incorrectly, that two lineages existed: a gracile and a robust. We know that niche divergence occurs in one of two ways. A part of the original population either begins to exploit new food resources, or it exploits the same resources in a new way. Because the ranges of the graciles and robusts in South Africa and in East Africa overlapped or were identical, the most likely reason for niche divergence was the exploitation of the same food in slightly different ways. The main difference between the strategy of the robusts and that of the graciles was that the graciles probably used culture. The use of tools, complex social structure, learning, and food-getting strategies eventually allowed this lineage to adapt culturally, rather than biologically, to their environment.

Many of the features we associate with more advanced hominids—particularly more efficient bipedalism, larger brains, and smaller teeth—are probably related to the growing influence of cultural behavior on hominid biology. Because of the great selective advantage tools would have given their makers, hands shaped and able to move in ways suited for toolmaking would also be an advantage. Thus, genes coding for hands capable of a precision grip and good eye-hand coordination would have become more common in the gracile population. If tools improved the chances of survival, then those qualities of the brain making possible the manufacture of tools would also be selected for. Thus the ability to control the finger, to translate concepts into tools, and to concentrate on a goal would tend to become more common in the population. The enlargement of areas of the brain that permit the integration of a variety of information from the senses and the use of symbolic verbal communication would be an advantage, as well. These abilities would make possible group organization for defense and food getting. The information relevant to group life and survival could be taught and learned through communication as well. Tool use and intelligence probably evolved in a feedback system. Each added to the advantages of having the others. Greater intelligence, for example, made possible the manufacture of better tools, which, together with changes in social organization, fostered the survival of the more intelligent hominids.

As the niche of the graciles was evolving toward that of *H. erectus,* the robust niche was also evolving. But the robusts came to depend on anatomical, rather than cultural, specializations. The relatively large early South African robusts may have given rise to the larger East

African robusts, whose powerful jaws and large molars and premolars were suited to the vegetable diet that was probably the basis of the animal's existence.

For at least 2 million years these two forms existed together. However, about 1 million years ago the robusts became extinct, as the later graciles were evolving into *H. erectus.* Although we have no direct evidence of how the robusts became extinct, the fact that tools were found with robust fossils at a site in Olduvai suggests to some that robusts were hunted by graciles. A more likely explanation is that the food resources of the robusts were being used more efficiently by the graciles. This could have slowly reduced the fertility of the robusts and finally led to their extinction. Unfortunately, although this theory makes sense ecologically, there is no archaeological evidence to support it. As more fossils are uncovered, however, we shall be able to draw more solid conclusions.

Summary

1. Physical anthropologists use *Homo sapiens* as a model for identifying fossils as hominids in their attempt to outline human evolution. But because the earliest fossils in the line leading to the modern great apes and the earliest hominids shared so many "apelike" and "humanlike" features, it is difficult to identify our earliest ancestors on the basis of our own features.

2. Frequently used criteria for hominid classification are: parabolic dental arcade, incisors set vertically in the jaw, thickly enamelled molars, large brain size, and changes in the shape of the vertebral column, pelvis, lower limbs and feet that permit erect posture and bipedal movement.

3. The hominid skull has features that changed as the stresses associated with strong vertical chewing forces diminished. The *mandible,* or lower jaw, is the only part that moves. The *temporalis muscles* are anchored at the top of the skull and run down the side of the head. The *masseter muscles* extend from the *zygomatic arch* to the lower jaw. The *sagittal crest,* to which the *temporalis muscles* are attached at the top of the head, and the *buttresses* that strengthened the inside of the lower jaw both disappeared as a modern, lighter-boned face evolved.

4. *Ramapithecus* may have been a hominid of the middle Miocene period. It inhabited usually wet environments, from subtropical to warm-temperate forests, but also adapted to the drier grasslands and wooded savannas of Miocene Eurasia and Greece.

5. Since *Dryopithecus* fossils are not found in savanna and steppe deposits, anthropologists think that only *Ramapithecus* made the adaptations necessary to move out into the new econiche at the forest edge as Eurasia became drier.

6. *Ramapithecus* adaptations include robust jaws and thickened tooth enamel for chewing tough foods. The canines may have been shorter than those of *Dryopithecus.* Scientists guess that the animal was 3½ feet tall and had an upright posture for defense, for carrying food, and for using tools. The hominid trend toward larger brains may be the result of greater reliance on the hands and mind than on teeth and brawn.

7. Fossil evidence of advanced primates living in the late Miocene and early Pliocene periods is very scanty. But the earliest African fossils that are definitely hominid have been dated at about 4 million years old.

8. Two groups of Plio-Pleistocene hominids have been found in South African *breccia* deposits—the graciles and the robusts.

9. South African graciles are distinguished from pongids by a larger brain-size to body-weight ratio, well-rounded foreheads,

more developed frontal and parietal lobes, and hominid teeth. The incisors are set vertically in the jaw, the molars are rounded, and the canines are short and incisorlike. The absence of a *sagittal crest* and the small cheekbones indicate smaller temporal and masseter muscles. A shorter pelvis, curved lower spine, and long legs show that the animal was bipedal.

10. South African robusts were much larger than the graciles. Other differences include larger molars, a more U-shaped dental arcade, more massive jaws and cheekbones, and the presence of a sagittal crest. Differences in the lower pelvis indicate that the robusts may have been stronger but slower and more clumsy bipedal walkers than the graciles.

11. East African robusts had larger teeth, broader molars, and a more well-buttressed face than either of the South African hominid forms. The size of the *sagittal crest* and the cheekbone show that the temporal and masseter muscles were also larger and stronger. Pieces of upper-leg bone show that East African robusts were fully bipedal and erect, but may have walked with a forward-leaning gait.

12. East African graciles had several characteristics in common with the South African: body size and weight, vertically set incisors, and shape of jaw. The cheek teeth were narrower, however, and the cranial capacity was largest among the hominids of this time. The thumb was capable of circular motion. Both gracile forms probably walked with a slightly bent knee.

13. There are three current theories as to how the early hominids should be classified. The *single-lineage hypothesis* proposes that humans evolved in a line from a single species that includes all of the Plio-Pleistocene hominids. Using living apes as a model, this hypothesis interprets differences between the graciles and the robusts as variations within one species with respect to age, sex, or geographical adaptation.

14. The *two-lineage hypothesis* classifies the graciles and the robusts in different species or genera. Some experts believe that the East African hominids evolved from the older South African forms. They classify the South African graciles as *Australopithecus africanus* and the East African graciles as *Australopithecus habilis.* The South and East African robusts would be *Australopithecus robustus* and *Australopithecus boisei,* respectively.

15. Leakey's *multiple-lineage hypothesis* suggests that one lineage of fossils, *Homo habilis,* is an ancient member of the human genus with many modern traits. The small teeth and jaw, lighter facial bones, and large brain of the East African gracile characterize *H. habilis. H. habilis* survived, while the *Australopithecus africanus, robustus,* and *boisei* lineages became extinct.

16. The robust hominids became extinct about 1 million years ago. Further evolution of the graciles toward *Homo erectus* was probably aided by the development of culture. Interactions between cultural behavior—use of tools, communication, and intelligence—and hominid biology formed a *feedback system,* in which each element stimulated the evolution of the others.

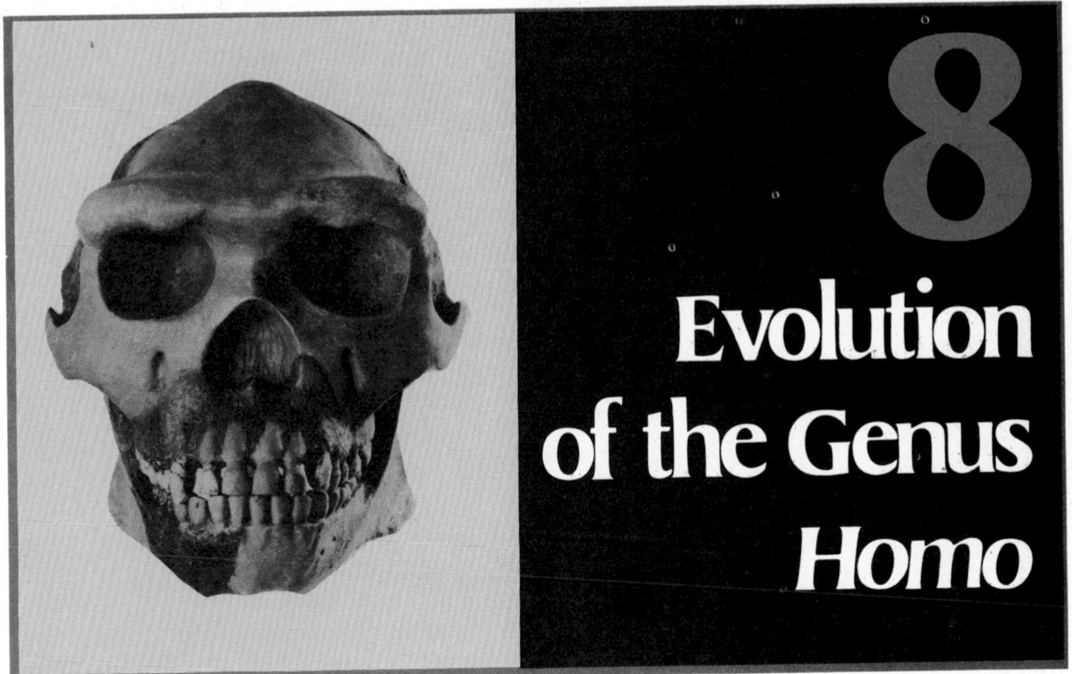

8 Evolution of the Genus *Homo*

FROM the early African hominids, we trace our ancestors into the Pleistocene Epoch, which began about 2 million years B.P. and ended only about 10,000 years ago. During this time, important physical changes occurred in facial form and in head size and shape. Brains became much larger and more complex than those of the earlier hominids. By the end of the epoch, the hominid brain, face, and skull were about the same shape and size as ours are today. The hominids that lived during most of the early and middle Pleistocene are called *Homo erectus,* or "erect man." The more recent, larger-brained forms that appeared in the late middle Pleistocene have been given the same label that we bear: *Homo sapiens,* or "intelligent man."

The hominids of the Pleistocene Epoch probably made up a single lineage, despite their broad geographical range. Cultural artifacts, mostly tools, suggest that the hominid toolmakers of the Pleistocene were the descendants of the early hominids from East Africa. The hunting technology they developed seems to be based on refinements of the crude tools found at sites at Lake Turkana and at Olduvai Gorge. Anatomical characteristics, too, seem to reflect gradual changes from the early East African hominid pattern.

There is, however, some question about the course of human evolution in the Upper Pleistocene Epoch. Some anthropologists claim that the European Neandertals of the late Pleistocene may have represented a separate species that later became extinct. But although some think that these Neandertals are a separate lineage, no one argues that they do not belong in the genus *Homo.* In this chapter we shall trace the gradual evolution of this genus in its biological aspect. Cultural evolution will be covered in detail in a later chapter.

The Pleistocene Time Scale

The time scale for this period is unusually confusing. Whenever possible, we will use absolute dates for fossil groups. But in some cases this is not possible, and we shall have to place fossils within the rather imprecise geological classification system (Lower, Middle, Upper Pleistocene) or within the sequence of glaciers that once covered a third of the earth. The Pleistocene Epoch is characterized by periods of glacial advances and retreats in North America, Europe, and the Himalayan region of Asia. Of these areas, Europe has until recently been the center of fossil and artifact hunting. European finds were traditionally placed according to the European alpine glacial sequence (Günz, Mindel, Riss, and Würm glacial advances, separated by interglacial periods of warmer weather). As fossils have been discovered gradually in other parts of the world, scientists have tended to use the European glacial sequences as a relative dating standard, even though Asian and African environmental events were largely unrelated to events in Europe. In Table 1, a few of the major Pleistocene fossils finds are tentatively placed in a framework that includes all three dating systems: absolute years, geological labels, and European glacial ages.

Major Trends of Hominid Evolution

During the early part of the Pleistocene Epoch, hominids began to live in areas far beyond Africa. Archaeological evidence suggests that they were developing cultural sophistication more rapidly than ever before. Migration and cultural evolution are linked to a growing emphasis on hunting. The earlier hominids probably lived mostly on vegetation, to some extent on small game or meat that they scavenged, and occasionally on large game animals such as mammoths that they killed (Isaacs, 1978). But as the Pliocene ended and the Pleistocene began, meat apparently became more important in the hominids' diet. Hominids probably began following herds of larger mammals into the tropics outside Africa and later into temperate regions. At the same time, they developed systematic hunting methods and rather advanced tools.

Changes in the Teeth and Jaws

The shift from limited meat-eating to big-game hunting and the cultural traits linked with it are also thought to have affected evolution of the human body, particularly the teeth, jaws, and skull. The dietary switch from vegetable to animal matter and the use of stone tools to prepare food, which earlier was done by the teeth, probably caused a gradual decrease in the size of jaws, teeth, and chewing muscles. Strength had been needed in these features for a diet that had consisted only of hard-to-chew raw vegetation (Bilsborough, 1976). The fact that later not as much crushing and grinding was done inside the mouth has often been offered to explain the increasingly smaller chewing apparatus of the Pleistocene hominids. There is not, however, complete agreement as to how to account for this change in size in terms of natural selection. The most likely explanation calls attention to the fact that the bone in which the teeth are set is not under rigid genetic control and is greatly influenced by chewing stresses during growth. The size of the teeth, however, is under fairly direct genetic control. Lightly stressed jaws would not develop the proportions needed to support relatively large teeth, which could result in crowding. Crowding makes it more likely that the person will have tooth or gum disorders, leading to impaction and infection. Such infections can weaken vision and other senses that are needed for hunting, and if the infection reaches the neural pathways leading to the brain, it can be fatal. This would place individuals possessing the genes for larger teeth at a disadvantage, thereby causing a gradual change toward smaller teeth among the population. As cheek teeth were becoming smaller, front teeth were increasing in size, only to decrease again beginning about 150,000 years ago. Possible explanations for this puzzling reversal will be discussed later in the chapter.

The Braincase

The bones of early Pleistocene hominids were much like us below the neck, although some hominids were more robust. But they had massive protruding jaws, thick facial bones, large teeth, and no chin. These features were largely dictated by their powerful chewing apparatus. As *H. erectus* evolved into *H. sapiens,* however, the shape of the hominid skull was determined more and more by the form and size of the brain (Wolpoff, 1975). The bony case protecting the brain of *H. erectus* was generally larger than that of the early African hominids. The average cranial capacity of the South African graciles, for example, was only about 440 cc. The 1470 skull found by Richard Leakey at Lake Turkana is an exception, with a cranial capacity of about 800 cc., larger than that of some early *H. erectus* forms. Nonetheless, the average capacity of *H. erectus,* 950 cc., was larger. A comparable figure for modern *H. sapiens* is 1330 cc. Part of this increase was related to the hominids increased overall size, which naturally produced proportionally larger parts. But the increase in the size of the braincase was relatively greater than the increase in the rest of the body.

Increases in brain size occurred slowly and gradually. The ever-increasing complexity was probably linked to greater cooperative behavior, ingenuity, skill in hunting large game, manual dexterity, and memory. The larger brains made possible a more sophisticated way of life—better tools, a wider range of habitation, more effective hunting techniques, and a more varied diet. Because each of these behaviors had its origin in the African hominids of the Pliocene, it is likely that the new patterns emerged gradually.

As we noted in Chapter 6, the part of the brain associated with vision grew larger early in primate evolution as reliance on the sense of smell declined. The later stages of human evolution were characterized by impressive growth of three other cortical areas—the frontal, temporal, and parietal lobes. Growth of these lobes allowed complex integration of many kinds of information and conscious control over behavior (Campbell, 1974). Large temporal and parietal lobes gave humans an unusually high, rounded skull shape, while the enlarged frontal lobe added a bulging, vertical forehead. The lobes also gave the top of the head its characteristic shape.

Early Homo Erectus

There are considerable structural differences among the fossils of the Pleistocene Epoch. As a means of organizing this varied group of fossils for study, we have divided our discussion of *H. erectus* fossils into those that existed before 700,000 B.P. (early *H. erectus*) and those that are dated to between about 700,000 and 200,000 B.P. (late *H. erectus*).

A variety of early *H. erectus* fossils have been found from Africa to China. Hominids seemed to have spread from East Africa to Indonesia (Java) and China by 1.7 million years

Table 1 The Pleistocene Time Scale

	Geological Age	Climatic Phase	Major Fossil Finds: Africa	Major Fossil Finds: Europe	Major Fossil Finds: Asia	Hominids
10,000	Holocene					Early Modern *Homo sapiens*
40,000	Upper Pleistocene	Würm or Weichsel glaciation	Saldana Bay	Neandertals	Skhul Shanidar	Late Archaic *Homo sapiens*
100,000		Riss/Würm or Eemian inter-glacial	Broken Hill Omo	Krapina Ehringsdorf Petralona	Solo (?)	Early Archaic *Homo sapiens*
	Middle Pleistocene	Riss or Saale Glaciation	Rabat Casablanca Temara		Ma-pa (China)	
200,000				Arago Cave Steinheim Swanscomb	Solo (?)	
300,000		Mindel/Riss or Holstein Interglacial				
400,000						

		Mindel or Elster glacial	Swartkrans ?	Vertesszöllös	Chou-kou-tien	Late *Homo erectus*
500,000		Günz/Mindel or Cromerian interglacial				
600,000		Günz Glaciation			Lantian	
		Donau-Günz or Tiglian interglacial				
700,000	Lower Pleistocene	Donau glaciation		Ternifine		Early *Homo erectus*
800,000				Heidelberg (?)	Sangiran (Trinil)	
900,000		Villafranchian				
1,000,000						
1,200,000			Hominid 9 (Olduvai)			
1,400,000			East Turkana		Djetis	
1,600,000						
1,800,000					Yuanmou	
2,000,000						

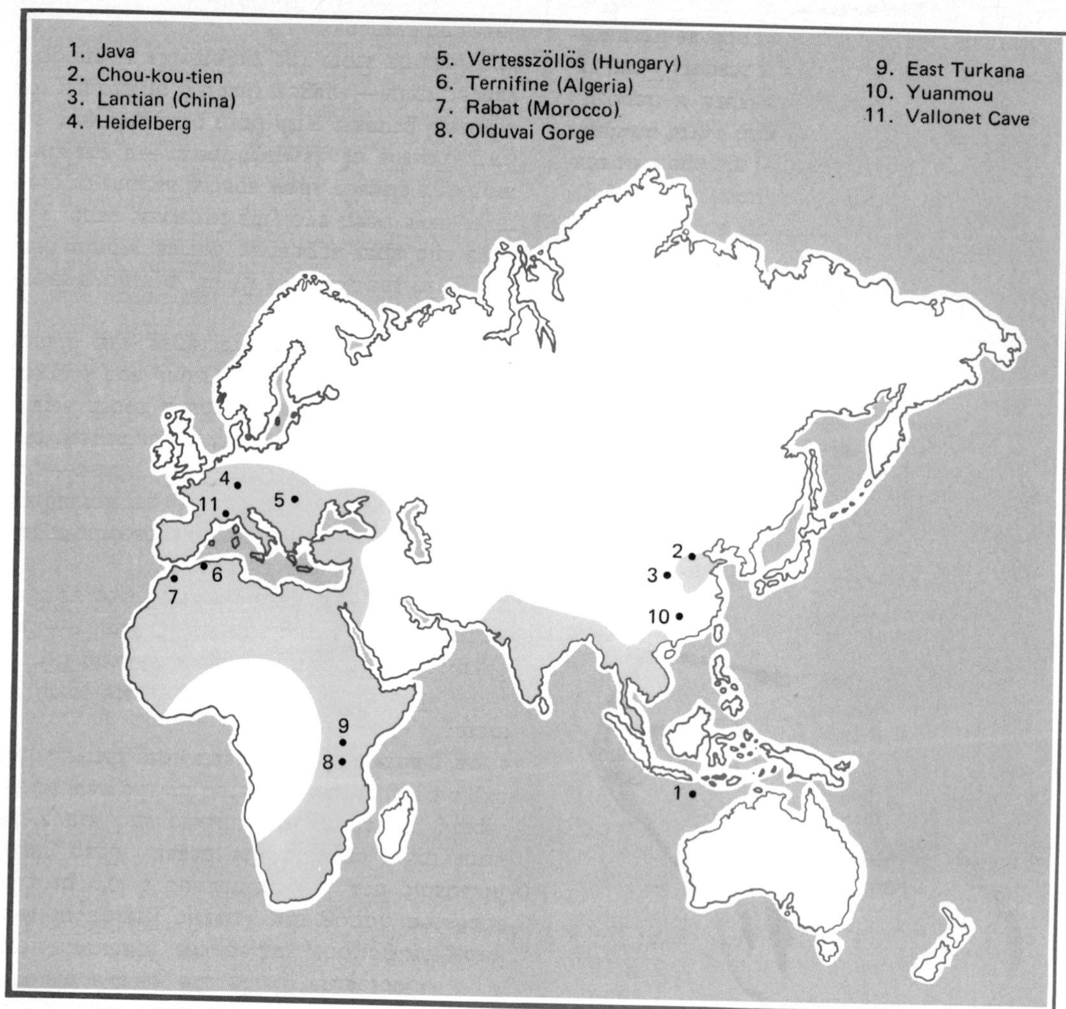

Figure 1 Distribution of *H. erectus* sites.
The colored area indicates the sites of early Paleolithic tool finds.

B.P. Tool finds suggest they appeared in Europe by about 800,000 years B.P.

The Fossils

Some early *H. erectus* fossils from the Lower Pleistocene come from Lake Turkana in Africa. They are dated at 1.6 million years B.P. (See Figure 1.) There, early *H. erectus* populations, represented by a cranium, mandibles, and assorted postcranial fragments, seem to have occupied the same sites as the East African robust hominids discussed in the last chapter. To the south, Olduvai Gorge has also yielded an early *H. erectus* (or erectine) fossil: a faceless skull with an enormous cranial capacity, called Olduvai Hominid 9. It has been dated at 1.2 million years B.P. (Leakey, 1971).

In Java, hominid material found in the Djetis beds is probably about 1.5 million years old, according to potassium-argon dating.

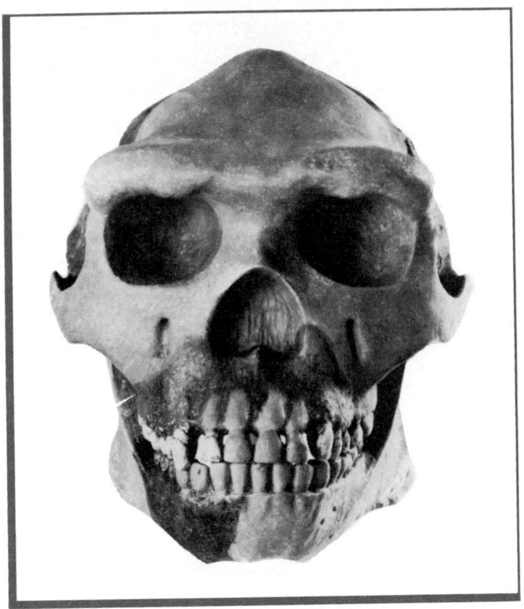

The skull of *H. erectus.* (Courtesy of the American Museum of Natural History)

Another Javanese site, Sangiran, has yielded many fossils, including the back of one individual's skull and some teeth, plus parts of a separate lower jaw. They are probably at least 800,000 years old. Also dated to about 800,000 years B.P. are a mandible and skull cap from the Lantian district in China. Some *H. erectus* teeth found near Yuanmou in the Yunnan Province of China are now dated at 1.7 million years B.P., about a million years before the earliest previously known *H. erectus* fossil in China *(The New York Times,* 2/6/78).

The presence of early *H. erectus* in Europe is less well documented. In 1907, some workers at a German gravel pit near Heidelberg uncovered an ancient lower jaw, complete with all its teeth. Though some paleontologists think it may be as old as 800,000 years (Bilsborough, 1976), others date it at about 500,000 years (Kretzoi & Vértes, 1965). And an early cultural site in Vallonet Cave, in southern France, has been dated to the end of the Lower Pleistocene. No early *H. erectus* remains have yet been discovered there among the crude tools and bones of rhinoceroses, horses, elephants, and even whales (Howells, 1974). But early *H. erectus* probably made the pebble and flake tools and killed the animals found at the site.

How did early erectines reach places as farflung as East Africa, Java, and China? One possible explanation is that they followed migrating animal herds. As hominids began to rely more and more on herds of large grazing animals for food, they followed the animals when they migrated. As the animals moved into new areas, so did the hunters. By the end of the Lower Pleistocene, hominids had developed the cultural sophistication—tools, knowledge, clothes, and fire—needed to move from their tropical or subtropical range into a variety of climates, including cooler northerly regions.

The Environment

The earliest Pleistocene hominids lived in tropical or subtropical environments. They seem to have preferred fairly open coastal areas and avoided dense tropical rainforests. They did not venture across the mountains of southern Europe and Asia into regions with extreme seasonal temperatures. The climate of the European sites, lived in much later than the others, was probably warm-temperate: Winters were cooler than summers, but temperatures were still fairly warm.

In Lantian, located in what is now a temperate region of China, hominids shared subtropical forests with saber-toothed tigers, huge deer, and giant macaques and shared grasslands with gazelles, early ruminants, and horses (Ju-kang, 1966).

In Africa, too, the climate was clearly tropical at both Olduvai Gorge and Lake Turkana. At the latter site, early *H. erectus* coexisted with such tropical animals as hippopotamuses, crocodiles, and assorted Old World monkeys (Maglio, 1971).

Few postcranial (below the skull) remains of early *H. erectus* have been found. But judging by the shape and position of the foramen magnum, the adjustments to upright posture and bipedalism were just about complete in the early *H. erectus* fossils. These early human ancestors probably stood and walked just about the same way we do. Our ancestors apparently had evolved all the changes necessary for a fully erect modern posture by the Middle Pleistocene (Bilsborough, 1976).

Two major trends distinguish early *H. erectus* fossils from Pliocene hominids: (1) the teeth and jaws became smaller, and (2) there was a dramatic increase in cranial capacity.

The trend toward smaller tooth size started with the molar teeth. The third molars (those farthest to the rear) of early *H. erectus* decreased the most at this time, though there were slight reductions in the second and first molars, too. Premolars did not become much smaller until the Upper Pleistocene. The front teeth were still large as well.

As back teeth began to decrease, the jaw changed, too. The heavily buttressed jaw became thinner and much more parabolic in shape. Although the early erectines were larger than the earlier hominids and had wider faces, their jaws were actually smaller. The part of the lower jaw that holds the teeth, for instance, had become lighter, and the vertical part had thinned out. These decreases in both grinding molars and jaws probably were associated with the gradual switch from unrefined vegetable foods to tool-chopped vegetation and meat (Bilsborough, 1976; Wolpoff, 1975).

The brain case underwent an expansion that nearly doubled its capacity. The relative proportions of different brain lobes also changed. (See Figure 2.) The parietal and occipital lobes became larger, broadening the face and the back of the head. There was also a trend toward greater thickness and strength in the braincase, and a series of buttresses developed on the surface of the skull. In the front, thick browridges stuck out over the eyes. They may have helped to distribute chewing stresses more evenly over the front of the cranium. At the back of the head, a bony swelling, or *torus,* developed, to which powerful neck muscles were attached. Both the torus and the neck muscles may have been necessary to counterbalance the massive faces of the early erectines (Bilsborough, 1976). (See Figure 3.)

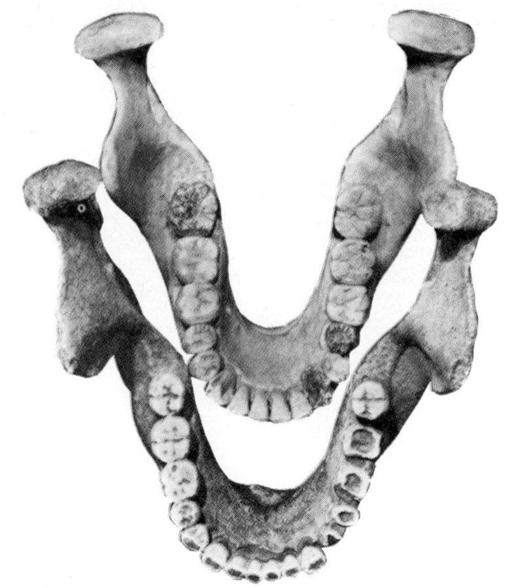

Models of the lower jaw of a South African gracile *(top)* and the jaw of Heidelberg Man, probably early *H. erectus.* Note the reduction in molar size and the change to a thinner, more parabolic jaw. (Courtesy of the American Museum of Natural History)

Late Homo Erectus

The Fossils

The fossil record during the Günz glacial period, beginning about 700,000 B.P., is very fragmentary, but many hominid fossils are

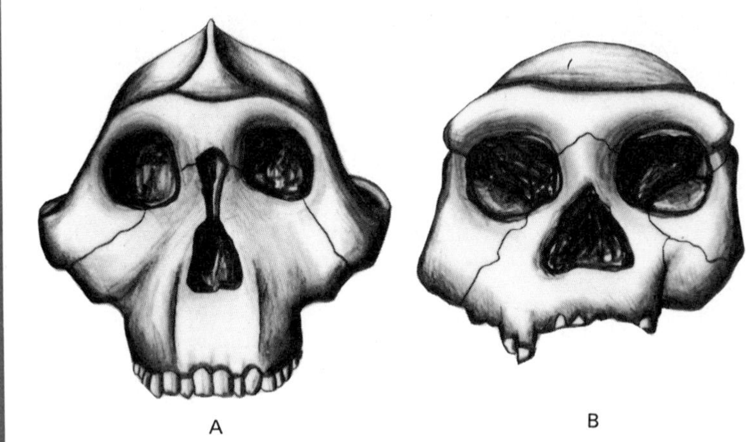

Figure 2 **Faces of an East African robust *(A)* and an early *H. erectus (B)*.** Enlargement of the braincase has led to an upper face much broader than even that of the East African robust, the broadest-faced of the earlier hominids.

found in strata dating to the Mindel glaciation, about 450,000 to 400,000 years B.P. The most spectacular discoveries from this period are skulls, jaws, teeth, and postcranial fragments from Chou-kou-tien, China.

For many centuries, enterprising traders had led annual expeditions to remote Asian caves and mountain gorges. They brought back tons of fossils of all sorts to supply the demand for "dragons' teeth" in Far Eastern cities. The fossils were sold to druggists, who ground them into powders thought to have great medicinal value. When paleontologists arrived on the scene in the nineteenth and twentieth centuries, they often did their "fieldwork" in drugstores. Among the fossilized bones waiting to be ground up was a humanlike tooth. Inquiries as to where it had been found led paleontologists to the site at Chou-kou-tien, near Peking. Workers dug through the debris there for 13 years during the 1920s and 1930s, unearthing 14 skulls, assorted other remains from at least 40 individuals, tools, and hearths where fires had been built. This priceless collection was somehow lost during World War II. Fortunately, however, detailed descriptions and good casts of the originals had been sent out of the country before the war. Recently, excavation of the cave has been renewed, turning up more hominid fragments.

The hominid represented by the Chou-

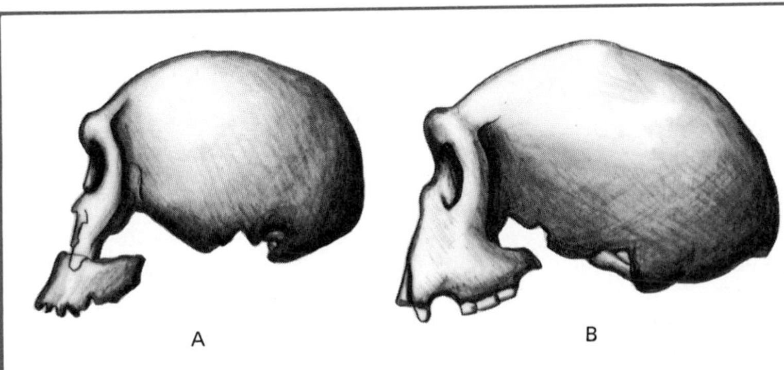

Figure 3 **An East African gracile *(A)* and an early *H. erectus (B)*.** Brow ridges have expanded in the latter to distribute chewing stresses over the front of the cranium. Note the torus at the back of skull *B*. It anchored the large neck muscles needed to balance the massive face.

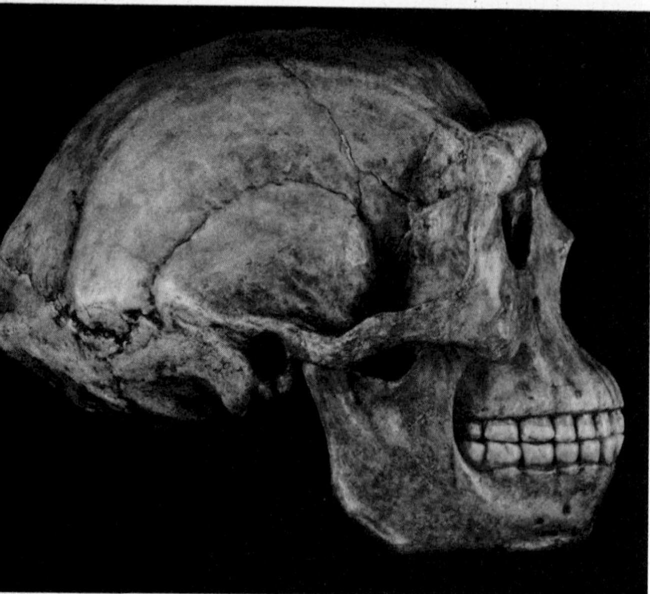

A side view of late *H. erectus,* from Chou-kou-tien. As in early *H. erectus,* the brow ridges are prominent, but cranial capacity is greatly expanded. (Courtesy of the American Museum of Natural History)

kou-tien fossils was once called "Peking Man." But it is now grouped by most anthropologists with similar African and European hominid fossils of about the same age. These include skull parts from Swartkrans Cave in South Africa that did not match those of the many earlier hominids found in the same cave. There are also many sites in the North African countries of Algeria and Morocco. And in Vertesszöllös, Hungary, in a valley cut by a former tributary of the Danube River, researchers have found ancient hearths, charred bones, a number of tools, and part of a skull and some teeth. They also seem to have belonged to a late *H. erectus* population (Kretzoi & Vértes, 1965).

Far more numerous than actual hominid fossils of this period are sites where late *H. erectus* populations left recognizable traces of their cultural activities. For instance, distinctive tools from the middle of the Mid-Pleistocene have been found in at least 31 locations, stretching from Spain and Morocco in the west to Java in the east (Collins, 1969). By the middle of the Holstein interglacial period (a time of fairly warm temperatures between glacial episodes) cultural sites were established all over Europe. Some have been found as far north as southern England.

The Environment

During the Middle Pleistocene, hominids continued to inhabit warm, open grasslands. But some began a definite tendency to live in more extreme environments. Both in Eastern Europe and at Chou-kou-tien in China hominids seem to have lived in the kinds of forests and steppes now found in cold areas farther north. When they were inhabited, the Chou-kou-tien and Vertesszöllös sites were about 1,000 miles from the ocean, thus subjecting them to the seasonal extremes of heat and cold typical of inland regions (Collins, 1969).

During the Holstein interglacial period, northern areas became warmer and more humid as the glaciers retreated. Silver firs replaced pines. These firs are now found mostly in the foothills of mountains in southern Europe. Their living requirements give us a good indication of what the Holstein climate must have been like. In what is now northern Europe, it was probably considerably warmer and wetter than that area is today. But the soils probably were not very rich, and the forests not very dense (Collins, 1969). In eastern Europe, forests expanded around the edges of the Eurasian steppe.

Physical Characteristics

Judging from the facial structure of late erectines, the stress of food-chewing continued to decrease. The front teeth of the late erectine fossils were smaller than those of the early erectines, and the trend toward smaller molars continued. The jaws became thinner and smaller, and the mouth area was reduced, giving the face a somewhat flatter appearance.

The chewing muscles also became smaller as did the skull areas to which they were attached. The neck muscles and the area at the back of the skull to which they were attached became smaller, possibly because they no longer had to counterbalance such a massive jaw.

At this time, the final adjustments to a fully magnum, at the base of the skull, ended its magnum at the base of the skull, ended its long-term movement in primate evolution. Rather than being located toward the rear of the skull base, as in quadrupedal animals, it is located toward the middle of the skull base, the most efficient position for balancing the head on the top of the spine. And muscle attachment points at the base of the skull became somewhat smaller, since the decreased mass of the jaws and face no longer required strong neck muscles for support, as in the early erectines.

Cranial capacity continued to increase. Only part of this growth can be accounted for by the increase in body size from early to late erectines. There were also structural changes that have nothing to do with body size. The most significant of these were in the frontal and parietal regions, which became higher in the skull as well as larger.

The marked changes in brain size and structure, as well as the smaller size of the teeth and jaws, suggest rapid evolution between the Lower and Middle Pleistocene as hominid populations radiated to new niches. Increasing cultural sophistication was probably the major factor making this possible.

Early Archaic Homo Sapiens

By the end of the Holstein warming trend, about 225,000 years B.P., the fire-using hunters of the Middle Pleistocene had given way to a more highly evolved hominid, *H. sapiens.* The division between *H. erectus* and *H. sapiens* is arbitrary, for the latter group evolved slowly from the former. Nevertheless, there are sufficient evolutionary differences in the form of the jaws, face, cranium, and brain to warrant using a new species name. By giving it the same genus name, we recognize its descent from the *H. erectus* forms. *H. sapiens* is further divided into four rather arbitrary groups: early archaic, late archaic, early modern, and modern. The early forms differ only slightly from their erectine forbears. And the range of variation in the early forms is significantly different from the range found in modern human populations (Wolpoff, 1975).

The Fossils

Early archaic *H. sapiens* fossils are those that date from the latter part of the Holstein interglacial period (late Middle Pleistocene) to the end of the Riss/Würm, or Eemian, interglacial period (early Upper Pleistocene). The time span represented is roughly 275,000 to 75,000 years B.P. The oldest fossils from this period are probably those from Steinheim (a warped skull found in a German gravel pit) and Swanscombe (a skull cap uncovered in an English gravel pit). Both may have been females (Brace, Nelson, & Korn, 1971). They are about 250,000 years old.

Other European hominid fossils from this period were found at Montmarin, Fontechevade, Abri Suard, and Arago Cave in France; Ehringsdorf and Steinheim in Germany, Petralona in Greece, and Krapina in Yugoslavia. This last find is made up of assorted bone and skull fragments of 14 or 15 individuals, five of whom were probably infants or children (Brace, Nelson, & Korn, 1971). Early Archaic *H. sapiens* is also represented by 11 faceless skulls and two tibia from the Solo River in Java. These fossils cannot be dated definitely because of poor excavation techniques. But their structural traits seem to place them at about this point in human evolution. African hominids during this period are represented by fossils found in Rabat, Temara, and Casablanca in North Africa and at Broken Hill in Rhodesia (Wolpoff, 1975). (See Figure 4.)

The Environment

The geographic distribution of early archaic *H. sapiens* seems to be about the same as that of the late *H. erectus* populations. In Europe, however, glaciation did not force the hominid populations to move south. Instead, they remained on the tundra, exposing themselves to greater cold than their ancestors had ever endured. Some sites in England and Germany may have been lived in when the edge of the Riss glacier was only a few miles away (Collins, 1969).

As the ice sheets moved south, game animals migrated to warmer areas. Instead of following them, some of our Pleistocene ancestors apparently learned to hunt mammoths, for these woolly creatures thrived in the tundra or cold steppe environments at the glacier's edge (Collins, 1969).

The cold of the Riss glaciation was followed by a warmer period—the Riss/Würm interglacial period. Just as their predecessors had done during the Holstein interglacial several hundred thousand years before, the early humans moved north as the glaciers receded.

Physical Characteristics

Many of the trends already established in the evolution of the human skull continued during this period. For instance, the lower jaws, molars, and chewing muscles were still smaller among these fossils than in late erectine populations. Internal buttressing of the lower jaw was further reduced, and some fossils began to exhibit external buttressing in the form of a weak chin (Wolpoff, 1975). But a reversal of some other trends shows up in the fossil record. The front teeth, upper jaws, and neck muscles of early archaic *H. sapiens* are noticeably *larger* than those of late erectines. This gives the newer forms a forward-projecting mouth area somewhat like that of more primitive hominids.

Wolpoff (1975) has an intriguing explanation for this enlargement of the front teeth. He speculates that these teeth were used as tools. In modern human groups, people have been seen using their front teeth to work animal hides, pull things, break thread, grip and twist objects, and even to pry the lids off gasoline drums. An uneven pattern of wear in some of these fossils suggests that the front teeth also were used to hold and manipulate objects. In doing so, new stresses were placed on their jaws. The crowns, roots of the teeth, and bones behind were pulled outward. The resulting projection of the upper jaw gave early *H. sapiens* a primitive look that their predecessors had almost lost. The need to counteract the pulling and gripping of the incisors and canines also apparently caused enlargement of the neck muscles. Larger teeth apparently were a selective advantage and became an increasingly frequent trait. Larger neck muscles, in part, probably developed during the life of the individual in response to stresses created by using the teeth as tools.

Despite the possible use of teeth as tools, cultural rather than biological adaptations seem to have been more important to the survival of the earliest *H. sapiens.* Evidence of complex hunting strategies, sophisticated tools, and semipermanent habitations suggests that human intellectual horizons were expanding. What anatomical evidence do we have that hominids were getting smarter? For one thing, the brain was clearly larger than in earlier hominids. Cranial capacity increased by about 21 percent over what it was in the later erectines (Wolpoff, 1975). Most of the difference seems to be associated with expansion of the frontal lobe. It began to expand above the browridges rather than behind them. And the whole skull became even higher and rounder to accommodate swelling in the occipital and

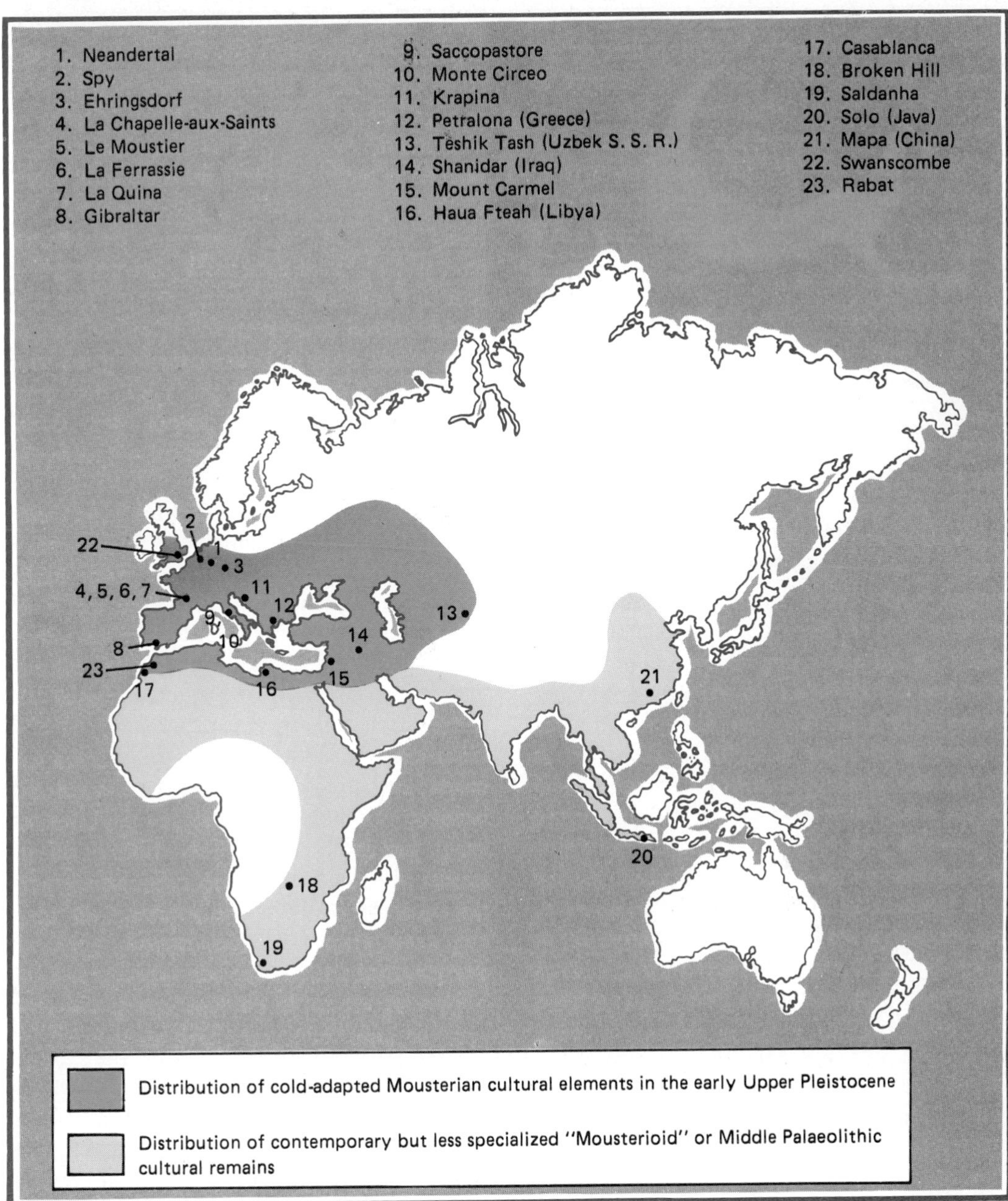

Figure 4 **Distribution of archaic *H. sapiens* sites.**
The colored area indicates the sites of Mousterian culture remains.

parietal lobes (Bilsborough, 1976). (See Figure 5.) The areas of the brain that were expanding most noticeably seem to be those that integrate sensory inputs and make speech possible. The frontal lobe coordinates muscle responses and conscious thought, and the occipital and parietal lobes integrate memory, perception, and vision.

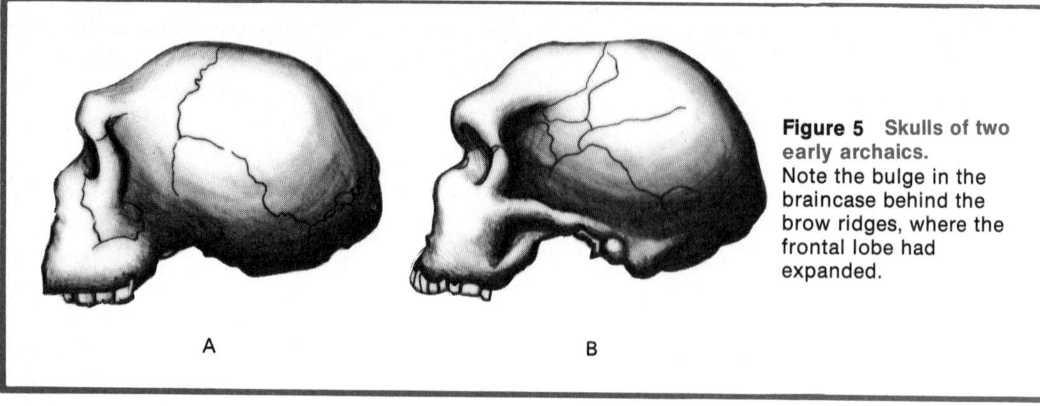

Figure 5 Skulls of two early archaics.
Note the bulge in the braincase behind the brow ridges, where the frontal lobe had expanded.

Late Archaic Homo Sapiens

The next hominid grouping covers only the first part of one glacial period—the Würm glaciation, which lasted from 75,000 to 10,000 B.P. Fossils of this age found in Europe have traditionally been referred to as "Neandertal." The label comes from skeletal fragments discovered in 1856 in a grotto in the Neander Valley, Germany.

The Environment

The geographic distribution of the late archaic fossils is close to that of the early archaics, although far more sites have been found from this period than from any earlier ones. Nearly 100 locations in Europe, Africa, the Middle East, and Asia have yielded specimens. And even more sites have contained tools, but no trace of the hominids that made them.

Within this broad area hominids were expanding into new environments. In Africa it seems that they were exploiting tropical rainforests for the first time. In Europe only a few early archaic sites have been found near areas that were never free from ice and snow. However, the tundra just south of the glaciers—from Spain and France in the west to the Ukraine in the east—seems to have been densely inhabited by the late archaics. Perhaps because of this advance into more marginal habitats, hominids were also more often making their homes in caves and rock shelters rather than out in the open.

Despite the cold weather late archaics must have faced in Europe during the Würm glaciation, the number of plant and animal remains found there suggests that the area was capable of supporting abundant life. In midsummer there were probably 16 hours of sunlight a day, and at least half that much in winter. In the south, great forests of pine and shrubs stretched from Southern Germany to Russia. In north central Europe the tundra was covered with a variety of plants that could exist in the cold, except in areas of perpetual snow. The tundra, like the savanna, supports few different kinds of plants. But because these few species were abundant during the Würm glaciation they supported large herds of mammoth, wooly rhinoceros, reindeer, elk, and bison. In the more forested regions south of the tundra, cave bears, hyenas, lions, and deer thrived. Although the hominids of this time fished and hunted game ranging from cave bears to small mammals and birds they must have been especially fond of reindeer. At one open-air site, almost three-fourths of the animal remains found are those of reindeer (Kennedy, 1975).

The Makeup of Archaic Populations

Since there are so many Würm fossils, we have enough data to apply population analysis techniques to extinct humans. Although we are not dealing with a biological population, enough individuals are represented to apply these techniques. Hominids from this period probably lived in bands of about 10 to 30 people. Some lived as nomads, following herds of game animals north into the tundra during the summer and south to the forests in winter. But in areas that had stable animal populations, hominids led a more settled existence.

Studies of age at death suggest high annual mortality rates and short lives. Very few lived to be older than 40; half of them died in infancy and childhood. Most women apparently died before they were 30, many in childbirth. Males probably outlived females, a trend that has been reversed probably only in industrial-age *H. sapiens* populations. It is possible that this sex ratio is inaccurate, however, because fragmentary skeletal remains make recognition of secondary sexual characteristics impossible. When analyzing such remains, researchers tend to assume that specimens with a heavy build are males rather than sturdy females (Kennedy, 1975).

Physical Characteristics

Although we shall refer to the late archaics as a single group with a single label, the fossils from this period show a broad range of anatomical variation. These are interpreted by some anthropologists as subspecific variations. Despite their broad geographical range and differences in environment, late archaic groups apparently had enough contact with one another and enough genetic similarity that they could still interbreed successfully. They did not become so genetically isolated that they evolved into separate species.

Some of the differences between late archaic fossils from Europe and those from other parts of the world may be related to time differences. For instance, while the early European fossils are over 50,000 years old, those from the Near East date mostly from 50,000 to 35,000 years B.P.

Some of the differences may also reflect anatomical adaptation to local environments. The late archaics from Europe—especially those from early in the Würm glaciation—may have developed specialized adaptations to the continual cold. The European fossils have extremely projecting faces, large nasal cavities, and somewhat short and stocky bodies. These characteristics were foreshadowed in earlier hominids and continued in other late archaic groups. But nowhere are they so noticeable as in the European fossils. All these characteristics can be seen as adaptations for retaining body heat. The projecting face, for instance, may have kept inhaled air as far as possible from arteries that supply blood to the brain, limiting the chance of chilling it. The large nose may have served to warm and moisten air as it is inhaled, and the large sinuses behind it may have acted as additional warming chambers. A short, stocky body would have reduced the amount of surface area over which heat could be lost (Wolpoff, 1975; Mann & Trinkaus, 1973).

Late archaics have, on the average, the largest front teeth of any fossil hominids. (See Figure 6.) This trend reached a peak during the first part of the Würm glaciation (about 65,000 to 50,000 years B.P.). During the middle part of the glaciation (about 48,000 to 40,000 years B.P.) the front teeth then began to get smaller. Neck muscles and their attachment points began to decrease in size even sooner.

According to Wolpoff's teeth-as-tools theory mentioned earlier, the development of specialized hand tools must have reduced the need to use the incisors to help grip and work

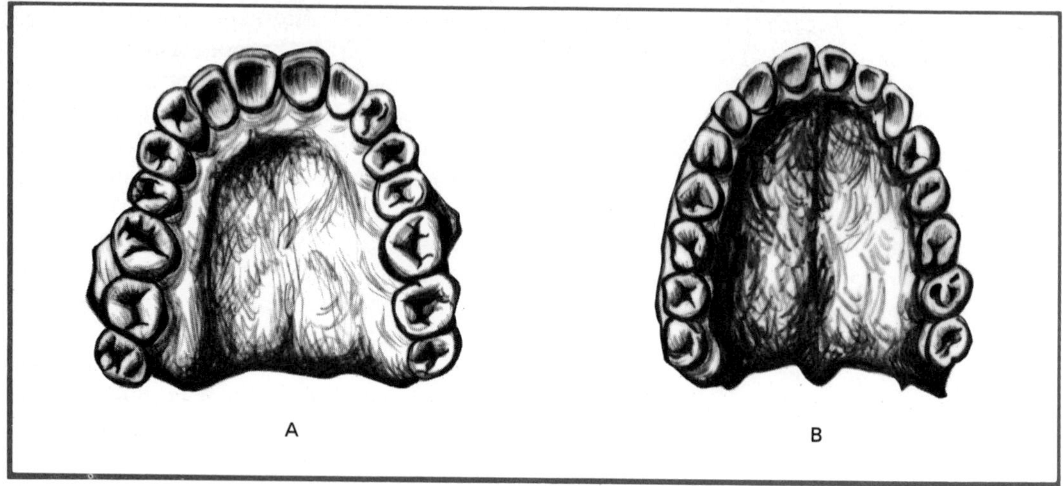

Figure 6 Dentition of a late archaic *(A)* and of a modern *H. sapiens (B)*. Incisors are larger than those of any other hominid. Molars of modern humans are smaller. (*A* is from Brace, Nelson, & Korn, 1971)

objects. The shift away from the use of teeth as tools is reflected first in smaller neck muscles. These are more affected than teeth by what goes on during a person's lifetime. Tooth size, a trait controlled largely by genetics, changes more slowly, in response to evolutionary pressures. It may be that the problems caused by the crowding of large teeth in a shrinking jaw were beginning to outweigh the selective advantages of having big front teeth (Wolpoff, 1975).

Elsewhere, the back teeth and jaws continued their long-term trend to smaller size. A slight chin was beginning to appear on many of the specimens from both Europe and other areas. Browridges were reduced. And the brain became so large that the average cranial capacity found in late archaic fossils—1470 cc.—is even greater than the average cranial capacity of modern humans—1330 cc. Whether these numbers say anything about how the intelligence of these hominids compares to our own is an open question. Brain size cannot be strictly correlated with intelligence, so the late archaics may not have had our mental abilities. However, evidence of burials and the appearance of ritual activity has prompted some anthropologists to argue that they were just as intelligent as we are.

Late archaics seem to have been able to use their hands independently—an indication of mental refinement of another kind. Tiny parallel scratches on their incisors suggest that they used stone knives to cut their meat before swallowing it. The direction of these cuts indicates that they habitually held onto the meat with their right hand, while cutting it with their left. Specialization in use of hands is a uniquely human trait. Some scientists associate it with the evolution of higher brain centers (Kennedy, 1975).

Another function of the higher brain centers is speech. Scientists are intrigued by the question of when language evolved. But as yet we have no way of knowing whether the late archaics could talk to one another. We know little of how their brain was structured, for only a few of their gross external features have been preserved as fossilized molds. Whether or not they had a localized "speech center" in their brains we cannot tell. However, some researchers have noted that these hominids had plenty of room to move their tongues around if they did try to speak, since the bony shelves had disappeared from the inside of their lower jaws. Philip Lieberman, a linguist, and Edmund Crelin, an anatomist, have determined that the larynx and brains of these early people were better equipped for speech than those of other primates. Their speech potential, Lieberman and Crelin suggest, was similar to that of modern human infants. And judging from their cultural advances, they probably used some primitive form of spoken communication. Lieberman and Crelin think that they could produce only a few vowel sounds, and their consonants were limited to *b*s, *d*s, and a few others. Fascinating as this theory is, however, it is based on very thin evidence—a single, possibly deformed, fossil. Alexander Marshack (1976) feels that Neandertal geometric designs indicate a symbolic ability that must have included a fairly sophisticated form of language.

Phylogenetic Interpretations

Although we have thus far treated late archaics as a single widespread group, anthropologists disagree as to how to interpret the variety within this group. Controversy centers on the late archaics. These fossils have been referred to traditionally as *Neandertals.* The use of this term has been particularly confusing. At different times, it has been used as a label for (1) the western European fossils contemporary with the Neander Valley skull, (2) an evolutionary grade (the "Neandertal" stage of biological and cultural evolution), and (3) the fossils from all over Europe, Asia, and Africa that date from the Würm glaciation. As a result, there is confusion as to which set of fossils the Neandertal label is being applied.

Why is "Neandertal" used for so many very different finds? Up to the mid-1950s, fossil collection and analysis was heavily influenced by a European bias on the part of western paleontologists. It seemed to them that the European fossils were the most important, since they were the most numerous. This is not surprising, because most of the fossil hunting went on in Europe. At any rate, the idea developed that Europe was central in hominid evolution. However, fossil finds accumulating from other parts of the world gradually made it evident that Europe was only a part of the evolutionary theater—and a rather isolated part, at that. Nonetheless, scientists continued to interpret these non-European fossils in terms of the European classification scheme. As anthropologist David Pilbeam has pointed out, calling fossils from Java "tropical Neandertals" makes no more sense than referring to modern populations living in Java as "tropical Europeans" (Pilbeam, 1970).

The lack of early data and often confused interpretations have combined to produce a number of theories for this period. The three major phylogenic theories are often referred to as the presapiens theory, the pre-Neandertal theory, and the single-lineage theory. In the past, the popularity of each has depended to a great extent on the popularity of its leading proponents.

The Presapiens Theory. This theory holds that the European Neandertals branched off from the hominid line at least as long ago as 250,000 years and finally became extinct, leaving no descendants. As the Neandertals evolved, another group of hominids was developing modern human anatomical traits. These hominids were the presapiens, for whom the theory is named. (See Figure 7.)

The presapiens theory has its origins in the end of the nineteenth century. Then, as now, interpretation of fossil discoveries was strongly influenced by the current climate of opinion. People were very unsympathetic to the idea that all life—including civilized Europeans—had evolved from more primitive forms. The newly found Neandertal remains, therefore, seemed to belong to a creature far more "brutish" than modern humans.

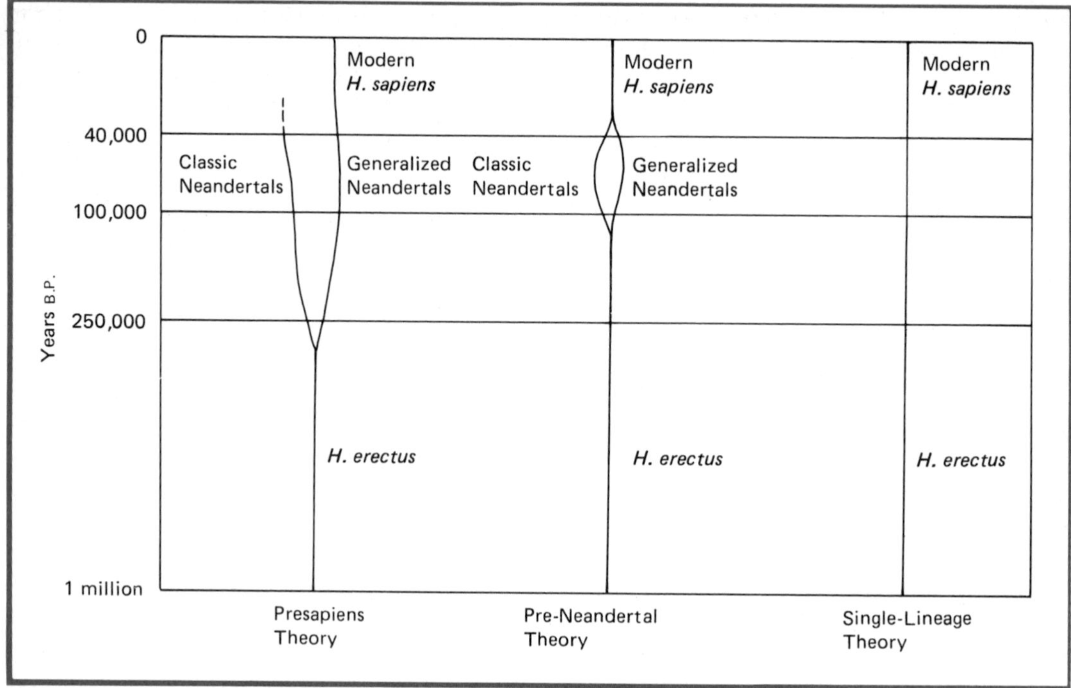

Figure 7 Theories of the evolution of early and late archaic *H. sapiens*. The presapiens theory suggests that the European Neandertal lineage diverged at least 250,000 years ago. According to the pre-Neandertal theory, two groups of late archaics evolved from the early archaic form more recently. The single-lineage theory proposes a single evolution line.

Since there was no known way to determine the age of the find, many scientists assumed that it was just an abnormal human.

As more European fossils resembling the Neandertal specimen were found, the notion that it was an isolated freak had to be discarded. But popular feeling still colored scientific interpretation. In 1908, the most complete set of bones of this type—the skeleton of an aging man found in La Chapelle-aux-Saints, France—was sent to Professor Marcellin Boule of the Museum of Natural History in Paris. The massive volumes this scholar turned out pictured the Neandertals as the kind of "cave men" we still see in cartoons. Very few people—including Boule—were willing to consider primitive creatures like the La Chapelle-aux-Saints fossil their ancestors. So Boule concluded that they were representatives of a line that had eventually died out, leaving no descendants. Their place was supposedly taken by more modern humans with "superior" traits, who invaded Europe from a hypothetical homeland somewhere else.

To support his theory, Boule presented evidence that the Neandertals and the modern forms that seemed to replace them in the geological record were far too different to be seen as evolutionary stages along a single line. Boule's theory influenced the classification of fossils for years. But in 1957 reexamination of the La Chapelle-aux-Saints remains showed that they had probably been distorted by a severe case of arthritis, making them seem more apelike than they were (Strause & Cave, 1957). Today the presapiens theory is generally discounted.

The Pre-Neandertal Theory. According to the pre-Neandertal theory, two groups of late archaics evolved from the preWürm early archaic form that had existed throughout Europe, the Middle East, and North Africa: the *generalized,* or *early, Neandertals* and the *classic Neandertals*. The traits of the generalized Neandertals were unspecialized enough that many experts think they evolved into modern humans. Holders of this theory believe that the modern form emerged everywhere except in Western Europe, where those who would become the classic Neandertals were isolated by glacial advances. Under the extreme natural selection caused by the cold weather, a specialized form that could survive in the harsh climate quickly evolved.

Supporters of the pre-Neandertal theory do not think that the classic and generalized Neandertals were different enough to warrant classification as separate species. They do, however, argue that with the retreat of the second Würm glaciation, modern-looking humans with new cultural techniques entered previously isolated Western Europe. There, they probably mixed with the classic Neandertals, and both groups contributed to the gene pool of modern humans.

The Single-Lineage Theory. The third theory—the *single-lineage theory,* proposes that in spite of some local variations, all hominids living around the world in the Würm glacial age are part of a single evolving line. The European Neandertals also contributed to the gene pool of modern humans, according to this theory.

What conclusion can we draw about these conflicting theories? There is a growing body of evidence that the presapiens theory is the product of a rather narrow focus on events in Europe, to the exclusion of the rest of the world. Reinterpretation of the fossil and archaeological data from the period suggests that European Neandertals were simply a localized population of a worldwide species, *H. sapiens.* The new evidence indicates that the Neandertals, along with other groups, evolved into early modern forms.

The presapiens theory was based on proving that rather modern humans appeared before Neandertals in the European fossil record. The traditional candidates for old but modern-looking humans have included the Piltdown skull and skullcaps found in Swanscombe, England, and Fontéchevade, France. Piltdown, of course, has been exposed as a hoax. Reexamination of the Swanscombe fossil shows that it is indeed older than the Neandertal finds. But its features do not fall within the range of variations seen in contemporary human populations as presapiens theorists had claimed.

As for the two Fontéchevade skullcaps, their apparent lack of browridges had been used as proof that they were closer to modern skull shapes than the Neandertals. But at least one of them belonged to a child and the other could have. Children at this time developed browridges as they aged. Therefore, the absence of browridges in these childlike skullcaps does not support the presapiens theory.

A fourth set of fossils—two individuals found in the Vertesszöllös cave—has recently been offered as evidence of a modern human line that predated the Neandertals. Again, these fossils are unquestionably older than the Neandertals. But their cranial characteristics are most similar to those of *H. erectus.* They cannot be interpreted as early *H. sapiens* (Wolpoff, 1971).

Finally, there is good biological and cultural evidence that the western European Neandertals gradually evolved in place into modern *H. sapiens* (Brose & Wolpoff, 1971). As Brose and Wolpoff point out, neither relative strata studies nor comparison of absolute dates reveal any signs that these people were suddenly replaced by more advanced forms. Instead, tools show a gradual improvement in technology at all sites. In anatomy, too, there appears to be a gradual transition from the Neandertal form to a more modern one. At both levels, however, there is a great deal of individual variation.

Early Modern Humans

During the latter part of the Würm glaciation, hominids having a nearly modern anatomy first began living in the Western Hemisphere and Australia. By 30,000 to 25,000 B.P., they had extended their range to all the areas now inhabited by humans. Though these people continued to live in rather small groups as hunters and gatherers, they rapidly advanced in both cultural and technological sophistication.

The Fossils

Far more fossils have been found from this period than from any that came before it. Because these hominids were often carefully buried, whole skeletons have been preserved. In Europe, for instance, twice as many fossils of early moderns have been found as fossils of late archaics. The density of archaeological sites from this period seems to indicate that population size had grown, too.

From modern-day France to the Soviet Union, early moderns hunted a wide assortment of game animals with a sophisticated variety of weapons—spears, harpoons, clubs, bows and arrows, and boomerangs. Their technology allowed them to survive in all but the most forbidding environments. Shelters ranged from caves and tents to skin-covered huts sunk into the ground.

Outside of Europe, there are not as many early modern fossils. A few have been found in Java, Japan, and China. Eastern Africa may have been heavily inhabited because it was a crossroads between the Nile Valley to the north, the rain forest to the west, and the grasslands to the south.

In Australia and the New World, hominid fossils appear for the first time during this period. How and when they got there we are not sure. Hominids may have island-hopped with small rafts or boats to reach Australia from the long-inhabited Java area. A fairly lengthy fossil record exists in Australia extending back to 25,000 years ago. Unfortunately, many fossils are hard to interpret. One find at Green Gully, near Melbourne, for instance, consisted of 3,900 scrambled bone fragments from a male and a female. As is still the practice among some Australian aborigines, their bodies had probably been left to rot for about a year before they were buried. Before being scooped into a single grave, their bones were probably mixed up and spread around by animal scavengers. Despite such paleontological nightmares, we are *certain* that there were fossil hominids in Australia before 24,000 B.P., and perhaps even as early as 32,000 B.P.

As in Australia, we have no direct evidence of how and when fossil hominids first reached the New World. Now, most scientists believe that they crossed a wide land bridge between Siberia and Alaska and then moved southward. When the Wisconsin glacier, the North American equivalent of the Würm glaciation in Europe, reached its peak about 40,000 years ago, it would have gathered so much sea water into its mass that the sea level might have been lowered by as much as 460 feet. This would have exposed a corridor of land across what is now the Bering Strait. This landbridge may have closed and reopened at times as the glacier periodically retreated and then advanced again, allowing migrants to cross in waves.

Physical Characteristics

These most recent of our ancestors looked very much like us. Their tooth structure and jaws are almost within the range of sizes seen in today's populations. Their faces became much flatter than those of earlier hominids. A chin was clearly in evidence on early modern fossils from all over the world. The cranial vault was higher but narrower than in earlier fossils, perhaps because reduced demands on the teeth allowed the skull to be shaped more by the expansion of the upper brain than by the need to provide robust anchor points for the jaw and neck muscles. (See Figure 8.) Finally, increasing use of specialized tools rather than muscle power in survival tasks decreased the need for heavy bone structure. All over their bodies, early moderns were generally less robust than their late archaic ancestors.

Although early moderns looked more like contemporary humans than any preceding group had, they were not fully modern. Compared to earlier groups, they had a higher incidence of "modern" characteristics (such as chins) and a lower incidence of "archaic" characteristics (such as strongly prognathous faces). In some traits, some of the fossils fall within the range of variations found in contemporary human populations. But taken as a whole, they are as different from living humans as they are from the late archaics (Wolpoff, 1975).

As one generation followed another under conditions of increasing cultural control over the environmental pressures of survival, the frequency of these primitive traits gradually declined, and more fully modern-looking humans emerged.

Summary

1. The major anatomical changes in hominids during the Pleistocene Epoch were reduction of the chewing apparatus and expansion of the brain. Both changes are the product of interacting biological and cultural forces.

2. We have divided the Pleistocene hominids into five groups: early *Homo erectus,* late *Homo erectus,* early archaic *Homo sapiens,* late archaic *Homo sapiens,* and early modern humans. With the possible exception of the Upper Pleistocene forms, these hominids probably represent a single lineage.

3. During the lower Pleistocene (2 million to 700,000 years B.P.) early *H. erectus* forms

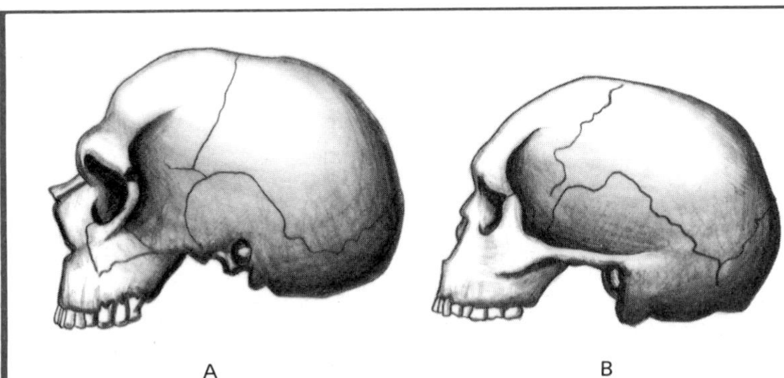

Figure 8 Skulls of a late archaic *H. sapiens* *(A)* and an early modern *H. sapiens* *(B)*. Cranial capacity is similar, although the skull of *B* is shorter (from front to back), narrower, and higher (from top to bottom) than that of *A*.

spread from Africa to warm parts of Java, China, and Europe, perhaps in pursuit of migrating animal herds. Compared to the early African hominids, these hominids had a more erect posture, lighter jaws, smaller molars, and bigger brains. But their broad faces and heavy neck muscles gave them a somewhat primitive appearance.

4. Fossil hominids are scarce from the period following 700,000 B.P., but reappear as late *H. erectus* from 450,000 to about 250,000 years B.P. These hominids inhabited harsher environments, aided by improved technology and expansion of brain centers responsible for conscious thought and sensory-motor integration. Chewing apparatus was further reduced.

5. In early archaic *H. sapiens* (ranging from about 225,000 to 75,000 years B.P.), the trend toward smaller jaws, molars, and chewing muscles continued. But their front teeth, upper jaws, and neck muscles were larger again, an evolutionary reversal that may have been a response to the use of the front teeth as tools.

6. Hominids from the Würm glaciation period traditionally have been referred to as Neandertals, but we call them late archaic *H. sapiens.* Classic Neandertals from western Europe were shorter and had a more projecting face and a relatively large nasal cavity compared to the generalized forms found elsewhere. Perhaps this is partly because their features were adaptations to the cold climate.

7. Explanations of the presence of late archaic variation fall into three main theories. The *presapiens theory* (today generally discounted) holds that the European Neandertals branched off from *H. erectus* stock as long ago as 250,000 years and became extinct, while another group of hominids developed modern human anatomical traits. According to the *pre-Neandertal theory,* the earlier *generalized Neandertals* and the later *classic Neandertals* evolved from earlier preglacial archaics. The generalized form later evolved into modern humans. The *single-lineage theory* proposes that all hominids of the Würm glaciation contributed to the gene pool of modern humans.

8. Early modern human fossils have been found in the New World and Australia, as well as in the long-inhabited areas—for example, Africa and the Far East. These fossils show the loss of the primitive characteristics of their predecessors. But their range of anatomical variations does not quite match that of modern humans.

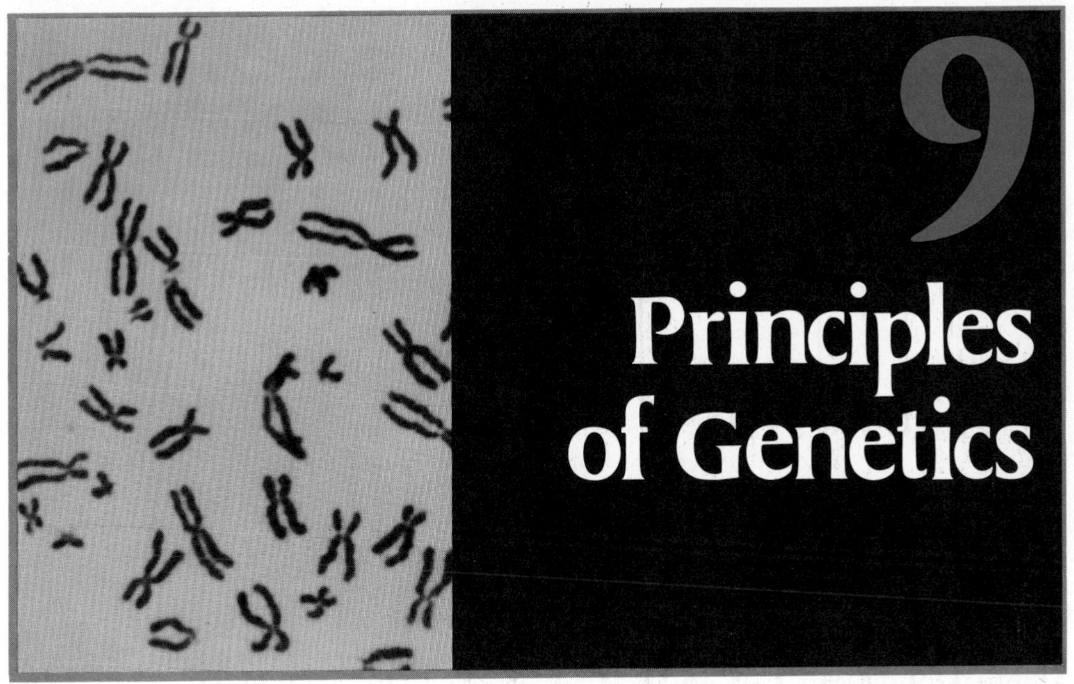

9 Principles of Genetics

THE fossil record can tell us part of the story of how we evolved. From it, we can see some of the ways in which the hominid body was changed in the course of time. Looking at the fossils, we can assume that the force responsible for these changes is natural selection and can construct hypotheses about the survival value of the various traits that have been preserved. But we can only theorize about how natural selection has been at work, because the fossil record consists of a small group of different individuals from different times and different places. And we cannot begin to study the process by which traits are inherited. To investigate the adaptive value of given traits and to understand genetics, we must continue our study of evolution among living organisms. Only by analyzing living individuals and populations can we gather the information we need to describe the genetic control of traits and changes in how frequently they appear in populations.

In this chapter we shall discuss the nature of heredity and how it has been applied to humans. In Chapter 10 we shall discuss how the forces of evolution have been studied and illustrated in living human groups.

Mendel's Laws of Inheritance

In his theory of natural selection, Darwin explained the nature of the major force that changes the physical makeup of populations from one generation to the next. But one question puzzled Darwin to his death: How are the traits of the individuals of a population passed on from parent to offspring? Darwin understood that some traits increase the chances of survival in a given environment, but he did not know the mechanism by which these traits are passed on to offspring.

The real operation of inheritance was being worked out by Gregor Mendel, an Austrian monk, at the time Darwin was writing *On the Origin of Species*. Mendal worked with pea plants that had a number of traits, each of which existed in one of two alternative forms. Stem length, for example, was either long or short. When he placed pollen from long-stemmed plants on short-stemmed plants, he found that the new plants (the so-called first filial, or F_1 generation) all had long stems. When the F_1 plants were crossed with one another, however, three-quarters of the second filial, or F_2 generation had long stems and one-quarter had short stems. (See Figure 1.)

To Mendel, these results suggested that the factors that controlled the traits must exist as separate particles in the plant cells. Each particle, he reasoned, must control one form of a given trait. These particles, whose presence was still only guessed at, were later named *genes*.

Mendel also had to explain why every plant in the F_1 generation had a long stem. First, he reasoned that each trait was controlled by two forms of the same gene. Second, he suggested that the form of the gene that controlled long stem was *dominant* over the form that controlled short stem. In other words, the dominant form of the gene for stem length (long) prevented the expression of the *recessive* form of the gene for stem length (short). In modern genetics, these different forms of the same gene are called *alleles*. The genetic makeup of an organism is called its *genotype*. When the genotype includes two alleles of the same type, it is said to be *homozygous*. When the genotype includes one allele of one type and a second allele of another type, it is *heterozygous*. The actual physical form controlled by the alleles of a gene is called a *phenotype*. Thus, the F_1 generation of Mendel's peas had a heterozygous genotype (one allele for long stem, one for short stem). The phenotype, however, was long stem.

Figure 1 Results of Mendel's cross of long-stemmed and short-stemmed pea plants

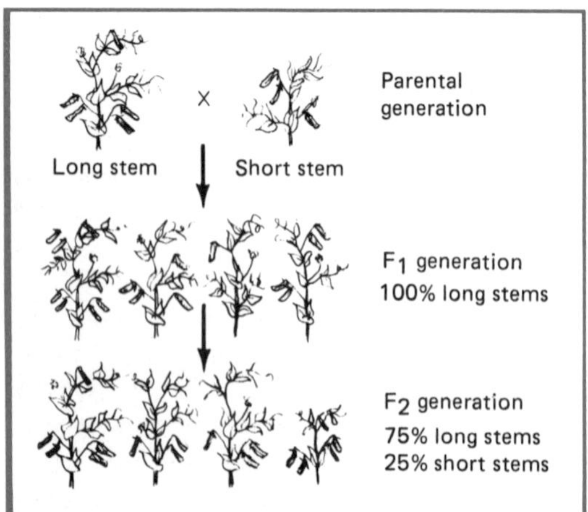

Table 1 Genotypes and Phenotypes of the F_2 Generation

Genotype	Phenotype
YY	Long stem, because only Y alleles are present
Yy	Long stem, because the Y allele is dominant over the y allele
yy	Short stem, because only recessive y alleles are present

Inside the Cell Nucleus

Improved microscopes and better techniques of tissue preparation in the late nineteenth century permitted scientists to find out what structures in the cell were active during its reproduction. It was known, of course, that all living organisms are made up of cells—the basic units of life. The rough outlines of cell structure were also known. Most of the billions of cells that make up the tissue of the body were known to have an area called the *nucleus* at their center.

Scientists had become fascinated by certain long, thin threads that appeared in the cell nucleus just before cell division. Techniques for studying the structure of cells included staining, and because these long, thin threads stained dramatically, they were called *chromosomes,* or "colored bodies." August Weismann (1834–1914), a German biologist, and others were able to find out that almost every cell in the body of an organism contains the same number of chromosomes and that chromosomes form the major part of the nucleus. Later, the process of chromosome duplication, which ensures that each body cell (that is, cells other than a sperm or an egg) has the same number of chromosomes was observed. The process of cell division, in which the chromosomes in the nucleus of a dividing body cell are duplicated and then transmitted to the nuclei of two new cells, was called *mitosis.* It provides each new daughter cell with the same genetic information as was in the parent cell. This process ensures the normal working of the body's *somatic cells*—cells other than the sex cells, sperm and eggs.

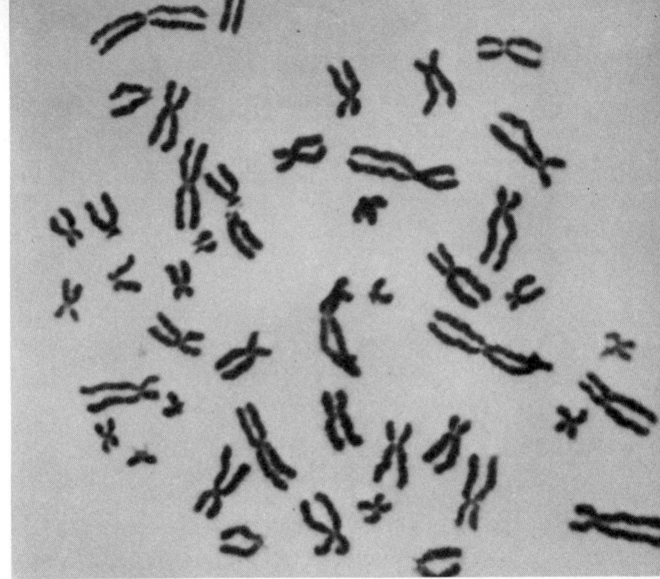

The chromosomes of a normal human somatic cell

Meiosis. The precise duplication of genetic material is necessary not only for the correct functioning of a living organism, but also for that of its offspring. The cell created by the union of gametes (the male sperm cell and the female egg) is called a *zygote.* This cell must have a normal number of chromosomes. Consequently, when sperm and eggs are formed from body cells in the testes and ovaries, the number of chromosomes in the gametes must be half that of the parental cells. If this halving did not occur, the number of chromosomes would double each generation. Two gametes, each having the normal number of chromosomes, would combine to form a zygote with twice the normal number. *Meiosis,* the division of cells to form gametes, therefore results in cells with half the normal number of chromosomes See Figure 2 for the deatils of meiotic division.

In fertilization, then, each parent contributes half a set of instructions for every characteristic in a new individual. But the half contributed by one parent must match the half contributed by the other. This can occur because, as researchers studying meiosis soon realized, chromosomes are paired by function. The unit that controls the same characteristics is known as a pair of *homologous chromosomes.*

Today, it is known that humans have a total of 46 chromosomes, which function as 23 pairs in the body cells. The sperm and the egg, it was realized, must each possess one member of every pair. Meiosis, then, not only reduces the number of chromosomes by one-half, but also distributes to each resulting gamete one member of each of the 23 homologous chromosomes.

An understanding of meiosis clarifies some of Mendel's observations of pea traits. For instance, if we think of the alleles for long stem and those for short stem as being located at the same position, or *locus,* on homologous chromosomes we can see why the factors con-

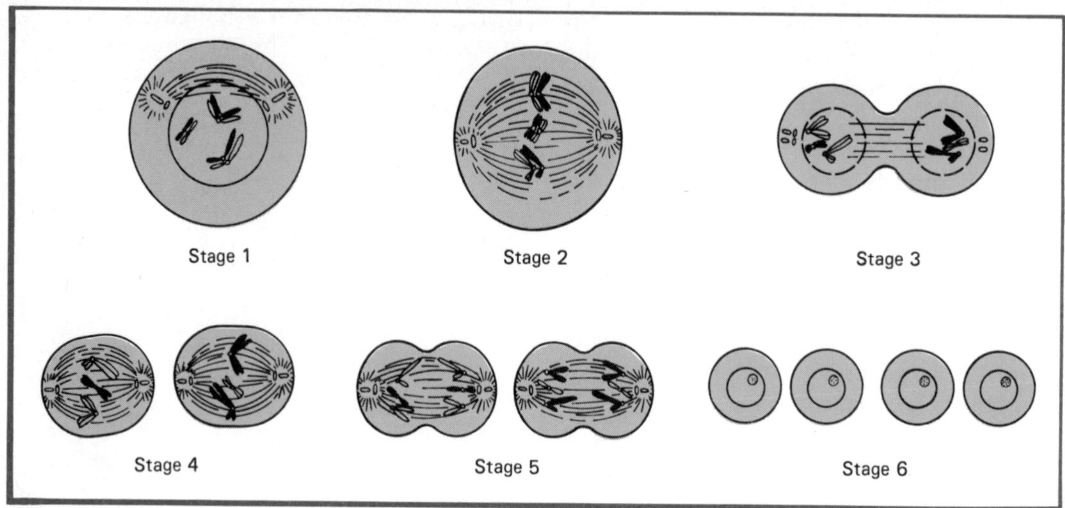

Figure 2 **Meiosis in an animal cell.**
Meiosis involves two sequences of cell division, creating four gametes. We shall explain meiosis in terms of six stages. Stage 1: Chromosomes have contracted, and homologous pairs have moved together. Stage 2: Each member of every homologous pair, having copied itself before Stage 1, becomes clearly double-stranded. The homologous pairs and their replicants line up at the center of the cell, and members of each pair and its replicant move to opposite poles. Stage 3: Two new cells form, each with one member of every homologous pair and its replicant. Stage 4: (Stages 4, 5, and 6 are a division exactly like that of mitosis.) The previously-formed duplicate pairs line up at the center of the cell. Stage 5: The pairs become unjoined and the two copies move toward opposite poles of the cells. Stage 6: Each cell forms two identical daughter cells, which are gametes.

trolling stem length seemed to Mendel to act as separate particles. The chromosomes separated during meiosis and entered separate gametes. In the F_1 generation, gametes containing the chromosome carrying a long-stem allele united with gametes containing the chromosome carrying the allele for short stem. A heterozygote long-stemmed plant was the result.

In the course of meiosis, alleles located on the same chromosome are copied and are incorporated into one of four gametes (see Figure 3). When the heterozygous F_1 plants were crossed with each other, half the gametes had a chromosome with the dominant allele and half had a chromosome with the recessive allele. Gametes with the dominant or the recessive allele therefore had an equal chance of forming the zygote. The resulting F_2 ratio of three long-stemmed plants to one short-stemmed plant could be predicted on the basis of the laws of probability.

The Chemistry of Genes and Their Activity

Biologists first gathered the information about genes presented in this last section almost entirely by inference. Later, however, much direct evidence was found to support the early theories. This evidence included detailed knowledge of the chemical makeup of

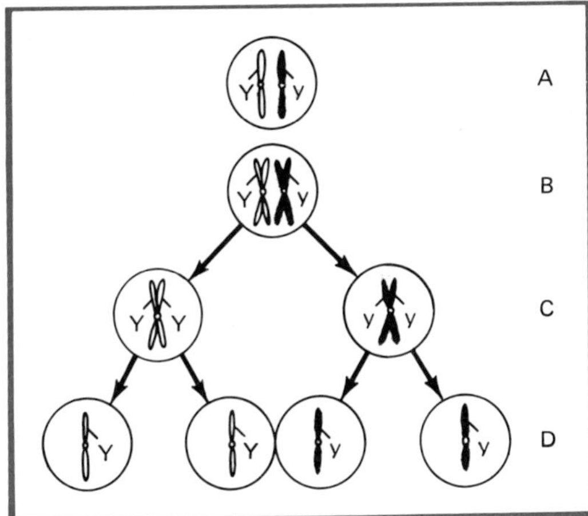

Figure 3 Segregation of alleles in meiosis. Meiosis in a heterozygous pea plant, genotype Yy. Y and y represent alleles on a homologous pair of chromosomes. Though pea plants have seven pairs of chromosomes, we shall focus only on the homologous pair having alleles Y and y. *(A)* parent cell with Yy pair; *(B)* in the process of chromosome duplication, the Y and y alleles are copied; *(C)* first reduction division separates the two double-stranded chromosomes, incorporating the Y alleles into one cell and the y alleles into the other; *(D)* second reduction division separates both the Y-carrying chromosome strand from its copy and the y-carrying strand from its copy, so that four cells exist, each carrying a chromosome with either the Y or the y allele.

the genes, how the chromosomes copy themselves, how they direct activities of the organism, and how they affect its characteristics.

A great deal of effort over a long period of time went into the chemical analysis of cell nuclei. By 1869, it was known that nuclei contain protein and an acid, now called *deoxyribonucleic acid,* or DNA for short. In the 1920s, workers using a stain that colors DNA bright red found that the DNA in the nucleus is located in the chromosomes. Then followed a long debate over whether it was the DNA or the protein in the nucleus that made up the genes. By the early 1950s, however, a number of experiments with bacteria had strongly suggested that the DNA was the genetic material. A few researchers began to put together what was known about the chemical composition of this molecule in an attempt to make a model of it. Finally, in 1953, James D. Watson and Francis H. C. Crick proposed the model of DNA structure that is commonly accepted today. Their model is perhaps the most important landmark in the history of biology to date, and they received a Nobel Prize for their work.

The Composition of DNA

DNA is a large molecule made up of a series of smaller molecules bonded together. The basic unit of DNA is a group of three molecules, called a *nucleotide.* As you can see in Figure 4, the three molecules are a sugar, a phosphate, and an organic base. The organic base can be one of two different types, either a purine or a pyrimidine. There are two purines: *adenine* (A) and *guanine* (G). There are also two pyrimidines: *cytosine* (C) and *thymine* (T).

The sugar of one nucleotide is bonded to the phosphate of the next, forming a long chain, as shown in Figure 5. As you can see in part B, the DNA molecule is formed of two such chains, which are linked together by weak bonds between the purines and the pyrimidines. The structure is like that of a ladder: the phosphate and sugar molecules forming the sides, and the two joined organic

Figure 4 A representation of a nucleotide, the basic unit of DNA. (Moody, 1975)

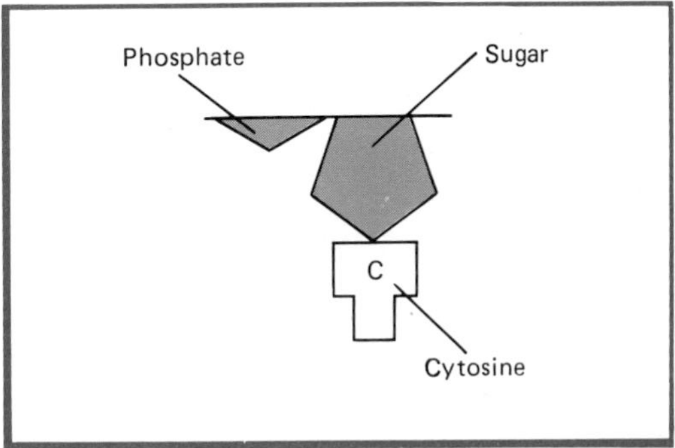

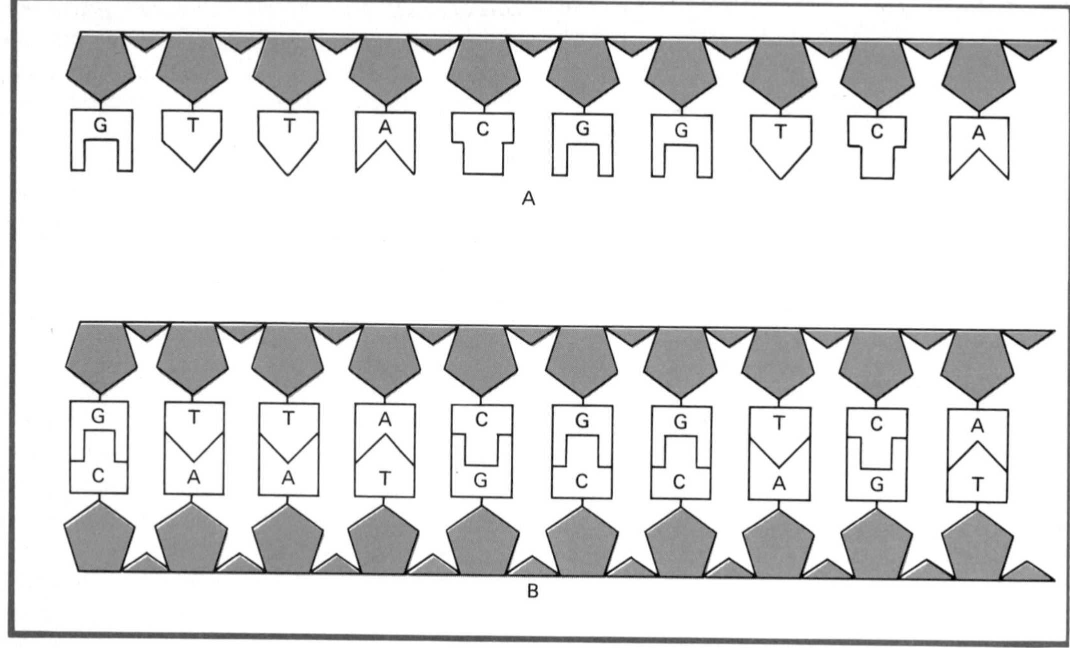

Figure 5 **DNA chains.**
Sugar of one nucleotide bonds to the phosphate of the next to form a long chain *(A)*. Two of these chains are linked *(B)* by purine-pyrimidine bonds. (Moody, 1975)

bases forming the rungs. In forming the rungs, adenine always bonds with thymine, while cytosine always bonds with guanine. The two organic bases are linked together by means of weak hydrogen bonds. Certain measurements led Watson and Crick to suggest that this ladder is a helix—that is to say, it is shaped like a spiral staircase (See Figure 6.) Research has shown this to be the structure of the DNA of all organisms.

DNA Replication. Knowing the structure of DNA helps us explain chromosome replication, or duplication, at the molecular level. The key to understanding this process is to remember the fact that adenine always bonds with thymine on the one hand, and cytosine always bonds with guanine on the other. During replication, the bonds linking the organic bases are broken, and the chain of nucleotides begins to "unzip." Then, the unbonded bases along each half helix immediately begin to attract free-floating nucleotides. An unbonded adenine base always attracts a free-floating nucleotide with a thymine base, and vice versa. An unbonded guanine base always attracts a free-floating nucleotide with a cytosine base, and vice versa. In this way, two new molecules are assembled after the original separates. The two new helixes have structures exactly like the original.

DNA and the Making of Proteins

Probably the only function of DNA is to direct the making of *proteins*. But this is a very complex task. Proteins are more intricate than any known compound, and are vital to the body's functioning as well as to its structure. Some proteins serve as *enzymes*, chemicals that start or speed up chemical processes in the body. Without enzymes, these reactions

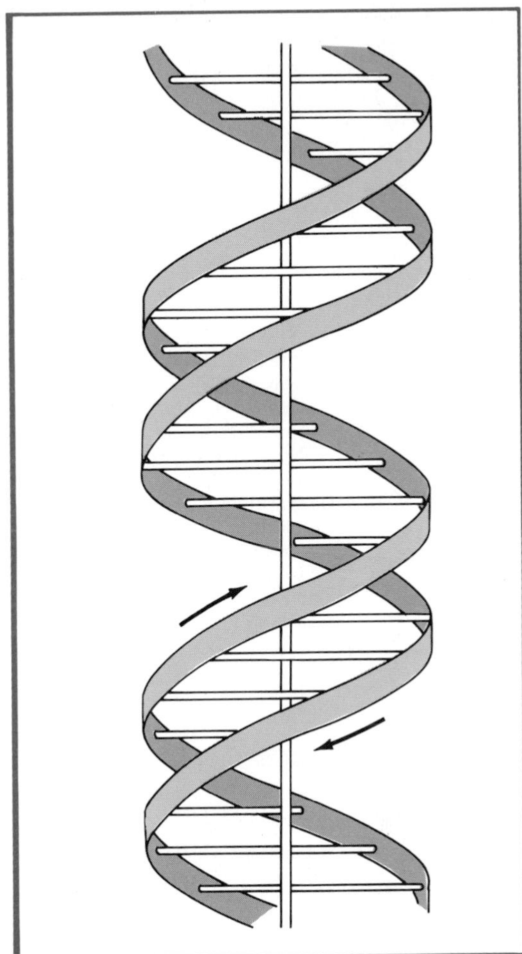

Figure 6 **DNA molecule.**
Measurements with x-rays led Watson and Crick to conclude that the DNA molecule is in the shape of a helix.

would either never begin or would occur so slowly that life would be impossible. Enzymes control the breakdown of nutrients into energy compounds or the synthesis of nutrients into large molecules of body tissue. The development of the embryo is also directed by enzymes. Proteins are also part of the structure of cells themselves. Cell membranes are made up of proteins, as are many of the internal cell parts.

The basic structural units of proteins are *amino acids.* These relatively simple molecules are organized into sequences called *polypeptide chains.* Proteins may be formed of one or more of these chains. Practically an infinite number of proteins, each with a different shape and different physical properties, can be formed from 20 known amino acids. This is true because single proteins contain anywhere from about 50 to 50,000 amino acids, and the number of variations in the order of amino acids is enormous.

There is strong evidence that the order of nucleotides in the DNA molecules forms the sequence of amino acids in proteins. But what combination of nucleotides contains the instructions (or codes) for properly ordering of the 20 amino acids? Geneticists have reasoned that the simplest possible code that could form all 20 amino acids is a group of three nucleotides. These groups of three, called *triplets,* can exist in 64 combinations, more than enough to code for the known amino acids.

DNA itself serves as a kind of storage place for information. It does not actively become involved in making proteins. Instead, it provides a blueprint that is copied by another type of nucleic acid called *ribonucleic acid* or RNA. RNA differs from DNA in two ways: (1) the sugar in each nucleotide contains one more oxygen atom, and (2) another organic base, uracil, replaces thymine as a bonding partner for adenine.

One kind of RNA, called *messenger RNA,* or mRNA for short, acts as a kind of go-between for the DNA. When protein synthesis is about to occur, part of the DNA helix "unzips." Next, a strand of mRNA is created similarly to the way that a duplicate strand of DNA is made. This time, however, only a small section of the DNA is copied by the mRNA.

After it is formed, the strand of mRNA leaves the unzipped section and, leaving the nucleus, enters the cytoplasm of the cell. In the cytoplasm it becomes associated with any

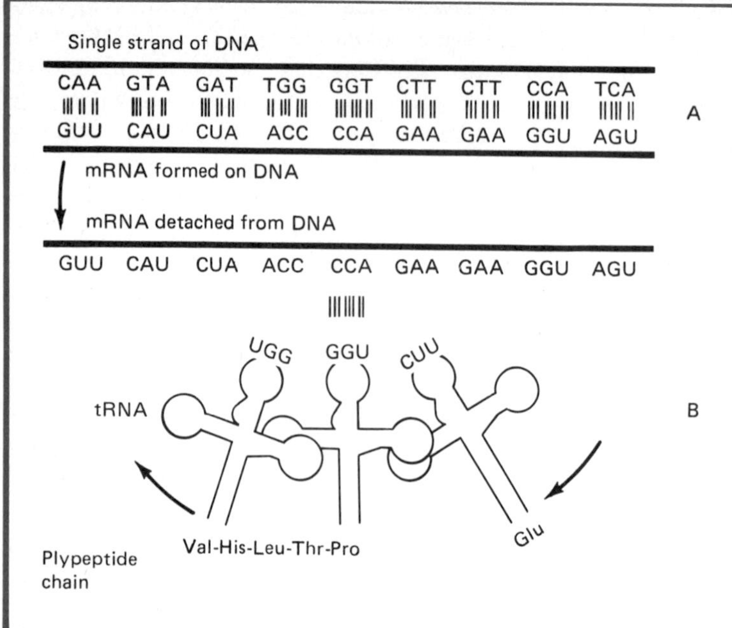

Figure 7 Highlights of protein synthesis. Messenger RNA (mRNA) is formed on a section of a DNA strand *(A)* before entering the cytoplasm and serving as a pattern for the making of a protein *(B)*. Transfer RNA (tRNA), carrying an amino acid, bonds to the mRNA, forming a polypeptide chain. (Moody, 1975)

of a number of small bodies, called *ribosomes*. In the ribosomes the mRNA serves as a pattern for lining up amino acids to produce a protein. This lining up is done by a second type of RNA, *transfer RNA,* or tRNA. This is a cloverleaf-shaped molecule that carries along one of the 20 amino acids in the cell. It can also link itself to a specific mRNA triplet. The tRNA nucleotides, already carrying their specific amino acids, enter the ribosomes and are bonded to that triplet on the mRNA strand for which it is matched (see Figure 7). The corresponding mRNA and tRNA triplets bond weakly, just long enough for the amino acid being carried by the tRNA to bond to amino acids carried by other tRNA molecules. In this way, polypeptide chains and, eventually, a whole protein are formed.

DNA thus contains all the genetic information for all the activities of all the body's cells. This information is carried from parent to offspring during meiosis and from cell to cell during mitosis. Thus, each cell contains the same genetic information. Yet cells obviously differ in their function. Nerve cells, for instance, secrete enzymes that allow electrical impulses to flow. Cells in the pancreas contain the same genetic information but specialize in making digestive enzymes. Cells first take on differing functions as the embryo develops, but the control process involved is not understood well.

Human Genetics

The application of the principles of heredity is not always straightforward. Human genotypes are complex, and it is difficult to study human groups over several generations. As a result, it is not possible to conduct experiments like Mendel's to determine the genetic control of human phenotypes. Other methods such as pedigree analysis and electrochemical techniques are therefore used to determine the number of alleles controlling a particular trait. These methods are also used to find out whether alleles are dominant or recessive and to determine the genotypes of individuals. Our knowledge of human genetics has been built up very slowly. We know most about *simple genetic traits*—those phenotypes controlled by only a few alleles at a single locus (or gene position) on one pair of homologous chromosomes. These traits include blood characteristics such as ABO blood groups.

We know much less about the genetic control of *complex genetic traits*—those phenotypes controlled by a large number of alleles at many loci. Most of the visible features of the body such as stature, weight, and skin color are controlled in this way. Although efforts are being made to understand the genetic control of such features, they are not completely understood for two reasons: (1) We cannot precisely identify the number of different genes involved, and (2) all of these phenotypes are influenced by the environment. In the sections that follow, we will examine how the genetics of simple and complex traits are studied.

Simple Traits

The study of the genetic basis of simple traits begins with an analysis of the phenotypes of the trait being studied. Since we cannot yet observe most genes directly, only the phenotype can actually be seen and measured. Once the various phenotypes are known, it is possible to figure out what genes are involved in their inheritance by constructing a *pedigree.* This is an analysis of the genotypes of related persons, based on a study of their phenotypes. Often done in the form of a diagram (such as the one in Figure 8), a pedigree shows the phenotypes and biological relationships of family members from at least two generations. Taking into account the number of alleles needed to explain the observed phenotypes and the possible presence of dominant and recessive alleles, it is possible to figure out the genotype of each individual.

ABO Blood Groups. The ABO blood groups were among the earliest traits to be analyzed in this way. Karl Landsteiner in 1900 noted that when blood cells of one individual were mixed with the serum of another, clumps formed in the mixture. This clumping was caused by an antigen-antibody reaction. *Antigens* are substances foreign to the host's body that may be part of a virus or bacterium. *Antibodies* are proteins that are formed specifically to attack foreign antigens that happen to find their way into an organism's body. In most cases, antibodies are formed only after foreign antigens enter the body. In the reac-

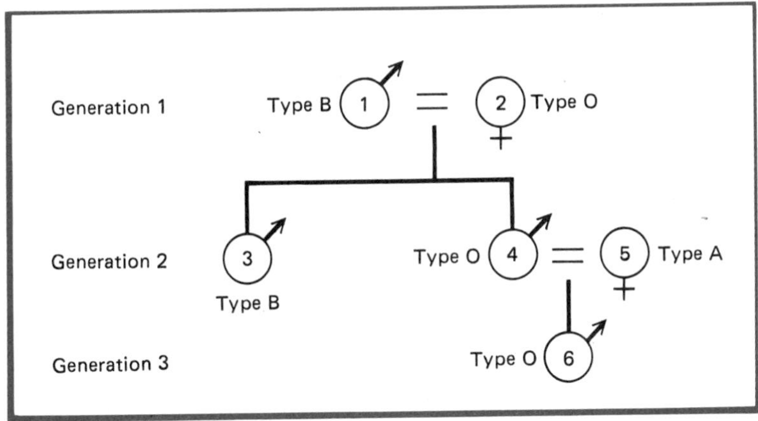

Figure 8 Pedigree showing blood type over three generations

tion that Landsteiner observed, antigens on the surface of the red blood cells were accompanied by antibodies in the serum in the blood. He isolated four distinct antigen groups based on the antigen-antibody reactions he observed. These groups are presently labeled A, B, AB, and O. The identification of the A, B, AB, and O phenotypes by antigen-antibody reactions is simple and straightforward (see Table 2).

Once the phenotypes were identified, scientists worked on determining the genes involved in the inheritance of these phenotypes. It was found that when type O persons mated with type A or type B persons, their children were more likely to be type A or B than O. The children of persons with A or B type showed phenotype AB. In 1925, the existence of three alleles was proposed: A, B, and O. Each individual possessed two of these alleles, one on each member of a single homologous chromosome pair. Thus, there were six possible genotypes: AA, AO, BB, BO, AB, and OO. But because O was not often expressed in the offspring of persons with type A or B it was assumed to be recessive to both A and B alleles. As a result, individuals with type AA or AO show A phenotypes, and individuals with type BB or BO show B phenotypes. Because A and B phenotypes were expressed together in some persons, it was assumed that A and B alleles were *co-dominant.*

Knowing the genetic basis of the ABO blood types permits us to find genotypes by identifying the phenotypes. Examine, for instance, the pedigree in Figure 8. We know that the genotype of all the type O individuals can only be OO, because the O allele is recessive. If the individual had one O and an A or B allele, then the phenotype would either be A or B. Thus, the O phenotype is expressed only in the homozygous condition. However, we do not know the genotype of the type A and the type B individuals. They could just as easily be AA or AO, BB or BO. To find out requires a simple application of the principle of segregation. Only one of the two alleles of any parent can become part of the genotype of the offspring.

The key to figuring out these ABO genotypes is knowing that type O parents can only contribute O alleles to the next generation. They do not have any other gene to give. Thus, #3 must have a BO genotype. To be type B, he must have received a B allele (in this case from his father, #1), but he can only receive an O allele from his mother (#2).

The genotype of #1 can be determined by noting that one of his sons (#4) is OO. Number 1 must therefore have BO genotype to be the source of one of #4's O alleles. Bv the same token, we know that individua number 5 must be genotype AO, because her son is genotype OO.

Using these same principles, human geneticists have devised models for many human traits. Our knowledge is particularly complete for blood characteristics. In addition to ABO, many other antigen-antibody systems in the blood have been identified. The Rh, or rhesus antigen-antibody reaction, is perhaps the best known of these. The structure of hemoglobin in the red blood cells, the structure of white blood cells, and proteins in the serum are all known to be controlled by relatively few alleles at single locii.

Abnormal Traits. Principles of genetics based on the study of blood traits has greatly expanded our knowledge of many other traits as well. Among the most important of these are abnormal, or pathological, traits. Many of these phenotypes seriously threaten the health of the individual, and may even cause an early death. The genetic basis of these conditions is determined in the same way as for normal traits—by making pedigrees of affected individuals.

Like many normal traits, some pathological traits are caused by a dominant allele. Huntington's chorea is such a case. This is a disorder in which mental deterioration is accom-

Table 2 Identification of Phenotype by Antigen-Antibody Reactions

Phenotype	Antigen	Antibodies	Reaction
A	A	B	Clumps when cells with B antigens are introduced
B	B	A	Clumps when cells with A antigens are introduced
AB	A and B	none	No clumping
O	none	A and B	Clumps when cells with A, B, or A and B antigens are introduced

panied by uncontrollable involuntary movements. Presently, its victims do not recover. But because the average age of onset is 35, those affected may pass the allelle on to their children before the disease occurs. Another disease controlled by a dominant allele is retinoblastoma, a cancer of the retina that occurs among children. It is quickly fatal unless the affected eye is removed. If children survive the disease, however, they too can pass on the responsible allele to their children.

More often, such traits seem to be controlled by recessive alleles. In this case, the disease is only manifested if the person is homozygous recessive for the affected allele. Cystic fibrosis is a recessive defect in which the glands do not work normally. The glands work properly if the individual has two normal dominant alleles (CC), or is heterozygous (Cc). However, among those individuals who possess two recessive alleles (cc) pancreatic enzymes may not be secreted, sweat may contain elevated salt levels, and there may be an excess of secretion of thick mucus in the lungs. The last complication is dangerous because the lungs' air passages can be blocked, resulting in death by suffocation. A large number of metabolic disorders are also caused by recessive alleles. In these cases, an enzyme controlled by a normal dominant allele is not produced. This stops the process by which cells break down more complex molecules, which then become poisonous as they collect in the body.

Sex-Linked Traits. Not all genes assort independently. As we mentioned earlier, independent assortment occurs only if the genes controlling different traits are located on different chromosomes. In many instances, genes controlling two or more traits are inherited together because they are on the same chromosome. The best studied forms of linkage in humans have to do with traits that are located on the sex chromosomes. Sex is determined by two chromosomes, the so-called X and Y chromosomes. Males develop when one X and one Y chromosome appear in the zygote, and females develop when two X chromosomes are present. The Y chromosome is a shortened form of the X chromosome, so that many of the loci on the X have no homologous site on the Y. This affects the way X-linked traits are inherited in the two sexes. Red-green color blindness is 1 of about 60 X-linked traits. Females may have one of three genotypes: X^CX^C, X^CX^c, or X^cX^c. Since the normal X^C allele is dominant, the dominant homozygote and the heterozygote are phenotypically normal. Only the recessive homozygote will show the trait. Males, however, have only one X chromosome, and the locus for the red-green color blindness does not occur on the Y chromosome. Among males, therefore, there are only two possible genotypes (X^CY and X^cY). The first is phenotypically normal and the second produces color blindness. As a result of this sexual difference in inheritance, recessive X-linked traits are more likely to appear among males than among females.

Mutation—The Source of New Traits. In most cases genes are inherited from the parents. In rare instances, however, the genetic material is altered spontaneously during meiosis. Thus, the individual may possess a feature controlled by an allele not part of either parental genotype. Such a change in the genetic material is called a *mutation.*

In general, mutations are caused when the genes are altered in the gametes, or when the chromosomes in the gametes are rearranged. Changes in the genes or chromosomes of body cells may also occur, but these modifications are not passed on to offspring during reproduction.

Changes in the nucleotide sequence of a DNA molecule are called *point mutations.* One base of the nucleotide triplet may be substituted for another, or bases may be added or deleted from the sequence. These three kinds of change—*substitutions, additions,* and *deletions*—are responsible for a variety of genetic mutations. For example, a single amino substitution has been found to cause an alteration in the ability of human hemoglobin to bind oxygen. This abnormal hemoglobin, in turn, provokes a disease known as sickle-cell anemia, which reduces the life expectancy of its victims. Although mutations occur, they are seldom detected. They usually occur in combination with a normal dominant allele, and a normal phenotype results. It is not until the mutant allele is inherited in the homozygous condition at some later time that it is expressed. Dominant mutations are either rarer or have such a disastrous effect on cell functioning that the embryo may be spontaneously miscarried early in pregnancy.

Chromosomal rearrangements involve changes in the structure or number of chromosomes. They are visible with a microscope and have notable phenotypic consequences. One type of chromosomal rearrangement, called *nondisjunction,* is the failure of paired chromosomes to separate completely during meiosis. (See Figure 9.) This causes both chromosomes, not just one, to enter the gamete. *Down's Syndrome* (sometimes called infantile mongolism) is the result of nondisjunction in humans. Individuals suffering

Figure 9 **Nondisjunction can occur in either of two ways**

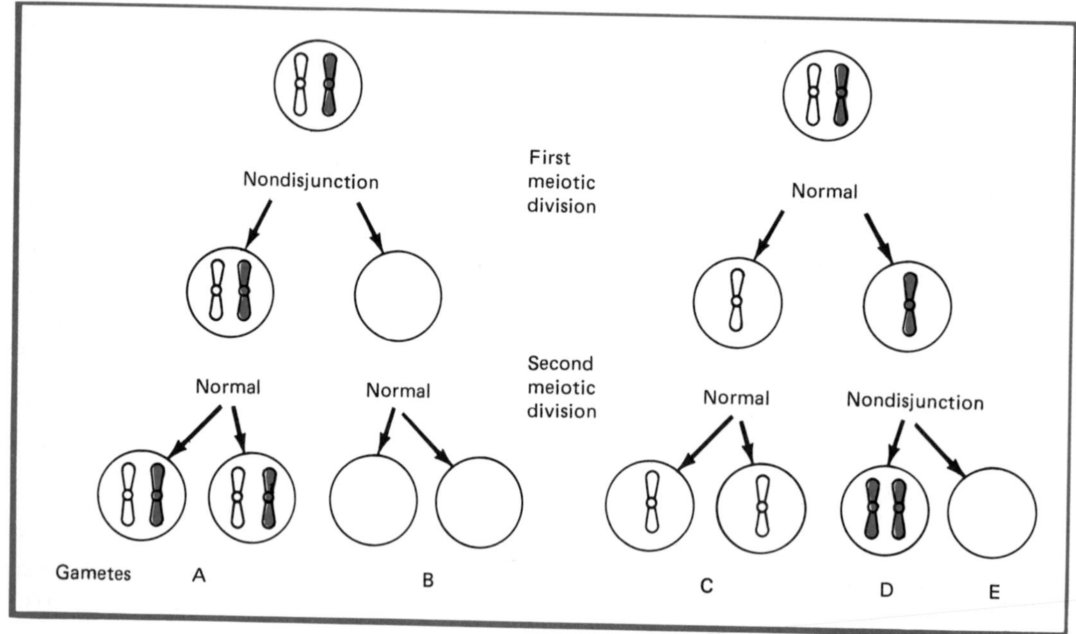

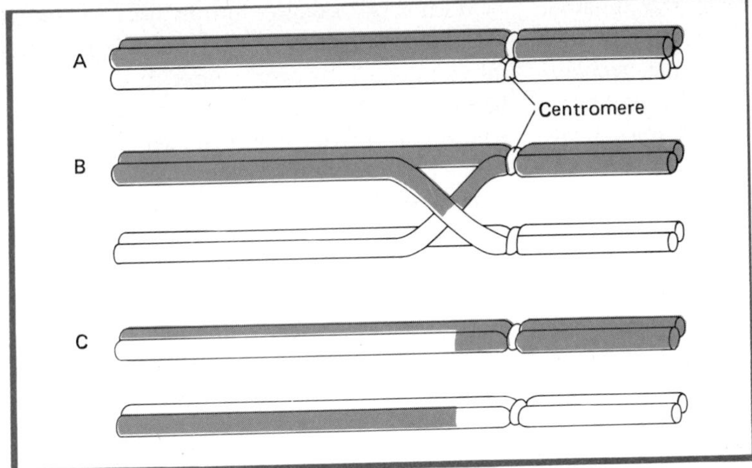

Figure 10 **Translocation.** (Moody, 1975)

from Down's Syndrome have 47 chromosomes instead of the usual 46.

Other types of chromosomal rearrangements include *translocation,* in which one chromosome is broken and then joined together with a piece from another chromosome. (See Figure 10.) *Inversions* occur when a segment of a chromosome is broken off, turned around, and reinserted backwards.

Much research has been devoted to the causes of mutations. X-rays and other radiation, and chemicals such as mustard gas (used as a weapon in World War I) and formaldehyde all contribute to mutation. Scientists have been very concerned about the effects of ionizing radiation, which arises not only from medical and dental X-rays but also from the operation of nuclear power plants and the detonation of atomic bombs. Studies on fruit flies and mice, for example, show that as dosages of radiation increase so do the number of mutations. The effects of radiation may also accumulate. A low dosage kept up over a long period of time can have the same effect as a large dosage occurring rapidly. Because sperm are produced continually but all eggs are created before birth, male gametes are more prone to show the effects of accumulated mutations. A type of dwarfism, and a certain disease causing skull and limb deformities are three to five times greater among the children of older males than they are among the children of younger males, regardless of the age of the mother (Vogel, 1965).

As we will discover in the next chapter, mutations are rather rare events. Even when they occur, they are usually not detectable. Most traits are controlled by alleles inherited from parents. They therefore follow the pattern of trait inheritance we have discussed in this chapter. Nonetheless, mutations provide an important source of new variation in all human populations.

Complex Traits

Complex traits are controlled by a large number of genes and can be strongly influenced by the environment. Thus, there is no direct correspondence between phenotype and genotype. It is impossible to identify all the alleles that control a given trait. Height and head shape, unlike blood type, are controlled by a number of interacting genes, and researchers may never be able to define the genetic basis of such traits.

Complex traits are of two kinds: They can be part of the physical structure of the body and measurable in terms of size, weight, and shape. These are *morphological traits.* Or they can be traits of body function, such as breathing or digestion. These are *physiological traits.* If we look at the lungs, for example, we can measure the dimensions of their tissues (morphological traits) and measure the amount of oxygen or carbon dioxide that passes through their membranes (physiological traits). Because function is so closely linked with structure, however, the distinction between the two is more an analytical convenience than a reality.

Heritability studies provide one way of finding the genetic component of complex traits. Pedigrees establishing the degree of biological relationship are just as important here as they are in the study of simple traits. In theory, all related individuals share some genetic material. But the actual number of shared genes can be determined more accurately for some relatives than for others. According to the principles of meiosis, for example, we know that each parent gives one member of every homologous chromosome pair to the zygote of an offspring. Therefore, one-half of the offspring's genetic material comes from and is identical to that of each parent. Each parent and an offspring thus "share" one-half of their genetic material. Monozygotic (identical) twins, on the other hand, share all of their genetic material. This occurs because the egg that has been fertilized divides by mitosis and thus creates two identical zygotes. These subsequently develop into individuals with exactly the same genetic material.

The amount of genetic material shared by other close relatives can only be determined on the basis of the laws of probability. Siblings, for example, share the same parents but are the results of two separate meiotic episodes. If an entirely random segregation of chromosomes occurs at the time of each meiosis, the amount of genetic material shared by two siblings will be one-half. Only one-quarter of the shared chromosomes will come from each parent.

With large samples, probability estimates are reasonable methods of estimating shared inheritance. However, these estimates are likely to be wrong when applied to one person. Some siblings may share more than one-half of their chromosomes, and some may share less. Because of this problem, we will concentrate on heritability studies comparing parents and offspring or monozygotic twins.

If the trait in question is controlled by genes that are equally dominant (and most seem to be), then we would expect the degree of similarity between relatives to approximate the amount of shared genetic material. That is, for a given complex trait, offspring ought to have a value somewhere intermediate between those of their parents, and identical twins ought to have the same values. Any deviation from these expected results can then be explained in terms of environmental influences.

As a result of this type of study, we know that some complex traits have high heritability, that is, they are under strong genetic control. Others have low heritability, that is, they are strongly influenced by the environment. The number of ridges on the fingertips, for example, has a heritability of about 95 to 97 percent (Holt, 1961). This means that 95 to 97 percent of the individual variation in the number of ridges is caused by genetic factors. Height also has a high heritability. Studies on identical twins raised apart showed a heritability of 90 percent (Bodmer & Cavalli-Sforza, 1976). Weight, on the other hand, has a low heritability. Studies on monzygotic twins raised apart show a heritability of only 77 percent. This means that a considerable amount of individual variation in weight is caused by environmental factors—most probably diet and disease.

In some cases, the existence of extreme as well as intermediate phenotypes permits a more precise estimate of the number of genes that control a complex trait. This is the case with skin color, which is measured in terms of the amount of light of certain wavelengths reflected from the surface of the skin. The skin color of children who have parents with dark and light skin, respectively, suggests that the trait may be controlled by three or four genes.

Heritability studies have also been used to estimate the genetic component of various diseases. Schizophrenia and multiple sclerosis have a very high heritability, diabetes has a somewhat lower heritability, and congenital heart disease and epilepsy have relatively low heritabilities (Newcombe, 1964). Studies of this sort are of great value in understanding whether diseases are caused by genetic or environmental agents.

Understanding the genetic basis of simple and complex phenotypes is the basis of our knowledge of how and under what circumstances biological evolution occurs in human populations. The evolutionary application of this knowledge is the focus of the next chapter.

Summary

1. The mechanism by which traits are passed from one generation to the next was first understood by Gregor Mendel, who performed his experimental work in the 1850s and 1860s. Mendel's experiments dealt with the inheritance of certain characteristics in garden peas.

2. When Mendel cross-pollinated plants with long stems and short stems, the offspring (the *F_1 generation*) had only long stems. But when members of the F_1 generation were bred together, the resulting plants, *(the F_2 generation)* were about 75 percent long-stemmed and about 25 percent short-stemmed. The fact that the short stem strait had reappeared after being absent in the F_1 generation suggested to Mendel that the factors controlling the inheritance of traits existed in the plant cells as particles that do not blend together. Later the particles hypothesized by Mendel were named *genes.*

3. Mendel also suggested that traits such as stem length were controlled by two forms. Furthermore, he determined that the form of the gene for long stem was *dominant* over the form of the gene for short stem, which was *recessive*. These different forms of the same gene are now called *alleles*.

4. The genetic makeup of an organism is called its *genotype.* The physical characteristics of an organism that are controlled by the action of alleles make up the *phenotype.* When the genotype includes two alleles of the same type, it is said to be *homozygous.* Two different paired alleles comprise a *heterozygous* genotype.

5. Mendel also proposed that the alleles of each genotype pair segregate, or separate, during reproduction and enter different gametes (or sex cells).

6. In the nineteenth century, improved microscopes and tissue preparation techniques allowed researchers to identify long, thin threads that appeared in the cell nucleus just before cell division. These structures, called *chromosomes,* were later found to carry the genes. Each gene position along a chromosome is called a *locus.*

7. There are two types of cell division. *Mitosis* is the type of division that occurs in *somatic* cells (cells other than those in the ovaries and testes). *Meiosis* is the division of cells to produce gametes.

8. In mitosis, the original cell divides, creating two new cells. Chromosomes duplicate and then separate so that both new cells receive the same number of chromosomes as the original cell. In meiotic division, four sex cells are produced. Chromosomes duplicate, but divide twice so that each of the gametes receives only one member of every homolo-

gous chromosome pair. In meiosis, the gametes receive one-half the number of chromosomes in the parent cell. At fertilization, the union of gametes forms a new cell (a zygote) with the full number of chromosomes.

9. On the chemical level, genetic material has been identified as *deoxyribonucleic acid (DNA)*, found in cell nuclei. The double-helix structure of DNA was established by Watson and Crick in 1953. This structure helps us to understand the nature of chromosome *replication*, or duplication. *Messenger* and *transfer ribonucleic acid (RNA)* organize chains of amino acids to form proteins. The messenger RNA is a copy of the DNA nucleotide sequence. Thus, DNA is the source of information for all protein synthesis.

10. *Simple genetic traits* are phenotypes controlled by a few alleles at one gene position (or *locus*). The genetic control of simple traits may be modeled by setting up *pedigrees*, or records of the traits and the biological relationships of family members.

11. A, B, and O blood types are simple genetic traits that have been studied with pedigrees. The alleles for A and for B blood types are dominant over the O allele.

12. *Sex-linked traits* are controlled by alleles located on the chromosomes that determine the sex of the individual. Red-green color blindness is an example of a sex-linked trait. Most sex-linked traits are more common among males than among females.

13. Two types of mutations provide a source of new traits: *point mutations* and *chromosomal rearrangements*. Changes in the nucleotide sequence, such as *substitution*, *addition*, or *deletion* of a base of the nucleotide triplet, are called point mutations. Chromosomal rearrangements include *nondisjunction*, *translocation*, and *inversion*.

14. Mutations have been linked to radiation and chemicals in the environment. The rate at which mutations occur is rather low, but mutations do provide an important source of new variants in human populations.

15. *Complex genetic traits* are determined by a number of genes and are strongly affected by the environment. *Morphological traits* are part of the physical structure of the body and can be measured in terms of size, weight, and shape. *Physiological traits* are related to body functions, such as breathing and digestion.

16. Heritability studies let us distinguish the genetic from the environmental aspects of complex traits. Heritability is that proportion of all variability in a trait that is under genetic control.

10 The Study of Human Diversity

IN earlier chapters we traced the gradual evolution of the early hominids from Miocene primates, and the emergence of humans from these hominids. In this chapter we shall study the evolution of humans today. This study must begin with an understanding of the origins and nature of the physical differences among people. In our coverage of genetics, we discussed the genetic basis of variation. Here, we shall talk about how the distribution of traits, and in some cases the genes that control them, can be measured in populations. We shall go on to explain how these measurements can be used as clues to the way evolutionary forces are molding the traits of human population in the present day.

Race and the Attempt to Classify Human Groups

Human groups have long been aware of the biological and cultural differences among human beings. The exploration and conquests of the ancient Greeks revealed to them that all people in the world do not share the same physical characteristics. This awareness is reflected in their art as well as in historic references to Pygmies, to black Africans, and to blonde Europeans. The Romans, Chinese, Egyptians, and people of other early civilizations also were aware of these differences.

After the fall of Rome, however, European contacts with different peoples were sharply reduced, and Western ideas of human diversity became rather limited.

Early Classifications

During the sixteenth century, at the beginning of the Age of Discovery, European explorers, merchants, and travelers once again made contact with groups having different physical features. At the same time, scientists grew restless from centuries of relying on the word of classical writers, and became interested in first-hand observation and classification of nature. Even so, most of the Europeans who first tried to classify humans did not venture abroad to study human populations. Instead they relied on descriptions and stories, added to by their study of skulls and by casual observations of foreigners who had found their way to Europe. As a result, early taxonomies, like that of Linnaeus published in 1735, were based on limited data. Linnaeus's classification of *Homo sapiens* divided the species into four groups, based on skin color and place of origin: black Africans, red-skinned Americans, darkish Asians, and white Europeans. These categories still form the basis of modern popular ideas of race in the West.

In 1775, J. F. Blumenbach (1752–1840), a German physiologist and anatomist, produced a racial taxonomy that influenced scientific racial classification for over 100 years. He based his taxonomy on many physical traits, but paid particular attention to the measurement of human skulls. He believed that skull features were the most important criteria of race.

Blumenbach identified five races: Caucasian, Asiatic, American, Ethiopian, and Malay. Although he knew that some humans would not fit into any one of these types perfectly, his classification had the effect of dividing humanity into units with sharp boundaries. Because most eighteenth- and nineteenth-century Europeans had only casual meetings with non-European groups and knew nothing of the subtle variations that can occur between neighboring groups, the idea of five distinct groups seemed reasonable. As awareness of human variation grew, however, the arbitrary nature of racial classification became more apparent. (See Figure 1.)

The Beginnings of the Scientific Study of Race

The precise measurement of skull features was the springboard for the systematic and scientific description of human differences. In the latter part of the nineteenth century, and through the first half of the twentieth century, the study of race had two basic goals: to develop a systematic racial classification for *H. sapiens* and to trace human races back in time.

The search for a workable classification system continued well into the twentieth century. Many different traits were used as the basis of these schemes. Skull shape and skin color were often employed, but other features were used as well. In 1889, for example, J. Deniker presented a system that made the texture and color of the hair the main distinguishing factor. On this basis, he proposed that humans could be divided into 29 races. But the groups identified by using one trait often did not correspond to those using another. People with straight black hair, for example, are equally likely to exist in Asia, America, and Europe. And people living in any one area are likely to have a variety of hair types.

To attempt to solve this problem, scientists developed racial groupings based on more than one trait. In 1930, for instance, A. C. Haddon (1885–1940), a founder of modern British anthropology, published a multiple-trait analysis that distinguished races primarily on the basis of hair texture, but also on skin color, height, and skull shape. Nordics were definable by their wavy hair, light skin and

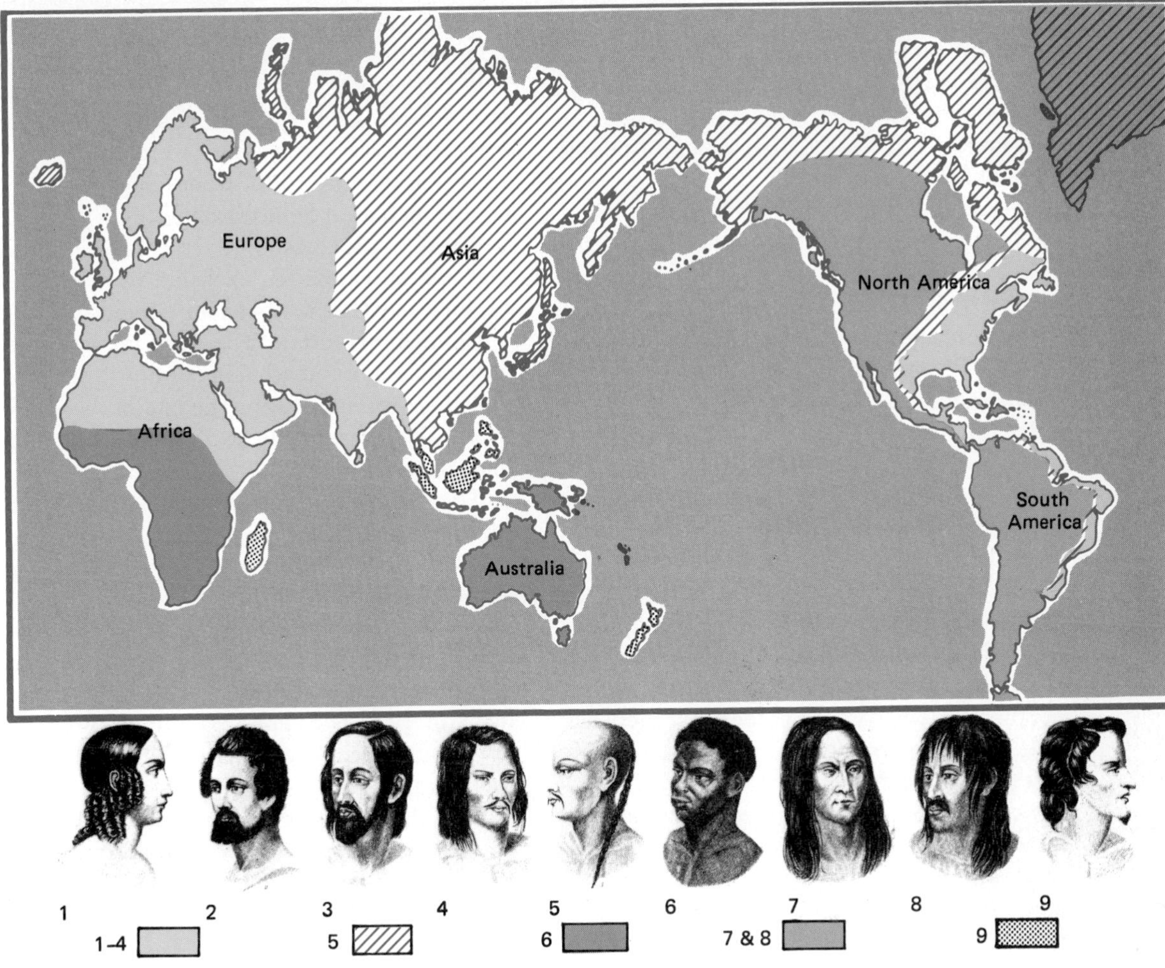

Figure 1 An early distribution of the world's races as defined by Blumenbach. The faces show "typical" members of each race. Numbers 1–4 are Caucasians; 5 is an Asiatic; 6 is an Ethiopian, 7 and 8 are American Indians, and 9 is a Malay.

hair, blue or gray eyes, tall stature, and rounded heads. Negroes had curly hair, short or tall stature, dark skin, and relatively long, thin heads. In this approach, it was only important that most of the individual traits match the definition. Thus, an individual with brown eye color could still have been classified as a Nordic if he or she fit the definition in all other ways.

Today, there is great debate among those who still use the concept of race. The multiple-trait approach has led many scientists to propose that there is a large number of small races, rather than a small number of large races. The larger the number of criteria, the fewer the people that satisfy all of them. One scientist who favors many small races restricts the definition of race to "a breeding population characterized by frequencies of inherited traits that differ from those of other populations of the same species" (Goldsby, 1977). Because this definition equates race with the local population, it is practially useless as a means of classification, since it would result in as many races as there are breeding groups—thousands.

Others see race as a large group of people who inhabit geographically definable parts of the world, but who share very few characteristics. Stanley Garn, for example, divides the world into nine races: American, Polynesian, Micronesian, Melanesian, Australian, Asiatic, Indian, European, and African (Garn, 1971).

Difficulties with the Concept of Race

There has never been, nor is there ever likely to be agreement on the number of races. There are two reasons for this that go beyond the superficial arguments about how many races there are and strike at the heart of the concept of race itself. First, in light of increasing awareness of the differences among people, it has become apparent that the isolation necessary to produce easily identifiable races has not been present in human evolution. Migration or the continual exchange of mates between groups creates subtle gradations that defy the creation of racial boundaries. Second, it has become clear that the variation in some features is caused by environmental influences that affect the growth process rather than genetic differences.

The problem raised by persons who fit neatly into none of the existing racial categories has been tackled with the suggestion that at some time in the past racial differences were more distinct and that migration only recently created mixed populations. It was assumed that early in the history of the genus *Homo,* human populations were isolated long enough for the basic differences among the primary races to evolve. For a long time these groups supposedly remained distinct from one another. But as humans developed the means to move long distances, composite races were created when members of two primary races mated. Some racial classifications of the 1930s and 1940s expressly divided the world into primary races and composite races (Comas, 1960). Even today racial maps show groups as they were thought to exist before A.D. 1500, when contact among people increased dramatically.

There is no reason to believe, however, that migration and the exchange of mates between groups has not been important throughout human evolution. The early migration of hominids out of Africa and the flow of people into the Americas during the end of the Pleistocene Epoch are only two examples of such mass movement.

The second problem with these racial classifications is that the most commonly studied features, especially those of the skull, are shaped to a significant degree by the environment. A classic study done by Franz Boas (1858–1942), an American anthropologist, dramatized this point (Boas, 1910). He found that American-born children of East European immigrants had significantly different head shapes than did their parents. If skull features do include such a large environmental factor, he reasoned, then they are not the genetically stable features on which racial classifications should be based.

Recent Attempts to Define Races

Scientists have since attempted to find workable racial criteria in traits that do not reflect environmental influence. In the late 1940s and early 1950s blood groups were first used as a means of racial classification. Blood type is directly controlled by a small number of alleles. There are no gradations of blood type caused by varying environmental influence. Researchers can easily determine a person's blood type and from this information figure out which alleles for blood type are present. Races could then be distinguished on the basis of differing gene frequencies.

However, even with the use of blood types

racial boundaries are impossible to draw. We would expect racially different groups to have sharply different gene frequencies. But maps of the frequency of alleles controlling blood type show that in some areas there are only gradual shifts of frequency from one population to the next. Here, the frequencies of blood group alleles form a *cline,* a gradual shift in gene frequencies over a stretch of territory. (See Figure 2.) Sometimes, however, the gene frequencies may differ radically from village to village. In the first case, very distantly related people could be placed in the same race because the populations of which they are a part share the same allele frequency. In the second case, persons who are quite closely related could be placed in different races because their populations have different allele frequencies.

In the last few years, researchers have expanded their study of traits that are not shaped by the environment. They have attempted to define how various kinds of groups differ in terms of a cluster of such traits. But because the groups under study tend to be large and defined in social or political terms, this research has not been very useful. Granted, multiple-trait analysis of national, ethnic, and religious groups has proved helpful as a means of measuring the degree to which they share various genes. But it tends to mask the variation within the groups it analyzes. Because these heterogeneous groups are defined in cultural terms before the research begins, the method cannot identify units of people who should be classed together on the biological basis that they share certain physical traits. While this technique has been used to indicate biological relationships, it has not proved to be a particularly effective or objective way of classifying humans.

Tracing the Origins of Races

During the first half of the twentieth century, many scientists turned to the fossil rec-

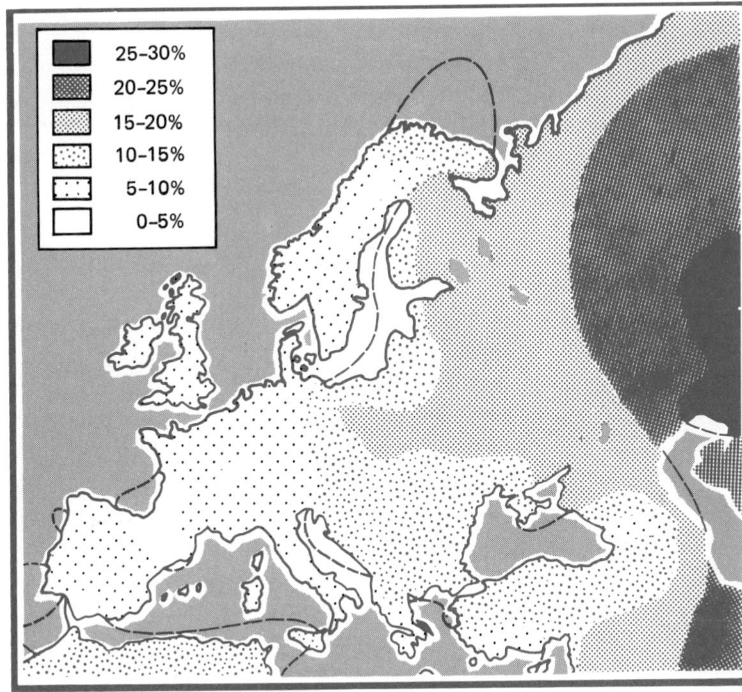

Figure 2 A cline of frequencies for the gene responsible for Type B blood. (Based on studies by A. E. Mourant)

ord for evidence of the origins of apparent racial differences. This idea has a sound biological basis if it can be proved that racial groups (however defined) have been isolated in the course of human evolution. Many notable physical anthropologists have been convinced of this idea and have attempted to look for the ancestors of modern "races" in the fossil record. The most recent attempt is that of Carleton Coon, which is presented in his book *The Origin of Races* (1962).

Such attempts are full of difficulties. The body parts that are preserved as fossils are features that could have changed as a result of interactions with the environment during the lifetime of the individual. In fact, we meet the same problems identifying ancient races that we do defining modern races. Even if these problems could somehow be overcome, the fossil record is still far from complete enough to supply evidence of the quality needed to establish the presence of clusters of traits that together define a race.

In addition, if it is impossible to isolate sets of physical features to define modern races, it should be equally impossible to do so among ancient peoples. As the physical form of the species has evolved, so too should its races. Some critics also point out that theories such as Coon's assume that racial populations remained reproductively isolated for a great stretch of time. But if races were separate biological entities for as long as Coon and others have suggested, why are humans not more than one species now? (Dobzhansky, 1963).

Race as a Cultural Concept

Why has it been impossible to agree upon a definition of race? The answer lies in the fact that the racial categories people use are often very revealing indicators of their social values. The way in which one sees other people is culturally conditioned. Recognizing the race of another is something one learns in the process of growing up in a culture. Some cultures recognize many more shades of skin color than do Americans, for instance, who tend to lump individuals into white or black. But Brazilians, who, like Americans, have a large black population, employ over 500 different racial labels (Kottak, 1967). Each label corresponds to some phenotypical trait. Because the gradations are so subtle, an individual whose skin becomes suntanned, for example, may automatically become a member of a race different from his or her previous one.

Concepts of race are so ambiguous and so much a product of cultural bias that *race,* as it is traditionally applied to humans, has no clear biological meaning. Thus, by using the term, one runs the risk of having it interpreted in ways that were not intended. No anthropologist would deny that race is an important way of organizing human variation in *cultural terms.* But these culturally defined categories cannot be translated into objective, clear biological categories. For this reason, physical anthropologists are abandoning the use of racial categories in studying human variation.

The Study of Human Populations

If we cannot use race to discuss and explain human variation, what can we use? Remember, we would like to define categories that will tell us something about the processes of evolution. The solution comes from combining genetics with the principles of evolutionary biology. All sexually reproducing animals must seek mates at some time, or make no contribution to the next generation. Mates are not sought randomly, but among those individuals living nearby. Long-term interactions between individuals develop that give the social group some permanence. Such behavior is very elaborate among humans, whose culture bind people together. It is in such interbreeding groups that evolution takes place. These groups are the populations we discussed in Chapter 3. A complete understanding of human variation must begin with an understanding of why local populations of humans may share certain traits.

A major goal of the study of modern human variation is to understand how, and in what directions, evolution is occurring at the present time among our own species. To do so, physical anthropologists must identify the forces at work and the way they operate to produce biological change. We have already discussed the genetic processes responsible for individual differences. In this section we shall apply the same genetic principles to the study of populations.

Defining a Human Population

A population is a group of individuals who are more likely to mate among themselves than among others of the same species. There are two factors that could restrict breeding with nongroup individuals:

1. Geographic factors can restrict the movement of people, thereby limiting possible mates to members of the local group. Although modern means of travel have somewhat reduced geographical obstacles, many groups still remain isolated because they cannot afford to, or do not choose to, migrate. The populations of many islands in the South Pacific are good examples.
2. Social factors such as marriage rules can prevent members of neighboring groups from mating with one another. In many areas of the world, people tend to marry residents of the same village. If the village is the breeding unit it becomes the focus of population studies. The breeding unit, or population, may be smaller or larger than a village, but it is always defined by a set of values, attitudes, and ideas of appropriate behavior. Thus, it is not surprising that the ethnographic concept of a culture as a group of individuals with a shared way of life is often synonomous with the biological concept of population.

Evolutionary Forces at the Population Level

Studies of modern human populations tend to concentrate on short-term biological changes because the human lifespan is long, and relevant data for previous generations often do not exist. By studying *microevolution,* or short-term biological change, we can gain a fairly clear understanding of how and why such change occurs. *Macroevolution,* in contrast, is physical change that has occurred over millions of years. The study of macroevolution tends to be more descriptive and less able to produce the sort of data needed to understand the action of all evolutionary processes.

Studies of microevolution have shown that biological differences among groups, and differences among stages of the same group at different times, are the result of four different kinds of forces: (1) mutation, the ultimate source of new genetic material, (2) gene flow, changes caused by migration,(3) genetic drift, random fluctuations affected by population size, and (4) natural selection. Of these processes, only natural selection produces a pattern of change in a population that is directed by the environment. Genes controlling nonadaptive traits become less and less frequent in the population, while those controlling adaptive features become more common over time. Changes in gene frequency caused by gene flow, genetic drift, and mutation, unlike those brought about by natural selection, occur randomly with respect to the environment. It is only by chance that they could produce a group of genes of great survival value to a population in a given environment. Instead, these forces seem to operate under the umbrella of natural selection. Selection reduces the effect of genes if they begin to increase the frequency of maladaptive traits or intensifies it if they begin to increase the frequency of adaptive traits. Although genetic drift, gene flow, and mutation contribute to evolution, their action is shaped in the long run by selection.

Simple Genetic Traits

Having identified the population, the next step is somehow to detect and measure the rate of biological change. If we are to assess the action of evolutionary forces, we must be able to measure change in a population. As we discussed earlier, simple traits are controlled by only a few alleles, and complex traits are controlled by large numbers of alleles. When studying a simple genetic trait we can determine the genotype responsible for the trait. (See Figure 3.) Once we know the genotype of each person in the population, the number of times a given allele appears in the population can be counted and compared over time. Changes in the number of times a particular allele appears from one generation to the next would be clear evidence of evolution.

The way to determine how widespread an allele is in a population is to figure its frequency. This number expresses the proportion represented by a given allele of all the alleles that occur in a population at the same locus on a chromosome pair. The first step in mapping the frequency is to determine all the genotypes possibly responsible for the observed phenotypes. In Table 1, for example, we have tested a population of 1,000 persons for their ABO blood phenotypes. We know that persons who are type AB must be genotype AB. That is, they must have one A allele and one B allele. Individuals who are phenotype O must have two O alleles. But we do not know the genotype of individuals who are phenotype A or B. As you will recall from the last chapter, it is difficult to find out the genotype because the dominant A and B alleles mask the presence of recessive O alleles. It is necessary to establish genotypes by figuring out a pedigree. This is done as described earlier.

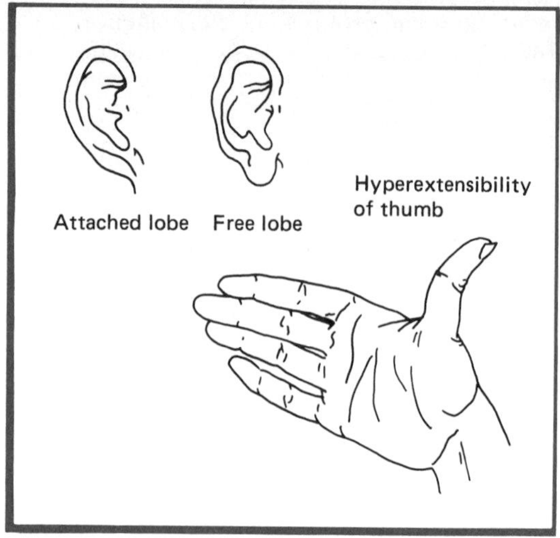

Figure 3 Three simple genetic traits

In our example, half of the A phenotypes were genotype AA and half were AO; 50 of the type B persons were genotype BB and 100 were BO. The next step is to count the total number of A, B, and O alleles in the population. In this case, there were a total of 450 A alleles, 350 B alleles, and 1,200 O alleles, for a total of 2,000 alleles. Dividing the number of each specific allele by the total number of alleles gives us the frequency of A, B, and O alleles.

In human populations, changes in the frequency of alleles controlling simple traits as a result of gene flow and genetic drift are the easiest to study. Mutation is somewhat more difficult to study, and demonstrating the action of natural selection on simple traits is the most difficult. All of these processes will be discussed below.

Gene Flow. Natural selection shapes the gene frequencies of a given population so that its members are adapted to local environmental

Table 1 Calculation of Gene Frequencies

- Assume we have a population of 1,000 individuals with the following genotype distribution:

AA = 100	These individuals are phenotypically type A	
AO = 100		
BB = 50	These individuals are phenotypically type B	
BO = 100		
AB = 150	These individuals are phenotypically type AB	
OO = 500	These individuals are phenotypically type O	
1000		

- We next must count the number of A, B, and O alleles in the population. Note that each individual possesses two alleles, so that there are a total of 1,000 (individuals) × 2 (alleles each) = 2,000 alleles in the population

- To count the number of alleles, the following scheme can be used:

	Number of				
	A alleles		*B alleles*		*O alleles*
100 AA individuals	200				
100 AO individuals	100				100
50 BB individuals			100		
100 BO individuals			100		100
150 AB individuals	150		150		
500 OO individuals					1,000
TOTAL (2,000 alleles)	450	+	350	+	1,200

- $\frac{\text{450 A alleles}}{\text{2,000 alleles}} = 22.5\%$ $\frac{\text{350 B alleles}}{\text{2,000 alleles}} = 17.5\%$ $\frac{\text{1,200 O alleles}}{\text{2,000 alleles}} = 60\%$

pressures. Gene frequencies, therefore, vary from one environment to the next. When members leave one population and mate with members of another, they are likely to contribute different genes to the new gene pool. *Gene flow* is the resulting movement of genes across population boundaries.

The degree to which genes from one population affect the gene frequency of a neighboring population depends on two factors:(1) the number of persons that migrate and (2) the degree of difference in gene frequencies that exists between the two populations. In many human societies, cultural rules promoting marriage with members outside the group ensure a steady flow of genes between populations. Male members of Bushman bands, for example, must seek mates in other bands. If mates are exchanged in this way for a long time, then the two groups become genetically similar.

Gene flow is the biological link that binds all human populations together. Genes that are introduced into a population by migrants can be taken to still other populations by their descendants. Because no group is isolated for very long from this web, we can assume that gene flow has been important in maintaining the unity of our species for the last million years or so. But when we talk of this unity, we are not implying that all groups have had equal opportunity to mate with members of all other groups. Eskimos do not marry Australian aborigines. The two groups are linked together by a large number of intervening populations, each of which exchanges genes with its neighbors. There is no break in the chain, and most genes are shared. Sometimes natural selection in a local area keeps a gene from becoming common in a population by rendering its migrant carrier less fit. Only in this case may gene flow be interrupted.

Genetic Drift. Genetic drift is a random change in gene frequencies that is associated with small population size. We can illustrate this kind of change by looking at a single trait. Say, for instance, that an individual has type B blood and possesses one B and one O allele. If that person has one child, the chance that the gamete producing the zygote will not contain the B allele is 1 out of 2. One has the same probability of getting heads or tails with a flip of a coin. If a person has 2 children, the chance that the B allele will not be passed on is the same as the chance that heads will not appear in two flips of the coin: $^1/_2 \times {}^1/_2 = {}^1/_4$. With 3 children, it is 1 chance out of 8; with 4 children, it is 1 chance out of 16. The greater the number of children, the greater the chance that the allele will be passed on.

In small populations, however, where the number of children that each individual has is relatively small, the chance that one of these alleles will *not* be passed on is quite high. As a result, random changes in the frequency of alleles may occur from one generation to the next. The larger the population, the less likely it is that genetic drift will occur.

How is genetic drift found and studied? The simplest method is to examine gene frequencies in small, isolated, but genetically related groups living in a similar environment. If the frequency of a given allele changes from population to population, it is possible that drift has occurred. Neighboring populations in the New Guinea highlands, for instance, often have dramatically different gene frequencies. Because the highland environment is uniform, the same selective forces would act on all the populations in the same way. Thus, it is unlikely that the differences in gene frequency are the result of differing selective forces. Natural selection is therefore probably not the cause of the genetic differences. Gene flow would increase similarity between groups. Mutation would not act with enough speed to produce the observed differences. So, by process of elimination, the genetic differences among the populations are attributed to genetic drift (Gajdusek, 1964).

Though it is fairly easy to name genetic drift as the source of variation in a population, it is much more difficult to spot it as it is happening. Only genetic data spanning many generations could provide conclusive evidence of genetic drift, and this kind of information is lacking for human populations (Morris, 1971). Still, information on random changes within the span of one generation can give evidence of special cases of genetic drift.

The *founder effect* is often considered such a special case. It occurs when the numbers of the original population are sharply decreased in some way. A natural disaster may wipe out a segment of the population randomly, or for cultural reasons the group might split up into subgroups that migrate. In either case the remaining population becomes the founder group. If this group is small, it will not accurately reflect the genetic makeup of the original group. Some alleles may be present in higher frequency than they were originally, and others in lower frequency. Thus, the founder group will probably differ biologically from the original population.

An excellent example of the founder effect has been documented among the Yąnomamö Indians of the Brazil-Venezuela border area. The mates most socially acceptable to Yąnomamö men are their *cross cousins*—daughters of either their mother's brother or father's sister. Mates are often drawn from a single lineage. As a result, gene flow is restricted, and different interbreeding lineages have unique gene frequencies. The Yąnomamö social system can only organize a limited number of people in a village structure. When the population grows beyond a certain point, rivalries cause the village to split. In the split, however, pairs of lineages that have been exchanging mates tend to remain together. When a village containing several of these pair lineages splits, new villages established by each of the pairs may have markedly different gene frequencies.

A phenomenon closely related to genetic drift is *inbreeding,* which results from the mating of biological relatives. Inbred individuals are born as the result of the mating of related persons. Because such persons share many genes, the effect of inbreeding is to increase the frequency of certain genotypes. The children of biologically related parents are more likely to be homozygous for any given allele.

Because inbreeding may increase the frequency with which harmful alleles appear homozygously, it may also reduce the fertility of the population. A study of the Goyigamas, a caste of Sinhalese-speaking Buddhists in Sri Lanka (an island in the Indian Ocean, southeast of India), shows that this group, among which there is a high degree of marriage among relatives, has a birthrate 16 percent lower than it was in the 1920s (Reid, 1976).

Mutation. Mutation rates are difficult to know with certainty. Many factors may intervene between a change in the DNA nucleotide sequence (a so-called point mutation) and a noticeable phenotype expression of the mutation. The most information is available for dominant mutation rates. These are determined simply by counting the number of persons whose phenotype reveals the presence of the mutation. Individuals with a variant known to be controlled by a dominant allele would be counted under this method if neither parent has possessed the trait. A recessive mutation, when paired with a dominant allele, goes unnoticed, because the dominant allele produces the phenotype. The only direct way to figure out the rate at which a recessive mutation occurs is to analyze the protein phenotypes of large numbers of people. Only in this way is it possible to detect the small number of mutant forms.

Studies of mutations in humans show that the rate of mutation varies from locus to locus. The gene that causes polycystic disease of the kidney is at least 10 times more frequent than the gene that causes retinoblastoma, cancer of the retina (Vogel, 1965). Studies have also shown that mutations are very rare. Their frequency is on the order of from one mutant allele for every 1 million to 10 million gametes.

Mutations do not by themselves change a population in any orderly way. And once a mutation occurs it is just as likely to change back into the normal form as it is to change in some new way. Mutations do, of course, provide a continuing source of new variation. Most mutations that affect the phenotype are not advantageous, however. More often than not, they disrupt the normal body function, placing the carrier at a definite disadvantage. Mutations thus have very little effect on gene frequencies.

Selection. One of the main problems we face in the study of selection in human populations is the length of our generation time—some 25 to 30 years. Direct study of the course of natural selection would call for observation over several human generations: This is difficult. Some long-term studies of gene frequencies on human populations have been begun, but the results are not yet clear. Perhaps in another generation or so such studies will yield valuable results.

Although we cannot now study the process of selection directly, we can look for evidence of how it has taken place in the past. There are two ways of doing this: (1) in *trait distribution studies,* we work with data from many populations to chart the frequency of a single gene and then look for correlations between its frequency and various environmental features; (2) in *single population studies,* we work with one human population and try to establish the environmental advantages offered by particular genes possessed by that group.

A Trait Distribution Study. This method has been applied to the study of sickle-cell anemia. Sickle-cell anemia is controlled by one of a number of alleles that code for the making of hemoglobin. Hemoglobin molecules in red blood cells help distribute oxygen to the cells of the body. Of the many different alleles that code for hemoglobin, we will be concerned with only two: the allele for normal hemoglobin (Hb^A) and the allele for sickle-cell hemoglobin (Hb^S). The structure of the two hemoglobins differs in only one amino acid. The difference probably first occurred as the result of a point mutation—a change in the nucleotide that controls the structure of only a very small part of the molecule.

Three phenotypic and genotypic combinations of these two alleles exist. The homozygous normal genotype (Hb^A Hb^A) produces hemoglobin than can transport oxygen from the lungs to the tissues under all normal conditions. The heterozygous normal—sickle cell genotype (Hb^A Hb^S) produces a mixture of cells with normal hemoglobin and cells with sickle-cell hemoglobin. The proportion of normal to sickle-cell hemoglobin may vary, but usually the homozygous normal and heterozygous phenotypes are difficult to tell apart. Severe exercise or a low level of oxygen in the atmosphere, which occurs at high altitudes, may cause some of the red blood cells of heterozygotes to collapse and form a sickle shape. These sickle-shaped cells may block small capillaries, thus cutting off the oxygen supply to the tissues in the affected area. Though severe pain results, the problem goes away with rest and removal of the stress.

The final genotype, the homozygous sickle-cell (Hb^SHb^S) produces red blood cells with almost 100 percent sickle-cell hemoglobin. These homozygous persons suffer from sickle-cell anemia. They can undergo a crisis after any sort of physical or emotional stress. Severe damage to the body tissues results from massive blockage of the capillaries. These persons tend to suffer serious damage to the spleen, lungs, and brain, and most die when they are very young.

Although scientists have been aware of the allele among American blacks since the 1920s, it was not until the late 1940s and early 1950s that its worldwide distribution was mapped. At this time, it was noted that the distribution of the Hb^S allele in central Africa seemed to go along with the distribution of malaria in the same area. (See Figures 4 and 5.) Malaria is caused by a parasite that spends part of its life cycle in the blood of human hosts. It breaks down the amino acids of hemoglobin molecules and takes them into its own structure. In so doing, it destroys large numbers of red blood cells.

Among people with normal hemoglobin who live in this area the number of malaria parasites in the blood is quite high, often causing early death. Among heterozygotes, however, the level of parasites is greatly reduced. This is of particular advantage to young children exposed to malaria for the first time and to pregnant women, whose placenta can be damaged by malaria. Homozygote sicklers, of course, have the same grave disadvantage in malarial environments as they do in nonmalarial environments. The reason for the heterozygote advantage is not entirely understood. The effect is clear, however. Because more heterozygotes survive, there is a high frequency of the Hb^S allele. There is, however, an upper limit on its frequency, because in each generation new sickle-cell homozygotes will be produced, only to die before the alleles can be passed on. If the heterozygote (rather than either of the homozygotes) is selectively advantageous, gene frequencies will stabilize, resulting in what is termed a *balanced polymorphism.*

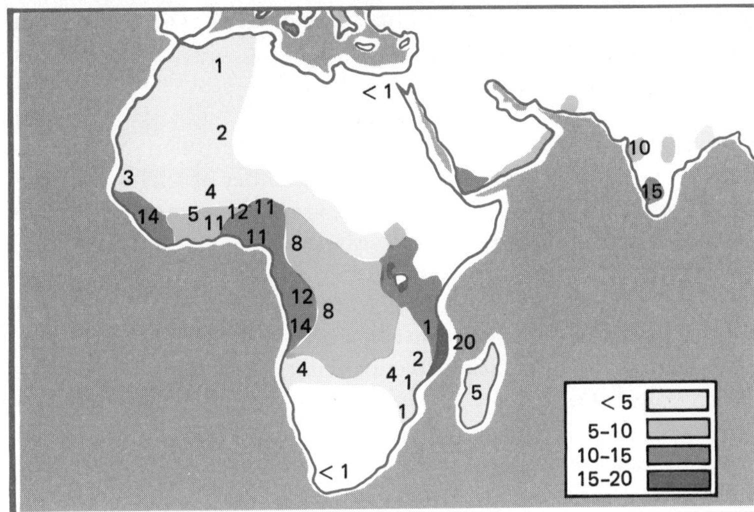

Figure 4 Distribution of gene frequencies for Hb^s allele in Africa and Southern Asia

Single Population Studies. This method studies natural selection by showing the selective advantage or disadvantage of a certain trait in a single population. Once again, blood groups are usually the focus of study. Vogel and Chakravartti (1971) have studied the relationship between smallpox and ABO blood groups in rural India. Their studies show a much higher incidence of the disease among people who have type A or AB blood. People with type B or type O blood show a much lower incidence. The major difference between these two groups is that the people with A and AB blood types possess no A antibodies, while those with B and O blood types do. Blood types B and O, as we mentioned earlier, clump when their A antibodies come into contact with the A antigen. The smallpox virus may be structurally and chemically similar to the A antigen. When it invades the body of people with type A or AB blood, the immunological response is weak;

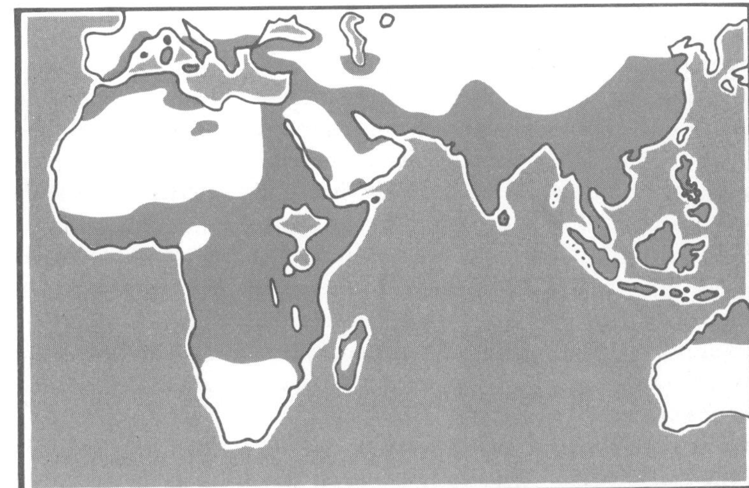

Figure 5 Distribution of malaria in Africa and Southern Asia. Its presence corresponds to high frequencies of the Hb^s allele, shown in Figure 4.

in type B and O blood the response is strong.

There are only a few examples where the exact nature of the selective advantage or disadvantage of a trait can be clearly shown. This is because a number of conditions must be satisfied if selection is to be detected: (1) the characteristic must have a simple genetic base, so that we can measure the impact of selection in terms of gene frequencies; (2) the trait must be studied easily, which means, in most cases, that it must be blood related; (3) the trait must give such an advantage or disadvantage that it directly affects the chances of survival of the person who has it.

The cases in which all three conditions are satisfied are few. Sickle-cell hemoglobin offers the perfect chance to study selection because (1) malaria directly affects a blood phenotype (hemoglobin) that is controlled by a simple genetic system; (2) the presence of the trait among heterozygotes increases the chance of survival, while its absence often means death from malaria; (3) the selective agent, the malarial parasite, lives in the bloodstream, where it is easily studied by researchers.

The Interaction of Evolutionary Forces. In our discussion of evolutionary forces, we have dealt separately with forces that normally act together. Gene flow, genetic drift, mutation, and natural selection shape the evolution of each human population. Among the Amish, for instance, a mutant recessive allele for the Ellis-Van Creveld syndrome, a kind of dwarfism, was contributed to the Lancaster county population by Samuel King or his wife, both of whom immigrated to Pennsylvania in 1744 (McKusick et al., 1971). Thus, a mutation that occurred outside the population was added to it by gene flow. Once in the gene pool, it increased in frequency because of the small breeding size of the population, an expression of genetic drift. Inbreeding caused a large number of persons who were homozygous for the condition to appear. But because these homozygotes mated infrequently, selection placed a ceiling on the total number of alleles for the condition in the population.

Complex Genetic Traits

Complex traits are controlled by the interaction of a large number of alleles at different loci on different chromosomes. Such traits are continuously distributed in the population. That is, they exist in as many forms as individuals. No two persons have exactly the same skin color, for instance. There are two reasons for this. First, the large number of alleles, as well as loci, that contribute to complex traits produce a much greater range of possible genotypic combinations than existed with, say, two alleles at a single locus. Second, most complex traits can be influenced by environmental factors during growth and development. The combination of these two phenomena makes it impossible to treat complex traits as if they fell into neat, easily definable phenotypes.

In order to analyze complex traits, then, we cannot use any of the techniques used to study simple traits. Instead, we employ a number of different statistical models.

In the American population, for instance, the weight of males ranges from about 42.5 kg to about 105 kg. Yet most men weigh about 62.5 kg (see Figure 6). A graph of all the weights in the population has approximately a bell shape, a pattern called a *normal distribution.* Traits that are distributed in this pattern can be compared between populations using statistical methods. In fact, this is one of the few ways population differences in complex traits can be studied.

Distinguishing Environmental from Genetic Influences. Because we cannot determine the genetic nature of complex traits, we can only indirectly assess the role of genes in forming them. We separate environmental effects from genetic effects by measuring the extent to which individuals' phenotypes are changeable. By studying the phenotypic ranges of which individuals in the population are cap-

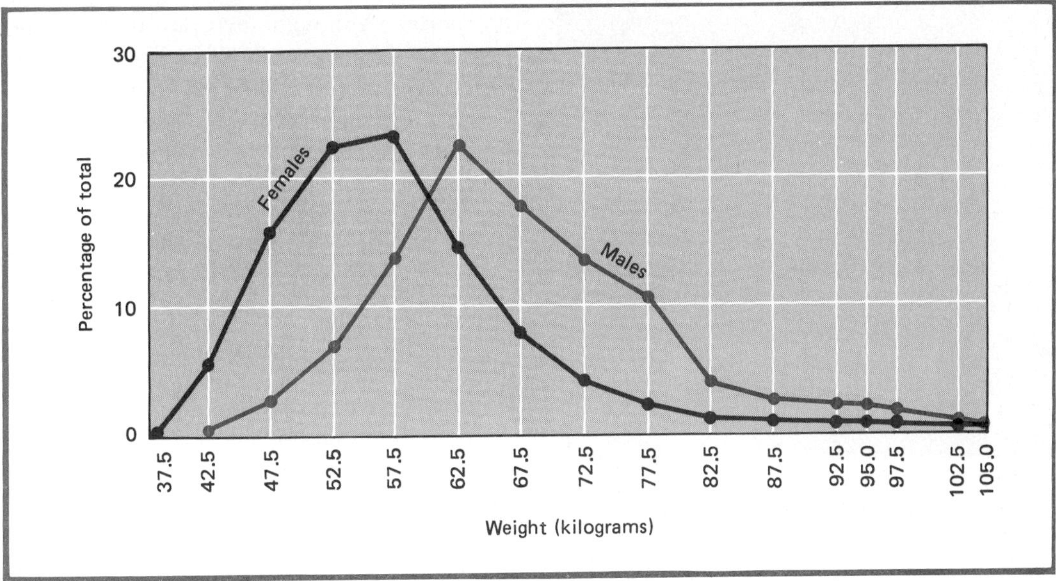

Figure 6 Distribution of the weight of males and females (average age is 17.5 years) in the United States.
Because weight is a complex trait, its distribution is in approximately a bell-shaped curve.

able we can begin to learn the degree to which differences among populations may be due simply to environmental influence.

Acclimatization. The ability of a phenotype to change in response to environmental forces is called *acclimatization.* All individuals are able to make quick adjustments to changes of temperature or diet, or to the presence of disease germs. If we could not increase our metabolic rate to respond to lower temperatures, we would not even be able to survive a cold night.

In general, physiological traits adjust rapidly to new environmental conditions. In hot weather, the circulation of blood through the skin quickens, and the perspiration rate increases almost immediately to keep the internal temperature of the body constant. Morphological traits respond somewhat more slowly. But after several weeks of hot temperatures, for example, weight loss will occur. Such short-term responses are most highly developed among mammals, probably because

Physical anthropologist Ivan G. Pawson measures Tibetan refugee children in Nepal as part of a high-altitude study. (Courtesy of I. G. Pawson)

The bodies of marathon runners have adapted to the stress of their sport in many ways. Muscles have become stronger and more efficient, and the functioning of nearly every organ in the body is improved. The heart, for example, is stronger and more coordinated. But because genes and long-term acclimatization vary, some runners finish before others. (Gerhard E. Gscheidle)

they live in varied environments or environments whose climate varies seasonally.

Other responses may develop over years of exposure to a particular stress. These *long-term acclimatizations* cause gradual changes that produce a phenotype more compatible with the environment. Among people who exercise often, there are changes in the tissues of the heart and the way they function. The muscles surrounding the right ventricle grow larger and push the blood with greater force through the lungs. Pumping efficiency increases, so that more blood is pumped per beat, and more oxygen can be carried to the body tissues. This process causes the low resting heart rates found among athletes.

Factors Affecting Acclimatization. If all humans had the same potential for acclimatization, it would be much easier to separate environmental from genetic influences. Unfortunately, humans vary by age and sex in their ability to adjust to stress.

Humans, unlike many other animals, are not marked by a high degree of sexual dimorphism. Although there are some differences in size and physiology, most of these differences do not appear until after puberty. At that time, males tend to become taller, heavier, and more muscular. Females remain shorter, and lighter, and have a higher percentage of fat. The known physiological differences, such as the greater ability of women to adjust to cold temperatures, is related to the morphological differences—in this case their larger proportion of body fat. Likewise, the difference between the sexes in the capacity to do physical work is related to differing proportions of muscle and fat.

We know a good deal about how acclimatization varies with age. This is because many workers have done careful research on growth spanning several generations in many different human populations. In humans, the growth period is the time during which people are shaped by environment to the greatest degree. This shaping is especially apparent when exposure to extreme conditions—such as high or low temperatures, poor nutrition, or disease—is prolonged. For example, American children who grow up in the hot tropical climate of Brazil are shorter and lighter than those growing up in the United States, even when nutrition and medical attention are good (Eveleth, 1966). These changes occur gradually as the children acclimatize to the heat stress of the tropics. Such changes are sometimes called *developmental acclimatization.*

As individuals age, their ability to acclimatize to environmental stresses is lessened. The elderly, for example, have rather poor metabolic responses to the cold. They must rely more heavily on restricting blood flow to the surface of the skin, thereby concentrating heat in the body core. Many older people have colder hands and feet during the winter as a result.

Control-Comparison Models. How can we tell to what degree a complex trait is genetically controlled and to what extent it is

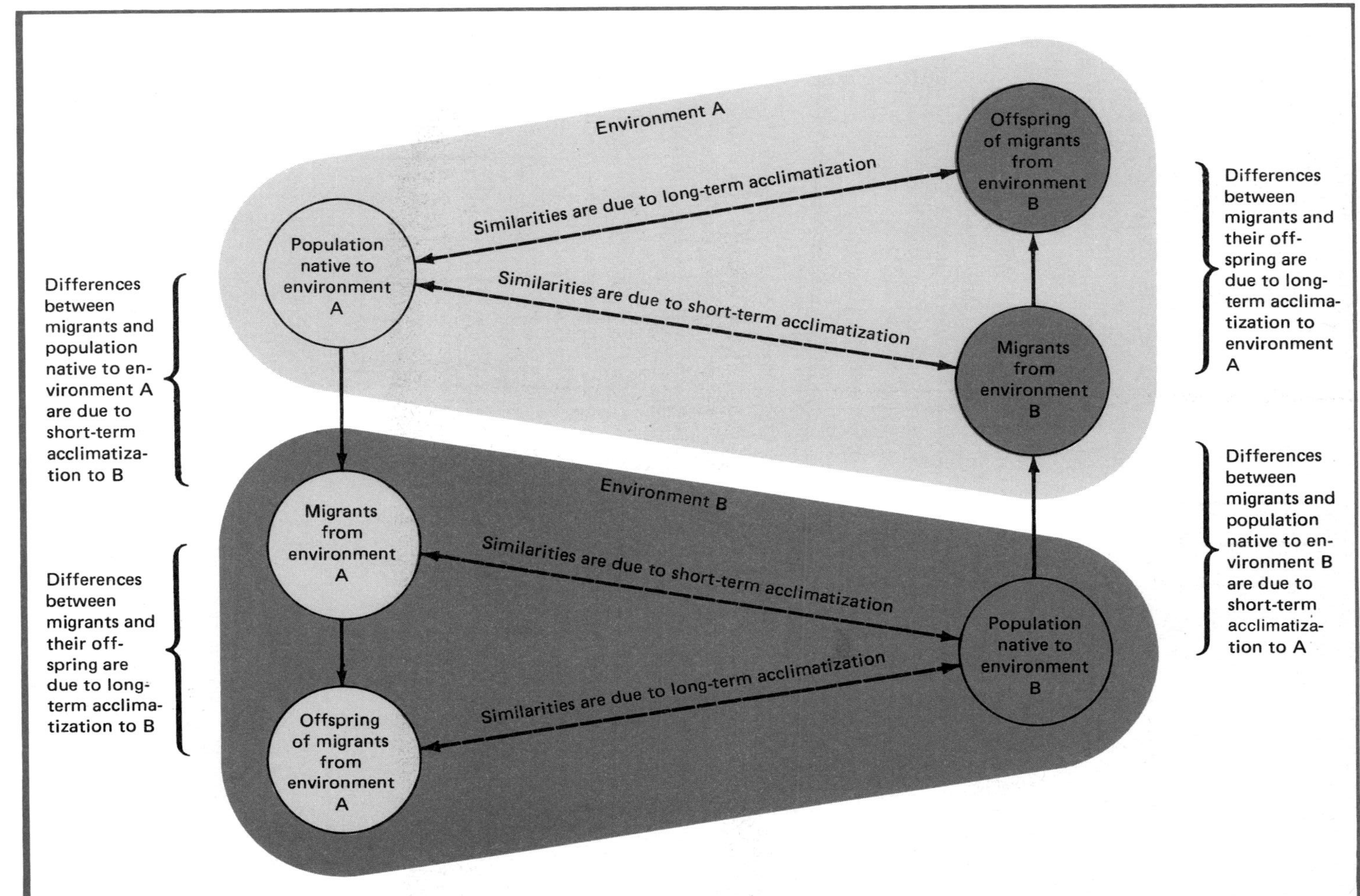

Figure 7 **A control-comparison model.** By comparing the traits of people native to an environment, migrants, and their offspring, physical anthropologists can distinguish genetic from environmental influences on complex traits.

shaped by the environment? The most useful device for this purpose is a control-comparison model, as shown in Figure 7. One study partly based on such a model focused on the stature of Japanese-Americans living in California (Greulich, 1957). These subjects were the children of migrants from Japan. The study showed that these children grew as tall as persons of European descent living in the same area. This similarity would suggest that differences in stature are the result of developmental acclimatization, probably related to differences in nutrition. The study, however, represents only half of the control-comparison model in Figure 7. The other half would consist of measuring offspring of Europeans growing up in Japan. Only then could the strong environmental influence in Japanese and European differences in stature be confirmed.

Despite the differences in stature, body proportions (for example, limb length as a proportion of height) in Japanese children and in Japanese-Americans remain the same after puberty, despite differences in nutrition. Thus, our model would suggest that the control of limb growth during adolescence must be associated more directly with genetic factors than height is.

Evolutionary Processes. Only when we can sort out the genetic and the environmental influences on a trait is it possible to see how evolutionary forces effect changes in the complex traits of a population.

Gene Flow. The flow of the genes controlling some simple genetic traits can be measured precisely by counting the number of new alleles that can be traced to migrants in a population. No such precision is possible in the study of the flow of genes controlling complex traits. Nevertheless, the effects of migration on traits such as head shape and height can be measured. One study of the people of the Swiss canton of Ticino showed that gene flow resulted in an increase in height among these people. Traditionally, the people of Ticino married people from their own village. During the twentieth century, however, this custom has fallen by the wayside, making possible comparisons of the offspring of couples in which both parents are from the same village and couples in which one parent is from a distant area. Those taking a spouse from outside the village are affecting gene flow, for the spouse introduces his or her genes into the gene pool of the population of Ticino. Sons of fathers who married outside the village have been shown to be an average of 5 cm taller than their fathers, whose fathers had married within the village (Hulse, 1968). This difference in height occurred independent of general increases in nutrition from one generation to the next. Sons of men who continued to marry within the village were also smaller than the sons of men who married outside their village.

Gene flow also often gives us the chance to study the effects of a new environment on two nearly identical gene pools. After some of the people of Ticino migrated to California, for example, their children were taller than those of their Swiss counterparts. Hulse (1968) explains this difference as the result of better diet among the Californians, who ate more meat, a greater variety of vegetables, and more fresh fruit.

Genetic Drift. Random change in the frequency of a single gene is very hard to detect, particularly when a trait is controlled by many genes. It is best studied only when a particular gene has a general effect on a trait that is controlled by many genes at more than one location on the chromosome. The lack of a single enzyme controlled at one locus can affect the production of the skin pigment melanin. This condition, known as albinism, is controlled by two recessive alleles. Small population size and inbreeding have combined to cause a high incidence of albinism among the Hopi Indians of New Mexico (Woolf & Dukepoo, 1959).

Mutation. Because we cannot count the alleles that affect complex traits, it is far more difficult to figure out the rate of mutations that bear on their expression. In some cases, a point mutation can have a strong effect if it prevents the other genes that affect the trait from functioning normally. For example, in children who have phenylketonuria, or PKU, the presence of a single mutant allele prevents the formation of an enzyme that prevents the normal functioning of an entire metabolic pathway. Information about the frequency of mutations among genes whose effect is not so persuasive is scanty, if not absent.

Natural Selection. Because it is fairly easy to study the effect of natural selection on complex traits, it is the best-studied evolutionary force. Researchers measure the variation in a population with respect to skin color, height, limb proportions, and the like. They then summarize their data in a graph like those in Figure 8. A given complex trait, as we have mentioned, is more common in certain forms than in others. Most of the population will fall within certain limits for the trait in question. In their study of complex traits, researchers assume that those forms of a trait that are most common in a population have the greatest selective advantage in the environment. The commonest form has in some way allowed its possessor to pass on the genes for the trait more effectively than those having less common variants of the trait. A study of male Harvard graduates, for example, has shown that those who are of average height had more children than did those who are extremely short or tall (Milton, 1975).

Just because one form of a trait is more common in a population than another does not mean that this distribution will remain unchanged. A change in environmental conditions could well be altering the makeup of a population as the investigator studies it. Assuming these changes are due to selection, one of three types may be operating. If selection is favoring the form of the trait presently found in the largest number of persons in the population, it is said to be *stabilizing* (see Figure 8). Then the rarer forms will remain about as rare as in the present and the most common forms will continue to be common.

If, however, some outside force upsets this equilibrium, one of two patterns may emerge. *Directional selection* favors individuals at one end of the curve. For some reason, a form of the trait other than that held by most of the population may become more adaptive, causing a gradual increase in the number of individuals having the advantageous form of the trait. Finally, selection may favor forms of the trait at extreme ends of the range in which it appears in the population. This is called *disruptive selection.* Again see Figure 8. Individuals in the center of the distribution are at a disadvantage in this case. Although it is not known how often this kind of selection occurs, it is thought to take place in varied environments, where one extreme is favored in one area and the other extreme is an advantage in another (Hartl, 1977).

As we saw in our discussion of selection and simple traits, researchers at this time can best study the results of selection, not the actual process. As is also the case in the study of simple traits, investigators have two options in their study of complex traits: They can study single populations or they can take a trait distribution approach.

Studies of Single Populations. A great deal of stress can be placed on a population with absolutely no evolutionary effect. This is true because humans, more than many other animals, can adjust their biological functioning according to the demands of the environment. For example, weight loss when food is scarce represents the use of energy stored in fat cells to maintain vital body functions. If food becomes available within a few weeks, the individual survives with no ill effects. A population of such individuals will undergo no shift toward an increased number of persons who can survive on small amounts of food.

When the environmental stress is continuous and severe, however, there is a good chance that the distribution of complex traits will be influenced by selection. Because selection is likely to be at work in extreme envi-

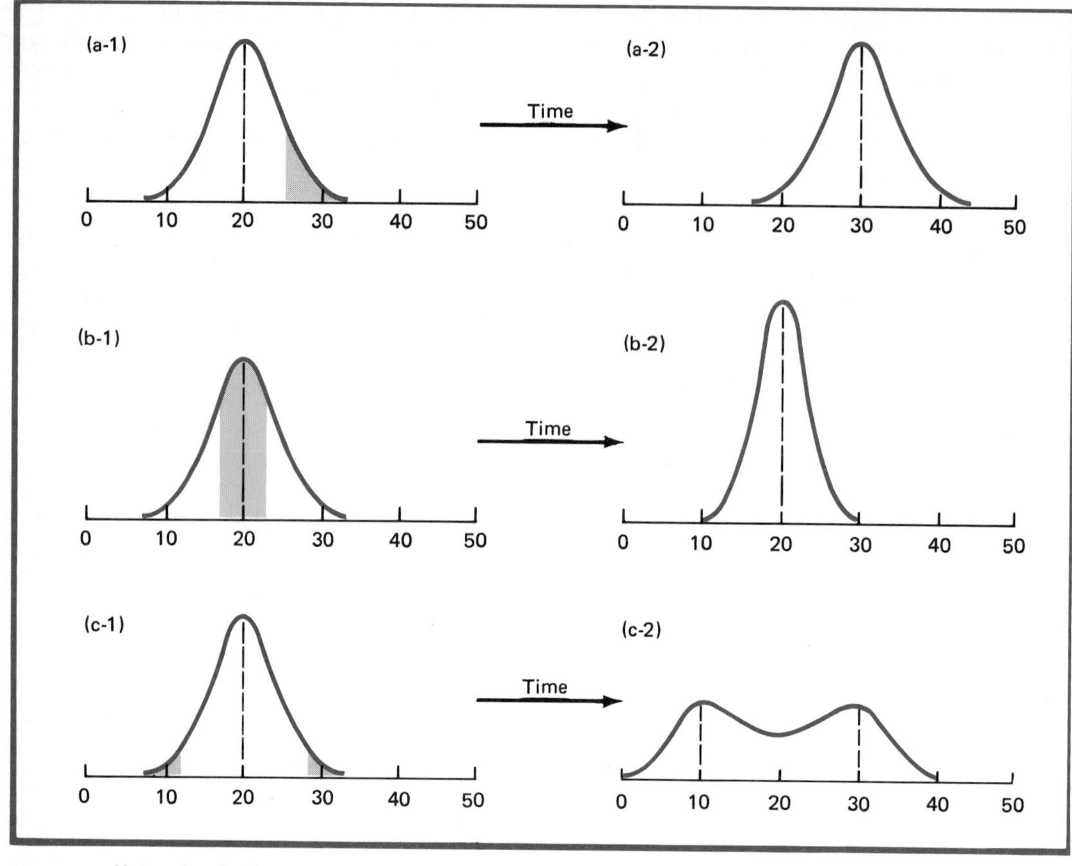

Figure 8 Natural selection can act on complex traits in three principal ways.
In *directional selection (a-1),* persons in the right-hand tail of the distribution are favored by selection. Ultimately, selection shifts the average of the population to the right *(a-2).* In *stabilizing selection (b-1),* individuals near the center of the distribution are favored and become more common *(b-2). Disruptive selection* favors extreme phenotypes *(c-1)* and increases their frequency *(c-2).* (Hartl, 1977)

ronments, many of the single-population studies of complex traits have focused on human populations living in harsh environments.

The most often studied environmental extremes are heat, cold, and high altitude. Studies of single populations often center on physiological rather than morphological adjustment.

Take, for example, the apparent adjustment by high-altitude dwellers in the Andes of South America and the Himalayas of Nepal to low levels of oxygen. Persons raised at low altitudes who rapidly ascend to heights of 3,000 m or more often suffer from altitude sickness for several days or longer. Symptoms include headache, shortness of breath, dizziness, and nausea. Pulmonary edema, which causes the air sacs of the lungs to fill up with fluid, and which can be deadly, is also caused by the low oxygen content of the air. Even in the absence of such severe symptoms, lowlanders are unable to perform normal activities as well as highlanders. But Peruvian and Nepalese natives are active and energetic. The Peruvian children play running games, and adults walk as much as 30 km to market.

A close examination of the phenotype of these people reveals several interesting differences from that of lowland dwellers. Physical growth of the Peruvian Indians is slow and lasts into the early twenties. Sexual maturation is late as well. There is also evidence that coordination between the brain and the muscles of the body develops more slowly. And the mountain dwellers have a larger chest and lung capacity, a greater marrow capacity of the long bones, where red blood cells are created, and the ability to deliver a larger amount of oxygen to the muscles during heavy work periods than do sea-level populations (Little & Baker, 1976).

Research shows that some of these differences can be explained in terms of poor nutrition, socioeconomic status, developmental acclimatizations to the colder temperatures of high altitudes, and particularly the low oxygen content of the air. Increased chest size, lung capacity, and the ability to do work at high altitudes are acclimatization developed during growth, not genetically controlled traits. Children migrating from sea-level homes to the mountains, for example, developed larger chests than the sea-level dwellers who remained behind (Little & Baker, 1976). There may be a genetic factor in the differences that Nepalese highlanders show. Here, children of mountain-dwelling parents kept the phenotype of their parents after growing up in a lowland environment with a higher oxygen content.

The Trait Distribution Approach. The other approach to the study of selection is to chart the variation in the expression of a trait from one environment to another. An example of this approach can be found in the studies of how the form of the body varies with the average temperature of areas around the world. In mammals, body tissue converts nutrients into heat through metabolism. Thus, animals with a large amount of tissues, or body mass, are capable of generating more warmth. At the same time, the larger the surface area of the skin, the more quickly body heat escapes into the air. Because large animals have a smaller surface area in proportion to their mass than do small animals, larger animals are probably better adjusted to cold environments and less well adapted to warm climates. This principle, that small animals will be found in warmer areas and large animals in colder areas is called *Bergmann's rule.*

Because disproportionately large amounts of the body's heat escape through the limbs, it was proposed that animals with shorter limbs would be more likely to be found in cold regions, and animals with long limbs would appear in warmer areas. This generalization is called *Allen's rule,* after J. A. Allen, an American zoologist, who suggested it in 1877.

Natives of the Altiplano region of Bolivia. Because their bodies are adjusted to the low oxygen content of the air, they can be as active at 3,500 m as lowlanders are in their own environment. (Gerhard E. Gscheidle)

A number of studies have attempted to apply these rules to human populations, and in general, the rules do seem to apply to humans. Eskimos, for example, with their short, stocky bodies and short limbs would seem to be adapted for minimum heat loss through the skin. Certain peoples of East Africa are exceptionally tall and thin and therefore have an ideal surface area-to-body mass ratio for their hot, tropical climate. In these areas the advantage of sweating is small because sweat will not evaporate in the humid air. Hence even slightly lighter individuals may have a selective advantage because their bodies produce less heat compared to their potential for radiating it through the skin.

Despite the general conformity of human populations to these rules, we know that many morphological traits found to vary with temperature—weight, fat content, limb length, and surface area-to-body weight ratio—are often influenced by local conditions other than temperature, such as nutrition and disease. The relation of these factors to temperature should become clearer when researchers have had the chance to study populations over the span of several generations.

In recent years the study of human diversity has become much more concerned with understanding the forces behind change than with cataloging human differences. Population genetics based on the study of simple traits has demonstrated that genetic drift and gene flow have a very significant effect on the evolution of human populations. Researchers have not been as successful in demonstrating the process of selection in populations, although we can show its consequences in macroevolutionary terms. When dealing with complex traits, we find that the most useful models involve selection. But many studies have emphasized the importance of local environmental features in causing differences due to acclimatization. It becomes a much more difficult enterprise to demonstrate gene flow and genetic drift.

Summary

1. In the study of human variation, racial classifications have had an important role, though they are less frequently used today.

2. An early racial classification proposed by Linnaeus in 1735 divided the human species into black Africans, red-skinned Americans, darkish Asians, and white Europeans. In addition to skin color, early classifications of race made use of skull features, the color and texture of hair, and height. As scientists realized that variation within human groups could be great, they relied increasingly on multiple-trait classifications to define races.

3. There are two flaws in traditional racial categories. First, the exchange of mates between groups in the course of human history has prevented the isolation necessary to evolve racial differences. Secondly, many traits, such as height and skull shape, are affected by the environment.

4. Racial classifications have been attempted recently on the basis of genetic traits, such as blood type. But changes in blood type often show a gradual shift from one population to another, rather than a sharp boundary.

5. Some attempts have been made to trace the evolution of racial groups, but the fossil record is incomplete, and the skeletal parts preserved are subject to environmental influence.

6. A more useful scheme for understanding human variation than race is the concept of population. A population is a group of interbreeding individuals.

7. Two factors can prevent members of a human population from mating with those of another population. First, geographical isolation may limit migration. Second, social factors such as class systems or marriage laws may limit the choice of marriage partners.

8. Studying the changes in *simple genetic traits* in a population provides one method for

measuring the action of such evolutionary forces as *gene flow, genetic drift, mutation,* and *natural selection.* Simple genetic traits are determined by a few alleles at one gene position. By finding the number of each allele in the population, the frequency of appearance of each different allele for a trait may be calculated. Changes in the frequency with which an allele appears give evidence of evolution in a population.

9. *Gene flow* is the movement of genes from one population to another. Gene flow has maintained the unity of the human species, even though not all populations have interbred.

10. *Genetic drift* occurs when small population size limits the number of genetic variations produced. It can sometimes be identified by process of elimination, when no other forces can explain variation in small groups living in the same environment. A special case of genetic drift is the *founder effect.* A small group of individuals that breaks off from a larger population and founds a new community will probably not have all the genetic variety present in the original group. Thus the new population will soon be quite different genetically from the original group.

11. *Inbreeding,* like genetic drift, limits the amount of genetic variation in a population. Also, inbreeding often causes an increase in the number of harmful homozygotes.

12. The frequency of dominant *mutations* can be found by counting the number of persons in the population whose phenotype reveals the presence of the mutation. Recessive mutation rates can only be determined directly using certain chemical tests.

13. One means of examining the process of natural selection is to map the distribution of a simple trait in many populations.

14. Another method of studying natural selection in humans is to focus on traits shown by a single population.

15. Studies of *complex genetic traits* have also provided information on gene flow, genetic drift, mutation, and natural selection. Complex traits, such as skull shape and height, are controlled by a number of alleles at different points on the chromosomes. Such traits may be partly determined by environmental factors.

16. To separate environmental and genetic effects, the ability of the phenotype of the members of a population to adjust to short-term environmental change may be measured. Such short-term adjustment is called *acclimatization.* Many physiological phenotypes of humans show rapid adjustment to new conditions. Adjustment formed over a long period of time is called *long-term acclimatization,* while that formed during growth is called *developmental acclimatization.*

17. Gene flow can also be studied using complex traits. When members of an isolated population in Switzerland began to take mates from outside the group, their offspring were taller than the children of those who married within the group.

18. Several types of natural selection have been noted in studies of complex traits. Stabilizing selection maintains the existing distribution. Directional selection causes a gradual shift in the most adapted phenotype. Disruptive selection causes extreme forms of a trait to become more common.

19. Complex genetic traits have been studied in single populations. For instance, expanded lung capacity is found in mountain dwellers. In Peru this large lung capacity may be long-term acclimatization to the low availability of oxygen at high altitudes.

20. Trait distribution studies have tended to confirm *Bergmann's rule:* Large animals are better adjusted to cold climates than are small animals. They have also given support to *Allen's rule:* Animals having short limbs are more likely to be found in cold climates, while long-limbed animals are more common in warm areas of the world. Short limb length aids in adjustment to the cold, apparently by preventing body heat loss.

PART TWO

Archaeology

11 Introduction to Archaeology

So far we have looked at mainly the biological aspects of human evolution and behavior. Now we shall focus on the cultural aspects of human evolution. This is the subject matter of *archaeology*. It can be defined as the study of the history, lifestyles, and processes of change in prehistoric human cultures. Although it began many years ago as a search for ancient objects and monumental architecture, archaeology is now a highly scientific search for information about past cultures.

Archaeologists limit themselves mostly to prehistory—to the study of human activity before written records were kept. Sometimes, however, archaeological techniques are applied to more recent peoples, to uncover information never recorded in writing.

As detectives of sorts, archaeologists have only the most decay-resistant remains of human activities as clues to everyday living patterns. Perishable items such as baskets and wooden implements are rarely preserved. But archaeologists have gained surprising amounts of information by analyzing everything from discarded tools and traces of once-cleared fields to fossilized human feces. As you will see, archaeology today, unlike the traditional discipline, regards these material remains as clues to the cultural behavior of the people who left them behind.

Traditional Archaeology

Archaeologists traditionally aimed their efforts at reconstructing past cultural sequences. They assumed that cultural elements—such as ways of working with stone to make tools—flow through space and time. That is, cultural elements spread from one area to another and

Machu-Picchu, or "the lost city of the Incas," was discovered in 1911 on a mountaintop in south central Peru, 2,045 m above sea level. Most of its excavation was carried out by archaeologists using traditional ideas and methods. (George Holton, Photo Researchers, Inc.)

from one generation to the next. Changes noted in *artifacts* (articles made or used by humans) and their distribution and frequency had to be explained in terms of historical factors, such as contact with another group whose ideas about toolmaking were different, and psychological factors, such as the personality characteristics that could lead people to adopt or reject the new ideas. But because psychological traits leave no obvious physical clues outside of records, and since archaeologists were not trained in psychoanalysis anyway, they were left with only partial explanations for cultural changes (Binford, 1972).

From the beginnings of systematic excavation early in the nineteenth century up until the 1950s, archaeology concentrated largely on finding and cataloguing things. The painstaking uncovering of buried artifacts yielded lists of culture traits—burial practices, stone tools, pottery types, methods of housebuilding—arranged by site and dated layers. This approach tended to obscure the nature of the human behavior responsible for the artifacts. Archaeologist Paul Martin (1972) for example, confesses that in his earlier work he had become so expert at cataloguing Southwestern pottery types that he could place any piece he was shown by site and date. But this pigeon-holing technique had blinded him to more general observations. For instance, he writes that he did not see that a certain kind of pottery might have been used only for rituals or burials, or that changes in artifacts might suggest something about patterns in human behavior. Martin's experiences were typical of what most archaeologists were doing prior to about 1960.

Despite the feeling of some archaeologists that they were not getting anywhere, traditional archaeology had made some important contributions. For instance, it was archaeologists who told us how long ago human tools first appeared and where. They also pieced together histories of ancient Greece and of groups mentioned in the Bible and described the origin of American Indians. In addition they found evidence of cultural evolution, described the beginnings of agriculture, and showed that there have been a number of sophisticated civilizations (Martin, 1972).

The New Archaeology

Twentieth-century archaeologists have been stung by criticisms that they have been doing little more than collecting miscellaneous relics and outlining major developments. They have also been influenced by a recent trend in many of the sciences toward reexamination of goals and methods. As a result, archaeologists have done a lot of soul-searching. Today there is general agreement that archaeology should have the following goals: (1) the reconstruction of culture history, (2) the detailed description of the way of life of earlier cultures, and (3) the analysis of the reasons for culture change.

Traditional archaeology specialized in the first goal—cataloguing the events of culture history. It traced the major trends of prehistory. Today archaeologists are interested in understanding social organization, the economics, and the religious and philosophical concepts of ancient peoples. Reaching the third goal, an understanding of change, requires a full understanding of how the people of an ancient culture lived their lives from day to day. Such detail brings to life the dynamics of the culture, upon which models for culture change can be based. Finally, of course, scientific hypotheses of how change occurred in a number of ancient cultures allows the writing of sound and detailed cultural history (Deetz, 1972).

Archaeologists have also become increasingly aware that if it is to be truly scientific, archaeology must have a more clearly defined theoretical framework. It must be designed both to generate and to test hypotheses about culture and culture change. As a result, there have been many recent attempts to define the basic ideas of archaeology and to clarify its procedures. Of particular interest has been the process of translating raw data from sites into statements about how the people who lived there behaved and why they changed.

The Shaping of Material Remains

Today archaeologists assume that objects people leave behind can be analyzed as clues to their patterns of behavior. For example, traditional archaeological research in the Santa Barbara Channel region in California revealed a change in seed-grinding tools—from heavy milling stones to small basket-sided mortars to large bowl-shaped mortars weighing several hundred pounds. This is probably an accurate description of a cultural progression, so far as it goes. But if the same artifacts, together with other parts of the system, are examined as clues to actual behaviors, they yield explanations that may give us a more detailed understanding of what went on.

The early milling stone stage at Santa Barbara, for instance, also had large shell *middens.* These were garbage dumps where shellfish were thrown away once their insides had been eaten. The few *projectile points* (rocks that had been altered for use in hunting) found during the early milling-stone stage suggest little emphasis on hunting. People apparently ate mostly plant and sea foods. And they probably did not move around much, a hypothesis that James Deetz (1972) suggested after noting the weight of the early milling stones. The large shell heaps, too, indicated a population that had stayed in the same place for a long time.

Relationships that he saw among a number of elements in the second cultural layer led Deetz to speculate that there had been a major change to a nomadic hunting lifestyle. The mortars with basketry sides probably involved an up-and-down seed-mashing motion, a form of grinding that did not require a large surface. Since these new tools were far lighter than the older millstones, they could be carried around. Furthermore, there was a decrease in the amount of shell middens and an increase in projectile points for hunting. Another clue that the people might have begun to travel lay in the similarity of the projectile points to those found in sites farther east. Deetz also speculated that examination of the geological record might reveal changes in the availability of shellfish. The early "settled" period might have corresponded to an abundance of sea life. A temporary decrease may have caused the switch to a nomadic lifestyle. Later, an increase in sea life could explain the return to the settled lifestyle noted for the third phase.

Culture and Patterns

We have looked at Deetz's example in some detail to show that artifacts can be examined as behavioral clues. It also illustrates another point: Culture is patterned in such a way that its parts fit together harmoniously and consistently. For a group to practice nomadic hunting but still try to retain its bulky, nonportable grinding stones would have been inconsistent. It would have upset the system because it would not have worked. A change to huge stone bowls for more efficient mortar-style grinding, however, was not inconsistent with the return to a sedentary way of life. At every site, archaeologists shape their theories to conform to the notion that cultural behaviors follow logical patterns (Hole & Heizer, 1973).

Culture Change

A final feature of the "new archaeology" is the attempt to formulate theories to account for culture change. Many archaeologists interpret changes in archaeological data as signs of adaptation to environmental or sociocultural pressures. The change to the second-stage set of culture traits at Santa Barbara, for instance, could perhaps be seen as an adaptation to a new ecological situation: not enough seafood to go around. Or evidence might be found of some kind of social pressure that forced many people to leave the camp to live as hunters.

The idea of adaptation is analogous to that used in evolutionary biology. In plant and animal populations, inability to adjust to the environment may make it impossible for all organisms to survive. Change occurs as selection permits individuals with adaptive traits to survive in new conditions. Many archaeologists feel that culture change may occur in the same way. Real or perceived change may begin to select from among the cultural options in a society a set that will offer the group a better chance for survival. There is some danger in applying this biological model of adaptation to culture change, though. Change in human cultures usually takes *extrasomatic,* or nonbodily, forms whereas adaptation in biology is largely based on physical changes in organisms (Binford, 1972). Culture change can be very rapid, while biological change tends to be slow. And there is no guarantee that all changes in human cultures will better adapt them than the old ways.

Also, people's actions are often prompted by culturally defined goals that may not be adaptive. In many agricultural groups a peasant, given the choice, would delay planting his crop in order to arrange for the marriage of a son or daughter. The marriage involves his prestige in the community. In human cultures, seeking and keeping prestige often takes precedence over subsistence, despite the fact that subsistence is linked more directly to biological survival.

Instead of regarding culture change as an adaptive process, then, some archaeologists have focused not on the reasons for change but on the processes that may result in culture change. Among them are random change, diffusion, invention, and accidental discovery (Hole & Heizer, 1973).

Random change occurs because children rarely learn to repeat the behavior of their parents perfectly. Some random differences between the generations may gradually emerge as changes in the way most people in a group behave.

Diffusion refers to change caused by cultural contact with different peoples. Today, for instance, we are seeing the widespread adoption of Eastern religions by Americans. And in a single generation the Manus Islanders in the Bismarck Archipelago north of New Guinea changed from a Stone Age culture to one with modern notions, after they made contact with people from industrial countries. It is partially this ability to adopt cultural material from outside groups that has made it possible for human cultures to change far more rapidly than biological systems.

Inventions, too, can profoundly change cultural patterns. The invention of motorized transportation devices and long-distance communication, for instance, has allowed members of extended family groups to remain in close contact while living half a continent apart. Some inventions are deliberate responses to unmet needs; some simply seem to grow out of people's delight in playing with new ideas and things.

The use of fire for warmth and cooking probably took place very gradually as our ancestors slowly realized that naturally occurring fires could be put to good use.

A population's ability to survive depends on its capacity to adjust to a changing environment. The processes we have just discussed must result in behavior that allows survival. Even cultural features that seemingly have no relationship to the environment cannot last if they begin to affect the resources upon which the population depends or the efficiency with which those resources are used.

Archaeological Techniques

Regardless of their theoretical orientation, all archaeologists go through the same general procedures in seeking data. They must locate a site and extract material from it, being careful to keep track of the precise position of each object. Then they describe everything they have found in such a way that it can be compared with material from other sites. Finally, they try to figure out what the material reveals about the lives of the people who left it behind (Deetz, 1972).

Stage One: Area Survey and Site Location

How do archaeologists know where to dig? It would be a waste of time for archaeologists to excavate at random. The first step, then, is to locate a *site,* a space of ground containing evidence of human occupation. In order to do this, archaeologists select an area and survey it.

The first step in surveying an area is to define its limits. Boundaries may be natural, such as a valley enclosed by a ring of hills. Or they may be arbitrary, perhaps a $^1/_4$ k. strip paralleling the sides of a river. After the area has been defined, one or more teams of ar-

Table 1 Types of Sites and Archaeological Remains

Types of Sites and Archaeological Remains
Monumental or fixed antiquities, usually found on the surface of the ground
Refuse heaps, in caves by the seashore, near ruins, etc.
Caches and storage pits for food, treasure, offerings, etc.
Hearths, firepits, temporary camp sites
House and village sites, tent rings, ruins, pile dwellings, etc.
Trails, portages, and causeways connecting the settlements, etc.
Workshops, smelters, foundries, etc.
Graves and cemeteries
Garden and field plots
Excavations, such as pitfalls for game, reservoirs, irrigation systems, quarries, mines, burial chambers, subterranean dwellings, artificial dwellings cut into loess, pumice, and limestone
Earthworks, including dams, ball courts, enclosures for field and for cattle, fortification walls, mounds, and pyramids
Megalithic and other stone structures in the form of menhirs or monoliths, cromlechs or stone circles, alignments, cairns, dolmens and trilithons, stone chambered mounds or barrows, cist graves, pyramids, shrines, temples, fortification walls, forts, treasure chambers, enclosures for fields and for cattle, fish weirs, boulder effigies, and gravestones
Petrogylphs and paintings on cave walls and exposed rock surfaces
Movable antiquities, ordinarily obtained only by excavation in either artificial refuse or natural earth deposits
Chipped stone work: tools, weapons, ornamental and ceremonial objects
Wood work: tools, weapons, boats and other means of transportation, ornamental and ceremonial objects
Bone work: tools, weapons, utensils, ornamental and ceremonial objects
Shell work: tools, weapons, utensils, ornamental and ceremonial objects
Skin, hair, and feather work: clothing, shelters, utensils, boats, and ornamental accessories
Wood fiber work: mats, baskets, oats, nets, clothing, hats, sandals, and ornamental accessories
Clay work: utilitarian, artistic, and ceremonial pottery, etc.
Grand stone work: tools, weapons, utensils, ornamental and ceremonial objects
Metal work: tools, weapons, utensils, ornamental and ceremonial objects

Hester, Heizer, & Graham, 1975 (as adapted from Nelson, 1938). Reprinted by permission of Mayfield Publishing Co.

chaeologists systematically search the area. They may scan the features of the land from the air with radar or infrared photography.

But a good bit of walking and looking forms the bulk of the work. The researchers may walk the entire area, or sample particular sections at random. In other instances, archaeologists may search a *transect,* a single strip crossing the area.

What do surveyors look for? This depends on the prehistoric period in which the surveyor is interested, and the area in which the survey is taking place. In the Near East and South Asia, modern villages may be built on top of mounds of accumulated refuse from thousands of years of human habitation. These mounds often yield much information about past agricultural activities. The plows of modern farmers may turn up pieces of ancient pottery, and erosion by wind or water may expose others.

The remains left by preagricultural populations tend to be less obvious, but the trained eye can find surface clues. Most often such sites are spotted by evidence exposed accidentally. Commercial mining and quarrying activities often turn up ancient tools and even an occasional hominid fossil. Here, too, erosion often exposes ancient tools or other clues of early cultures. Other times, archaeologists, lacking visible clues, may play hunches about where early human groups have lived. Possibilities include sites near water sources, in caves, and on cliff tops. Sometimes areas are chosen for archaeological investigation simply because they are about to be destroyed. The damming and flooding of a valley, for instance, may destroy signs of ancient human life. The study and removal of material from such an area is called *salvage archaeology.*

In general, sites that have been disturbed the least are the ones most likely to be chosen for excavation. At many sites, however, geological processes, animals, and humans may have scrambled or carried off remains, making interpretation very difficult.

Theoretical considerations influence site selection, too. Someone who wants to trace the history of a single culture will look for a site that was long inhabited. Researchers interested in processes of culture change look for sites of a certain age that bear on a train of events. If the problem is the effects of agriculture, for instance, sites immediately preceding and following its appearance can be analyzed for material evidence of how this cultural change altered living patterns. And if the researcher is interested in reconstructing the culture of a particular past group—such as the Maya—extensive, well-preserved sites like the Tikal ruins may be the best choice (Hester, Heizer, & Graham, 1975).

Each site located is carefully described and photographed, and a grid is marked out over the area. Sample artifacts on the surface that would help to date the sites may be removed after their location is accurately recorded. And in sophisticated operations, test pits may be sunk to sample what lies below the surface. The goal of these procedures is to choose a site or sites for more extensive excavation.

Stage Two: Recovery of Material

At the excavation stage, too, what goes on depends on what the archaeologist is looking for. In the search for grand buildings or precious museum pieces, archaeologists of the past probably passed up material that would be of great interest today for its information about the way people once lived.

In general, archaeological sites are excavated in strata, just as paleontological sites are. The same assumptions apply. Younger deposits, for instance, are presumed to lie on top of older deposits unless there is some sign that the normal sequence has been scrambled. Strata may be defined by layered changes in cultural remains. Or they can be defined by geological layers, indicated by visible differ-

Archaeologists of the Illinois Museum and the University of Wisconsin uncover a line of Indian palisades at a site in Illinois. In an area excavation such as this one, trenches are dug in a grid pattern to allow precise measurement of the artifact positions in all parts of the site. (United Press International Photo)

ences in soil type or composition. If neither kind of layering is apparent, the site may be excavated in layers of an arbitrary depth, such as 10 cm.

To get to lower layers, excavators often have to destroy the upper layers. It is therefore very important that they carefully and accurately record everything in each layer. Even if what they find does not happen to pertain to the problem they are working on, the information may be of value to other researchers.

Excavators may use shovels or even bulldozers to dig down to the level at which cultural materials begin. But once there, they switch to more delicate tools—trowels, whisk brooms, paintbrushes, jackknives, screens. As they proceed they may do the following:

1. Locate artifacts and the remains of organisms, record their location on a grid map of the horizon (see Figure 1), photograph them, and perhaps remove them for laboratory study.
2. Look for the outlines of perishable objects such as shelters or the holes of poles that may have supported tents whose shape may be preserved as soil of a different color.
3. Collect samples of soil, pollen, or seeds as clues to the environment.

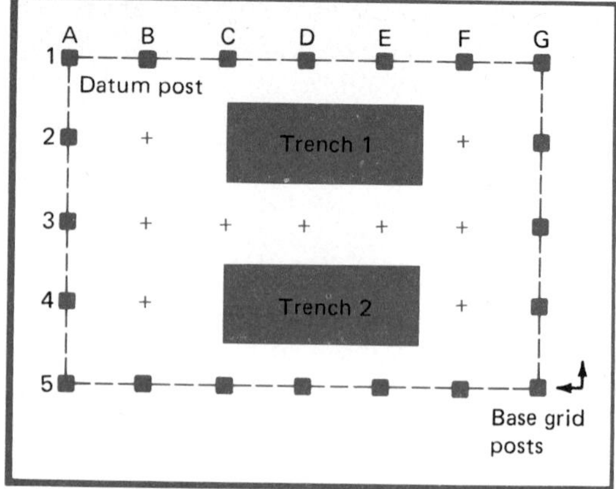

Figure 1 A site grid. Such a grid is used to lay out the trenches and then to fix the position of finds in terms of three dimensions. Two measurements locate the object's position in the grid, and a third gives its depth.

4. Look for things that may help to date the site.
5. Seek clues to the time sequence in the strata.

Archaeologists who are interested in reconstructing the way of life of the people who left a group of artifacts may also look in as many places as possible for clues to the activity patterns of the people who once lived there.

Environment makes a great difference in whether traces of the past will remain intact.

Anthropologists from Michigan State University excavating a burial ground of the Mitchigami Indians, who lived near the present town of Prairie du Rocher, Illinois, from 1730 to about 1770. (United Press International Photo)

The dark, round discolored patches surrounding the piles of rock and shells show the locations of post holes from a seventeenth-century Dutch stockade uncovered in Kingston, New York. (United Press International Photo)

Things found under the sea are likely to be unusually well preserved. Tropical areas, on the other hand, probably offer the worst opportunities for preservation. Their combination of frequent rainfalls, acid soils, warm climate, lush vegetation, thriving insect populations, and erosion can destroy almost anything humans have made. The best conditions for preservation are continual wetness, continual dryness, or continual cold. Excavations at the Pazyryk burial mounds in Siberia, for instance, uncovered the bodies of warriors who had been buried one summer about 2,300 years ago in tombs 12 feet deep. They froze so thoroughly in the intense winters that followed that everything was perfectly preserved—fragile silks, wood, leather, metal, even the men's richly tattooed bodies.

Stage Three: Analysis

After archaeologists have unearthed and recorded an assortment of artifacts, fragmented skeletons, and minute traces of pollen and plants, the enormous task of figuring out what they are and what they mean begins. This involves examining and dating them, organizing them into some sort of classification scheme, and then interpreting them.

Technical Examination. The range of information that can be gotten by close examination of archaeological materials expands every year. For example, the stones of which certain artifacts are made can be linked to specific quarries by their trace element patterns. The 47-foot-high statues of Pharaoh at Thebes are made of giant quartzite blocks that were somehow brought there from a quarry 676 km down the Nile. This kind of data is useful in testing theories about the use of natural resources or trading patterns.

Analysis of animal remains is particularly important to researchers who are trying to reconstruct the diets and lifestyles of hunting peoples. Animal bones can tell us what people usually ate and how much, where they hunted and when, whether or not an animal had a ritual significance, and whether the animals had been domesticated by humans. They also can tell us about the climate of the time, how many persons lived at the site, and for how long.

Dating. Figuring out the age of a site is another important aspect of its analysis. Most of the methods paleontologists use to date remains, discussed in Chaper 6, are best for very old things. Uranium-lead dating, for instance, cannot be used to date objects younger than 10 million years. Archaeologists have a different set of dating techniques that are better for fairly recent periods (10,000 years to the present).

Dendrochronology. In certain areas tree-ring analysis, or *dendrochronology,* can be used

The dry climate of what is now Israel contributed to the preservation of these fragments of a "Dead Sea Scroll," found in a cave about 2,300 years after it had been hidden there. (S. Weiss, Rapho/Photo Researchers)

to date artifacts very accurately. In temperate zones, trees add on new rings of cells to their circumference every year. To figure out how old such a tree is, we can cut it down and count the rings on the stump.

To apply this commonly known method to archaeology, we examine the rings in ancient timbers. Features of the climate such as rainfall influence the size of the yearly ring; in a wet year the ring will be larger than in a dry year. All trees of the same species in an area, therefore, tend to develop matching ring patterns. To make use of this phenomenon in dating, we try to match the pattern of wet and dry years in the youngest rings of an old house timber with the oldest rings on a slightly younger timber in a newer dwelling. These in turn may overlap with the patterns in a newly cut tree. See Figure 2. We can thus count backwards through the overlapping sequences to figure out when the original dwelling was first built. In the American Southwest this technique can be used to date artifacts as old as 2,000 years.

Carbon 14. This dating method has been popular with archaeologists since the 1950s. It involves measuring how much of the heavy carbon isotope C^{14} is present in organic material. During an organism's life, it takes in radioactive Carbon 14 and stable Carbon 12 from the environment in a constant ratio (about 1 molecule of $C^{14}O_2$ to every 1 trillion molecules of $C^{12}O_2$). The radioactive carbon is constantly decaying back to Nitrogen 14, the gas it came from, but it is continually replaced. After the death of the organisms the radioactive carbon continues to decay, while the amount of C^{12} remains the same. By measuring the ratio of C^{12} to C^{14}, scientists can estimate how long it has been since a tree was burned for fuel, or an animal was eaten, or an antler was shed. One of the great advantages of Carbon 14 dating is that it can be used to date most organic materials, such as charcoal, shells, and paper. And sometimes it can even date inorganic items, such as pottery and iron.

Early users of the C^{14} method rarely considered possible sources of error, of which

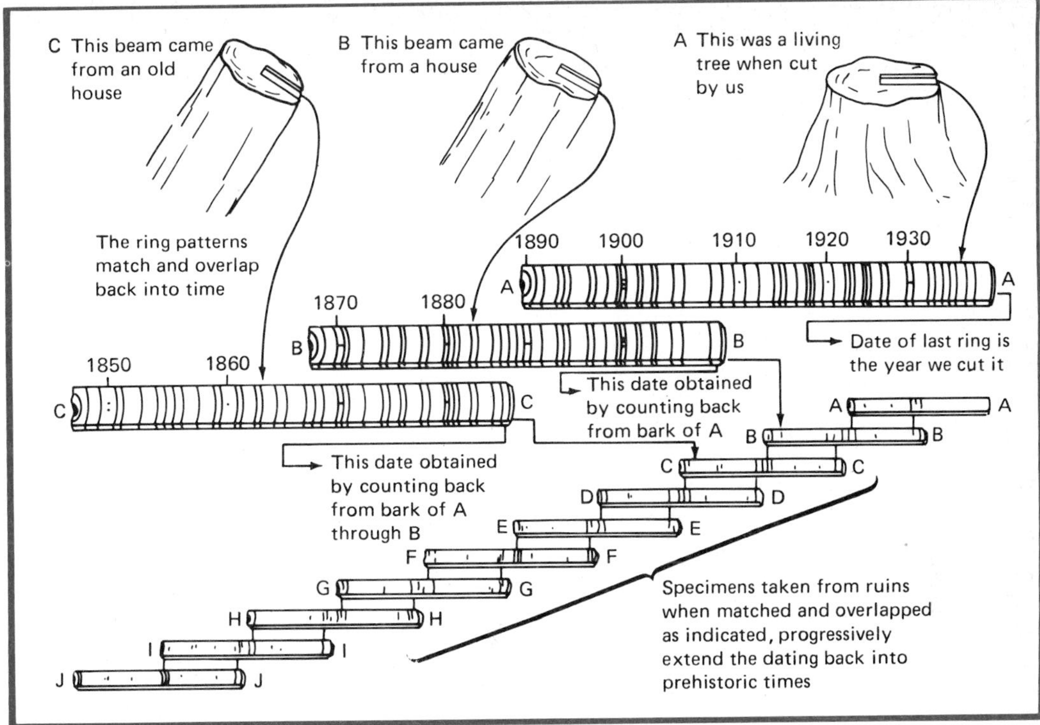

Figure 2 Dendrochronology. (Adapted from Stallings, 1939, Laboratory of Anthropology, School of American Research)

there are several. They assumed that C^{14} decays at a steady rate. Unfortunately, it does not. Radiocarbon dates for relatively recent samples—those about 3,500 years old or younger—are fairly accurate. But radiocarbon dates for older samples may be 20 to 30 percent too young. The margin of error varies unpredictably. Although C^{14} can be used to give good relative dates for samples up to 50,000 years old, the absolute dates it yields should perhaps be expressed as radiocarbon years rather than calendar years.

Another source of error is possible contamination of a sample by contemporary radiocarbon. For instance, in the past archaeologists unknowingly introduced new radiocarbon into their samples by packing them in paper boxes or coating them with organic preservatives before sending them to a laboratory to be dated. Natural processes in the soil may contaminate finds, too. But rigorous new collecting and cleaning methods have greatly reduced these chances of error.

Thermoluminescence. Four other archaeological dating techniques are used to date only cultural artifacts. The first of these is *thermoluminescence*—a means of measuring the amount of light released by a piece of pottery when it is heated. Small amounts of radioactive elements in the pottery give off particles that are absorbed at a known rate by minerals nearby in the clay. These minerals, when struck by the particles, give off electrons, which are trapped in a state of higher energy in the ceramic material. When the pottery is heated quickly, the excess energy in the electrons is released in the form of light and measured. Although this method is not at present wholly reliable, research is underway at a number of institutions to perfect it.

Archaeomagnetic Dating. As we mentioned in our discussion of paleomagnetic dating, the earth's magnetic poles have periodically reversed themselves many times in the history of the planet. In addition to these radical changes, there have been frequent shifts in the direction and intensity of the magnetic field.

When certain clays are fired, magnetic minerals in them align according to the direction and intensity of the earth's magnetic field. Thus, we can date ceramic material that has not changed its position since it was fired. Pottery left untouched in the kiln, the kiln itself, ovens, and hearths can all meet this requirement. If a sequence of fired clay can be found in successive layers, the variations can be plotted against time. The magnetic properties of isolated pieces found within a thousand-mile radius can then be compared with this master chart to estimate their age. As the sequence of magnetic shifts in more and more areas is worked out and dated with other methods, archaeomagnetic dating will become more useful.

Obsidian Hydration. Stone implements of *obsidian,* a glasslike black or banded igneous rock, can sometimes be dated by the characteristics of their worked edges. When an obsidian surface is freshly exposed, it absorbs water from the atmosphere, forming an outer layer. This hydration layer deepens slowly over the years. Researchers can measure the thickness of the hydration layer of an obsidian artifact to measure its age. But since the rate at which this layer is formed varies from one area to another, separate hydration scales must be worked out for each region studied. Although there are many such obstacles to its widespread use, obsidian hydration dating has the important advantage of being quick and cheap.

Seriation. Far older than the new laboratory methods is the relative dating of artifacts by their outer characteristics. The basic assumption here is that artifact types change with time. Archaeologists excavating many-layered sites have found much proof of this. For instance, on a very broad scale, European sites show a stratified progression from stone tools to bronze and then to iron. In a more limited frame of reference, a part of a kind of artifact, such as the handle of a kind of pot, may gradually change in form. The frequency of a given form varies with the time. Today, frequencies of visible characteristics are worked out by computer analysis in sophisticated techniques. But the basic object remains the same: to work out the temporal sequence of changes in artifacts. This is basically a relative dating method, showing whether one artifact is older or younger than another. But it can sometimes be keyed to other dating systems to give the absolute age.

Traditional Organization. In order to understand the cultural activities that led to the creation of artifacts, the activities must first be classified in some orderly way. The basic unit of the traditional organizational system is the *type.* All pots, for example, that look alike in certain specified respects such as shape, size, material, or decoration can be grouped together as a type. An average-looking specimen of each type is chosen as its representative and then used as a standard for categorizing other finds. Sometimes a period in the history of a culture is named on the basis of one kind of artifact typical of it. Such a period is called a *phase* in the traditional system. Agricultural phases, for example, have been identified most often by their characteristic pottery.

Even though modern archaeologists work with a concept of culture strongly influenced by the definitions of cultural anthropologists, the traditional definition of culture in archaeology has been somewhat different. An *archaeological culture* is defined as a grouping of artifacts that reappears consistently in a number of similar dwellings or sites. The people responsible for the archaeological culture are presumed to be a group that shared a cultural system. In this book, when the anthropological concept is meant, the word *cul-*

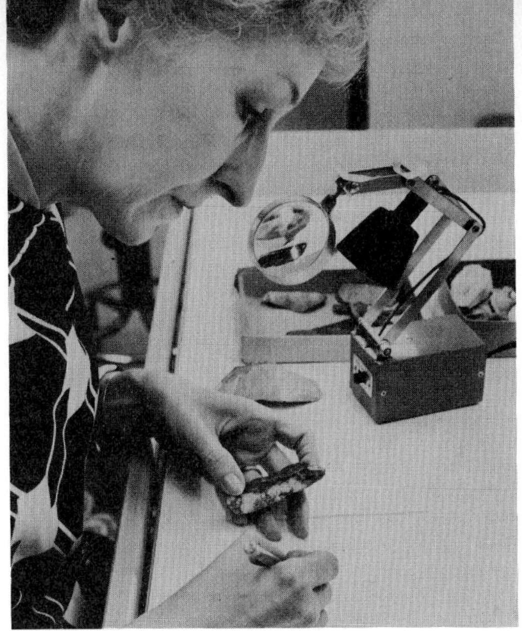

Artifacts must be examined and classified carefully if organization of remains by attribute or by type is to succeed. Here an archaeologist draws marks identifying a projectile point on a record sheet. (Hugh Rogers, Monkmeyer)

ture will be used. When the archaeological concept is intended, the term *archaeological culture* will be used.

Attribute Analysis. New methods of organization are designed to produce information about the nonmaterial aspects of a culture. One new method is called *attribute analysis.* An *attribute* is a significant trait of an object made by humans (an artifact). It could be a decorative pattern or a shape. These traits are like those that together made up a type. But the new method does not simply group objects according to how closely their traits match an ideal type. It focuses not on the artifact as a basic unit of analysis, but rather on the attribute. First, the range of all the possible ways an attribute can be expressed is found. Then the cultural beliefs that caused the artifact-maker to choose the particular set of traits in a given artifact can be inferred. This method, unlike typology, gives insight into at least some of the beliefs and values of an ancient culture (Deetz, 1972).

Archaeologists have various ways of organizing their information for study. These organizational schemes are designed to produce data for the kind of interpretation the archaeologist wants to make. Recently, archaeologists have been interested, as we have mentioned, in drawing conclusions about the behavior of people in past cultures. One organizational system that is widely used for this purpose has been suggested by James Deetz. Each level of Deetz's system matches a level of behavioral patterns in the culture under study.

At the most basic level is the attribute. (See Figure 3.) When an individual makes an object, he or she often follows a consistent pattern of behavior in fusing its various parts into a whole. The pattern may be a set way of doing things developed by the individual. Or it may be influenced by a behavior pattern of the family or other small groups. This pattern is preserved in the finished artifact.

By studying the way in which artifacts appear together, archaeologists can make inferences about the shared cultural behavior of larger subgroups of the culture. A group of artifacts reflecting a particular behavior of such a group is called a *subassemblage.* The kinds of knives, projectile points, and scrapers used, for instance, tell us something about how hunting was done. A group of subassemblages together show the influence of cultural patterns in an entire community. Such a group is called an *assemblage,* and might consist of artifacts used in hunting, agriculture, war, shelter, and religious ceremonies. Finally, if an assemblage is found at several sites in the same form, then it can be assumed that the consistencies are there because the artifacts were made by members of the same society in accordance with a shared set of techniques, rites, or styles. Deetz calls such a group of artifacts an *archaeological culture* (Deetz, 1967). This is admittedly an arbitrary framework for classifying differences among artifacts. But it is useful in isolating the cause of changes and variations.

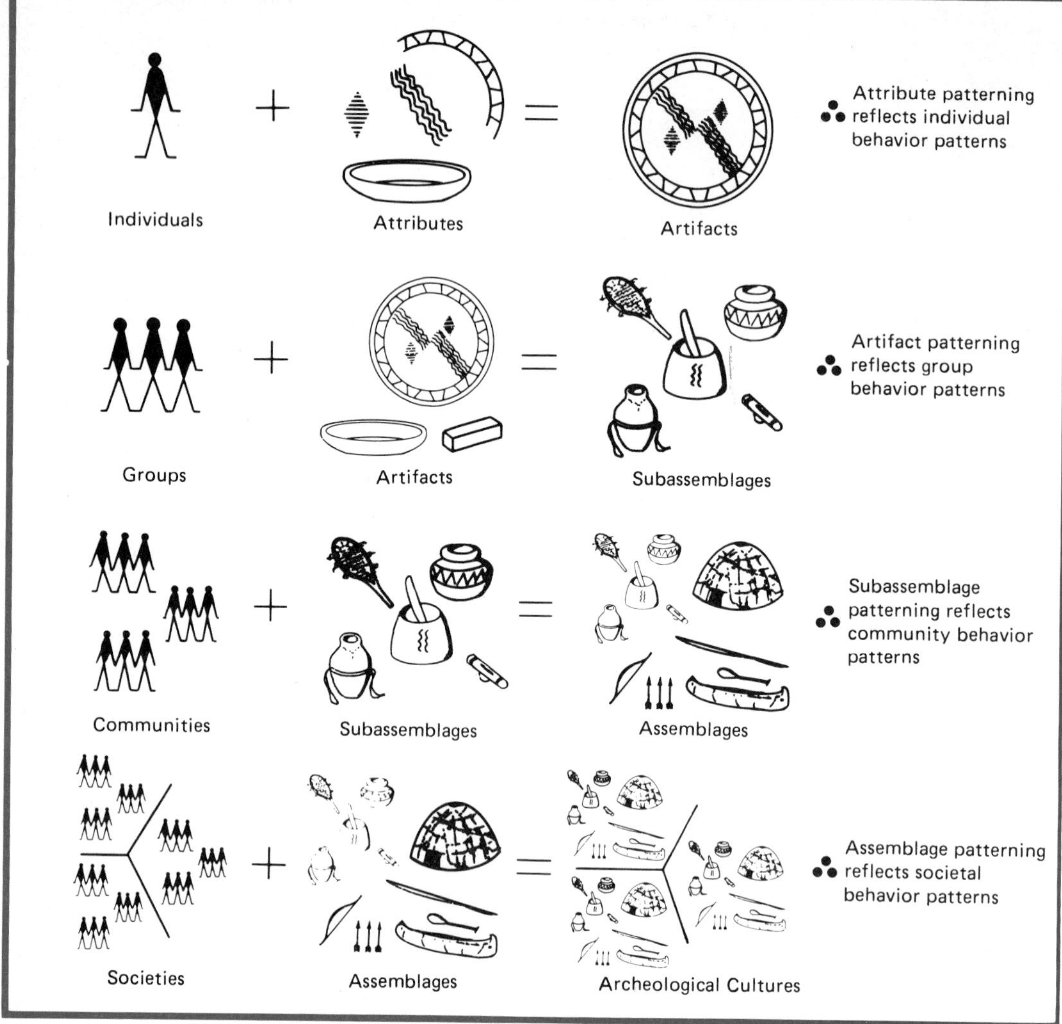

Figure 3 **A representation of Deetz's organizational system, showing levels of social organization *(left),* archeological units patterned at each level *(center),* and the level at which the pattern can be seen *(right).*** (Adapted from Deetz, 1967)

Stage Four: Interpretation

The final step is explanation or interpretation of the data. In traditional approaches, this step has often been omitted. The organization of data—perhaps as changing phases in artifact manufacture—has been considered an end in itself. Sometimes traditional archaeologists have speculated about the reasons for the changes they chronicle. But the data are not organized to make detailed inferences about the behavior of ancient peoples.

Analogies with Existing Cultures. In the "new archaeology," on the other hand, attempts are made to find relationships between artifacts and behavior, rather than between artifacts and artifacts. To explain them, archaeologists often turn to studies of living cultures. Those most useful for the interpretation of preagricultural sites are the few remaining hunting and gathering groups whose material possessions resemble those found in archaeological sites. Their economy, social structure, and artifact manufacture can be intensively observed and cautiously applied to prehistoric peoples by *ethnographic analogy.* Traditional archaeologists used it to figure out what unfamiliar artifacts might have been used for. But it is now being extended to include new areas of interest. These include the process of adaptation by a culture to the resources of its environment, and what their refuse patterns reveal about their subsistence strategies.

The Use of Models. Another important interpretive tool is the model—a tentative reconstruction of a culture and its elements, that can be tested by data analysis. So far, no one model has been generated that can be used to explain all data at all sites. In fact, there are almost as many interpretive models in archaeology as there are archaeologists.

To get an idea of how archaeologists use models, we will look in detail at just one kind: *spatial models.* These models are attempts to reconstruct the economic, social, and environmental systems revealed in the spacing of sites. The form the model takes depends on a researcher's assumptions. *Anthropological spatial theory,* for example, is based on the theory that spatial patterns are the result of culturally established beliefs about how a society should organize itself. And *economic spatial theory* assumes that, in the long run, societies tend to develop spatial patterns that minimize costs and maximize profits (Clarke, 1977).

These broad theoretical approaches have generated a number of subtheories. Economic spatial theory, for example, has produced, among others, the *central place* subtheory. German geographer Walter Christaller hypothesized that in urban communities with rather sophisticated economies, least-cost distribution of goods and services will dictate the development of a network of smaller sites spaced in a hexagonal pattern around a large central site. This model seems to fit some urban-suburban population centers in our own society. And it has been tested and supported at various archaeological sites, including the settlement patterns of the ancient lowland Maya. On the Yucatán Peninsula of Mexico, Joyce Marcus found an elaborate settlement hierarchy in which four large regional centers each served hexagonal networks of smaller secondary centers. Each of these in turn was surrounded by villages and hamlets whose position shifted in a circular pattern around the second-level sites to accommodate the long fallow periods required by their slash-and-burn agricultural practices. The Maya apparently were unaware that they had spaced themselves into a network of roughly hexagonal nested cells. As the central place theory predicts, the pattern apparently simply evolved as a result of the need for efficiency in service, travel, and carrying of goods (Marcus, 1973).

Models should be testable. In the case of spatial models, the location of sites can be tested by surveys and mapping. Models based on the system of ideas thought to characterize a culture, however, cannot be tested unless written records were kept that can be deciphered. But ecological models that explain patterns and change in terms of adaptation to the environment are increasingly popular because they can be tested. Material remains of subsistence activities (such as hunting and food-preparing implements) can be combined with clues to what the environment was like and how it changed to see if people were behaving in ecologically efficient ways. This is what Deetz was beginning to do in his interpretation of the changes in mortar styles in the Santa Barbara region.

Summary

1. *Archaeology,* the study of the history, lifestyles, and processes of change in prehistoric cultures, focuses on cultural, rather than biological change, though it must take the latter into account.

2. Traditionally, archaeology tried to reconstruct cultural sequences from prehistory. The emphasis on finding and cataloging *artifacts,* things made or used by humans, tended to obscure the human behavior responsible for the artifacts.

3. The *"new archaeology"* has stressed two new goals in addition to the old one of reconstructing culture history: (1) the detailed description of the way of life of earlier cultures, and (2) the analysis of the reasons for culture change. In addition, archaeologists have clarified their ideas and methodology to facilitate the generation and testing of hypotheses.

4. When they make inferences from artifacts about the way of life of ancient peoples, archaeologists assume that the various aspects of the culture fit together logically and harmoniously. And in studying culture change, archaeologists often draw analogies between biological adaptation and cultural adaptation. The most adaptive cultural options probably survived better than less adaptive options. Archaeologists explain the process of change in terms of *random change, diffusion, invention,* and *accidental discovery.*

5. Archaeological techniques can be broken down into the following stages: (1) *area survey* amd *site location,* (2) *recovery of material,* (3) *analysis* of the site, and (4) *interpretation* of the data.

6. To locate a *site,* a space of ground showing evidence of human occupation, archaeologists pick an area and *survey* it by defining its boundaries, walking over it looking for evidence of human occupation, and finally by entering all finds on a grid map.

7. Excavation of a site is done layer by layer, and all finds are recorded on a grid map of each layer. The environment affects how well materials are preserved: the sea preserves many things well, but very little survives in tropical areas.

8. Analysis of material from sites involves examining and dating it and organizing it into some sort of classificatory scheme.

9. Some archaeological dating techniques are based on organic remains. These include *dendrochronology* (tree-ring analysis), *paleontology* (relative dating of animal fossils), and *Carbon 14* (measurement of the amount of radioactive carbon left in organic remains and artifacts).

10. Other dating techniques focus solely on manufactured items. These methods include *thermoluminescence* (measurement of energy built up in ceramic materials by radioactive particles), *archaeomagnetism* (analysis of changes in the earth's magnetic field as reflected in pottery samples), *obsidian hydration* (measurement of the depth of the water-absorbing layer in obsidian tools), and *seriation* (relative dating by sequences of related artifacts).

11. To organize the remains of an *archaeological culture*—a grouping of artifacts that reappears consistently in a number of similar dwellings or sites—traditional archaeologists simply grouped them into sequence of types. In the "new archaeology," organization is based instead on *attribute analysis.* In this method, each *attribute,* or significant trait of an artifact, is regarded as a clue to culturally patterned behaviors, and therefore to possible reasons for the culture change implied in a sequence of remains.

12. Attempts to interpret patterns and changes in artifacts may be based on analogies with living cultures and on theoretical models. Models are tentative reconstructions of a culture and its elements, against which data can be tested.

12 Early Hominid Cultures

IN past chapters we presented humanity's biological development up to the present. In the next few chapters, however, we will start over again with the early hominids, tracing the beginnings of their cultural traditions. Distinguishing culture from biology in this manner is somewhat artificial, but it is a useful way of organizing the material remains of past societies. Although artifacts are often not found with biological remains, they provide clues to such traditions as toolmaking, hunting, pair bonding, food sharing, labor dividing, social grouping, home building, clothes making, art, speech, and religion. Some of these—such as the making of crude tools and the presence of sex- and age-related activities—are found among certain other animals as well. But only humans, with their self-awareness, prolonged childhood, and their large and complex brains, have ever come to depend so much on learned behaviors to meet the problems of survival. And as knowledge and customs grew over the millenia, humans became so good at manipulating their environment that culture began to shape biological evolution in important ways.

The Stages of Prehistory

In the past, prehistoric cultures have been divided into four stages: the Paleolithic, Mesolithic, Neolithic, and Metal Ages. These terms for chunks of prehistory are often thought inadequate today, because they are based on the toolmaking sequence found in western Europe. They have little to do with what was going on elsewhere in the world or in other aspects of cultural evolution. But since they are so familiar, we will use them as a rough guide to major cultural stages.

The *Paleolithic,* a term still commonly used by archaeologists (literally, the "Old Stone Age"), initially referred to the stage in which humans made chipped stone tools. Now, however, it stands for the period of cultural development that began during the late Pliocene Epoch and lasted through the glacial advances and retreats of the Pleistocene Epoch. Since this covers such a long time span, it is often divided into thirds: the Lower, Middle, and Upper Paleolithic. These have no connection with the geological subdivisions Lower, Middle, and Upper Pleistocene. Instead, the long Lower Paleolithic is defined as simply everything in cultural evolution that preceded the Middle Paleolithic. The Middle Paleolithic, in turn, refers to the state of human culture in western Europe during Neandertal times. And the Upper Paleolithic has traditionally been defined as the time during which blades, long, thin stone tools with parallel sides, and burins, tools used to cut and shape wood and bone, were used. It is difficult to date this sequence because cultural evolution proceeded at different rates in different areas. Consequently, the dates presented in this chapter will be area specific.

In this framework, the *Mesolithic* (the "Middle Stone Age") refers to the gap between the Paleolithic and the Neolithic in Europe. It is less often used today. The period is transitional between the last Upper Paleolithic cultures and the first cultures having agriculture. In Europe and the Near East it is a very short period just before the emergence of agriculture. With the exception of the Archaic period in North America, it is doubtful that a similar sequence appears elsewhere. Once again, the dates for this period vary. In Europe and the New World, it began about 8,000 to 10,000 years ago. In the Near East, it began somewhat earlier.

During the *Neolithic* (New Stone Age), humans began making tools by grinding and polishing rather than by chipping. A more recent definition of this cultural stage is the period from the invention of agriculture to the invention of metalworking. This stage, or ones like it, have been identified in Europe, Asia, Africa, and the Americas.

The Neolithic was followed, at least in Western Europe, by the *Bronze Age* and the *Iron Age.* Bronze and iron were the chief metals used in the art of metallurgy, which developed at this time. Toward the end of the Iron Age, people began to keep written records, ending millions of years of prehistory.

Various other frameworks have been suggested. One is based on the means of food procuring. This framework divides prehistory into two chunks: the food-gathering stage and the food-producing stage. During the first, hominid societies were organized to efficiently gather plants and to hunt animals. In the second major phase, humans began to assert more control over resources by domesticating plants and animals. The larger populations that could be supported by this process eventually led to the development of complex political structures.

The question of which system is best to analyze cultural stages is subject to considerable debate. Many archaeologists switch back and forth, depending on the time and the archeological culture they are discussing. Both systems break up a continuous line of cultural evolution. Thus, as long as the types of cultures to which we refer are clear, it does not matter which system we use.

In this book we have chosen the traditional terms. The term *Paleolithic* will be used to mean that period during which humans hunted and gathered. It was during this long period that humans spread from their tropical origins to all parts of the world. The term *Neolithic* will be used to mean that period during which agriculture emerged. And *Mesolithic* will stand for the transitional episode between the Paleolithic and the Neolithic.

Table 1 Cultural Stages of Human Prehistory

Years (B.P.)	Geological Scale	Cultural Stage	Stone Industry	Cultural Achievements
3,000	Holocene	Iron Age Bronze Age		Writing in the Near East
10,000		Neolithic Mesolithic	Upper Paleolithic	First agriculture
	Upper Pleistocene	Upper Paleolithic	Mousterian	Blade technology begins Oldest burials
100,000		Middle Paleolithic		Hand axes widely used
200,000	Middle Pleistocene		Acheulean	Oldest dwellings made by humans
500,000		Lower Paleolithic		Oldest evidence of fire Oldest biface tools
1 million	Lower Pleistocene		Pebble culture	
2 million				
2.6 million				Oldest stone tools

Although we have given some rough dates for these segments of human prehistory in Table 1, cultural development did not proceed at the same speed everywhere. Agriculture, for instance, apparently appeared independently at various places at different times and then spread slowly. Some societies still have not adopted this means of feeding themselves. For Eskimos and people of the Australian bush, for instance, hunting and gathering is still the only means of survival in regions where crops will not grow.

In this chapter, we shall explore cultural evolution during the Paleolithic period. It is by far the longest of the major toolworking stages, for it lasted from about 2.6 million to 10,000 years B.P. in the Near East. It persisted even later in Europe and the New World. Its history can be seen as a tale of cultural diversification. At the earliest and simplest level, stone tool assemblages were remarkably similar at sites throughout Africa, Europe, and the Near East. In the next stage, there were two major toolmaking traditions. By the late Middle Paleolithic, traditions were still more diversified. And by the Upper Paleolithic, there were a large number of specialized local cultural traditions.

The Oldowan Culture

The first signs that primitive hominids had begun to shape their environment by learned patterns of behavior, rather than just adapting to it biologically, are the crude stone tools found at very ancient sites. We can barely tell some of them apart from ordinary rocks. Perhaps the deliberate making of stone tools was preceded by finding and using stones whose edges were sharp enough to be better than human hands for certain chores (Bordes, 1968). Just what these chores were is hard to say for sure, but it is widely assumed that they mostly involved food getting. Perhaps sharp stones were used in cutting up carcasses or splitting bones to get at the marrow. Perhaps they were used for making points on sticks so they could be used in digging. Whatever their use, the discovery that sharp stones made certain tasks easier was important for the survival of early hominids.

Stones were not the only material aspects of early cultures. Sticks and bones must have been available, too. But wood is rarely preserved, and crude bone tools are often hard to recognize as tools. The wood and bone tools that have lasted show that until rather recent times they were cruder than stone tools (Clark, 1977).

The earliest stone tools have been grouped together in the *Oldowan tradition,* so named because tools of this type were first uncovered in the lower beds at Olduvai Gorge. These tools were made by striking one pebble against another rock to knock off enough flakes to form a single crude edge.

The Range of the Oldowan Culture

The earliest Oldowan tools known do not come from Olduvai. They were found in another part of the great Rift Valley System of East Africa. Here 10 to 12 million years of prehistory have been preserved in natural basins by sedimentary deposits. Shifts in the tectonic plates below have since exposed them. Anthropologist Glynn Isaac recently discovered stone tools that may be 2.6 million years old at the Koobi Fora formation, a peninsula that cuts into Lake Turkana in the northeast corner of Kenya.

Tools found at Koobi Fora are similar to those found in sediments at Olduvai Gorge that date from 1.89 million to about 400,000 years B.P. (M. Leakey, 1975). Early stone tool traditions probably spread from East Africa to southern and northern Africa, and then were carried to the tropical and subtropical zones of Asia as hominids moved out of Africa. Later these tools were used by early inhabitants of temperate zones in Europe. By about 700,000 years B.P., the same kind of crude tools appeared in Vallonet Cave on the shore of the Mediterranean in southern France (Bordes, 1968).

Just who made these tools is not yet clear. There may have been several species of bipedal hominids on the African scene at the time the earliest tools appeared. At least one species began to carry stones about and to sharpen their edges when the need arose. Most anthropologists think the stone carriers and sharpeners were probably the East African gracile hominids, who may have been meat eaters. The unspecialized tooth pattern of the graciles is often cited in support of the notion that tools took over some dental functions, such as the preparation of food before eating it. Tools may also have expanded the number of different types of foods that could have been eaten. Their less-advanced neighbors, the robusts, were probably highly spe-

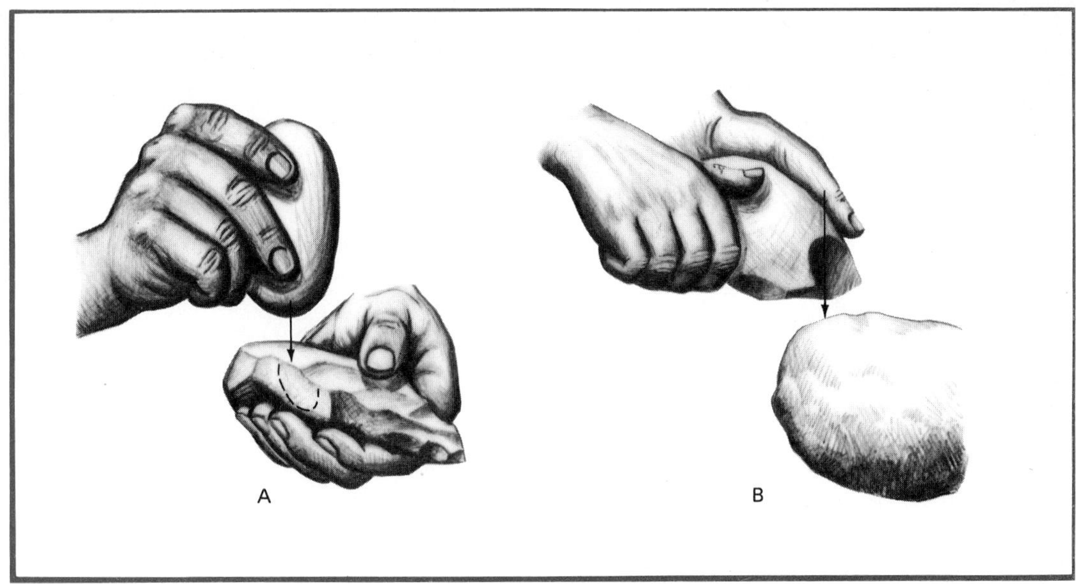

Figure 1 **Two kinds of percussion flaking.**
In *A,* a hammerstone is being used to strike flakes from another rock to form an edge. The finished tool will be a chopper. In *B,* flakes are chipped from a rock by striking it against an "anvil." (Adapted from Fagan, 1977.)

cialized vegetarians and therefore less likely to have made tools. As we mentioned in Chapter 7, their specializations suggest that the robusts were part of a separate evolutionary lineage that did not contribute to later hominid evolution. The presence of dental specialization suggests that cultural adaptations to the environment either were not made or were used in only a limited way. Although graciles seem to have been the stone toolmakers, the controversy over the number of gracile species and their names continues. It is therefore not possible to say for certain whether the toolmakers were gracile australopithecines or early members of the genus *Homo* (Isaac, 1978).

Technology of the Oldowan Culture

We know that early hominids carried stones suitable for making tools rather than gathering them on the spot. Many have been found in places where the naturally occurring stones are no larger than peas (Isaac, 1978). The favorite stones of these early hominids seem to have been water-worn pebbles about the size of a tennis ball (R. Leakey, 1977). These were given a sharp cutting edge by knocking a few flakes off one part of the rock with another rock, called a *hammerstone.* (See Figure 1.) Sometimes the stone being flaked was struck against another rock, called an *anvil.* Both methods of using one stone to strike off flakes from one or both sides of another are called *percussion flaking.*

The small flakes themselves make effective cutting or scraping tools if held between the thumb and fingers and were probably used this way. What is left of the pebble after the flakes have been removed is called a *chopper.* (See Figure 2.) We are not sure what they were used for, but modern researchers who have experimented with choppers find them very effective in cutting up game animals (Fa-

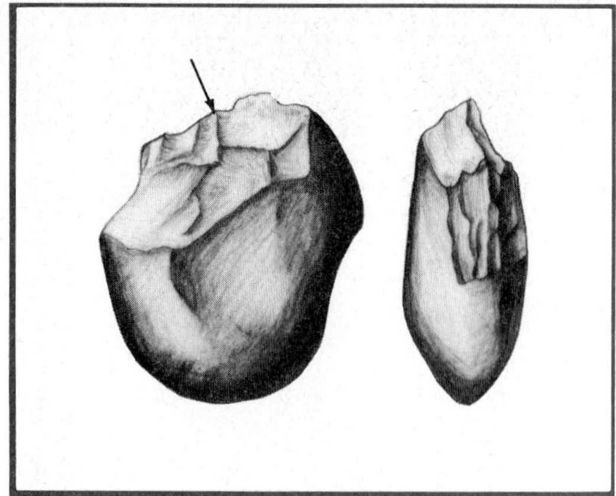

Figure 2 Front and side view of an Oldowan chopper from Olduvai Gorge.
The arrow shows the worked edge. The drawing is about 3/5 actual size. (Adapted from Fagan, 1977.)

gan, 1977). As the period progressed, tools of quartzite, such as hide-scrapers and burins, increasingly appeared in the Oldowan assemblages as well (M. Leakey, 1975).

The Econiche of the Early Hominids

Habitat. The hominids of the Oldowan culture seem to have been part of a savanna ecosystem. Although they did hunt animals that lived in the savanna-forest fringes and along watercourses, their diet included a large number of grassland plants and animals. These hominids usually camped near bodies of water—lakes, rivers, or streams. They may have preferred these sites for a number of reasons. For one thing, they offered a ready supply of water before anybody invented things to carry it in (R. Leakey, 1977). Water would have drawn many animals that could be preyed upon when they came looking for water (Butzer, 1971). And the trees around these areas would have provided shade, fruits, and a means of escape from predators. Isaac suggests that in using tree-lined streams for campsites, early hominids kept their ancestors' means of security in an arboreal environment even as they began exploiting the more varied resources of the open grasslands (Isaac, 1975).

Food Resources. Our earliest ancestors were mainly vegetarians. They lacked the large flesh-ripping canines of other carnivorous animals. It was a cultural solution—toolmaking—rather than a biological change that allowed them to tear through the fur and skin of animals to get at the meat inside. The gradual switch from a diet of vegetation to one that included a variety of animals probably added to their success in making use of the food resources of tropical areas. It may also have made possible their later move to colder climates, where plant foods were only available in certain seasons (R. Leakey, 1977).

Meat probably became part of the early hominid diet in a gradual way. When hominids first began to eat meat, they ate mostly small, easy-to-catch animals. The bones of creatures such as rodents, birds, bats, lizards, turtles, and fish are most common at their living sites. Judging from the diets of modern hunting and gathering tribes, vegetation probably continued to provide about two-thirds of what they ate. But occasionally they seemed to have fed on big game, such as hippopotamuses. Some of the remains suggest that they chased large animals into swamps and then clubbed or stoned them to death. They may also have taken meat from carcasses killed by other animals, a practice still present in some primitive tribes (Butzer, 1971).

Social Patterns

Artifacts from the beginnings of hominid culture reveal very little about social behaviors. To help reconstruct such behaviors, archaeologists also draw on an awareness of the behaviors of modern primates and hunting-and-gathering groups. The evidence has convinced archaeologists that late Pliocene and early Pleistocene hominids must

East African savanna. The early African hominids exploited a similar environment, camping near tree-lined lakes and streams. (Cannon, Anthro-Photo)

already have been diverging from nonhuman primates in social *and* biological ways.

Like some modern primates, early hominids probably lived in small bands. The members of the bands were probably fairly young, for the probability of surviving until adulthood was low (Mann, 1968). Food sharing and the cooperative behavior in food getting may have been the forces most responsible for group cohesion. There are growing signs in the fossil record that systematic hunting was an important part of this behavior. Thus, the hunting hypothesis put forth over 10 years ago by S. Washburn and C. S. Lancaster seems more relevant than ever (Washburn & Lancaster, 1968).

According to this hypothesis, hunting may have given rise to division of labor, a behavioral trait that is unique in the animal world: males probably left a base camp to hunt in bands, while females gathered plants, shellfish, eggs, and the like. Care of the young, while probably still mainly a female activity, may also have been performed part-time by males. This is the case among many nonhuman primates and human societies. It is true that open-country primates such as baboons do have a highly evolved division of labor for defense and social control. But the cooperation involved in splitting up to gather different kinds of food and then bring them back to the base camp to share would be something new. Food sharing is almost unknown among the other primates, for they forage as individuals and eat as they go. Only chimpanzees share food, and they do so rarely. When they have meat, they allow some scrounging by other members of the troop. The hypothesis that hominid hunters and gatherers brought food back to camp to share with one another is supported by sites that have piles of the remains of many different animals. According to Isaac, it is unlikely that they were all killed and eaten at the same spot. Instead, they were probably killed here and there and then carried to a butchering or camping site for the group to eat (Isaac, 1978).

Some camps may have been built near lakes and rivers during the dry season when water elsewhere was scarce. While there, the hunters killed large numbers of turtles and grazing animals, the same kinds of animals hunted by modern bushmen during the dry season. During the rainy season, Oldowan hominids moved on to other areas, about which we know little.

Hominids may have evolved permanent pair bonds between males and females to reduce aggression between males and to allow their integration into a cooperating band. Pair

A female chimpanzee, whose arm is visible at top right, begs for a piece of bushbuck being eaten by two brothers. Chimpanzees tolerate scrounging for food and sometimes hunt and use tools. These behaviors, however, are not integrated into a coherent behavioral pattern, such as food sharing at a base camp. This pattern, together with a division of labor by sex, is thought by Glynn Isaac to be the most basic innovation of human society. (Nancy Nicolson, Anthro-Photo)

bonding presumably would have lessened sexual jealousies by limiting promiscuity. Males would also help to protect and get food for mothers and their offspring.

Finally, to make all this cooperative behavior possible, hominids may have developed a communication system that was more advanced than those of the other primates. Although we have no way of knowing when language appeared, it seems logical that group planning called for some way of talking about objects, times, and places. By contrast, primate communication is largely limited to responses to objects in the immediate environment. Nonhuman primates cannot express abstractions well enough to communicate about the future or make plans.

Forces for Change

Although the cultural achievements of these early hominids were limited, they represent a landmark in our evolutionary history. At this time, hominids began to assert conscious control over their environment. They could begin to change the environment with their behavior or, if this were impossible, change their behavior to suit the conditions. Culture, in effect, created a new niche for the hominids, in which natural selection began to favor the best culture users. Smart hunters and tool users were the most fit because of their better survival strategies.

These strategies in turn probably began to select for a more complex brain. Hunting depends for its success on the ability to remember the nature and location of environmental features, as well as the habits of animals. Refinements in the coordination of hand and eye facilitated the making and use of tools. And perhaps simple language was necessary for teaching the young the basics of culture, or to plan the hunt. All these activities required the culture bearer to process sensory data, to remember it, and to integrate new perceptions with those stored in the memory. Hominids with the best brains were probably also the most adept at using culture and therefore more likely to pass on their genes. Eventually these selective pressures produced the extremely complex brain of the members of the genus *Homo.*

Early Migrations from Africa

As we noted earlier, Oldowan tools have been found not only in Africa but in other tropical and subtropical areas of the Old World as well. It is possible that they were invented separately at each location. But since the tools found at Koobi Fora and Olduvai Gorge are older than any found elsewhere, most archaeologists believe that the earliest hominid toolmakers originated in East Africa.

The earliest hominids to exploit the plants and animals of grasslands outside Africa were probably *Homo erectus.* It is not yet clear what kind of pressure led to this expansion. One theory is that early hunters followed herds of savanna herbivores in their migrations to these new territories. Both in Africa and elsewhere, this movement was accompanied by increases in technological sophistication. These, in turn, allowed hominids to move into colder and colder regions. Probably during the Günz and during the Mindel glaciations of the Middle Pleistocene (from about 600,000 to about 400,000 years B.P.) some lived in temperate environments in Europe. And during the Riss glaciation (roughly 220,000–150,000 years B.P.) some populations seemed to have lived in perpetually cold areas of Europe.

During this time, the carriers of the Oldowan culture split into two different cultural and geographical groups. The two traditions were more or less separated by a mountain barrier made up of the Himalayas in the east, the Caucasus and Zagros Mountains in southwest Asia, and the Carpathians in southeast Europe. To the east and north of this mountain barrier was an elaboration of the Oldowan tradition called the *chopper-tool culture.* People to the west and south of this string of mountain ranges evolved the life-style and way of making tools, specifically hand axes, known as *Acheulean culture.* (See Figure 3.)

The Acheulean Tradition

The Acheulean toolmaking tradition first appeared about 1.2 million years B.P. at Olduvai Gorge, long before Oldowan technologies died out. It is also found throughout much of Africa, persisting until about 60,000 years B.P. at one Rhodesian site, Kalambo Falls. Acheulean tools have also been found in the Middle East, India, and Java. They are common in southern Europe as well, but were replaced there about 100,000 to 70,000 years B.P. by the beginnings of the next cultural tradition, the Mousterian.

Acheulean Technology

The tool most characteristic of Acheulean assemblages is the *hand ax.* It is considered a logical improvement over the Oldowan chopping tool, for instead of one sharpened edge it has two. These edges meet to form a point that added to the usefulness of the tool (see Figure 4). The base, or butt, is broad for easy gripping. We are not sure how *H. erectus* used the hand ax. Recent experiments show that these tools may have had a number of functions, such as skinning, butchering, and digging.

A variation on the hand ax, the *cleaver,* is also bifacially worked, but instead of a point there is a third cutting edge (see Figure 4). The cleaver could have been helpful in chopping, hacking, and prying apart carcasses. Retouched flake tools, made from stone flakes chipped from a core, commonly appear in Acheulean assemblages.

The transition from Oldowan to Acheulean stone-working technology seems to have happened in several stages. Some of the early Oldowan choppers had been worked on both sides. Gradually, however, early hominids flaked more and more of the surface of the stone, making the tool more slender and symmetrical. By the end of the Acheulean tradition, the whole tool, including the butt, was shaped, often to the point that the original shape of the stone is unrecognizable.

At first this flaking was done with a hammerstone, as in the Oldowan industries. But eventually Acheulean toolmakers discovered that they could control the size and shape of the flake better by using a bone or a stick as a hammer. This method is called the *soft-hammer* technique. In this technique, a bone, antler, or piece of wood was used to strike off shallow flakes from the sides of core tools. The use of this technique is marked by thinner axes, from which many more flakes have been removed to create a sharper edge (Bordes, 1968; Butzer, 1971).

A further development was an increasing

sophistication in the production of flakes. In Oldowan industries, flakes were merely useful by-products of making choppers. Probably recognizing that a well-designed flake could be more functional than one randomly struck, later Acheulean toolmakers prepared some stones with an eye toward the shape of the flake, rather than the shape of the parent stone, or core. The chief intent in this aspect of toolmaking was to prepare the core in such a way that flakes of predictable size and shape could be struck from it.

Stone was not the only material Acheuleans used for their tools. Bone and wood artifacts occasionally appear in their assemblages as well, but they are much rarer than stone tools. Bones were shaped and trimmed for specific purposes. They may have been used as picks, axes, and cleavers, or perhaps for activities that humans no longer carry on. Wood is oc-

Figure 3 Distribution of cultures with and without hand axes. The two cultures are separated by a chain of mountain ranges extending from the Himalayas in the east to the Pyrenees in the west. Note the overlap in central Europe. (Adapted from Bordes, 1968.)

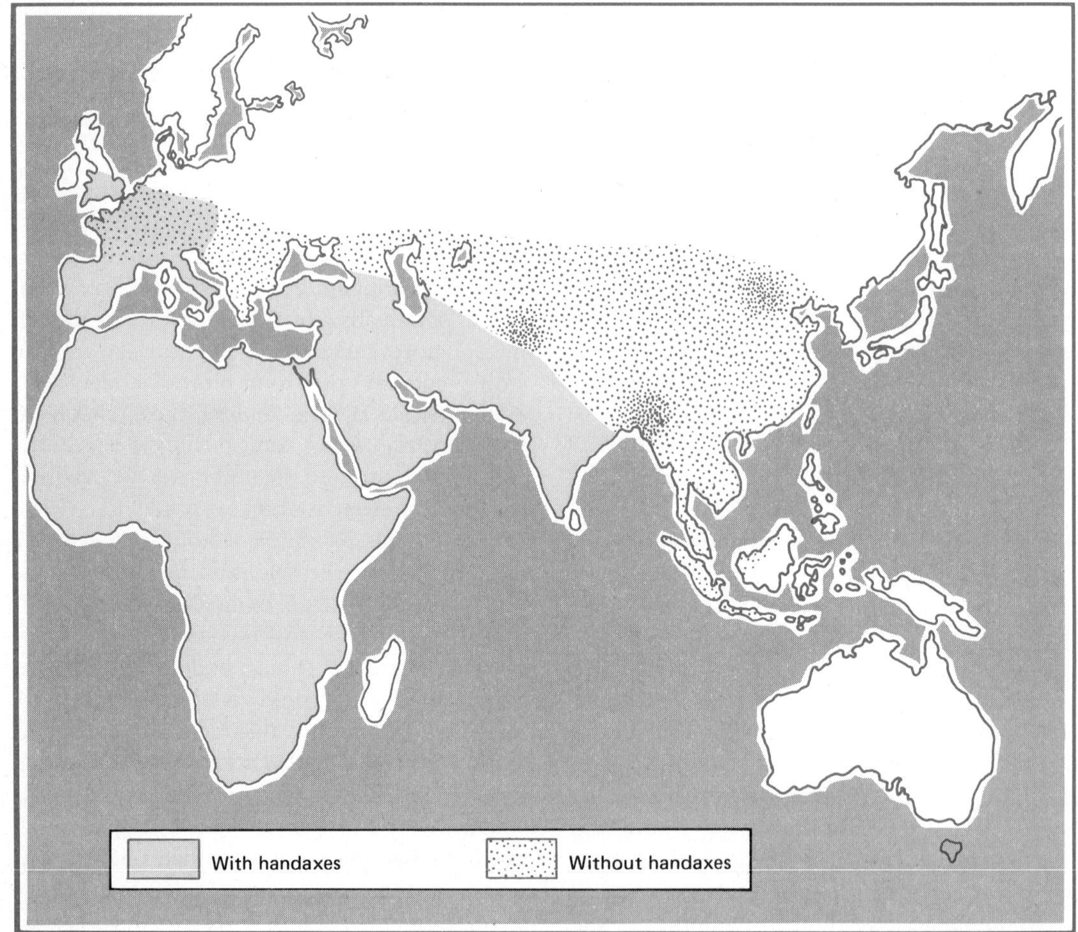

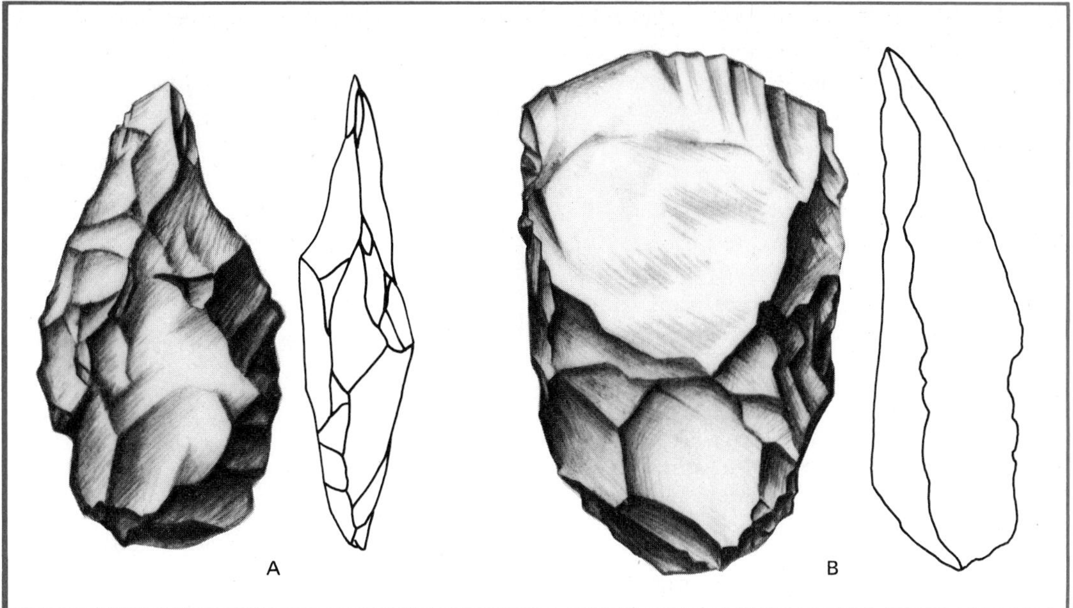

Figure 4 An Acheulean hand ax *(A)* from Olduvai Gorge and an Acheulean cleaver *(B)* from Baia Farta, Angola.
The hand ax is 3/4 the actual size; the cleaver is 1/2 the actual size. Acheulean toolmakers worked a much greater portion of the stone than Oldowan people had. (Adapted from Fagan, 1977.)

casionally preserved in the shape of what appears to be a spear. The Acheuleans may also have used wood as clubs, throwing sticks, and tools to dig for roots and bulbs, as primitive peoples do today (Butzer, 1971).

Econiche

In the main, Acheulean sites seem to have been located within grassland environments. These grasslands probably provided an optimal environment for the large and medium-sized animals that they regarded as food. Until the end of the middle Paleolithic, Acheulean groups avoided both the dense tropical rainforests of west-central Africa and the barren deserts elsewhere on that continent. For most of this time, they lived in tropical or subtropical latitudes, rarely venturing farther north than southern Europe, which had a warm-temperate environment. But toward the end of the Acheulean period, particularly during the Riss glaciation (220,000–150,000 years B.P.), they moved into progressively colder regions. In some cases, the cold came to them, in the form of advancing glaciers. For instance, instead of retreating southward ahead of the European ice sheets, as did the elephants they had been hunting, the Acheuleans in southern Europe stayed in place, culturally adapted to the cold, and started hunting the mammoths that thrived on the tundra (Collins, 1969).

One cultural innovation that would play an increasingly important part in humans' ability to survive in cold climates was the controlled use of fire for warmth and cooking. Fire clearly was used at a chopper-tool site, Vertésszöllös, about 450,000 years B.P. It can also be seen in the bits of charcoal and charred bone at Torralba, in Spain. The use of fire spread slowly to warmer climates, not reaching Africa until the end of the Pleistocene.

Shelter, too, was becoming more important as another cultural adaptation to the cold weather. In Europe, signs of crude windbreaks and huts with stake walls reinforced by stone piles have been found. There is also evidence that caves were being occupied. But some sites seem to have no shelters at all, suggesting that people did not build them unless the weather was bad or a long stay was expected. Judging from the lack of debris at their campsites, the Acheuleans seem to have moved about a great deal, possibly because they followed the seasonal movements of animal herds. But a few of the sites seem to have been occupied for weeks or months by bands of about 20 to 30 adults plus children.

The dismembered carcasses and smashed animal bones that litter Acheulean sites leave little doubt that these bands were also becoming increasingly systematic hunters. Animal protein was probably very important in cold climates where vegetation was seasonally scarce. Although Acheulean hunters may have eaten scavenged meat, as the Oldowans did, they had more refined methods of downing large animals. For instance, stone bolas on hide thongs were probably hurled at the legs of running prey. Prey varied from elephants and rhinos to baboons and reptiles, but some local populations seem to have concentrated on a single species (Butzer, 1971).

The Chopper-Tool Culture

Another distinct cultural tradition seems to have existed during roughly the same period as the Acheulean. Dates for this chopper-tool culture are not as well determined, however. Chopper-tool assemblages lacked hand axes, and are found over a different geographical and environmental range than the Acheulean. Except for northern Europe, where they were intermixed somewhat with the Acheulean, chopper-tool culture sites are all located north and east of the Acheuleans—in east Asia, southeast Asia, and in India east of the Indus River.

Technology. Non-Acheulean tool kits are

Figure 5 A chopping tool *(A)* and a cleaverlike tool *(B)*, both of the chopping-tool culture.
These implements were found in the same bed as *H. erectus,* at Chou-kou-tien. (Adapted from Bordes, 1968.)

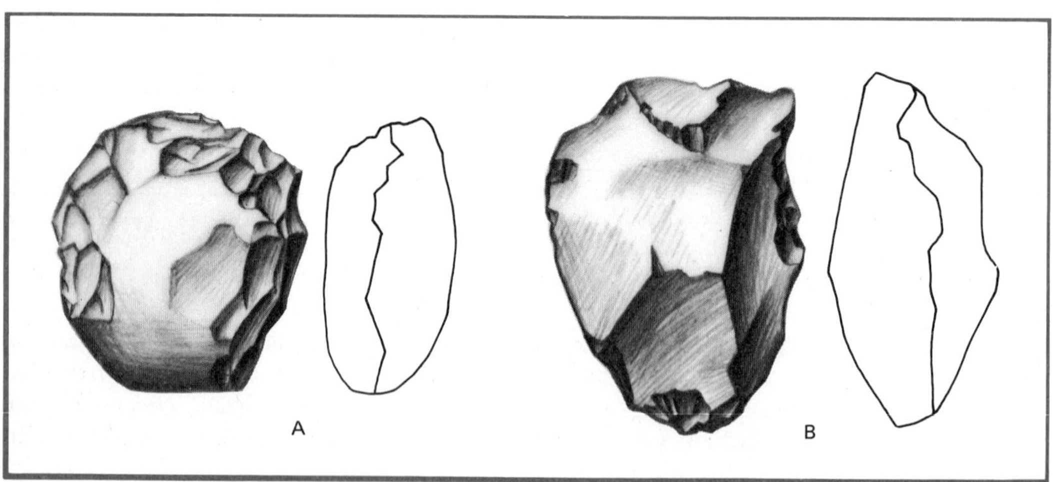

easier to define by what they lack—the hand axes that are so typical of Acheulean assemblages—than by what traits they have. Some assemblages seem to consist mostly of flakes removed by striking a stone held against an anvil. This was *bipolar* working, for it produced percussion effects at both ends of the flake. The edges of some of the flakes were then chipped to form a variety of rather refined tools, some with teeth and notches. Choppers and chopping tools (with cutting edges worked on both sides) were also present. (See Figure 5.)

The origins and spread of this toolmaking tradition are obscure. But French archaeologist François Bordes suggests that it may have appeared first in southeast Asia 475,000 to 425,000 years B.P. as an elaboration on the Oldowan tradition and then spread to the west as far as England. Chopper-tool sites there have been dated to the Holstein Interglacial, which began about 425,000 years B.P. (Bordes, 1971).

Food Resources. Despite the relative crudeness of their tools, Eurasians of this period managed to kill and butcher a great variety of animals. The bones of deer are most common in their food debris, but elephants, rhinos, bison, water buffalos, and many other animals were eaten as well. They may even have enjoyed an occasional meal of their own species. At Chou-kou-tien, near Peking, cannibalism may have occurred. Some of the long bones of hominids found there were split, possibly so that the marrow could be reached. Some skulls seem to have been cracked open so that the brains could be removed (Clark, 1977).

Econiche

The chopper-tool complex is found at sites that are on the northern edge of the Eurasiatic mountain chain. Compared to Acheulean sites, they were located in more wooded and colder areas, farther from the ocean.

Acheulean and chopper-tool sites were, for the most part, clearly separated. In northern Europe, however, they do overlap in time and, in some cases, space. One explanation is that the sites attributed to the two different cultures simply represented different activities—and therefore different types of tools—of the same population. But a closer look at the environmental range and toolmaking technology of these two cultures shows that they were really quite different. Desmond Collins (1969) has suggested that the chopper-tool complex was organized to exploit wooded terrain and a greater variety of food resources than the Acheulean. The latter specialized in the sorts of game herds that lived in more open, grassland environments. Because of this difference, the chopper-tool culture was the first to colonize northwestern Europe sometime during the Holstein Interglacial (420,000–220,000 years B.P.). Until the Riss, the glacial period following the Holstein Interglacial, Acheulean populations may only have existed in open areas or during warmer periods in larger river valleys in the north. During the Riss, however, Acheulean populations seem to have adjusted to the tundra parkland near the glaciers—particularly exploiting the large mammoth herds. But even at this time the types of environments exploited by the two cultures would have remained distinct. Because of this aparently distinct adaptive difference, it is likely that two separate culture types existed at this time.

Cultures of the Late Middle Paleolithic

By the beginning of the Würm glaciation, at about 80,000 years B.P., and perhaps even a little before then, populations in many parts of the world began to make a greater variety of more specialized, more sophisticated tools. Hominids intensified their efforts to exploit the environment, managed to survive in extremely cold conditions, and showed many social features of modern human cultures.

This late middle Paleolithic cultural period is roughly contemporary with the archaic *H. sapiens* (or Neandertal) period of human biological evolution. In Europe, where the time sequence is best known, it lasted from 80,000 or 100,000 years B.P. to about 40,000 years B.P. The major tool tradition associated with this time period is the Mousterian. Its characteristic assemblages are found throughout Europe and in the Near East, western Russia, south Asia, and northern Africa.

Technology

Mousterian assemblages are not identified by a single tool—as Acheulean sites are characterized by the presence of hand axes—or even by a single toolmaking tradition. Different sites may have very different tool kits. Perhaps these differences represent increasingly sophisticated adaptations to differing environments. Or they may indicate different sets of cultural notions about how tools should be made, and what kind. In general, though, they are more complex than anything that existed before.

Mousterian artifacts are often *composite tools,* having several parts. Earlier tools were made in one part from a single piece of raw material. A Mousterian spear might have a wooden shaft, a stone point, and a bone handle. Another indication that the toolmaker's art was becoming more advanced was careful preparation of a core so that flakes could be struck in precise, preshaped forms. This method, called the *Levallois technique,* produced longer, sharper cutting edges than previous methods. (See Figure 6.)

There was considerable local variety in Mousterian assemblages. Bordes (1968) sees five distinct general toolmaking traditions in Mousterian France. They correspond to some extent to assemblages found in similar environments elsewhere in the world.

Figure 6 The Levallois technique.
During the Middle Paleolithic, stoneworkers refined the technique of preparing a stone core from which many flakes of a given shape could be struck. One such form was a Levallois core. The worker first trimmed the sides of a piece of flint *(1),* then the top *(2)*. Next, an edge was chipped at one end *(3)* so that a flake could be struck from the top *(4)*. The process was repeated to produce additional flake tools. (Adapted from Fagan, 1977.)

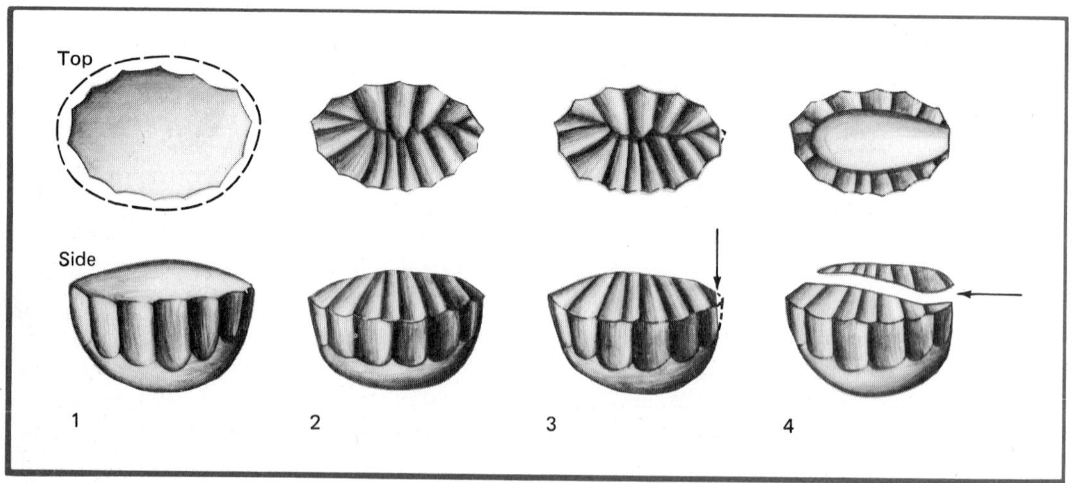

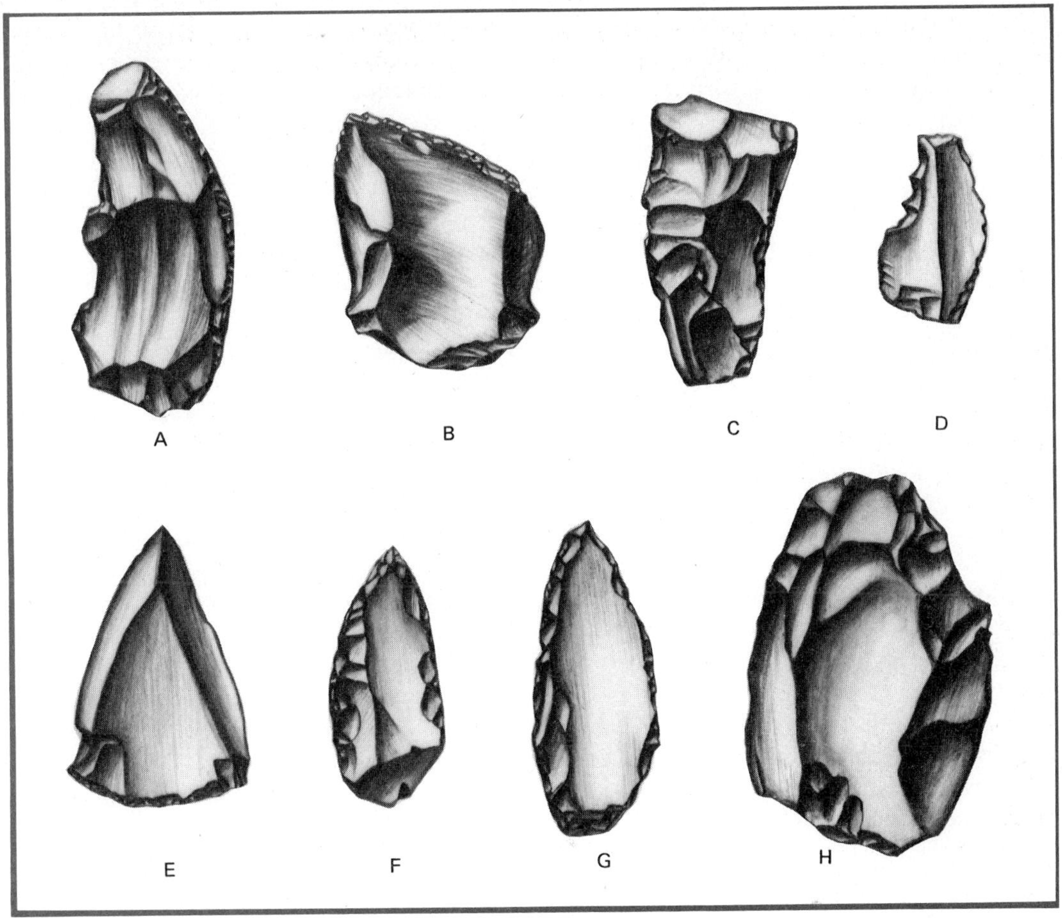

Figure 7 Mousterian tool types.
A–C are scrapers, *D* is a notched tool (notches are along the upper left edge), *E–G* are points, and *H* is a Levallois flake. (Adapted from Bordes, 1968.)

1. *Typical Mousterian* assemblages rarely contain hand axes. Tools probably used as scrapers are plentiful, and points on other tools are made with care.
2. *Quina-Ferrassie* (or Charentian) assemblages are dominated by scrapers. Some are apparently designed for extremely specialized functions.
3. *Denticulate Mousterian* assemblages are rich in fine-toothed (or "denticulate") tools. But hand axes, points, and scrapers are either altogether lacking or of poor quality.
4. The fourth tradition, *Mousterian of the Acheulean tradition,* evolves from an earlier to a later form. Type A has numerous hand axes and varied flake tools, including a number of scrapers. Type B, on the other hand, has few hand axes or scrapers, but many denticulates and knives.
5. The last tradition, *Micoquian,* is characterized by lance-shaped hand axes, often with concave edges and thick bases.

Although Bordes interprets the differences among these assemblages as distinct cultural traditions, some archaeologists see them as the products of a single culture, occupying varying environments and carrying on different activities.

Econiche

The econiche occupied by the late archaics is best understood in Europe, which was densely settled during Mousterian times. Sites dating from the Würm have been excavated intensively in modern times. Despite the cold weather that hominids must have faced in Europe during the peak of glacial activity, the number of plant and animal remains found there suggest that the area could support abundant life. Ample amounts of sunlight helped. In midsummer, there were probably 16 hours of light a day, and at least half that much in winter. Except in areas of perpetual snow, northern Europe was covered with a variety of plants that were adapted to the cold. Wooly mammoth, wooly rhinoceros, elk, bison, and many other animals were numerous. The environment must have been like the tundra meadow and forest areas of northern Canada and Alaska—a region that today supports large herds of elk and moose.

The European hominids of this time apparently took full advantage of the high biomass of the tundra. Although they seemed to be capable of bagging everything from cave bears to fish, they must have been very fond of—or good at following and killing—reindeer. At one open-air habitation site in northern Germany, for instance, almost three-fourths of the animal remains found are those of reindeer (Kennedy, 1975).

To make use of this rich ecosystem, humans continued to rely on traditional hunting tools such as spears and bolas. Bows and arrows, fishhooks, and harpoons were still unknown. It is possible, though, that since Mousterians made graves with digging sticks, they also probably used pits to trap game. And the increasing inventory of tools may have been used to fashion a variety of weapons made of wood, bone, and plant fibers.

Adaptations to the cold may have included anatomical changes, as we saw in Chapter 8. (The larger noses of the Neandertals may have helped them to bear better the bitterly cold air of the glacial period.) Cultural solutions included continued use of fire. Rock shelters and caves were now systematically used for dwellings for the first time, sometimes on a semipermanent basis. Branches or skins may have been draped across the openings to keep out the cold, and fires were burned for warmth. And even in open-air sites some groups seemed to have built weather-tight shelters covered with skins. The many scrapers found in Mousterian assemblages suggest that these people were also scraping animal hides, possibly for use as blankets or clothing, though we cannot be sure of this (Clark, 1977).

Another way in which some of these archaic humans adapted to the Würm cold was to migrate with the seasons, as did the animals they hunted. In the summer they traveled north into the open tundras; in the winter they came south to take refuge in the forests. This kind of life continued to favor small group size. Campsites are not large enough to suggest any social organization more complex than a band.

Outside of Europe archaic *H. sapiens* populations were expanding into new ecosystems, from tropical rainforests to subarctic regions. They were also developing technologies more specifically aimed at making use of local food sources and building materials. In the African rainforest, for instance, there was a seeming emphasis on tools for working wood, for this material was abundantly available (Butzer, 1971).

Glimmers of Modern Culture

At the same time that they were refining their toolmaking arts and living in new ecosystems, some groups seemed to be developing a more modern capacity for self-awareness and symbolic thought. We know that their brains were large, at least as large as ours, though this trait cannot be directly linked with intelligence. By this time, their cultural traditions were so rich that they must have been using some form of speech. Our only evidence of their ability to speak, however, is indirect. We know little of how their brain was structured, for only a few of their external features have been preserved in endocranial casts. Whether or not they had a localized "speech center" in their brains we cannot tell. Some researchers have noted that these hominids had plenty of room in which to move their tongues if they did try to speak, since the bony shelves had disappeared from the insides of their lower jaws. Philip Lieberman, a linguist, and Edmund Crelin, an anatomist, determined that the larynx and brain of these early people were better equipped for speech than those of other primates. The two scientists built a model of the vocal tract of a European fossil dated to the early part of the Würm. They then designed a computer program to analyze what kinds of sounds it could have made. The result: although the late archaics could make more differentiated sounds than other primates could, they could produce only a few vowel sounds, and their consonants were limited to *b*s, *d*s, and a few others. Fascinating as this theory is, however, it is based on very thin evidence—a single fossil of a very old male.

In some areas, the late archaics had begun to practice such uniquely human social customs as ritual burial. Sixty thousand years ago, in a cave located in modern-day Iraq, a child was buried on a bed of flowers. A youth found buried at Le Moustier, France, was buried with animal bones and stone tools. And at La Chapelle-aux-Saints, another individual was laid to rest in a small grave carved out of the rocky floor of the cave. The body was surrounded by bits of quartz, jasper, and red ochre. Perhaps these were personal possessions; perhaps they were symbolically linked with a belief in an afterlife. We have no way of knowing. We do know, however, that ochre was increasingly used in burials and other rituals, suggesting that it carried some kind of symbolic meaning. One anthropologist thinks that the red of the ochre was linked to the life-giving connotations of blood (Wreschner, 1976).

Some of the earliest ornamental objects yet found may have been made by Mousterian groups. Most were things worn on the body—necklaces and beads made of animal teeth, bones, and even 50-million-year-old fossilized shells. Whether these were used as ornaments, symbols, or perhaps even as magical tokens is not clear (Marshack, 1978; Clark, 1977). But strange groupings of cave bear skulls and bones have been interpreted as strong evidence for some kind of magical or religious beliefs (Kennedy, 1975). For some reason, the Mousterians also made symbolic marks—such as zigzags—on bone plaques and then covered them with red ochre (Marshack, 1976).

Such rare discoveries are extremely exciting to contemporary archaeologists, for they push back by tens of thousands of years the possible beginnings of symbolic, rather than strictly functional, behavior. And for all we know, Mousterians may have had elaborate myths, songs, and dances that will remain forever lost to us because they have left no material traces (Marshack, 1976).

The Upper Paleolithic

Up to about 40,000 years ago, culture had evolved rather slowly. The Oldowan tradition lasted 1.5 million years, overlapped to some extent by the Acheulean, which persisted for over a million years. The pace of change increased somewhat during the Mousterian, which in Europe lasted only 40,000 to 60,000 years (Butzer, 1971). By the Upper Paleolithic, people apparently had the technology and the background of accumulated knowledge to rapidly improve and specialize their toolmaking techniques. They organized themselves into larger groups and translated their perceptions of one another and the animals they hunted into surprisingly good works of art. And, exploiting many different environments, they crossed geographical barriers to enter the last frontiers of the habitable world: the Americas and Australia.

Technology

Upper Paleolithic toolmaking traditions are complex and confusing. The best-known sequences exist in Europe. But even there, they are poorly worked out except in France. Some archaeologists speculate that southeastern Europe and southwestern Asia may have been areas in which for some reason there were many cultural innovations. These traditions then spread to other regions (Klein, 1974). Others, like Bordes (1968), suspect that technological changes were taking place independently at many different locations, rapidly increasing cultural diversity throughout the world. Rather than try to follow the changes in each region, we will focus on only two: France and the Paleo-Indian cultures of the New World.

In France, deposits show a gradual transition from Mousterian to *Perigordian* industries. This culture existed from about 35,000 to about 18,000 years B.P. It probably evolved from the Mousterian of Acheulean tradition. At about the same time, however, another culture appeared in France that did not seem to have originated there. This was the *Aurignacian,* which lasted from about 33,000 to 25,000 years B.P. Its origins and spread are still a mystery, though some archaeologists suspect that it may have been introduced from the Middle East. During the third Würm glaciation (Würm III), these two cultures seem to have coexisted without affecting each other much more than the various Mousterian traditions of the earlier Würm did.

Whatever the relationship between the Perigordian and Aurignacian, only the former existed between about 25,000 and 18,000 years B.P. After 18,000 years B.P. the late Perigordian was replaced in France by the short-lived *Solutrean.* The Solutrean lasted only 2,000 years, but during that time flint-working techniques advanced to a new peak. The origin of the Solutrean is not at all clear. It may have been a holdover from some Mousterian tradition that had continued to evolve in an isolated region before it spread across a rather limited area of Europe.

Roughly 16,000 years ago, the Solutrean vanished as mysteriously as it had appeared. It was quickly replaced by the very different tools of the *Magdalenian* tradition. The Magdalenian lasted until about 10,000 years ago, when it was replaced by the so-called Mesolithic Period (or Middle Stone Age). As we shall see in the next chapter, the Mesolithic lasted until the onset of agriculture in Europe (Bordes, 1968).

Despite their differences through time, Upper Paleolithic assemblages have one unique technological feature: They are rich in *blades.* These are long, thin flakes with parallel sides. Blades may have been produced in at least three different ways: (1) hammering a chisel-like instrument against a stone that was steadied on top of a large rock (see Figure 8), (2) punching vertical slices out of a prepared rock with a long pointed tool steadied against the toolmaker's chest, or (3) traditional stone-against-stone percussion flaking. The blades that resulted were of predictable, standardized shapes. With a little retouching, they could readily be made into specialized tools. The keen edge of these tools probably made it

A blade, characteristic tool of Upper Paleolithic assemblages. (Courtesy of the American Museum of Natural History)

possible to work material other than stone, such as hides, wood, and bone.

Among the specialized Upper Paleolithic blade tools are what archaeologists call *borers.* Their sharp points were probably used to drill holes into wood, shell, bone, or skins. The flattened ends of burins may have been used to chisel grooves in wood, bone, and antlers. *End scrapers* were sharpened on both ends, rather than one side (as in the Mousterian side-scrapers). They were probably used in hollowing out bone and wood or removing bark, as well as in scraping skins. *Notched blades* may have been used to shave wood in fashioning the shafts of arrows or spears.

Upper Paleolithic assemblages also contain *backed blades,* with one purposely dulled edge and one sharpened one, useful in general cutting and scraping. Bows and arrows appear for the first time during this period. *Shouldered points* were probably affixed to spears or arrows for fighting or hunting. Laurel-leaf blades were so delicately chipped and thin that they may have been used as ceremonial items, rather than as weapons.

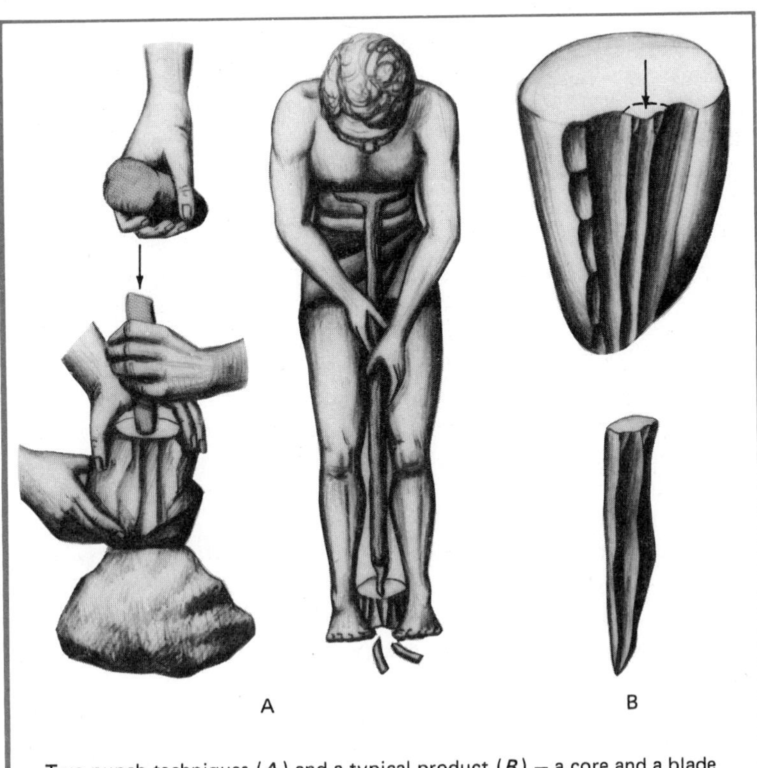

Two punch techniques (*A*) and a typical product (*B*) – a core and a blade struck from it. The dotted line and arrow show the point at which the next blade will be struck off from the core

Figure 8 (From Fagan, 1977.)

A Solutrean laurel leaf blade.
(Courtesy of the American Museum of Natural History)

In addition to blade tools, Upper Paleolithic assemblages—especially the Magdalenian—contain elaborate tools made of bones and antlers. Magdelenian bone and antler spear-throwers, barbed fish-hooks, harpoon heads, thong or shaft straighteners, and needles testify to the specialized uses to which materials other than stone were put. These objects were not only efficient tools but also showed the artistic talent of their makers. Many are even handsomely decorated with engraved pictures (Fagan, 1977; Butzer, 1971).

Econiche of European Upper Paleolithic Populations

Upper Paleolithic tools made possible a more efficient use of food resources. In Europe, Upper Paleolithic populations occupied roughly the same tundra and forest ecosystem in which Mousterian populations had lived. But there are far more Upper Paleolithic sites, some apparently the ruins of permanent or semipermanent camps of over a hundred people. This suggests that more successful adaptations to extreme cold allowed population density to increase greatly. Their more settled existence and larger group size probably called for some form of political authority, a theory that is borne out by evidence that some people were buried with greater ceremony than others. The informal political structure of small bands becomes a less effective way of organizing large groups of people. In larger groups leadership roles were probably performed by persons who could influence others through the force of their personalities.

Like their predecessors, the Upper Paleolithic peoples of Europe continued to rely on tundra and forest game. There is no sound evidence that they were beginning to domesticate the herds that they followed, though herd management may have appeared at about this time in the Middle East with selective killing of the young (Patterson, 1973). But their ways of capturing game were becoming far more effective than ever before. Spear-throwers and bows and arrows increased the accuracy and speed with which projectile points could be directed at prey. Judging from large piles of bones at the base of some cliffs, herds apparently were driven over precipices to their death. Cave drawings show the use of various traps, pitfalls, and enclosures. And fishing was greatly improved by the invention of harpoons and primitive fishhooks. All these advances led to what was probably the highest standard of living ever known anywhere before the onset of agriculture (Butzer, 1971).

For the first time, humans were having a significant effect on the environment. The increasing use of large game animals like the mammoth may have contributed to their extinction, though climate changes undoubtedly played a part in this, too. Upper Paleolithic groups may have changed the vegetation as well. Frequent evidence of forest fires in layers of this age has been interpreted by some archaeologists as an indication of intentional burning by humans. Fires may have made it easier to sight and trap game. Fires also caused plants eaten by game species to grow, and helped the growth of berries and other vegetation probably eaten by humans (Butzer, 1971).

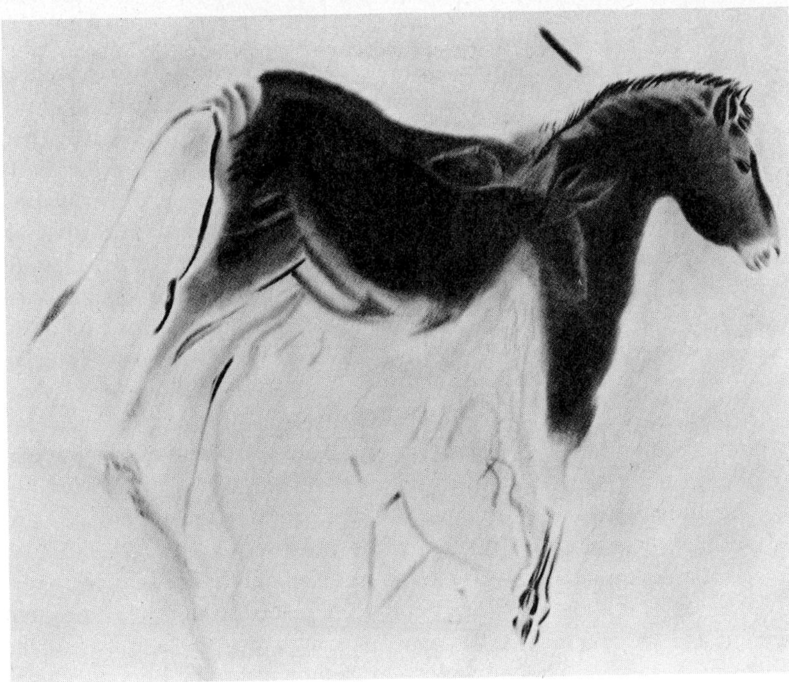

An Upper Paleolithic cave painting from Altamira, Spain, showing a horse with a deer superimposed on it. (Courtesy of the American Museum of Natural History)

Art

Improved hunting-and-gathering techniques may have provided Upper Paleolithic peoples with enough free time to develop artworks of extraordinary quality. Especially in France and Spain, engraved bone and antler implements, low-relief clay sculptures, carved statuettes, cave drawings, and multicolored paintings reached a peak of sophistication during the Magdalenian.

Observers once tended to dismiss these pieces as bored cave dwellers' way of distracting themselves. But the current trend is to see the paintings as meaningful products of a patterned intelligence. Some of the realistic representations of game animals might have been used repeatedly in rituals designed to encourage the success of the hunt, cure sickness, mark births or deaths, or celebrate the onset of spring. Exquisite "Venus" statues of women—many of them apparently pregnant—might have been fertility symbols. Various abstract signs—such as rectangles, rows of dots, barbed lines, and ovals—might have symbolized males, females, and their relationships. Some marks might be attempts to keep track of time, distance, or quantity. If so, they predated by thousands of years the first recognizable calendars, rulers, and systems of writing and arithmetic. Consistencies in the location of various animals in the cave paintings suggest that whatever the explanation, it was intentional and orderly rather than random. Many archaeologists are now excitedly studying them as symbolic traditions that, if deciphered, could provide a wealth of clues to how these early people lived, thought, and perhaps spoke (Leoroi-Gourhan, 1968).

Migration to the New World

Except for its bitterly cold climate, eastern Siberia was probably fairly attractive to Stone Age hunters. With open park vegetation feeding an abundance of animals, it probably supported more people than it does today. By late Paleolithic times, humans apparently had adjusted to cold by wearing warm, fitted clothing and shoes (Bricker, 1976) and by living in rather large heated dwellings.

Perhaps because of the increasingly successful adaptation to this environment, Upper Paleolithic groups may have increased in number beyond the ability of the area to support them. At any rate, about 30,000 years ago various groups began to migrate into the previously untapped ecosystems of *Beringia,* the land mass that connected eastern Siberia and western Alaska.

This continental land mass was temporarily exposed as expanding glaciers trapped normally circulating water as ice and caused sea levels to drop. The first human immigrants probably followed grazing herds onto Beringia and eastern Alaska not long after their ancestors reached Siberia, perhaps between 32,000 and 28,000 years ago. These migrations were cut off about 10,000 years B.P., as the last glacial maximum ended and sea levels rose, covering the landbridge.

Alaska and the Yukon were probably even richer in plant and animal life than Siberia. This new area had never been covered by glaciers. Instead, it was dotted with streams, lakes, and a variety of forest, grassland, and tundra ecosystems. A similarly rich and varied environment lay to the south, and when gaps appeared between the major eastern and western Canadian ice sheets, some humans followed animal herds down through these unglaciated corridors. They probably reached what is now the continental United States by at least 18,000 years B.P. and South America by at least 16,000 years B.P.

The Paleo-Indian Hunters of North America

The earliest known humans in the New World—the so-called *Paleo-Indians*—brought with them technologies and living patterns taken from Old World cultural traditions, especially those of eastern Siberia. After they made their way south of the ice sheets, they spread rapidly and diversified as they adapted to new ecosystems.

The unusually rapid movement into these new ecosystems may have been caused partly by sheer human curiosity to see what lay over the horizon. But perhaps it can also be explained by the dynamics of population growth in a new environment. According to one model (Patterson, 1973), populations probably increased as they moved into areas of previously untapped resources. As their numbers grew, the Paleo-Indians began to exhaust some of these resources—food, water, fuel, shelter, toolmaking materials—making it necessary for some of the population to migrate. The rest probably stayed behind to live at a density that could be supported by the resources of the area. Those who moved out probably settled in virgin territory nearby, increased in number, and then split again. At each stop, the features of the environment changed to some degree. Therefore these migrants would have had to abandon the use of traditional resources and invent ways to make use of the new ones.

As a result of this continuing process, the material cultures of the New World became very diverse. The *Llano* culture, for instance, first appeared among mammoth hunters in what is now the western United States. Llano people soon spread across the northern United States to the northeast coast, hunting mammoths. But as mammoth populations declined, those back in the temperate grasslands of the Great Plains and Rocky Mountain valleys began hunting bison instead, using smaller points called *Folsom points.* In the East, on the other hand, Paleo-Indian groups turned to more intensive fishing and plant gathering and to hunting smaller mammals such as deer, which were plentiful in their temperate forest ecosystem (Butzer, 1971).

Paleo-Indian tool assemblages of North America are classified by age and projectile-point style into three traditions—the Llano, Folsom, and Plano. The Llano tradition, for instance, is identified by what seems to be an American innovation in stone tool technology: a small blade at either side of the base of a lance-shaped projectile point, perhaps designed to improve the way it fit into a wooden shaft (Bordes, 1968). Characteristic of this tradition are the so-called Clovis and Sandia points. Clovis points in particular are widespread in the American West and Northeast. The Llano tradition lasted from about 11,600 years B.P. to about 10,900 years B.P. in the West and until 10,500 B.P. in the East.

The Llano tradition was replaced in the area just east of the Rocky Mountains by the Folsom culture. It lasted from 10,800 to 10,000 B.P. and seems to have marked a shift from dependence on mammoth to bison.

About 10,200 years B.P., the Folsom gave way to the Plano tradition, which existed between Mexico and Canada and from the Rockies to the Midatlantic Coast. It reflected a growing diversity of local traditions, suggesting great cultural complexity (Butzer, 1971).

A major area of controversy in the study of Paleo-Indian cultures is whether or not they were responsible for the widespread mammal extinctions that occurred not long after their arrival. Almost a third of the genera of mammals in North America became extinct at the end of the Pleistocene, from about 13,000 to 7,500 years B.P. They covered a wide range of econiches, from open-country grazers (mammoths, wild horses, camels, llamas, bison, antelopes, yaks) to forest browsers (such as mastodons and ground sloths).

It is hard to blame their extinction on climatic or environmental changes, partly because they had such differing habitat requirements and partly because in many cases their favorite habitats never disappeared and are still widespread in North America today. But as Butzer (1971) points out, it is hard to see how Paleo-Indian groups could have caused this much damage, either. They moved in relatively small bands spread over an enormous area, never staying in any one place for long and never hunting any animals intensively except mammoths and bison. And even the far more numerous and efficient Indian hunters of later times killed many fewer buffalos each year than the herds' annual increase in population. Instead of accusing the Paleo-Indians of single-handedly causing "Pleistocene overkill" in America, some archaeologists now think that human hunters simply pushed already precarious animal populations over the brink of extinction. There is evidence that even before human predators appeared, these animals' numbers were already marginal. Better-adapted competitors, and animals newly arrived from Beringia and Alaska by way of the Canadian corridor, may have reduced the native fauna. Severe reduction of grazing lands caused by glacial advances or arid periods and the loss of young when bitter cold occurred in the springtime may also have contributed to the mass extinctions.

Human hunters in the Americas adjusted to the loss of these animals by making use of a large number of different food resources, including many plants. Except for a limited number of agriculturalists, most North Americans were still following this diversified food strategy when European settlers arrived.

Summary

1. Prehistory can be divided into four cultural stages. The *Paleolithic* lasted from the late Pliocene, when the first tools were made, almost to the end of the Pleistocene, about 10,000 years B.P. It is often divided into three parts: the *Lower Paleolithic,* which preceded the *Middle Paleolithic*—the state of culture in Neandertal times—and the *Upper Paleolithic,* during which *blades* appeared in large numbers. The *Mesolithic* Age is transitional between the Paleolithic and the first appearance of farming. During the *Neolithic,* humans made tools by grinding and polishing stone rather than solely by flaking and began to pro-

duce food as well. Finally, the *Bronze* and *Iron Ages* of the *Metal Age* were marked by the smelting of the metals for which they are named.

2. Experts think that the earliest stone tools that form the *Oldowan tradition* were made by one of the early gracile hominids, although they do not know by which one. Percussion flaking—the process of using one stone, a *hammerstone,* to strike flakes from another—was employed to make the *chopper,* the characteristic tool of the tradition. A chopper is a pebble of which one edge has been sharpened.

3. The early hominids were probably part of a savanna ecosystem, ate more vegetable matter than meat, and lived in small bands that shared food that was probably gathered by the women and hunted by the men.

4. As the carriers of the Oldowan tradition migrated into Europe and through southern Asia to the Far East, two new tool traditions evolved: the *Acheulean tradition* and the *chopper-tool culture.* The Acheulean lasted from about 1.2 million years B.P. in Africa to about 100,000 years B.P. in Europe and is marked by the common use of the *hand ax* and the *soft hammer technique.* The chopper-tool culture, generally found to the north and east of the Acheulean, may have arisen 475,000–425,000 years B.P. and lacks a hand ax. The two cultures are probably the separate adaptations of different populations to different environments.

5. The major tool tradition of the late middle Paleolithic is the *Mousterian,* which in Europe lasted from about 100,000 to about 40,000 years B.P. Mousterian tools vary greatly but are more complex than earlier tools. The *Levallois technique* was used to prepare stone cores so that preformed flakes could be struck.

6. The European Mousterians adapted to the tundra by hunting big game and probably by building open-air shelters and sewing clothes from animal hides. Aspects of modern culture began to appear at this time. Limited speech may have been possible, and Neandertals buried their dead, made ornaments, and may have engaged in rituals.

7. During the *Upper Paleolithic,* (40,000–10,000 years B.P. in Europe) population densities increased, making necessary more efficient use of food resources. As a result, tool types and styles became more complex in response to the demands of local environments. *Borers, end scrapers, notched blades, backed blades, bows and arrows, spear throwers,* and *fishhooks* are among the new tools. Like the Mousterians, Upper Paleolithic peoples exploited a forest and tundra ecosystem, but they lived in larger groups, possibly of greater political complexity than those of earlier people.

8. Sculpture, drawings, and painting became advanced during the Upper Paleolithic. Art may have played a role in ritual, though consistencies in the location of cave art can only tell us for sure that its placement was often not random.

9. Some time between 32,000 and 28,000 years B.P., Siberian hunters, whose numbers may have increased beyond the ability of eastern Siberia to support them, probably followed herds of big game into the New World. These people migrated across *Beringia,* a land bridge now covered by the Bering Strait. By at least 18,000 years B.P. they had reached the continental United States.

10. The three major early archaeological cultures of North America are the *Llano,* the *Folsom,* and the *Plano* traditions. The Llano precedes the other two and was adapted to hunting mammoths. The Folsom was designed for smaller game and was succeeded by the diverse and widespread Plano tradition.

13 The Origins of Agriculture

BETWEEN the end of the Paleolithic Age, with its Pleistocene big-game hunting and stone-tool traditions, and the beginning of the Neolithic Age, with its sedentary farming villages and pottery traditions, there was a transitional period. Archaeologists have named this period the Mesolithic Age.

The Mesolithic Age

While not clearly defined in all areas of the world, there is evidence of the Mesolithic in Europe, the Near East, and North America. In general, the Mesolithic Age coincided with the warming trend that followed the retreat of the last glaciation some 10,000 years ago.

Along with the post-Pleistocene warming trend came the extinction of the animals that had lived together in large herds on the *tundras* that had covered most of Europe. These game-rich tundras were gradually replaced with modern temperate forests. The new forest ecosystems supported a larger number of different species, but the density of each species was less than in the Pleistocene period.

Smaller, and in some cases less abundant, game animals caused people to live and hunt in smaller social groups, or bands, and to use new weapons and tools. A greater variety of food was consumed, and each source of food was exploited more fully. In the Near East, Mexico, and probably China, as we shall see later in this chapter, these Mesolithic adaptations ultimately led to the domestication of plants and animals. Traditionally, the beginning of food production marks the end of the Mesolithic Age, so its length varies in different parts of the world. Perhaps the best-studied Mesolithic period is that from Europe.

In fact, the term *Mesolithic* was originally used to describe the European remains from the end of the Magdalenian, or "reindeer" period, about 10,000 years ago, until the adoption of agriculture about 6,000 years ago.

The game available to European Mesolithic peoples included elk, wild pig, bear, small mammals such as wild cat, fox, and marten, and wild fowl. These people also leaned heavily on fresh- and saltwater fish and shellfish (Clark, 1977). One unusually well-preserved site at Starr Carr in England includes a birch platform at the very edge of a lake. There, the inhabitants may have fished through holes cut in the ice while preying on the red deer that wintered not far from the site (Clark, 1972).

The tools of the European Mesolithic differed greatly from the long, fluted, leaf-shaped stone points of the Paleolithic. Small blades usually less than an inch long, called *microliths,* were used especially as tips and barbs for arrows. These weapons were well suited to hunting the small game of this time. Other tools included flint and polished stone adzes for breaking earth and chopping trees, antler and bone-headed spears and harpoons, bone fishhooks and needles, and nets, dugout canoes, and paddles (see Figure 1). The artifacts left by different peoples in different environments show great variety and suggest to some archaeologists that Mesolithic peoples lived in very specific econiches (Binford, 1968).

Some experts see the Mesolithic as a "cul-

Figure 1 Some Mesolithic tools. Mesolithic people developed implements designed for hunting small game. One such tool was the bow *(A)* and arrow tipped with a microlith *(B).* In Northern Europe heavy stone tools designed for felling timber were produced. Some, such as this adze *(C),* were chipped, and others were ground *(D).* Bone tools, such as the Natufian needles *(E),* fishhooks *(F),* and harpoon point *(G)* shown here, were fashioned. And people wore bone ornaments such as this Natufian necklace *(H).* (*A–D* from Braidwood, 1975; *E–H* from Clark, 1977)

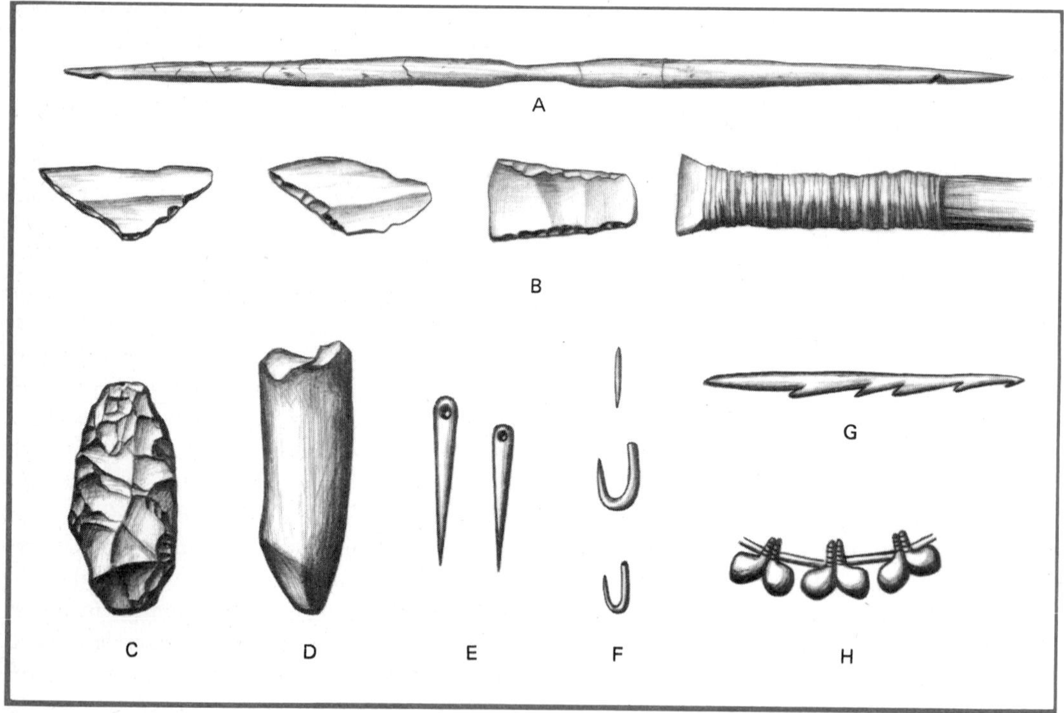

tural degeneration when compared with the Upper Paleolithic" (Binford, 1968). They cite the fact that there was no representational art as evidence. Others, however, remind us that the highly stylized drawings of humans and animals common in the art of this time are not inferior to representational art. Clark (1977), for example, suggests that the abstract drawings may have been the forerunners of Neolithic pottery designs.

North America

In North America the Mesolithic Age has been divided into two parts, according to time and place: (1) the *desert tradition,* which began about 9,000 years ago in the arid western regions of North America and lasted until European contact; and (2) the *archaic tradition* of the Eastern woodlands, which began about the same time and lasted until about 4,000 to 3,000 years ago.

The Desert Tradition. The desert tradition evolved in the extremely arid Great Basin, an area that includes Nevada and parts of Utah, California, Oregon, Idaho, and Wyoming. There American aborigines, especially the Paiute, roamed while making use of seasonal resources such as piñon and other nuts, seeds, and berries, as well as bison, deer, antelope, and other smaller animals (Willey, 1966).

The people of the desert tradition are considered Mesolithic because they depended on modern plants and animals, used microliths, and lived in bands. Small, seminomadic bands were most effective in making use of scarce resources. At most, any one location could support only 25 to 30 people at a time. The wide variety of resources called for a variety of portable, easily made tools. These included microlith projectile points for hunting, and baskets and milling stones for collecting and grinding up plants (Willey, 1966).

The Archaic Tradition. The archaic tradition of the Eastern woodlands and river valleys arose in an environment more like that of Europe. Like the European people, the Indians of the archaic tradition also relied on fish, shellfish, small game, and wild plants. This tradition extended as far west as the Great Plains, where its remains are somewhat like the tool assemblages of the desert tradition. However, ground- and polished-stone tools, especially adzes, axes, and gouges for working wood, were specifically an archaic adaptation. Like members of the desert culture, archaic tradition peoples were seminomadic. But later, perhaps due to a greater wealth of resources, they gave up their seasonal wandering for a more settled existence (Willey, 1966).

In Europe, and in North America north of Mexico, the Mesolithic did not lead to the independent development of agriculture. It is likely that plants and animals that could be domesticated were absent in these areas. In addition, population densities may never have been so high as to make food production necessary (Clark, 1967).

The Neolithic Age

The story of plant and animal domestication is the subject of the so-called *Neolithic Revolution.* This term is used to describe the change from a hunting-and-gathering economy and a flaked-stone-tool technology to an economy based on farming and a technology that included polished stone tools, pottery, and weaving (Clark, 1977; Perkins & Daly, 1974).

The Neolithic Revolution has been considered as important as the Industrial Revolution. Indeed it is probably more so, since without agriculture there never would have been an Industrial Revolution. But the use of the word "Revolution," while helping to show the importance of the change, is misleading. The Industrial Revolution spanned about 100 years, but the Neolithic Revolution took at least 3,000-4,000 years. And although we associate the Industrial Revolution with specific inventions, such as the steam engine, the domestication of plants and animals was not an invention, but a very gradual process in which humans began to manipulate the traits of plants and animals for their own advantage. Unlike a political revolution, with its abrupt, often violent change, the development of agriculture production was a slow, continuous change.

In what ways, then, was the development of food production revolutionary? The answer lies in its profound impact on all other aspects of life. The domestication of plants and animals allowed people to produce more food on a given area of land and thus to support larger populations (Clark, 1977). Permanent settlements were formed near the fields, and people began to hold title to pieces of land and call them their own. Conflicts arose over property, territory, and resources. And some groups within a farming society came to have higher prestige and more property and benefits than other groups. Food production may have begun over 10,000 years ago, but we are still dealing with its effects today.

Not only did agriculture begin fairly recently, but it also spread very rapidly, compared to the rate of change in the Paleolithic and Mesolithic. Between about 10,000 and 2,000 years ago, agriculture had almost everywhere replaced hunting and gathering as the main way of life. Modern studies of living hunters and gatherers suggest that this change did not occur because agriculture provided a better standard of living than hunting and gathering. Despite old myths of half-starved hunters scrounging from day to day, anthropologists now know that contemporary hunting-and-gathering peoples frequently eat better, work less, and live more securely than farming people, to whom a blight or a drought spells disaster and the waste of countless hours of labor. Why, then, did most human beings change from hunting and gathering to agriculture? Before answering this question we shall first study the nature of domestication and its effects on wild plants and animals. Then we shall look at some of the cultures in which agriculture first arose.

The Domestication of Plants and Animals

When humans first began to cultivate wild plants and raise wild animals, they caused a kind of evolution, a change in gene frequencies over time, to occur. Perhaps the most potent force causing changes in genetic makeup is selection. In the case of domestication, humans were the selective agent.

Plants or animals with small chance of success in the wild but with features desirable to humans were often chosen for sowing or breeding by early domesticators, thus increasing their presence in the population. As a result, the frequency of genes responsible for these traits increased. Plants and animals whose traits were an advantage in the wild, but a liability under domestication, however, may have been less well protected by humans or purposely prevented from reproducing.

Human beings may have produced some of these changes without knowing it at first. Merely changing the environments of plants and animals by moving them to different areas or by protecting them from weeds, drought, or predators permits more mutants and variants to survive and reproduce. Deliberate saving of seed for future crops may have been a major step in domestication, since it probably led to planting in new environments and to further changes in the selective pressures acting on the crops' genetic composition (Patterson, 1973). The soil of a new environment could differ in terms of moisture and nutrients. Such changed conditions might favor traits not previously selected for.

Obstacles to Domestication. Wild plants and animals are adapted to surviving and reproducing in their natural environment. Often they have traits that make it difficult for human beings to use them effectively.

Plants. According to archaeologist Kent Flannery (1965), wild grains posed three major problems:

1. The brittle *rachis* of wild wheat and barley breaks easily and helps scatter seeds. The rachis is the fiber by which the seed is attached to the stem of the plant. This adaptation helps the wild plant survive and multiply, but makes harvesting very difficult.
2. Wild grains have tough, inedible *glumes,* or husks, which hold the kernels tightly, despite vigorous threshing.
3. Wild grain grows in scattered patches on hillsides, not in concentrated stands suitable for easy reaping.

According to one expert (Helbaek, 1959), the earliest farmers overcame the problem of a fragile rachis by selectively reaping grains with a tough rachis. But the argument can be made that selective reaping of grain with a tough rachis would favor an increase in the number of the brittle-stemmed plants. Grain with a tough rachis would be eaten, while the grain from the brittle-stemmed plants would remain in the field to sprout. Only deliberate sowing of the tough-rachis plants could lead to their domestication.

The problem of the tough glumes was solved in two ways. First, roasting the grains made the husks brittle enough to be ground off on stone slabs. Also, early farmers could have sorted out and planted certain mutant forms. For example, polyploidy, a genetic trait of many plants that permits the number of chromosomes to increase from one generation to the next, may have created new strains of easily harvested wheat. Hybrid forms, created by crossing two different kinds of plants, may have produced grain having "naked kernels," which are easily threshed free of their husks (Flannery, 1965).

The problem of grain being difficult to harvest was overcome through a mutant form of barley better adapted to the drier spring weather of the level Mesopotamian plain. This mutation resulted in a barley with six fertile kernel rows instead of only two. The harvesting of barley therefore became both easier and more productive when it was planted in dense stands in lowland fields. (See Figure 2.)

Mutations and human-directed changes in the frequency of genes controlling valued traits resulted in domesticated species that were physically different from wild species. As they became adapted to new, human-dominated environments, they became dependent upon human intervention for survival. In the case of wheat and barley, the tough stems that made harvesting easier also made natural seed dispersal impossible. Modern corn is also totally dependent on human beings for its reproduction. Unlike the extinct tiny wild maize from which it evolved, modern corn has seeds entirely enclosed by husks. Thus, it cannot reproduce itself without human help. Both consciously and unconsciously, human beings became an important selective agent in the evolution of domesticated plants.

Animals. Early domesticators had to overcome several problems in keeping wild animals. First, animals must be either aggressive or good at escaping to survive in the wild. Wild cattle, for example, were large and powerful, and had long horns for protection (Isaac, 1971). Nor were adult boars and sows particularly docile. Other animals, such as fowl, could easily escape their human captors. The earliest would-be herders, then, had to handle animals that could be quite dangerous or difficult to keep.

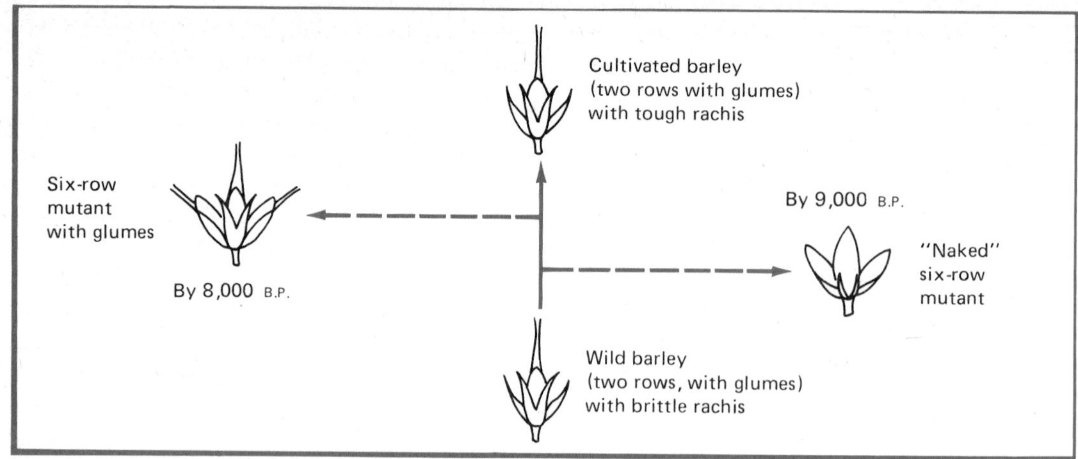

Figure 2 Diagram showing some of the changes in barley after it was first domesticated. Each of the three domestic forms shown represents the elimination by early farmers in the Near East of an obstacle to the domestication of the original wild barley. (Flannery, 1965)

Furthermore, some animals that were kept probably competed with humans for food. It is likely, for example, that pigs were never economically important in the Near East because, unlike cattle, goats, and sheep, they competed with humans for grain. The other animals ate fodder (Perkins & Daly, 1974).

By studying the archaeological record and comparing wild strains with domestic strains scientists have found that domestication has changed certain plant species in a number of ways.

Captive animal herds in the Neolithic Near East had sex and age compositions different from those of wild herds. Early farmers slaughtered young animals for food, while keeping the adults for breeding. More young males were butchered, since females would be valuable for breeding. An excess of female goats and sheep may have proved a further boon in later winter and early spring when the lambing season brought forth a flow of milk (Flannery, 1965).

Other differences between wild and domestic strains are known primarily by comparison of living varieties. Sheep and goats have two kinds of hair follicles: *primaries,* which produce the straight hairs of the visible coat, and *secondaries,* which make up the wooly undercoat. Wild animals have mostly straight hair. Mutation and selective breeding resulted in animals having many more secondaries, thus producing the familiar wooly coat of domestic sheep and goats. (See Figure 3.). Wooly hair probably first appeared as a random mutation some 2,000 years after sheep had been domesticated. We know that wool may have been spun as early as 8,000 years ago in Turkey.

Some genetic changes in domesticated animals seem to have no adaptive advantage. For example, the twisted horns of domesticated goats are unknown in the wild variety (Flannery, 1965). In addition, just as domesticated plants become more and more dependent on humans for their survival, so, too, do domesticated animals. Animals lacking powerful defensive traits could also only survive in domestication (Isaac, 1971). Thus, although domesticated animals (unlike grains) have retained the ability to reproduce without help from humans, they cannot protect themselves from predators as well as wild animals can.

Theories of the Origins of Agriculture

Why did people start sowing wild plants and go to the trouble of subduing unruly animals in the first place? This is a hard question to answer, because to do so we must imagine the thoughts and motives of Neolithic humans.

Archaeologists have nevertheless developed a number of hypotheses explaining the kinds of pressures that may have motivated the earliest farmers. In this chapter, we shall discuss a few of the most prominent of these theories and then briefly review the evidence of agricultural development in the Near East, China, and Mesoamerica.

Childe's Oasis Model

V. Gordon Childe (1892–1957), one of the most distinguished British anthropologists of the early twentieth century, spent much of his life studying the Neolithic people of the Near East. In his *New Light on the Most Ancient East* (1952), he published a theory linking the drying trend that presumably affected much of the world as the glaciers withdrew at the close of the Pleistocene period to the domestication of plants and animals. His theory, unlike previous ideas, presented a series of hypotheses specific enough to be tested by archaeological data. According to Childe, as the Mesopotamian climate grew drier, already dry grasslands turned into deserts, dotted here and there with oases. People, animals, and plants were concentrated in these areas. This climatic crisis forced humans to domesticate plants and animals, since killing them would have left the oasis-dwellers with no sources of food. These inhabitants of the oases domesticated animals by (1) letting them eat the fodder remaining in their fields after harvest, (2) protecting them from predators, and (3) selecting for docility by killing aggressive animals for food.

In the long run, archaeological data has not supported this theory. Rainfall and vegetation in such key early agricultural sites as Jarmo and Karim Shaher were at least as heavy at that time as they are now. Moreover, these and many other early villages clustered not in Childe's alluvial oases, but in upland areas, where there was enough rainfall for cultivation.

Finally, Childe's theory has been attacked as being logically unsound. As Braidwood (1967) has remarked, "There had also been three earlier periods of great alpine glaciers, and long periods of warm weather in between. Thus, the forced neighborliness of men, plants, and animals in river valleys and oases must also have happened earlier. Why didn't domestication happen earlier, then?"

Braidwood's Nuclear Zone Theory

Braidwood believes that when people had acquired an in-depth knowledge of the environment they lived in, they were ready to begin food production. They were culturally receptive to domestication. The other prerequisite for food production was an area rich in animals and plants that could be domesticated. In such an area, called a *nuclear zone,* people worked out the techniques of domestication. Braidwood identified several possible nuclear zones in the hills of the Near East. Knowledge of agriculture later spread from these zones to surrounding areas.

Unlike Childe, Braidwood does not explain agriculture as a new adaptation in the face of environmental pressures. Instead, Braidwood believes that the ability to experiment with and manipulate the environment has long been part of human nature. These abilities were gradually being improved in the course of human evolution, and only the right envi-

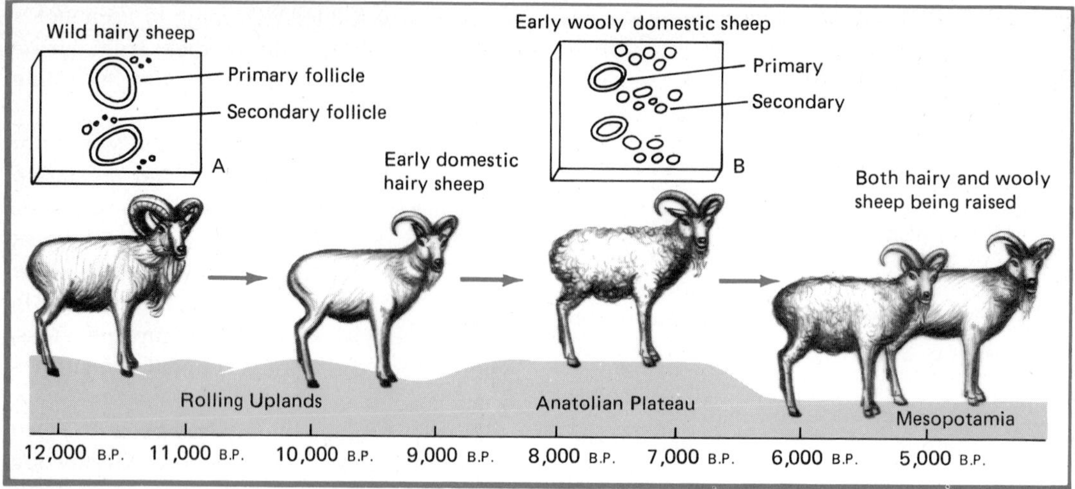

Figure 3 The evolution of wooly domestic sheep from wild hairy sheep. *(A)* is a section of the skin of a wild sheep, as seen through a microscope, showing the pattern of primary (hair) and secondary (wool) follicles. *(B)* shows a magnified section of the skin of a wool-bearing domestic sheep. Note that there are many more secondaries and that they form clusters away from the primaries. (Adapted from Flannery, 1965)

ronment, that of a nuclear zone, was needed to stimulate agriculture. As Braidwood admits, however, it is very difficult to see the archaeological traces of an "atmosphere of experimentation" (Braidwood, 1967).

Braidwood's hypothesis has been attacked because it does not explain enough. He implies that the various events of cultural evolution were the natural expression of emerging human traits. The evolution of human qualities controlled the sequence of culture history. To explain why agriculture had not occurred in between periods of glaciation in the Pleistocene, he said that "culture was not ready to achieve it" (Braidwood & Willey, 1962). Thus the reason that agriculture developed is that culture was ready for it to develop. But, as archaeologist Lewis Binford has pointed out, "Trends which are observed in cultural evolution require explanation; they are certainly not explained by postulating emergent human traits which are said to account for the trends" (Binford, 1968).

Population Models

Over the past 20 years, several theorists have suggested that population growth beyond the land's ability to support the human biomass is responsible for the development and spread of agriculture. In other words, when there were not enough preferred foods, people were forced to experiment with and eat secondary (and probably less desirable) foods.

Archaeologists disagree as to the most likely source of disruption of preagricultural human ecosystems. Some think that environmental changes reduced food supplies, while others believe that an increase in human populations came first.

Lewis Binford has suggested that the balance between the food resources of the land and the needs of a given population can only be disturbed by a change in the environment. He argues that long before people in a group whose numbers were expanding would have allowed themselves to starve for lack of food, certain cultural restraints would have been placed on fertility. The killing of infants, abortion, and taboos on intercourse during lactation have all been used by twentieth-century hunter-gatherers as a brake on population growth.

If preagricultural groups did limit population growth to numbers below the carrying capacity of the environment, then outside conditions that could have led to food production are of two kinds: (1) a change in the physical environment that reduced the available food; and (2) an increase in population density beyond the environment's carrying capacity, as a result of immigration. The first condition is essentially Childe's oasis theory, with which Binford disagrees (Binford, 1968). In favoring the second option, Binford suggests that people from relatively sedentary, heavily populated areas in which fish and shellfish were very plentiful migrated to less favored inland areas already populated by more mobile groups. In this "tension zone," the balance would have been upset, and people would have had to use new methods of getting food, such as agriculture (Binford, 1968).

There are two main problems with Binford's theory: First, it is too specific in requiring sedentary forager-fishing villages as the "donor groups." Secondly, by specifying that the source of imbalance must be population pressure caused only by immigration, it seems too restrictive.

Another group of theorists believes that human populations naturally increase to the limit of the ability of the environment to support them. William Sanders and Barbara Price (1968), for example, suggest that in the Tehuacán Valley of Mexico, *geographical circumscription*—the condition occurring when a population is surrounded by physical features of the land that make emigration difficult—may have led to food production. High mountain walls and tropical jungles block the exit of the valley into the coastal plain. The growing population in the valley turned to farming to increase the food supply because the excess population could not leave (Sanders & Price, 1968).

Esther Boserup (1965) has suggested that on a worldwide basis, human populations have grown steadily, and that growth has forced changes in technology and subsistence—in particular, the development of agriculture. Anthropologist Mark Cohen (1972) offers detailed archaeological evidence from the Old World and North and South America to show that by the end of the Paleolithic, hunters and gatherers had spread to all parts of the world that could support them. In doing so they had expanded the number and variety of wild resources used for food in order to feed growing populations. As migration became more difficult, Paleolithic peoples had to gather a wider variety of less preferred foods.

In the period between 9,000 and 2,000 years ago, populations around the world were using nearly all the available edible foods. But their numbers continued to increase relentlessly. As a result, people were forced to increase the supply of those foods that could be domesticated. These were not necessarily the most tasty foods to be had. In fact, Cohen thinks that the earliest plants to be sown and harvested were generally undesirable foods. Hungry populations used them because other food sources were not enough (Cohen, 1977).

The Development of Agriculture

Argument continues on the question of why agriculture began. Most archaeologists would agree, however, that some combination of population pressure, ecological change, and population movement is responsible for its origin. In the next section we shall look at

Table 1 Selected Sequences at the Beginnings of Food Production

Years Ago	Near East	China	Tehuacán	Central Peru
3,000				Pottery enters region
4,000			Purron Phase: Pottery	Permanent agricultural villages
5,000			Abejas Phase: Larger, more permanent settlements; agriculture firmly established	Domestication of alpaca, llama, and many plants
6,000		Cultivation of millet; domestication of pigs and dogs; small settlements	Coxcatlán Phase: Early cultivation of maize, beans, aramus, squash, and chili	Early cultivation of quinoa and squash
7,000				
8,000	Ceramic Jarmo pottery	Intensive plant gathering	El Riego Phase: Intensive plant gathering	Seasonal pattern of intensive plant gathering
9,000	Prepottery Neolithic B: domestication of plants and animals			
10,000	Prepottery Neolithic A. early cultivation of barley and wheat; permanent settlements			
11,000	Natufian: intensive plant gathering; possible early herding			
12,000				

three areas in which the archaeological sequences are well worked out: the Near East, China, and Mesoamerica. To a significant degree, archaeologists working on the origins of food production in these areas have oriented their research to test different aspects of the preceding hypotheses. When it is appropriate, therefore, we shall point out data that support or refute the different theoretical models.

The Near East

We shall begin with the Near East, where agriculture first developed.

Environment. For the purposes of this discussion, we can limit the geographical extent of the Near East to modern-day Iran, Iraq, Turkey, Syria, Lebanon, Israel, and Jordan. Within this area, it is possible to distinguish several ecological zones, as shown in Figure 4:

1. The *Levant,* the narrow eastern and southern coasts of the Mediterranean, containing evergreens and plants adapted to this warm, temperate environment.
2. *Mesopotamian alluvium,* the swamps, desert, and desert-steppe surrounding the Tigris-Euphrates river systems, much of which is unsuitable for agriculture.
3. *High mountains and the Iranian plateau,* the high Zagros mountains, too rugged for normal farming; and, to the north and east, the central plateau of Iran, a desert basin.
4. Foothills and valleys in between mountains, *the oak and pistachio woodland belt* of foothills and valleys that flank the Zagros mountains to the southwest. In this zone, with its ample streams, rivers, and rainfall, were present all plants and animals that could be domesticated, such as wild emmer wheat, barley, oats, and wild sheep, goats, pigs, cattle, and horses.
5. *Steppe-piedmont,* rolling hills and natural winter grasslands that lie between the Zagros foothills and the Mesopotamian alluvium. This zone includes wide, farmable floodplains and pastures that could have supported wild or domesticated herds (Flannery, 1965; Braidwood et al., 1960).

The Developmental Sequence. In the Near East, there were both wild plants (emmer wheat and barley) and herd animals (sheep and goats) that could be domesticated. Near Eastern Mesolithic populations migrated from area to area as resources became available seasonally. As a result, they could make use of food resources of different habitats. Compared to the Paleolithic big-game hunters,

Figure 4 Map of the Near East, showing the environmental zones mentioned in the text. (Flannery, 1965)

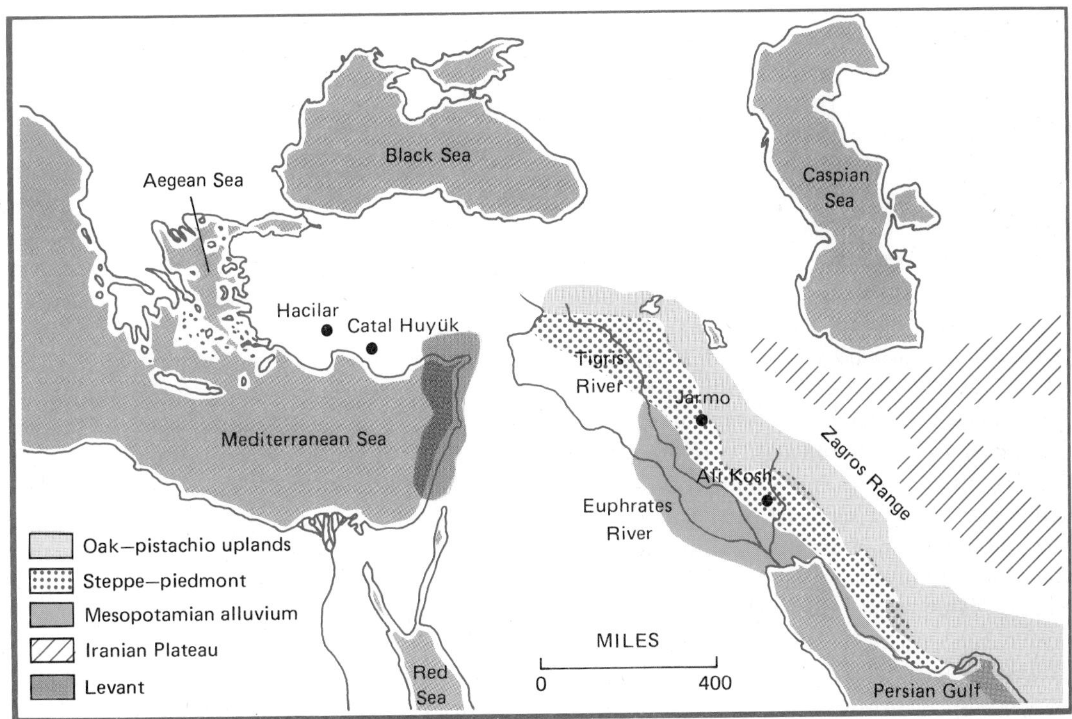

Near Eastern Mesolithic populations depended on smaller animals and more plants. These adaptations occurred at the same time as increasing population densities, a tendency to settle in one place, and, finally, about 9,000 years ago, the development of agriculture (Cohen, 1977).

Domesticated plants and animals did not develop at the same time in each of the Near East's major geographic zones. The earliest evidence of changing patterns comes from the Levant and from the Zagros highlands. As early as 13,000 years ago, populations seem to have been concentrating on a few animal resources. Wild goats and gazelles seem particularly favored at sites associated with the *Kebaran* culture in the Levant; wild cattle, goats, and sheep are associated with the *Zarzian* culture in the Zagros highlands. It is possible that this reflects a subtle shift toward herding—perhaps to ensure a constant source of food for a growing population. People still lived in caves or in open-air camps, with no sign of permanence (Mellaart, 1975).

The Natufian Culture (12,000–10,000 Years B.P.). About 12,000 years ago in the Levant, the Kebaran culture gradually gave rise to the *Natufian* culture. The Natufians seem to have preferred to live in the belt of oak and pistachio forests that was bordered by the Mediterranean coast to the west and the desert to the east. This area of coastal foothills had more water than it does today and supported stands of wild emmer wheat and barley. As during the Kebaran culture, there is some evidence that herds were being kept (Mellaart, 1975). Natufian sites show a high proportion of bones from immature gazelle and goats. This is a sign that Natufians slaughtered young animals for food, while keeping the adults for breeding (Clark, 1977).

The Natufians seem to have lived in large settlements on cave terraces, near springs, or alongside lakes and rivers. Although there is evidence of growing *sedentism,* or settling in villages, archaeologists disagree about the extent to which this was happening. Clark (1977) regards their sites as base camps from which the Natufians migrated to follow seasonally available animal and plant resources. Perkins and Daly (1974), however, argue that the Natufians lived in permanent villages, with large populations supported by much wild grain and other crops.

Whoever is correct, the archaeological evidence makes it clear that the Natufians did harvest and grind grains, possibly wild barley and wheat. The many reaping-knife handles made of bone and antler, and flint sickle-blades showing the sheen that comes from cutting stalks, indicate that cereal grasses were harvested. Stone mortars and pestles were used to grind these and possibly other plant foods. Other stone tools included many microliths, burins, borers, and scrapers. Antler and bone fishhooks suggest that the Natufians also fished (Clark, 1977).

Pre-pottery Neolithic A and B (10,000–8,000 Years B.P.). Between about 10,300 and 10,000 years ago in the Levant, experiments with plant domestication led to the first farming communities (Mellaart, 1975). Excavation of a number of Near Eastern sites shows that during the next 2,000 years humans came to depend almost entirely on domesticated plants as well as animals. By about 8,000 years ago, for example, the farming village of Jarmo depended on domestic sheep and goats for 95 percent of its meat.

Because it is used to prepare and store food, pottery generally appears in the same strata as the first signs of agriculture. In the Near East, however, early domestication of wild plants and animals occurred for at least 2,000 years before the appearance of pottery. Archaeologists break up this span into the pre-pottery Neolithic A and B.

Pre-pottery Neolithic peoples manufactured a large number of stone tools, especially of flint and obsidian. These included microliths and flaked and side-notched points. Barbed spearheads and projectiles tipped and

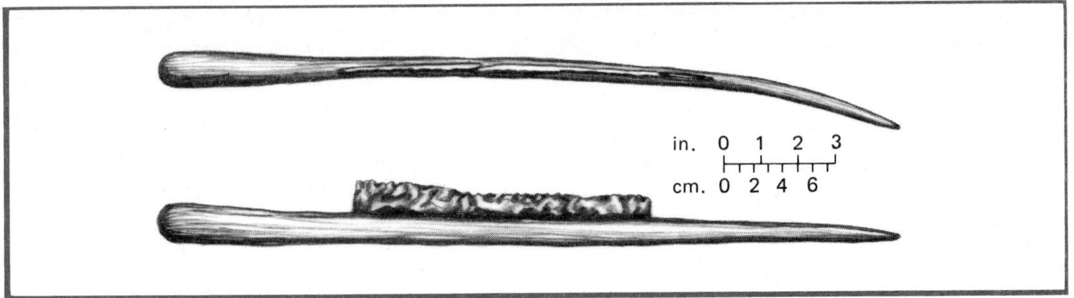

Figure 5 Mesolithic sickle made by fitting flint blades into a wooden haft. Sickles such as this were used by Natufian people to harvest stands of wild grain. (Cole, 1965; reprinted by permission of the trustees of the British Museum of Natural History)

barbed with microliths were used for hunting.

Domesticated emmer wheat and barley appeared in the pre-pottery Neolithic A level of Jericho, and during the B period domesticated einkorn wheat and legumes such as lentils, peas, and horse beans were added. In Syria and Turkey the earliest evidence for farming villages occurs at dates contemporary with pre-pottery Neolithic B in the Levant (Mellaart, 1975). Here and in the Zagros mountains, people began to grow many of the same crops at about the same time.

Fully Developed Village Farming. Beginning at about 8,000 years B.P., there were fully developed farming villages and small towns in the Near East. Most of these permanent communities held several hundred peasants, a considerable increase over the approximately two dozen households that normally made up pre-pottery Neolithic settlements. The relative uniformity of house size, construction, and layout show an absence of social hierarchies, although there may have been some specialized crafts. In general, houses had a main living space with sitting and sleeping benches, a fireplace, a corner or wall oven, a nearby mortar, and several small storage areas. Buildings were usually one story, although two-story kilns were used to fire the high-quality pottery that came out of this region. Passages, yards, and courtyards separated houses, but with the later building and rebuilding that occurred in these villages, such spaces tended to fill up.

The outstanding addition of this period to the Neolithic tool kit was pottery. The people of the pre-pottery Neolithic period had used clay in ritual cults to make figurines, and to coat skulls that were buried separately from bodies. But they did not use clay to take the place of their stone, wooden, and woven vessels. The appearance of pottery probably is linked to a fully sedentary lifestyle. Pottery is well suited to the storage and preparation of grains and vegetable foods. However, pottery is fragile, and thus is liable to break if moved from place to place. It is not surprising, then, that it first developed in various areas of the Near East, usually by 8,000 years B.P., when fully developed village farming arose.

Pottery is an especially useful clue for archaeologists, since they can trace the spread and sometimes origins of various cultures by the styles of pottery manufacture and especially decoration. The earliest Near Eastern pottery was both plain and decorated, and found at such sites as Jericho in the Levant, Çatal Hüyük and Mersin in southwest Turkey, Jarmo in the foothill zone, and Hassuna in the steppe-piedmont zone. The earliest pottery included dishes, bowls, flasks, and some vessels with bucketlike handles (Clark, 1977).

In this period there was less and less hunting as domesticated animals made more populations self-sufficient (Perkins & Daly, 1974). Some sites, such as Erbaba in Turkey, show a complete absence of hunted animals such as pig or red deer. But at other sites, such as Djeitun in the U.S.S.R., north of Iran, antelope and goat were still an important part of the diet (Clark, 1977). In areas with enough rainfall, such as northern Mesopotamia, grains were cultivated without irrigation. Primitive irrigation was used near the Zagros foothills, and, in the Sumerian south, elaborate irrigation projects were undertaken.

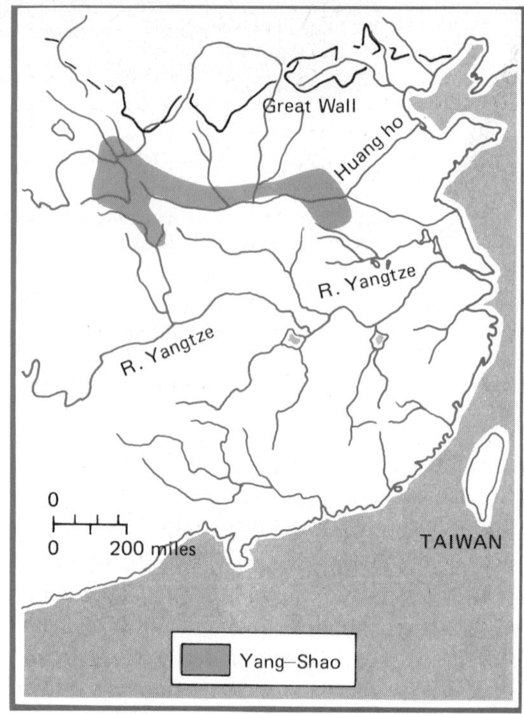

Figure 6 The distribution of the Yang-shao, the first food-producing culture of China. It arose in the valley of the Wei and Huang-ho Rivers. (Clark, 1977)

China

Archaeologists know much less about how agriculture began in China. Although it evolved about 2,000 years later in China (around 7,000 years B.P.) than in the Near East, archaeologists believe that it was an independent development. The idea of domestication probably was not imported from elsewhere.

Paleolithic people to the north in Siberia had hunted the mammoth, bison, rhinoceros, and other big-game animals common in the Pleistocene. By about 12,500 years B.P., however, much of the big game had become extinct, and human populations had begun to move south from the *steppes* (vast, level, treeless plains) into the *taiga* (a forest region dominated by spruce and fir). Here they made use of a wide variety of food resources. Mesolithic people of China relied on fishing and the hunting of single forest animals. Vegetable foods also became important, and after about 7,000 years B.P. permanent settlements appeared, often near streams and bays. Tools from this preagricultural period include grindstones for vegetable foods, fishing equipment, and stone spades (Cohen, 1977; Clark, 1977).

The Yang-Shao Culture. The earliest Chinese farming took place on the fertile loess soil along the Yellow (or Huang Ho) River in the Chung-yuan region of north-central China. (See Figure 6.) By about 6,000 years B.P., peasants of the Yang-shao culture were raising millet (a hardy, drought-resistant cereal grain) and brown corn. Rice was first domesticated in Thailand, and was not grown in China until several hundred years later—about 5,000 years ago. Archaeologists believe that the Yang-shao farmers engaged in slash-and-burn agriculture—a type of shifting agriculture involving the periodic clearing and burning of forest land to create new fields. Thus the terrain, the crops grown, and the agricultural techniques that arose in China were quite different from those in the Near East. However, like the Near Eastern agriculturalists, the Yang-shao peasants also kept dogs, hunted wild cattle, horse, deer, and other er animals, fished, and collected wild seeds and plants. Later Farmers also raised cattle, sheep, horses, and water buffalo (Clark, 1977).

Yang-shao villages consisted of some 50 round or rectangular dwellings. Often built partly underground, these shelters had wattle-and-daub (woven twigs and plaster) walls, thatched, slanted roofs, stamped-earth or plastered floors, and hearths. As in the early Near Eastern Neolithic settlements, no sign of social hierarchy is evident from these structures. Yang-shao villages also lacked elaborate defensive works, suggesting that important village differences in wealth did not exist (Clark, 1977).

There is evidence from at least one site that pottery may have occurred before agriculture among settled hunting-and-fishing populations. By Neolithic times Chinese pottery was already impressive. The Yang-shao peasants made ceramic bowls, dishes, jars, and other vessels, and probably used them for cooking, serving, and storage. Yang-shao peasants also engaged in weaving, basketry, leather-work, and carpentry. Stone was worked into axes and adzes for cutting and shaping wood, and projectile heads and knives, especially reaping blades, were made of polished stone. Fish-hooks, arrowheads, and a variety of craft tools were fashioned out of bone (Clark, 1977).

Mesoamerica

Domestication of plants and animals also arose independently in Mesoamerica—central and southern Mexico and the northern part of Central America. As in China, it occurred at least 2,000 years later than in the Near East. Domestication did not begin with one population in one area. Instead, it first appeared separately at various times and places in Mesoamerica.

As in the Old World, New World peoples domesticated local wild plants and animals. These were different from Old World types and included corn, squash, peanuts, potatoes, chili peppers, and kidney beans. In all, as many as 150 different kinds of plants may have been cultivated. Also unlike the Old World, the New World had far fewer animals that could be domesticated. Consequently, animals were much less important to farming in the New World. Only the Andean populations, which raised llamas and alpacas, made heavy use of animals. Four other species of animals were domesticated in the New World—dogs, turkeys, guinea pigs, and ducks.

The Tehuacán Valley. Among the most important regions for early agriculture were the central highlands of Mexico. The Tehuacán Valley, located about 150 miles southeast of Mexico City, has provided vital data about the beginnings of agriculture in the highlands. Here archaeologists have painstakingly reconstructed the sequence of events leading to the development of agriculture and have provided detailed information about its origins.

The valley itself, at an elevation of about 6,000 feet above sea level, is surrounded by mountains rising about 5,000 feet above the valley floor. These peaks block precipitation and restrict annual rainfall to about 20 inches. The valley is not only dry but also quite warm, with temperatures ranging from 55° to 92°F. The floor of the valley is semiarid and spotted with scrub and cactus (Willey, 1966). Once it contained a mesquite grassland inhabited by deer, jackrabbits, gophers, and quail. Along the edge of the valley, small side canyons extend in among the mountains. Here deer lived and wild avocados and maguey (a fleshy, spiny-leafed plant) flourished.

Archaeologists have been able to trace a sequence of continuous habitation in the Tehuacán Valley, from a Paleo-Indian hunting-and-gathering culture to full-fledged settled villages and ceremonial centers supported by irrigation agriculture. As in the Near East, agriculture developed very gradually in Mesoamerica. Archaeologist Richard MacNeish (1964) has described nine phases in the Tehuacán Valley sequence.

Ajuereado Phase (12,700–9,200 Years B.P.). During this time, wandering bands of no more than four to eight persons lived a hunting-and-gathering life. Hunters, trappers, and food gatherers moved from place to place, as resources in different parts of the valley became available. They hunted big game such as antelopes and horses, as well as rodents, turtles, and birds. Wild plants were a smaller part of their diet. Tools included leaf-shaped flint knives and projectile points, choppers, and scrapers. Life must have been difficult, for these valley dwellers had fairly few resources on which to draw in the hot, dry environment.

El Reigo Phase (9,200–7,200 Years B.P.). The population of the valley grew slightly larger, and there was a greater emphasis on collecting wild seed plants than there had been in the earlier phase. The culture at this time has been likened to the desert culture tradition of the American Southwest. Various wild plants were available only in certain seasons, which determined the activities of the *tehuacanos,* the inhabitants of the valley. During the dry winter months (from October to March) small bands hunted game animals, which gathered around the springs and streams that did not dry up. These bands also trapped smaller animals and collected maguey leaves and roots from certain other plants. Plants were scarce during this time of the year. As a result, deer and peccary, a nocturnal animal related to and resembling the pig, made up about 75 percent of the total food eaten at this season.

During the rainy season, from mid-March through mid-September, the *tehuacanos* gathered in larger groups and harvested various plants as they ripened. Prickly pears were gathered first, then wild grasses and mesquite, and toward the end of the rainy season wild fruits could be picked. Wild varieties of squash, chili, and avocados were collected as well. Plant foods probably made up about 65 percent of the diet during this season.

The *tehuacanos* of this period used pestles and mortars to grind seeds. They also fashioned wood and wove baskets and blankets. Scrapers and choppers were used to work skins and to process vegetable foods.

Coxcatlán Phase (7,200–5,400 Years B.P.). It is from this phase that we have the earliest clear evidence of agriculture. In the past only 10 to 20 people had lived in the valley; during this time the population increased tenfold. Domesticated plants took on a minor but important role in meeting the added need for food.

In an excavation of a cave located in the valley wall, Richard MacNeish uncovered the oldest maize cobs, the forerunner to modern strains of corn, known anywhere in the world. The ears are tiny and podlike, looking vastly different from the foot-long cobs of today's hybrid corn. The cobs have been dated to about 7,000 years B.P., a date that strongly suggests that the maize plant was first domesticated in Southern Mexico (Willey, 1966). The Coxcatlán cobs are thought to represent the very earliest stages of domestication of this species.

There is also evidence that chili peppers, squash, beans, and gourds were being planted at this time. The canyons opening on the valley were favored planting grounds. Later wild fruit trees, such as avocados, were planted around springs and along the banks of streams and rivers. The first trees and maize planted in the valley were probably native to the area. Later arrivals such as gourds and squash, however, were imported from neighboring areas (Patterson, 1973).

The shift from hunting and gathering to agriculture involved a fundamental change in the way the *tehuacanos* saw their environment. Before, they had thought about the land in terms of the kinds of plants they could find there. Now, however, they evaluated the land in terms of its ability to support the various

Corn as we know it today evolved from the tiny maize cob at the left. This cob, the earliest known domesticated maize, was uncovered in Coxcatlan Cave of the Tehuacán Valley in a layer dating from 7,000 years ago. Selective breeding over the course of about 4,000 years increased the number and size of cobs on a plant and resulted in more fragile husks. (Courtesy of Paul Mandgelsdorf & R. S. MacNeish)

plants they could transport and farm there (Patterson, 1973).

Agriculture also brought with it a tendency for people to remain in one camp for a longer period of time. Although the valley dwellers still followed their ancient pattern of wandering with the seasons in search of food, their groups were becoming larger and their base camps more permanent.

Abejas Phase (5,400–4,300 Years B.P.). The trend toward sedentism continued during this phase. Less dependence on hunting and gathering was made possible by genetic changes in maize and other crops that resulted in a higher yield. Maize was crossed with a variety of wild grass to produce a hybrid corn with larger cobs. Pumpkins, beans, cotton, and dogs were domesticated for the first time, as well.

Purron (4,300–3,500 Years B.P.) and Ajalpan (3,500–1,100 Years B.P.) phases. Agriculture increasingly became a fulltime job carried out by the people living in settled villages during this time. The appearance of the earliest-known pottery in Mesoamerica dates from the Purron; it made possible long-term storage of vegetable foods. During the Ajalpan, settled villages of 100 to 300 grew hybrid corn, various squashes, gourds, amaranths, beans, chili peppers, avocados, and cotton.

These crops were planted during the spring and the early summer, and harvested in the fall. In autumn, however, the *tehuacanos* ate the newly ripened fruit, thus saving their crop plants for the dry season in the late fall and winter. Eventually, they became good enough farmers to supply themselves with adequate food to last year round (Patterson, 1973). More productive strains allowed more people to settle permanently in small villages.

During the next three phases, the population of the valley increased dramatically. Irrigation enlarged the land area on which crops could be farmed, and, by the later phases, commerce with other areas supplemented the domestically produced food supply. Villages with temples expanded into citylike ceremonial centers, dominated by monumental architecture. At this time sedentism and almost total dependence on agriculture had long been established.

The Spread of Agriculture

Some ecosystems cannot easily maintain the sort of changes required by agriculture or herding. As mentioned earlier, it is a myth that simple farming is necessarily more productive than hunting and gathering for any given population. Had certain Indian groups in central California adopted agriculture, they would have had less—not more—food to eat. Small wonder, then, that they resisted its introduction (Patterson, 1973).

Today, of course, sophisticated irrigation networks and refined fossil fuels used for tractors have made the central valley of California one of the most productive agricultural areas in the world. Without this technology, the soil would be easily depleted, and crops would soon die in the semiarid environment.

In some areas, so much food grows wild that food production is simply unnecessary. People tend to choose the economic strategy that is most effective in their area.

There is good reason to believe that population pressure led to the widespread diffusion and acceptance of agriculture practically throughout the world, and in a relatively short period of time. According to Mark Cohen (1977), populations at the end of the last glaciation throughout the world had become as large as the resources of their ecosystems would allow. In his view, population growth, which first resulted in territorial expansion and the entering of untapped areas, gradually made farming necessary when there were no more virgin areas to which to migrate (Cohen, 1977). In this section we shall look at how agricultural know-how was spread throughout Europe, Africa, and coastal Peru.

Europe

Agriculture probably was brought to Europe from the Near East. Many of the plants and animals that were eventually domesticated were introduced from Asia. And not only did the earliest farmers use reaping and milling tools similar to those that were used in the Near East, but they also raised livestock that had no wild ancestor in the region (Clark, 1977).

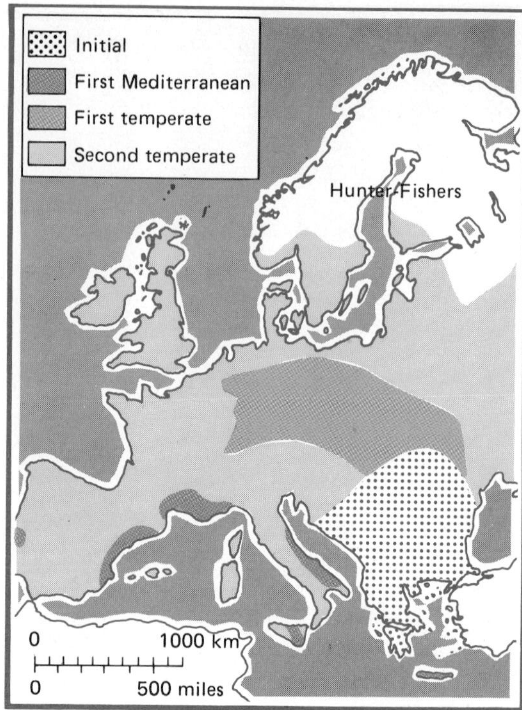

Figure 7 The four stages of the spread of agriculture in Europe. (Clark, 1977)

The most important route for the spread of agricultural ideas was by way of Greece into central, south, southeastern, and northern Europe. No doubt sailors and traders who came to Europe by way of the Mediterranean also helped spread seeds and the techniques of agriculture. Greece and the south Balkans were farmed first, about 8,000 to 7,000 years ago. They are the closest to the Near East, and because climate and soil there were most similar to those of the Near East, it was easier for the imported plants and animals to survive (Clark, 1977).

During this first phase in the spread of farming across the continent, peasants lived year-round in settlements consisting of a small cluster of shelters made with sun-dried mud.

They grew barley, lentils, beans, and several kinds of wheat. They also raised sheep, goats, and pigs. These early peasants made pots, baskets, polished stone axes, and adze blades for felling timber and woodworking. They reaped crops using knives of chert, a flintlike mineral, and obsidian blades set in antler or wood handles. This way of life continued for 2,000 to 3,000 years without any major changes. The population and settlement density grew steadily, and farming gradually spread into nearby areas (Clark, 1977).

Between 7,000 and 6,000 years ago, European agriculture expanded beyond its early zone into several areas along the Mediterranean coast and into Central Europe as far west as France and as far east as southwest Russia (see Figure 7). In this temperate area, the peasants practiced slash-and-burn agriculture. After harvesting crops for a few years, the clearings lost their fertility and the small villages were temporarily abandoned, to be reoccupied some years later. Centuries of this activity were probably the major force responsible for the reduction of the forests that once covered most of Europe.

Between about 6,000 to 5,000 years ago, a second phase of expansion spread agriculture throughout the rest of Europe's temperate zone. However, the inhabitants in the North, beyond the deciduous forest, kept a hunting, fishing, and foraging economy. In Western Europe, the earlier Mediterranean settlement seems to have expanded into Spain, France, part of Switzerland, and the British Isles. In these areas, peasants grew wheat and barley and raised cattle and pigs. In south Britain, a crude plough was used to till the soil. Hunting became fairly unimportant except in rugged Alpine areas (Clark, 1977).

Farther east, in the south Balkans and central Europe, the peasants developed a copper industry. In south Russia, the use of wheels on ox-drawn carts and wagons eased the burden of peasant transportation, and between 5,000 to 4,000 years B.P. such vehicles spread to northern and western Europe. Later, the domestication of the horse in south Russia made it an important military tool (Clark, 1977).

In northern Europe hunting, fishing, and gathering remained the basic economy. Because the climate north of the deciduous forest did not favor agriculture, hunting, fishing, and gathering remained the basic source of food (Clark, 1977).

Africa

Knowledge of agriculture in Africa is limited by a lack of research and, because of climatic conditions, poor preservation of archaeological clues. Consequently, firm evidence is lacking as to whether agriculture arose there independently or spread southward along the Nile from the Near East. The earliest reliable evidence of domestication in Africa is in the Fayum Oasis in Egypt, where grains of emmer wheat, barley, and flax were preserved from about 6,500 years B.P.

The earliest certain evidence of African agriculture outside Egypt is from Dhartichitt in Mauritania. There, due to a drying trend, hunting and fishing became impossible. As a result a farming economy grew up within a few hundred years around 3,000 years B.P. The lateness and speed with which the grains raised there took hold point to the introduction of a grain that had been previously domesticated elsewhere (Cohen, 1977).

A number of African food crops may have been domesticated independently at several places in the zone south of the Sahara and north of the Equator. These crops include African rice, millet, yams, and watermelon. This domestication might have resulted from high population densities and the southward expansion of the Sahara Desert. Displaced peoples may have placed pressure on the carrying capacity of the savanna south of the desert. Domestication may have been the solution to this problem (Cohen, 1977).

Other archaeological evidence of domestication in Africa south of the Sahara, especially in West Africa and eastern and southeastern Africa, is relatively late—sometime around 1,500 years B.P. Crops included several types of wheat, melons, legumes, and cowpeas. It is thought that the spread of agriculture south of the Equator occurred with the movement of iron-using, Bantu-speaking peoples (Cohen, 1977). Possible reasons for the late occurrence of Neolithic technology in West Africa include: (1) lack of incentive due to an environment rich in meat and plant food; and (2) ecological obstacles, such as a heavy tropical summer rainfall unsuited to the crops grown in Egypt and North Africa. A long period of experimentation was needed to transform local wild varieities into crop plants (Clark, 1970).

Coastal Peru

In South America, food production arose independently in Peru and diffused gradually into neighboring areas. The first clear evidence of the domestication of plants dates from between 7,500 and 6,200 years ago in the Ayachucho region of Central Peru. Here, the seeds of domesticated quinoa (an Andean grain) and squash have been uncovered. By 4,500 years ago, the list of domesticates had expanded to include potatoes, corn, gourds, common beans, and perhaps cocoa. All except corn appear to have been domesticated indigenously (MacNeish, Patterson & Browman, 1975). About the same time crop plants appeared, tamed llamas and probably alpacas seem to have existed in the Huancayo region of Central Peru, which, like Ayachucho, is an area of mid-altitude. One region to which the idea of food production diffused was the Ancón-Chillón area of the desert coast of Peru.

The Consequences of Agriculture

Within a few thousand years after people first began to raise animals and crops, agriculture had set in motion a series of events that completely changed human culture and altered the natural environment. Much of this transformation can be traced to one fact: Agriculture supplied enough food to make it possible for larger groups of people to live in smaller areas. A hunting-and-gathering way of life had usually meant moving in small groups with the seasons in search of food. But when people evolved to a more settled existence in villages, more complex governments were required for social control. Trade and conflict grew, health worsened, and new technologies were invented.

Demographic Effects

During the Mesolithic Age, most environments could support only small groups of people. It is true that some environments rich in resources have fed hunting-and-gathering settlements with large populations. The best-known examples are the large communities of the American Northwest coast, which thrived on fish and shellfish. But the carrying capacity of most environments kept human groups small. The population of the entire Tehuacán Valley before about 9,000 years ago, for instance, is thought to have been no more than 12 to 24 people (MacNeish, 1964). Twelve thousand years ago, the world population was perhaps 5 to 10 million. When seen against the background of the gradual increase throughout the 2 million years of the Pleistocene, the last 12,000 years represent a population explosion.

Agriculture led not only to population

growth but also, far more importantly, to increased population density. Hunter-gatherers generally needed a large range in which to draw on a variety of foods. Agriculture concentrated the food in nearby fields in the form of crop plants that were much more productive than wild varieties. This allowed settlements to become larger and closer together.

The adoption of agriculture not only raised the ceiling on population size, but also may have reduced the death rate among infants and the elderly. Soft foods such as animal milk and cereal mush added to the possible diet of the toothless. There is not, however, any firm evidence that life expectancies improved during the Neolithic. Men lived an average of 31 to 34 years, and women lived an average of 28 to 31 years (Smith, 1972).

Changes in Social Organization

The advantage of being able to store surplus food tended to lead, according to some theorists, to increasing inequality in agricultural societies. In early agricultural groups there was a change in the way food was gotten and surplus food redistributed among the members of the group. Hunter-gatherers tend to have less complex political systems—members of the group have more equal access to available material and social rewards (Harner, 1970). Among hunter-gatherers food sharing is based on kinship. But in agricultural groups some people, perhaps on the basis of their age or position within the kin group, began to take charge of food distribution. The more productive the society, the more complex the redistribution system, and the more control the leader(s) attained. As populations grew, the leadership, because of prestige and power associated with the role, became more powerful. The position also became institutionalized—that is, the leader became dependent for power not on personal traits, but on custom and the office itself.

With agriculture came not only more complex governments and economies, and greater differences in power within a society, but also a change in the division of labor. In hunting-and-gathering societies sex, age, and natural ability were probably the only factors affecting how work was divided. In larger groups, however, other factors, such as inherited status, began to play a role. Some people in farming groups spent part of their time at crafts such as pottery making or woodworking. In more complex societies the most skilled workers became full-time specialists.

Agriculture ultimately influenced the role of the sexes in society, as well. At first the division of labor by sex was probably not much affected. Men continued to perform the most strenuous tasks such as hunting and adopted forest clearing, herding, and plowing. The women probably added weeding, harvesting, and food preparation to the task of plant collecting (Smith, 1972). But as population pressures increased the need for more intensive cultivation, the role of women in agriculture decreased. With it, status may have fallen as well. The status of women tends to be high when they do most of the agricultural work, as among the Iroquois Indians of the American Northeast before the European invasion. Where women are less active, they are valued as mothers only (Smith, 1972). One study (Sanday, 1974) suggests that when women's contribution to subsistence is about equal to that of men, their status is highest.

Conflict and Trade

As population densities increased, and people began to produce more food and goods, war and trade among different groups became more common. Although there was almost certainly conflict in prefarming days, groups were too spread out for the violence to become systematized warfare. But the massive walls of Jericho, probably built soon after it became a farming settlement, and the cliff dwellings in the American Southwest show how much early farmers felt they needed to be defended. For warriors, the incentives to launch raids were greater than ever before. The spoils of war took the form of food, slaves, animals, and resources such as mines and irrigated land (Smith, 1972).

As the demand for the products of farming communities increased, so did peaceful means of obtaining them. Trade became more elaborate and, for the first time, institutionalized. Markets were set up, and middlemen, who sold the goods carried by others, appeared on the scene. It was not long before flint, amber, obsidian, food, and manufactured goods such as pottery were traded between regions and communities (Smith, 1972).

War and trade both helped bring about radical changes in the distribution of the physical traits of the world's populations. More contact between people increased gene flow and began to break down group differences. The trend heightened as food producers grew in number and expanded their territory, displacing or intermingling with other cultures.

Inventions and New Technologies

Continual population pressure resulting from the production of more and more food provided an incentive to find still more efficient ways of using the land and other resources. News of discoveries and breakthroughs spread relatively quickly because of the increased travel of this time due to trade and war. As a result, the rate of innovation rose dramatically (Smith, 1972).

Inventions of the age include the wheel and sails, both of which were present by at least 5,300 years B.P. in Mesopotamia. Animals were harnessed for transportation and for plowing the fields. And pottery allowed long-term storage of some foods. It also expanded the variety of foods that could be eaten, since they could now be prepared and cooked in a number of new ways.

Numerous new technologies were developed at this time, as well. Irrigation greatly improved crop yields. In canal irrigation, channels several feet deep brought water from rivers to the field. In pot irrigation, pots were used to draw water from shallow wells for use in watering the crops.

In some regions, new, heavy cutting and chopping tools such as axes, adzes, hoes, and other tools used in felling trees and tilling the soil were developed. And just about everywhere, new ways of changing the properties of natural substances were found. Kilns transformed clay into wear-resistant pottery. Metals were produced after the basics of smelting were learned. And people discovered how to change fruit and grain into delightful drinks by allowing the raw materials to ferment.

All of these inventions and technologies, except possibly the last, contributed to an enormous increase in the efficiency with which humans could change their environment to support themselves. As this ability increased, so did population, thus redoubling the pressure to invent and to discover.

Summary

1. The *Mesolithic Age* coincided with the warming trend and the extinction of herds of large game animals following the retreat of the last glaciation of the Pleistocene Epoch. The period is distinguishable in Europe, the Near East, and North America. Smaller game animals were hunted with small blades called *microliths*. The relative scarcity of food caused Mesolithic people to exploit a greater variety of food resources.

2. The *Neolithic Age* is marked by a change

from a hunting-and-gathering economy and a technology dominated by flaked-stone tools to an economy based on farming and new technologies, such as polished stone tools, pottery, and weaving.

3. In *domestication,* humans, acting as a selective force, brought about evolutionary change in the frequency of traits of plant and animal populations. Domestication not only made plants and animals more productive sources of food, but also made them dependent on humans for their existence.

4. Kent Flannery has proposed three obstacles to the domestication of grain: (1) the brittle *rachis* of some grains broke easily under the impact of the sickle, scattering the grain and making it hard to harvest; (2) wild grains had tough husks, or *glumes,* which encased the edible kernels; (3) wild grain grew in difficult-to-harvest patches scattered on hillsides. These obstacles were overcome in the Near East when early farmers deliberately began to sow plants with a tough rachis, developed "naked kernel" hybrids, and planted mutant six-row barley in lowland fields.

5. The primary obstacle to the domestication of animals was the aggressiveness of the wild forms and the ease with which they could escape. By breeding less aggressive animals, herders reduced the number of unmanageable animals in their flocks and herds. Other changes resulting from domestication were the rise in frequency of wooly-haired sheep and goats and of goats with twisted horns.

6. The major theories explaining the origins of farming covered in the text are *Childe's oasis model, Braidwood's nuclear zone model,* and various *population models.*

7. V. Gordon Childe proposed in his oasis model that a drying trend in Mesopotamia during the Mesolithic turned grasslands into deserts dotted with oases. Humans were forced to domesticate the animals and plants concentrated in the oasis, since killing them would have eliminated all sources of food. Archaeological data have discredited this theory.

8. According to Braidwood's nuclear zone theory, the human ability to experiment with and manipulate the environment had by the Neolithic advanced to the point that, given a zone rich in domesticable species, humans would naturally begin to produce food. This theory has been attacked for its lack of explanatory power.

9. Various population models propose that an imbalance between population size and food resources provided the stimulus to produce food. Some experts feel that populations tend culturally to limit their numbers to a level beneath the carrying capacity of the environment. Lewis Binford, for example, argues that external factors such as a change in the physical environment or immigration create pressure for food production. Others, however, like Esther Boserup and Mark Cohen, argue the populations have tended to grow large enough to exceed the food supply, making farming necessary.

10. Archaeological sequences pertaining to the origins of food production are well worked out in the Near East, China, and Mesoamerica.

11. Food production first appeared in the *Near East* in the Levant between 10,300 and 10,000 years ago, although signs of herding predate this by at least 2,000 years.

12. In *China,* farming settlements began to appear by about 6,000 B.P., when people of the *Yang-shao* culture were planting millet and keeping pigs and dogs.

13. In *Mesoamerica,* native plants and a few animals were domesticated separately at different times and places. Natives of the Tehuacán Valley of central Mexico hunted and gathered in seasonal patterns until around 7,000 years B.P. Then, steady population growth may have forced the planting of *maize,* the ancestor of modern corn.

14. Persistent worldwide population growth among hunter-gatherers is the most

likely reason for the spread of agricultural techniques. Agriculture spread from the Near East throughout Europe in several stages. Farming did not reach parts of northern Europe until some 3,000 to 4,000 years B.P. By 6,500 years B.P., wheat, barley, and flax were being planted in North Africa, but southward diffusion was slow due to already plentiful food supplies and ecological obstacles. And in the Ancón-Chillón coastal area of Peru a rising population forced domestication of some plants by about 4,000 years B.P.

15. Agriculture transformed human life by allowing people to live permanently in much larger and more densely settled communities than ever before. Higher densities made necessary more complex forms of social control, and some groups gained greater access to wealth and prestige than others. Demand for the goods and food of settlements was satisfied peacefully by means of trade and violently in wars. Growing populations provided an incentive to use resources more efficiently. Inventions such as sails and the wheel, and technologies, including irrigation, pottery-making, metalworking, and brewing helped bring about more effective exploitation of resources.

14 The Emergence of Cities, States, and Civilizations

FOR more than 99 percent of our history, humans have lived in simple egalitarian societies (societies whose members were nearly equal in prestige and access to resources). As the population of agricultural societies grew, increasingly complex political structures evolved to coordinate the activities of a larger number of people. The first societies in which some groups had more power than others appeared in the Near East about 5,500 years ago. In some parts of the world the change from a egalitarian social structure to more complex forms is still occurring, spurred by pressures from more advanced states.

Before we begin to explore where, how, and why complex societies emerged, we must define three basic terms: *city, state,* and *civilization.*

Some Definitions

The City

A *city* can be defined as a central place that performs economic and political functions for the surrounding area. The first cities probably developed around political bureaucracies that became the seat of political power in a region. When the bureaucracies began to attract people who performed special services for rulers and people who wanted to become part of the ruling structure, the first true cities probably were formed. The process by which cities are formed is called *urbanism.* As urbanism progresses, cities become composed of new people with more diverse talents and cultural backgrounds.

Not everyone, however, agrees to this reconstruction of how cities arose. Jane Jacobs (1970) holds that cities emerged before rural settlements, and that they in fact stimulated the development of agriculture. The first cities, she believes, were trading centers. The basic techniques of agriculture arose as city dwellers experimented with wild plants and animals brought in by traders in return for obsidian or other valuable items. The techniques that came out of such experimenting later diffused to nearby farming villages, which exchanged food for the goods of the city. Jacobs' theory is considerably weakened, however, by traces of agricultural activity that have been dated back to between 10,000 and 9,000 years B.P., well before the earliest cities.

The State

A *state* can be defined as an independent political unit that includes many communities in its territory, with a centralized government that has the power to collect taxes, draft citizens for work and for war, and enact and enforce laws (Carneiro, 1970). States are socially *stratified*—some groups of citizens have greater access either to wealth, status, or both than do other groups. States are also economically diversified, which means that only a part of the population produces food—other members may be artisans, traders, priests, rulers, or other specialists (Flannery, 1972). In early states, organized religion merged with the state and its leadership, making both objects of worship.

Civilizations

Civilization is the most difficult of the three concepts to define, partly because it is used in so many different ways. A precise definition has been offered by E. R. Service (1975): Civilization "can be accurately used to mean that the society was characterized by the presence of cities or large towns and that the inhabitants were citizens of some kind of legal commonwealth." But civilization carries with it many connotations other than that of cities of people bound together in a government based on laws. Some think of civilization as a flourishing of the arts. Others associate it with the development of philosophical concepts to a very high level. Others have identified writing as the distinguishing feature of civilization.

Perhaps the best-known list of criteria for civilization is that of V. Gordon Childe. It is presented here in Service's summary (1975):

1. Urban centers (of between 7,000 to 20,000 people)
2. A class of full-time specialists working in the cities
3. A ruling class of religious, civil, and military leaders
4. A surplus of food produced by the peasants for use by the government
5. Monumental public buildings, symbolizing the concentration of the surplus
6. Use of numbers and writing
7. Arithmetic, geometry, and astronomy
8. Sophisticated art
9. Long-distance trade
10. An institutionalized form of political organization based on force, called the *state*

Excavation has turned up evidence against Childe's list. Seldom have all of these traits appeared together in the earliest cultures that we think of as civilizations. It is often argued, for instance, that cities do not have to exist for there to be civilization. Most people would agree that the Maya were a civilization, in spite of the fact that cities did not exist. And while the Inca culture did display most of Childe's characteristics, there was no system of writing.

The term *civilization* has become more and more vague as it has been applied to societies that have different characteristics. Because *state* can be more clearly defined, we shall treat this concept as the center of our discussion. Nevertheless, *civilization* is often useful as a word meaning a society with sophisticated artistic, architectural, philosophical, economic, and political features.

The development of states and the emergence of cities are the main consideration of this chapter. We shall explore different types of political organization and then consider a number of theories of state formation. Finally, we shall present some of the archaeological data that are the basis of the definitions and theories we have presented.

From Bands to States

States did not spring fully formed from anarchy. Archaeologists have identified several stages through which human societies passed before states appeared. Our knowledge of these stages comes from the archaeological record and from observations of present-day societies. Unfortunately, in trying to distinguish the earliest states from less complex societies such as chiefdoms, we must arbitrarily break up what was a continuous process of evolution. But with this in mind, the contrasts between three different levels of pre-state social organization can be seen.

The Bands

Before about 12,000 years B.P., the basic unit of human social organization was a small, egalitarian society called a *band.* The only subunit of the band was the family, or a group of related families held together by kinship and marriage bonds. Leadership was informal, probably not resting for very long with any one person. The leader's power came from force of personality rather than from laws or traditions defining the role and naming the person to assume it. Bands were and are the usual form of society among hunting-and-gathering people, who do not have a strong sense of territoriality (that is, the need to define and defend one's own land). Owning and defending land would not make sense for people who were often moving from one area to another.

The Tribes

About 9,000 years B.P., a slightly larger, more complicated form of social organization called the *tribe* can be inferred from the archaeological record in the Near East. It appeared in Peru about 5,000 years B.P., and in Mesoamerica by 3,300 years B.P., The *tribe* was larger than a band; it was made up of groups of families related by common descent or by membership in a variety of kinship-based groups such as clans or lineages (Flannery, 1972). The power of leaders was weak, with individual family heads being more important than any one leader. Kinship groups seem to have been bound together for different reasons in different cultures. Among primitive farmers, the kin group probably held land in common. Farming brought with it territoriality, since land was now an important resource. Lines of ancestral descent were becoming an important part of tribal life—evidence includes the skulls of many generations found buried under the floors of their descendant's houses in Near Eastern villages (Flannery, 1972). There was little or no stratification, and division of labor was still largely by age and sex.

The Chiefdom

A third stage of pre-state social organization, the *chiefdom,* first appeared in the Near East around 7,500 years B.P. Chiefdoms were probably theocracies, with the ruler or a member of his family serving as a high religious official (Service, 1975). For the first time, the position of leader existed apart from

Table 1 The Cultural Evolution of Societies

Type of society	Some institutions, in order of appearance	Ethnographic examples	Archaeological examples
State	Stratification; Kingship; Codified law; Bureaucracy; Military draft; Taxation	France England India United States	Classic Mesoamerica Sumer Shang China Imperial Rome
Chiefdom	Ranked descent groups; Redistributive economy; Hereditary leadership; Elite endogamy; Full-time craft specialization	Tonga Hawaii Kwakiutl Nootka Natchez	Gulf Coast Olmec of Mexico (3,000 B.P.) Samarran of Near East (7,300 B.P.) Mississippian of North America (3,750 B.P.)
Tribe	Unranked descent groups	New Guinea highlanders Southwest pueblos Sioux	Early formative of inland Mexico (3,400–3,000 B.P.) Pre-pottery Neolithic of Near East (10,000–8,000 B.P.)
Band	Local group autonomy; Egalitarian status; Ephemeral leadership; Ad hoc ritual; Reciprocal economy	Kalahari. bushmen Australian aborigines Eskimo Shoshone	Early Archaic of United States and Mexico (12,000–8,000 B.P.) Late Paleolithic of Near East (12,000 B.P.)

Flannery, 1972. Reproduced with permission from the *Annual Review of Ecology and Systematics*, Vol. 3. © 1972 by Annual Reviews, Inc.

the person who occupied it. That is, his power came not from his personality, but from his position or role as leader. When a chief died, the role was filled by someone from a particular line of descent.

No longer were all family groups or lineages of equal rank. There is further evidence that some kin groups may have owned the best farm land or enjoyed other marks of status. Perhaps the best evidence that certain groups enjoyed higher status from birth is the discovery of the remains of children who had been buried much more elaborately than most other people at the time. At Tell es Sawwan, Iraq, from about 7,500 to 7,000 years B.P., children were buried with alabaster statues and turquoise and copper ornaments. At La Venta, Mexico, from about 800 B.C., children were buried with jade articles in basalt-columned tombs. These children, having died so young, could not have achieved a status worthy of such attention. Their status had to be inherited (Flannery, 1972).

Chiefdoms were characterized by large villages, among which some craft specialization existed. Some villages in the Near East, for example, worked only on pottery; others produced large amounts of copper goods. In Mesoamerica, some villages made magnetite mirrors, while others made shell ornaments. But within each village, there were no groups of people who worked only on these goods. All villagers seem to have worked part-time at crafts as well as at farming: Signs of both activities can be found in the remains of houses whose members were part of a chiefdom.

Chiefdoms exist today in many parts of Africa, as well as in South Pacific Islands such as Fiji and Tahiti. Until they were disturbed by Europeans, the Hawaiians and the Kwakiutl and Nootka of the Pacific Northwest were also chiefdoms (Flannery, 1972).

The Emergence of States

Why some bands developed into tribes and others did not, or why some tribes became chiefdoms and others did not are questions that concern many anthropologists. In this chapter we shall limit our discussion to the transition from chiefdoms to states. Along the way, we shall examine the role the formation of cities has played in this transition.

The first question we must ask is what features allow us to distinguish a chiefdom from a state. The answer lies partly in the types of changes that occur as states emerge. Most anthropologists would agree that the following events mark the transition from chiefdom to state.

1. Complex chiefdoms break up and collapse.
2. Regulatory organizations change, and a formal, centralized, legal apparatus for governing emerges.
3. Specialized economic activities become the function of particular groups.
4. Territorial expansion follows the emergence of the state.

This list may tell us what happens in the state formation and provide clues that archaeologists can look for. But it cannot tell us why the process occurs in the first place. Since we were not present to observe these causes, their nature can only be approached by hypothesis. Two basic types of hypotheses exist. Some experts have proposed universal causes of state formation. These so-called *prime mover* theories tend to focus on single causes. Others have decided that such a complex evolution cannot be explained in terms of a single cause. They look to a combination of factors. We shall examine some of the most important theories of state formation in this section.

Irrigation

In his *hydraulic theory,* Karl Wittfogel (1957) has suggested that states first arose in dry areas when large-scale irrigation became a necessity. The body of officials needed to manage the building of canals and to operate them evolved into the strong government of the state. Wittfogel assumes that village farmers saw the advantages of large-scale irrigation and chose to join in a larger political unit to get them. The state grew larger as it took over the functions of smaller administrative units.

The hydraulic theory has been weakened by evidence uncovered since it was put forth. Excavations in China, Mesopotamia, and Mexico—three areas originally cited in support of the theory—have shown that these states arose long before there was large-scale irrigation. Furthermore, some states, such as the ancient Mayan, grew in areas where irrigation was always of minor importance.

Trade

In some areas of the world, the lack of certain vital raw materials required that communities trade with one another. For example, southern Mesopotamia needed building stone, wood, and metal. The Petén region of Guatemala lacked salt, obsidian, and stone for maize-grinding tools. To get such goods, these communities had to trade with people outside their immediate areas (Flannery, 1972). This trade called for a way to organize the production of the resources traded, as well as communication and recordkeeping. All of these activities are thought to be important in the formation of states.

Unfortunately, not all emerging states depended on trade. Raw materials were abundant in the Valley of Mexico, for example. There trade began after the state had already developed.

Population Growth

As we mentioned in the last chapter, many experts feel that population growth was the prime mover that gave rise to farming and to complex societies. Excavation has clearly shown that population increases are linked with (1) the beginnings of food production and (2) the appearance of complex societies. There is a great deal of disagreement, however, as to whether population growth preceded or followed the other two trends.

Some authorities hold that the development of agricultural techniques caused population growth. Knowledge of how to produce food led to food surpluses, which made possible concentrations of people and gave some the time to specialize in nonfarming pursuits. One such pursuit was government. Full-time administrators dependent on the food produced by others supervised the activities of an increasingly powerful central government in the emerging state.

In the 1960s another group of experts, foremost among whom was Esther Boserup, proposed (1965) that population growth itself forced humans to look for more and more efficient means of supplying food. Population growth preceded farming, in their view. The class of officials who oversaw food production and other activities formed the basis of the state's bureaucracy.

It remains to be shown, however, why population increased in the first place. Studies have revealed that many human groups behave in such a way as to keep their numbers below the resource limits of their environment. This is especially true of hunter-gatherers. Sexual abstinence and socially prescribed killing of the young and old may have occurred during periods of environmental stress. But these may only have proved effective within limited periods. Over the longer periods archaeologists deal with, some gradual population increase may have occurred.

Circumscription and Warfare

Robert Carneiro's *circumscription theory* (1970) can be seen as a modification of the idea that population pressure acted as a prime mover in the rise of the state. According to him, there is evidence of war during the early stages of the formation of all the major states. Growing populations fought one another for land, and in some cases states were formed. But, because war does not necessarily lead to the birth of a state, it must do so only under certain conditions. To define these conditions, Carneiro sought factors common to the times and places in which states have formed.

The one common condition he found is *circumscription.* In *geographical circumscription* an area is set off by mountains, seas, or deserts, which severely limit the land that people can occupy and farm. In Egypt, for instance, the state arose in the narrow strips of fertile land that flank the Nile River. The river valley was virtually isolated by deserts and other geographical features.

Similarly, in *social circumscription* people may be prevented from moving by the surrounding populations. Napoleon Chagnon found social circumscription in a study (1965)

This relief, from Persepolis, the capital of ancient Persia, shows a procession of officials from Media, a territory that was conquered and incorporated into the empire. The officials are paying tribute to Darius, the founder of the empire. Here, as elsewhere, government grew and became more complex as the state expanded. (Georg Gerster, Photo Researchers)

of the Yąnomamö of the Amazon River Basin. He observed that at the center of Yąnomamö territory, villages are much closer together than elsewhere in the territory. Migration from these central villages is difficult, because to do so would mean encroaching on another village's territory.

According to Carneiro, war produces greater centralization and, eventually, states. As populations in the circumscribed Nile River Valley increased, crop-producing land became more scarce and valuable. Consequently, villages began to war with one another for land. Because defeated villages could not move, they had to choose between death or political subordination. As chiefdoms collected taxes, drafted armies, and administered more and more villages, they grew stronger. Warfare among the two great chiefdoms of the upper and lower Nile ultimately led to state formation.

At the same time warfare need not inevitably lead to state formation. Although the Yąnomamö are socially circumscribed and have probably engaged in warfare for many generations, they are clearly not a state—or even a chiefdom.

It should be clear that each of these prime-mover theories explains more in some areas than in others. This fact is not lost on many archaeologists, who feel that different combinations of factors caused state formation in different areas.

Flannery's Process Model

Kent Flannery (1972), for instance, feels that different combinations of the prime movers we have just discussed act in different areas to set in motion the processes of state formation. When a society is subjected to stress—as it is, for example, during war or as a result of population pressure, the demands of large-scale trade, or any combination of prime movers—it either collapses or changes. Flannery believes that the mechanisms of change leading to state formation are universal, although the events and conditions that set them in motion are not. For this reason, none of the prime movers alone is enough to explain the rise of states.

An understanding of Flannery's view of society is helpful in comprehending his model of the processes that make societies more complex. He sees human society as a series of subsystems arranged hierarchically, from lowest and most specific to highest and most general (Flannery, 1972). Each level controls the one below it by comparing the performance of the latter to goals defined by the needs of subsistence and to ideological and religious values. A low level of government, for instance, might direct the planting and harvesting of crops in the field with specific commands. A middle level might control the distribution of harvests and surpluses by means of rituals or general policies that set goals and guidelines.

Flannery's explanation of the rise of the state centers on the processes by which such a system becomes more complex. He defines complexity in terms of the degree to which two processes have occurred. The first, *segregation,* is the extent to which various administrative tasks are split up among separate units of the bureaucracy. The second, *centralization,* is the "degree of linkage between the various subsystems and the highest-order controls in society." He then proposes two mechanisms that affect the level of segregation and centralization in a society. *Promotion* is the elevation of a preexisting institution to a higher level or the elevation of one role of an existing institution to the status of a new institution. *Linearization* is the bypassing of lower-order controls by higher-order controls.

Promotion may embody one aspect of the function of an earlier institution in a new institution specializing in that one task. Thus, aspects of the office of the director of public works might be split into several offices. The director of irrigation and the director of public monuments, for example, might be promoted to become heads of their own departments. As more administrative units are created, each function becomes regulated more closely. Promotion, therefore, adds to increasing segregation, because it creates new institutions.

Linearization typically occurs when higher-order systems have to take on the regulatory activities of a lower level because the latter fails to perform its function. For instance, states may initially tax only local chiefs, who then assess their followers. If this arrangement is later replaced by direct payment of taxes by each citizen, linearization has occurred. As you can see, linearization increases centralization.

Modern archaeologists recognize that the main value of each of these hypotheses is that they can be tested in the field. That is, the data that archaeologists find can be used to support, reject, or modify hypotheses so that a clearer understanding of what underlies the formation of states can be developed. With this in mind, in the rest of this chapter we shall review the archaeological evidence from four ancient states—Mesopotamia, Egypt, China, and Mesoamerica. As we describe the evidence, we shall take note of which, if any, of the theories we have just presented is the most applicable.

State Formation in the New and Old Worlds

Mesopotamia

The first state emerged in the area between the Tigris and Euphrates Rivers in what is now Iraq, Syria, and Iran. In our account of its rise we shall draw primarily on the work of Robert Service (1975).

Bands of hunters and gatherers had roamed

Table 2 The Chronology of State Formation

Years Ago	Mesopotamia	Egypt	China	Mesoamerica
1,000				Militaristic period
		Militaristic period	Militaristic period	
2,000	Militaristic period			Initial empire
				Regional centers
3,000			Initial empire	Formative
4,000			Regional centers	Early agriculture
	Initial empire			
5,000		Initial empire		
			Formative	
	Regional centers			
			Early agriculture	
6,000				
	Formative			
7,000		Early agriculture		
	Early agriculture			
8,000				
12,000				

the highlands of the Zagros mountains since Neolithic times but had rarely wandered into the arid lowlands to the southeast. Around 10,000 years B.P., however, some of these people began settling as herding and farming tribes on the Assyrian steppe between the mountains and the lowlands. There, as we mentioned in the last chapter, during the late Neolithic they developed a basic knowledge of irrigation, which in time allowed them to move into and farm the arid lowlands.

Formative Era (7,000–5,000 years B.P.). Before irrigation, lowland inhabitants had depended to some degree on hunting and gathering. This, of course, made some seasonal migration necessary. After upland peoples introduced irrigation, the dry lowlands of the Tigris-Euphrates lowland system could for the first time support settled villages.

Several geographical factors also influenced the social evolution of lowland culture. Many villages lacked certain basic resources, forcing them to acquire these materials through trade. They traded food for wood to build boats and stone for tools and construction with people living in the highlands. The easily navigable rivers aided the movement of goods and people, and, equally important, the movement of ideas, inventions, and discoveries.

Another important trend of this period is the gradual evolution of a separate herding culture in the highlands. Highlanders became more specialized as herders, trading with lowland people for what they could not grow. At times the herders raided lowland communities, and their mobile way of life led to a military superiority that later became an important factor in the social evolution of the area.

The most advanced culture of the late formative era appeared in the far south, on the alluvial plain of Sumer. Here, farmers lived in self-sufficient, politically independent villages. Excavation of a site named Al Ubaid shows the presence of an advanced chiefdom. As in other chiefdoms, religion and government fused in the chief. At Al Ubaid, imposing temples built during the late formative period served as a place of worship, a palace, a storage place, and a center for the gathering and redistribution of goods. The Sumerians were clearly placing the temple and its priests at the core of their social and political organization.

There is also evidence of full-time specialization in the crafts. The building of temples alone probably required the full-time labor of a large number of people. As the class of specialists grew, so did the power of the temple administrators who saw that they were fed and controlled the trade of the goods produced.

Formation of Regional Centers (5,500–5,000 years B.P.). During this time large towns, each controlled by a chiefdom, became the religious and economic focus for whole regions. Warka, on the Sumerian plain, is typical of these regional centers.

The Warka site is dominated by a temple that was probably the religious and economic life of the settlement. The temple was a 40-foot-high ziggurat—a stepped pyramid with outside staircases and a shrine at the top. Adams (1966) estimates that if all the hours spent by those building the temple were added together, the total would come to 7,500 years worth of work. Evidently, the priestly administrators could command enormous amounts of labor. There is evidence that the temple redistributed both manufactured goods and raw materials over wide distances. Wood and metals brought from distant areas are among the evidence found at the site. The ability of the chiefdom to control the distribution of goods may suggest that, at this time, economic influence was more important than political controls.

Still, loyalties seem to have been to local political and social institutions. A centralized bureaucracy, which is typical of states—specialized to administer a number of governmental functions at several levels—had not yet emerged.

Era of Multiregional States (5,000–3,500 years B.P.). The development of multiregional states out of regional centers was gradual. The first step is a fairly brief but important dynastic era (4,900–4,500 years B.P.). It was characterized by a lessening of the influence of religion in the government, the build-up of cities, and an increase in the social differences among various classes of people. Warfare was almost constant. Highland dwellers and herders living on the fringe of settled lowland areas stepped up their raids on the cities. And the expanding cities fought one another over land needed for farming, water, and trade routes. Military leaders replaced priests as the most vital decision makers. In time, these military leaders were able to keep power within their families, resulting in the first dynastic kingdoms. Because of the constant threat of warfare, many villagers moved into the larger towns, which were more easily defended. As a result, major cities grew up. Warka, for instance, may have had 20,000 to 30,000 inhabitants at this time.

The growth of social stratification is evident from burial sites. Before 5,500 years B.P., such sites show almost no distinction in the wealth or prestige of the deceased. As Warka became a regional center, differences become more apparent; during the dynastic era, they are marked. At the bottom level were slaves, who as captives of war were assigned work such as weaving cloth. Most of the population were farmers, some of whom owned their own land. There was also a class of craft work-

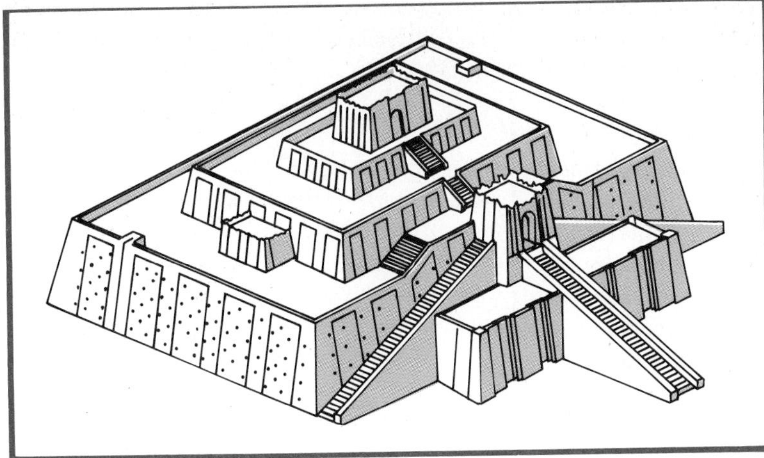

Figure 1 The Ziggurat of Ur. Temple-towers such as this required the organization of large labor forces over a long period of time—a feat most easily accomplished by a state. (Adapted from Mallowan, 1965)

ers, who are difficult to describe in terms of status because it varied from one craft to another. The ruler and his family were the leaders of the society, although we cannot tell for sure to what degree wealth was concentrated among them.

The first empire uniting all the separate regional centers of Mesopotamia was founded around 4,500 years B.P. by Sargon, who, it was said, began his political career as a cupbearer to the king of Kish, in northern Sumer. After becoming a successful military leader, he founded and set himself up as ruler of the city of Akkad, which was in a strategic location between the steppes and the lowlands. Further conquests brought the sophisticated, theocratic regional centers of Sumer to the south under his control.

Akkad attracted a diverse population—older, more refined, religious Sumerians and rougher, secular Semites from the hill country. Akkad of course was a secular city, having been founded by a military leader instead of evolving from a long period of priestly rule. Under Sargon, farming techniques such as irrigation were applied by managers who had been tribal chieftains. These men had once been in charge of flocks but now directed the activities of workers in the irrigation system. Thus, the combination of government by chieftains and the technologies of Sumer led to a bureaucratic government unlike any other previous system. As the empire changed during the four generations that it existed, local rulers and priests were replaced by members of the royal family and trusted friends, thus making the bureaucracy more and more loyal to the ruler.

The local loyalties upon which the earlier city-states were based were replaced by loyalties to the larger, more impersonal, multiregional state. At the top of the bureaucracy was the hereditary ruler (the king, or emperor) who performed judicial, administrative, and legislative functions. Sargon himself took important steps toward a rule by law, one of the characteristics of the state, as we have defined it. He gained the right to enforce agreements and oaths among people in the empire.

Examining the Theories. It is hard to pinpoint the precise period at which a Mesopotamian state emerged. By the time regional centers were being formed (5,500 years B.P.), however, all 10 of Childe's characteristics of civilization were, in varying degrees, present in Mesopotamia. Least evident were full-time specialists, except the priest-rulers and other temple officials. Political organization based on force was not very evident until the dynastic era. True states probably did not emerge until the beginning of the dynastic era.

No one factor can explain the emergence of the state in Mesopotamia, which makes it necessary to think in terms of a multiple-factor theory. Without irrigation, significant settlement—let alone the formation of a state—could not have occurred in the arid lowlands. But irrigation began in the steppe region long before the formation of states. Thus, irrigation was a necessary precursor to state formation but did not directly cause it. Gradually, irrigation became an important source of the state's control of the population, until control of irrigation was taken over completely by the state. Flannery's idea of centralization by linearization is helpful in describing this process.

Circumscription and warfare did not bring about state formation, but they played crucial roles in building nonreligious rule and in the later emergence of multiregional states. Nor can agricultural surplus explain the creation of the state. The soil of Mesopotamia was fertile because annual floods deposited silt in the floodplain. The resulting abundant harvests produced a food surplus that enriched the state but was not a primary factor in creating it.

Trade was vital because of the lack of raw materials, and its control undoubtedly also added to the development of central authorities. The larger empires, like that of Sargon, included varied geographic areas, and the planned exchange of certain goods was clearly important to the integration of these areas.

Population growth during the formative period probably caused some important changes in the structure of the society. Growth may have led to increasing competition for resources, which finally resulted in the increasing militarism and secularization of the dynastic period (Adams, 1972).

Thus, it is obvious that a number of factors contributed to state formation in Mesopotamia. Population growth, leading to circumscription and warfare, may have started the process. But along the way trade, agricultural surpluses, and management of irrigation enlarged the scope and power of the state.

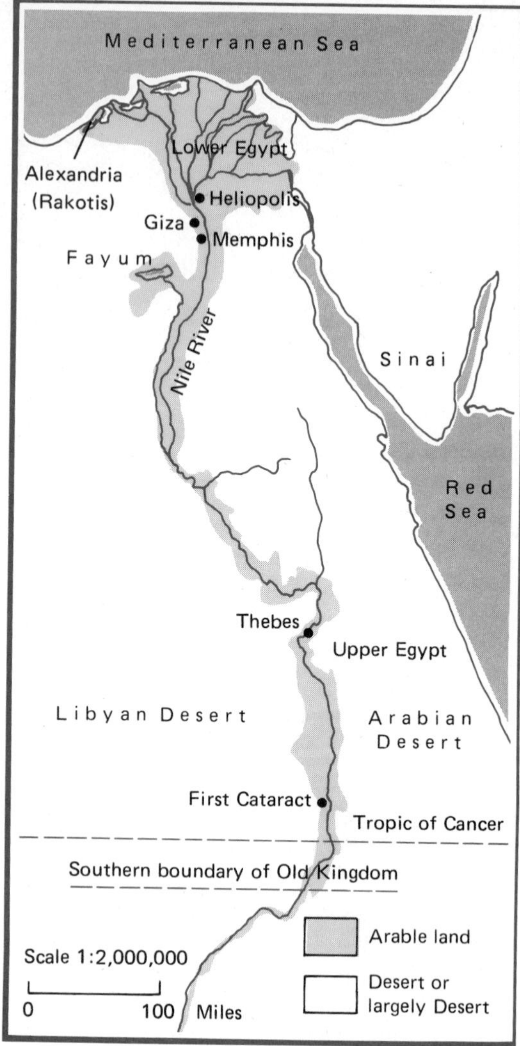

Figure 2 Ancient Egypt

Egypt

Egypt is rightly called the Land of the Nile, for that great river dominates the area through which it flows. For most of its length the Nile is bounded by deserts to the east and west. Waterfalls limit travel south into the interior of Africa, while to the north the broad delta of the Nile fans out into the Mediterranean. Every year the Nile floods its narrow valley. The rise and fall of the river takes place over a period of months, renewing the soil without eroding it. The Nile also provides easy transport for raw materials, goods, and information. All these factors eventually helped shape the state that arose there.

Formative Era (6,000–5,350 years B.P.). People first began to farm in Egypt by at least 6,000 years B.P., when scattered villages supporting themselves by floodwater farming appeared throughout the Nile's floodplain. These villages were organized into local districts called *nomes.* Although these local governments were independent, like those of the cities of Sumer, they were much weaker. Small temples seem to have been a major feature of these nomes, but religious leaders did not command much political power, because the local chieftain, priest, or priest-king was not looked on as the earthly representative of the local gods, as was the case in the cities of Sumer. Later, after the state arose, the pharaoh could be seen as the unrivalled god of the whole valley, Unification of the valley was made easier than if localities had been strong. Finally, complex urban bureaucracies did not develop, partly because there was not yet any long-distance trade that needed regulation by bureaucrats (Service, 1975).

Formation of Regional Centers (5,350–5,050 years B.P.). At this time the difference between Lower Egypt (the delta region of the north) and Upper Egypt (the southern Nile valley) became important. The two regions shared a common language, a similar culture, and a political structure based on the nome. Lower Egypt, however, was more culturally advanced, while Upper Egypt was more disciplined politically. The ambition of the rulers of the southern region led them to extend their power over more and more of the Nile area, until they had joined the rival nomes under a unified government.

Era of Multiregional States (5,050–3,970 years B.P.). Tradition holds that Menes, a chief of Upper Egypt, conquered the lower Nile around 5,200 years B.P. and established the First Dynasty of the Egyptian empire. Most likely the unification actually occurred over several generations. Even so, it appears to have been accomplished with relative ease, probably because of the weakness of the nomes.

In many respects Egypt during the first few dynasties was more like an elaborate chiefdom than a state. The pharaoh held sway over all the nomes of the valley, with little if any bureaucracy in between. Unlike the earlier chiefs, he was both emperor and god. It was not until the Fourth Dynasty that a separation of powers in the theocracy appeared. Then a top official took over secular matters such as trade, the treasury, and food production.

Apparently the organization of communal projects such as land reclamation, flood control, and irrigation did not come about on a really large scale in Egypt until a political system of centralized rule under the pharaoh had been established. The attitude of awe felt toward the pharaoh by his subjects continued during much of the Old Kingdom (established with the Third Dynasty and lasting from 4,636 to 4,110 years B.P.) and helped to make possible the enormous projects (such as pyramid-building) the state undertook for its rulers. It was believed that the pharaoh could make those officials who pleased him immortal. Their devotion created peace and made possible a powerful state (Service, 1975; Aldred, 1965).

The Old Kingdom started out with a fairly simple governmental structure. But by the Fourth Dynasty, which began about 4,563 B.P., the pharaoh governed by means of a vast

Seated figures of Aemonophis III, the only remains of his funerary temple. The awe pharoah's subjects felt toward him helped make possible the enormous undertakings of the Egyptian state. (George Holton, Photo Researchers)

bureaucracy. The structure of Old Kingdom society resembled a pyramid, with the pharaoh at the top. Members of the royal family held the top positions in the bureaucracy. This structure controlled all important trade of the country, collecting and redistributing goods in accordance with the wishes of the royal court. The pharaoh held a virtual monopoly on the trade of the empire. Some pharaohs expanded trade routes to reach along the Mediterranean coast to the Levant.

Below the bureaucrats were the artists and craft workers, who were organized into guilds on a hereditary basis. The vast majority of citizens, however, were simple farmers. They worked in the fields during part of the year and supported the bureaucracy with the surplus they produced. At other times, they were drafted to help in the huge building projects of the state.

Examining the Theories. The history of the rise of the Egyptian civilization seems to contradict Childe's idea that cities are essential to civilization. Although most of Childe's 10 characteristics of a civilization were present, even in the times when regional centers were being formed, the most notable exception is the presence of cities. In Egypt, urbanism neither preceded nor accompanied the formation of the state: It came long after. The first true cities did not appear until after the Old Kingdom.

The theory of geographical circumscription seems to provide the best explanation for Egyptian development. The Nile River Valley can be seen as an area circumscribed by deserts and the sea. As a result, the unification of the South and the North by Menes was easier than it would have been otherwise. The nomes never produced strong leaders because the need for strong bureaucratic control of irrigation and defense never arose. Annual floods made extensive irrigation projects unnecessary. And enemies could not easily reach Egypt early in its history. Thus, there was little need for local military organization. As a result, the weak nome leaders could offer little resistance to the northern conquerors. Because the area was circumscribed, the people had little choice but to accept the rule of Menes. Gradually, the dynastic rulers provided the centralization from which the state emerged.

China

Complex political organizations first grew up in northern China around the lower and middle Huang Ho River. The area is a basin bounded on the north and west by plateaus, and on the south by plateaus and mountains. To the east it opens on a large plain. As in Egypt, the state that arose here seems to have been formed without the influence of outside forces.

Formative Era (5,000–4,600 years B.P.). Farming villages were first established during this time. Each village apparently was a moderate-sized, self-contained tribal community. Social stratification was not pronounced, nor was warfare frequent (Chang, 1976).

Formation of Regional Centers (4,600–3,850 years B.P.). During this stage, the people of the Lung-shan culture were able to increase rapidly their agricultural production. This seems to be associated with increased population density, and larger, more permanent settlements.

Because basic agricultural methods do not seem to have undergone any great improvement during the time of the Lung-shan culture, the growing productivity must be explained in terms of a social change. The archaeological evidence points to increasing specialization and to the beginnings of differences in status among the population. The presence of potter's wheels and excellent craftsmanship suggests that there were full-time potters. And jade objects concentrated at one site indicate the presence of specialists in jade-working. Activities, when performed by specialists whose work is directed by officials, are carried out much more efficiently than when done on a part-time basis. Thus the rate at which goods and food were produced rose.

Population pressure probably caused farmers from the original settlements to spread out into new territories. Then, for several reasons, the Lung-shan culture split into a number or regional stylistic traditions. One of the traditions, probably the Honan, was the base of the earliest Chinese state (Chang, 1976).

Period of Multiregional States (3,850–3,050 years B.P.). At the beginning of this period the communities of the lower and middle Huang Ho River were joined under the control of the Shang dynasty.

The change from Lung-shan culture was gradual and was marked by an intensification of long-term trends. Population density increased, and status and role differentiation became greater. Increasingly, central settlements governed political and economic affairs of the surrounding area. Communication was no longer a haphazard process carried out by individuals. Institutions put their messages into writing, and trade was carried on by organizations, which made communication between groups more regular and dependable.

Perhaps the most evident trait of the Shang dynasty is the presence of networks of build-

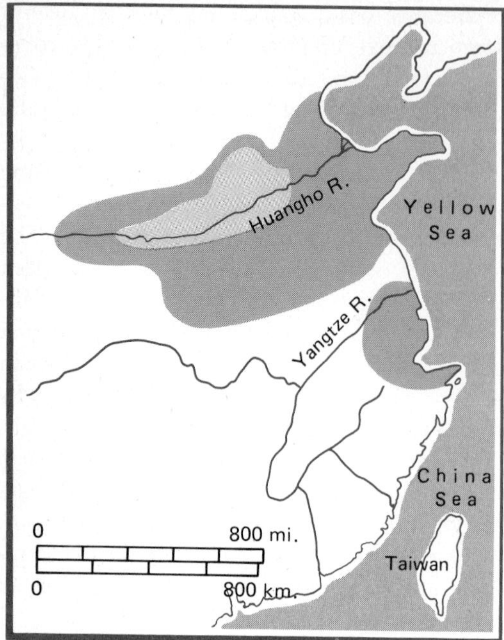

Figure 3 **The distribution of the Lung-shan (darker-shaded areas) and Shang cultures (lighter-shaded area)**

ing clusters. The networks were most concentrated at the center, and spread out to fill an area of between 30 and 40 square kilometers. The Lung-shan communities had been self-contained, with little contact with other villages. During the Shang dynasty, however, these villages became part of the administrative web that surrounded central clusters. From these centers officials and priests directed and organized political and economic activities. They in turn obeyed the ruler-god, whose position was inherited. Local villages were administered by relatives of the ruler, other high officials, or local leaders under the control of the ruler (Chang, 1976).

Examining the Theories. Early in the development of regional centers, China showed evidence of all 10 of Childe's characteristics of a civilization, except possibly monumental buildings. Many of the early Chinese structures were made out of wood, apparently a preferred material. Because they did not survive, we have little information about the kinds of structures that were built.

In the development of the state, circumscription and warfare were significant factors. It appears that state formation and development could not have occurred without the use of force. The people of the Huang Ho River Basin were not geographically circumscribed, but they may have been socially circumscribed. Land was either controlled by urban centers or left undefended to nomadic invaders. As populations increased, warfare among neighboring populations in competition for resources increased. In order to migrate, a defeated village would have to enter the territory of hostile neighbors. Instead, they were absorbed into expanding states.

Neither irrigation nor other technologies were crucial to the development of the state in China, although flood control and irregular rainfall could have brought about some river control. Trade, although widespread, was not well developed, probably because there were no great regional differences in goods that were produced.

Mesoamerica

Archaeologists use the term *Mesoamerica* when referring to the area in Central America in which several native Indian civilizations arose. The region consists of the highlands and lowlands of central and southern Mexico and Guatemala, and the lowlands of San Salvador, Belize, and part of Western Honduras. (See Figure 4.) The highlands, centering around the Valley of Mexico (where Mexico City now stands), are dry, with irregular rainfall. The lowlands, particularly the Yucatán Peninsula of Mexico and the Petén region of northern Guatemala, are covered by dense tropical rainforests. Mountain ranges, large lakes, and the Gulf of Mexico produce great

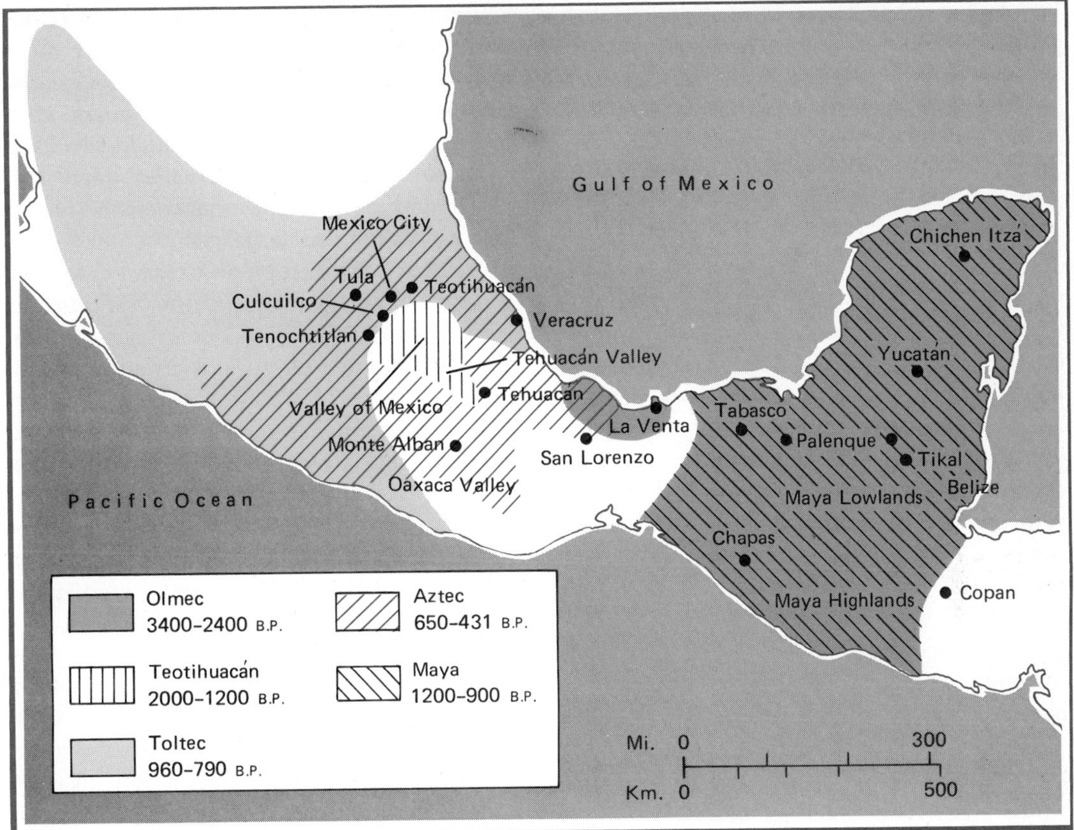

Figure 4 **The major civilizations of Mesoamerica**

geographic and climatic variation within both of these regions.

The best way to understand the complex societies that emerged in Mesoamerica is to consider the area as a unit. In this way we can gain a perspective and ability to generalize that is not possible in a discussion limited to one regional center. We shall use the same framework we used to describe the development of the state in the Near East, in Egypt, and in China.

The Formative Era (3,450–2,750 years B.P.). Complex societies first emerged in the Mesoamerican lowlands and spread from there to the highlands. The earliest complex society of the lowlands was that of the Olmecs, who lived on Mexico's southeastern Gulf coast, north of the Yucatán Peninsula. The Olmecs, with their distinctive art forms, imposing architecture, complex calendar, and writing, foreshadowed the more sophisticated states of the highlands.

The Olmecs are best known for their *ceremonial centers,* clusters of earthworks that seem to have been designed for religious purposes rather than as dwelling places. The largest of these centers, at a site named La Venta, took an estimated 800,000 days of human labor to build (Coe, 1962).

The ceremonial center appears to have been separated from the villages in which the population lived. There is no evidence that people lived in the centers, except perhaps a small number of priests. People probably grew their crops elsewhere and supported the priests with the surplus.

The extent of the power the priests had can be seen in the labor force they could get for the construction of sites like La Venta, which was redone, expanded, and repaired over a period of 400 years. The stone carvings of the Olmecs are striking as well. Characteristic of the art style are "baby-faced" sculptures and jaguar motifs. These motifs are seen at many Mesoamerican sites and are testimony to the influence that the Olmecs must have had on other Mesoamerican cultures. Moving huge stones upon which human faces were carved offers further testimony to the priests' power to mobilize people for work. But, in both cases, there must have been a strong element of religious activity in this work. Time and effort were probably gladly given to fulfill religious obligations.

Formation of Regional Centers (2,750–1,850 years B.P.). Three main regional centers began to emerge at this time: one in the Valley of Mexico, another in Oaxaca (a valley to the south of Mexico City), and a third in the Mayan lowlands of Yucatán.

The Valley of Mexico. The earliest farmers of the Valley of Mexico (probably migrating from the South) seem to have been organized into large tribal villages. In time, however, population size grew, and chiefdoms seem to have arisen. The largest of the chiefdoms were at Teotihuacán, a village in the northeastern part of the Valley, and Cuicuilco, a village at the southwestern part of the Valley. Around 2,150 years B.P., both Teotihuacán and Cuicuilco had at least 4,000 inhabitants, and both used irrigation to aid farming (Sanders, Parsons, & Logan, 1976).

Oaxaca. Oaxaca is a flat-bottomed, semiarid valley with three wings (see Figure 4). In each of these three parts of the valley independent, theocratic chiefdoms were developing during this time. The leaders of these growing societies were powerful enough to draft workers to build large monuments. They also controlled populations that lived in the mountains surrounding the valley, regulating the trade that had grown between the mountain and valley people. Like the centers of the Near East, the ceremonial center probably functioned as a regulator of trade, a religious center, an administrative center, and a center that redistributed the surplus produced by the area's farmers. Also like other chiefdoms, those in Oaxaca supported a growing number of craft specialists (Service, 1975; Wright, 1977).

Mayan Lowlands. Before this period began, Mexico's Yucatán Peninsula and northern Guatemala and Belize were settled by people who were related to the Olmecs. The first people in this area to live by farming, they practiced a slash-and-burn system, as did the Olmecs. At the beginning of this period the Maya were beginning to form themselves into political groups and to build the type of ceremonial centers that were to characterize their later development.

The Mayan ceremonial centers were arranged in a hierarchy. Each hamlet had a small ceremonial center or platform at which the important local rituals were performed. These small centers also acted as the administrative centers for the hamlets. Ten to 15 hamlets together would support a minor ceremonial center, which probably coordinated the activities of the local inhabitants. Major centers were supported by the inhabitants of 10 to 15 minor centers. The major chiefs probably lived in or near these larger centers. But at this time, large ceremonial centers were inhabited by only a few people. The bulk of the population lived in scattered settlements (Bullard, 1960).

Formation of Multiregional States (1,850–1,300 years B.P.). This is really the story of

Teotihuacán—of its growth and ultimately its influence or direct rule (we do not know which) over the rest of Mesoamerica.

About 1,900 years ago, Teotihuacán's rival for dominance in the Valley of Mexico, Cuicuilco, was destroyed by a volcano. Teotihuacán may have absorbed some of the displaced population. In any case, its population increased rapidly. By 1,850 years ago, the city contained at least 10,000 people, about half the population of the Valley (Parsons, 1976). By about 1,800 years ago, the city's broad north-south and east-west avenues had been laid out, and the Pyramid of the Sun—the largest construction in Pre-Columbian America—was built. Traders from as far away as Tajin, a center in the northern Veracruz lowlands, came seeking obsidian (which was mined nearby) and other products of Teotihuacán.

Whether or not Teotihuacán was actually an empire is open to question. It did not conquer other communities in the Valley of Mexico: It swallowed up their populations like the center of a vast whirlpool. There is also little evidence of militarism at Teotihuacán, so that military conquests probably did not occur. More likely, cities far beyond the Valley of Mexico were attracted to Teotihuacán as a religious and economic center. The influence on them was probably like the effect that powerful modern economies, such as that of the United States, have on other nations.

By 1,350 years B.P., perhaps as many as 200,000 people lived within the 8 square miles of Teotihuacán (Millon, 1976), making it one of the largest and most populous preindustrial cities of the world. Aside from the city itself, the Valley contained only a few small villages that served special functions. Some were salt- or lime-mining towns, and there were three ceremonial centers of no more than 3,000 inhabitants each. Possibly these were used only in certain seasons (Sanders, Parsons, & Logan, 1976).

The central role of religion in the Teotihuacán state never faltered. The priesthood was as powerful, if not more powerful, than the aristocracy. Militarism and the secularization that often were associated with power in other states did not develop until perhaps the very last stage of Teotihuacán's influence. Military figures do not appear in art until about 1,300 years ago (Millon, 1976).

Militaristic Period (1,300–430 years B.P.). The urbanism that was part of Teotihuacán's greatness also added to its decline. The city had become too large to be supported by local or even valley-wide farming. Drought years must have had terrible effects. Cutting down the forests for firewood, boats, and building materials may have caused soil erosion (Patterson, 1973). Competition in trade may also have eroded the city's economic base. Finally, nomadic raiders from the north may have sacked the city around 1,150 years B.P. (Service, 1975). The city was not abandoned, but the population gradually moved away into smaller communities. None of these towns developed into a major city.

The collapse of Teotihuacán also had an effect on its tributaries. Work on the structures in some Mayan sites seems to have been stopped between 1,416 and 1,352 years B.P., perhaps signaling the end of Teotihuacán's influence in the lowlands (Willey, 1977). The Oaxacan state collapsed around 1,050 years B.P.

The Maya. For a time, the power vacuum left by the decline of Teotihuacán was filled by Tajin. However, the major state in Mesoamerica after Teotihuacán's collapse appeared in the Mayan lowlands. For about 300 years, until about 1,050 years B.P., the Mayan civilization was able to support a number of extremely elaborate ceremonial centers. Some of these centers, like Tikal, were apparently "supercenters" that were supported by a large number of other major centers (Sanders & Price, 1968).

The centers themselves and the Mayan re-

The temple of the Giant Jaguar at Tikal, one of the large ceremonial centers of the Maya. It was built about 1,300 years B.P. by piling up rubble and encasing it with limestone blocks. (George Holton, Photo Researchers)

ligion were directed by a highly organized priesthood. Priests played a major role in government and were custodians of astronomy and astrology. Relationships between centers were also controlled by the priests. The members of the ruling class at this time differed from those of earlier periods in that they were probably hereditary secular leaders. These leaders were probably involved in the growing militarism that is apparent after 1,300 years B.P. Wall murals and stone carvings show that conflicts between the supporters of different ceremonial centers had become a fact of life at this time.

In the eleventh century B.P., the lowland Mayan sites were abandoned one by one. The most satisfactory model of the "collapse" of Mayan civilization emphasizes the fact that the Mayan social-political system was too rigid to deal with the onset of a number of problems, including disease, drought and soil depletion, trade disruptions, and war. By 1,041 years B.P., the last of the great Mayan centers had been abandoned to the jungles (Willey, 1966; Willey & Shimkin, 1973).

The Toltecs. Toward the end of the twelfth century B.P., the Toltecs emerged as the dominant power in Central Mexico. Their capital, Tula, about 60 kilometers north of the Valley of Mexico, became the center of an empire that covered a large part of the same region that was earlier controlled by Teotihuacán. Unlike Teotihuacán, whose influence was primarily economic, there is no doubt that the Toltecs captured and kept their empire by force. At Chichén Itzá in the northern part of the Yucatán Peninsula, murals and carvings show Toltec warriors defeating, capturing, and being honored by Mayan warriors (Willey, 1966).

The Toltecs were probably brought down by a combination of internal rebellion and a series of disastrous droughts (Coe, 1962). After Tula was abandoned, the Valley of Mexico once again returned to a collection of city-states.

The Aztecs. The last of the great militaristic empire-builders, the Aztecs, migrated into the Valley of Mexico beginning about 750 years ago, and for at least 100 years were vassals of the existing city-states. They settled on a series of islands in the middle of Lake Texcoco.

About 550 years ago they began to systematically conquer and control their neighbors. Within a century they controlled most of Mesoamerica, except for the Yucatán Peninsula. Among the Aztecs, as among the Toltecs, warfare was of great importance. One of the most important of the Aztec gods was the fierce Huitzilpochtli, the god to whom perhaps 25,000 people a year were sacrificed (Harner, 1977).

Part of a mural at Bonampak. Two Mayan chiefs dressed in jaguar tunics pass judgment on captives. These murals supplied the first evidence that warfare played a role in the formation of the Mayan state. (Avis Tulloch, in Thompson, 1954)

When the Spanish arrived (431 years B.P.), the great Tenochtitlan, with perhaps 300,000 inhabitants, was a thriving city. It was dotted with pyramids and plazas interspersed between masonry apartments and even parks.

The social order of the Aztecs was rigid. At the top were the nobility, chief priests, and war officers. Together these groups ruled society. This class elected the emperor, who reigned for life. In the eyes of the Aztecs, the emperor was linked to the gods. And in a more secular sense he was also the richest of the Aztecs. Below the nobility were the commoners. This, by far the largest group, was organized into 20 clans that lived in separate parts of the city. Each clan erected a small temple and built and maintained markets in their section of the city. Below the commoners were serfs and bondsmen who worked on the lands of the nobility. At the bottom of Aztec society were slaves and war captives, many of whom were ritually sacrificed and often eaten (Harner, 1977).

When the Spanish finally conquered Tenochtitlan in 431 B.P. they brought an end to the indigenous development of the state in Mesoamerica.

Examining the Theories. Trade probably contributed to the multiregional aspect of Teotihuacán culture. Its importance as a trading center probably grew as a side effect of its importance as a religious center. Why and how Teotihuacán grew as a religious center is still being investigated by archaeologists.

Because the city was located in a small side arm of the Valley of Mexico, it may have been geographically circumscribed. The organization of local resources could have created the bureaucracy that coordinated the state. As elsewhere, the process of urbanization was linked with population increases and increasing cultural diversity. The society may have failed ultimately because agricultural production failed to keep pace with population growth. It has been learned that irrigation systems had been developed while Teotihuacán was competing with Cuicuilo—probably to cope with a growing population in a geographically limited area. The state did not survive partly because it could not develop a truly complex irrigation system, as the Aztecs would do in the same area many centuries later.

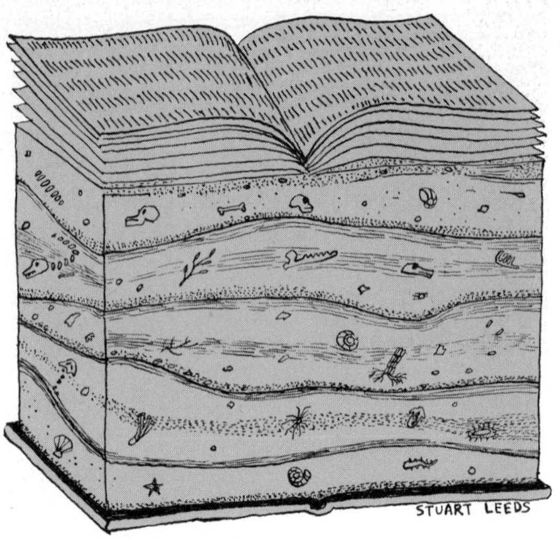

We have already observed that warfare did not play a major role in the formation of the Teotihuacán state. But some sort of conflict may have been significant in the evolution of the early state in Oaxaca. Wright (1977) notes that the collapse of chiefdoms in the three arms of the Oaxacan valley occurred before the first Oaxacan state emerged—the same thing that happened in Mesopotamia.

We know that Teotihuacán was a highly segregated city and that centralization would have had to increase as the city grew. But it is not clear how much promotion and linearization occurred over time. Perhaps the city's internal structure was too rigid to be able to react positively to the problems of expansion. In spite of its enormous size, in the end it was unable to overcome internal shortages, competition, and hostile forces.

Of the other civilizations that emerged in Mesoamerica, the Mayan has most intrigued archaeologists. The lowlands were neither geographically circumscribed nor dependent on irrigation. Warfare, while common during the height of the civilization, was little in evidence as the basic features of Mayan life were being formed. Population growth did not lead to urbanism—indeed, there may have been no true urbanism. But trade was important, perhaps crucial, to state formation. The organization of long-distance trade may have required the sort of bureaucratic structure from which more complex political organizations could have emerged (Rathje, 1970). In addition, contact at the formative stage with the Olmecs and at later stages with the Valley of Mexico was vital in introducing and encouraging the centralization that would have affected state formation.

In using a process model for studying the Mayan state, it would be especially interesting to analyze what went wrong in the period of their collapse. Besides two constructive mechanisms, Flannery's model proposes two destructive mechanisms. These include *usurpation,* in which a subsystem is elevated to a higher status for self-serving purposes, and *meddling,* the unnecessary, unproductive bypassing of lower-order controls (Flannery, 1972). An increasingly ingrown, withdrawn, insular elite, perhaps more concerned with achieving greater power and prestige, could have caused great damage to the traditional Mayan political system, and thus made it unresponsive to changing social and economic conditions.

Summary

1. A *city* is a central place that performs economic and political functions for the surrounding area. The process by which cities are formed is called *urbanism.*

2. A *state* is an independent political unit that includes many communities in its territory, with a centralized government that has the power to collect taxes, draft citizens for work and for war, and enact and enforce laws. States are *stratified* (some groups of citizens have greater access to wealth and status, or both) and *economically diversified.*

3. *Civilization* refers to a society having large cities or towns whose residents are bound together in a legal commonwealth. Some authors, such as Childe, have defined the term more broadly, and it remains an ambiguous concept.

4. Archaeologists have arbitrarily defined the stages of human social evolution from simple to complex as follows: band, tribe, chiefdom, state.

5. Before about 12,000 years ago, humans lived in small egalitarin groups called *bands.* Force of personality is the basis of the leader's power, and there is probably little if any sense of property.

6. *Tribes* appeared in the Near East about 9,000 years B.P. A tribe is made up of groups of families related by common descent. The leader is weak. In tribes that farm, land is considered property, though stratification is minimal.

7. *Chiefdoms* were present by 7,500 years B.P. in the Near East. Chiefdoms are often theocracies, and the position of chief is institutionalized. Stratification is present in some degree, as are large villages and part-time craft specialization.

8. As states are formed (1) chiefdoms collapse, (2) centralized legal apparatus for governance emerges, (3) certain activities become the full-time function of particular groups, and (4) the emerging state expands its territory.

9. Holders of *prime-mover* theories think state formation stems from a single cause.

10. Karl Wittfogel, in his *hydraulic theory,* proposes that the state arose from the body of officials needed to manage irrigation works in dry areas. The state grew as surrounding areas opted for extension of irrigation into their land.

11. Other theorists think the state grew out of the need to organize and regulate *trade* and production of goods in areas that lacked vital raw materials.

12. Still others think *population growth* has been a prime-mover. Expanding populations led to food production and eventually to a food surplus, upon which a group of officials could draw, while administering more and more political and economic activities.

13. According to Robert Carneiro's *circumscription theory,* growing populations in areas that are geographically or socially circumscribed, making migration difficult, collide and war over resources. Because defeated people cannot migrate, they are absorbed into an expanding state.

14. Kent Flannery's *process model* is one theory that allows for a number of interacting factors in state formation. Flannery believes that the mechanisms of change that produce a state are universal, but the events and conditions activating the mechanisms are not. Flannery names two mechanisms of state formation: *promotion* and *linearization.* The first produces greater *segregation,* and the second increases *centralization,* both of which are present to a high degree in states.

15. The first multi-state empire emerged in *Mesopotamia* about 4,500 years B.P., when Sargon united Sumer and northern Mesopotamia. Before this time, villages in the Tigris-Euphrates river valley expanded as trading centers and were governed by chiefdoms. By

5,000 years B.P. multi-regional centers such as Warka redistributed goods and administered other activities over a wide area. In the next 500 years some of these centers developed a strong enough political organization to be called states.

16. Unlike in Sumer, large independent cities were not present before the formation of the *Egyptian state.* Tradition holds that Menes united upper and lower Egypt to form the first empire there about 5,200 years B.P. Scattered villages had appeared by 6,000 years B.P. and were organized into weak political units called *nomes.* These units were easily united, first in regional governments and then in the empire. Irrigation, circumscription, and warfare seem to have contributed to state-building in Egypt.

17. About 3,850 years B.P., villages along the lower and middle Huang Ho River were united under the Shang dynasty, *China's* earliest known state. Tribal farming villages, which had first appeared about 5,000 years B.P., gave way to larger, partly stratified and economically diversified settlements during the Lung-shan culture (4,600–3,850 years B.P.). By the time of the Shang, settlements had become urban clusters controlling large surrounding regions. Circumscription and warfare were certainly factors in the rise of the Shang.

18. In Mesoamerica, the *Olmecs,* with their ceremonial centers, their ability to draft large labor forces, and their arts, foreshadowed later Mesoamerican societies. Several regional centers emerged in the period 3,750–1,850 years B.P. after the Olmec decline: Teotihuacán and Cuicuilco in the *Valley of Mexico, Oaxaca,* and the *Mayan lowlands.* Populations grew, and chiefdoms were able to organize the building of elaborate ceremonial centers. Between 1,850 and 1,300 years B.P., *Teotihuacán* emerged as the dominant religious and economic force in central and southern Mexico. After the city's collapse, which occurred around 1,150 years B.P., the *Mayan state* became strong, supporting a number of large ceremonial centers directed by priests. First the *Toltecs* and then the *Aztecs* succeeded the Maya as empire builders after the decline of the Maya, beginning about 1,100 years B.P.

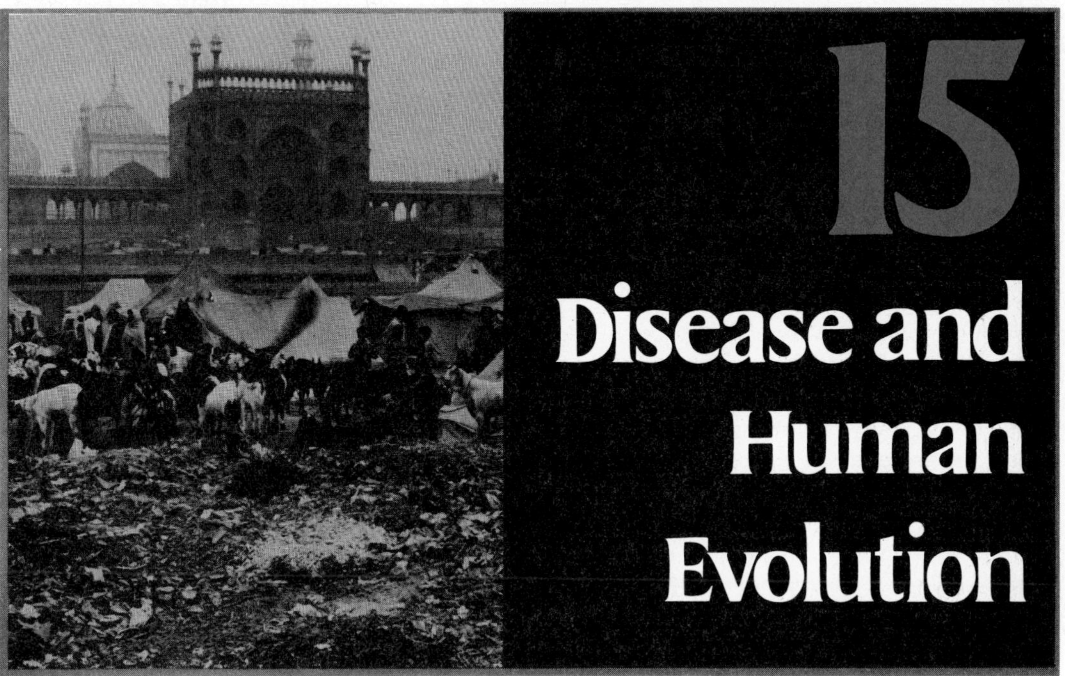

15 Disease and Human Evolution

CULTURAL patterns often influence human biological evolution, as earlier chapters have suggested. Marriage rules may state which individuals are suitable marriage partners and which are not, thus influencing the genetic makeup of the next generation. Or, to take another example, urban societies like our own encourage a high degree of mobility in their members. As a result, there is a great deal of marriage between members of different groups, and gene flow is very high.

Culture shapes not only our social environment but also the physical environment. In the course of its evolution, the hominid line has increased its ability to change the living and nonliving parts of its environment. First, hunting became an important part of the econiche of early hominids, thereby altering their position in local food webs. Then came more complex tools, which permitted a larger variety of foods to be exploited more effectively, and survival strategies, which increased the environmental range of early hominids. Radical new technologies such as agriculture and industrialism followed. Each of these events heralded a greater rearrangement of environmental forces, until today they are controlled largely by cultural behavior. This has meant that culturally-modified environmental conditions, as well as socially-defined behavior, are exerting progressively greater influences on human biology.

To give you an idea of how human culture has affected our past biological evolution and how it may influence change in the future, we shall focus on the relationship between cultural practices and the disease microorganisms or food resources of an environment. Any changes in these conditions can greatly affect the health, or biological well-being, of native populations. In the course of their evolution, humans have changed their environments in ways that have created new disease and dietary stresses. Because the members of a population vary in their ability to survive such stresses, disease and diet act as selective forces.

In this chapter, many different types of disease will be discussed. So it is useful to proceed with a classification of disease in mind. Such classifications reflect the viewpoint of the classifier. Non-Western people often explain disease in terms of social or magical factors, which cannot be detected through the senses. In this chapter, however, we will use a Western classification of disease. *Disease* is a state in which any two of the following conditions are present: (1) a recognizable agent or agents causing the disease; (2) a group of symptoms; or (3) a consistent change in the structure of the body or its functioning.

Diseases may be broken down into a number of different categories. Our classification is fairly simple. It contains only five disease types: genetic, degenerative, parasitic, nutritional, and infectious. *Genetic diseases* are inherited diseases resulting from genetically-caused changes, often in protein structure and function. These changes hinder the body's ability to use food for energy and growth. *Degenerative diseases* involve a change in cells, tissues, or organs that inhibit or destroy their function. The normal aging process may cause such changes, such as those connected with degenerative cardiovascular diseases. Other degenerative diseases such as cancer may be caused by the buildup of environmental agents.

Infectious diseases are caused by microorganisms that invade and multiply in the body. Modern medicine has had great success dealing with infectious diseases, such as measles, poliomyelitis, and so on. A useful way to discuss infectious disease as a selective agent is to look at the interaction of the environment, the *pathogen* (the disease-carrying agent), and the host. The host, in this case humans, may meet new pathogens when moving into a different environment. Or the size and the density of human populations may determine which pathogenic organisms can survive. Finally, the genetic makeup of individuals or entire populations may give them resistance or make them more susceptible to pathogens.

Parasitic diseases are caused by a variety of small, single-celled and many-celled organisms that get their nourishment from part of the human body. Some, such as tapeworms, can occur in the gut, while others, such as Plasmodia (malarial parasites), live in the blood.

Nutritional diseases are caused by the lack of one or more of the following food stuffs: fats, carbohydrates, proteins, minerals, or vitamins. The severity of the effect of poor nutrition depends on the length and degree of food shortage as well as the kind of food that is in short supply. Deficiencies of long duration can slow down the development of fetuses as well as the growth or cell replacement in children and adults. A poor diet can cause disease or increase susceptibility to viral infections and can prevent people from functioning normally in society.

These categories are merely convenient ways of talking about the great variety of ailments that have afflicted humans. A given individual, however, may possess more than one type of disease. Indeed, many disease conditions are only understandable as an interaction of a number of different types of diseases. Inadequate nutrition quite frequently makes people vulnerable to infectious diseases. Allergies may be triggered by a virus or other environmental agent. So when we talk about a certain type of disease, we do not mean to imply that it always occurs in isolation from others. We are merely trying to isolate its general effect for explanatory purposes.

In this chapter, we shall look at the changing pattern of disease in human evolution. We shall attempt to trace what some people feel is a gradual shift in the evolutionary impact of different types of diseases: from parasitic and perhaps occasionally nutritional and infectious diseases among hunters and gatherers to common infectious and nutritional disorders among farmers to genetic and degenerative diseases in modern Western society.

Basically, there are three sources of information available for studying the history of human disease and nutrition:

1. Direct observation of the health of modern groups with different technologies. Such groups include modern hunters and gatherers (Australian aborigines, bushmen of the Kalahari Desert in southern Africa, and Eskimoes), nonindustrialized farmers, and present-day urban societies as well.
2. Archaeological evidence may be examined. Studies of skeletal remains have provided important data on illnesses that affected earlier human populations. Studies of fossilized excrement, along with skeletal analyses can provide information on ancient diets.
3. Written records such as ancient Egyptian medical texts or historical accounts left by explorers and settlers in the New World may yield information on some periods in the history of human health and nutrition.

This chapter will focus on the interaction of culture change and health as it has occurred in the major stages of cultural development outlined in the last three chapters. We shall begin with the hunting-and-gathering stage, which lasted until the Neolithic Period, when settled agricultural villages were formed. We shall continue with the appearance of preindustrial cities and industrialized cities, and we shall conclude with a discussion of the present and the future.

Hunters and Gatherers

Until about 10,000 years ago, human populations were made up of small bands of perhaps 25 to no more than a few hundred persons, who survived by hunting and gathering. These were mostly seminomadic groups that migrated as the seasons changed, searching for edible plants or following herds of game. During this period of the human past, the population of the entire world was probably not above 10 million. Because of the low population density, contagious diseases that require fairly large host populations to survive would probably not have taken up long-term residence in human groups (Black, 1975). Such diseases include influenza, smallpox, and poliomyelitis.

A member of a band of about 15 Hoti Indians gathers wild fruit in the Guiana Highlands of Venezuela. Studies of groups that, like the Hoti, live in small, scattered bands and depend mostly on hunting and gathering suggest that contagious diseases have had little impact on preagricultural populations. (Jacques Jangoux, Peter Arnold, Inc.)

Additional support for the idea that many infectious diseases did not persist in hunters and gatherers has been gained by studying living groups. Blood serum tests of Alaskan Eskimos done in the 1940s showed that a high proportion of older members of the population had a polio virus antibody, suggesting a history of polio epidemics earlier in the twentieth century. The epidemics must have quickly killed or immunized the entire population of this hunting-and-gathering society. Once it had killed off all its potential hosts, the virus died out. Similar infections, it is thought, would have worked in the same way in prehistoric populations (Black, 1975).

If the small size of such populations reduced the threat of contagious diseases, what diseases were common in ancient hunters and gatherers, and how did these illnesses arise? Some authorities have suggested that the sources of disease in early humans were twofold. Some organisms that depend on primate hosts may have adopted the earliest humans as substitute hosts. Parasites such as lice and pinworms, and bacterial diseases such as yaws, today afflict nonhuman and human primates alike. Second, the earliest humans were probably susceptible to microorganisms transmitted by insect bites or those living in contaminated foods, especially in uncooked meats. Sleeping sickness, tetanus, trichinosis, and tularemia are among the diseases of this type (Armelagos & Dewey, 1970).

The nature of the environment determined what kinds of infections afflicted the earliest humans. Both tropical rainforests and deserts, for example, can support hunting-and-gathering societies. But the tropical rainforest is a very complex environment with many species of plants and animals, including a wide variety of pathogenic microorganisms and parasites. The desert, on the other hand, is a fairly simple environment and supports far fewer pathogens. A recent survey of worms and intestinal parasites among populations living in these different environments has confirmed that there is a greater diversity in the number and intensity of infections encountered among hunters and gatherers living in tropical rainforests than among those living in deserts (Dunn, 1968).

Diet has been another factor affecting the health of hunting-and-gathering groups. Nutritionists who have studied the habits of nomadic bushmen in the Kalahari Desert of Africa have found that the usual menu of nuts, vegetables, and meat on which these modern hunters and gatherers live provides them with a well-balanced diet and an adequate intake of calories. Because of the variety of foods they eat, the bushmen rarely suffer from vitamin deficiencies. Blood serum tests show that the members of the tribe rarely have deficiencies of iron, folic acid, or vitamin B_{12}, for example (Kolata, 1974).

Some experts, after studying a variety of modern hunters and gatherers, have concluded that birthrates among ancient hunters and gatherers were generally high, but populations were kept in check by parasitic diseases, warfare, and attacks from animals. Thus, with so many causes of death in the environment, the life expectancy of the ancient hunters and gatherers was very low. A result of this low life expectancy was that hunters and gatherers did not often suffer from the degenerative diseases, such as cancer and heart attacks, that usually occur in older humans (Dunn, 1968).

Settled Villages and the Beginnings of Agriculture

Throughout the hunting-and-gathering stage of human history the health problems faced by humans were probably little different from those of other mammals. At this stage humans could not alter their environment enough to bring about changes in the life cycle of natural disease agents. In fact, their low population density, nomadic existence, and generally balanced diet may have protected early humans from many infectious diseases, sanitary problems, and prolonged nutritional deficiencies. But when human populations

Rice paddies in central Java. Farming has made humans a part of the niche of many disease microorganisms for the first time. Malaria-bearing mosquitoes, for example, have thrived in expanses of still water like this. (Bernard Wolff, Photo Researchers, Inc.)

began to practice agriculture and to settle in villages, they began for the first time to change significantly the natural environment. In so doing, they began to include themselves in the niche structures of microorganisms that had never before affected them. As a result, infections and deficient diets became much more important factors in the health and well-being of the species.

When farmers began to locate their communities along rivers or near swamps, where water for irrigation was plentiful and the soil was fertile and easily tilled, they probably met such pathogenic agents as the malaria-bearing mosquito. It is likely that the beginning of agriculture in these wet environments also marked the beginning of malaria as an important factor in human evolution.

The story was similar in other environments. Studies of modern-day primitive farmers show that when these groups clear forested areas they often contract new diseases or increase their rate of infection for diseases that were already active. For example, by exposing themselves to the bites of parasite-carrying insects as they work in newly cleared fields, farmers may contract scrub typhus more often then they would otherwise.

Another health hazard developed for early farmers as they began to domesticate animals such as pigs, sheep, and cattle. Humans walking barefoot over fecal soils probably became hosts to animal parasites such as the ascaris worm, a roundworm that lives in the intestinal tract. When humans ate poorly preserved meat, bacteria that cause food poisoning, such as salmonella, may have been a frequent problem. In addition, animal products, including milk, hides, and wool, may have been the route by which other diseases, among them anthrax and tuberculosis, were passed to humans (Armelagos & Dewey, 1970).

Researchers generally agree that, beginning with a settled village stage of history, infectious disease became a chief selective factor in human evolution. Some scientists have

Frequent contact with livestock and their wastes has exposed primitive agriculturalists like these Indian villagers to parasites and disease bacteria. (Philippa Scott, Photo Researchers)

suggested that the results of these numerous new infections were catastrophic. No genetic factors providing resistance to the new diseases would have been built up in the preceding hunting-and-gathering stage. Thus, when early farmers met with these infections, epidemics would have destroyed large parts of the population. Only the variety of genes in the gene pool ensured that parts of the population survived. Genes that afforded resistance apparently were present in the gene pool; and individuals having them produced more children than those who did not.

Other investigators, however, have questioned this "disaster theory" of infection among early farmers. They argue that most of the infectious diseases caught by early farmers occasionally would have been found in humans before the settled agricultural stage. And the development of agriculture took place over several thousands of years. During this time, human populations trying to domesticate animals probably became exposed gradually to the biological consequences. Thus natural selection due to these infections would have operated slowly, eliminating some genetic traits and favoring others over a fairly long period of time (Armelagos & Dewey, 1970).

When humans took up farming they produced their own food, bringing its availability under closer control. At the same time, however, early farmers ran the risk of famine if their crops failed or if the animals they raised were stricken with disease. Farmers who depended on only one kind of crop were very vulnerable. Insect pests (which of course were adapting to make use of abundant new food resources so thoughtfully provided by humans) probably increased in number. Selection probably favored those insects that could best exploit these new food resources. Therefore, insect populations improved their power to ruin crops. Thus, although the early farmers had "tamed" their environment to some extent, they had also become more vulnerable to disease and undernutrition. Hunters and gatherers, on the other hand, were able to gather a variety of natural foods, at least some of which were available even in poor years.

Unlike hunters and gatherers, farmers stored the foods they produced. Storage posed new health hazards. Mention of certain kinds of plagues in Babylonian and Assyrian records suggests that contamination of grain by ergot (a deadly growth) may have had serious effects on the health of early farmers (Brothwell, 1972).

Agriculture also affected the balance of protein, carbohydrate, fats, vitamins, and minerals in human diets. Grains such as barley, wheat, and corn were probably the most common crops and provided the basis of the early farmer's diet, which was sometimes supplemented with meat and milk. This fairly unvaried diet probably led to vitamin deficiencies and anemias. Examination of deformities in the skeletons of Maya Indians has yielded evidence for such deficiencies. In turn, the unbalanced diet would have produced people who were not physically strong enough to engage in normal work or who caught other diseases easily (Saul, 1973).

Another possible consequence of the change in diet that occurred when humans began farming was an increase in fertility and, thus, in population size. The Kalahari bushmen discussed earlier were also studied during the period in which the group settled in villages and took up farming. The women in this settled population showed an increase in the rate at which they gave birth. Experts have suggested that this increase in fertility may be due to an increase in body fat provided by their diet, which is rich in cereals and milk (Kolata, 1974).

The extensive skeletal and mummified remains of ancient Egyptians, together with ancient Egyptian documents dealing with disease, provide the most detailed picture of human health problems of ancient farmers. The analysis of teeth and skeletons from Egyptian burials indicates that the life expectancy was about 39 or 40 years for the nobility and probably less for lower classes. This short life span may mean that the Egyptians were afflicted with many fatal infectious diseases. Among the infections for which there exists evidence in skeletal or mummified remains are tuberculosis and schistosomiasis (a parasite-caused condition that can damage the liver, produce bleeding and diarrhea, and lead to a lowered resistance to other diseases). There are also signs that leprosy, smallpox, and pneumonia afflicted some members of the civilization (Sandison, 1968).

Today, as in the past, irrigation projects have greatly increased the incidence of certain diseases. The construction of the Aswan Dam on the Nile River and associated irrigation canals has greatly increased the range of water snails, which can live only in still water. These snails carry the schistosomiasis parasite, which can infect humans who bathe or work in the water. The finding of schistosomiasis in ancient Egyptian mummies suggests that similar irrigation projects undertaken by the ancient Egyptian state could have had similar effects in the past.

Only a few examples of the far-reaching results of the increasing ability of humans to change their environment have been presented here. The point should be clear, however, that at this stage in cultural evolution, humans had begun to alter radically their environment. As they did so they and other organisms were inevitably exposed to new selective pressures. Agriculture had inadvertently caused the spread of infectious and parasitic diseases and had changed human nutrition. Although an increased food supply carried with it many benefits, it created the conditions that from time to time led to devastating famines and epidemics. The selective action of these events no doubt changed the makeup of most human populations and profoundly influenced the course of further cultural evolution as well.

Preindustrial Cities

As large populations clustered in small areas to form the first urban centers, the impact

A goat market near a mosque in New Delhi, India. As human populations became concentrated in cities, sanitation became a problem, and diseases requiring large numbers of hosts thrived. (Bernard Wolff, Photo Researchers, Inc.)

of disease and nutrition on human biology grew. Maintaining supplies of clean drinking water and disposing of human wastes became major problems for early cities. Water polluted by human excrement was a potential carrier of new diseases such as cholera and dysentery. No doubt epidemics of these diseases were frequent and disastrous. Another new factor in the action of disease as a selective agent was the birth of social classes. As privileged classes emerged, so too did differences in access to food, medicine, adequate housing, and sanitary conditions. Members of the lower classes were probably stricken in greater numbers than were members of the upper classes.

Archaeological evidence suggests that human intelligence was quickly applied to solving at least some of these problems. In places where population density was high, sewage systems were designed. Excavations of Mohenjo-daro, an early city of the Indus Valley that flourished about 4,500 B.P., show that each house had a drain that was part of a municipal sewage system. In addition, each house in the community seems to have had a rubbish chute for easy garbage disposal (Brothwell, 1972).

Another result of the high density of city populations was a change in the way certain infections were transmitted. For example, the bacillus responsible for plague was originally spread by fleas carried by rodents. When the fleas bit humans, they passed on the bacillus. But the most deadly epidemics occurred in cities in which close contact between infected and uninfected persons occurred frequently, and the plague bacillus began to be transmitted directly through the air.

It has also been hypothesized that syphilis, an infectious disease caused by microorganisms known as spirochetes, was not spread by sexual contact until human populations became urbanized. Crowded conditions, changes in family structure, and increased sexual promiscuity would have made sexual intercourse the easiest means of transmission of the syphilis spirochetes (Armelagos & Dewey, 1970).

Preindustrial cities also concentrated large enough numbers of people in small areas to make possible the spread of diseases requiring large numbers of hosts. Measles, for example, probably did not become a permanent disease threat to humans until populations of 1 million or more were available. This is the minimum number necessary for the disease always to have new hosts to infect.

One of the most significant historical events that took place during the age of preindustrial cities was the discovery of the New World. For the native populations of the Americas, 1492 marked the beginning of both contact with Europeans and a long series of epidemics introduced by the newcomers. These outbreaks of disease were probably more important in reducing native populations than all the wars that were waged between the Indians and the white settlers in the course of four centuries.

Prior to the European conquests the populations of the New World seem to have been free of the sorts of infectious diseases that had ravaged the Old World. Measles, mumps, smallpox, and tuberculosis were introduced by the Spanish conquerors. Typhus was carried from the Cape Verde Islands to the Pacific Coast of America by the men sailing under Sir Francis Drake, and English settlers brought malaria to northeastern America. Yellow fever, too, was probably introduced from Africa by slaves (Crosby, 1972; Cockburn, 1963). The impact of these diseases on native American Indians, who were biologically and culturally unable to resist them, was enormous. Although the exact population of central Mexico at the time of the Spanish conquest is not known, estimates have placed it at about 25 million (Crosby, 1972). It is thought that the population declined by 25 percent in the first decade following the conquest (Cook & Woodrow, cited in Crosby, 1972). Only a small fraction of these people died in battle; most fell victim to the virulent new diseases.

The deadly effect of tuberculosis on native Americans, compared to its fairly milder impact on Europeans, may suggest a genetic difference in susceptibility. Apparently, native American populations had never been exposed to tuberculosis before they came in contact with European explorers and settlers. Once they got the disease, however, the symptoms were usually acute, and the deathrates were higher than among Europeans. This fact suggests that among populations in the Old World, where tuberculosis had been active for centuries, resistance to the disease may have been selected for gradually. Since this selection process had never had a chance to operate in the New World, the disease had much more drastic effects on the native populations. Nevertheless, it should be noted that some of these severe effects may have been due to the different nutritional and sanitary practices of the native Americans, rather than to purely genetic factors (Armelagos & Dewey, 1970).

The Birth of Industrialism

Beginning in the middle of the eighteenth century, technological advances in iron smelting and textile production, together with the development of a workable commercial steam engine by James Watt, brought about a series of far-reaching economic changes usually called the Industrial Revolution. Centered in Great Britain at the start, the Industrial Revolution owed its success not only to new technologies, but also to a large supply of workers. Women and children as well as men worked in the new mines and factories. Population growth was rapid, and growth of the industrial cities was explosive. It is estimated that the British population increased by about 30 percent every generation during the Industrial Revolution. The population of Manchester, an industrial city in central England, grew from 12,000 in 1760 to 100,000 by 1801 and to 400,000 by 1850. Most of this demographic change was due to migration from towns and rural areas to the cities. Of the people living in London in 1850, less than half had been born there (Weber, 1972).

Along with these shifts in the size and distribution of population came a restructuring of the social system. The industrial cities were the home of large, generally poor, working-class populations and smaller middle-class and upper-class groups. The workers, with few legal safeguards and little or no organization, were forced to accept wages so low that survival was difficult. It is not surprising that the working-class slums in industrial cities were the scene of frequent outbreaks of infectious disease due to poor sanitation. Furthermore, the workers were poorly nourished, which weakened their resistance to numerous diseases. To a great extent, good health in the large industrial cities was related to social class and wealth. Thus, a survey made in Paris in the 1820s found that people who paid higher taxes were likely to be taller than poorer people. In other words, the higher a person's economic standing, the better nourished and the better developed physically he or she was likely to be. Furthermore, deathrates in the poorer parts of the city were twice or three times the rates in wealthier districts (Weber, 1972).

One outcome of the poor diet and hard work of industrial laborers seems to have been a decline in birthrate. This decline began in England after 1870, following a century of industrial growth and a rapidly expanding population. The fall in birthrate may have been caused by a short reproductive span due to poor nutrition, hard physical work, and poor living conditions. Food supplies had not kept pace with the exploding population in the 1800s because so many farm workers had come to cities looking for employment. Poor nutrition caused both men and women to arrive at sexual maturity at a later age. Poor health is likely to have caused decreased sperm count and sperm mobility among males, while women had a greater frequency of miscarriage and stillbirth than did better-nourished women. As a result, fewer children were born into the working classes than into other, better-fed classes (Frisch, 1978).

The poorer classes were also exposed to health hazards in the factories and mines. These hazards helped lower the birthrate by killing potential parents. As early as the middle of the eighteenth century it had been noted that workers at lead refineries in Scotland could become chronically ill as a result of absorbing particles of metal into their systems. Lead poisoning, which results in anemia or more serious symptoms such as convulsions and coma, was also found in workers at ceramic factories, where lead glazes were used to finish the pottery (Wilcocks, 1965).

Occupational disease and poor nutrition were significant factors in shortening the lives of workers in the early stage of the Industrial Revolution. A textile worker in Lille, France, during the early part of the nineteenth century, for example, could expect to live to the age of 22 (Weber, 1972). Only later, as workers organized to demand improved conditions, and employers recognized the higher productivity of healthy workers, were measures taken to prevent work-related sickness and to correct poor diets.

Chiefly responsible for the high deathrate among the urban poor were infections such as cholera, smallpox, typhus, diphtheria, and yellow fever. Ironically, it may have been the frequency of epidemics in industrial cities that led to better understanding of the diseases, the adoption of preventive measures, and finally the development of vaccines. A London doctor named John Snow studied an outbreak of cholera that occurred in his city in 1848 and found that those who had gotten the disease were all users of water from a certain well that had been contaminated by nearby cesspits. With the relationship between polluted water and cholera transmission established, the value of good sanitation could be seen (Wilcocks, 1965).

In the nineteenth century, humans came to value the control they could exert on environmental forces through public health and medicine. Toward the end of the century, advanced experimental techniques allowed scientists to identify many of the microorganisms that caused infections.

Together with the isolation of disease-causing microorganisms and the production of vaccines, the nineteenth century saw improvements in hospital care. Before the mechanism of bacterial infection was understood, hospital sanitary practices were naturally quite poor, and deathrates from infection were often high.

Similar advances were also being made in understanding the importance of good nutrition. Officers in the British Navy had for a long time noticed that sailors on long voyages usually got scurvy, a disease causing gum inflammation and general weakness. However, when fresh fruits and vegetables (especially citrus fruits) were added to the seamen's diets, there was no scurvy. As we now know, scurvy is due to a deficiency of vitamin C in the human diet, and citrus fruits, a good source of this vitamin, were a remedy for the disease.

The fact that fewer persons died because of the new ways of treating and preventing disease has had far-reaching biological consequences. When natural selection acts unchecked by human cultural intervention, the poorly-adapted members of a population survive in fewer numbers than the better adapted. Effective medical protection (a cultural trait of some societies), however, means that deathrates have declined greatly. Better sanitation, improved diet, drugs, and vaccinations began to give larger numbers of people an equal chance to survive, no matter what their genotype. Thus, certain genes that normally would have been selected against have increased their frequency in human populations. A further effect of the drop in deathrate has been an increase in the world population. In recent years, growth in the world population has created some acute problems, as we shall see in the next section.

Health in the Modern World

A discussion of human disease in the modern world must begin by pointing out that there are really two worlds existing side by side on our planet today: the highly developed, industrialized nations of Europe, North America, Japan, and the Soviet Union and the underdeveloped nations of Asia, Africa, and South America. Just as social standing was a large factor in determining the health of a person in the industrialized cities of the 1800s, so today the place of birth—in the industrialized or the underdeveloped world—plays an important role in determining the diseases and dietary problems that a person will encounter. At present, the major causes of death in underdeveloped countries are infectious and parasitic diseases that produce chronic ill health and decrease the productivity of workers as well. These diseases include malaria, schistosomiasis, and tuberculosis—probably the same infections that humans faced 10,000 years ago when they first settled in farming communities. In the industrially developed countries on the other hand, good sanitation and nutrition, together with immunization and advanced medical care, have eliminated most infectious disease and given people a life span of 70 years or more. In this half of the world degenerative disease such as cancer, heart attacks, and emphysema (a chronic lung ailment) are among the chief causes of death. These degenerative diseases result in part because people can now live long enough to become susceptible to them. The pathogenic substances found in the environments of industrialized cultures also contribute to the prevalence of degenerative diseases. Thus, the elimination of fatal infectious diseases has let many humans live long enough to die from the byproducts of their wealthy societies (Miller, 1975).

Of course the underdeveloped and the developed nations cannot be regarded as two totally separate regions. International agencies such as the World Health Organization of the United Nations have waged successful immunization campaigns in the underdeveloped nations against diseases such as smallpox. But as medical technology does away with infectious disease in underdeveloped societies, unexpected side effects may appear. Cultures in which infections have regularly killed a large percentage of the population often show a dramatic increase in population growth. This happens because cultural values supporting high birthrates are kept long after medical care has reduced the deathrate. Many people are concerned that the ability of the land to produce enough food to support the growing population may be severely taxed. Therefore, it has been proposed that birth control programs accompany campaigns to combat infectious diseases in underdeveloped nations (Armelagos & Dewey, 1970).

There are many ways in which sudden modernization may disrupt the ecology of underdeveloped populations. When irrigation canals were constructed in a rural area of northwest Pakistan the deathrate increased sharply, due to a series of extremely severe smallpox, cholera, and influenza epidemics. One explanation for this rise in the rate of infection is that irrigation canals provided new econiches for parasites—particularly malaria—capable of infecting the farmers. It is also likely that the expanded transportation links established to take the surplus farm produce to cities served as transmission routes for diseases. City populations were large enough to support persistent infections of many diseases, while the sparser rural populations were free of a number of these sicknesses. When transportation improved, contact between infected individuals from the cities and susceptible individuals from the rural areas increased,

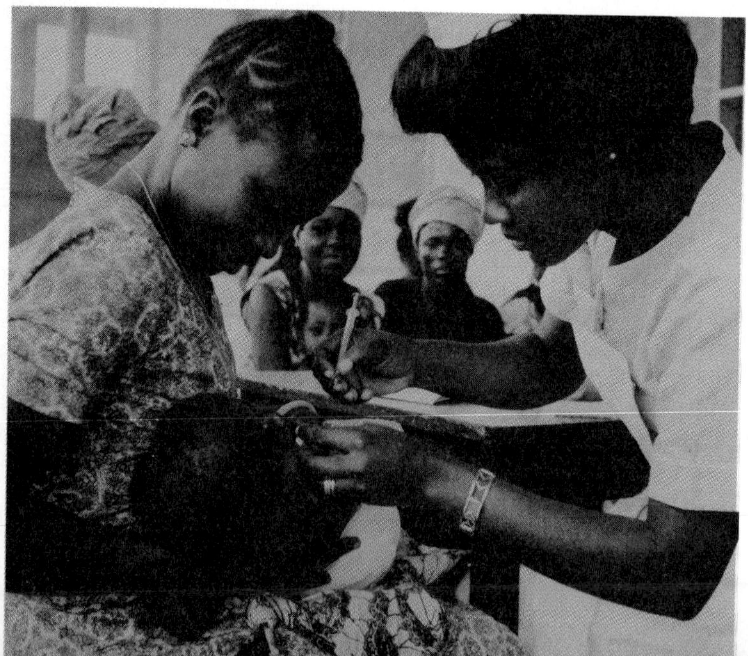

Child being immunized against tuberculosis in the West African country of Sierra Leone. Medical technology has eased the high deathrate due to infectious disease and thereby increased the birthrate in many underdeveloped areas. (Bernard Wolff, Photo Researchers, Inc.)

leading to higher rates of disease and death in previously isolated farming communities.

The ability to control the environment by means of technology has never been greater than it is today. With our machines and know-how, we can change the elements of our environment to suit our needs. For example, we can change the temperature to which our bodies are exposed with our architecture, increase access to water by means of irrigation and water supply systems, and change the nutrient content of the soil. With pesticides and other chemicals, we can orchestrate ecosystems for our own purposes. The extermination of insect populations to protect crops is but one example. Power provided by gasoline and other fossil fuels allows us to carry on this kind of change. But even though technology has given humans more power, it has also given rise to new threats, not the least of which are disease-causing chemicals. Degenerative diseases—cancer, heart disease, and emphysema—may be linked to pathogenic substances in the environment. The exact nature of this link is not always known. According to one theory, a combination of genetic factors and higher levels of pathogenic substances in the surroundings may be responsible for many cases of degenerative disease. When concentrations of these pathogens reach a certain critical level, or threshold, the disease is triggered.

Studies have shown that a susceptibility to some cancers is controlled by the genes to a large degree. Susceptibility can therefore be inherited. Cancer of the stomach seems much more common among persons with type A blood than among those of other blood types. Cancer of the breast is more common in European populations than in Asiatic populations. Although a genetic link is clearly indicated in such cases, its precise nature is obscure. The environmental agents are equally hard to isolate.

The incidence of some cancers seems to be related to the amount and intensity of contact with certain substances. A 1964 report by the U.S. Surgeon General said that cigarette smoking is linked to lung cancer. Since then, statistical evidence has made it increasingly clear that the more a person smokes, the more likely he or she is to have lung and heart diseases. But the exact way in which the nicotine, tobacco tar, and carbon monoxide in cigarette smoke causes these diseases is still being studied.

The effect of air pollution also seems to depend on the density of the pollutant and how long one is exposed to it. Significant rises in deathrates during episodes of heavy air pollution in urban areas have shown the harmful effects of such atmospheric contaminants as sulfur dioxide. The long-term effects of lower levels can only be guessed at. The 150 million tons of sulfur dioxide released into the world's atmosphere every year come mostly from burning fossil fuels (oil and coal). Without using these fuels, many factories could not operate, and many homes would have no lighting. Developing other sources of power (such as solar or nuclear energy) safely and in sufficient quantities and finding ways to remove sulfur from oil and coal before burning are the complex tasks that must be taken up in order to reduce sulfur dioxide pollution.

It is ironic that a number of chemicals that are useful to humans may also be harmful or deadly in the long run. The pesticide DDT was widely used to kill off malaria-bearing mosquitoes between 1945 and 1970. An estimate by the World Health Organization suggests that the lives of about 5 million people were saved during that time. DDT has also helped to control insects that feed on crops, and has thus aided in increasing our food supply. But with more than 1 billion tons of pesticides being produced every year in the United States, concern has grown over the long-term effects of these chemicals on the health of humans (Miller, 1975). Furthermore, higher and higher doses of pesticides are needed to kill insects that have developed resistance to these chemicals. Thus, as these poisons make their way up the trophic pyramid, their concentration may be reaching levels at which disease is triggered in humans. Obviously, the benefits and possible harm from pesticides combine to make the question of their continued use a difficult issue to resolve.

Our Biological Future

Given our knowledge of human cultures today and the evolutionary principles we discussed earlier, what predictions can we make about the course of human biological evolution? Many of the crucial variables that could influence change in the future are not well understood; others are probably not known at all. But let us make a few guesses based on the evidence we have.

It is safe to assume that human culture will continue to shape human biological evolution. As a result, the influence of natural selection as a shaper of human biological evolution will gradually diminish. There are two reasons for this. First, Western medicine aims to allow each person to survive for as long as possible. Indeed, almost everyone born in modern industrial societies survives through reproductive age. In 1973, about 92 percent of all males and 95.5 percent of all females survived to age 45. Medicine has allowed people to live who otherwise would have died without reproducing. Medicine has thus blunted the evolutionary effects of differing deathrates for possessors of different traits.

A second, equally important reason for the lessening role of natural selection is a widespread shift in the notion of ideal family size. In recent years, more and more couples have chosen to have small families or no children at all. The trend has caused a great decrease in the fertility differences among couples. Although some pairs may be biologically able to have a large number of children, they no longer want a large family. As differences in fertility and in the likelihood of dying before having children lessen, the importance of natural selection as an evolutionary force must inevitably decrease as well.

Degenerative diseases may have little effect on this process, because most occur after the reproductive period has ended and thus do not affect fertility. But if the alarming increase in cardiovascular diseases and cancers among young people continues, these diseases could pose a threat. Certain people may have genetic traits that make them more vulnerable to one or more of these diseases. If so, natural selection may be reducing their numbers in the population, simply because an early death limits their contribution to the next generation.

We cannot determine the mutation rates in future human populations. If, however, the mutagenic effect of radiation, drugs, and chemicals is as great as feared, the mutation rate must increase. We are literally bombarded with radiation. Our color televisions and microwave ovens, x-rays, sun lamps, and many other sources of ionizing radiation, for example, may all increase the rate of mutation. Although we cannot tell how this will affect our biological future, the very fact that we cannot predict the effects of increasing mutation rates is a strong argument for caution.

Gene flow will probably continue to have an increasing effect on human biological evolution. Technology making travel easier and cultural values promoting geographic mobility will inevitably reduce the number of isolated breeding populations in countries like ours. If national populations become more heterogeneous, the pool of possible mates will increase, and the effect of genetic drift, which acts most strongly in small groups, willdiminish.

The ability to shape humans or human populations by designing genotypes or by manipulating fertilization is probably further

As modern technology allows more and more people to travel, human gene pools will become increasingly uniform. (Joyce Wilson, Design Photographers International)

in the future than most people realize. Recently, scientists fertilized a human egg outside the mother's body and placed it in the uterus, where it was successfully brought to term. The random nature of fertilization remained unchanged, however. The selection of an egg and the sperm that fertilized it occurred at random, the same way it would have happened in the womb. We cannot match a sperm with certain genetic traits with a specified egg. In fact, geneticists have only recently developed the ability to identify a specified gene from among the millions in a human cell. Presently, the gene that controls the making of hemoglobin can be found, and abnormalities leading to anemia can be identified. Within a few years, experts probably will be able to identify many more common defects before birth. This technique is expected to make possible the cure or correction of many abnormalities, or at least their early detection.

The final answer to the question of what we will become lies more and more with ourselves. There is a growing awareness that technology, guided by cultural values, can structure the biological future of the species. What we do with this awareness is up to us.

Summary

1. When changing human cultural patterns cause alterations in the environment, new health hazards may arise. Such hazards include infectious diseases, dietary deficiencies, and harmful substances or pollutants. All of these hazards have probably acted at one time or another as agents of selection in human evolution.
2. A helpful way of understanding infectious disease in humans is to study the interaction of three elements: the environment, the pathogen (disease-carrying agent), and the host.
3. Three principal sources are used in studying human disease through history: observations of societies still existing today, archaeological evidence, and historical records.
4. The history of human health can be divided into these stages: hunting-and-gathering, settled farming villages, preindustrial cities, early industrial cities, and the present.
5. The health problems of hunters and gatherers were probably little different from those of other mammals, since they could not change the environment radically enough to alter the niche of disease germs.
6. Because of small population size (usually no more than a few hundred individuals), hunting-and-gathering groups were not suitable long-term hosts for pathogenic organisms causing measles, influenza, smallpox, polio, and other infectious diseases. Parasites and or-

ganisms that cause diseases such as yaws probably afflicted early human groups as they had their primate ancestors.

7. The wide variety of foods eaten by hunters and gatherers gave them a balanced diet. Vitamin deficiencies and malnutrition were probably rare. But lack of rich foods such as cereals and milk may have limited fertility.

8. The beginning of agriculture 12,000 years ago introduced humans to serious infections of malaria and schistosomiasis. These infections were contracted when farming brought humans into constant contact with stagnant water. Malaria became an important selective factor for humans, as shown by the rise of the protective sickle-cell traits in some human populations.

9. Diseases passed from animals to humans and vitamin deficiencies due to an unvarying diet also presented important health problems for early farmers.

10. The higher level of carbohydrates provided by farming caused population growth in the settled villages of 10,000 years ago. This growth may later have been checked by cultural and environmental factors.

11. Increased crowding in preindustrial cities led to sanitation problems. Cholera, dysentery, and plague were significant diseases in this period.

12. The transmission of infectious diseases was also aided by the changed social structure in urban centers. In addition, populations became large enough to serve as long-term hosts for infections such as measles.

13. Infectious diseases were passed on to native populations in the Americas by European explorers and settlers. The resulting high deathrate among the native societies may indicate genetic differences in resistance to disease.

14. The large populations drawn to cities by the Industrial Revolution proved to be a breeding ground for epidemics. Social class determined the quality of diet and sanitation available to a person and thus affected susceptibility to disease.

15. By the end of the nineteenth century, much progress had been made in isolating pathogenic microorganisms and developing vaccines.

16. Occupational medicine came into being to deal with sickness created by harsh working conditions. Lead poisoning and silicosis were two significant occupational illnesses during the Industrial Revolution.

17. In the modern world the populations of underdeveloped nations still suffer mainly from infections such as malaria and schistosomiasis. In developed nations degenerative diseases such as cancer, heart attacks, and emphysema are among the chief causes of death.

18. Sudden elimination of infectious diseases in underdeveloped nations may lead to population explosions if high birthrates are not reduced at the same time.

19. Pathogenic substances created by industrial nations have been linked to cancer, heart disease, and other degenerative conditions. Controlling the spread of these harmful substances in the environment is made more difficult by the fact that many of these pathogens (such as pesticides) are also of great benefit to humanity.

abiotic features the nonliving parts of the environment, including temperature, precipitation, humidity, soil types, and solar radiation.

acclimatization the ability of an individual's phenotype to change in response to environmental forces.

Acheulean tradition a toolmaking tradition that first appeared about 1.2 million years B.P. in the Olduvai beds and persisted until about 100,000–70,000 B.P., when it was replaced by the Mousterian tradition. It is characterized by the hand ax and the soft-hammer technique.

adapids Eocene primates, probably ancestral to modern lemurs.

adaptation the process whereby a population changes genetic composition in response to environmental change.

adaptive radiation rapid speciation, which often occurs as organisms adapt to environments where there are many potential but unoccupied niches.

Aegyptopithecus an arboreal Oligocene primate with both primitive and advanced traits that suggest it is on or near the line leading from the omomyids to modern apes and humans.

allele any of the genes controlling alternative forms of the same trait, as the genes for green and yellow pea color in pea plants. Alleles are found at the same locus on homologous chromosomes.

Allen's rule the principle that short-limbed animals are more likely to be found in cold climates, while animals with long limbs are more commonly found in warm climates. Trait distribution studies have given support to Allen's rule.

allopatric speciation speciation that occurs when part of an expanding population moves to a new area, thereby creating geographic separation between the new and the old groups.

amino acids simple acids that form the basic structural units of proteins.

anagenic evolution the persistence of a population as a single evolutionary unit through time.

anaptomorphids a varied mixture of Eocene primates that ate both insects and fruit.

angiosperms flowering plants, shrubs, and trees.

Anthropoidea a suborder of the order Primates, whose members include monkeys, apes, and humans.

anthropological spatial theory a spatial theory based on the premise that spatial patterns are the result of culturally established beliefs about how a society should organize itself.

anthropometry the study of the measurements of the human body.

anvil a rock against which a stone being flaked is struck.

arboreal tree-living.

archaeological culture a grouping of artifacts that reappears consistently in a number of similar dwellings or sites.

archaeology the study of the history, lifestyles, and processes of change in prehistoric human cultures.

archaeomagnetic dating a method for dating the age of cultural artifacts involving an analysis of changes in the earth's magnetic field as reflected in the orientation of minerals in pottery samples.

archaic tradition one of two major traditions of the Mesolithic Age in North America. The archaic tradition began about 9,000 years B.P. in the Eastern woodlands of North America and lasted until about 4,000–3,000 years B.P.

artifact an article made or used by humans.

assemblage a group of subassemblages that show the influence of cultural patterns in an entire community.

attribute a significant trait of an object made by humans.

attribute analysis a method for organizing the remains of an archaeological culture involving the analysis of the significant traits of each artifact, which are regarded as clues to culturally patterned behaviors.

Aurignacian tradition an Upper Paleolithic toolmaking tradition of unknown origin, that lasted from about 33,000 to 25,000 years B.P.

Australopithecus africanus the earliest of the African gracile hominids, found in South Africa and probably in East Africa as well.

Australopithecus boisei a later East African robust hominid.

Australopithecus habilis the gracile East African hominid. Holders of the two-lineage hypothesis place it in the same genus as *A. africanus.*

Australopithecus robustus An African robust hominid found at Swartkrans and in East Africa as well. Thought by some to have been an ancestor of *Australopithecus boisei.*

autecology the study of the growth and aging of the individual, and its interactions with the environment.

baboon any of a largely terrestrial group of Old World monkeys found throughout Africa and on the Arabian peninsula.

backed blade a specialized Upper Paleolithic blade tool with one dulled and one sharpened edge, useful in general cutting and scraping.

balanced polymorphism the stabilization of the frequency of contrasting alleles that occurs when a heterozygote is advantageous to the population.

band the basic unit of human society that existed before about 12,000 years B.P. The only subunit of these egalitarian groups was the family or groups of related families held together by kinship and marriage bonds. Leadership was not institutionalized.

behavioral system a set of activities that have a functional relationship to one another. Examples are feeding and communication.

Bergmann's rule the principle that large animals are better adjusted to cold climates than small animals. Trait distribution studies have tended to confirm Bergmann's rule.

Beringia the continental shelf beneath the Bering Strait that was temporarily exposed as expanding glaciers trapped normally circulating water as ice and caused sea levels to drop. Upper Paleolithic groups apparently migrated across Beringia from Siberia to Alaska.

biomass the total mass of living tissue at a given trophic level.

biospecies a reproductively isolated population of living organisms capable of breeding successfully with one another.

biotic diversity the number of different kinds of life forms in an area.

biotic features the living parts of the environment.

bipedalism use of only the two back limbs in locomotion.

bipolar working a method of removing flakes by striking a stone held against an anvil, producing percussion effects at both ends of the flake.

blade long, thin flake with parallel sides characteristic of the Upper Paleolithic toolmaking tradition.

borer a sharp-pointed Upper Paleolithic blade tool probably used to drill holes in wood, bone, shells, or skins.

B.P. an abbreviation for the phrase "before present." Anthropologists have established the year 1950 as the "present," or base, year for their calculations.

brachiation arboreal locomotory type in which the animal swings from branch to branch, using only its hands and arms for support.

breccia a matrix of fossilized bone and limestone. Many of the South African hominid fossils have been found in this material, which makes them hard to date.

Bronze Age the prehistoric period immediately following the Neolithic Age. It was characterized by the use of bronze as the chief metal in the art of metallurgy, which developed during that time.

burin tool characteristic of the Upper Paleolithic, used to cut and shape wood and bone.

buttress a thickening of the bone as an adaptation to greater strength. The human lower jaw, for example, is buttressed with the structure forming the chin.

canines cone-shaped teeth between the incisors and the premolars, used to grip food during mastication and for threatening displays.

carbon 14 dating a method used for dating the age of an archaeological site. It involves measuring how much of the heavy carbon isotope C14 is present in an archaeological sample.

carnivore a flesh-eating animal.

Carpolestidae a late Paleocene family of the superfamily *Plesiadapoidea.*

Catarrhini one of two infraorders in the suborder Anthropoidea, consisting of the Old World primates: Old World monkeys, apes, and humans.

catastrophism Georges Cuvier's ninteenth-century theory that periodic catastrophes killed all existing species, preserving their remains as fossils, and allowing the earth to be populated again by new divine creations.

centralization part of Flannery's explanation of state formation. Centralization refers to the degree to which the various subsystems of the society are linked to the highest controlling bodies.

central place subtheory a subtheory of the economic spatial theory based on the premise that in economically sophisticated urban communities, least-cost distribution of goods and services will dictate the development of a network of smaller sites spaced in a hexagonal pattern around a large central site.

Cercopithecoidea a superfamily in the suborder *Anthropoidea,* consisting of the Old World monkeys.

cerebellum the center of muscular coordination, which lies at the base of the brain.

cerebral cortex the heavily convoluted outer layer that overlies the rest of the human brain. It is the center of motor control, speech, memory, association of new experiences with old, and the integration of sensory information.

ceremonial center typically a cluster of temples and related buildings that seem to have been designed for religious purposes rather than as dwelling places for a large number of people. Ceremonial centers were a feature of Mesoamerican civilizations.

chiefdom a form of prestate social organization that first appeared in the Near East around 7,500 years B.P. Chiefdoms are often theocracies with a ruler or member of his family serving as a high religious official. The leader's power is a function of his position rather than his personality. Social stratification is present, as is part-time economic specialization.

chimpanzee largely arboreal ape found in western and central Africa.

chopper a heavy, primitive pebble tool having one or two edges used for chopping.

chopper-tool culture one of two different cultural traditions that emerged from the Oldowan tradition.

chromosomes the long threadlike structures in the cell nucleus that contain the genetic material in the form of DNA.

chronometric dating dating that measures a deposit's distance in time from the present. Also called *absolute dating.*

circumscription theory Robert Carneiro's explanation of the evolution of complex societies. When growing populations that are geographically circumscribed (set off by geographical barriers that severely limit the population's access to other lands) or socially circumscribed (prevented from moving by the surrounding populations) fight one another for scarce resources, defeated populations become part of a larger state.

city a central place that performs economic and political functions for the surrounding area.

civilization a society characterized by the presence of cities or large towns that are inhabited by people who are citizens of some kind of legal commonwealth. Civilization has also been more vaguely defined as a society with sophisticated artistic, architectural, philosophical, economic, and political features.

cladogenic evolution evolution in which the original population splits into two or more distinct biological units.

classic Neandertals one of two groups of late archaics referred to in the pre-Neandertal theory. According to the theory, classic Neandertals were isolated by glacial advances in Western Europe and developed into a specialized form that could survive in the harsh climate.

cleaver a variation on the Acheulean hand ax. The cleaver has three cutting edges and may have been used in chopping, hacking, and prying apart carcasses.

cline a gradual shift in gene frequencies over a stretch of territory.

Clovis tradition the earliest tradition of points in the New World. Also called the Llano tradition.

coevolution an evolutionary association between two populations so close that a change in one niche immediately redefines the other.

community a group of interrelated populations that exist in a definable area.

comparative anatomy the systematic comparison of the bodily structures of organisms. The discipline is useful to physical anthropologists in reconstructing fossils, inferring structure-function relationships, and ascertaining phylogenetic relationships among species.

complex genetic trait a phenotype controlled by a large number of alleles at many loci.

composite tools tools having several parts. Such tools were first used during the Mousterian Era.

consumer an organism that gets its energy from complex compounds. Primary consumers get these compounds by eating plants; secondary consumers eat primary consumers.

continental drift the gradual movement of land masses on plates of the earth's crust, beginning approximately 200 million years ago.

convergence evolutionary trend that occurs when two unrelated species or groups of species independently evolve similar biological and behavioral characteristics because of the similarity of their niche structure.

craniometry the descriptive analysis of skulls.

Cretaceous Period the period in the earth's history extending from about 145–65 million years B.P. and dominated by dinosaurs.

cusps points on premolars and molars that aid in grinding and shearing.

decomposer an organism such as a bacterium that breaks down the remains of organisms, recycling organic and inorganic compounds.

dendrochronology a method of dating archaeological sites based on a sequence of tree rings established for the area.

dental arcade the arch formed by the rows of the teeth.

dental comb structure found in many prosimians, formed by projecting incisors and canines and used for grooming the fur.

denticulate Mousterian tradition one of five distinct general toolmaking traditions in Mousterian France. Tool assemblages found during this period are characterized by fine-toothed tools. Hand axes, points, and scrapers are either missing from this period or of poor quality.

desert tradition one of two major traditions of the Mesolithic Age in North America. The desert tradition began about 9,000 years B.P. in the arid western regions of North America and lasted until European contact.

developmental acclimatization adjustments to the environment that occur during the growth period of the individual.

directional selection a form of selection that favors a trait held by a minority of the population at one end of the distribution curve.

disruptive selection a form of selection that favors the forms of a trait found at extreme ends of the trait distribution curve. The form presently most common is now at a disadvantage.

diurnal active during the day.

DNA deoxyribonucleic acid. A large double-stranded molecule that controls the making of proteins in the cell. It is the main component of the chromosomes.

dominant gene gene that masks the effect of recessive alleles, so that the trait it controls becomes the phenotype.

Dryopithecus a genus of Miocene apes, believed by many to have been ancestral to both modern apes and humans.

early archaic *Homo sapiens* the earliest form of *Homo sapiens,* which dates from about 275,000 to 75,000 years B.P. Important physical characteristics include a mouth area that is noticeably larger than that of late erectines.

early *Homo erectus* the form of *Homo erectus* that existed before 500,000 B.P. Early *Homo erectus* fossils have been found in Africa and tropical and subtropical parts of Java, China, and Europe. These hominids had a more erect posture, lighter jaws, smaller molars, and bigger brains than the early African hominids.

early modern humans hominids having a nearly modern anatomy that appeared during the latter part of the Würm glaciation. By 30,000 to 25,000 B.P., early modern humans were found in all areas now inhabited by humans. Their features—including reduced tooth and jaw sizes, flatter faces, and generally less robust bone structures—resemble those of contemporary humans.

East African gracile any of a group of small, omnivorous, bipedal hominids thought to have evolved into *Homo erectus.* It has been classed as *Australopithecus habilis* and as *Homo habilis.*

East African robust Any of a lineage of human-sized, bipedal, vegetarian hominids, the earliest of which have been classed as *Australopithecus robustus,* and the evolved forms of which are named *Australopithecus boisei.*

ecology the study of the relationships between organisms and their environments.

econiche sum of all the interactions occurring between a population and its biotic and abiotic environments. Also called *niche.*

economic spatial theory a spatial theory based on the premise that, in the long run, societies tend to develop spatial patterns that minimize their costs and maximize their profits.

ecosystem the interaction of a biotic community and the physical environment of an area.

electrophoresis a method for determining rates for recessive mutations.

endocranial cast mold made of the inside of the skull in order to approximate the shape of the brain.

end scraper a specialized Upper Paleolithic blade tool characterized by sharpened surfaces on both ends. End scrapers were probably used in hollowing out bone and wood or in removing bark, as well as in scraping skins.

Eocene Epoch the second epoch of the Cenozoic Era, 58–36 million years B.P.; prosimians proliferated and diversified during this time.

epoch the major subdivision of a period.

era major geological division of the history of the earth.

ethnographic analogy the process of making inferences about prehistoric cultures based on observations of living groups whose cultures are presumed to be similar in some way.

ethology the scientific study of animal behavior.

evolution continuous biological change in frequencies of genetically determined traits in a population over generations.

extrasomatic adaptation nonbiological forms of change that characterize culture change.

family taxonomic category ranking above genus and below order.

faunal succession the principle that animal species change with time, without regression to earlier forms. This assumption helps paleontologists date strata in relative terms on the basis of index fossils.

first-order behavior the mechanical actions of an organism's body that make up functional complexes such as feeding and locomotion.

fission-track dating a method of chronometric dating based on measurement of the short tracks made in rock by particles of radioactive uranium atoms as they decay.

Flannery's process model an attempt to explain the transition from chiefdoms to states that centers on the processes by which a society becomes more complex.

Folsom tradition tradition of the southwestern and western United States, dating from about 11,000 to about 9,000 B.P.

foramen magnum the opening in the base of the skull through which the spinal cord passes.

fossil the preserved remains of an organism that lived in the past.

founder effect a special case of genetic drift that occurs when a small part of a larger population founds a new population. The founders do not have the genetic variety of the original group. Thus the genetic makeup of the founder group and its descendants may differ from that of the original population.

frontal lobes in humans, the seat of initiative and concentration.

gametes the reproductive cells that join in fertilization to produce a zygote. In humans, the male gametes are sperm and the female gametes are eggs.

gene the basic unit of inheritance, located on the chromosomes.

gene flow the movement of genes from one population to another through interbreeding.

generalized characteristics primitive traits inherited early in the evolution of a lineage and modified by later specialized adaptations for particular niches. Primate dental and limb structures are generalized characteristics of the order.

generalized Neandertals one of two groups of late archaics referred to in the pre-Neandertal theory. According to the theory, generalized, or early, Neandertals evolved from the preglacial, early archaic form that spread throughout Europe, the Middle East, and North Africa. Holders of the theory believed that this group evolved into modern humans.

genetic drift a random change in gene frequencies from one generation to the next. Drift is most likely to occur in small populations.

genotype the genetic composition of an organism.

genus biological grouping that ranks below the family and that may include one or more related species.

geographical circumscription a condition in which a population in an area isolated by geographical barriers is severely limited in its access to other lands.

gibbon mostly arboreal, Southeast Asian ape, whose long and powerful arms and shoulders make it the most skilled brachiator.

Gigantopithecus large, ground-living pongid descendant of *Dryopithecus* that became extinct in the Pleistocene Epoch.

glume any of the tough, inedible husks found on wild grains that hold kernels tightly, despite vigorous threshing.

Gondwana the southernmost of the two supercontinents formed as Pangaea broke apart.

gorilla large terrestrial ape, inhabiting tropical rain forests of central Africa.

guenon any of a group of arboreal Old World monkeys (genus *Cercopithecus*).

hammerstone a rock used to strike flakes from another rock to produce an edge.

hand ax the tool most characteristic of the Acheulean tradition. It has two chopping edges that meet to form a point and a broad base for easy gripping. *Homo erectus* may have used the hand ax for such functions as skinning, butchering, and digging.

herbivore a plant eater.

heterozygous having different alleles at the same locus on homologous chromosomes.

home range the area within which an adult organism normally moves.

hominid member of the family Hominidae, which includes humans and their extinct direct ancestors.

Hominoidea superfamily containing the gibbons, the apes, and humans.

Homo erectus an early hominid ("erect man") that lived during most of the early and middle Pleistocene. Fossils have been found with Oldowan and Acheulean tools.

Homo habilis the East African gracile hominid thought by holders of multiple-lineage theories to have been the earliest fossil hominid in the genus *Homo.*

homologous chromosomes the members of a chromosome pair made up of the contribution of the female and male parent and containing the same gene loci.

Homo sapiens "intelligent man," the species of modern humans that first appeared in the late middle Pleistocene.

homozygous having the same allele at the same locus on homologous chromosomes.

ilium the large bone forming the top part of the human pelvis.

inbreeding a phenomenon closely related to genetic drift, resulting from the mating of biological relatives. Inbreeding limits the amount of genetic variation in a population and increases the probability homozygous pairs will occur.

incisors teeth in the front of the jaw that are generally used to seize and cut food.

index fossil a fossil common to a broad geographical area and used to compare the age of remains at different sites.

infraorder taxonomic category ranking above suborder and below superfamily.

intrusion the presence of younger remains in the same geological layer as older ones, due to a process such as burial or an earthquake.

Iron Age the prehistoric period that was characterized by the use of iron as the chief metal in the art of metallurgy. Toward the end of the Iron Age, written records, which ended the prehistoric period, began to appear.

langur any of a group of slender, long-tailed, Asiatic monkeys in the subfamily Colobinae.

late archaic *Homo sapiens* the second earliest group of *Homo sapiens,* which dates from 75,000 to 40,000 years B.P. Fossils of this age found in Europe have traditionally been referred to as "Neandertal," and are associated with the Mousterian culture.

late *Homo erectus* the form of *Homo erectus* that is dated between 500,000 and 275,000 years B.P. These hominids were characterized by expanded brain centers and reduced chewing apparatus.

Laurasia the northern continental land mass, consisting of what would become North America, Europe, and Asia, according to the principle of continental drift. It became distinct about 180 million years B.P.

law of independent assortment Mendel's principle that the inheritance of one trait is not affected by the inheritance of others. In fact, linkage causes genes on the same chromosome to be inherited together.

law of particulate inheritance Mendel's principle that genes exist in the cells as separate particles.

law of segregation Mendel's principle that the alleles of a pair separate to become part of gametes, which contain one allele or the other.

learning the acquisition of experience in the course of growth. The results of learning are stored in the brain, not in the genes.

Lemuriformes infraorder of the suborder *Prosimii,* whose members include indrises, aye-ayes, and lemurs.

Levallois technique a Mousterian toolmaking technique that involved the careful preparation of a core so that flakes could be struck in precise, preshaped forms. This method produced longer, sharper cutting edges than previous methods.

limbic system part of the brain, located below the cortex; translates sensory stimuli into states of arousal or emotion.

lineage the line of descent of a group of organisms from a form arbitrarily defined as the earliest.

linearization part of Flannery's explanation of state formation. Linearization refers to the process by which lower-order controls are bypassed by higher-order controls.

Llano tradition toolmaking tradition of the United States, associated with the hunting of large and small game and the Clovis point.

locus the position of a gene on the chromosome.

long-term acclimatization gradual change that occurs during years of exposure to a particular stress and produces a phenotype more compatible with the environment.

Lorisiformes infraorder of the suborder *Prosimii,* whose members include lorises and galagos.

Lower Paleolithic the first of the three periods of the Paleolithic Age. It was the time of the Oldowan, Acheulean, and chopper-tool traditions.

Lung-shan culture a stage in Chinese civilization (4,600–3,850 years B.P.) characterized by rapidly increasing productivity, increased population density, larger, more permanent settlements, the beginnings of social stratification and role specialization, more frequent warfare, and the spread of farming villages into new areas.

macaque largely terrestrial Old World monkey similar to baboons, but found in a range from India to Japan.

macroevolution refers to physical change that has occurred over millions of years. The study of macroevolution tends to be more descriptive than the study of microevolution and less able to produce data needed to understand the action of all evolutionary processes.

Magdalenian tradition an Upper Paleolithic toolmaking tradition that appeared about 16,000 years B.P. and replaced the Solutrean tradition. It lasted about 6,000 years.

mandible the lower jaw.

mangabey any of several species of Old World monkeys (genus *Cercocebus*) native to the tropical rain forests of Africa.

masseters a set of facial muscles that attach to the zygomatic arch and move the lower jaw.

meddling One of Flannery's mechanisms destructive of complex societies. It is the unnecessary, unproductive bypassing of lower-order controls.

meiosis the division of sex cells to form gametes, each with half of the number of chromosomes contained in a body cell.

Mesoamerica region that now encompasses central and southern Mexico and Central America.

Mesolithic Age a term whose literal meaning is the "Middle Stone Age." It refers to a very short transitional period between the last Upper Paleolithic cultures and the Neolithic period, and represents a time just before the emergence of agriculture.

Metal Age a prehistoric period made up of the Bronze Age and the Iron Age.

Micoquian tradition one of five distinct general toolmaking traditions in Mousterian France. Tool assemblages found during this period are characterized by lance-shaped hand axes often with concave edges and thick bases.

microenvironment environment that has been modified by means of culture.

microevolution refers to short-term biological change. The study of microevolution can include an examination of how and why evolutionary changes occur.

microlith any of a variety of small blades that appeared during the European Mesolithic Age. Microliths (usually less than an inch long) were used alone, as tips for arrows, and as part of a number of other tools. Such tools were often well suited to the hunting of small game.

midden an accumulation of refuse around a dwelling.

Middle Paleolithic the second of the three periods of the Paleolithic Age.

Miocene Epoch the fourth epoch of the Cenozoic Era. The earliest hominid probably appeared during this epoch, which ranges from 22–6 million years B.P.

mitosis the process of cell division in which the genetic material of body cells is duplicated and distributed equally to the two daughter cells.

molars large rear teeth equipped with cusps and shearing ridges for grinding and shearing food before swallowing.

Mousterian of Acheulean tradition One of five distinct toolmaking traditions in Mousterian France. Tool assemblages of this tradition have two forms: Type A includes numerous varied hand axes and flake tools including scrapers. Type B includes many denticulates and knives but few hand axes or scrapers.

Mousterian tradition a tool tradition that lasted from about 100,000 years B.P. to about 40,000 years B.P. and is marked by the presence of hand axes, flakes, points, and burins.

mutation spontaneous alteration of the genetic material. Genetic mutations affect a single nucleotide sequence on a chromosome, while chromosomal mutations involve rearrangements of long sequences on whole chromosomes.

Natufian culture a Near Eastern culture that

took the place of the Kebaran culture about 12,000 years B.P. The Natufians lived in the coastal foothills that were part of the Levant. There is some evidence of herding, harvesting of wild grains, and growing sedentism.

natural selection the process by which nature acts on the variation within a population so that the better-adapted contribute their genes to the next generation more successfully than the poorly adapted. This mechanism of evolution allows a population to adapt to a changing environment.

Neandertal traditional label for late archaic *Homo sapiens* fossils found in Europe. The label comes from skeletal fragments discovered in 1856 in a grotto in the Neander Valley, Germany.

Neolithic Age a term whose literal meaning is the "New Stone Age." It refers to the prehistoric period beginning with the invention of agriculture and ending with the invention of metal working.

Neolithic revolution a term used to describe the change from a hunting-and-gathering economy and a flaked-stone-tool technology to an economy based on farming and a technology that included polished stone tools, pottery, and weaving.

new archaeology the modern form of archaeology, characterized by the pursuit of three goals: (1) the reconstruction of cultural history, (2) the detailed description of the way of life of earlier cultures, and (3) the analysis of the reasons for cultural change.

New World monkey any member of the extremely varied infraorder *Platyrrhini,* including the marmosets and the cebid monkeys.

niche see *econiche.*

nocturnal active at night.

nome any of the local districts scattered along the Nile Valley in Egypt that appeared around 6,000 years B.P.

normal distribution a distribution that, graphically represented, takes the form of a bell-shaped curve.

notched blade a specialized Upper Paleolithic blade tool, perhaps used to shave wood in fashioning the shafts of arrows or spears.

nuclear zone theory Braidwood's theory of the origins of agriculture. According to him, human culture at the end of the Mesolithic was ready to begin food production. In certain Near Eastern zones, the presence of animals and plants that could be domesticated provided the needed stimulus.

nucleotide the basic unit of DNA, consisting of a sugar, a phosphate, and an organic base.

oasis model theory proposed by V. Gordon Childe to explain the origins of food production. Childe thought domestication became a necessity in oases in which humans, plants, and animals were concentrated during a post-Pleistocene drying trend.

obsidian a glasslike black or banded igneous rock often used by prehistoric people in the manufacture of tools.

obsidian hydration a method for dating the age of obsidian tools, based on the measurement of the depth of the water-absorbing layer in obsidian.

occipital lobe the posterior lobe of the cerebral cortex in which the visual cortex is located. Analysis of visual images takes place here.

Oldowan tradition a name for the earliest stone tools, which were made by striking one pebble against another to form a single crude edge. Tools of this type were first uncovered in the lower beds at Olduvai Gorge in East Africa.

Old World monkey any member of the superfamily *Cercopithecoidea,* including colobus monkeys, langurs, guenons, mangabeys, baboons, and macaques.

olfactory lobe the part at the forward end of each cerebral hemisphere responsible for the reception of sensory inputs from the nose.

Oligocene Epoch the third epoch of the Cenozoic Era, 36–22 million years B.P., in which primitive monkeys and apes first appeared.

Oligopithecus an early generalized Oligocene primate, possibly ancestral to the Miocene pongids.

Omomyid a tarsier-like member of the anaptomorphid subfamily. May have been a direct ancestor of the catarrhines, and therefore of the hominids.

opposability the ability to move the thumb opposite the other fingers, allowing manipulation of objects.

orangutan an arboreal ape found in Borneo and Sumatra.

order taxonomic category ranking above family and below class.

osteology the study of bones. Physical anthropologists apply it to the study of variation among prehistoric human populations.

paleoanthropology the study of fossils and their environment as they bear on the evolution of hominids.

Paleocene Epoch the earliest epoch of the Cenozoic Era, 65–58 million years B.P. Primates probably first became a clearly distinct order during this epoch.

Paleo-Indians the original human inhabitants of the New World.

Paleolithic Age a term whose literal meaning is the "Old Stone Age." It initially referred to the culture stage in which humans made chipped stone tools. Currently, the term stands for the period of cultural development during the glacial advances and retreats of the Pleistocene Epoch. The Paleolithic Age is often divided into three parts: the Lower, Middle, and Upper Paleolithic.

paleomagnetic dating a method of chronometric dating based on the history of the reversal of the earth's magnetic field. The orientation of the field at a given time is indicated by the pattern of metallic particles in the rock.

paleospecies anatomically similar extinct animals.

palynology the analysis of pollen as a method of relative dating or as a means of reconstructing prehistoric environments.

parallelism an evolutionary trend that occurs when two closely related species or groups of species begin to exploit similar but geographically separate ecosystems in similar ways.

Parapithecus a small Oligocene primate presumed to be an early Old World monkey.

parietal lobes areas of the cerebral cortex that receive and integrate auditory, somatic, and visual information from other parts of the brain.

Paromomyidae a family of the superfamily *Plesiadapoidea.* Members include *Purgatorius,* Paleocene, and Eocene representatives.

pedigree an analysis of the genotypes of related persons, based on a study of their phenotypes.

Peking Man original name for the *Homo erectus* fossils found near Chou-kou-tien, China.

pentadactyly five-finger, five-toe pattern.

percussion flaking method of using one stone to strike off flakes from one or both sides of another. The hammerstone and anvil were used in percussion flaking to produce Oldowan tools.

Perigordian tradition an Upper Paleolithic toolmaking tradition that existed about 35,000–18,000 years B.P. It probably evolved from the Mousterian of Acheulian tradition.

period major subdivision of an era.

phase a period in the history of a culture that is named on the basis of one kind of artifact typical of it.

phenotype the physical and physiological traits of an organism. The phenotype is the result of genetic composition and environmental forces.

phylogeny a history of the evolution of a group of genetically related organisms.

phylum taxonomic category more general than class and less general than kingdom.

Plano tradition the Paleo-Indian cultural tradition of the New World, which succeeded the Clovis and Folsom traditions and was found throughout North America.

plate tectonics the study of the motion of the continental plates of the earth's crust.

Platyrrhini one of two infraorders in the suborder *Anthropoidea,* consisting of the New World monkeys.

Pleistocene Epoch a geological epoch extending from about 1.9 million years B.P. to about 10,000 years B.P., marked by a cool climate and periodic glaciation.

Plesiadapidae a family of the Paleocene superfamily *Plesiadapoidea.* Many of its traits foreshadow those of later primates.

Plesiadapoidea superfamily whose members include early primates of the Paleocene Epoch.

Pliocene Epoch a geological epoch extending from about 6 to 1.9 million years B.P., during which the first undisputed hominids evolved.

polypeptide chain a chain of amino acids bonded one to the next.

Pongidae one of three families in the superfamily *Hominoidea,* whose living members include chimpanzees, gorillas, and orangutans.

population an interbreeding group of relatively similar individuals who share the same environment; the level at which evolutionary processes work.

population ecology the study of the interactions of populations with other populations and with the abiotic features of the environment.

population genetics a branch of genetics that studies evolutionary processes in populations by testing statistical models of change in gene frequency.

potassium-argon dating a method of chronometric dating based on the decay of unstable potassium isotopes into inert argon.

power grip a grasp in which the fingers and thumb clamp an object tightly against the palm.

precision grip a grasp in which the index finger is placed against the thumb, allowing fine manipulation of objects; characteristic of monkeys, apes, and humans.

precocial strategy reproductive pattern in which fairly mature young are born in small litters after a long gestation period. Primates follow this strategy.

prehensility the ability to grasp.

premolars teeth found behind the canines, used for grinding and shearing.

pre-Neandertal theory one of three major theories explaining the presence of variation in late archaic human fossils. This theory holds that two groups of late archaics—the generalized, or early Neandertals and the classic Neandertals—evolved from the preglacial, early archaic form. Many experts believe that the generalized Neandertals evolved into modern humans.

prepottery neolithic A and B a 2,000-year period in the Near East (between about 10,000 and 8,000 years B.P.) in which wild plants and animals were domesticated but pottery had not yet appeared.

presapiens theory one of three major theories explaining the presence of variation in late archaic human fossils. This theory, which is generally discounted by modern anthropologists, holds that the European Neandertals branched off from *Homo erectus* stock as long ago as 250,000 years B.P. and became extinct at the end of the Würm glaciation, while another group of hominids developed modern human anatomical traits.

primary follicles one of two kinds of hair follicles found on sheep and goats. Primary follicles produce the straight hairs of the visible coat.

primate a member of the order *Primates,* which includes prosimians, monkeys, apes, and humans.

Primates mammalian order that includes prosimians, monkeys, apes, and humans.

primatology the study of the biology and the behavior of nonhuman primates.

prime-mover theory an attempt to explain the transition from chiefdoms to states in terms of a single initial cause.

producer an organism (such as a green plant) that produces its own organic compounds from inorganic materials. Many producers are food sources for other organisms.

projectile point rock or pebble altered for use as the tip of a spear or arrow.

promotion part of Flannery's explanation of state formation. Promotion refers to the elevation of a preexisting institution to a higher level or the elevation of one role of an existing institution to the status of a new institution.

Prosimii one of two primate suborders; it includes the *Tarsiiformes, Lorisiformes,* and *Lemuriformes.*

proteins large, complex molecules that are made up of amino acids and that serve as enzymes and basic components of cell structure.

Purgatorius the earliest known primate, dated to the late Cretaceous Period.

quadrupedalism use of all four limbs in running or walking.

Quina-Ferrassie tradition one of five distinct general toolmaking traditions in Mousterian France. Tool assemblages are dominated by scrapers, some of which were designed for extremely specialized functions.

rachis the fiber that connects the seed to the stem of the plant. The rachis found on wild wheat and barley is brittle, making harvesting very difficult.

radiocarbon dating a method of absolute dating frequently used to date items up to 50,000 years old. It is based on the decay of the radioactive carbon isotope C^{14}.

radiometric dating dating techniques based on the rate of decay of radioactive isotopes in the rocks surrounding fossil finds.

Ramapithecus a Miocene primate more evolved than dryopithecine apes, but of questionable hominid status.

random culture change change brought about because of children's imperfect repetition of their parent's behavior. Some random differences between the generations gradually show up as changes in the way most people in a group behave.

recessive gene gene whose effect is masked by a dominant allele, and whose phenotype is expressed only in the homozygous condition.

relative dating dating that determines whether one deposit is older or younger than another. Methods include stratigraphy and analysis of the fluorine, nitrogen, or uranium content of remains.

releaser a stimulus that serves as a trigger of instinctual behavior.

reproductive isolation the absence of interbreeding between two populations.

ribosomes small bodies that are found in the cytoplasm and are the site of protein synthesis.

RNA ribonucleic acid. A nuclear acid active in transferring genetic information from DNA to the ribosomes for use in protein synthesis. Messenger RNA and transfer RNA are active in this process.

sagittal crest bony ridge along the top of the skull in some nonhuman primates.

salvage archaeology the study and removal of material from an area that is about to be destroyed, or disturbed.

Scala Naturae an arrangement of nature in a scale of perfection, from the divine (most perfect) to humans, apes, simpler animals, plants, and inorganic matter. Also called the Great Chain of Being.

secondary follicles one of two kinds of hair follicles found on sheep and goats. Secondary follicles produce hairs found on the woolly undercoat.

second-order behavior interaction between individuals and between populations. Social behavior and communication are examples.

sedentism the process of settling in permanent villages inhabited year round.

sedimentary rock rock formed of bits of other rock transported from their source and deposited in water.

segregation part of Flannery's explanation of state formation. Segregation refers to the extent to which various administrative tasks are split up among separate units of the bureaucracy.

seriation a method of relative dating based on arrangement of samples of a kind of artifact (such as a vase or coin) in a chronological sequence.

sexual dimorphism the presence of a difference in form between the males and females of a species.

Shang Dynasty the earliest Chinese state (3,850–3,050 years B.P.) for which there is archaeological evidence. The Shang Dynasty comprised the communities of the lower and middle Huang Ho River and was characterized by networks of building clusters, increased population density, and more sophisticated communications techniques.

shouldered point an Upper Paleolithic tool probably affixed to spears or arrows for fighting or hunting.

sickle-cell anemia disease resulting from the homozygous occurrence of the gene Hb^s, which causes the red blood cells to take an abnormal "sickle" shape.

simian shelf bony structure behind the front teeth in the front part of the lower jaw of apes.

simple genetic trait a phenotype controlled by a few alleles at a single locus.

single population study a method for studying the process of selection in human populations. Anthropologists work with one population and try to establish the advantages offered by particular genes possessed by that group.

site a space of ground containing evidence of human occupation that archaeologists select for their dig.

Sivapithecus a late Miocene primate, thought to have descended from dryopithecine apes, and a possible hominid ancestor.

social circumscription condition in which a population is prevented from moving by surrounding hostile populations.

socialization social learning, by which individuals adjust their own behavior to fit into group life.

social stratification the condition in which some groups of citizens have greater access either to wealth, status, or both than other groups.

sociobiology the scientific study of the genetic basis of behavior and its evolution.

soft-hammer technique a technique, part of the Acheulean toolmaking tradition, in which a bone or a stick was used to flake away edges of a stone. This technique became popular when people discovered that they could use it to control the size and shape of the flake better than with the hammerstone, used to make Oldowan tools.

Solutrean tradition an Upper Paleolithic toolmaking tradition that replaced the Perigordian and Aurignacian traditions about 18,000 years B.P. This tradition lasted only about 2,000 years and was known for its fine flintwork, especially in laurel-leaf blades.

South African gracile an early bipedal, omnivorous, Plio-Pleistocene hominid generally classified as *Australopithecus africanus.*

South African robust a specialized hominid, mainly bipedal and probably a vegetarian, that was about twice as heavy as the South African gracile. Often classified as *Australopithecus robustus.*

spatial model a reconstruction of the economic, social, and environmental systems as revealed in the spacing of archaeological sites.

specialized characteristics adaptations not shared by all members of a lineage.

speciation the splitting of a population into one or more new biological species.

species a group of organisms whose shared biological background permits individuals to mate with one another and to produce fertile offspring.

stabilizing selection a form of selection that favors a trait with the highest frequency in a population.

state an independent political unit that includes many communities in its territory, with a centralized government that has the power to collect taxes, draft citizens for work and for war, and enact and enforce laws. Social stratification is present.

steppe any of the vast, level, treeless plains of southeastern Europe or Asia.

stereoscopic vision vision in which images from

each eye overlap to allow perception in three dimensions.

stratification the layering of sedimentary deposits.

stratigraphy the study of layers of sedimentary deposit and their sequence.

subassemblage a group of artifacts reflecting a particular behavior of a subgroup of a community. Studying the knives, points, and scrapers, for instance, can tell us something about how the hunters of a culture hunted.

superfamily taxonomic classification ranking above family and below infraorder.

superposition the principle that a given sedimentary layer is younger than the layer beneath it.

sympatric speciation speciation that occurs when parts of an original population no longer interbreed, though they coexist in the same area.

synthetic theory of evolution the currently accepted theory of evolution, which combines theories of natural selection, Mendelian genetics, mutation, and population genetics.

taiga a subarctic forest region dominated by spruce and fir that begins where the tundra ends.

tarsiids small Eocene primates ancestral to today's tarsiers.

Tarsiiformes infraorder in the suborder Prosimii, whose only remaining member is the tarsier.

taxonomy the science of classifying extinct and living organisms according to biological similarity and evolutionary relationship. Also, the classification system itself.

temporal muscles facial muscles that attach to the top of the skull and move the lower jaw.

terrestrial ground-living.

thermoluminescence a method used for dating artifacts. It involves the measurement of the amount of light released by pottery when heated.

torus a bony swelling such as that at the back of the head of early *Homo erectus.* Powerful neck muscles were attached to the torus.

traditional archaeology archaeology as it was practiced from the early nineteenth century until the 1950s. It concentrated largely on finding and cataloguing things, and using these things to reconstruct cultural history. Even though the artifacts uncovered by traditional archaeologists revealed a variety of cultural traits, this method obscured the nature of prehistoric human behavior.

trait distribution study a method for studying the process of selection in human populations. In trait distribution studies, anthropologists work with data from many populations to chart the frequency of a single gene and find correlations between its frequency and various environmental features.

transect a single strip of land crossing an area possibly containing an archaeological site. Archaeologists may search a transect rather than survey the whole area.

tribe a form of social organization that existed by about 9,000 years B.P. Larger than a band, a tribe is made up of groups of families related by common descent or by membership in a variety of kinship-based groups such as clans or lineages. There is little or no social stratification, and central leadership is often weak.

triplet a group of three nucleotides that together control the synthesis of a specific amino acid.

trophic hierarchy a series of categories, each of which is broadly defined in terms of how the organisms that belong to it get their energy.

tundra large, level, treeless plain characteristic of cold climates.

type the basic unit of the traditional organizational system for classifying artifacts.

typical Mousterian tradition one of five distinct general toolmaking traditions in Mousterian France. Hand axes are rarely present, but scrapers are common.

uniformitarianism the theory that existing processes, acting as they do today, were responsible for all change in the past.

Upper Paleolithic the last of three periods of the Paleolithic Age, characterized by pressure flaking and cave art.

uranium-lead dating a method of chronometric dating based on analysis of the decay into lead of certain unstable isotopes of uranium.

urbanism the process by which cities are formed.

usurpation One of Flannery's mechanisms destructive of complex societies.

varve analysis a method of relative dating in which varves (layers of silt deposited by glacial runoff annually in lakes) are placed in sequence.

vertical clinging and leaping method of locomotion employed by some prosimians; consists of leaping from tree to tree and clinging to the vertical trunks between leaps.

Wittfogel's hydraulic theory an attempt to explain the transition from chiefdom to states in terms of the need for large-scale irrigation in dry areas. Village farmers, dependent on an adequate water supply, joined in a larger political unit that could build and operate irrigation canals.

Yang-shao culture a culture of about 6,000 years ago that existed along the Huang Ho River in the Chung-yuan region of north-central China. The earliest Chinese farming occurred during this cultural period.

zygomatic arch a bony extension of the cheekbone in the human skull, running along the side of the face.

zygote the cell created by the union of the male and female gametes in fertilization.

ADAMS, R. E. W., & CULBERT, T. P. The origins of civilization in the Maya lowlands. In R. E. W. Adams (Ed.), *The origins of Maya civilization.* Albuquerque: University of New Mexico Press, 1977.

ADAMS, R. McC. *The evolution of urban society.* Chicago: Aldine, 1966.

ADAMS, R. McC. Developmental stages in ancient Mesopotamia. In S. Struever (Ed.), *Prehistoric agriculture.* Garden City, N.Y.: Natural History Press, 1971.

ADAMS, R. McC. Patterns of urbanization in early southern Mesopotamia. In P. J. Ucko, R. Tringham, & G. W. Dimbleby, (Eds.), *Man, settlement and urbanism.* London: Duckworth, 1972, pp. 735–749.

ALDRED, C. *Egypt to the end of the Old Kingdom.* New York: McGraw-Hill, 1965.

ALEXANDER, B. K., & BOWERS, J. M. The social structure of the Oregon troop of Japanese macaques. *Primates,* 1967, *8,* 333–340.

ARMELAGOS, G. J., & DEWEY, J. R. Evolutionary response to human infectious diseases. *Bioscience,* 1970, *157,* 638–644.

AUSTIN, D. *Heat stress and heat tolerance in two African populations.* Unpublished doctoral dissertation, Pennsylvania State University, 1974.

BAKER, P. T. Human biological diversity as an adaptive response to the environment. In R. H. Osborn (Ed.), *The biological and social meaning of race.* San Francisco: W. H. Freeman, 1971.

BEHRENSMEYER, A. K. Taphonomy and paleoecology in the hominid fossil record. *Yearbook of Physical Anthropology,* 1975, *19,* 36–50.

BILSBOROUGH, A. Patterns of evolution in Middle Pleistocene hominids. *Journal of Human Evolution,* 1976, *5,* 423–439.

BINFORD, L. R. A consideration of archaeological research design. *American Antiquity,* 1964, *29* (4), 425–441.

BINFORD, L. R. Post-Pleistocene adaptations. In S. R. Binford & L. R. Binford (Eds.), *New perspectives in archaeology.* Chicago: Aldine, 1968.

BINFORD, L. R. Archaeological systematics and the study of culture process. In M. P. Leone (Ed.), *Contemporary archaeology: A guide to theory and contributions.* Carbondale: Southern Illinois Press, 1972.

BLACK, F. L. Infectious diseases in primitive societies. *Science,* 1975, *187,* 515–518.

BLACK, R. M. *The elements of paleontology.* New York: Cambridge University Press, 1970.

BOAS, F. *Changes in bodily form of descendants of immigrants.* Partial report on the results of an anthropological investigation for the U.S. Immigration Commission. Washington, D.C.: U.S. Government Printing Office. (Senate Document No. 208, 51st Congress, 2nd Session.)

BODMER, W. F., & CAVALLI-SFORZA, L. L. *Genetics, evolution and man.* San Francisco: Freeman, 1976.

BORDES, F. *The old stone age.* New York: McGraw-Hill, 1968.

BOSERUP, E. *The conditions of agricultural growth: The Economics of agrarian change under population pressure.* Chicago: Aldine, 1965.

BOUGHEY, A. S. *Ecology of populations* (2nd ed.). New York: Macmillan, 1973.

BOURKE, J. B. Trauma and degenerative disease in ancient Egypt and Nubia. *Journal of Human Evolution,* 1972, *1,* 225–232.

BRACE, C. L. Sexual dimorphism in human evolution. *Yearbook of Physical Anthropology,* 1973, *17,* 283–252.

BRACE, C. L., NELSON, H., & KORN, N., *Atlas of Fossil Man,* New York: Holt, Rinehart & Winston, 1971.

BRAIDWOOD, R. J. *Prehistoric men* (7th ed.). Glenville, Ill.: Scott, Foresman, 1967.

BRAIDWOOD, R. J., et al. *Prehistoric investigations in Iraqi Kurdistan.* Studies in Ancient Oriental Civilization, *31.* Chicago: University of Chicago Press, 1960.

BRAIN, C. K. The Transvaal ape-man-bearing cave deposits. *Transvaal Museum Memoir,* 1958, No. 11.

BROSE, D. S., & WOLPOFF, M. H. Early Upper Paleolithic man and Late Middle Paleolithic tools. *American Anthropologist,* 1971, *73,* 1156–1194.

BROTHWELL, D. The question of pollution in earlier and less developed societies. In P. R. Cox & J. Peel (Eds.), *Population and pollution.* London: Academic Press, 1972.

BROWN, L. R. Human food production as a process in the biosphere. *Scientific American,* 1970, *223,* 162–163.

BUETTNER-JANUSCH, J. *Origins of man.* New York, Wiley, 1966.

BUETTNER-JANUSCH, J. *Physical anthropology: A perspective.* New York: Wiley, 1973.

BUETTNER-JANUSCH, J., & HILL, R. L. *Molecules and monkeys.* In H. K. Bleibtreu, *Evolutionary anthropology.* Boston: Allyn & Bacon, 1969.

BULLARD, W. R. Maya settlement pattern in northeastern Petén, Guatemala. *American Antiquity,* 1960, *25,* 355–372.

BUTZER, K. W. *Environment and archaeology.* Chicago: Aldine, 1971.

BYERS, D. S. The region and its people. In D. S. Byers (Ed.), *The prehistory of the Tehuacán Valley* (vol. 1), Austin: University of Texas Press, 1967.

CAMPBELL, B. G. *Human evolution* (2nd ed.). Chicago: Aldine, 1974.

CARNEIRO, R. L. The theory of the origin of the state. *Science,* 1970, *169,* 733–738.

CARTMILL, M. *Primate origins.* Minneapolis: Burgess, 1975.

CHAGNON, N. A., *Proceedings, 111th International Congress of Anthropological and Ethnological Sciences,* 1965, *3,* 251.

CHAGNON, N. A. Tribal social organization and genetic micro-differentiation. In G. A. Harrison & A. J. Boyce (Eds.), *The structure of human populations.* Oxford: Clarendon Press, 1972.

CHAGNON, N. A., NEEL, J. V., WEITKAMP, L., GERSHOWTIZ, H., & AYERS, M. The influence of cultural factors on the demography and pattern of gene flow from the Makiritare to the Yanomama Indians. In F. Hulse (Ed.), *Man and nature.* New York: Random House, 1975.

CHANG, K. C. *Early Chinese civilization: Anthropological perspectives.* Cambridge, Mass.: Harvard University Press, 1976.

CHILDE, G. V. *Man makes himself.* New York: New American Library, 1951.

CHURD, C. H. *Man in prehistory.* New York: McGraw-Hill, 1969.

CLARK, G. *The Stone Age hunters.* New York: McGraw-Hill, 1967.

CLARK, G. *World prehistory.* New York: Cambridge University Press, 1977.

CLARK, J. G. D. *The prehistory of Africa.* New York: Praeger, 1970.

CLARK, J. G. D. Star Carr: A case study in bioarchaeology. *An Addison-Wesley Module in Anthropology,* 1972, *10.*

CLARK, W. E. L. *History of the primates.* Chicago: University of Chicago Press, 1965.

CLARKE, A. D. B., & CLARKE, A. M. Some recent advances in the study of early deprivation. *Child Psychology and Psychiatry,* 1960, *1,* 26–36.

CLARKE, D. L. Spatial information in archaeology. In *Spatial Archaeology.* New York: Academic Press, 1977.

COCKBURN, T. A. *The evolution and eradication of infectious diseases.* Baltimore: Johns Hopkins University Press, 1963.

COE, M. D. *Mexico.* New York: Praeger, 1962.

COE, M. D., & FLANNERY, K. V. Microenvironments and mesoamerican prehistory. In S. Struever (Ed.), *Prehistoric agriculture.* Garden City, N.Y.: Natural History Press, 1971.

COHEN, M. *The food crisis in prehistory.* New Haven, Conn.: Yale University Press, 1977.

COLLINS, D. Culture traditions and environment of early man. *Current Anthropology,* 1969, *10*(4), 267–296.

COMAS, J. *Manual of physical anthropology.* Springfield, Ill.: Charles C. Thomas, 1960.

COON, C. S. *The origin of races.* New York: Knopf, 1962.

CROSBY, A. W. *The Columbian exchange: Biological and cultural consequences of 1492.* Westport, Conn.: Greenwood, 1972.

DARWIN, C. *The descent of man* (1871). (Facsimile of the first edition.) New York: International Publications, 1962.

DARWIN, C. *On the origin of species by means of natural selection* (1859). (Facsimile of the first edition with an introduction by L. Mayr.) Cambridge, Mass.: Harvard University Press, 1964.

DAY, M. H. Femoral fragment of a robust Australopithecine from Olduvai Gorge, Tanzania *Nature,* 1969, *221,* 230–233.

DEETZ, J. *Invitation to archaeology.* New York: Doubleday, 1967.

DEETZ, J. F. Archaeology as a social science. In M. P. Leone (Ed.), *Contemporary archaeology.* Carbondale: Southern Illinois Press, 1972.

DE VORE, I., & HALL, K. R. L. Baboon ecology. In I. De Vore (Ed.), *Primate behavior.* New York: Holt, Rinehart & Winston, 1965, pp. 20–52.

DIETZ, R. S., & HOLDEN, J. D. The breakup of Pangaea. *Scientific American,* 1970, *223,* 30–41.

DOBZHANSKY, T. *Mankind evolving.* New Haven, Conn.: Yale University Press, 1962.

DOBZHANSKY, T. Genetic entities in hominid evolution. In S. L. Washburn (Ed.), *Classification and human evolution.* Chicago: Aldine, 1963, pp. 347–362.

DOLHINOW, P. J. (Ed.). *Primate patterns.* New York: Holt, Rinehart & Winston, 1972, pp. 352–382.

DOLHINOW, P. J., & BISHOP, N. The development of motor skills and social relationships among primates through play. In P. J. Dolhinow (Ed.), *Primate patterns.* New York: Holt, Rinehart & Winston, 1972, pp. 312–337.

DUNN, F. L. Epidemiological factors: Health and disease in hunter-gatherers. In R. B. Lee & I. DeVore (Eds.), *Man the hunter.* Chicago: Aldine, 1968.

EIBL-EIBESFELDT, I. Ethological perspectives on primate studies. In P. C. Jay (Ed.), *Primates: Studies in adaptability and variability.* New York: Holt, Rinehart & Winston, 1968, pp. 479–486.

EIBL-EIBESFELDT, I. Phylogenetic adaptation as determinants of aggressive behavior in man. In J. de Witt & W. W. Hartrup (Eds.), *Determinants and origins of aggressive behavior.* The Hague: Mouton, 1974, pp. 29–54.

EIMERL, S., & DE VORE, I. *The primates.* New York: Time-Life, 1965.

EISELEY, L. *Darwin's century.* New York: Doubleday, 1961.

EVELETH, P. B. The effects of climate on growth. *Annals of the New York Academy of Science,* 1966, *134*(2), 750.

FAGAN, B. *In the beginning.* Boston: Little, Brown, 1975, p. 149.

FAGAN, B. *People of the earth* (2nd ed.). Boston: Little, Brown, 1977.

FLANNERY, K. V. The ecology of early food production in Mesopotamia *Science,* 1965, *147, 1247*–1255.

FLANNERY, K. V. The vertebrate fauna and hunting patterns. In D. S. Byers (Ed.), *The prehistory of the Tehuacán Valley* (vol. 1). Austin: University of Texas Press, 1967.

FLANNERY, K. V. The cultural evolution of civilizations. *The Annual Review of Ecology and Systematics,* 1972, *3,* 399–425.

FLINT, R. F., & SKINNER, B. J. *Physical geology* (2nd ed.). New York: Wiley, 1977.

FRAYER, D. W. A reappraisal of *Ramapithecus. Yearbook of Physical Anthropology,* 1974, *18,* 19–29.

FRISCH, J. E. Individual behavior and intertroop variability in Japanese macaques. In P. C. Jay (Ed.), *Primates: Studies in adaptation and variability.* New York: Holt, Rinehart & Winston, 1968, pp. 243–252.

FRISCH, R. E. Population, food intake and fertility. *Science,* 1978, *199,* 22–30.

GAJDUSEK, D. C. Factors governing the genetics of primitive human populations. *Cold Spring Harbor Symposia on Quantitative Biology,* 1964, *29,* 121–127.

GARDNER, R. A., & GARDNER, B. T. Teaching sign language to a chimpanzee. *Science,* August 15, 1969, 664–672.

GARN, S. M. *Human races.* Springfield, Ill: Charles C. Thomas, 1965.

GOLDSBY, R. A. *Race and races.* New York: Macmillan, 1977.

GOODALL, J. Chimpanzees of the Gombe Stream Reserve. In I. De Vore (Ed.), *Primate behavior.* New York: Holt, Rinehart & Winston, 1965, pp. 458–461.

GREULICH, W. W. A comparison of the physical growth and development of American-born and native Japanese children. *American Journal of Physical Anthropology,* 1957, *15,* 489–515.

HALL, K. R. L. Social learning in monkeys. In P. C. Jay (Ed.), *Primates: Studies in adaptation and variability.* New York: Holt, Rinehart & Winston, 1968, pp. 383–397.

HAMILTON, T. H. *Process and pattern in evolution.* New York: Macmillan, 1967.

HARLOW, H. F. The nature of love. *American Psychologist,* 1958, *13,* 673–685.

HARLOW, H. F., & HARLOW, M. Learning to love. *American Scientist,* 1966, *54,* 244–272.

HARLOW, H. F. et al. From thought to therapy: Lessons from a primate laboratory. *American Scientist,* 1971, *59,* 538–549.

HARNER, M. The ecological basis for Aztec sacrifice. *American Ethnologist,* 1977, *4,* 117–33.

HARRISON, G. A., & WEINER, J. S. Some considerations in the formulation of theories of human phylogeny. In S. L. Washburn (Ed.), *Classification and human evolution.* Chicago: Aldine, 1963, pp. 75–84.

HARTL, D. L. *Our uncertain heritage.* Philadelphia: Lippincott, 1977.

HELBAEK, H. Domestication of food plants in the Old World. *Science,* 1959, *130,* 365–372.

HESTER, T. R., HEIZER, R. F., & GRAHAM, J. A. *Field methods in archaeology.* Palo Alto, Cal.: Mayfield, 1975.

HOCKETT, C. D. The origin of speech. *Scientific American,* 1960, *203,* 88–96.

HOLE, F. Questions of theory in the explanation of culture change in pre-history. In C. Renfrew (Ed.), *The explanation of culture change.* (Models in prehistory.) London: Duckworth, 1973.

HOLE, F., & HEIZER, R. A. *An introduction to prehistoric archaeology.* New York: Holt, Rinehart & Winston, 1973.

HOLLOWAY, R. L. The casts of fossil hominid brains. *Scientific American,* 1974, *231,* 106–115.

HOWELLS, W. W. Neanderthal man: Facts and figures. *Yearbook of Physical Anthropology,* 1974, *18,* 7–18.

HRDY, S. B. Infanticide as a primate reproductive strategy. *American Scientist,* 1977, *65,* 40–49.

HULSE, F. S. Migration and cultural selection: in human genetics. *The Anthropologist,* (Special Volume), 1968, 1–21.

Human teeth in China dated at 1.7 million years, *The New York Times,* February 6, 1978.

ISAAC, E. On the domestication of cattle. In S. Struever (Ed.), *Prehistoric agriculture.* Garden City, N.Y.: Natural History Press, 1971.

ISAAC, G. L. Early hominids in action: A commentary on the contribution of archeology to understanding the fossil record in East Africa. *Yearbook of Physical Anthropology,* 1975a, *19,* 19–35.

ISAAC, G. L. Stratigraphy and cultural patterns in East Africa during the middle ranges of Pleistocene time. In K. W. Butzer & G. L. Isaac (Eds.), *After the australopithecines.* The Hague: Mouton, 1975b.

ISAAC, G. L. The food-sharing behavior of protohuman hominids. *Scientific American,* April, 1978, 90–108.

JACOBS, J. *The economy of cities.* New York: Vintage, 1970.

JAY, P. C. The common langur of north India. In I. De Vore (Ed.), *Primate behavior.* New York: Holt, Rinehart & Winston, 1965.

JENKINS, F. A. *Primate locomotion.* New York: Academic Press, 1974.

JOHANSON, D. C., & BRILL, D. Ethiopia yields first "family" of early man. *National Geographic,* December 1976, 790–811.

JOLLY, A. *The evolution of primate behavior.* New York: Macmillan, 1972.

JOLLY, C. J. The seed-eaters: a new model of hominid differentiation based on a baboon analogy. *Man,* 1970, *5,* 5–26.

JU-KANG, WOO. Mandible of Sinanthropus Lantianensis. *Current Anthropology,* 1964, *5*(2), 98–101.

JU-KANG, WOO. The skull of Lantian man. *Current Anthropology,* 1966, 7(1), 83–86.

KAY, R. F., The functional adaptations of primate molar teeth. *American Journal of Physical Anthropology,* 1975, *43,* 195–216.

KENNEDY, K. A. R. *Neanderthal man.* Minneapolis: Burgess, 1975.

KETTLEWELL, H. B. D. The phenomenon of industrial melanism in *Lepidoptera. Annual Review of Entomology,* 1961, 6, 245–262.

KOLATA, G. B. !Kung hunter-gatherers: Feminism, diet and birth control. *Science,* 1974, *185,* 932–934.

KOTTAK, C. P. Race relations in a Bahian fishing village. *Luso-Brazilian Review,* 1967, *4,* 35–52.

KRETZOI, M., & VÉRTES, L. Upper Biharian (Inter-Mindel) pebble-industry occupation site in Western Hungary. *Current Anthropology,* 1965, 6(1), 74–87.

KURTEN, B. Continental drift and evolution. *Scientific American,* 1969, *220,* 54–64.

KUMMER, B. K. F. Functional adaptation to posture in the pelvis of man and other primates. In R. H. Tuttle (Ed.), *Primate functional morphology and evolution.* The Hague: Mouton, 1975.

LASKER, G. W. Human biological adaptability. *Science,* 1969, *166,* 1480–1486.

LEAKEY, M. D. *Olduvai Gorge* (vol. 3). Cambridge: The University Press, 1971.

LEAKEY, M. D. Cultural patterns in the Olduvai Sequence. In K. W. Butzer & G. L. Isaac (Eds.), *After the australopithecines.* The Hague: Mouton, 1975.

LEAKEY, M. D., HAY, R. L., CURTIS, G. H., DRAKE, R. E., JACKES, M. K., & WHITE, T. D. Fossil hominids from the Laetolil beds. *Nature,* 1976, *262,* 460–466.

LEAKEY, R. E. F. Evidence for an advanced Plio-Pleistocene hominid from East Rudolf, Kenya. *Nature,* 1973, *242,* 447–450.

LEAKEY, R. E. F. *Australopithecus, Homo erectus* and the single species hypothesis. *Nature,* 1976, *261,* 572–576.

LEAKEY, R. E. F. *Origins.* New York: Dutton, 1977.

LEAKEY'S find—tracks of an ancient ancestor. *Time,* March 6, 1978, 75.

LEGROS CLARK, W. E. *An introduction to the study of fossil man* (5th ed.). Chicago: University of Chicago Press, 1965.

LEOROI-GOURHAN, A. The evolution of Paleolithic art. *Scientific American,* February, 1968.

LIEBERMAN, P. On the evolution of language: A unified view. In R. H. Tuttle (Ed.), *Primate functional morphology and evolution.* The Hague, Paris: Mouton, 1975, pp. 203–212.

LIEBERMAN, P., & CRELIN, E. S. On the speech of neanderthal. *Linguistic Inquiry 2,* 1971, 203–222.

LITTLE, M. A., & BAKER, P. T. Environmental adaptation and perspectives. In P. T. Baker & M. A. Little (Eds.), *Man in the Andes.* Stroudsburg, Pa.: Dowden, Hutchinson & Ross, 1976.

LITTLE, M. A., & MORREN, G. E. B., Jr. *Ecology, energetics, and human variability.* Dubuque, Iowa: William C. Brown, 1976.

MACNEISH, R. S. Ancient mesoamerican civilization. *Science,* 1964, *143,* 531–537.

MACNEISH, R. S., PATTERSON, T. C., & BROWMAN, D. L. *The central Peruvian prehistoric interaction sphere.* Phillips Academy, Andover, Mass.: Papers of the Robert S. Peabody Foundation for Archaeology, 1975, (Vol. 7).

MAGLIO, V. J., Vertebrate fauna from the Kubi Alfi, Koobi Fora and Ileret areas, east Rudolf, Kenya. *Nature,* 1971, *231.*

MANGELSDORF, P. C., MACNEISH, R. S., & GALINAT, W. C. Domestication of corn. *Science,* 1964, *143,* 538–545.

MANN, A. *A paleodemography of Australopithecus.* Berkeley: University of California Press, 1968.

MANN, A., & TRINKAUS, E. Neandertal and Neandertal-like fossils from the Upper Pleistocene. *Yearbook of Physical Anthropology,* 1973, *17,* 169–193.

MARCUS, J. Territorial organization of the lowland classic Maya. *Science,* June 1, 1973, 191–195.

MARGALEF, R. *Perspectives in ecological theory.* Chicago: University of Chicago Press, 1968.

MARSDEN, H. M. Antagonistic behavior of young rhesus monkeys after changes induced in social rank of their mother. *Animal Behavior,* 1968, *16*(1), 38–44.

MARSHACK, A. Some implications of the paleolithic symbolic evidence for the origin of language. *Current Anthropology,* 1976, *17,* 274–282.

MARTIN, P. S. The revolution in archaeology. In M. P. Leone (Ed.), *Contemporary archaeology.* Carbondale: Southern Illinois Press, 1972.

MARTIN, R. O. Strategies of reproduction. *Natural History,* 1975, *84,* 49–57.

MASON, W. A. Naturalistic and experimental investigations of the social behavior of monkeys and apes. In P. C. Jay (Ed.), *Primates: Studies in adaptation and variability.* New York: Holt, Rinehart & Winston, 1968, pp. 398–419.

MCDERMOTT, W. C. *The ape in antiquity.* Baltimore: Johns Hopkins University Press, 1938.

MCKERN, T. W. *The search for man's origins.* An Addison-Wesley Module in Anthropology, Module #53. Reading, Mass.: Addison-Wesley, 1974.

MCKUSICK, V. A., HOSTETLER, J. A., EGELAND, J. A., & ELDRIDGE, R. The distribution of certain genes in the Old Order Amish. *Cold Spring Harbor Symposium on Quantitative Biology,* 1964, *29,* 99–114.

MELLAART, J. *The Neolithic of the Near East.* New York: Scribner's, 1975.

MICHELS, J. W. *Dating methods in archaeology.* New York: Seminar Press, 1973, p. 4.

MILLER, G. T., Jr. *Living in the environment: Concepts, problems and alternatives.* Belmont, Cal.: Wadsworth, 1975.

MILLON, R. Social relations in ancient Teotihuacán. In E. Wolf (Ed.), *The Valley of Mexico: Studies in prehistoric ecology and society.* Albuquerque: University of New Mexico Press, 1976.

MILNER, R. B., & PROST, J. H. The significance of primate behavior for anthropology. In N. Korn & F. Thompson (Eds.), *Human evolution* (2nd ed.). New York: Holt, Rinehart & Winston, 1967, pp. 125–136.

MILTON, J. B. Fertility differentials in modern

societies resulting in normalizing selection for height. *Human Biology,* 1975, *47,* 189–200.

MOODY, P. A. *Genetics of man* (2nd ed.). New York: Norton, 1975.

MORRIS, D., & MORRIS, R. *Men and apes.* London: Hutchinson, 1966.

MORRIS, L. N. *Human populations, genetic variation and evolution.* San Francisco: Chandler, 1971.

MURAYAMA, M., & NALBANDIAN, R. M. *Sickle cell hemoglobin.* Boston: Little, Brown, 1973.

NAPIER, J. R. Fossil hand bones from Olduvai Gorge. *Nature,* 1962, *196,* 409.

NAPIER, J. R. *Monkeys without tails.* New York: Taplinger, 1976.

NAPIER, J. R., & NAPIER, P. H. *A handbook of the living primates.* London: Academic Press, 1967.

NELSON, N. C. *Prehistoric archaeology.* In F. Boas, *General anthropology.* Boston: Heath, 1938, pp. 146–148.

NEWCOMBE, H. B. In M. Fishbein (Ed.), *Papers and Discussions of the Second International Conference on Congenital Malformations.* New York: International Medical Congress, 1964.

PARSONS, J. R. Settlement and population history of the basin of Mexico. In E. Wolf (Ed.), *The Valley of Mexico: Studies in prehistoric ecology and society.* Albuquerque: University of New Mexico Press, 1976.

PATTERSON, T. C. *America's past: A New World archaeology.* Glenview, Ill.: Scott, Foresman, 1973.

PERKINS, D., & DALY, P. The beginning of food production in the Near East. In R. Stigler, Holloway, R. Solecki, D. Perkins, & P. Daly (Eds.), *The Old World: Early man to the development of agriculture.* New York: St. Martin's, 1974.

PIANKA, E. R. *Evolutionary biology.* New York: Harper & Row, 1974.

PILBEAM, D. *The evolution of man.* London: Thames & Hudson, 1970.

PILBEAM, D. *The ascent of man.* New York: Macmillan, 1972.

PILBEAM, D. Adaptive response of hominids to their environment as ascertained by fossil evidence. *Social Biology,* 1972, *19,* 115–127.

PILBEAM, D., MEYER, G. E., BADGLEY, C., ROSE, M. D., PICKFORD, M. H. L., BEHRENSMEYER, A. K., & SHAH, S. M. I. New hominoid primates from the Siwaliks of Pakistan and their bearing on hominoid evolution. *Nature,* 1977, *270,* 689–695.

PREMACK, A. J. *Why chimps can read.* New York: Harper and Row, 1976.

PREMACK, D. "Language and Intelligence in Ape and Man," *American Scientist,* 1976, *64,* 674–683.

RATHJE, W. L. Socio-political implications of lowland Maya burials: Methodology and tentative hypotheses. *World Archaeology,* 1970, *1,* 359–374.

REID, R. M. Effects of consanguineous marriage and inbreeding on couple fertility and offspring mortality in rural Sri Lanka. In B. A. Kaplan (Ed.), *Anthropological studies of human fertility.* Detroit: Wayne State University Press, 1976.

RICKETSON, O. G., & RICKETSON, E. B., Uaxacton, Guatemala group—1926–1931. Washington, D.C.: Carnegie Institution of Washington, 1937, publication #477.

ROBINSON, J. T. *American Journal of Physical Anthropology,* 1952.

ROBINSON, J. T. *Early hominid posture and locomotion.* Chicago: University of Chicago Press, 1972.

ROE, D. *Prehistory: An introduction.* Berkeley: University of California Press, 1970.

ROSEN, S. I. *Introduction to the primates: Living and fossil.* Englewood Cliffs, N.J.: Prentice-Hall, 1974.

SALTHE, S. N. *Evolutionary biology.* New York: Holt, Rinehart & Winston, 1972.

SANDERS, W. T., & PRICE, B. T. *Mesoamerica: The evolution of a civilization.* New York: Random House, 1968.

SANDERS, W. T., PARSONS, J. R., & LOGAN, M. H. Summary and conclusions. In E. Wolf (Ed.), *The valley of Mexico: Studies in prehistoric ecology and society.* Albuquerque: University of New Mexico Press, 1976.

SANDISON, A. T. Pathological changes in the skeletons of earlier populations due to acquired disease, and difficulties in their interpretation. In D. R. Brothwell (Ed.), *The skeletal biology of earlier human populations.* New York: Pergamon Press, 1968.

SARICH, V. M. The origin of the hominids: An immunological approach. In S. L. Washburn & P. C. Jay (Eds.), *Perspectives on human evolution.* New York: Holt, Rinehart & Winston, 1968, pp. 94–119.

SAUL, F. P. Disease in the Maya area: The pre-Columbian evidence. In T. P. Culbert (Ed.), *The classic Maya collapse.* Albuquerque: University of New Mexico Press, 1973.

SAWKINS, F. J., CHASE, C. G., DARBY, D. G., & RAPP, G. *The evolving earth.* New York: Macmillan, 1974, p. 11.

SCHALLER, G. B. The behavior of the mountain gorilla. In I. De Vore (Ed.), *Primate behavior.* New York: Holt, Rinehart & Winston, 1965.

SCHOLANDER, P. F., LANGE ANDERSON, K., KROG, J., VOGT LORENTZEN, F., & STEEN, J. Critical temperature in Lapps. *Journal of Applied Physiology,* 1957, *10*(2), 231–234.

SCHULTZ, A. H. *The life of primates.* New York: Universe Books, 1969.

SERVICE, E. R. *Origins of the state and civilization.* New York: Norton, 1975.

SHEPRO, D., BELANARICH, F., & LEVY, C. *Human anatomy and physiology: A cellular approach.* New York: Holt, Rinehart & Winston, 1974.

SHIMER, H. W. *An introduction to the study of fossils.* New York: Macmillan, 1924.

SIMONS, E. L. The early relatives of man. *Scientific American,* July 1964, 56.

SIMONS, E. L. *Primate evolution: An introduction to man's place in nature.* New York: Macmillan, 1972.

SIMONS, E. L. *Ramapithecus. Scientific American,* 1977, *236,* 28–35.

SMITH, P. E. *The consequences of food production.* Addison-Wesley Module in Anthropology, Module #31, 1972.

STALLINGS, W., JR. *Dating prehistory ruins by tree rings.* Santa Fe, N.M.: Laboratory of Anthropology, School of American Research, General Series, Bulletin 8, 1939.

STERN, T., & OXNARD, C. E. Primate locomotion: Some links with evolution and morphology. *Primatologie, 4.* Basel: S. Karger, 1973.

STRAUS, W. L., & CAVE, A. J. E. Pathology and posture of neanderthal man. *Quarterly Review of Biology,* 1951, *32,* 348–363.

SWINDLER, D. R. *Dentition of living primates.* London: Academic Press, 1976.

SZALAY, F. G. Systematics of the Omomyïdai. *New York Bulletin of the American Museum of Natural History,* 1976, *156*(3), 420.

SZALAY, F. S. A review of some recent advances in paleoprimatology. *Yearbook of Physical Anthropology,* 1973, *17,* 39–59.

TEMPLE, S. A. Plant-animal mutualism: Coevolution with dodo leads to near extinction of plant. *Science,* 1977, *197*(4306), 885–886.

TERRACE, H. S., & BEVER, T. G. What might be learned from studying language in the chimpanzee? The importance of symbolizing oneself. *Annals of the New York Academy of Sciences,* 1976, *280,* 579–587.

THENIUS, E. *Fossils and the life of the past.* Heidelberg: Springer-Verlag, 1973.

TOBIAS, P. The Taung skull revisited. *Natural History,* 1974, *88,* 38–43.

TOBIAS, P. V. Brain evolution in the hominoidea. In R. H. Tuttle (Ed.), *Primate functional morphology and evolution.* Paris: Mouton, 1975.

TROTTER, R. J. From endangered to dangerous species. *Science News,* 1976, *109,* 74.

TURNBULL, C. The lesson of the pygmies. *Scientific American,* 1963, *208,* 28–37.

VALENTINE, J. W. *Evolutionary paleoecology of the marine biosphere.* Englewood Cliffs, N.J.: Prentice-Hall, 1973.

VAN LAWICK-GOODALL, J. *In the shadow of man.* New York: Dell, 1971.

VOGEL, F. "Mutations in man." From *Genetics today, proceedings of the XI international congress of genetics.* New York: Pergamon, 1965.

VOGEL, F., & CHAKRAVARTTI, M. R. ABO blood groups in a rural population of West Bengal and Bihar (India). In C. J. Bajema (Ed.), *Natural selection in human populations.* New York: Wiley, 1971.

VOGET, F. W. *A history of ethnology.* New York: Holt, Rinehart & Winston, 1975.

VOLPE, E. P. *Understanding evolution* (3rd ed.). Dubuque, Iowa: William C. Brown, 1977.

VORZIMMER, P. J. Darwin and Mendel: The historical connection. *Isis,* 1968, *59* (196, Part 1).

WASHBURN, S., & LANCASTER, C. S. The evolution of hunting. In R. B. Lee & I. De Vore (Eds.), *Man the hunter.* Chicago: Aldine, 1968.

WATSON, R. A., & WATSON, P. J. *Man and nature: An anthropological essay in human ecology.* New York: Harcourt Brace Jovanovich, 1969.

WEBER, E. *Europe since 1715: A modern history.* New York: Norton, 1972.

WEINER, J. S. *The natural history of man.* New York: Universe Books, 1971.

WHITE, L. A. *The evolution of culture.* New York: McGraw-Hill, 1959.

WHITE, T. D., & HARRIS, J. M. Suid evolution and correlation of African hominid localities. *Science,* 1977, *198.*

WILCOCKS, C. *Medical advance, public health and evolution.* New York: Pergamon Press, 1965.

WILLEY, G. R. *An introduction to American Archaeology* (vol. 1). Englewood Cliffs, N.J.: Prentice-Hall, 1966.

WILLEY, G. R. The rise of Maya civilization: A summary view. In R. W. Adams (Ed.), *Origins of Maya civilization.* Albuquerque: University of New Mexico Press, 1977.

WILLEY, G. R., & SHIMKIN, D. B. The Maya collapse: A summary view. In T. P. Culbert (Ed.), *The classic Maya collapse.* Albuquerque: University of New Mexico Press, 1973.

WILSON, E. O. *Sociobiology: The new synthesis.* Cambridge, Mass.: Harvard University Press, 1975.

WITTFOGEL, K. *Oriental despotism: A comparative study of total power.* New Haven, Conn.: Yale University Press, 1957.

WOLPOFF, M. H. Sexual dimorphism in the Australopithecines. In R. H. Tuttle (Ed.), *Paleonanthropology: Morphology and paleoecology.* Paris: Mouton, 1975.

WOLPOFF, M. H. Some aspects of human mandibular evolution. In J. A. MacNamara, Jr. (Ed.), *Determinants of mandibular form and growth.* Ann Arbor, Mich.: Center for Human Growth and Development, 1975.

WOOLF, C., & DUKEPOO, F. Z. Hopi Indians, inbreeding, and albinism. *Science,* 1959, *164,* 30–37.

WRESCHNER, E. The red hunters: Further thoughts on the evolution of speech. *Current Anthropology,* 1976, *17,* 717–718.

WRIGHT, H. T. Recent research on the origin of the state. *Annual Review of Anthropology,* 1977, 379–97.

ZUCKERMAN, S. *The social life of monkeys and apes.* New York: Harcourt, Brace, 1932.

Indexes

Name Index

Note: Numbers in italic refer to pages on which the respective subject is illustrated.

Subject Index